Main Currents of Marxism

ITS ORIGINS, GROWTH AND DISSOLUTION

LESZEK KOLAKOWSKI

*

2. THE GOLDEN AGE

Translated from the Polish by P. S. Falla

Oxford New York Toronto Melbourne

OXFORD UNIVERSITY PRESS

1981

Oxford University Press, Walton Street, Oxford OX2 6DP

London Glasgow New York Toronto
Delhi Bombay Calcutta Madras Karachi
Kuala Lumpur Singapore Hong Kong Tokyo
Nairobi Dar es Salaam Cape Town
Melbourne Wellington

and associate companies in
Beirut Berlin Ibadan Mexico City

First published 1978 by Oxford University Press
First published as an Oxford University Press paperback 1981

British Library Cataloguing in Publication Data

Kolakowski, Leszek
Main currents of Marxism.
Vol. 2: The golden age
1. Communism – History
I. Title   II. Falla, Paul Stephen
335.4'09'034   HX21   78-40247
ISBN 0-19-285108-X

Printed in the
United States of America

Main Currents of Marxism

1. THE FOUNDERS
2. THE GOLDEN AGE
3. THE BREAKDOWN

'the discussion as a whole is unique and unparalleled in the entire literature on Marx and Marxism, and should dominate the field for decades to come'

Tom Rockmore, *Man and World*

'a deeply impressive examination of the entire Marxist tradition, marked by lucid and accurate exposition, sustained and high-level analysis, and a passionately committed point of view which ... distorts neither exposition nor analysis'

Steven Lukes, *New York Review of Books*

MAIN CURRENTS OF MARXISM is a handbook and a thorough survey of the varieties of Marxism. Leszek Kolakowski describes the development of Marx's own thought and the contributions of his best-known followers. No survey of the doctrines of the Marxist tradition could fail to be controversial, but Kolakowski's treatment is detached and pluralistic, and he does not attempt to identify a pure or essentially Marxist strand in the tradition as a whole. There is no better example of the variety of Marxism than the diversity which results from the tension between the Utopian and fatalist impulses in Marx's thought. In the author's own words, 'The surprising diversity of views expressed by Marxists in regard to Marx's so-called historical determinism is a factor which makes it possible to present and schematize with precision the trends of twentieth-century Marxism. It is also clear that one's answer to the question concerning the place of human consciousness and will in the historical process goes far towards determining the sense one ascribes to socialist ideals and is directly linked with the theory of revolutions and of crises.'

LESZEK KOLAKOWSKI was for many years, until March 1968 when he was expelled for political reasons, Professor of the History of Philosophy at the University of Warsaw. He is now a Fellow of All Souls College, Oxford, and has been a visiting Professor at the universities of Montreal, Yale, and California, Berkeley.

CONTENTS

BIBLIOGRAPHICAL NOTE   ix

I. MARXISM AND THE SECOND
   INTERNATIONAL   1

II. GERMAN ORTHODOXY: KARL KAUTSKY   31
   1. Life and writings   32
   2. Nature and society   34
   3. Consciousness and the development of society   40
   4. Revolution and socialism   43
   5. Critique of Leninism   50
   6. Inconsistencies in Kautsky's philosophy   51
   7. A note on Mehring   57

III. ROSA LUXEMBURG AND THE
    REVOLUTIONARY LEFT   61
   1. Biographical information   61
   2. The theory of accumulation and the inevitable collapse
      of capitalism   65
   3. Reform and revolution   76
   4. The consciousness of the proletariat and forms of political
      organization   82
   5. The national question   88

IV. BERNSTEIN AND REVISIONISM   98
   1. The concept of revisionism   98
   2. Biographical information   100
   3. The laws of history and the dialectic   102
   4. The revolution and the 'ultimate goal'   105
   5. The significance of revisionism   111

V. JEAN JAURÈS: MARXISM AS A
   SOTERIOLOGY   115
   1. Jaurès as a conciliator   115
   2. Biographical outline   117
   3. The metaphysics of universal unity   120
   4. The directing forces of history   125
   5. Socialism and the republic   125
   6. Jaurès's Marxism   138

VI. PAUL LAFARGUE: A HEDONIST
MARXISM   141

VII. GEORGES SOREL: A JANSENIST
MARXISM   151

1. The place of Sorel   151
2. Biographical outline   154
3. Rationalism versus history. Utopia and myth. Criticism of
   the Enlightenment   156
4. *Ricorsi*. The separation of classes and the discontinuity of
   culture   162
5. Moral revolution and historical necessity   164
6. Marxism, anarchism, Fascism   170

VIII. ANTONIO LABRIOLA: AN ATTEMPT AT AN
OPEN ORTHODOXY   175

1. Labriola's style   175
2. Biographical note   177
3. Early writings   179
4 Philosophy of history   183

IX. LUDWIK KRZYWICKI: MARXISM AS AN
INSTRUMENT OF SOCIOLOGY   193

1. Biographical note   194
2. Critique of the biological theory of society   197
3. Prospects of socialism   198
4. Mind and production. Tradition and change   201

X. KAZIMIERZ KELLES-KRAUZ: A POLISH
BRAND OF ORTHODOXY   208

XI. STANISLAW BRZOZOWSKI: MARXISM AS
HISTORICAL SUBJECTIVISM   215

1. Biographical note   217
2. Philosophical development   219
3. The philosophy of labour   223
4. Socialism, the proletariat, and the nation   231
5. Brzozowski's Marxism   236

XII. AUSTRO-MARXISTS, KANTIANS IN THE
MARXIST MOVEMENT, ETHICAL
SOCIALISM   240

1. The concept of Austro-Marxism   240
2. The revival of Kantianism   243

3. Ethical socialism   245
4. Kantianism in Marxism   247
5. The Austro-Marxists: biographical information   254
6. Adler: the transcendental foundation of the social sciences   258
7. Adler's critique of materialism and the dialectic   268
8. Adler: consciousness and social being   272
9. What is and what ought to be   274
10. The state, democracy, and dictatorship   276
11. The future of religion   282
12. Bauer: the theory of the nation   285
13. Hilferding: the controversy on the theory of value   290
14. Hilferding: the theory of imperialism   297

XIII. THE BEGINNINGS OF RUSSIAN MARXISM   305

1. Intellectual movements during the reign of Nicholas I   305
2. Herzen   311
3. Chernyshevsky   313
4. Populism and the first reception of Marxism   316

XIV. PLEKHANOV AND THE CODIFICATION OF
MARXISM   329

1. The origins of Marxist orthodoxy in Russia   329
2. Dialectical and historical materialism   336
3. Marxist aesthetics   345
4. The struggle against revisionism   347
5. The conflict with Leninism   350

XV. MARXISM IN RUSSIA BEFORE THE RISE OF
BOLSHEVISM   354

1. Lenin: early journalistic writings   356
2. Struve and 'legal Marxism'   362
3. Lenin's polemics in 1895–1901   373

XVI. THE RISE OF LENINISM   381

1. The controversy over Leninism   381
2. The party and the workers' movement. Consciousness and
   spontaneity   384
3. The question of nationality   398
4. The proletariat and the bourgeoisie in the democratic
   revolution. Trotsky and the 'permanent revolution'   405

XVII. PHILOSOPHY AND POLITICS IN THE
BOLSHEVIK MOVEMENT   413

1. Factional struggles at the time of the 1905 Revolution   413
2. New intellectual trends in Russia   419

3. Empiriocriticism   424
4. Bogdanov and the Russian empiriocritics   432
5. The philosophy of the proletariat   441
6. The 'God-builders'   446
7. Lenin's excursion into philosophy   447
8. Lenin and religion   459
9. Lenin's dialectical Notebooks   461

XVIII. THE FORTUNES OF LENINISM: FROM A THEORY OF THE STATE TO A STATE IDEOLOGY   467

1. The Bolsheviks and the War   467
2. The Revolutions of 1917   473
3. The beginnings of socialist economy   481
4. The dictatorship of the proletariat and the dictatorship of the party   485
5. The theory of imperialism and of revolution   491
6. Socialism and the dictatorship of the proletariat   497
7. Trotsky on dictatorship   509
8. Lenin as an ideologist of totalitarianism   513
9. Martov on the Bolshevik ideology   517
10. Lenin as a polemicist. Lenin's genius   520

SELECTIVE BIBLIOGRAPHY   529

INDEX   537

BIBLIOGRAPHICAL NOTE

Sources of quotations used in the text:

LENIN, V. I., *Collected Works*, 45 vols., Lawrence & Wishart, London. 1960–70.

McLELLAN, D., *Karl Marx: Early Texts*, Blackwell, Oxford, 1971.

MARX, K., *Capital*, Lawrence & Wishart, London, 1974.

SOREL, G., *Reflections on Violence*, trans. T. E. Hulme and J. Roth, The Free Press, Glencoe, Ill., 1950.

TROTSKY, L., *The Defence of Terrorism*, Labour Publishing Co. and Allen & Unwin, London, 1921.

CHAPTER I

Marxism and the Second International

THE period of the Second International (1889–1914) may be called without exaggeration the golden age of Marxism. Marxist doctrine had been clearly enough defined to constitute a recognizable school of thought, but it was not so rigidly codified or subjected to dogmatic orthodoxy as to rule out discussion or the advocacy of rival solutions to theoretical and tactical problems.

Certainly the Marxist movement cannot, at this time or at any other, be identified simply with the ideology of the socialist parties that belonged to the International. The many sources of European socialism had by no means dried up, though they seemed of little importance compared with the apparently self-consistent, universally applicable theories of Marx. Only in Germany was it possible, despite the strong tradition of Lassalleanism, to frame and maintain for a considerable time a uniform ideology based on Marxist premises, or what were generally regarded as such. The French party led by Guesde could lay claim to orthodoxy inasmuch as its programme had been drawn up under Marx's own auspices and with his assistance; but the French socialist movement was in a state of disruption for some time, and the Marxist tradition was more lively in some sections than in others. In Austria, Russia, Poland, Italy, Spain, and Belgium, and wherever else there was a working-class socialist movement, its ideology was permeated by Marxism to a greater or lesser degree. The influence of Marxism was least strong in Britain, the country in which its basic doctrine had been formulated: British socialism owed far more of its character to the ideas of Owen, Bentham, and J. S. Mill. In Europe generally, to be a socialist was not necessarily to be a Marxist, but, except in Britain, socialist theory was in general the work of men who called themselves Marxists, though each understood the term in his own way. There was no clear distinction between theorists and practical socialists: in addition to the many theoreticians, party leaders such as Bebel, Guesde, Victor Adler, and Turati, who were not intellectuals and had no ambition to develop socialist theory on their own account, were nevertheless educated men and quite capable of joining in theoretical discussions. The general intellectual calibre of party leaders never again reached such a high level, either among social democrats or communists. Marxism seemed to be at the height of its intellectual impetus. It was not the religion of an isolated sect, but the ideology of a powerful political movement; on the other hand, it had no means of silencing its opponents, and the facts of political life obliged it to defend its position in the realm of theory.

In consequence, Marxism appeared in the intellectual arena as a serious doctrine which even its adversaries respected. It had redoubtable defenders such as Kautsky, Rosa Luxemburg, Plekhanov, Bernstein, Lenin, Jaurès, Max Adler, Bauer, Hilferding, Labriola, Pannekoek, Vandervelde, and Cunow, but also such eminent critics as Croce, Sombart, Masaryk, Simmel, Stammler, Gentile, Böhm-Bawerk, and Peter Struve. Its influence extended beyond the immediate circle of the faithful, to historians, economists, and sociologists who did not profess Marxism as a whole but adopted particular Marxist ideas and categories.

The main characteristics of Marxist doctrine were of course connected with its social situation and political function. There were many factors which contributed to its development as an ideology of the workers' movement, but at the same time, as that development was affected by current political pressures, its scope was in some respects limited. The quarter-century of the Second International saw the publication of many important theoretical works on the general problems of historical materialism, the Marxist interpretation of particular ages and historical events, and the economics of imperialism. A Marxist school of aesthetics and art criticism came into being (Plekhanov, Lafargue, Mehring, Klara Zetkin, and Henriette Roland-Holst), and works were published on the theory of religion and ethnology (Cunow, Krzywicki, and Kelles-Krauz). There was, however, no such efflorescence in the more strictly philosophical fields of epistemology and anthropology. Those who considered themselves Marxists may be divided into two groups according to their attitude towards the philosophical premisses of Marxism. One group took the view that Marxism was a theory of social development and especially of capitalist society and its inevitable collapse, and that this theory could without inconsistency be supplemented and enriched by philosophical doctrines derived from other sources, in particular Kantianism and positivism. They thus attempted to link historical materialism with Kantian ethics (as in ethical socialism) or empirio-critical epistemology (for example, the Russian Machists and Friedrich Adler). The orthodox majority, however, maintained that Marxist doctrine itself contained the answers to all or most of the problems of philosophy, and that Engels's works, in particular the *Anti-Dühring* and *Ludwig Feuerbach*, were the natural completion of Marx's economic and sociological theories. Those who thus regarded Marxism as a single, uniform theoretical whole—for instance, Kautsky, Plekhanov, and Lenin—did not add much to Engels's popular philosophy and were generally content to echo his summary conclusions or apply them to the criticism of new idealistic trends. After Engels's death the German socialists published many of Marx's works that were not previously known—such as *The Theory of Surplus Value*, part of *The German Ideology*, correspondence with Engels and others, and the doctoral dissertation—but other texts of great philosophical value remained unpublished, for instance the Paris Manuscripts of 1844, the *Critique of Hegel's Philosophy of Right*, and the *Grundrisse*. Attempts were made, by Sorel and Brzozowski among others, to distinguish the materialism of Engels from Marxian anthropology, but these were not in the main stream of Marxism and played no decisive role. On the whole, therefore, Marxism as a general philosophical theory remained a dead letter or took the form of eclecticism, despite the vast body of literature interpreting the premisses of historical materialism. The *Theses on Feuerbach* were known and quoted, but rather as pieces of rhetoric than as statements to be seriously analysed. Categories such as alienation, reification, and praxis, which are today so frequently met with, received scarcely any mention in Marxist literature.

The Second International was not a uniform, centralized organization with an elaborate body of doctrine acknowledged by all its members, but rather a loose federation of parties and trade unions, working separately though united by their belief in socialism. Nevertheless, the International seemed to be the first true embodiment of Marx's dream, which was also Lassalle's, of a marriage between socialist theory and the workers' movement, between the class struggle and the scientific analysis of social processes—two phenomena of independent origin, condemned to impotence unless they could achieve this state of symbiosis or identity. Although non-Marxist traditions of socialism had not lost their strength (Lassalleanism in Germany, Proudhonism and Blanquism in France, anarchism in Italy and Spain, utilitarianism in Britain), it was Marxism that stood out as the dominant form of the workers' movement and the true ideology of the proletariat. Unlike the First International, which was an ideological centre rather than an organization of the workers' movement, the Second was an assemblage of parties representing the masses.

What, however, did it mean to be a Marxist in the twenty-five years preceding the First World War? In relation to the stereotypes of the period, the notion of Marxism may be most simply defined by enumerating some classic ideas that distinguished Marxists from the adherents of all forms of utopian socialism and anarchism, and *a fortiori* from liberal and Christian doctrines. A Marxist was one who accepted the following propositions:

The tendencies of capitalist society, in particular the concentration of capital, have activated the natural tendency of the historical process towards socialism, which is either the unavoidable or the most probable consequence of the processes of accumulation.

Socialism involves public ownership of the means of production and thereby the abolition of exploitation and unearned income, of privilege and inequality deriving from the unequal distribution of wealth. There must be no discrimination of race, nationality, sex, or religion, and no standing armies. There must be equal opportunities for education, democratic freedom for all —freedom of speech and assembly, popular representation at all levels—and a comprehensive system of social welfare.

Socialism is in the interest of all mankind and will make

possible the universal development of culture and welfare, but the standard-bearer in the fight for socialism is the working class as the immediate producer of all basic values and as the class most strongly and directly interested in abolishing wage-labour.

The advance towards socialism calls for an economic and political struggle on the part of the proletariat, which must fight for the short-term improvement of its lot within the capitalist system and must make use of all political forms, expecially parliamentary ones; in order to fight for socialism, the proletariat must organize itself into independent political parties.

Capitalism cannot be radically altered by the accumulation of reforms, and its catastrophic consequences of depression, poverty, and unemployment are unavoidable. Nevertheless, the proletariat must fight for reforms in the shape of labour legislation, democratic institutions, and higher wages, since these make conditions more tolerable and also provide training in class solidarity and in the technique of battles to come.

Capitalism will finally be swept away by revolution, when economic conditions under capitalism and the class-consciousness of the proletariat are ripe for this. The revolution, however, is not a *coup d'état* to be carried out by a handful of conspirators, but must be the work of an overwhelming majority of the labouring population.

The interests of the proletariat are identical on the world scale, and the socialist revolution will come as an international event, at all events in the advanced industrial societies.

In human history, technical progress is the deciding factor in bringing about changes in the class structure, and these changes determine the basic features of political institutions and the reigning ideology.

Socialism is not only a political programme but a world-view based on the premiss that reality is susceptible of scientific analysis. Only rational observation can reveal the nature of the world and the meaning of history. Religious and spiritualist doctrines are the expression of a 'mystified' consciousness and are bound to disappear when exploitation and class antagonisms are abolished. The world is subject to natural laws and not to any kind of Providence; man is the work of nature and is to be studied accordingly, although the rules that govern his being cannot be simply reduced to those of the pre-human universe.

The main lines of Marxist doctrine as thus formulated were, however, open to important differences of interpretation, and in certain conditions these led to the formation, within Marxism, of political movements and theoretical positions that were radically hostile to one another. Within the framework of the general definition it was possible to hold quite different views as to, for example, the degree of validity of historical materialism or the relationship between the 'base' and the 'superstructure'. Socialism might be regarded either as a 'natural inevitability' or as a possibility within the historical tendency of the capitalist economy. The struggle for reform might be treated as valuable in itself or merely as training for the revolution to come. It was possible to advocate the political exclusivism of socialist parties or to admit, with greater or less freedom, the legitimacy of alliances of various kinds with non-socialist movements. The revolution could be envisaged either as a civil war or as the result of non-violent pressure by the majority. It was possible to hold either that the socialist world-view was an all-embracing, self-contained system providing the answer to every important philosophical question, or that philosophical criticism might draw freely on pre-Marxist or non-Marxist thought in respect of questions that Marxism itself did not decide one way or the other. All these differences were of great importance in defining the objectives and policy of socialist parties. The latter were not mere discussion groups but had to take many practical decisions. They were constantly confronted by situations which Marx's doctrine had, so to speak, not foreseen; this obliged them to draw particular conclusions from the master's principles, and they did not always agree as to the mode of doing so.

From the doctrinal point of view the most important stages of theoretical development in the Second International may be reduced to three: the struggle against anarchism and revisionism in the first and second phases respectively, and the conflict between orthodoxy and the left wing after the Russian Revolution of 1905. From the point of view of the fate of Marxism and the socialist movement the decisive conflict was of course that waged against revisionism in all its ramifications. (In these introductory remarks we take no account of Russia, which requires separate and more detailed treatment.)

The most important factors of the European situation affecting the development of socialist thought during the period of the Second International may be summarized briefly as the retreat from liberalism in ideology and economic practice; the democratization of political institutions, especially the introduction of equal and universal suffrage in many European states; the economic expansion of Western Europe; and the growth of imperialist tendencies.

The decline of liberalism was expressed above all in the abandonment of two principles that had been fundamental to liberal social philosophy. The first of these laid down that the main function of state institutions was to protect the safety, freedom, and property of the individual: questions of production and exchange lay outside their competence and should be left to private initiative, which gave the best assurance of prosperity. The second, more specific principle was that the relationship between the employer and the wage-earner was a particular kind of free contract between free individuals and must be left subject to the laws of such contracts: it was an infringement of freedom for the law to interfere in labour agreements or for trade unions to exert collective pressure on employers to improve conditions. These two principles, expressing what may be called the 'pure' doctrine of capitalism and free competition, were scarcely defended by anyone in the closing years of the nineteenth century. This was partly the result of socialist propaganda and partly because changes in the world economy had made the ideal of unrestricted free trade unworkable. Socialist ideas had effectively destroyed the fiction that the employer and the wage-earner met on equal terms, and most liberal theorists had also abandoned this position. It was consequently recognized as the right and duty of legislative bodies to regulate the system of wage contracts and restrict certain forms of exploitation, and it was equally conceded that workers were entitled to form associations for the collective defence of their interests against employers.

The recognition of the principle of state intervention between workers and employers, and the possibility of exerting pressure through freely elected legislative bodies, faced the socialist parties of Western Europe with a situation to which Marxist strategy provided no clear-cut answer. If socialists became members of bourgeois parliaments and helped to pass laws in the working-class interest, were they not participating in the reform of capitalism? The anarchists charged them with doing so and admitting, by implication, that capitalism was remediable, whereas Marx had stated the contrary. To this the orthodox replied that capitalism could not be reformed in the sense that it would cease to be capitalism and evolve of its own accord into a socialist order, but it was nevertheless essential to fight for the improvement of workers' conditions under capitalism so as to develop their class-consciousness. Workers who were left to the mercy of capitalists, deprived of education and stupefied by toil, would never be capable of playing their part in the socialist revolution.

The dilemma was especially acute as regards temporary alliances with non-socialist parliamentary groups. If the socialists refused, on principle, any association with parties of the centre, they lost all hope of obtaining concessions in the interest of the working class and were in practice favouring the conservatives and the right wing. But if they agreed to such associations it meant co-operating with the bourgeoisie to improve the capitalist system, and thereby blunting the edge of class antagonism. In countries such as Russia, where the parliamentary system either did not exist or was ineffectual from the socialist point of view, this problem scarcely arose: parliament might be a sounding-board for propaganda, but could not be looked to for effective social reform. But where such reforms proved to be practicable, it was hard to draw a line between the struggle to improve conditions and 'reformism' in the pejorative sense. The anarchists held that any form of political action, especially in parliament, demoralized the workers by suggesting that capitalism was changing for the better; the distinction drawn between one bourgeois party and another obscured, in the eyes of the proletariat, the basic cleavage between hostile classes. To this the orthodox retorted that it was not a matter of indifference to the future of socialism whether the workers lived in an empire, a tyranny, or a republic. It was not contrary to the principles of the class struggle to defend republicanism and bourgeois democracy against reaction, clericalism, and military cliques: a bourgeois republic could not itself carry out the socialist programme, but it provided better conditions for the proletariat to carry on the fight.

The history of the socialist movement is that of a continuing debate between these two points of view. Either side could find statements by Marx supporting its attitude. If it were held that the proletariat does not belong to bourgeois society and cannot amend that society, but only destroy it—that the natural laws of capitalist production operate against the workers, and that this state of things can no more be altered than physical bodies can be made to fall up instead of down—then any struggle for reform, any temporary parliamentary alliance, any distinction between one bourgeois party and another is a betrayal of the proletariat and an abandonment of the revolution. But, on the other hand, did not Marx expressly reject Lassalle's view that all the non-proletarian classes form a single reactionary mass? Did he not approve of the proletariat fighting not for total revolution but for democratic rights or factory laws, and did he not condemn the absurd principle 'The worse, the better'?

The anarchists, and particularly the anarcho-syndicalists, set their faces against parliamentary tactics and any idea of reforming capitalism or coming to terms with the bourgeoisie. The older generation of orthodox socialists, such as Guesde, and the young German Left accepted the need for political action but were against temporary alliances, and they regarded the struggle for reforms as valuable not in itself but only in relation to the ultimate aim. The orthodox of the centre persuasion accepted political alliances provided the working-class party remained fully independent, and they recognized the fight for short-term objectives as valid in itself. The right wing (Jaurès, Turati) were not only prepared to come to terms with anyone in the immediate interest of the proletariat, but regarded reforms within capitalist society as having a socialist significance, i.e. as implanting elements of socialism in the midst of bourgeois reality. There was a clear divide between the syndicalists and the rest of the movement, as there was between the socialism of Jaurès and the orthodox position. Between intermediate schools of thought the barriers were more fluid and made themselves felt occasionally, in particular controversies.

Throughout its existence the Second International was dominated by German social democracy. The German socialist movement was the most numerous and uniform and the best equipped doctrinally. Lassalle's party founded in 1863 enjoyed considerable support among the workers even after the death of its leader, but it did not produce any outstanding theoreticians or men of action. It held dogmatically to the views of its founder, who thought the social question could be solved by establishing producer co-operatives with the help of the state and gradually eliminating the system of hired labour. For this purpose Lassalle believed that the working class would first have to gain a parliamentary majority, and the prospect of this was so remote that the party's programme seemed devoid of practical content. A new party, the Sozialdemokratische Arbeiterpartei, was formed in 1869 at Eisenach under the aegis of August Bebel and Wilhelm Liebknecht. Bebel (1840–1913) was a turner by occupation and spent some years in his youth as a travelling journeyman, but at an early age became active in workers' associations at Leipzig. There in 1864 he met Liebknecht (1826–1900), who acted as a mentor to his younger friend and introduced him to Marxist theory. Liebknecht had lived abroad for a dozen years after the 1848 Revolution: he met Marx and Engels in England and adopted their social theories. Bebel and Liebknecht were subsequently elected to the Reichstag and opposed the war with France and the annexation of Alsace and Lorraine. Bebel was not a theoretician, but his chief work apart from memoirs, *Die Frau und der Sozialismus* (1883; translated as *Woman under Socialism*), was popular with two or three generations of socialists: its importance was that it led the socialist movement as a whole to embrace the cause of women's emancipation and equal rights. Bebel enjoyed moral authority in the German and European socialist movement and displayed tactical skill in the intricate disputes that arose within the party. He was concerned above all to preserve unity, and it was mainly thanks to his influence that the later conflict with revisionism did not disrupt the party organization.

In 1875 the Lassalle and Eisenach parties united at Gotha to form the Socialist Workers' party. The Gotha Programme, severely criticized by Marx, was a compromise between Lassalle's strategy and Marxism, in which the former's basic principles were maintained; in practice, however, the influence of Marxism was increasingly strong. Neither Bebel nor Liebknecht was a doctrinaire by nature: they accepted the fundamental principles of Marxian socialism, but were not interested in the absolute correctness of theoretical formulas without direct application to the practical struggle. They believed that socialism would eventually conquer by revolutionary means, but this was more a general hope than a political directive. Between them they organized the German socialist movement into a powerful force which set an example to the rest of Europe.

In 1878 Bismarck used the pretext of an attack on the Emperor's life to enact an emergency law prohibiting socialist meetings and publications and dissolving local party organizations. Many leaders were forced to emigrate, but the party did not give in and, as was seen in due course, managed to maintain and extend its influence. At this time Kautsky founded at Stuttgart the monthly *Die Neue Zeit*, ostensibly a private venture, which became a focus for the whole European Marxist Movement. Bernstein at Zurich edited the *Sozialdemokrat*, a less theoretical publication which became one of the chief organs of party life during the period of repression. The Anti-Socialist Law was repealed in 1890, and in that year the party obtained a million and a half votes at the polls and 35 seats in the Reichstag. In the following year the Congress at Erfurt adopted a new programme drafted by Kautsky and Bernstein: this was purged of Lassalleanism and faithfully reflected Marxist doctrine in the current version approved by Engels. It asserted that capital was bound to become more concentrated, squeezing out small businesses and accentuating the class struggle. It spoke of the exploitation of the proletariat, economic crises, and the growing incompatibility between private ownership of the means of production and the efficient use of existing technology. The programme set out the need to fight for reforms in preparation for the revolution which would bring about the socialization of property and the subordination of all production to social needs. It also declared the unity of proletarian interests on a world scale. A second section dealt with practical objectives: universal and equal suffrage, a direct, secret ballot, proportional representation; replacement of the standing army by a people's militia; freedom of speech and assembly; equal rights for women; secular, free, and compulsory education; religion to be treated as a private matter; free legal aid, election of judges and magistrates; abolition of the death penalty; free medical care; progressive taxation; an eight-hour working day; no child labour under fourteen years of age; supervision of working conditions.

It soon became evident that the relationship between the practical and the theoretical part of the programme was far from clear. The dispute between the orthodox and the revisionists may be reduced to the question which part of the Erfurt Programme truly expressed the party's mind and policy.

The second pillar of the International was France. French socialism had a richer and more varied tradition than that of Germany, but was in consequence more subject to ideological disputes, and Marxist doctrine did not enjoy a monopoly position. The Parti Ouvrier Français led by Guesde was fundamentally closer to German social democracy. Jules Guesde (1845–1922; real name Jules Bazile) grew up under the Second Empire, which he hated from his early years, and soon became a republican and atheist. From 1867 he worked as a journalist for various republican publications, and in 1870 he helped to found *Les Droits de l'homme*, a democratic but not socialist journal. Sentenced to five years' imprisonment for supporting the Commune, he escaped to Switzerland, where he encountered Bakuninist groups and spread anarchistic ideas among French *émigrés*. He was still an anarchist while at Rome and Milan in 1872–6, but after returning to France became a Marxist and the chief organizer of the party founded on Marxist doctrine. In 1877–8 two workers' congresses were held in France, both dominated by reformist tendencies. The third, held at Marseilles in October 1879, adopted the main premisses of Marxian socialism and decided upon the creation of a workers' party. In May 1880 Guesde went to London to discuss the party programme with Marx, Engels, and Lafargue. This document, to which Marx himself wrote the theoretical introduction, was less elaborate than the subsequent Erfurt Programme, but embodied similar practical objectives. It was adopted with small amendments at a congress at Le Havre in November 1880, but it soon became clear that the party was by no means unanimous as to its interpretation. Some argued that the party should adjust its programme to real possibilities and only set itself tasks that could be carried out in the foreseeable future: these members were called 'possibilists' by their orthodox revolutionary opponents, and retorted by calling the latter 'impossibilists'. The former group was not interested in direct action towards the 'ultimate goal', but preferred to concentrate on local and municipal issues as the proper field of party activity. A split took place in 1881–2: the adherents of the Parti Ouvrier Français under Guesde took the line of awaiting a global revolution which would sweep away capitalism, while the possibilists in the Parti Socialiste Français set their sights on immediate objectives. The former emphasized the purely proletarian character of the movement and were basically opposed to alliances with non-socialist radicals, while the latter aimed to increase their influence among the petty bourgeoisie and were ready for local and tactical alliances of all kinds. There soon came into being a new group of possibilists led by Jean Allemane, which was essentially revolutionary but in the manner of Proudhon rather than Marx: unlike the followers of Guesde, this group disbelieved in the effectiveness of political action, but it was also opposed to the pure reformism of the possibilists. Meanwhile Blanqui had formed a group of his own, which was led after his death in 1881 by Édouard Vaillant. The Blanquist group eventually joined the Guesdists, but Vaillant continued to insist on the division between himself and the Marxists. Besides these four groups there were, at a later stage, independent socialists such as Jaurès and Millerand.

At the beginning of the twentieth century French socialism was divided into three main streams: the Parti Socialiste Français, with Jaurès as its chief ideologist, the Parti Socialiste de France (Guesdists and Blanquists), and the syndicalists. Of the first two groups, the Guesdists were concerned with proletarian purity and were opposed to tactical understandings with non-socialist parties, or to intervention in disputes within the bourgeois camp. They disbelieved in the value of reformist action and firmly rejected the idea that any reforms within the existing system could be of significance for socialism. Jaurès and his followers, on the other hand, while they saw the transition to socialism in terms of revolution, believed that some socialist institutions could be established and maintained in bourgeois society, as socialism was not the negation of republicanism but a development of its principles. They were also prepared to contract alliances with non-socialist forces in the interests of any cause currently defended by the socialists. The syndicalists, the least important of the three groups, were opposed in principle to all political activity and especially to parliamentary action. Their periodical, the *Mouvement socialiste*, was edited from 1899 to 1914 by Hubert Lagardelle, and the chief ideologist of the movement, although he stood outside it, was Georges Sorel. The Guesde and Jaurès groups united in 1905, but this did not put an end to ideological differences within French socialism.

Marxism, however, did not produce any important theoreticians in France during the period of the Second International. Guesde was not a scholar, and Lafargue, no doubt the chief French Marxist in the 'classic' sense of the term, was more of a popularizer than an independent thinker. Jaurès and Sorel, who were genuinely original writers, could only be called Marxists in a very loose sense, but both influenced French intellectual life by their different interpretations of Marxism as well as in other ways.

British socialism, as already mentioned, was hardly affected by Marxian doctrine. Strictly speaking, there is nothing in the ideological basis of Fabianism that can be called specifically Marxist. *Fabian Essays in Socialism* (1899), which struck the keynote of British socialism for generations to come, comprised a programme of reform which was either contrary to Marxist theory or rooted in principles drawn from the general arsenal of nineteenth-century socialism. The Fabians were not interested in social philosophy unless it was directly related to feasible reforms. Their main ideals were equality and rational economic planning, and they believed that these could be achieved by democratic pressure within the framework of existing political institutions and their gradual improvement. They accepted that the concentration of capital created the natural economic preconditions of socialism, but they believed that social reform and the gradual limitation of unearned income would make it possible to give this process a socialist sense without the revolutionary destruction of the existing state. It would seem that in the course of time the idea of rational, scientific social organization and economic efficiency came to loom larger in Fabian ideology, at the expense of democratic values. Despite the great importance of the British movement in the history of socialism, it made no significant contribution at this time to the evolution of Marxist doctrine, except of course for the British role in the formation of European revisionism.

The Belgian socialist movement was more Marxist than the British, but less doctrinally consistent than the German. The Parti Ouvrier Belge, formed in 1885, had as its chief theoretician Émile Vandervelde (1866–1938), chairman of the International from 1900 to 1914. He considered himself a Marxist, but felt free to diverge on points of theory that he regarded as doctrinaire: Plekhanov, for one, denied that he was a Marxist at all. But he was not a leader of the type, common in the Second International, that was interested in doctrine only for its direct relation to political and reformist action. On the contrary, he strove after an 'integral' world-view and regretted that socialism, unlike Catholicism, had not evolved one. In *L'Idéalisme dans le marxisme* (1905) he gave an extremely loose interpretation of historical materialism, retaining only the general idea of the 'reciprocal influence' of all historical circumstances—technical, economic, political, and spiritual: a position which almost everyone at that time accepted, but which left no room for Marxian monism. He also argued, following Croce, that the term 'historical materialism' was misleading. No type of historical change was absolutely 'prior' to any other, and in different circumstances different kinds of change might give the initial impetus. Demographic processes or changes of geographical environment might of themselves affect social developments. Nor was it true that spiritual phenomena were simply the consequence of changes of economic structure: they could not exist outside that structure, just as a plant had to have soil in which to grow, but it was absurd to say that the soil was the cause of the plant. Technical development was itself conditioned by man's intellectual activity, which was a spiritual phenomenon. Moral factors, too, played an independent part in historical change: Marx and Engels, in attacking capitalism, had been moved by moral considerations. Historical materialism was a useful device for seeking out the hidden causes of social ideas and institutions, but it was wrong to regard it as providing the sole cause of the entire historical process. Arguing in this way Vandervelde rejected the determinist aspect of the doctrine, while accepting that the general tendency of capitalist economy led towards the socialization of industry. This did not mean that he accepted the theory of 'increasing misery', or of socialism as requiring the transfer of all production to public ownership, or, above all, the inevitability of revolution. On the contrary, all the signs were that socialism would come about gradually, in different ways and not necessarily in the same form everywhere. Socialization was not the same as nationalization: one of its most essential elements was the gradual elimination of political authority centralized in the state. The development of socialism was more likely to be aided by local groupings and forms of self-government which permitted genuine social control over the productive process. Vandervelde was not an outstanding theorist, and his views on theoretical questions are generally cursory and commonsensible. In politics he stood perhaps closest to Jaurès, but he had not the latter's analytical mind or rhetorical gifts.

The Austrian socialist movement was, next to the German, the most active from the theoretical point of view. The social democratic party, formed in 1888, was led for many years by Viktor Adler (1852–1918), a doctor by profession. He was not an original theorist, and on important questions generally took up a position near the centre of German orthodoxy. The great achievement of the Austrian party was the enactment of universal suffrage in 1907, an event helped to a large extent by the Russian Revolution. In the multinational Habsburg monarchy the social democrats had to cope incessantly with conflicts between nationalities, both in the state and in the party, and their ideologists naturally spent much time analysing the national problem from a Marxist point of view. The best-known writings on this subject are by Otto Bauer and Karl Renner. Both were leaders of so-called Austro-Marxism, a movement generally regarded as including also Max Adler, Rudolf Hilferding, Gustav Eckstein, and Adler's son Friedrich. The Austro-Marxists produced important theoretical works which, for the most part, were looked on askance by the orthodox, as they refused to treat Marxism as an all-embracing system and had no hesitation in combining it with other sources: in particular (though they were not alone in this) they sought to incorporate Kantian moral and epistemological categories into the Marxist philosophy of history. Most of them belonged to the generation born in the 1870s, as did Lenin, Trotsky, Rosa Luxemburg, and many other leaders of Russian socialism. Scarcely any of this generation were orthodox Marxists of the stamp of Kautsky, Plekhanov, Lafargue, and Labriola; the polarization which took place as a consequence was to be the ideological cause of the division of socialism into two hostile camps.

In Italy the workers' movement, after some false starts, achieved separate existence in opposition to anarchism in 1882, but it was not until 1893, after two changes of name, that it adopted a socialist programme in the Marxian sense. Its chief leader was Filippo Turati (1857–1932), who was not a theoretician but stood for a decidedly reformist policy, or 'gradualist' as it was then called. The only important Marxist theoreticians at this period of Italian socialism were Antonio Labriola and Enrico Ferri. The former represented the main stream of Marxist orthodoxy, while the latter was even more of a 'Darwinist' than Kautsky.

Poland, too, was an important centre of the Marxist movement. It may in fact be said that it was here that socialism for the first time split up in accordance, more or less, with the principles that subsequently divided social democracy from communism. The Social Democratic Party of the Kingdom of Poland (i.e. Russian Poland) and Lithuania, known from its Polish initials as SDKPiL, was the first independent party of communist type inasmuch as it emphasized the purely proletarian character of the socialist movement, refused to have anything to do with Polish (or any other) nationalism, and professed absolute fidelity to Marxian doctrine. On the other hand, it lacked the features which were to distinguish Lenin's form of social democracy, viz. the idea of the party as vanguard and the use of peasant demands as a weapon in the revolutionary struggle. The party's co-founder and chief theoretician was Rosa Luxemburg, but although of Polish birth she belongs essentially to the German socialist movement. Another theoretician of the SDKPiL was Julian Marchlewski, who studied the history of the physiocrats and also the theory of art. However, the main stream of Polish socialism was represented by the Polish Socialist party (PPS), which as a whole can hardly be considered Marxist; its chief Marxist theoretician was Kazimierz Kelles-Krauz. Ludwik Krzywicki, an unorthodox Marxist and the most eminent sociologist of his generation in Poland, was also close to the PPS. Another writer who belongs in part to Polish Marxist literature is Edward Abramowski, a philosopher and psychologist and a theoretician of the anarcho-cooperative movement. Finally a special place in the history of Marxism belongs to Stanisław Brzozowski, who made a highly original and unorthodox attempt to interpret Marx in terms of voluntarism and collective subjectivism.

The Dutch socialist movement began as a struggle on two fronts, being opposed on the one hand to Catholic trade unions based on the doctrines of Leo XIII's *Rerum Novarum* and, on the other, to a strong anarchist tendency whose chief exponent was Domela Nieuwenhuis. As in Poland, a strong leftist group arose within Dutch social democracy and eventually formed an independent party, the nucleus of the future Communist party. Its chief ideologist, Anton Pannekoek (1873–1960), was an implacable opponent of the 'parliamentary delusion' and the pitfalls of reformism, insisting that socialism required the violent overthrow of the bourgeois state machine and could not be built piecemeal in capitalist conditions. Pannekoek sided with Lenin at the Zimmerwald Conference in 1915, and later belonged to the left-wing, anti-parliamentary section of the Dutch Communist movement.

Although larger or smaller groups of Marxists were active in almost every European country, it is more or less true to say that the Marxist movement was a phenomenon of Central and Eastern Europe. The Second International can be called Marxist only in a very approximate sense, nor was it ever centrally organized and directed like the Comintern. The criteria for membership of the International were not clear-cut, as in some countries there was no clear division between political parties and trade union movements. Nevertheless, its inaugural congress at Paris in July 1889 was attended by the whole élite of European Marxism including Engels, although he had expressed in letters his misgivings at setting up an international organization. Strictly speaking, the conflict between the Guesdists and possibilists meant that the founding congress broke in two from the beginning, a fact which led to general confusion. Yet it was only the Marxist congress that really mattered to the subsequent history of socialism. Among the twenty countries represented were Germany (Bebel, Liebknecht, and others), France (Guesde, Vaillant), Russia (Plekhanov, Lavrov), Austria

(Viktor Adler), Britain (William Morris), Belgium, Poland (Mendelson, Daszyński), and the Netherlands. Resolutions were passed concerning the eight-hour day, the replacement of standing armies by a general militia, the First of May holiday, the fight for social legislation and universal suffrage as a means to the seizure of power. From 1889 to 1900 the International had no real existence except in the form of successive congresses; at the fifth of these a permanent organ was set up, the International Socialist Bureau, but this was only a clearing-house for information, not a directive body. The list of congresses between 1889 and 1914 is: Brussels 1891, Zurich 1893, London 1896, Paris 1900, Amsterdam 1904, Stuttgart 1907, Copenhagen 1910, and Basle 1912.

The crucial issue during the first phase of the International, up to the London Congress, was the controversy with the anarchists. The latter had done much to break up the First International but, partly because of their own ideology, did not set up a lasting independent organization. Accordingly, the anarchist wing of the First International soon ceased to exist. In the early 1880s an anarchist association (the Alliance Internationale Ouvrière) came into existence, numbering among its members Kropotkin, Malatesta, and Élisée Reclus, but it had no precisely agreed doctrine or means of co-ordinated action. The anarchist movement was largely defined in negative terms, there being about as many sub-groups as there were individual writers or political activists. Their main common ground was the belief that human beings left to their own inclinations were capable of forming harmonious communities, but that the root of all evil lay in impersonal institutions and particularly the state. It might seem that the opposition of actual individuals to faceless institutions was in accordance with Marx's social philosophy, but the two cases are not the same. Marx believed that socialism would restore man's individual life in all its fullness and would do away with autonomized political organisms, thus replacing sham forms of community by the direct association of individuals. But he also held that the return to an 'organic' community could not consist in the mere liquidation of existing institutional forms, but required the reorganization of civil society on the basis of the technique and organization of labour created in the capitalist world. The state as an instrument of coercion would become superfluous, but not the centralized administration of material resources and production. In Marx's view the overthrow of the state and political authority did not imply the destruction of social and industrial organization; but he believed that the socialization of property would prevent the organization of society from degenerating into an apparatus of violence and a source of inequality. If the state were destroyed and the processes of production were at the same time handed over to the unco-ordinated initiative of groups or individuals, the result would be bound to be a return to capitalism in all its forms.

This view of Marx's implies the existence of certain natural laws governing a commercial economy independently of the will of individuals. The anarchists, on the other hand, generally believed that the aptitude of human beings for friendly co-operation would prevent all injustice once the institutions of tyranny were swept away. Kropotkin, in his *Ethics* and in *Mutual Aid, a Factor of Evolution*, argued in opposition to the Darwinists that within a given species the law of life is not force and rivalry, but aid and co-operation: from this he drew the comforting conclusion that the natural inclinations of individuals would ensure the harmony of society. Only a few anarchists professed absolute egoism *à la* Stirner: the majority thought there was no basic conflict between individual interests, and that disputes would come to an end when men perceived their own nature and threw off the religious and political mystification and cor-ruption that tyranny imposed upon them. Hence the anarchists often attacked Marxist socialism as a new form of tyranny designed to replace that of the bourgeoisie. The Marxist claimed that their objective was a social organization in which all forms of democracy would not only be preserved but would come into their own for the first time, as legal democracy was reinforced by democratic production; the state, however, as a means of organizing production, exchange, and communication could not be abolished without destroying society. To this the anarchists retorted that a 'democratic state' or a 'state based on freedom' was a contradiction in terms, since any form of state was bound to give rise to privilege, inequality, and violence. In the same way the anarchists were opposed to agitation for reforms such as the eight-hour day, since small concessions of this sort only served to strengthen and perpetuate the organization of oppression.

Political action, too, in the sense of socialist parties engaging in current rivalries, elections, parliamentary contests, etc., was a fraud at the expense of the downtrodden classes. To seek the verdict of the ballot was to endorse the legality of existing political institutions. Thus the anarchists were equally opposed to the political struggle and to the economic struggle for immediate ends. They rested their hopes either on a transformation of the moral consciousness of the oppressed which would cause the breakdown of coercive institutions, or on a violent revolution engineered by a terrorist conspiracy. Their ideal was complete equality and the abolition of all organizational forms beyond the range of immediate democracy, i.e. the complete decentralization of public life. In addition the anarchists, and especially the syndicalists, were mistrustful of middle-class intellectuals in the revolutionary movement, as they suspected them of seeking to dominate the workers. Some anarchist groups professed violent hatred of intellectuals as such, of the whole body of scientific knowledge and art: it was the duty of the working class, they believed, to sever all continuity with culture as it had hitherto existed. This tendency was represented only by a few writers and groups, but it is in accordance with the spirit of a movement which sought to begin human history anew, to go back to the sixth day of creation and restore mankind to a state of paradisal purity.

The anarchists were influential in France, owing in part to Proudhonist tradition. They were stronger still in Spain and Italy, and had active groups in Holland and Belgium; they were least firmly rooted in Germany. At the Zurich and London congresses they were finally excluded from the International, since a rule was adopted confining membership to parties which accepted that political activity was indispensable.

In 1896–1900, between the London and Paris congresses, events took place which brought to light or exacerbated profound differences within the socialist movement: the Dreyfus case, the controversy over Millerand joining the Waldeck-Rousseau government of 1899–1902, and the debate over revisionism in Germany. The agitation over Dreyfus and 'ministerialism' might appear purely tactical, but in fact these issues involved fundamental questions of the class interpretation of the French socialist movement. Those who, headed by Jaurès, demanded that the party commit itself without reserve to the defence of Dreyfus argued that socialism, as the cause of all mankind and of the moral values created throughout history, must take up arms against injustice wherever it appeared, even if the victim was a member of the governing class. Guesde and his followers objected that if the party sprang to the defence of a particular member of the military caste it would blur the distinction between the proletarian party and bourgeois radicalism and, by weakening class-consciousness, would play into the hands of the bourgeoisie. The dispute, although it was not so formulated, can be seen as reflecting two different interpretations of Marxism. Marx himself, especially after his polemic with German 'true socialism', held that although socialism is the affair of all humanity and not just of a single class, the advance towards socialism is the concern of the working class and must therefore be inspired by its class-interests and not by humane moral values in general. This could be interpreted to mean that socialists should not get involved in conflicts that did not affect proletarian interests, especially those between different sections of the bourgeoisie who, by definition, could not be upholders of socialist values. It was possible, following Guesde, to defend the political exclusivism of the working class and treat the possessing classes as essentially a single, uniform, hostile camp. (Some socialists also pointed out that the party would suffer needlessly at the polls if it came out too strongly for Dreyfus, but Guesde rejected this consideration as unworthy.) But strategic and theoretical arguments could also be advanced, from a Marxist point of view, in the opposite direction. Marx did not accept the over-simple and ruinous principle that it was all one to the proletariat what kind of system prevailed until the day of revolution: on the contrary, he and Engels repeatedly distinguished between reaction and democracy, royalists and republicans, clericals and radicals in the political groupings of the propertied classes. As they were well aware, for the working class to look on passively while the bourgeois quarrelled among themselves not only brought the revolution no closer but condemned the workers to impotence. (A basically similar dispute, though more clearly articulated, was that between Russian Marxists on the role and participation of the working class in a bourgeois revolution.)

Jaurès, however, based himself on other grounds which were

more doubtful from the Marxist point of view: viz. that the party must take an active part in all conflicts involving universal moral values because by defending those values it was building socialist reality in the midst of bourgeois society. While the *ouvriérisme* professed by Guesde and his followers was no doubt a false and over-simplified interpretation of Marxism, Jaurès was guilty of unorthodoxy when he represented the party's moral commitment as itself a realization of socialism. In Marx's view the socialist revolution was to be a violent breach of continuity with bourgeois institutions, and could certainly not be realized in whole or in part within bourgeois society. To an orthodox Marxist, then, it would seem that support for Dreyfus might be justified on strategic or tactical grounds but not on moral ones. On the other hand, it was hard to find a text in Marx stating that the revolution meant a breach of moral as well as institutional continuity. If Marx had taken this view, it would have implied that socialists enjoyed complete moral freedom *vis-à-vis* bourgeois society. But had not Engels on this very ground condemned Bakunin for treating all moral precepts as strategic weapons, holding, for instance, that the sanctity of contracts was a bourgeois prejudice? Here again, it was difficult to judge the question unequivocally by appealing to the fathers of scientific socialism.

The problem of Dreyfus was, however, less acute than it might have been inasmuch as none of the socialists found it necessary to pose the question 'For or against?' Moreover, not even Guesde proposed that the party should ignore the *Affaire* completely. The opponents of Dreyfus stood for black reaction, militarism, chauvinism, and anti-Semitism, and there were no two opinions about them in the socialist camp. The Millerand issue was a more delicate one, raising the question whether, and on what conditions, a socialist was justified in joining a bourgeois cabinet—in the present case, a cabinet which included among its members General Galliffet, the bloodthirsty suppressor of the Paris Commune. Those who defended Millerand's action argued that the presence of one socialist in the government could not alter its class character but might help to curb the more reactionary elements and promote reforms within the existing system, a policy which enjoyed the party's basic approval. The opponents of this view replied that the participation of a socialist confused the proletariat by giving the impression that the party was throwing in its lot with those in authority; moreover, it would mean that the party bore some responsibility for the actions of a bourgeois government.

The Millerand question was debated at the Paris Congress of the International in 1900, where Vandervelde, like Jaurès, argued that agreements between socialists and other parties were justifiable in defence of democratic freedoms (the issue of the Italian emergency laws) or the rights of the individual, or for electoral purposes. The Congress adopted a compromise resolution by Kautsky to the effect that socialists might join a non-socialist government in exceptional circumstances provided they remained under party direction and that their action was not treated as a partial transfer of power.

The dispute over revisionism was the most important event in the ideological history of the Second International and calls for a separate discussion. The International was less concerned with the theoretical sources of antagonism between the revisionists and the orthodox than with the question of reformism and the significance of reforms, which from the theoretical point of view reflected more fundamental divergences. The German social democrats passed a resolution against revisionism at their congress in Dresden, and at the Amsterdam Congress Guesde proposed that the International adopt the same resolution. On this occasion Jaurès made his famous speech declaring that the doctrinal rigidity of the German socialists was only a mask for their practical ineffectiveness (the French socialist movement was in fact much smaller, but also much more militant, than the German). The anti-revisionist resolution was adopted by a majority, but the revisionist movement continued to grow. The German party did not expel its revisionists: neither Bebel nor Kautsky wanted a split, and the strength of revisionism lay not in Bernstein's theoretical arguments but in the practical situation of the German working class. Those party activists who supported Bernstein were not interested in his critique of the dialectic, or even in the theory of value or the concentration of capital, but rather expressed that state of mind of the workers' leaders who saw a gulf between the austere revolutionary formulas of the party's programme and its actual policy, and who could no longer ascribe a practical meaning to traditional

Marxist dogmas. In theory, of course, neither the increased importance of parliamentary institutions (which was much greater in Britain, France, or Belgium than in Germany) nor the achievement of labour legislation and other social reforms should have affected the revolutionary outlook of the proletariat. According to the doctrine, everything the working class was able to secure under capitalism, in the way of social reforms or democratic freedoms, should have helped to awaken the revolutionary consciousness, and no orthodox Marxist could admit that this was not so. But the crisis over revisionism emphasized the problem of the social significance of reforms and gave an impetus to the study of the theoretical premises of Marxism in this area. It soon became clear that the dispute affected, directly or indirectly, many of the basic categories of Marxism. The idea of revolution, classes, and the class struggle, the continuity and discontinuity of culture, the state, historical inevitability, historical materialism, and the meaning of socialism itself—all these were called in question. Once the debate on revisionism was engaged, orthodox Marxism was no longer the same as before. Some of its adherents held by the old positions, but new forms of orthodoxy gradually supplanted the 'classic' Marxism of Kautsky, Bebel, and Labriola.

The last years of the Second International were overshadowed by the approach of war. The threat of a European conflict and the problem of socialist policy were discussed many times, especially at the Stuttgart Congress in 1907. The question was closely bound up with that of nationalities and self-determination. Some general principles were accepted by all socialists. All but a group of the German social democrats were opposed 'in principle' to militarism and colonialism, and all opposed national oppression. But this did not suffice to determine a common attitude towards war or particular international conflicts. The International had condemned militarism in general terms at Brussels in 1891, and at London in 1896 it adopted a resolution for the replacement of standing armies by peoples' militias. But as the respective socialist parties were organized on national lines and were obliged in the event of war to take up a position in view of the policy of their own governments, such resolutions had no tangible consequences for any of them. As regards the discussions of war and peace, the following general points may be singled out.

Guesde, faithful as ever to his dogmatic Marxism, was un-
enthusiastic about any special anti-war campaign: wars were
inevitable under capitalism, and the way to stop them was to
abolish it. This was in effect a repetition on the international
plane of Guesde's position in regard to the Dreyfus case.
Socialists should not interfere in disputes among the possessing
classes; imperialist war is an instance of such a dispute, and is not
the proletariat's concern. This was also the view of some German
social democrats, but it meant abandoning all hope of exerting
a socialist influence on events. If war broke out, a large part
of the proletariat was bound to be mobilized and take part in the
general slaughter, and if the socialists stood aside in the name
of doctrinal purity they would in practice be endorsing the
actions of governments. Several leaders accordingly urged that
the International should adopt a definite policy of preventing
war. Jaurès and Vaillant were for active resistance, including
rebellion if necessary; but they also held that if a country was
attacked it had a right to defend itself and it was the duty of
socialists to take part in the defence. At Stuttgart in 1907
Gustave Hervé proposed a resolution calling for a general strike
and mutiny in the event of war; but the Germans opposed this,
chiefly for fear that their party might be outlawed. Even the call
to strike and rebel was within the bounds of a 'reformist' policy;
the left wing, represented by Lenin, Rosa Luxemburg and
Karl Liebknecht, put forward more radical proposals. In their
view the business of socialists, should a war break out, was not
to attempt to stop it, whether by means of strikes or invoking
international law, but to use it to overthrow the capitalist system.
The resolution adopted at Stuttgart spoke in general terms of
acting to stop a war or using it to hasten the downfall of
capitalism, but these were purely ideological statements and
comprised no specific plan. The idea of taking advantage of the
imperialist conflict could be interpreted, as it afterwards was by
Lenin, in the sense of turning it into a civil war, but the great
majority of socialist leaders were not thinking on these lines. At
the Basle Congress in 1912, although the First Balkan War had
broken out, the mood was one of concord and optimism. A
further anti-war resolution was passed, the slogan 'war on war'
was vociferated, and the delegates dispersed in the conviction
that the socialist movement was strong enough to prevent the

carnage plotted by imperialist governments.

The International was also divided, though along different lines, on the question of national self-determination. National oppression was of course condemned by all, but neither this nor Marxist theory provided a solution to the complicated ethnic problems of Central and Eastern Europe. In general it was accepted that while national oppression and chauvinism were contrary to socialist ideas, the former was only a 'function' of social oppression and would vanish along with it; the nation-state was likewise associated with the development of capitalism, and there was no reason for Marxists to regard it as a guiding principle. The Austrian Marxists put forward the idea of cultural autonomy within a multinational state: there was no need for the state to be organized on a national basis, but every ethnic community was entitled to maintain its cultural traditions and language without interference. Rosa Luxemburg violently attacked the principle of self-determination on the ground that socialism would do away with national quarrels in due course: while the fight for socialism was going on, to raise the national question as a separate problem would distract the proletariat from its proper objective and assist the bourgeois policy of national unity. Lenin and the left wing of the Russian social democrats upheld the right of every nation to form a state of its own. Rosa Luxemburg's dogmatism on this issue was similar to the rigid attitude of Guesde towards other disputes: as all important historical processes were determined by the class struggle there was no such thing as a separate national problem, and in any case it was not a proper object of attention for the working-class movement. As for Lenin, he did not advocate the idea of the nation-state for its own sake, but regarded national tension and oppression as a powerful source of strength that could be exploited in the interest of the social struggle.

The collapse of the International in the face of the 1914 war was the more unexpected and depressing as the socialists had built such high hopes on the strength of their movement. The left wing did not expect it either: Lenin at first refused to believe that the German social democrats had obeyed the fatherland's call to arms. In every country of Europe the great majority had instinctively adopted a patriotic attitude. Even among the Bolshevik *émigrés* in the West, a large number did so without hesitation. Plekhanov, the father of Russian Marxism, had no doubt that Russia must be defended against invasion, and almost all the Mensheviks thought likewise. At the beginning of August the large social democratic party in the Reichstag voted for war credits: a minority which had been outvoted at a previous party meeting conformed to the majority line. At the next Reichstag vote in December, Karl Liebknecht alone broke the ranks of party solidarity. During the next two years the number of active dissidents rose to the point at which there was a split: the opponents of war were expelled and, in April 1917, formed the Independent German Socialist party (USPD), which drew its members from all parts of the German Socialist party (SPD). The war brought about new political divisions: the USPD included orthodox centrists like Kautsky and Hugo Haase (chairman of the SPD since Bebel's death in 1913), revisionists like Bernstein, and the left wing, which had formed itself into the Spartacus League at the beginning of 1916 and now joined the USPD in a body. In France the anti-patriotic opposition was if anything even weaker than in Germany. Jaurès, who might have hesitated, was murdered on the eve of the war. Guesde and Sembat joined the war government, as did Vandervelde in Belgium. Hervé, the most radical of French anti-war agitators, changed almost overnight into an ardent patriot. The International was in ruins.

In the summer of 1914 the socialist movement suffered the greatest defeat in its history, when it became clear that the international solidarity of the proletariat—its ideological foundation—was an empty phrase and could not stand the test of events. Both on the side of the Entente and on that of the Central Powers attempts were made to justify the upsurge of patriotism on Marxist grounds. Marx had often denounced Russia as a bulwark of barbarism and reaction, and a war against her could well be represented as defending European democracy against Tsarist despotism. On the other hand, Prussian militarism and feudal survivals in the German lands had traditionally been the object of socialist attack from Marx onwards, and it was easy to present France's struggle as that of republicanism against reactionary monarchy.

Lenin and the later Zimmerwald Left attributed the collapse of the International to treachery and opportunism on the part of the social democratic leaders. None of the Marxists posed the question whether the débâcle of the socialist movement in the face of national conflicts was of any significance for Marxist doctrine itself.

The summer of 1914 saw the beginning of a process whose consequences are still with us and whose final outcome cannot be foreseen. Two fundamentally different interpretations of social-ism, which for years had made themselves felt in a variety of questions, had suddenly collided with such force as to destroy the International. Marxists at the time did not clearly examine or decide the question whether, and in what sense, socialism is a continuation of human history and in what sense it represents a breach with all that has gone before; or, to put it another way, how far and in what sense the proletariat is part of bourgeois society. Different answers to these questions were implicit in the philosophical conflicts within the socialist movement, and Marx's doctrine was by no means unambiguous on the point. In some important respects it supported the view of revolu-tionaries who refused to have any dealings with existing society or to attempt to reform it, but who counted on a great historical apocalypse that would sweep away oppression, exploitation, and injustice and begin history anew on the ruins of capitalism. On the other hand, Marx did not envisage socialism as something built in the void, and he believed in the continuity of civilization, both technical and cultural. He thus provided support to those who regarded socialism as the gradual increase of justice, equality, freedom, and community of ownership within the present system. The workers' movement, organized into parties adhering more or less strictly to Marxist ideology, had obtained real successes in the fight for labour legislation and civil rights: this seemed to show that existing society was reformable, whatever the doctrine might say, and thus to knock the bottom out of revolutionary programmes. The idea of socialism as a radical break was more natural in countries such as Russia, the Balkans, and Latin America, where there was little or no prospect of improving conditions by gradual pressure for reform. In Western Europe it was hard to argue that the proletariat was a pariah class with no place in society or the national community and no expectation of better conditions under the present system. Marxism had in fact helped on its own dissolution as an ideological force by contributing to a workers' movement that had achieved successes under capitalism and so refuted the view that the latter was incapable of reform.

This is of course a simplified schema, and does not take account of the intricate changes that took place in the socialist movement after the collapse of the Second International. It gives an idea, however, of the subsequent polarization leading to a state of affairs that still exists: on the one hand, reformist socialism bearing only a tenuous relation to Marxism, and, on the other hand, the monopolization of Marxism by Leninism and its derivatives. The latter, despite the traditional doctrine, displays its main strength in parts of the world that are backward from the technological, democratic, and cultural points of view— countries that are only on the threshold of industrialism and where the main pressure comes from non-proletarian claims, especially those of the peasants and subject nationalities. This polarization appears to have shown that the classic version of Marxism which held the field up to the First World War is untenable as a practical ideological force. From this point of view the present situation is, in spite of all changes, essentially the outcome of the drama that took place in the summer of 1914.

CHAPTER II

German Orthodoxy: Karl Kautsky

THE figure of Karl Kautsky dominates the theoretical development of Marxism for the whole period of the Second International. While certainly not an outstanding philosopher, he was the chief architect and, so to speak, the embodiment of Marxist orthodoxy. He defended it against all extraneous influences popularized it skilfully and intelligently, and applied it successfully to the interpretation of past history and to new phenomena connected with the evolution of capitalist imperialism. He played the main part in creating a stereotype of Marxism which, especially in Central and Eastern Europe, held the field for decades and has only begun to give ground to other stereotypes in the last ten or fifteen years. Generations of Marxists were brought up on his books, which became classics of Marxist literature and—doubtless a unique case—remained so even after Lenin had denounced their author as a renegade for attacking the October Revolution. Kautsky was not orthodox in the sense of feeling obliged to defend every particular thought expressed by Marx or Engels, or of treating quotations from their works as arguments in themselves; indeed, no theoreticians of his generation were orthodox in this sense. In some matters, not of the first importance but not wholly trivial either, he criticized Engels's views, for example by maintaining that the state most frequently comes into existence as the result of external violence. But he was pedantically orthodox in the sense that Marxism as a theory and a method of historical investigation was the only system that he regarded as valid for the analysis of social phenomena, and he opposed all attempts to enrich or supplement Marxist theory by elements from any other source, except Darwinism. Thus, while not a strict dogmatist in respect of all Marx's or Engels's ideas, he was a rigorous defender of doctrinal purity. It was thanks to his interpretative work that the stereotype known as scientific socialism—the evolutionist, determinist, and scientistic form of Marxism—became universally accepted in its main lines.

1. Life and writings

Karl Kautsky (1854–1938) was born in Prague of a Czech father and a German mother. As a youth in Vienna he became acquainted with socialist ideas by reading the novels of George Sand and the historical works of Louis Blanc. He entered the University in 1874, and joined the social democratic party in the following year. He studied history, economics, and philosophy and was attracted by Darwinism as an explanation of the general principles governing human affairs. His first book, *Der Einfluss der Volksvermehrung auf den Fortschritt der Gesellschaft* (*The Influence of Human Increase on Social Progress*, 1880), was a critique of the Malthusian view that poverty is the result of overpopulation.

While still a student Kautsky wrote for the socialist Press in Vienna and Germany and met Liebknecht and Bebel. In 1880 he moved to Zurich, where he became a friend of Bernstein and worked for the German-language periodicals *Sozialdemokrat* and *Jahrbuch der Sozialwissenschaft und Sozialpolitik*. In 1881 he spent some months in London, where he met Marx and Engels. In the following year he returned to Vienna, and at the beginning of 1883 founded the monthly (later weekly) *Die Neue Zeit*, which he edited until 1917 and which was, throughout this period, the chief Marxist journal in Europe and therefore in the world. No other periodical did so much to popularize Marxism as the ideological form of the workers' movement in Germany and the rest of Europe. Many articles by socialist theoreticians that appeared in *Die Neue Zeit* later became part of the Marxist canon. The journal was first published at Stuttgart, but was subsequently transferred to London owing to the anti-socialist laws. After the laws were repealed Kautsky returned to Stuttgart at the end of 1890, and moved to Berlin seven years later.

The Erfurt Programme adopted at the German social democratic congress in October 1891—the first party programme based strictly on Marxist premises—was the work of Kautsky and Bernstein, the former being responsible for the theoretical section. Kautsky attended every congress of the German party and of the International, defending his conception of orthodoxy against the anarchists, Bernstein, the revisionists, and the left wing. In matters of political strategy he was the chief exponent of what was then usually called the centre point of view, opposing the reformist idea that socialism could be introduced into capitalist society by way of gradual reforms and co-operation between the proletariat, the peasantry, and the petty bourgeoisie; at the same time he opposed the revolutionary theory that the party's proper task was to prepare for a single violent upheaval at a moment dictated by political circumstances. In the same way, when the war came and the International fell apart Kautsky took up a middle position between the nationalism of the German party as a whole and the revolutionary defeatism of the left wing. His sharp criticism of the October Revolution in Russia caused him to be branded as a traitor by Lenin and his followers. In the 1920s he returned to politics and took a prominent part in drafting the programme adopted by the German social democratic party at Heidelberg in 1925. He lived in Vienna until shortly before the Anschluss, and died at Amsterdam.

Kautsky's writings cover all the important problems that confronted Marxism and the socialist movement in his time. Amid his huge output of books and articles those on history and economics achieved the most permanent reputation. In 1887 he published *Karl Marx's ökonomische Lehren* (*The Economic Doctrines of Karl Marx*)—in effect a summary of Volume I of *Capital*, which served for some decades as a handbook of Marxist economic theory for beginners. Four historical works, applying the Marxist method of class analysis to the study of ideology and political conflict, are perhaps the most important part of his theoretical activity: these are *Thomas More und seine Utopie* (*Thomas More and his Utopia*, 1888; English translation 1927); *Die Klassengegensätze von 1789* (*The Class Antagonisms of 1789*, 1889); *Die Vorläufer des neueren Sozialismus* (*The Forerunners of Modern Socialism*, two volumes, 1895); and *Der Ursprung des Christentums* (*The Foundations of Christianity*, 1908). The first of these works analysed the state of England under Henry VIII and the life and best-known work of Thomas More in terms of the class conflicts of the age of primitive accumulation. The third work is a historical review of socialist ideas from Plato's *Republic* to the French Revolution, with particular attention to revolutionary anabaptism; while the fourth is concerned with the historical significance of early Christian ideas.

Kautsky's most important work of general theory published before 1914 is *Ethik und materialistische Geschichtsauffassung* (*Ethics and the Materialist Interpretation of History*, 1906), which contains a history of ethical doctrines and an exposition of Darwinist and Marxist views on the biological and social significance of moral ideas and behaviour. Works dealing directly with political theory and the strategy of social democracy are his extensive commentary on the Erfurt Programme (*Das Erfurter Programme in seinem grundsätzlichen Teil erläutert*, 1892); and polemics against Bernstein and the Left on the reformist-revolutionary dilemma (*Bernstein und das sozialdemokratische Programm*, 1899; *Die soziale Revolution*, 1907, translated 1909; *Der politische Massenstreik*, 1914; *Der Weg zur Macht*, 1909). His criticism of the Russian Revolution can be found in *Die Diktatur des Proletariats* (1918, translated 1918, 1964); *Terrorismus und Kommunismus* (1919); and *Von der Demokratie zur Staatssklaverei* (1921). In 1927 he summed up his theoretical ideas in *Die materialistische Geschichtsauffassung* (*The Materialist Interpretation of History*). This vast work had far less influence than his earlier treatises, on account of its size and because its popularity suffered from the ban pronounced on Kautsky by the highest authority in the Communist world. Moreover, the social democrats, having broken with the Communists, were less interested in the philosophical foundation of socialist ideas and their own links with the Marxist tradition. Marxist doctrine had been almost monopolized by the Leninist and Stalinist brand of socialism, in which there was no longer room for Kautsky's later ideas. In consequence, the most impressive exposition of historical materialism ever written had virtually no audience and no effect on those it was meant for.

2. Nature and society

Kautsky's views changed remarkably little in the course of his career. In his youth he had embraced Darwinism and a naturalistic view of the world; he soon discovered historical materialism, and wove the two elements into an integral whole which satisfied him for the rest of his life. Having written his commentary on the Erfurt Programme in 1892 he could still reaffirm its validity not only in 1904 but also in the preface to the seventeenth edition in 1922, after the European war, the Russian Revolution, and the disintegration of international socialism. His last, monumental work contains scarcely anything by way of modification or correction of the views he expressed in the preceding fifty years. This early rigidification and satisfaction with his own conclusions made him insensitive to new political and philosophical ideas. However, he preserved the spirit of inquiry and intellectual honesty, which enabled him to remain clearsighted in polemics: he eschewed demagogy and the replacement of logic by insult, and marshalled his vast knowledge of history into convincing arguments. His writing is marked by pedantry and a hankering after systematization: when he sets out to explain the Marxist view of ethics he begins by attempting (with very poor success) to give a compressed history of ethical doctrines and the whole history of manners and customs. Denouncing the terrorism of the Russian Revolution, he traces the history of France's Revolution of 1789 and the Paris Commune. He always goes back to first beginnings, is imbued with didactic purpose, and attaches great importance, as did Lenin, to the correct formulation of the theoretical basis of the socialist movement.

A striking feature of Kautsky's work is the complete lack of understanding of philosophical problems. His remarks on purely philosophical subjects do not go beyond what may be read in the summary essays of Engels: from his comments on Kant it is clear that he had no idea of the true meaning of the latter's philosophy. The key problems of metaphysics and epistemology, including the epistemological basis of ethics, are unknown to him. The strongest aspects of his intellect are seen in his analysis of past events and social conflicts in the light of Marxist theory.

The peculiar nature of Kautsky's thought is best seen by comparing him with a writer like Jaurès. To Jaurès, socialism, and Marxism as the modern theoretical expression of socialism, was above all a moral notion, a value-concept, the highest expression of man's eternal longing for freedom and justice. To Kautsky, Marxism was primarily the scientific, deterministic, integral apprehension of social phenomena. Kautsky was fascinated by Marxism as a coherent theoretical system by which the whole of history could be comprehended and its events reduced to a single schema: he was a typical child of the scientist era in which he grew up, inspired by Darwin and Herbert Spencer and the advance of physics and chemistry. He believed in the unlimited capacity of science to synthesize knowledge into a more and more extensive yet concentrated system of facts and explanations. The scientistic and positivistic version of Marxism developed in Engels's later writings was adopted by Kautsky without modification; his world-view was dominated by scientific rigour devoid of sentiment and value-judgements, a belief in the unity of scientific method, the strictly causal and 'objective' interpretation of social phenomena, the world of men considered as an extension of organic nature. Thinking in this way, he naturally regarded the Hegelian origins of Marxism as a historical accident of small importance; like Engels, he saw no more in Hegel's contribution to the Marxist tradition than a few banal reflections on the interdependence of all phenomena, the development and variability of the universe, etc.

Thus the foundation of the scientific world-view was, in Kautsky's eyes, strict determinism and a belief in unchanging universal laws. Even more strongly than Engels he emphasized the 'natural necessity' (*Naturnotwendigkeit*) of all social processes. He was not a 'social Darwinist' in the sense of denying the specific character of human society or reducing social conflicts and class struggles to a mere Darwinian fight for survival. But his reservations concerning the reduction of human society to the level of animal communities are of far less importance than the analogy that he sees between them. All specifically human characteristics, i.e. those that appear throughout history, are shared by mankind with other animals: this is a frequent motif in Kautsky's works, from the *Ethics* to *The Materialist Interpretation of History*. Kautsky adopted without reserve Darwin's view of evolution as a process resulting from chance mutations that permit the survival of the individual best adapted to its environment. Nature has no purpose in the sense either of a conscious force governing evolution or of a definite over-all tendency. Organisms that undergo favourable mutations transmit their power of adaptation to their descendants, and this process accounts for the whole course of evolution. All typically human functions can be found in the animal world: intelligence, sociability, social instincts, and moral feelings. Intelligence is a weapon in the struggle for existence, and the cognitive faculty has no other purpose than to ensure the preservation of the species. Animals show a knowledge of natural laws and the relations of cause and effect, and human knowledge is a development and systematization of this.

Kautsky does not ask himself how it is that a purely biological ability to associate events and to express this association in terms of 'natural laws', articulated in the form of language, can claim the status of a discovery of the truth about the universe, or how the idea of knowledge as truth can be derived from its role as an instrument of adaptation. Two basic instincts, those of self-preservation and the preservation of the species, are a sufficient explanation of the whole range of animal and human behaviour, both moral and cognitive. The instinct for co-operation within the species is what, in the human race, we call the moral law or the voice of conscience. Among human beings as among animals, it is often in conflict with the instinct of self-preservation. It is therefore not the case that man is 'naturally' egoistic or altruistic, since both tendencies, though they may conflict in particular cases, coexist in him as in all the higher animals. The division of labour and the use of tools are observable among beasts in embryonic forms, as is production in the sense of transforming the environment to suit one's purposes. In short, human beings are in no way different from animals as cognitive, moral agents and producers. There is nothing in specifically human nature that cannot be found also in the non-human universe. The specific powers achieved by man, or rather specific developments of animal powers, can be explained by adaptation and the interaction of the organism with its environment. These powers —namely language and the invention of tools—have fostered each other's development, making possible the accumulation of thought, experience, and ability; but they are no more than the prolongation of animal faculties. The whole progress of civilization can be explained by the working of the same laws of adaptation. When primitive man emerged from the jungle into open country he had to make clothing, build houses, discover fire and the art of cultivation. Language was a strengthener of social ties and co-operation within the tribe, but it led to differences of speech and social groups and hence to the peculiarly human institution of wars within a single species.

The division of labour, a continuation of the process begun in animal communities, made it possible to produce in excess of essential needs: this led men to fight for control of such surpluses, and also to the formation of class divisions based on the possession of means of production. Technical developments determined the changing forms of such divisions, but these were also determined in part by other factors, especially the natural environment. Class divisions take one form where centralized irrigation works are required, for example in the Nile delta, another where the chief problem is to ward off the attacks of neighbouring tribes; they will be different among mountaineers and in coastal settlements. In all cases, however, the principle of adaptation to the environment determines specific forms of human behaviour, governed by the unvarying instincts of self-preservation and co-operation.

The delusion that there are eternal and absolute values that humanity finds ready-made or, at any rate, preserved throughout history arises from the fact that for thousands of years social progress was extremely slow, so that particular commands and prohibitions remained unchanged until they came to be regarded as valid for all time and in all circumstances. In reality the only immutable factors of this sort are general biological instincts, whereas specifically human moral norms and values are all dependent on modes of production. It is true that in the struggle carried on by the oppressed classes throughout history certain uniform circumstances can be discerned, and hence a similarity in the values created by those classes. But this similarity is more apparent than real. In primitive Christianity, equality meant an equal distribution of goods, while freedom meant idleness; in the French Revolution, equality meant an equal right to property and freedom meant the free use of one's possessions. Under socialism, however, equality means an equal right to use the products of social labour, while freedom is the reduction of necessary labour, i.e. the gradual shortening of the working day.

It can happen, indeed, that opinions or values outlive the conditions from which and in which they arise, and in which case they act as a clog on social progress. As a rule, however, human behaviour in society is not determined by ideals but by the material exigencies of life. A moral ideal 'is not an aim, but a weapon in the social struggle'. In general no ideals can be ascertained by scientific observation, which is by definition morally neutral and concerned only with necessary connections in nature and human history. Scientific socialism demonstrates the in-evitability of a classless society as a result of economic laws, but it cannot erect this into a moral purpose. This fact, however, does not detract from the greatness and sublimity of the vision of a socialist world for which the working class is fighting, impelled by irresistible economic necessity.

Kautsky appears to have failed to understand the epis-temological problem of moral values or the fact that, when a historical process has been presented as inevitable, the question of its value remains open. Hence his criticism of Kant and of ethical socialism is beside the point. As Cohen, Vorländer, and Bauer pointed out, from the fact that something is necessary it does not follow that it is desirable or valuable. We need a special cognitive faculty to tell us that socialism is not only historically necessary but also a good thing; Marx having demonstrated the former proposition, Kantian ethics might show us a way to believe the latter. Kautsky replied, however, that values are outside the province of science. He agreed with the neo-Kantians that Marxism proved the historical necessity of socialism, and this, in his view, was all that required to be shown. The working class was bound to develop a consciousness that would regard socialism as an ideal, but this attitude of mind was itself no more than the consequence of a social process. The question why a person should regard as desirable what he believes to be inevit-able is ignored by Kautsky, who gives no reason for not answer-ing it. He maintained that Kant's categorical imperative rested on a delusion, in the first place, because it purported to be in-dependent of experience, whereas it presupposed the existence of other people, which could only be known empirically to the philosopher. (In actual fact the categorical imperative is in-dependent of experience in the sense that it cannot be logically derived from empirical data, but not in the sense that it can be effectively formulated without any empirical knowledge.) Secondly, Kautsky declares, the categorical imperative is un-workable in a society torn by antagonisms and conflicting loyalties. In fact, however, it is presented by Kant as a formal norm constituting the necessary condition of any concrete rule, and not an empirical assertion excluding moral conflicts or pre-supposing the existence of a harmonious society; nor does it purport to be a sufficient basis for the construction of a moral

code. The extent of Kautsky's failure to understand Kant is
shown by a remark in his *Ethics* to the effect that the Kantian
precept of treating every individual as an end and not as a means
is realized among animals, with the proviso that the community
protects only those individuals whose survival is advantageous
to the species. Kautsky does not notice that this proviso is contrary to the whole principle of the intrinsic value of the individual, who is treated, in this case, not as an end in himself but as
a means to the preservation of the species.

3. Consciousness and the development of society

The principle of strict determinism, and the belief that human
history is a continuation of natural history and can be explained
by the same laws, led Kautsky to a purely naturalistic interpretation of human consciousness. Kautsky does not regard consciousness as an 'epiphenomenon' (as critics of Marxism frequently
assert), i.e. as a phenomenon that is not part of 'objective' history
but appertains only to the perception, true or false, of historical
events. On the contrary, he regards it as an essential link in
the chain of necessary processes; but, he says, there is no such
thing as a human consciousness differing from that of animals.
Human consciousness consists of intelligence, knowledge, and
moral sensibility, all of which evolved at the pre-human stage as
organs of adaptation. It is therefore wrong to say that conscious
processes are an inessential 'extra' without which human history
would be exactly the same as it is now. But this is also true of pre-
human history, which in the case of higher animals involves
conscious processes enabling them to survive in a hostile environment. From this point of view, he declares, the human species,
despite its faculties of language and tool-making, is no different
from other intelligent beings. In particular—and here Kautsky
seems to be mistaken in imagining that he is faithful to Marx's
ideas—the necessity of the downfall of capitalism and the
transition to socialism is no different from the necessity whereby
technological progress has in the past brought socio-economic
systems into existence. Of course Marx's idea that socialism will
be consciously brought about by the organized working class,
when it has acquired knowledge of social processes, remains in
force. But neither Kautsky nor his neo-Kantian adversaries

realized the true sense of Marx's attempt to transcend the opposition between necessity and freedom, between description and prescription. Neither the Kantians nor the determinists assimilated the Marxian eschatology involving the identification of the subject and the object of history—the idea of man's return to his 'species-nature', and the theory of alienation which is inseparable from it.

Marx, as we have seen, did not regard socialism merely as a new system that would do away with inequality, exploitation, and social antagonism. In his view it was the recovery by man of his lost humanity, the reconciliation of his species-essence with his empirical existence, the restoration to man's being of his 'alienated' nature. History up to the present time involved the participation of human beings and their conscious intentions, but was subjected to its own laws, which were valid whether or not they were consciously apprehended (as in fact they could not be, at all events not completely). But in the consciousness of the working class we have not merely to do with the increased knowledge of social processes, which, like any other knowledge, can be used to transform society in the same way as it transforms technology. The consciousness of the working class actually *is* the process of the revolutionary transformation of society: it is not a reservoir of information, first acquired and then put into practical use, but is the self-knowledge of the new society, in which the historical process coincides with awareness of that process. Socialism is necessary in the sense that capitalism, like all previous systems, is fated to lose control over the technological conditions it has itself created; but the necessity of socialism realizes itself as the free, conscious activity of the working class. Since the consciousness of the proletariat is the self-awareness of humanity recovering its lost nature (a nature that really exists, not a normative ideal), this consciousness cannot be divided into a descriptive or informational aspect and a normative or imperative one. The act by which men become aware of their own being, or return to their own essence, is a self-affirmation of humanity and, as such, cannot be reduced to awareness of the natural inevitability of the historical process, or to a normative ideal, or to a combination of these two. Marx's specifically Hegelian belief in 'essence' as something more real than empirical reality, and not simply an imagined ideal, was ignored in the argument between the determinists and the Kantists. The latter's position was that Marx had shown that socialism was an objective necessity, and they held that awareness of this fact must be supplemented by the socialist norm of value. Kautsky contended that Marx had shown socialism to be an objective necessity, and that one factor in this necessary process was the proletariat's awareness and approval of that necessity: this awareness and approval were inevitable, and nothing more was required. Marx's real view, however, was that the consciousness of the proletariat, being the consciousness of humanity returning to its own essence, was identical with that return as an objective process: in the revolutionary activity of the proletariat, the opposition between necessity and freedom ceased to exist.

To put it another way: Kautsky, following Engels, took a naturalistic and positivistic view of consciousness as knowledge which, being itself the result of the necessary development of society, was part of that development inasmuch as it provided the indispensable basis for effective social technology. Knowledge of society, and the practical application of that knowledge, were distinguished from each other in the same way as in any technology. Hence the specific meaning of the term 'scientific socialism': socialism was a theory that could only be the result of scientific observation and not of the spontaneous evolution of the proletariat. Socialist theory was bound to be the creation of scholars, not of the working class, and must be introduced from outside into the workers' movement as a weapon in the struggle for liberation. This theory, later adopted by Lenin, of socialist consciousness implanted in the spontaneous working-class movement from outside is a direct consequence of the naturalistic interpretation of consciousness and the Darwinist interpretation of social processes in general. It also became a political instrument by supplying a theoretical basis for the new idea of a proletarian party directed by intellectuals versed in theory—a party expressing the authentic, scientific consciousness of the proletariat, which the working class was unable to evolve for itself. Kautsky drew different consequences from the theory of 'scientific socialism' than did Lenin; but in his case, too, the view that the proletarian class-consciousness can only take shape outside the proletariat, in the minds of the intelligentsia, was a reflection and theoretical justification of a socialist party transforming itself into a party of professional politicians and manipulators.

4. Revolution and socialism

Belief in historical necessity, and in particular the 'objective' necessity of socialist society, was to Kautsky the corner-stone of Marxism and the essential difference between scientific and utopian socialism. (In fact, however, the opinion that socialism is objectively inevitable is not exclusively Marxist: it can be found in the works of some utopians, for example the Saint-Simonists.) Kautsky was especially careful to remain faithful to Marx's doctrine on this point, and he never ceased to emphasize that political fantasy is no substitute for economic necessity: socialism can only proceed from the economic maturity of capitalism and the resulting polarization of classes. Kautsky's political attitude was essentially determined by this principle of 'maturity', which indeed was accepted by all theoreticians of the Second International except the Leninist wing: it appeared to follow as a matter of course from the anti-utopian and anti-Blanquist elements in Marx's teaching.

Both in his criticism of utopian socialism and of revisionism Kautsky emphasized the difference between the class division of society and its division according to criteria of consumption, i.e. participation in the national income; in this he was fully in accord with Marx. The proletariat's struggle is not the result of poverty but of class antagonism, and the condition of socialist victory is not the absolute impoverishment of the working class but the sharpening of class antagonism, which is not the same thing. At various points in his historical analyses Kautsky shows that the class struggle may become more acute in cases where the exploited workers' lot is improving, so that its intensity is not a function of poverty. On this ground he rejects all revisionist arguments showing that the workers were relatively better off and predicting that class antagonism would therefore diminish. The theory of the absolute pauperization of the working class was thus, in Kautsky's view, not an essential part of Marxist doctrine, such that the latter would have to be abandoned if the theory proved to be untrue. What was essential, however, was the view that class polarization would increase and that the middle class would be squeezed out by the concentration of capital. Kautsky was uncompromising on this point, and strove to refute Bernstein's contention that in spite of the concentration process the middle class, and especially the small owners, were not becoming less numerous. In his polemics with the revisionists and in his exposition of the theoretical portion of the Erfurt Programme Kautsky argued that the development of bourgeois society was bound to eliminate small enterprises; when told that statistics did not confirm this, he replied that the new owners were not petty bourgeois but men thrown out of work by the concentration of capital, who strove to keep afloat by establishing small workshops and co-operatives. He admitted that in agriculture the disappearance of small holdings was not proceeding so fast as had been predicted, but here too he thought it was bound to come about in time.

Kautsky held that the collapse of capitalism would not be a result of the fall in the profit rate, which was compatible with a rise in the absolute level of profits. Capitalism would break down because private ownership of the means of production did not permit the efficient use and development of the techniques that humanity had evolved. Capitalism could not avoid anarchy, recurrent crises of overproduction, and mass unemployment; moreover, it was bound to develop the consciousness of the working class, which was organizing itself not only to obtain short-term improvements but to seize political power and establish public ownership of the means of production for the good of society.

On the two basic question of the relation between the political and the economic struggle, and that between fighting for reforms and awaiting the revolution, Kautsky's position was that of orthodox Marxism. As to the first question, he opposed the Marxist viewpoint to the equally false extremes of Proudhonism on the one hand and Blanquism on the other. The Proudhonists were not interested in the political struggle, for they held that the conquest of political power by the proletariat would not do away with exploitation: as long as there was capitalism the proletariat would gain nothing by democracy, as political democracy would not bring economic liberation. The workers must therefore have nothing to do with political and parliamentary issues, but concentrate on freeing themselves by organizing production independently of capitalism. The Blanquists, on the other hand, were interested only in the conquest of political power, irrespective of economic conditions. Marx, as Kautsky explains, avoided both these one-sided views and adopted the only position consonant with the scientific method, viz. that the proletariat's assumption of political power is the necessary condition and means of economic liberation, but this power can only be used to overthrow capitalism when the latter is ripe for destruction. If the moment is premature from the economic point of view the seizure of power cannot lead to the overthrow of capitalism, for objective economic laws cannot be overruled by decrees or violence. An example of this is the Jacobin dictatorship, which Kautsky regarded as a dictatorship of the proletariat. The Terror was supposed to smash profiteering and keep up the revolutionary enthusiasm of the masses, but it only brought fear and disillusionment. When the Thermidor reaction came, the Jacobins had no support and the revolution returned to the base established for it by economic conditions, i.e. the rule of the bourgeoisie. The Paris Commune was bound to collapse for the same reason.

Kautsky, however, was unable, or did not try, to explain precisely how the ripeness of capitalism for political revolution was to be recognized. He maintained against the reformists that socialism could not simply develop as a natural continuation of capitalism, by partial reforms and concessions on the part of the possessing classes. A revolution, in the sense of a conscious seizure of political power by the organized proletariat, was an essential and inevitable precondition of socialism. But social democrats must not tie their hands by any precise definition of the character and duration of the revolutionary process. In particular it need not signify a once-and-for-all act of violence, an armed rebellion or a bloody civil war. On the contrary, the more the proletariat was capable of organized action, aware of historical processes and trained in the working of democratic institutions, the more likely it was that the revolution would take a non-violent form. The precise situation, however, was hard to predict. As for the social democratic party, since it could not itself create the economic conditions that made revolution possible, it was, in Kautsky's words, a revolutionary party but not a party that was making or preparing a revolution. For a revolution could not simply be made at will or from purely political ingredients. The social democrats rightly rejected the absurd doctrine of 'The worse, the better': the struggle for social and political reforms under capitalism was in the highest interest of the proletariat and of its eventual victory, developing its class-consciousness and enabling it to gain experience of economic administration and political life. Reforms were not a substitute for revolution, but they were a necessary preparation for it. It was contrary to Marxist strategy either to set a course towards catastrophe or to rely on co-operation between classes in the hope that capitalism would turn into socialism by gradual evolution.

Kautsky was certainly faithful to Marx when he insisted that the revolution could not be enacted by decree, and that the mere transfer of political power would not bring about the economic liberation of the proletariat unless capitalism were economically and technically ripe for the change. But he seems to have over-looked the fact that the strategy, tactics, and organization of the worker's movement would have to be quite different according to whether it set about preparing for a political upheaval or chose to await the conditions, whatever they were exactly, for the economic collapse of capitalism. Kautsky's refusal to prejudge the character and duration of the revolution was quite reasonable on the premiss that the proletariat must wait for the ripening of conditions under capitalism. But a party that calls itself revolutionary cannot act rationally if, on what-ever grounds, it refuses to prejudge the meaning of the term 'revolution'. If it signifies a peaceful process, perhaps lasting for decades, in which the proletariat gradually gains control of political institutions, the party's educational and organizational tasks must be quite different than if the revolution is to be a once-and-for-all act of violence. The party, therefore, cannot in practice refrain from choosing on the mere ground that historical events are unpredictable. It may leave both alternatives open in its programme, but in political life it is bound to opt for one or the other. For this reason Kautsky's centrist position, based on his scientific attitude and reluctance to take decisions without rational foundation, amounted in practice to acceptance of the reformist standpoint. The theory of a revolution prepared by capitalism itself and not by the proletariat was a reflection, in Kautsky's doctrine, of the practical situation of the party, which adhered to revolutionary phraseology in its programme but took no action suggesting that it meant what it said. Bernstein was quite right when he observed that German social democracy was in actual fact a reformist organization and that the revolutionary elements in its programme were at variance with its actions and even with the practical objectives set forth in the programme itself. The eventual defeat of centrism—as a matter of practice, not of phraseology—and the party's dissolution into a revolutionary and a reformist wing were due to the fact that centrism, under the appearance of scientific open-mindedness, was a philosophy of indecision and was incapable of taking up a clear position on questions that had to be decided—and that were decided, if not in the party programme, at all events in political life. This fault was not obvious while the party was peacefully building up its strength, and so Kautsky's orthodox Marxism prevailed over the reformist programme at congresses although the party continued in practice to take a reformist line. The inconsistency came fully into view at the moment of crisis, which swept away the foundation of Kautsky's policy.

The idea that the revolution must await the ripening of economic conditions appeared to Kautsky a perfectly natural consequence of the Marxist theory of historical processes. It was not his view that in the relationship between the 'base' and the 'superstructure' the former alone played an active role and the latter was a mere adjunct. On the contrary, he emphasized, following Engels, that the division between the two was not identical with that between 'material' and 'spiritual' factors in the historical process. The base, which he regards as including means of production and tools, develops in accordance with the advance of knowledge and comprises all human productive faculties including 'spiritual' resources. The superstructure, on the other hand, i.e. legal and political relationships and socially formed opinions, has a great deal of influence on economic conditions. There is thus a continuing process of reciprocal influence, and the 'primacy' of the base *vis-à-vis* the superstructure applies only 'in the last resort'—a phrase which Kautsky, like Engels before him, does not explain precisely. He only adds that technological progress and the accompanying changes in property relations do not account for every detailed change in the superstructure, though they do account for the appearance of new ideas, social movements and institutions. Having thus limited the interpretation of the 'primacy' of the base, Kautsky still does not explain how the new is to be distinguished from the old, or how we can be sure that ideas or institutions that may come into being long after the relevant changes in technology or property relations are in fact a consequence of these.

In interpreting single events in the history of the revolutionary movement Kautsky suggests many convincing explanations, but in the case of more extended processes his suggestions often appear arbitrary. He argues, for instance, that the Kantian principle of treating every human being as an end and not a means is the expression of a bourgeois protest against personal dependence in a feudal society. But the opposite ethical principle voiced by the utilitarians of the Enlightenment is equally characteristic of the rising bourgeoisie, asserting its epicureanism against the asceticism of Christian morality. On the other hand, epicureanism is also typical of the declining aristocracy, while Kant's principle is rooted in Christianity; and again, the liberal doctrine of the survival of the fittest is of bourgeois origin. It is easy to see that if the sense of intellectual phenomena can be manipulated thus freely it is possible to defend any interpretation of them in class or economic terms, which in itself shows up the weakness of the theory. If, as Kautsky argues, Christian ethics reflected the misery of the oppressed classes in ancient Rome and also the situation of the decadent aristocracy of those times, and if it could then be an instrument of the rulers of feudal society, and later an inspiration of protest against that society; or if the bourgeois mentality could equally well be expressed by Kant's personalism, Bentham's utilitarianism, and Calvin's asceticism—then the theory is certainly capable of accounting for all historical phenomena and is covered against falsification, but only because it is arbitrary and lacking in precise criteria for the correlation of spiritual phenomena with their material origins.

In Kautsky's evolutionist doctrine there is of course no room for eschatology or any belief in the general 'meaning' of history. Like Marx, he regards socialism as the cause of all mankind and not merely of a class, but he also follows Marx in insisting on the class character of the movement that is to bring socialism about. The working class may conclude temporary alliances with the bourgeoisie or lower-middle class to secure political or social reforms, but it would be lost if it did not at the same time preserve its independence and separate character. (Kautsky was especially mistrustful of any alliance with the peasantry, which he regarded, above all in Germany, as a pre-eminently conservative class.) Socialism is in the interest of all, but the fight for socialism is in the interest of the working class alone. This idea (not formulated by Kautsky in so many words, but expressing his teaching and that of Marx) is self-consistent on the assumption that only the proletariat is so privileged by history that its immediate and ultimate aims are in harmony with each other, whereas the short-term objectives of the peasantry and the lower-middle class, not to mention the bourgeoisie, are contrary to the interest of all humanity embodied in the idea of a socialist society. The contradiction does not lie in the doctrine, but in the interests of the possessing classes.

Socialism signifies emancipation for the whole human race: this is true, first and foremost, because public ownership of the means of production and control of the production process in accordance with social needs will shorten the working day and give people more time to develop their personal aptitudes and aspirations. Socialism does not mean the abolition of the state, as the anarchists would have it, or a return to small self-contained communities, which would revive all the consequences of anarchic production and competition. The state, transformed into an organ of the social administration of things as opposed to people, must be centralized and capable of looking after the whole range of material production; artistic and intellectual production, on the other hand, will develop in perfect freedom. Kautsky, like most Marxists of his time, saw no conflict between the central regulation of trade and industry and the independence of culture. Democracy, freedom of the spoken and written word, the right of assembly, and cultural freedom were generally regarded by Marxists as automatic features of socialist organization. Kautsky often expressed his view on this subject, and always in the same sense. Although, as a matter of history, democratic freedoms have been secured by the bourgeoisie fighting feudal oppression, they belong to the permanent achievement of progress, and socialism without democracy would be a parody of its own first principles. For this reason socialism must never be imposed by a revolutionary minority, for it would then contradict itself. It must be the undisputed work of a majority, which should respect the right of the minority to express and advocate different opinions.

5. *Critique of Leninism*

Kautsky's basic conviction that socialism could not prevail until economic conditions were right for it, and his belief that socialism entailed democracy, combined to make him firmly opposed to the October Revolution and the Leninist conception of the dictatorship of the proletariat.

Like most of Lenin's socialist critics Kautsky held that Lenin was wrong in claiming Marx's support for the idea of the dictatorship of the proletariat as a particular form of government, opposed to democratic forms: to Marx and Engels, he maintained, it signified not the form of government but its social content. This was shown by the fact that Marx and Engels used the term 'dictatorship of the proletariat' to describe the Paris Commune, which was based on democratic principles, a multi-party system, free elections, and the free expression of opinion. In resolving to build socialism in a backward country by means of terror and oppression the Bolsheviks were in opposition to the views of Marx and Engels—who, for instance, had sharply criticized the Bakuninists for attempting to start a Communist rising in Spain in 1873—and also to those of Russian Marxists like Plekhanov and Akselrod, who hold that a revolution in Russia could only be of a bourgeois character, even if the proletariat played a decisive role in it. The destitution of the Russian people and the chiliastic hopes that went with it, the brutalization caused by war, and the general backwardness of the proletariat meant that socialism, if introduced there, was bound to turn into its opposite. Instead of organizing the proletariat for practicable aims and raising it to a higher level the Bolsheviks had incited it to take revenge on individual capitalists, destroyed all elements of democracy, and allowed the immaturity of the movement to bear fruit in universal savagery and banditry. They were trying ineffectually, like the Jacobins before them, to cure economic difficulties by mass terror and forced labour, which they falsely called the dictatorship of the proletariat. Thus, as Kautsky wrote in 1919, there was growing up amid despotic conditions a new class of bureaucratic exploiters, no better than the Tsarist chinovniks; and the workers' future struggle against tyranny would be even more desperate than under traditional capitalism, when they could exploit divergences of interest between capital and the state bureaucracy, whereas in Bolshevik Russia these two had coalesced into one. This kind of regimented socialism could only maintain itself by denying its own principles, which it was most likely to do, given the Bolsheviks' notorious opportunism and the ease with which they changed their tune from one day to the next. The most probable result would be a kind of Thermidor reaction which the Russian workers would welcome as a liberation, like the French in 1794. The original sin of Bolshevism lay in the suppression of democracy, abolition of elections, and denial of the freedom of speech and assembly, and in the belief that socialism could be based on a minority despotism imposed by force, which by its own logic was bound to intensify the rule of terror. If the Leninists were able to keep their 'Tartar socialism' going long enough, it would infallibly result in the bureaucratization and militarization of society and finally in the autocratic rule of a single individual.

6. Inconsistencies in Kautsky's philosophy

Next to Engels, Kautsky was certainly the chief exponent of the naturalist, evolutionist, determinist, Darwinist version of Marxism. At first glance his philosophy appears to form a consistent whole and to be reducible to a few main principles covering the whole history of nature and of mankind. All development is the result of interaction between organisms and their environment; those that are best adapted survive and transmit their characteristics to the next generation; the competition among species creates universal instincts of aggression and intra-species solidarity; the human race has achieved a special place in nature owing to its ability to make tools and to the power of articulate speech; the development of tools led to the origin of private property and classes fighting each other for the appropriation of surpluses; this in turn leads to the concentration of capital and class polarization; private ownership prevents further technical progress and intensifies the antagonism between the exploiting minority and the exploited majority; and this process is bound to end in the establishment of public ownership and of a new society which will preserve the technical and social achievements of capitalism, especially the democratic way of life, but will de-antagonize the process of socialization, restore the solidarity of the human race, do away with basic social conflicts, and enable individuals to develop without restraint.

On closer inspection, however, the theory proves to be full of gaps and inconsistencies, some of which are peculiar to the evolutionist brand of Marxism as opposed to that contained in Marx's early writings, while others are common to the naturalist and anthropocentric versions.

In Kautsky's view the whole development of the organic world, and human history as a subdivision of natural history, are to be explained by the interaction of organisms with their environment. Kautsky regards this theory of interaction as the true, rational content of the dialectic, and for this reason he criticizes the idea of the dialectic as the theory of the dichotomy of Being, due to its latent inner contradictions: self-negation as an explanation of development is, in his view, a survival of Hegelian idealism. Changes in nature and history are not brought about by a self-generated movement of contradiction but by the inter-action of distinct elements of the universe. There is no such thing in reality as the paradigm of human nature returning into itself after an age-long state of fission and restoring the unity between the object and subject of history. We are the spectators of a necessary process of changes which have no 'meaning' in themselves and cannot reveal any to scientific investigation, for science has nothing to do with values and is only concerned with necessity or the 'laws' of nature.

This naturalistic determinism, which is not fully worked out from the philosophical point of view, gives rise to important in-consistencies, or arbitrary assumptions, affecting the whole of Kautsky's thought. To begin with, it is not clear whether 'historical necessity' comprises every detail of history or only its general direction. If the former, then, leaving aside the arbitrari-ness of this form of determinism, it must be the case that each particular event or process is inevitable and predetermined in exactly the same sense. It follows that there is no point, for example, in Kautsky criticizing the Russian Revolution, for this was a no less necessary event than the transformation of a commodity economy into capitalism. Human volition may indeed be a necessary link, but its nature and effect are as much determined as everything else, and it is no different in function from any other factor of historical change. It is meaningless to criticize a revolutionary movement for taking no account of whether the situation is ripe, since its ripeness is demonstrated by the movement's very success. If, on the other hand, historical necessity is only a matter of general tendencies, while the particular form of events is subject to unconditioned human volition, then the criticism is meaningless for another reason. Since we cannot say precisely what constitutes 'ripeness' for the change-over to socialism, and since conscious human activity may bring the favourable moment closer, no one can say for certain at what time the moment has in fact arrived. Hence Kautsky's criticism of Blanquism and Leninism is not justified, as it purports to be, by his theory of historical determinism.

Furthermore, as scientific consciousness arises independently of the social movement that leads to socialism and must be introduced into that movement from without, there is no reason not to draw the same conclusion from this state of affairs as Lenin did. The truly proletarian, i.e. the scientific, consciousness can develop independently of the actual proletariat, and the political organism which possesses that consciousness is entitled to regard itself as embodying the 'will of history' whatever the actual working class thinks of the matter. Lenin's theory of the party as a vanguard was based on the doctrine formulated by Kautsky and cannot be accused of inconsistency. In Marx's own thought the problem does not arise, as he identifies the scientific doctrine that arises in the minds of scholars with the movement which makes that doctrine its own. In Marx's view the scientific consciousness is an articulation of the elemental consciousness: it is not simply awareness of a process that is going on outside it, but is itself that process; in the consciousness of the proletariat the object and subject of history coincide, and the proletariat, by becoming aware of itself and thus of the whole historical process, *ipso facto* transforms the historical situation. In the proletarian consciousness knowledge of the (social) universe and political activity are not two separate things, like the knowledge of natural laws and the application of that knowledge to technological purposes; they are one and the same.

For the same reason, as already stated, there is no problem

for Marx of the dichotomy between facts and values, or knowledge and duty. As, in this particular case, the act of cognizance of the world is the same as the act of changing it or of taking a practical part in the cognitive process, there is no room for the dichotomy to manifest itself, for there is no question of a perception followed by a separate act of evaluation. But since Kautsky, like his neo-Kantian opponents, regards knowledge as independent of its application and free from any value-judgement, he does not really come to grips with his critics' objections but fends them off with general statements, without perceiving the real nature of the problem. If men are convinced by scientific knowledge that socialism is a historical necessity, they must then ask themselves why they should help to bring it about: the mere fact that it is necessary does not answer this question. For Marx there is no problem, as humanity personified in the proletariat becomes aware of the necessity of the revolution in, and only in, the very act of bringing it about—theoretical awareness of the revolutionary movement *is* that movement. But Kautsky's deterministic philosophy makes it necessary to cope with the difficulty that the Kantians formulated but Kautsky himself failed to perceive. He also failed to notice that approbatory terms such as 'humanism', 'liberation', the 'greatness' or 'sublimity' of the socialist ideal—all of which he often employed—were inadmissible on his own premises.

Kautsky was profoundly attached to democratic values; he hated violence and war, and, while recognizing that future forms of the class struggle could not be foreseen, he hoped that mankind would advance into the realm of socialist freedom as a result of peaceful pressure, without violence or bloodshed. He tried to provide a theoretical backing for his hopes, but here too his doctrine is not free from essential weakness. The case for democracy, in his view, was based on the incurable limitation of human knowledge. No group or party could claim a monopoly of truth; all knowledge was partial and subject to change, and it would impede progress if any party were to reserve the exclusive right to express its views and to suppress criticism and discussion. These are sound arguments from the common-sense point of view, but they are combated by Kautsky's own theory of the social basis of knowledge. He maintained that there is no such thing as classless knowledge, at any rate in social questions, but that a true understanding of social processes can only be had by adopting the proletarian viewpoint. This raises epistemological problems that Kautsky never faced: if all knowledge of society is class-conditioned, how can knowledge acquired from the proletarian viewpoint in particular lay claim to universal validity? If it cannot, however, then all the scientific pretensions of Marxism are baseless; at best it can only rate as the formulation of a particular interest, albeit the interest of humanity in general, but it cannot, in addition, claim superiority over all other theories as the possessor of 'objective truth'. If, however, the proletarian viewpoint also entails a purely cognitive superiority, i.e. if it alone makes it possible to apply universal criteria of knowledge and if all other attitudes are not only class-conditioned but inevitably lead to the distortion of reality, then the demand for democracy, pluralism, free speech, etc. is groundless; for the party of the proletariat has, by definition, a monopoly of truth as against every other political organism, and all the privileges it claims and the despotism it imposes are fully justified in the interest of truth itself. But on this point too Kautsky failed to notice his own inconsistency.

Again, it is not clear why despotism and violence should be condemned from the point of view of Kautsky's historiosophy, although undoubtedly he himself was opposed to them. If mankind, unlike the rest of nature, has evolved various forms of intra-species aggression as a result of the very factors to which its pre-eminence is due, if man is endowed by nature with an aggressive instinct as well as an instinct of solidarity with his fellows, and if he has given free rein to the former instinct throughout his history, why should this state of things suddenly come to an end? Why should we believe in a law of history tending to lessen the use of coercion in intra-human relations? Even if we accept that capitalist forms of appropriation and the sharing of the surplus product must give way to public ownership, it does not follow that the same struggle will not be continued by other means in a socialized state, since the instincts that caused it will still be there. Kautsky's faith in the gradual elimination of violence and the increase of human solidarity is no more than faith, and cannot be vindicated by his theoretical principles.

Kautsky's position is also ambiguous as to the relation between reform and revolution. At first sight he appears in general to follow Marx in holding that there is no contradiction between the prospect of revolution and the policy of fighting for reforms; social progress, the shorter working day, greater prosperity for the workers, and democratic rights enabling them to defend their interests collectively, are all ways of developing class-consciousness and training the workers to take over the state in due course. But the consistency of this position is only apparent. The real question is whether reforms are *only* of value in relation to the coming revolution, or whether they are also valuable in themselves since they improve the lot of the proletariat. Kautsky took the latter view, holding that the intrinsic value of reforms was quite consistent with their value as an instrument of the revolutionary struggle. The course of practical politics, however, was to show that this supposed consistency was an illusion. A party which treated the struggle for reform seriously and which was successful in its efforts naturally became a reform party, its revolutionary slogans surviving only as embellishment. Kautsky was able to show that there were cases in history when the class struggle had intensified although the lot of the exploited workers was at the same time improving. But he was wrong in thinking that the improvements obtained by the working class through economic pressure were, as a general principle, without effect on the sharpness of class conflict and the state of revolutionary ardour. No doubt revolutionary situations are always the result of an unexpected coincidence of many circumstances, and better conditions for the workers do not rule out such situations *a priori*. But the practical difficulty is that a party which works for reforms instead of for revolution, which achieves reforms and therefore treats them as a serious objective, will find that its revolutionary theory becomes atrophied, and when the moment for revolution arrives the party will be incapable of seizing its opportunity. The objectives of reform and revolution can be reconciled in general doctrinal formulas, but not in social and psychological reality. Hence a socialist movement that achieves success in the economic struggle and in reformist endeavours tends inevitably to turn into a reform movement. As Bernstein saw but Kautsky did not, the achievements of German social democracy meant that it virtually ceased to be a revolutionary party.

The keynote of Kautsky's philosophy and that of the Marxists who thought like him is the 'naturalization' of human consciousness, i.e. its complete subordination to natural determinism, so that it plays the part of a mere factor of organic evolution. The main features of Kautsky's political theory and historiosophy are determined by this Darwinian version of Marxism: belief in the gradual and continuous evolution of capitalism to the point at which it destroys itself; confidence in historic inevitability, perceived from outside by the theoretical consciousness; dichotomy between theoretical awareness and the social process to which it is directed; the notion of a proletarian consciousness imported from without, and the rejection of the eschatological spirit of socialism. Kautsky's policy may be summed up as: 'Let us improve capitalism for the time being; socialism is guaranteed by the law of history in any case. It does not matter that we cannot prove separately the moral superiority of socialism: it simply so happens that what is necessary is also what appears desirable to me and to other persons of good sense.' Having introduced into Marxism the Enlightenment belief in continuous progress and the Darwinian view of consciousness as a biological organ, Kautsky was insensitive to the dramatic reversals of progress and failed to realize that consciousness itself is the cause of breaches of historical continuity that can easily be explained with the aid of hindsight, but which no one is ever able to foresee.

7. *A note on Mehring*

Franz Mehring (1846–1919) was, after Kautsky, the principal pillar of orthodox German Marxism. He became a social democrat in middle age, in the early 1890s, having made a considerable name as a publicist and writer for the liberal Press. From then on he devoted his vast historical knowledge and literary skill (in which he stood foremost among the orthodox writers) to the cause of socialism. His works include the voluminous classic *Geschichte der deutschen Sozialdemokratie* (*History of German Social Democracy*, 1897–8); a no less classic, though somewhat hagiographic, life of Marx (*Karl Marx, Geschichte seines Lebens*, 1918; translated 1936); *Deutsche Geschichte vom Ausgange des Mittelalters* (*History of Germany from the End of the Middle Ages*, 1910–11); and *Die Lessing-Legende* (1893), perhaps the finest work of Marxist historiography of the period. He also left many studies of literary history and criticism, and helped to create the Marxist theory of literature (articles on Schiller, Heine, Tolstoy, and Ibsen). From time to time he dealt with the general principles of historical materialism, for example in the appendix to *Lessing*, in different parts of his book on German social democracy, in the life of Marx, and in critical articles against the neo-Kantists. On these occasions he showed a leaning towards very simplified or 'reductionist' formulations—a fact to which we owe Engels's famous letter of 1893, in which the patriarch of scientific socialism corrected 'one-sided' interpretations of historical materialism and the rather crude formula which he himself and Marx had employed on occasion for purposes of controversy. Mehring's historico-literary analyses also contain some remarkable simplifications, as when he says that the *Oresteia* merely reflects the victory of the patriarchal principle over the matriarchal, or that the whole of classical German literature— Klopstock and Lessing, Goethe and Schiller—represents 'nothing but' the fight of the bourgeoisie for emancipation. If this is so, it is hard to see how Aeschylus can be read with pleasure and understanding by people who have not the faintest interest in the conflict between the patriarchate and the matriarchate in ancient Greece, or why Goethe and Schiller are still part of German culture although the political struggles of the last century have been forgotten. But it would be unfair to judge Mehring purely on the strength of such utterances. As a theoretician of historical materialism he did not, it is true, contribute anything to the evolution of Marxism, but he was of great importance as a historian and literary critic who, when it came to particular analyses, shook off the stiffness of doctrinal generalizations. The *Lessing-Legende* is not only a work about Lessing, but a review of the conventional views of German historians on the Enlightenment and an attack on the idolators of Frederick the Great and those who called Lessing the 'scribe of the Prussian monarchy'. Mehring tries to show that Lessing embodied in the most perfect and radical form all the virtues and progressive aspirations of the German bourgeoisie in its most militant and therefore creative period. His work has also an ideological purpose: it ends by declaring that Lessing's legacy 'belongs to the proletariat', as the bourgeoisie has jettisoned all his enlightened ideals.

Mehring joined issue with Marx on one point, namely his opinion of Lassalle. He recognized that Marx stood far above Lassalle as a scholar, writer, and revolutionary, and that Lassalle had his faults both as a historian and as a man of action, but he regarded Marx's judgement of him as offensive and largely due to personal prejudice. In Mehring's opinion, Lassalle had done a permanent service to German socialism both by his work as a theoretician and by creating a workers' party.

In his works on literature Mehring generally endeavoured to show that the greatness of a writer was measured by his success in presenting the aspirations and ideals of the class which he historically represented. But he did not identify artistic value with the class standpoint or with the social function that served to explain it. He held that no artistic values or tastes were permanent irrespective of history, but that all were relative to social situations. What he called 'emergent classes', i.e. those that were just beginning to fight for their social rights, tended in his opinion to show similar tastes in literature and art, in the shape of a desire for truth and realism. But naturalism, which had once been a weapon of the progressive bourgeoisie, had at times degenerated into the slavish imitation of casual reality and had deprived literature of the greatness that comes from a historical perspective. Naturalism had shown, sometimes very convincingly, the horrors of capitalism, but given its class origin it could not offer any way of escape from the bourgeois predicament. It had therefore given place to neo-Romanticism, which was an escape from the unfeeling world into capricious subjectivism and a capitulation before social problems. Along with historical perspective, the bourgeoisie had lost its spiritual creativity and no longer produced great works of the mind. Contemporary art and literature were alien to the proletariat, which turned to the great classics for the sound of warfare, the passion and fighting spirit by which it was itself animated. The art which would express specifically proletarian ideals and aspirations was still in an embryo state. Mehring did not believe, however, that sympathy for the workers' cause sufficed to produce literature of high quality: he did not identify artistic value with a correct political tendency, but more than once deprecated any such 'reduction'. Good intentions were not a substitute for artistic ability. Thus, although Mehring emphasized the value of art that expresses the proletarian point of view (Freiligrath's poems, Hauptmann's *Die Weber*), he was mistrustful of proletarian literature produced for direct political or propaganda ends and detached from the classical literary tradition.

It is not clear, however, how there can be a 'scientific aesthetic' such as Mehring desiderates, since he declares on the one hand that art cannot be evaluated by its social genesis and intentions, and, on the other, that there can be no purely aesthetic, non-historical criteria. Mehring was a well-read and percipient critic and quite aware of the difference between great and mediocre art. He defined the greatness of a work of art by the success with which it reflected the conflicts of its time, but he also questioned the possibility of other criteria than those based on the genesis of the work. On this basic point it is hard to clear him of inconsistency. For if all works of literature are born of class conflict, their genesis cannot permit us to distinguish good works from bad. The fact that a work expresses the tendencies of the 'progressive' class is also not enough. There is still a need for criteria independent of the genetic explanation; but according to Mehring there cannot be any such criteria, for in that case we should have to acknowledge that there were non-historical standards of beauty, which would mean falling into Kantianism or worse.

Here again, however, Mehring should not be too severely blamed for inadequacies that he shared with all contemporary Marxist writers on this subject. The value of his work does not consist in theoretical generalizations but in particular analyses in which he explained, skilfully and convincingly, the social background of creative literature. The genetic approach remains legitimate even when it is not clear exactly how it relates to artistic evaluation.

Kautsky, Mehring, and Heinrich Cunow were the most eminent theoreticians of orthodox Marxism as it was understood in their day. During and after the war, however, their political paths diverged. Kautsky maintained his 'centrist' position, Mehring declared for Spartacus, and Cunow for the right wing of the party. There was no direct correlation between theoretical orthodoxy on the one hand and politics on the other.

CHAPTER III

Rosa Luxemburg and the Revolutionary Left

ROSA LUXEMBURG occupies an ambiguous place in the tradition of socialist thought. She was the principal theoretician of the small revolutionary group which combated both revisionists and orthodox centrists, but she differed from the Leninist wing on certain important points. The group in question, the left wing of German social democracy, had no real prolongation in the later history of the socialist movement, in the time of polarization after 1918. Rosa Luxemburg's uncompromising revolutionism, and her violent criticism of the treachery of most of the socialist leaders in 1914, separated her completely from reformist social democracy. At the same time her sharp attacks on Lenin's programme and tactics meant that, in spite of dying a martyr's death, she was never quite admitted to the Communist pantheon. Verbal tribute was paid to her as a revolutionary and critic of revisionism, but from a practical point of view she was disregarded.

None of her writings is expressly philosophical: she was a theoretician of socialist strategy and tactics and of political economy. One may, however, regard 'Luxemburgism' as a particular variant of Marxism which, though not possessing an articulate philosophical basis, occupies a place of its own in the history of socialist doctrine, including its theoretical foundations.

1. Biographical information

Rosa Luxemburg, a Polish Jewess, was born at Zamość in 1870. Although she spent very little of her adult life in Poland she maintained close links with the Polish revolutionary movement, as a pillar of the Social Democratic Party of the Kingdom of Poland and Lithuania and, indirectly, as one of the founders of the Polish Communist party. Her links with socialism began in her early youth. After leaving high school in Warsaw in 1887 she joined a clandestine socialist youth group and, to escape arrest, fled to Switzerland in 1889. She studied at Zurich University and lived there till 1898, when she moved to Berlin and became one of the most active theorists and leaders of German social democracy. In Zurich she met the Polish socialists Warski, Marchlewski, and Tyszka-Jogiches, and wrote for the Paris paper *Sprawa Robotnicza* (*The Workers' Cause*), which became the organ of SDKPiL when the latter was founded in 1894. From 1893 onwards she took part in all the congresses of the Second International except the final one at Basle, and afterwards in all those of the German social democratic party. From the outset she devoted much time to combating the Polish Socialist party and its programme for the independence of Poland. In 1897 she wrote a doctoral thesis at Zurich on Polish industrial development (published as *Die industrielle Entwicklung Polens*, 1898): this formed the historical background to her future tactics, which were unalterably opposed to any attempt at reconstituting an independent Polish state. Her argument was that the development of capitalism in Russian Poland was mainly the result of the conqueror's policy, which had linked the fate of the Polish bourgeoisie with the Tsarist empire and its economic expansion to the east; plans for an independent Poland, as she maintained in subsequent writings, were contrary to the 'objective economic trend' which had irrevocably drawn Polish capitalism into the Russian orbit. Rosa Luxemburg's opposition to the movement for Polish independence supplied the main ideological theme of SDKPiL in contrast to that of the PPS.

From the time she settled in Berlin Rosa Luxemburg's career was linked with the German socialist movement, but she remained active in the leadership of SDKPiL, carried on political propaganda in Prussian Poland, which she visited several times, and wrote for Polish socialist papers; *Przegląd Socjaldemokratyczny* (*Social Democratic Review*), published legally at Cracow, and the illegal Warsaw journal *Czerwony Sztandar* (*Red Flag*). From 1895 she wrote for *Die Neue Zeit*, the *Leipziger Volkszeitung*, and other German socialist organs. From 1898, when the world of German social democracy was dominated by the controversy over Bernstein's views, Rosa Luxemburg's writings and speeches were largely devoted to combating revisionism as advocated by Bernstein and other reformists. Her most important theoretical work of this period was the pamphlet *Sozialreform oder Revolution?* (*Social Reform or Revolution?*) published in 1900 (second edition 1908), containing the fullest expression of her disbelief in the possibility of reforming capitalism and her conviction that any struggle for economic reform must be of purely political significance.

Up to 1906 revisionism was attacked by all orthodox German socialists, but the first Russian revolution caused, or rather brought to light, a divergence of view resulting in the formation of a left-wing group with Rosa Luxemburg as its chief theorist; other members were Karl Liebknecht, Clara Zetkin, and Franz Mehring. It was not until 1910, however, that the differences between the radicals and the centre took on an acute form and led to a new balance of political forces within the party, with the centre group (Bebel and Kautsky) in general closer to the Right than to the revolutionaries.

The events in Russia prompted Rosa Luxemburg to work out a new idea of revolution in the light of the spontaneous uprising of the workers of the Tsarist empire. At the end of 1905 she went illegally to Warsaw to take part in the revolutionary movement. Arrested after two months, she was released on bail in July 1906 and returned to Berlin via Finland. In a pamphlet *Massenstreik, Partei und Gewerkschaften* (1906) she attempted to draw conclusions from the events of the past year. Apart from this, both before and after the 1905 Revolution she expressed her views on matters related to the state of socialism in Russia. In articles published in *Die Neue Zeit* in 1903–4 she criticized the 'opportunism' of Lenin's ultra-centralist policy and his distrust of the workers' movement. At the same time she defended the Bolsheviks against the charge of Blanquism that was brought by Plekhanov and the Mensheviks. Like Lenin she opposed the doctrine that, in view of the bourgeois character of the coming Russian revolution, the socialists should not attack the liberals but should allow them to gain power without hindrance; this issue was debated, for example, at the London Conference of the Russian Social-Democratic Workers' Party (RSDWP) in May 1907. Rosa Luxemburg believed that the defeat of the Russian revolution was only temporary, that the revolutionary process would continue and that Russia was a pattern for the German working class as well—which Bebel and Kautsky both denied. The centrists and the radicals, however, were agreed in their attitude towards militarism and the threat of war, until it actually materialized. At the Stuttgart Congress of the Second International in 1907 Rosa Luxemburg caused the anti-war resolution to be amended in the sense that if war did break out despite the efforts of the working class, it should be transformed into an anti-capitalist revolution.

In 1912 she wrote her principal theoretical work *Die Akkumulation des Kapitals* (published in 1913; English translation, *The Accumulation of Capital*, 1951), which analysed the process of reproduction and demonstrated the economic inevitability of the collapse of capitalism. In 1913, with Marchlewski and Mehring, she founded the *Sozialdemokratische Korrespondenz*, a revolutionary organ of the German Left. She was sentenced to a year's imprisonment in 1914 for anti-war speeches, but was not actually imprisoned until later. The outbreak of war, the action of the social democrats in voting for war credits, and the dissolution of the International had placed the internationalist Left in the position of a helpless minority; but Rosa Luxemburg continued the struggle, convinced that the revolutionary potential of the world proletariat would eventually turn the war into a social upheaval. Sentenced to another year's imprisonment in February 1915, she wrote in her cell a pamphlet analysing the causes of the war and condemning the social democratic leaders for destroying the socialist movement by accepting the *Burgfriede* ('civic truce') and supporting the imperialist war. She went on to define the basis on which the workers' movement should be revived: wars, imperialism and militarism could not be abolished as long as capitalism lasted, but could only be overcome by a socialist revolution; the most urgent task was to free the proletariat from the state of spiritual dependence on the bourgeoisie in which it had been placed by its time-serving leaders. This work, published under the title *Die Krise der Sozialdemokratie* but generally known as the 'Junius pamphlet', was the ideological foundation of the Spartacus League, which was formed early in 1916 and was the nucleus of the future German Communist party (KPD). In 1917 the League, while remaining a separate body, joined the left wing of the social democrats who had formed the USPD: after the war the USPD dissolved, its members joining either the KPD or the reconstituted SPD.

Rosa Luxemburg was released from prison in February 1916 but was arrested again less than four months later for taking part in anti-war demonstrations; she remained in gaol until the last days of the war (8 November 1918). While there she wrote a reply (the *Antikritik*) to criticisms of her *Accumulation of Capital*, and an unfinished analysis of the October Revolution in Russia. The latter work was first published in 1922, after Rosa Luxemburg's death, by her friend Paul Levi, a former member of the Spartacus League and a leader of the KPD, who, however, was afterwards expelled from the latter and returned to the SPD. The pamphlet, entitled *Die russische Revolution*, hailed the events in Russia as a sign that world revolution was close at hand, but attacked the Bolsheviks for their policy towards the peasants and the national question, and above all for their despotic rule and suppression of democratic freedoms. It was chiefly on account of this work that Rosa Luxemburg became a *bête noire* of the Stalinists (who never quoted it, however). In general the pamphlet was little known before the Second World War, and was only translated into other languages after 1945 (English version 1959).

Rosa Luxemburg was set free by the German revolution, but did not enjoy her liberty for long. She imagined that the revolution would at once develop into a socialist phase, but the attempted rising by the Spartacus League, which was weak in itself and had scarcely any roots in the working class, was a fiasco. During the rising the League transformed itself into the KPD, while the Workers' and Soldiers' Councils formed the basis of the social democratic government of Germany. On the night of 15–16 January 1919 the two chief Communist leaders, Rosa Luxemburg and Karl Liebknecht, were murdered by *Freikorps* troops, and two months later Leo Tyszka-Jogiches met a similar death at the hands of the police. The lectures on economics which Rosa Luxemburg had delivered at the party school and written up while in prison were published posthumously in 1925 (*Einführung in die Nationalökonomie*).

2. The theory of accumulation and the inevitable collapse of capitalism

Although Rosa Luxemburg's chief theoretical work was not published until 1913, its main ideas can be found in many earlier texts, including *Social Reform or Revolution?*, and most of her theoretical and political opinions derive logically from her views on accumulation, which we shall therefore begin by examining.

The theory expounded in *The Accumulation of Capital* is commonly referred to as that of the 'automatic collapse of capitalism'. This term, however, was coined by Rosa Luxemburg's opponents, chiefly Leninists and Stalinists: it does not occur in her own work, and it is misleading in so far as it suggests that capitalism will collapse by virtue of its own contradictions and irrespective of the political struggle of the proletariat. Far from taking this view, Rosa Luxemburg believed that the revolution would overthrow capitalism long before the latter's economic possibilities were exhausted. She held, however, that the capitalist system could only work as long as it had at its disposal a non-capitalist market, whether internal or external, and, as it was in the nature of the system to destroy its non-capitalistic environment, it was inevitably preparing its own economic ruin. There could be no such thing as 'pure capitalism' on a world scale: if the capitalist economy developed to that extent it would cease to exist.

Marx had maintained that capitalism was bound to destroy itself by its own contradictions, especially those connected with the concentration of capital and the impoverishment of the working class, but he never defined the exact conditions under which capitalism would become an economic impossibility. Rosa Luxemburg set out to do this, partly by supplementing Marx's views and partly by modifying them.

The starting-point of her theory of accumulation consists in the schemata of reproduction set out in Volume II of *Capital*. This is the most arduous and the least-read portion of Marx's work, but from Rosa Luxemburg's point of view it was fundamental to the crucial question of scientific socialism, viz. 'Why is capitalism doomed to destruction on economic grounds?'—or, to put it the other way round, 'Can the process of compound reproduction (*erweiterte Reproduktion*) as it exists in capitalism develop, theoretically, to infinity?' Rosa Luxemburg's argument is as follows.

According to Marx the value of any commodity consists of three components, expressed in the formula $C + V + S$. C (constant capital) stands for the value of the means of production, i.e. tools and raw materials, that have gone into making the product; V (variable capital) represents wages, and S (surplus value) is the increase of value due to the unremunerated portion of wage-labour. In contrast to previous systems in which reproduction was governed by social needs, capitalism is concerned only with the maximum increase of surplus value, and therefore tends constantly to increase production irrespective of need. Accumulation, or the conversion of surplus value into fresh, active capital, belongs to the nature of capitalist production. It is a condition of compound reproduction, however, that the goods produced should be converted into money: for this purpose further quantities of goods must be marketed, a process over which the individual capitalist has little influence. Let us assume that the annual production is expressed in the proportion:

$$40C + 10V + 10S = 60$$

In this formula the amount of constant capital is four times that of variable capital, and the rate of surplus value, or rate of exploitation, is 100 per cent. The value of the commodities produced is 60 units. If the capitalist now devotes 5S, or half the surplus value, to increasing production, i.e. adds it to his constant capital, then, the organic composition of capital remaining the same, the next phase of production will be expressed by the formula

$$44C + 11V + 11S = 66$$

This process can go on as long as the capitalist can get hold of sufficient means of production and labour force and secure an outlet for his goods. Hence, if in conditions of simple reproduction money plays only the part of an intermediary in the exchange of commodities, under capitalism it is an element in the circulation of capital: for accumulation to be possible, surplus value must assume a monetary form. In addition capitalism tends naturally to drive wages down to subsistence level, so that S tends to increase in relation to V.

If, following Marx, we divide the whole of social production into two 'departments'—I production of means of production, and II production of consumption goods—then we see that the two are interdependent, i.e. they must remain in a specific proportion so that the process of production may continue harmoniously. Department I produces means of production for both departments I and II, while department II produces consumption goods for the workers and capitalists of both departments. The necessary proportion is illustrated by the following pattern:

$$\text{Department I: } 4,000C + 1,000V + 1,000S = 6,000$$
$$\text{Department II: } 2,000C + 500V + 500S = 3,000$$

For simple reproduction the value of the products in department I, i.e. 6,000, must equal the value of the constant capital of both departments (4,000 + 2,000), while the value of the products of department II, i.e. 3,000, must equal the combined income of workers and capitalists in both departments, i.e. 1,000 + 1,000 + 500 + 500. This is so in the above example, but it is not so in capitalist reality, which is based on 'compound reproduction', i.e. the capitalization of a part of S in both departments. If we have

$$\text{Department I: } 4,000C + 1,000V + 1,000S = 6,000$$
$$\text{Department II: } 1,500C + 750V + 750S = 3,000$$

it will be seen that the value of the production of means of production (6,000) exceeds by 500 the value of the means of production used in the given productive cycle (i.e. 4,000 + 1,500), while the value of consumption goods (3,000) is 500 less than the total incomes of capitalists and workers in both departments (1,000 + 1,000 + 750 + 750). The application of this unconsumed portion of S to the new productive cycle, the proportion between the two departments remaining the same, causes a corresponding increase in all elements of the value of the totality of commodities. For this, however, the commodities must first be transformed into money. Accumulation depends on an increasing demand for the goods produced, and the question is, how does this demand arise? Industry cannot go on creating its own market *ad infinitum*; what is produced must in the end be consumed. An increase of population does not solve the problem of demand, for the numerical increase of the capitalist class is included in the absolute magnitude of the consumable portion of surplus value, while working-class consumption is limited by the wage-level; non-producing sections of the population, such as landowners, civil servants, soldiers, professional men, and artists, are maintained either from surplus value or from wages. Nor does foreign trade provide the solution, for the analysis of compound reproduction applies to world capitalism, for which all countries are an internal market. In other words, for the surplus value of both departments of production to realize itself in money-form, there must be a market external to both departments and capable of absorbing goods at a rate increasing with the rate of accumulation.

Marx, according to Rosa Luxemburg, did not come to grips with this problem. He believed that capitalists collectively provide a market by buying one another's means of production; but they cannot increase surplus value indefinitely except by increasing the rate of consumption, and the workers cannot help towards this end, since all they have is their wages, which figure in the equation already. Marx, it is true, never stated that accumulation can go on to an unlimited extent: his schemata are only designed to illustrate the proportion between accumulation in the two departments and their dependence on each other. But, as he never answered the basic question, For whom does compound reproduction occur?, the schemata may be falsely interpreted as indicating that production is capable of absorbing the whole increase of surplus value: the industry of department I expands to increase production in department II, and the latter is increased so as to maintain the growing army of workers in both departments. Thus the Russian Marxists—Struve, Bulgakov, and Tugan-Baranovsky—use the Marxian schemata to infer that capitalist accumulation can go on increasing indefinitely. But to admit this is to give up the whole idea of scientific socialism. For if there is no limit to accumulation within capitalist forms of production, it follows that capitalism is economically invincible, that it is an inexhaustible source of economic and technical progress; socialism is not a historical necessity, and there is no economic reason for the collapse of capitalism. (The idea that capitalism would collapse because of the falling rate of profit seemed to Rosa Luxemburg absurd. It was impossible to imagine the scenario of this breakdown, the more so as the tendency for the profit rate to fall was quite compatible with an absolute increase in total profits; it was hard to suppose that capitalists would one day cease production because the profit rate was too low, even though they were making larger profits than before.)

Thus, in Rosa Luxemburg's opinion, Marx overlooked the

question which is vital to the existence of scientific socialism, viz. that of the precise economic reason why capitalism is bound to destroy itself. He wrote, indeed, that the increase of productive power conflicts increasingly with the limited possibilities of consumption, but his schemata of compound reproduction do not reveal the contradiction between the creation of surplus value and its realization. The schemata presuppose that capitalists and workers are the only consumers, i.e. they assume for theoretical purposes a fictional society of 'pure' capitalism, consisting of capitalists and workers only. Such a fiction is admissible in the analysis of individual capital but not, Rosa Luxemburg argues, in regard to capital as a whole: for it conceals the fundamental point that compound reproduction takes place in a world in which there is still a non-capitalist market, and the social classes or countries that live outside the capitalist system are necessary to the latter as consumers of its surplus production in both departments I and II. The surplus value must realize itself outside the sphere of capitalist production, in pre-capitalist spheres such as backward countries, the rural economy, and handicrafts: mature capitalism depends on the existence of non-capitalist classes and countries. But capitalist expansion tends inexorably to eliminate pre-capitalist economic forms by drawing peasants and craftsmen into its own orbit. Capitalism thus unconsciously prepares its own downfall by destroying the forms on which it depends. When capitalism succeeds in assimilating the whole of production, accumulation will become impossible and capitalism will be economically unfeasible. 'Pure capitalism' is incapable of surviving. At the present time there are many non-capitalist areas of the world, and the struggle to possess these as sources of raw materials and cheap labour, and above all as outlets for European goods, takes the form of imperialism. The field for expansion still exists, but it is contracting rapidly. By the fight for markets capitalism is steadily destroying all remnants of the pre-capitalist environment which is the condition of its own being.

It is noteworthy that although Rosa Luxemburg's intention was to establish once and for all the economic inevitability of the collapse of capitalism, none of the Marxist theoreticians who believed in the historical necessity of socialism endorsed her argument, and the most important of them opposed it—

Hilferding, Kautsky, Gustav Eckstein, Otto Bauer, A. Pannekoek, Tugan-Baranovsky, and Lenin. Tugan-Baranovsky held that the anti-human character of capitalism, and the fact that it makes increased production an end in itself instead of a means of satisfying social needs, meant that accumulation could go on indefinitely, as industry was able to provide itself with outlets by continuing to increase production, absorbing more and more of the means of production, employing more and more workers, and so forth. No one denied, of course, that capitalism was beset by marketing difficulties that resulted in crises of overproduction, cut-throat competition, the struggle for markets, and imperialist wars, and that militarism, beside the immediate purpose of conquering markets, itself afforded a sphere of capital accumulation. But Marxists generally took the view that although capitalism would eventually be destroyed by its own manifold contradictions, it was not possible to predict the exact economic circumstances in which this would happen; and they were inclined to attach more importance to the concentration of capital, the pauperization of the working class, and the extinction of the middle class than to any insufficiency of demand, which capitalism seemed able to remedy in various ways despite its undoubted difficulties and crises. Rosa Luxemburg's Leninist critics were suspicious of the theory of accumulation precisely because it seemed to imply that capitalism would break down automatically. If capitalism was bound to destroy itself by its own expansion, irrespective of the political role of the proletariat, this would encourage a policy of passive expectation and would tend to relax the party's zeal instead of spurring it to revolutionary activity. Rosa Luxemburg herself never drew this conclusion from her theory. The critics also objected that she underrated the possibility of compound reproduction thanks to the armaments industry and military expansion, and this has been confirmed by the later development of capitalism.

In general it appears that the theory of accumulation involves assumptions concerning capitalism that were either unreal or have been disproved by subsequent events.

Rosa Luxemburg frequently makes the point that she is concerned with capitalism as an all-embracing system, a single worldwide market, and for this reason she ignores any modifications that might be due to external markets. Capitalism in a single country may be able to survive by expanding into the non-capitalist world, but if capitalism is worldwide there are no markets to expand into. But for 'pure capitalism' to exist in this sense, it is not sufficient for capitalist production to embrace every country in the world. It is necessary in addition for the rate of profit to be the same throughout the world: for, on Rosa Luxemburg's theory, the developed countries may expand into areas which, although capitalist, are backward and where the rate of profit is therefore higher. In other words, her schema presupposes a world in which there is no difference in economic development between the Congo and the U.S.A. One may imagine a world as uniform as this, but it scarcely affords a solid basis for economic predictions. Not only is the prospect remote and unreal, but it ignores the fact that the gap between developed and backward nations is getting larger rather than smaller. This being so, to assert that capitalism will break down when this prospect becomes a reality is no less arbitrary than, for example, to suppose that capitalism can content itself with simple reproduction and could therefore survive if there were insufficient outlets to permit of compound reproduction. Rosa Luxemburg derides those who believe that the fall in the profit rate will lead to the collapse of capitalism, on the ground that one cannot see the capitalists committing suicide because their profit rates are less high than they used to be. But she fails to observe that her own theory is open to the same taunt: if capitalists one day find they cannot market an increased volume of goods, will they hang themselves sooner than be content with simple reproduction? The answer to this in Marxian terms is of course that it is in the nature of capitalism to seek after compound reproduction; but if 'nature' is not a purely metaphysical entity, we may ask whether capitalism is really unable to change its spots as an alternative to complete destruction. Such a hypothesis is no less extraordinary than Rosa Luxemburg's imaginary world in which all countries are at the same level of industry, technology, and civilization.

From today's standpoint we can see how far her theory of accumulation was based on a false estimate of the future development of capitalism. This estimate, however, unlike her specific theory of the collapse of capitalism, was shared by most of her Marxist contemporaries. The theory of accumulation assumed a growing class polarization approximating to the condition in which society consisted exclusively of capitalists and workers. As we know, things happened differently; not only were small businesses not squeezed out, but, above all, in the more developed countries the proportion of workers in the population has tended to decrease, while there has been a huge increase of what Marx called non-productive workers, i.e. those engaged in trade, administration, education, services, etc. Rosa Luxemburg disposes of these non-productive elements by saying that they are remunerated either from the uncapitalized portion of surplus value or out of wages, but that there is always a portion of surplus value that is turned into capital and so increases production in the next cycle. But it is not clear why the increased consumption of the non-productive workers should have no effect on the realization of surplus value, even if we accept Marx's increasingly doubtful distinction between productive and non-productive labour and suppose that the latter is 'in the last resort' paid out of surplus value created by the working class.

Another false assumption of the theory of accumulation is that wages under capitalism would always be close to subsistence level: the argument being that although the laws of exploitation might be weakened from time to time they would 'in the last resort' always prevail over working-class resistance, so that a genuine increase in workers' consumption was unlikely to occur.

Further, Rosa Luxemburg did not believe that a state controlled by the bourgeoisie could regulate the process of accumulation to any important extent. But the evolution of capitalism has shown that she was mistaken. Even if, following Marx, we regard the state as a whole as the political embodiment of global capital, experience has shown that this state can play the part of an organizer, using economic and legal means to affect the distribution of investment resources, and that it can, under political pressure for instance, enlarge the internal market. That is to say, it can act as a socialist state in so far as it controls the process of production in accordance with social needs, instead of leaving everything to the 'wolfish greed for surplus value' as the sole motive force of capitalist production.

For the above reasons Rosa Luxemburg's theory of accumulation cannot, in its literal form, be accepted as an explanation or forecast of the economic development of capitalism. It does not follow, however, that her work was of no effect. As Michael Kalecki observes in the collective work (in Polish) *The economic theories of Marx's 'Capital'* (1967), the rival theories of reproduction put forward by Rosa Luxemburg and Tugan-Baranovsky were both erroneous but both helped to illustrate certain features of economic growth under capitalism. Tugan-Baranovsky held that there are no absolute barriers to capitalism in the form of limited outlets, and that its output can be marketed at any level of consumption as long as the ratio of consumption to investment is maintained. There is nothing absurd, in capitalist terms, in production being undertaken simply in order to increase production: on the contrary, production regardless of need is the strength of the system. But, Kalecki observes, Tugan-Baranovsky overlooked the fact that a system which entirely ignored the level of consumption would be very unstable, since any drop in investment would mean a decrease in the use made of the existing apparatus of production, hence a further drop in investment, and so on in a vicious spiral. On the other hand, Rosa Luxemburg's theory that compound reproduction depends wholly on non-capitalist markets has been refuted by our experience of the state's power to create, in the form of arms production, a huge market that may have a decisive effect on economic growth. In addition she was wrong in supposing that the whole volume of goods exported to non-capitalist markets contributes to the realization of productive surpluses, whereas what actually counts is the excess of exports—both goods and capital, but especially the latter—over imports; for imported goods also absorb purchasing power. However, in a limited sense the two theories supplement each other: one shows up the absurdity of a system whose viability depends on producing for profit instead of need, while the other demonstrates the importance of foreign markets for capitalist growth. At the same time, neither theory provides a sufficient explanation of the process of compound reproduction.

To Rosa Luxemburg, however, the theory of accumulation was of fundamental importance not only as the sole possible scientific vindication of Marx's prophecy of the downfall of capitalism, but also as an ideological weapon: for it meant that capitalists could do nothing to avert the destruction of their class and that no human power could prevent the final victory of socialism, which, as she and all Marxists believed, would replace capitalism.

This belief was, it would seem, based on a more general conviction by which her thought was permeated—an unshakeable, doctrinaire fidelity to the concept of iron historical laws that no human agency could bend or break. The belief in historical laws is, of course, a classic theme of Marxism, and all Marxists at the time professed it, but some held it more uncompromisingly than others. Most of them attenuated the literal sense of the doctrine, for instance by invoking Engels's formula of the 'relative independence of the superstructure', or, like Lenin, emphasizing the role of 'subjective' factors—i.e. organized will-power—in hastening social change; or again, pointing out in a common-sense fashion the many social conflicts that do not fall into the general category of 'contradictions of capitalism' yet undeniably do affect history. Rosa Luxemburg, however, was determined to find a single key to all historical problems and believed that Marx's analysis of the dynamics of capitalism provided this key, at any rate when supplemented by an exact account of the conditions of reproduction. Her adamant refusal to believe in any individual or even collective human actions that were not predetermined by the 'laws of history' was manifested in all important questions in which she took a different stand from her fellow Marxists. Just as no capitalist efforts could hinder the blind anarchic forces of accumulation that were bringing the whole system to ruin, so too it was impossible for any organized movement to bring about a revolution by artificial means. Men and women were instruments of the historical process, and their task was to understand it and their own part in it. No purely ideological phenomena could of themselves affect the course of history; in particular, national ideologies were powerless to deflect history from its progress towards the great transformation of all time, the worldwide socialist revolution.

Owing to this doctrinaire belief Rosa Luxemburg was frequently blind to the empirical reality of social events and showed an extraordinary lack of political understanding in regard to national questions and to the revolution itself. Her writings show a theoretical consistency of the kind which can only come from extreme dogmatic rigidity and insensitivity to facts.

3. *Reform and revolution*

If Rosa Luxemburg had believed in the 'automatic breakdown' of capitalism in the sense imputed by her critics, it would have been in glaring contradiction to the position she took up in the debate on 'reform versus revolution'. But, although she held with Marx that capitalism was condemned to self-destruction in that it would sooner or later become a brake on technical progress and economic growth, it did not follow that capitalism would collapse without the need for revolutionary action. It was rather the case that imperialism must develop to a point at which it would awaken the revolutionary consciousness of the proletariat, without which capitalism could not be overthrown. Its overthrow was a historical necessity, but so was the revolutionary movement that must bring it about. This view was shared by Rosa Luxemburg and other orthodox Marxists of her time.

The question of the significance and prospects of 'reformist' action—i.e. the workers' economic struggle for better conditions, and the campaign for democratic measures within bourgeois society—was, in Rosa's Luxemburg's opinion, vital to the whole socialist movement. Her position was essentially the same as Marx's: the value of reforms was not that they brought an alleviation of conditions but that the struggle itself afforded the proletariat the necessary practice for the decisive battle. Those who regarded reforms as an end in themselves were denying the prospect of socialism and turning their backs on the ultimate goal.

Many orthodox Marxists took the view that the revolution would come when economic conditions were ripe and that meanwhile their task was to fight for democracy in public life and better conditions for the working class. The reformists, while not expressly abandoning the hope of revolution, were vague about the time and circumstances in which it would occur. The essence of Rosa Luxemburg's position (like that of all the left wing of the International, including Lenin) was that she combated both these views, although her opposition to the orthodox viewpoint took shape at a later date. In the controversy with Bernstein and those party leaders and trade unionists who supported him in practice though without evolving any special theoretical views—for example, Georg von Vollmar, Wolfgang Heine and Max Schippel—Rosa Luxemburg in effect directed her attack not only against 'revisionist' reformism but also against the orthodox variety. Her main point was that reforms were meaningless if they were not a means to the conquest of power; they must not be treated, even partially, as an end in themselves, and those who did so, whatever their professions, were abandoning the revolutionary cause. Any struggle for reform that was not subordinated to the coming revolution was a hindrance rather than a help to socialism, whatever its immediate outcome might be. As Rosa Luxemburg declared at the party congress at Stuttgart in 1898, the unions' fight for better terms for the sale of labour-power, pressure for social reform and democratic methods were forms of activity within the capitalist system and therefore had no specifically socialist meaning except as part of the struggle for the ultimate conquest of political power. To Bernstein's dictum that 'The goal is nothing, the movement everything' she replied with the opposite formula: 'The movement as an end in itself, unrelated to the ultimate goal, is nothing to me; the ultimate goal is everything.' Concentration on short-term effects led reformists like Schippel to support militarism, as the growth of armies and war production would reduce unemployment and prevent crises by increasing purchasing power. This, Rosa Luxemburg said, was absurd economically, as crises were not due to an absolute imbalance between consumption and production, but to the inherent tendency of production to exceed the possibilities of the market, and military costs would be borne in one way or another by the working class. But the theory was also politically dangerous, as it suggested that the workers could or should give up their principal aims for the sake of temporary gains that would finally be to their detriment ('Miliz und Militarismus', *Leipziger Volkszeitung*, February 1899).

Rosa Luxemburg's most general treatment of this question is in her pamphlet *Social Reform or Revolution?* There is no opposition, she declares, between the struggle for reform and the struggle for political power: the former is a means, the latter an end in itself. Social democracy is distinguished from bourgeois reformism by its awareness of the ultimate goal. To treat reforms as an end in themselves means accepting the indefinite continuance of capitalism, enabling it to escape destruction at the cost of a few modifications. For example, Konrad Schmidt held that the workers' political and economic struggle would lead in time to public control over production and would limit the role of capitalists. But in fact the workers' influence on capitalist production could only have a reactionary effect: it would hold up technical progress, or align workers and capitalists against consumers. 'In general,' Rosa Luxemburg wrote in 1900, 'the trade union movement is not moving into a period of victorious development but into one of increasing difficulties. When the development of industry reaches its zenith and worldwide capitalism begins to go downhill, the unions' task will be doubly difficult. In the first place the objective state of the labour market will be worse, as demand will increase more slowly and supply more rapidly than now. Secondly, capital will be even more unscrupulous in seizing that part of the product which is the workers' due, so as to recoup its losses on the world market.' The state cannot intervene in any other interest than that of capital, since it is an organ of the capitalist class and can only pursue general policies in so far as they accord with the interests of that class. This applies equally to democratic political institutions, which the bourgeoisie will maintain as long as, and to the extent that, it suits them to do so. Hence no amount of reform can overthrow capitalism or achieve revolutionary objectives by degrees. The proletariat's economic and political struggle can only help to bring about the subjective conditions of revolution; it does not, as Bernstein argues, lead objectively towards socialism or restrict exploitation. What the struggle achieves is not the transformation of society but the transformation of the consciousness of the proletariat. To treat short-term successes as ends in themselves is contrary to the class viewpoint and can only breed illusions; 'in the capitalist world, social reform is and always will be a nut without a kernel'. In despite of Bernstein, Marx's predictions concerning the development of capitalism are being fulfilled to the letter. The fact that there are no crises of overproduction at the moment does not invalidate his views or signify that capitalism is changing or is capable of adaptation. The crises that Marx knew at first hand were not the same as those he predicted: the former were crises of the growth and expansion of capitalism, not its exhaustion—the real crises of overproduction have yet to come. The system of share capital is not, as Bernstein maintains, a sign that small capitalists are on the increase: it is a form of the concentration of capital and therefore intensifies contradictions instead of curing them. The proletariat cannot avert or invalidate the laws of capitalist economy: its defensive struggle for the right to sell labour-power on normal terms is a Sisyphean task, though necessary to prevent wages falling still more. But, whatever the workers' efforts, their share in the wealth of society must diminish 'with the in-evitability of a natural process, as the productivity of labour increases'.

Thus revolution and reform are different in nature, not merely in degree: reform does not amount to a gradual revolution, or revolution to a telescoped reform. To think otherwise is to believe that capitalism need only be amended, and that its overthrow is unnecessary.

Rosa Luxemburg's refusal to admit that reforms had any value in themselves, and her mistrust of any conspicuous success in the proletariat's economic struggle, inclined her to make pessimistic forecasts and to disparage the results obtained. Her revisionist adversaries, such as Bernstein and David, regarded Britain as a model country as far as the workers' struggle was concerned; she, on the other hand, saw in it a pernicious example of how the proletariat could be corrupted by temporary gains. In an article in the *Leipziger Volkszeitung* in May 1899 she declared that the British trade unions had achieved successes by abandon-ing the class viewpoint and bargaining within the framework of the capitalist economy. The British proletariat had adopted bourgeois ideas and sacrificed class objectives for immediate gain. But we are now at the end of this period, and the class struggle—in the true, not the reformist sense—is about to begin again.

All this is fully in accord with Marx's theory, but not with the celebrated text from Engels on which the reformists relied. At the first congress of the German Communist party on 30 December 1918 Rosa Luxemburg made no attempt to interpret Engels in a sense favourable to her own views, but criticized him for taking a reformist line in the Introduction to Marx's *The Class Struggles in France*, under pressure, as she claimed, from Bebel and the social democrats in the Reichstag. The text in

To discussion
of Marx's own theory
a *priori* premises

80 *Rosa Luxemburg and the Revolutionary Left*

question had done harm to the socialist movement by providing a permanent excuse to those who based their hopes on purely parliamentary action and in practice ignored the prospect of revolution.

Rosa Luxemburg did not speculate deeply as to the basis of Marx's view that the working class, by virtue of its position, must evolve a revolutionary consciousness. Marx formed this opinion in 1843 on purely philosophical grounds, and never abandoned it. Its only basis at that time, however, was the conviction that because the working class is subject to the maximum of dehumanization it cannot liberate itself as a separate class but only as a movement restoring the humanity of mankind as a whole. This is scarcely a cogent argument. Because a particular class is oppressed, exploited, and dehumanized it does not follow *a priori* that that class must aspire to world revolution, still less that its aspiration will succeed. In any case, the modern working class is no more dehumanized than the slaves of antiquity. In his later writings Marx used what appeared to be more pragmatic arguments. The capitalist system would soon lose control over technological progress, and the working class stood for a society that would remove obstacles to such progress and subordinate production to human needs instead of to the multiplication of value for its own sake. But this argument involves premises which are far from obvious. It assumes that indefinite technical progress is in the nature of things, or rather that the desire for technical improvement is an inseparable part of human nature— for technical progress is a human activity: as Lévi-Strauss puts it, one axe does not produce another. But Marx did not make this assumption; on the contrary, he believed that the urge for technical improvement was peculiar to capitalism and had not existed in other economic systems. Thus, if he was right in holding that capitalism was bound to lose the power to improve technology, the consequence would be that capitalism would cease to exist in its present form, i.e. as characterized by technical progress; but it would not follow that its role would be inherited by the working class, still less that the working class would inherit the ability to control technical progress and that this ability would ensure its political triumph. It could equally well be supposed that capitalism would go on existing in a stagnant form or be replaced by another society that might not necessarily depend on the continual improvement of productive forces and need not be socialist in Marx's sense.

This, it is true, was not the whole of Marx's argument. He also thought that the historical prelude to the proletarian revolution would be the increasing polarization of classes, the disappearance of the intermediate class, the increasing size of the 'reserve army' and of the proletariat, and the development of the latter's class-consciousness. But even on Marx's premisses these events are not sufficient to justify belief in the inevitability of a proletarian revolution. Poverty does not in itself produce a trend towards revolution, nor does the preponderance of the exploited class, nor, least of all, the fact that justice is on its side. On the other hand, according to Marx the growth of revolutionary consciousness depends on social conditions 'objectively' tending towards revolution: it is not a spontaneous mental phenomenon, but must be the reflection of an actual historical trend. In order to know whether to expect an upsurge of revolutionary consciousness, we must first find out whether a socialist upheaval is on the way in accordance with the historical process. But it has not been shown that this condition is fulfilled, since the proletarian revolution as predicted by Marx has not yet occurred anywhere and there is no reason to expect it soon, or indeed at all.

Neither Marx nor Rosa Luxemburg makes it clear which statement logically comes first: that capitalism cannot be reformed, or that the working class is bound to destroy it by revolution. Since the two propositions are not the same, either they must be proved independently or one must follow from the other. In her polemics with the reformists, Rosa Luxemburg appears to make most use of the former proposition. Her theory of accumulation supplies proof (which, according to her, Marx failed to give) that for purely economic reasons capitalism cannot go on indefinitely. But even if we accept that theory for the sake of argument, it is not clear how it follows that there must be a proletarian revolution. Assuming that capitalism must collapse because private ownership of the means of production leads to overproduction and crises, it is still not proved that the system of ownership must be transformed in that particular way. The conclusion is more likely, though still not certain, on the further assumptions that society is coming closer to a state in which it consists of nothing but the bourgeoisie and the proletariat, that the latter's situation cannot be really improved, and that the bourgeoisie is bound to resist any attempt to break its monopoly of the means of production. But of these three additional assumptions, only the last is credible.

Since, however, Rosa Luxemburg believed unalterably that the working class was revolutionary by nature, her account of social reality was often based more on theory than on observation. She was convinced that revolutionary consciousness was on the increase, and when the facts belied this she was more inclined to blame the leaders' opportunism than objective circumstances. Believing that the workers were 'essentially' revolutionary, she placed more hope in an elemental outbreak than in organized party action.

4. *The consciousness of the proletariat and forms of political organization*

The question of spontaneity versus party organization was the crux of Rosa Luxemburg's most violent disagreement with the Bolsheviks; but she saw similar dangers in every branch of social democracy. Lenin, Kautsky, Jaurès, and Turati were all guilty in her eyes of underrating the spontaneity of the masses and tending to discourage it by the doctrine of 'leadership'. Here again, she was almost the only one of her opinion in the social democratic movement.

By spontaneity, however, she did not mean a blind impulse devoid of ideological self-awareness. Not only had Marx predicted the proletarian revolution, but his prediction must itself become part of the proletarian consciousness in order for the revolution to come about. 'It is fundamental to the historic upheaval as formulated in Marx's theory that this theory should become the form of the working-class consciousness and, as such, a historical factor in its own right' (article on Marx in *Vorwärts*, 14 March 1903). Since the revolutionary consciousness that is to be, or is now taking shape, has already been formulated in terms of theory, the working class has every opportunity to become aware of its own destiny, and there is no need of leaders to educate the masses or look after their consciousness for them. Lenin's ultracentralism was a piece of opportunism, typical of the intelligentsia—so Rosa Luxemburg declared in 'Problems of the organization of Russian social democracy' (*Die Neue Zeit*, No. 42–3, 1903–4). According to Lenin, the Central Committee could arrogate to itself full power *vis-à-vis* party organizations, turning the whole party into a mere passive instrument.

The centralization of social democracy, based on these two principles —firstly the blind subjection of all party organs and their activity, down to the minutest detail, to a central authority which thinks, acts and decides for everyone, and secondly the strict separation of the organized core of the party from the surrounding revolutionary *milieu*, as Lenin would have it—seems to us no more or less than a mechanical transference of the Blanquist principles of the organization of conspiratorial groups to the social democratic movement of the working masses. Lenin has defined his own point of view more trenchantly, perhaps, than any of his opponents could have done when he speaks of his 'revolutionary democrat' as a 'Jacobin linked with an organization of the proletariat conscious of its class interests'. But social democracy is not 'linked' with the organization of the working class, it is itself the working-class movement.

Lenin failed to distinguish the mindless discipline of the barrack-room from conscious class-action, and his centralism was imbued with the 'sterile attitude of a night-watchman'. Revolutionary tactics could not be invented by leaders, they must develop spontaneously: history came first, leaders' consciousness second. The effect of the Bolshevik policy was to paralyse the free development of the proletariat, deprive it of responsibility, and make it an instrument of the bourgeois intelligentsia. The agency of revolution must be the collective mind of the workers and not the consciousness of self-styled leaders. The errors of the true workers' movement were more fruitful than the infallibility of a Central Committee.

The Russian Revolution of 1905 convinced Rosa Luxemburg that mass strikes were the most effective form of revolutionary action. In her view, that revolution afforded a pattern for other European countries: an elemental outbreak without a leader, a plan, or a co-ordinated programme, and not initiated by any political party. In 1914 Kautsky, in *Der politische Massenstreik*, decried Rosa Luxemburg's views as an aberration: how could she suppose that a few months of accidental, disorganized strikes, without a unifying idea or plan, could teach the workers more than thirty years of systematic work by parties and trade unions?

But this was precisely what Rosa Luxemburg believed; and she held that the revolutionary potential of the working masses was indestructible, though it might be temporarily stifled by arrogant leaders. This did not mean that the party was superfluous, however. The concept of an advance guard of the proletariat was a sound one; but it should be a group of active members, not a sovereign body. The party's task was not merely to await the revolution but to hasten the course of history; this, however, was not a matter of conspiracies and *coups d'état*, but of cultivating the revolutionary consciousness of the masses, who would in the end decide the fate of socialism without help from their leaders.

Although Rosa Luxemburg criticized Lenin for his barrack-room ideas and manipulation of the socialist movement, she did not join issue directly with Kautsky's doctrine which Lenin adopted as the basis of his theory of the party, viz. that revolutionary consciousness should be instilled into the workers' movement from without. Lukács, in his article 'Rosa Luxemburg as a Marxist' in *Geschichte und Klassenbewusstsein* (*History and Class-Consciousness*, 1923), maintained that she herself accepted this doctrine, as she held that the party was the vehicle of the proletariat's class-consciousness and that its task was to turn theory into practice by imbuing a spontaneous movement with the truth already implicit therein. Rosa Luxemburg would probably have agreed with this formulation, but she would not have gone on to say that the intelligentsia was the prime source of the consciousness of the proletariat, or that the party in its role of standard-bearer could be replaced by a group of leaders. To her the party was the self-organizing proletariat, not the proletariat organized by professional functionaries of the revolution. In her comments and criticisms she maintained the position that Marxism was not merely a theory of the historical process but an articulation of the consciousness, latent though it might be as yet, of an actual workers' movement. When that consciousness took shape, i.e. when the spontaneous movement achieved theoretical self-knowledge, the distinction between theory and practice would cease to exist: the theory would become a material force, not in the sense of being a weapon in the struggle, but as an organic part of it. There is in this sense a kind of pre-established harmony between Marx's doctrine and the revolutionary movement that was to make it its own. Marx did not 'invent' the

philosophy of history: he expressed the content of the proletariat's self-awareness, which was still dormant, and was, one
may say, the instrument by which that content was first manifested.

This account of the matter is consistent with Marx's view of
his own theory and with Rosa Luxemburg's dominant idea, but
she did not herself use this or similar language. It is clear that
the above interpretation does not remove the difference between
Leninism and Rosa Luxemburg's philosophy of the party, but
is compatible with either of them. If the party's function is to
inspire a spontaneous movement with the truth that is immanent
in that movement, we are still free either to accept Lenin's view
of the party as a manipulator or to agree with Rosa Luxemburg
that the workers' movement is always a spontaneous process and
that all the party has to do is to explain to the workers their
true objectives as laid down by history.

Rosa Luxemburg's belief that the workers' movement should
not be manipulated or forced into a tactical mould by party
leaders was the basis of her criticism of the Bolsheviks after their
first year of rule in Russia. This fell under three main heads:
their policy towards the peasants and towards the nationalities,
and the question of democracy in the state and party.

Rosa Luxemberg criticized Bolshevik tyranny in the same way
as Kautsky, but not for the same reasons. Kautsky defended
democracy on general grounds that were not specifically Marxist
but might also be recognized by liberals, whereas Rosa
Luxemburg was actuated by her Marxist faith in the unique
value of the spontaneous political activity of the masses. She
brushed aside the arguments of Kautsky and the Mensheviks
about Russia's economic backwardness and the desirability of a
coalition with the liberal bourgeoisie. This, she said, would be a
desertion of the revolutionary cause. The Bolsheviks had been
right to start the revolution when they did and to bank on its
spreading to the rest of the world. Here Rosa Luxemburg was in
agreement with Trotsky and Lenin: the party should seize power
when it was politically feasible to do so, regardless of doctrinaire
objections about economic maturity—always on the assumption,
which was generally accepted, that a socialist revolution in
Russia could only succeed if it touched off a revolution throughout Europe. She also rejected the social democratic principle

that the party must first gain a majority and only then think about taking power. This was 'parliamentary cretinism': the proper course was to use revolutionary tactics to gain a majority, not the other way round.

This did not mean, however, that the party, having seized power despite the majority of the population, should maintain itself by terror and reject all normal forms of political freedom and representation. The turning-point of the Russian Revolution was the dispersal of the Constituent Assembly. Lenin and Trotsky had done away with general elections altogether, basing their power on the Soviets. Trotsky declared that the Assembly summoned before October was reactionary and that universal suffrage was needless as it did not truly reflect the state of feeling of the masses. But, Rosa Luxemburg replied, the masses could influence their representatives after the elections and make them change course, and the more democratic the system, the more effective such pressure could be. Democratic institutions were not perfect, but to abolish them was much worse, as it paralysed the political life of the masses. The restriction of the suffrage to those who worked for their living was absurd in the general state of chaos, with industry in ruins and unemployment on a huge scale. The curbs on the Press and on the right of assembly turned the rule of the masses into a fiction. 'Freedom only for supporters of the government, only for members of a single party, however numerous—this is not freedom. Freedom must always be for those who think differently' (*The Russian Revolution*). Socialism was a live historical movement and could not be replaced by administrative decrees. If public affairs were not properly discussed they would become the province of a narrow circle of officials and corruption would be inevitable. Socialism called for a spiritual transformation of the masses, and terrorism was no way to bring this about: there must be unlimited democracy, a free public opinion, freedom of elections and the Press, the right to hold meetings and form associations. Otherwise the only active part of society would be the bureaucracy: a small group of leaders would give orders, and the workers' task would be to applaud them. The dictatorship of the proletariat would be replaced by the dictatorship of a clique.

For Lenin and Trotsky, Rosa Luxemburg wrote, democracy was the opposite of dictatorship, as it was for Kautsky. Because of this opposition Kautsky thought the proletariat should give up the power it had seized in an unripe situation; because of it, Lenin and Trotsky decided that power should be wielded by means of coercion. But the proletariat is supposed to exercise the dictatorship of a class, not of a party or a clique, and it should do so openly, in democratic conditions. 'If we have revealed the bitter kernel of inequality and slavery beneath the husk of formal equality and freedom, it is not in order to throw the husk away, but to persuade the working class not to be satisfied with it but to press on to the conquest of political power and fill it with a new social content ... Dictatorship is not a matter of abolishing democracy but of applying it correctly' (ibid.). True, the Bolsheviks had come to power in circumstances in which full democracy was impossible. But they were now making a virtue of necessity by seeking to impose their own tactics on the whole workers' movement, turning the distortion of an exceptional situation into a universal rule. They were to be commended for' seizing power in Russia, but the socialist cause was a matter for the whole world and not for a single country.

Rosa Luxemburg's criticism of the Bolshevik dictatorship was consistent with her earlier critique of Leninism. In 1906 she wrote that 'the very idea of socialism excludes minority rule' ('Blanquism and social democracy', *Czerwony Sztandar*, 27 June). She also said at that time that when the Tsardom was overthrown the Russian proletariat, after seizing power, would hand it over to a government elected by a majority of the population, and, as the proletariat was a minority in Russia, this government could not be predominantly social-democratic. It is not clear how she imagined the Bolsheviks could keep themselves in power in 1918 while allowing free elections, since the proletariat was only a minority and it could not by any means be supposed that the whole of it would vote for them. Martov and Kautsky did not have to meet this difficulty in their criticism of the Bolshevik dictatorship, since they took the view that authority must derive from general representative institutions, so that there could only be a government of the proletariat if the latter constituted the bulk of society. Rosa Luxemburg, on the other hand, seemed to believe that the Bolsheviks could have held on to power by democratic means under a system of popular representation. This strange notion could only be based on her mythical, unshakeable belief in the innate revolutionary character of the masses, which, left to themselves, were bound to evolve socialist forms of public life. Lenin and Trotsky were a good deal more circumspect and realistic than this.

5. *The national question*

The question of nationality was a permanent, unsolved theoretical difficulty of Marxism and a practical difficulty of socialist movements. It was not easy to reconcile the principle that class divisions were fundamental to social analysis and prediction and to problems of practical policy, with the historical fact that people were and always had been divided on a national basis. Ethnic units were divided by quite other criteria than those of class, and a nation was historically a unit transcending class; how then could a purely class viewpoint be combined with the traditional recognition of the right of nations to independence? The brotherhood of peoples against their exploiters had been a popular slogan in the mid-nineteenth century and no doubt expressed the natural attitude of the democratic revolutionaries of the Age of Emancipation, but on inspection it clearly failed to solve the inveterate problems of national frontiers and minorities and colonial exploitation. When countries were ruthlessly exploiting their colonies it was hard to show in despite of all practical experience that the interests of the subject peoples were 'in the nature of things' identical with those of the metropolitan population.

Marx and Engels left nothing that could be called a theory of the nationality question. Their attitude to the problem was a mixture of Hegelian reminiscences, the slogans of 1848, and their personal likes and dislikes, which they expressed forcibly at times, especially in letters. Their views are marked by a strong European orientation and by contempt for small 'unhistorical' peoples, which are doomed to destruction as nations and are meanwhile supporters of darkest reaction and puppets of great-power intrigue. Marx was systematically hostile to Russia, believing that the desire for world domination was the mainstay of her policy; he suspected the British government of conniving at Russian expansionism, and regarded Britain's part in the Crimean War as due to proletarian pressure. He was little interested in ancient civilizations other than that of Greece, dismissing them as infantile periods of spiritual weakness and barbarism: both India and China were written off in this way. He once wrote in a letter that the Orient had given us nothing but religion and the plague. He had no doubt that socialism was the mission of the advanced and dominant countries. By creating a world market the bourgeoisie was setting the stage for revolution, and when it took place in the developed countries the rest would follow. Engels welcomed the United States' conquest of territory from Mexico and the French colonization of Algeria: the Bedouin were a race of bandits anyhow. Marx emphasized Britain's revolutionary role in India, roused by colonization from its millennial slumbers. In a letter of 9 August 1882 he rebuked Bernstein for taking a sentimental view of Egyptian nationalism. Engels made no secret of his contempt for the Balkan peoples: the Bulgarians were a race of swineherds who would do best to keep quiet under Turkish rule pending the European revolution. All these small nations were allies of the Tsar and enemies of the developed West. The 'historic' peoples—Germans, Poles, Hungarians—should rule over the other Slavs (except Russia); Poland should be restored to her pre-1772 frontiers, including Lithuania, White Russia, and a large part of the Ukraine. The Hungarians were entitled to rule over the Slovaks and Croats, the Austrians over the Czechs and Moravians. All these small subject peoples had played no part in European history and would never be independent. France should rule over Belgium, Alsace, and Lorraine; Germany over Schleswig. In general the higher civilization should prevail over the lower, progress over barbarism and stagnation. Both Marx and Engels were especially interested in the Polish question. Engels thought the Poles had done more for the revolution than Germany, Italy, and Hungary put together. Both men regarded the partition of Poland as the corner-stone of European reaction: the freeing of Poland from Russian rule would be the first step towards overthrowing the Tsardom and destroying reaction throughout the world.

Engels's distinction between historical and non-historical peoples is a reflection of the mood of 1848 rather than a deliberate historical theory, and the same may be said of his sympathy for Poland and his belief that it would play a key part in the revolution. Marx, however, towards the end of his life became seriously interested in the prospect of a revolution in Russia; he also thought the Irish question might hasten the revolution in England. However, national questions in general played no part in his theory of revolutionary strategy.

The socialists of the Second International, especially those from the multinational empires of Russia and Austria-Hungary, could not fall back on general formulas and summary classifications of nations into 'progressive' and 'reactionary', especially as they canvassed for support from the proletariat of the subject nationalities. It was thus natural for the Russians, Poles, and Austrians in particular to endeavour to find a socialist solution to the national question. Lenin, Otto Bauer, Karl Renner, Stalin, and Rosa Luxemburg all in their different ways sought to integrate the national problem into the corpus of Marxist doctrine.

The theme is one which naturally recurs incessantly in Rosa Luxemburg's correspondence. The SDKPiL proclaimed itself first and foremost, in opposition to the PPS, to be against the policy of Polish independence. Not that Rosa Luxemburg was indifferent to the oppression of one nation by another, but she regarded it as a consequence and a function of the rule of capital. After the socialist revolution the problem would solve itself, as socialism by definition would do away with all forms of oppression. In the meantime it was no use fighting for national independence, and it would be harmful to the revolutionary cause as it would divide the movement into sections, destroy the international solidarity of the proletariat, and divert its attention to nation-building, which was supposed to be the concern of the whole nation and not only of the oppressed classes. In general, concern over the national question as a separate problem was the result of bourgeois infiltration and tended to undermine the class viewpoint which was the *raison d'être* of social democracy. Marx's attitude towards Poland was understandable as a matter of policy in his time, but it was outdated or erroneous and in conflict with Marxist theory, which forbade the labelling of Poland and Russia, regardless of class divisions, as respectively progressive and reactionary. The attempts of Limanowski, continued by the PPS, to link the cause of socialism with that of an independent Poland were reactionary in the highest degree. The PPS sought to involve the international workers' movement in the cause of a reconstructed Polish state by foisting on it the traditions of the

Polish nobility's struggle for independence. As early as 1896 Rosa Luxemburg protested against the introduction of a 'Polish' resolution at the London Congress of the Second International, arguing that it was not true that Russia's strength depended on the subjugation of Poland and that the Tsardom would collapse if she were freed. The strength of the Tsardom depended on conditions inside Russia, and the development of capitalism would lead to its downfall in due course.

The idea of restoring Poland was not only reactionary inasmuch as it tended to destroy the class solidarity of the proletariat in the Tsarist empire, but it was utopian and hopeless as well. In all her writings Rosa Luxemburg never ceased to emphasize that Polish capitalism was an integral part of Russian capitalism; two-thirds of Polish exports went to the east; the irreversible process of economic integration could not be arrested by childish patriotic dreams. No social class in Poland was interested in independence: neither the bourgeoisie, whose livelihood depended on Russian markets, nor the gentry, fighting desperately to preserve as much as they could of their way of life, nor the proletariat, whose concern was the class struggle, nor the majority of the petty bourgeoisie, nor the peasants. At the most, some small groups of the intelligentsia who lacked social advancement, or of the reactionary petty bourgeoisie threatened by the rise of capitalism, dreamt impotently of an independent Poland. In general, national problems had no significance of their own; national movements were always in the interest of particular classes. Since there was no class that could represent the national cause on the basis of strong, irrefutable economic principles, that was the end of the matter: an independent Poland was an impossibility. What was true of Russian Poland applied equally to the provinces ruled by Prussia and Austria. Polish capitalists attempted to turn the workers' thoughts to ideas of independence so as to cloud their minds and persuade them that the enemy was not capitalism but the Germans and the Hakata (an organization for eroding Polish rights in the Poznań province).

Holding these views, Rosa Luxemburg combated from the outset the principle of national self-determination that figured in the programme of the Russian social democrats; she inclined instead to the Austro-Marxist idea of cultural autonomy as a solution to the national question after the revolution. Her opinions were set out in an article 'The nationality question and autonomy' in *Przegląd Socjal-demokratyczny* (No. 6, August 1908), and in her pamphlet on the Russian revolution. In the former she states that the right of self-determination is a slogan of bourgeois nationalism, implying that every nation has an equal right to decide its own destiny. In fact, national movements are progressive or reactionary according to historical circumstances. This was recognized by Marx and Engels when they emphasized the reactionary character of national aspirations on the part of the southern Slavs and Czechs, the Swiss revolt against the Habsburgs in the fourteenth century, or the separatism of Scots, Bretons, and Basques; many of these movements supported reactionary monarchies against republicans. The natural tendency of history was for small nations to be absorbed by larger ones; cultural and linguistic unity was bound to be the ultimate goal, and it was reactionary and utopian to seek to reverse this process. 'Can one speak seriously of "self-determination" for the Montenegrins, Bulgars, Romanians, Serbs and Greeks, or even to any real extent of the Swiss?' In any case a nation was not an integrated social whole, but a congeries of hostile classes opposing one another in everything.

Rosa Luxemburg held that the recognition of the right of nationalities to self-determination was one of the Bolsheviks' gravest mistakes. This so-called right was 'no more than an idle petty-bourgeois phrase and humbug': the Bolsheviks had hoped by it to secure the support of the non-Russian peoples of the empire, but the result was that the Poles, Finns, Lithuanians, Ukrainians, and the peoples of the Caucasus used their freedom to combat the revolution, though formerly they had been active in its cause. Instead of defending the integrity of the Russian state, now .the bulwark of the revolution, and 'crushing separatism with an iron hand', the Bolsheviks had allowed the bourgeoisie of the non-Russian peoples to decide their own fate and had even stirred up national feeling among peoples like the Ukrainians, who had never been a nation.

The acerbity with which Rosa Luxemburg fought the idea of national independence, especially for the Poles, brought her and the Leninists into sharp opposition, but it must be emphasized that this was a question of strategy and not of different views as to the intrinsic value of nations and national culture. Lenin's attitude on this point was the same as Rosa Luxemburg's. He conceded the right to self-determination, but he regarded it as the duty of socialists to fight against the separatism of their own nation; in any case self-determination was far less important than the interest of the revolution, i.e. of keeping the Bolsheviks in power. The proletariat of a nation should speak for it as regards separation versus integration, and the mouthpiece of the proletariat was its party, which expressed the most progressive tendencies of any national group. Lenin's disapproval of the brutality of the Soviet occupation of Georgia in 1921 had no practical effect, and the party's programme afforded ample justification of the violent measures by which most of the Russian patrimony was regained. However, Rosa Luxemburg's quarrel with the PPS was a fundamental one. With hindsight it may appear incredible that she could be so blind to social realities, but this was not the only instance of its kind: she was a doctrinaire intellectual through and through. Her accounts of social phenomena are deductions from a Marxist schema, with the minimum of correction in the light of experience. Since capitalist society was in the nature of things divided into hostile classes, and as the interest of each class was identical throughout the world, at least as far as the class war was concerned, it was a theoretical impossibility for any nation 'as a whole' to aspire to independence, for aspirations on the national plane simply could not exist. Rosa Luxemburg was not shaken in this opinion by the outburst of nationalism in 1914 and the resulting collapse of the International: she merely blamed the social democratic leaders for betraying international ideals. Like many doctrinaire Marxists, she ceased to think in terms of social analysis when experience failed to bear out her theoretical presuppositions; instead, she looked for 'guilty men' and blamed the discrepancy on subjective factors. Since nations did not exist as integrated communities, there could be no such thing as a true national movement. If there appeared to be, it was a case of 'bourgeois fraud' or 'revisionist treachery', and the Marxist schema remained unscathed. The working class was essentially revolutionary, and any appearance to the contrary must be due to corrupt leaders instilling reformist ideas in the workers: the disparity between the essence of things and superficial experience could be ignored or attributed to individual bad faith, or explained as a 'dialectical contradiction'. Reasoning in this way, Rosa Luxemburg was able to preserve her views unaltered even though her predictions were almost always falsified by events.

Lenin for his part criticized Rosa Luxemburg on the ground that by one-sidedly combating Polish nationalism she was favouring the more dangerous nationalism of Great Russia. Others who criticized her were the PPS theorists, Feliks Perl and Kazimierz Kelles-Krauz. The latter wrote in 1905 that the 'economic conditions' that were supposedly an obstacle to Polish independence were no more than a matter of trade between provinces, and that Rosa Luxemburg was in effect advocating that the proletariat should adapt its activity to the temporary requirements of the bourgeoisie. National states were in the natural interest of capitalism, but independence was also necessary to the working class, as it was a necessary condition of democracy.

The Polish Communists, on the other hand, wholeheartedly accepted Rosa Luxemburg's doctrine on the subject of national independence. The later criticism of 'Luxemburgism', which was of a general and summary character, accused her of 'underestimating' the bourgeoisie's interest in the internal market and that of other classes in the national cause. But this criticism never went so far as to call in question the principle that the class struggle is 'in the last resort' the only decisive historical conflict; national questions are either transient, unimportant issues or a disguise for 'real', i.e. class, interests, or else they represent a potential source of revolutionary energy that must be used for tactical reasons but can hardly be taken seriously 'in a historical perspective'. In short, Marxism in its Communist version never came to terms with national realities.

Rosa Luxemburg is an outstanding example of a type of mind that is often met with in the history of Marxism and appears to be specially attracted by the Marxist outlook. It is characterized by slavish submission to authority, together with a belief that in that submission the values of scientific thought can be preserved. No doctrine was so well suited as Marxism to satisfy both these attitudes, or to provide a mystification combining extreme dogmatism with the cult of 'scientific' thinking, in which the disciple could find mental and spiritual peace. Marxism thus played the part of a religion for the intelligentsia, which did not prevent some of them, like Rosa Luxemburg herself, from trying to improve the deposit of faith by reverting to first principles, thus strengthening their own belief that they were independent of dogma.

Rosa Luxemburg's main theme was the theory of accumulation, linked closely with her belief that capitalism must bring about increasing class polarization. (All orthodox Marxists shared this belief, and in Kautsky's view Marxism would have collapsed without it.) She endeavoured to give Marxism a final consistent shape by defining the circumstances in which capitalism becomes an economic impossibility. Marxism was to her the universal key to the meaning of history, enabling the mind to reject as insignificant trifles any adventitious factors that might disturb its course. In this way historical materialism could be looked on not as an extreme impoverishment of reality but as a process of scientific abstraction, preserving the essence of things and eliminating what was merely accidental. No one seemed to notice, however, that this meant treating the whole of actual history as a series of unimportant contingencies, leaving science to contemplate only the general framework of the transition from one economic system to another. All the rest—wars, national and racial conflicts, constitutional and legal forms, religions, artistic and intellectual life—was relegated to the scrap-heap of 'accidents', of no concern to the theoretician brooding over the majestic phases of 'great' history. In this way the barrenness of simplistic schemata was endowed with a false sublimity.

The fate of Rosa Luxemburg's writings illustrates the tragedy of the attempt to preserve the integrality of Marxism while rejecting the only means of doing so, viz. an institutional body with authority to distinguish finally between truth and error. Rosa Luxemburg sought to be the champion of orthodoxy, but instead of regarding the party as the infallible fount of orthodoxy she preferred to believe in the revolutionary mission of the masses as the spontaneous source of truth. Lenin was not guilty of this inconsistency, and his form of Marxism was effective in practice because its doctrine was made the exclusive property of an organization of professional revolutionaries. In the case of Rosa Luxemburg, strange results followed from believing absolutely in the predetermination of history and also in the 'essentially' revolutionary character of the masses. In her pamphlet on the Russian revolution she urged Lenin to introduce unfettered democracy and at the same time to crush all nationalist movements with an iron hand, not suspecting for a moment that there might be any inconsistency in these two demands.

On the basis of her theory of accumulation Rosa Luxemburg foresaw increasing market difficulties and pressure of capital on wages, the radicalization of the working masses, and the class polarization of society. This is why she attached no practical importance to national and peasant movements, whose effect must diminish as capitalism expanded, and she neglected the role of colonial territories as theatres of revolution. In short, she believed in a proletarian revolution in the classic Marxian sense, whereas Lenin realized that no 'pure' proletarian revolution would ever occur and that as capitalism approached the 'ideal' of two-class society the socialist revolution became less probable, not more. Thus Rosa Luxemburg opposed Lenin on three points, each of which was a necessary precondition of the Bolsheviks' success in 1917: their policy towards the peasants and the nationalities, and their military conception of the party.

In an article written in 1922 and published posthumously in 1924 Lenin drew a picture of Rosa Luxemburg which was accepted as definitive by the Communist movement: she was an 'eagle of the Revolution', but she had been wrong in her opinions concerning accumulation, the national problem, the Mensheviks and Bolsheviks, and the October Revolution itself. (Her ideas on 'spontaneity' and the role of the party do not figure in this list of her mistakes.) The German Communists, after their failure to bring about a rising in 1920 and 1923, blamed their miscalculation on the ideology of 'Luxemburgism': prominent in this were Ruth Fischer and Maslow, the former of whom compared Rosa Luxemburg to a syphilis germ. The whole tradition of the Spartacus League was written off as a series of theoretical and tactical errors. In 1926, when factional and personal conflicts in the Soviet party leadership brought the so-called 'rightists' to power in the German Communist party, Rosa Luxemburg was rehabilitated for a brief period, while Ruth Fischer and Maslow lost their influence; but soon the old stereotypes were revived and intensified. In an article in 1931 Stalin closed the discussion by stating that Rosa Luxemburg was responsible for the theory of 'permanent revolution', later adopted by Trotsky in opposition to the doctrine of 'socialism in one country'.

In consequence, all that was distinctive in Rosa Luxemburg's political and theoretical views became a dead letter, and she was remembered only in verbal tributes by Polish and German Communists commemorating her martyrdom for the revolution. Her critique of revolutionary despotism was not noticed until long after the Second World War, when such criticism had become current coin, and was treated as a historical curiosity rather than an incentive to change. In the 1960s, however, some interest in her ideas was shown by the so-called 'New Left' in its search for an alternative model of Marxist orthodoxy which, while rejecting Lenin's theory of the party, would set its face against revisionism and continue to rely on the inexhaustible revolutionary potential of the proletariat.

CHAPTER IV

Bernstein and Revisionism

1. The concept of revisionism

THE term 'revisionism' has never been precisely defined, but has been used in a wider or narrower sense according to circumstances. In present-day Communism it is no more than an arbitrary label affixed to any group or individual who in any way criticizes the policy, programme, or doctrine of a particular party; but at the turn of the century 'revisionism' existed as a specific phenomenon, though with fluid boundaries, in Central and East European socialism. The term denoted those writers and political figures who, while starting from Marxist premises, came by degrees to call in question various elements of the doctrine, especially Marx's predictions as to the development of capitalism and the inevitability of socialist revolution. 'Revisionists' were not people who abandoned Marxism completely or had never been Marxists, but those who sought to modify the traditional doctrine or who held that some of its essential features were no longer applicable in the present state of society. Jaurès, for instance, was seldom called a revisionist, because he never set up to be an orthodox Marxist in the German sense. Later the term was also applied to those who attempted to supplement Marxism on Kantian lines. In general, however, revisionism is typically found within the parties that insisted on their fidelity to Marx's theory, i.e. especially those of Germany, Austria, and Russia.

Strictly speaking, revisionism was regarded as a theoretical position, but its articulation by Bernstein in the later 1890s was preceded by political tendencies which led to the same direction. The first sign of the revisionist crisis in the German party appeared in a discussion of the agrarian question in the early 1890s. At the Frankfurt Congress in 1894 the Bavarian social-democratic leader Georg von Vollmar (1850–1922) urged that the party should defend the interests of peasants as well as workers. This appeared to be a purely tactical question, but it involved an essential point of theory. The orthodox, following Marx and Engels, held that agriculture under capitalism must develop on broadly the same lines as industry, i.e. that fewer and fewer owners would hold more and more of the land, and that small peasant proprietors would be squeezed out of existence. Hence Kautsky and those who thought like him were against taking up the cause of the small farmers, who were doomed to extinction as a class and were therefore 'reactionary' in the eyes of history. This meant, however, that the socialists could never enlist peasant support, a fact which greatly weakened them in electoral terms, especially as most of the Prussian peasants allied themselves with the reactionary Junkers against the bourgeoisie. But the issue was not only a tactical one: it was also a question of whether the expected concentration of agriculture was really taking place. Eduard David (1863–1930), a socialist expert on agricultural questions, argued that it was not, and that the family farm was the ideal form of rural production. Kautsky disputed both these points, but agreed many years later that David was right in holding that there was no 'necessary' process of concentration in landownership.

It soon appeared, however, that the correctness of Marx's predictions could be doubted with regard to industry as well as agriculture. The traditional doctrine was that capitalism involved the increasing polarization of classes and concentration of capital, the ruin of small concerns, and the proletarianization of the masses, and that this was an irreversible process: all reforms within the framework of capitalism were superficial and impermanent, and the main task of socialists was to organize their forces for the coming revolutionary conflict. But the growth of mass socialist parties, parliamentary successes, and social reforms prompted a large section of the leadership to see their task in terms of immediate advantages to the working class, and to lose sight of the prospect of a final decisive battle. This 'reformist' attitude was widespread in practical socialism before Bernstein gave it a theoretical basis. Note was taken of the record of British socialism, which had no revolutionary doctrine but had scored undoubted successes over the years. Thus the revisionist doctrine, when it came, fell on fertile ground among party and trade union leaders. Their practical revisionism had various motives and took various directions. Parliamentarians were interested in forming alliances with non-socialist forces for electoral or reformist purposes, and all such alliances were suspect from the orthodox point of view. Local party and union representatives were less interested in electoral tactics, but they were also generally indifferent to the 'ultimate goal' of socialism and the whole theoretical side of the party programme. Among the leaders their way of thinking was represented by Ignaz Auer (1846–1907). Others again, such as Schippel and Heine, questioned the party's anti-militarist and anti-colonial programme on grounds of nationalism and in the belief that a strong army and the acquisition of colonies and markets were in the interest of the German proletariat. In general, the practical basis of this loosely formulated revisionism was that socialists should build the new society 'by degrees', concentrating on day-to-day improvements and not merely waiting for a revolution. Bernstein's theories could never have had such an earth-shaking effect if they had not been a crystallization of ideas which were already in the air.

2. *Biographical information*

Eduard Bernstein (1850–1932) was born in Berlin, the son of an engine-driver; both his parents were non-practising Jews. After leaving the Gymnasium at an early age he worked in a bank from 1869 to 1878. He joined the Eisenach party in 1872 and took part in the Gotha Congress of 1875. For a time he adhered to Dühring's philosophy, but was put off by the latter's dogmatic intolerance and anti-Semitism. Engels's *Anti-Dühring* (1878) converted him to Marxism, and he became a zealous exponent of orthodoxy as then understood. After the anti-socialist laws were promulgated he went to Lugano and then to Zurich as secretary to Karl Höchberg, a rich German who sympathized with the social democrats and helped them financially, though not himself a Marxist. In Zurich Bernstein wrote for the *Sozialde-mokrat*, and became its editor from 1880 to 1890. He also met Kautsky, who came from Vienna with Höchberg's help, and the Russian socialist *émigrés*. The *Sozialdemokrat* was an orthodox revolutionary journal and played an important part in maintain-

ing the party's continuity in conditions of illegality or semi-
legality. In 1880 Bernstein accompanied Bebel to London, where
he met Marx and Engels. He visited Engels again in 1884 and
they maintained a lively correspondence, which Bernstein did
not publish until 1925. In 1887 he published in Zurich a work on
the Chartists (*Die Chartisten-Bewegung in England*). In the middle
of 1888 he was deported from Switzerland and went to London;
he was one of Engels's closest friends for the next few years, and
was an executor of his will.

Bernstein remained in England till the beginning of 1901. His
stay there fundamentally altered his views on Marxism and the
philosophy of socialism: he was much influenced by the Fabians,
with whom he remained in close contact. His experience of conditions in England convinced him that the idea of a once-and-for-
all break-up of capitalism was a doctrinaire illusion, and that
socialists should place their hopes in gradual social reforms and
socialization as the result of democratic pressure. These conclusions soon took the form of an entire system in which many of the
philosophical and political premisses of Marxism were modified.
Bernstein's critique had much in common with the *Katheder-
sozialismus* of Brentano, Schulze-Gävernitz, and Sombart, who
attempted to combine socialism with liberalism and looked to
social legislation as a means of reform instead of a single
'qualitative' jump from capitalism to socialism. Bernstein
expounded his views in a series of articles entitled 'Problems of
Socialism' which appeared in *Die Neue Zeit* from the end of 1896,
and later in a book *Die Voraussetzungen des Sozialismus und die Aufgaben der Sozialdemokratie* (*The Premisses of Socialism and the Tasks
of Social Democracy*, 1899), which became the fundamental revisionist text and the object of innumerable polemics. Bernstein
replied to the first attacks in a letter to the party congress at
Stuttgart, which he could not attend as he was still wanted for
trial in Germany. His views were denounced at the congress by
Kautsky, Clara Zetkin, and Rosa Luxemburg, and soon the
whole of the European social democratic movement was involved in a debate which led finally to the crystallization of two
opposing tendencies. In spite of the succession of anti-revisionist
resolutions and condemnations, and although Bernstein was opposed by most of the party theorists, his influence was already
clearly increasing within the party and the trade unions.

Bernstein returned to Germany in 1901, and was elected to the Reichstag in 1902 as member for Breslau. He ceased to contribute to *Die Neue Zeit* but wrote frequently for *Sozialistische Monatshefte*, which Julius Bloch edited from 1897 and which became the chief theoretical organ of reformism. He was not expelled from the party (only a small group of radicals pressed, unsuccessfully, for the expulsion of the revisionists), and as time went on his adherents secured more and more influential posts in the party administration.

From then on Bernstein divided his activity between parliamentary work (he was a deputy to the Reichstag from 1902 to 1918 and again from 1920 to 1928) and writing and publishing. In London he had published works by Lassalle, and a complete edition in twelve volumes subsequently appeared in Berlin. He endorsed the programme for a mass political strike (*Der politische Massenstreik und die politische Lage der Sozialdemokratie in Deutschland*, 1905), wrote a three-volume history of the Berlin workers' movement (*Geschichte der Berliner Arbeiterbewegung*, 1907–10), collaborated with Bebel in publishing the correspondence of Marx and Engels in four volumes, and founded and edited the periodical *Dokumente des Sozialismus* (1902–5). He criticized Marxism more and more outspokenly, and in the last few years before 1914 was closer to the liberal reformers than to the Marxists. During the war he belonged to the anti-war minority of the party and joined the USPD along with Kautsky and Haase. He rejoined the SPD after the war and took part in drafting its first programme. He was the real founder of the social democratic ideology as that term was generally understood between the wars, in opposition to Communism. He died in Berlin.

3. *The laws of history and the dialectic*

In Bernstein's opinion, it was the misfortune of Marxist theory that it derived from Hegelianism. Marx, he thought, had never quite shaken off the Hegelian tendency to make deductions about social conditions from abstract, *a priori* dialectical schemata, with insufficient regard to actual facts. This had led him to believe in historical determinism and in a single factor governing the course of history, in relation to which human beings were merely instruments or organs. But Engels had considerably attenuated the original formulas of historical materialism by his doctrine of 'ultimate causes', which implied that there were also mediate causes affecting history: the more numerous and varied these were, the less absolute must be the preponderance of the 'ultimate causes'. This was confirmed by experience: the multiplicity of forces affecting society limited the sphere of necessity and enabled human beings to exercise increasing influence on social processes. This being recognized, Marxism could no longer be regarded as a purely materialist doctrine, still less as teaching that history was absolutely governed by the 'economic factor'; though Marx deserved immense credit for having shown the importance of changes in technology and production methods for the understanding of history.

Hegel was also responsible for the Blanquist element in Marxism, the belief in total revolution and the creative role of political violence. *The Communist Manifesto* made no mention of Babeuf among the socialist authors whose views it criticized. The Address of the Central Committee to the Communist League made in March 1850 was Blanquist in spirit: it appeared to assume that the will to revolution and the organization of terrorism were sufficient to provide the driving force of a socialist upheaval. In general, Marx had tried to find a compromise between two socialist traditions. The first was constructive and evolutionary: it had been developed in utopian literature and in nineteenth-century socialist sects and workers' associations, and aimed at emancipating society by means of a new economic system. The second principle was destructive, conspiratorial and terrorist, and its aim was to transform society by the political expropriation of the governing classes. Marxism was rather a compromise than a synthesis of the two principles, and Marx's thought oscillated between them, presenting different features at different times.

Bernstein's view that Hegel was to blame for the Blanquist elements in Marxism was, it may be noted, the opposite of Plekhanov's opinion. The latter held that Hegel's tradition, with its anti-utopian trend and its emphasis on the natural 'logic' of history, was the most effective weapon against political adventurism, Blanquist conspiratorial tactics, and the expectation of a lightning leap to socialism, before the relations of production under capitalism had matured to the point where an organic change was possible.

Another blemish in Marx's philosophy, according to Bernstein, was his theory of value, suggesting as it did that value as defined by labour-time was a real phenomenon governing the terms of exchange and not merely a convenient expository device. Value in Marx's sense was unmeasurable and was at best an abstract conceptual instrument, not an economic reality. Engels had held that in the Middle Ages goods were still exchanged according to their value, but Parvus had shown that even then there were various factors limiting the effect of value on prices. The law of value was truly in force only in primitive societies. The rightness or wrongness of Marx's theory in this respect was not essential to the analysis of surplus value, but here too the doctrine was misleading: by identifying the rate of surplus value with the rate of exploitation, he gave the impression that the former was the index of social injustice. This was incorrect, for the workers' standard of life was not directly geared to the rate of surplus value—they might be in a state of destitution when the rate was low, or comparatively well off although it was high; moreover, socialism could not be justified by the fact that wages did not equal the full value of the product, since they could not do so anyway.

In his later articles Bernstein took issue even more emphatically with the theory of value expressed in *Capital*. The point that Marx's definition of value was an expository device and not a real social phenomenon had made previously by Schmidt and Sombart, and in his main treatise Bernstein followed their argument. Later he went further and declared that value in Marx's sense did not exist; price was the sole economic reality, and commodities had value because they had a price. Marx had underestimated the use-value of commodities, and his concept of value was useless because it was not quantitative: one of the reasons for this was that one can measure labour-time but not the intensity of labour.

Bernstein's critique of the philosophical basis of Marxism and its derivation from Hegelianism is summary in the extreme. He does not in fact seem to have known any more of Hegel's work than he could gather from the absurd simplifications of Engels. In this he was not alone among his contemporaries: the Marxists knew next to nothing of Hegel, and the latter's contribution to Marx's world-view was reduced to a few platitudes or ignored. (Labriola and Plekhanov were among the few who mentioned the dependence of Marx on Hegel, but Plekhanov's view of Hegel was also simplified out of all recognition.) The general trend of Bernstein's critique of Marx is clear, however. It is an attack on all speculative systems which purport to explain history by a single abstract principle, and on the 'philosophic' mentality which, instead of studying empirical economic tendencies, subordinates all to the expectation of a single tremendous qualitative change which is to transform and save the world.

Bernstein did not endeavour to show that he was faithful to Marx's views: he openly criticized what he regarded as the 'negative' element of Marxism, the belief in speculative historical schemata and in the advent of socialism as a complete break with the previous history of mankind.

4. *The revolution and the 'ultimate goal'*

The critique of Hegelian blemishes in Marx's thought would not in itself have been a grave threat to party ideology, but the brunt of Bernstein's attack lay elsewhere. He argued that Marxist predictions as to the concentration of capital were erroneous, as was the theory of class polarization and a single revolutionary change sweeping away the existing order; that the task of social democracy was gradually to socialize political institutions and property, and that the party had already accepted this in practice, though it had not the courage to jettison the time-honoured revolutionary theory. Such was the true substance of the revisionist doctrine, which was clearly inconsistent with the letter and spirit of Marxism and with the theoretical section of the party programme.

Marx's statements concerning the falling rate of profit, overproduction, crises, concentration and the periodical destruction of capital were undoubtedly based on fact, Bernstein observed, but he ignored or underrated the contrary tendencies that were to be found in capitalism. The concentration of enterprises was not the same as the concentration of wealth: the former was taking place, but not the latter. Owing to the joint-stock system, the growth of large industrial concerns did not mean the corresponding growth of large fortunes. On the contrary, the number of property-owners was increasing in both relative and absolute terms. Thus, if the prospects of socialism depended on the concentration of wealth, social democracy would be fighting against an objective economic process. In reality, however, the chances of socialism did not depend on the validity of the theory of concentration. As Bernstein emphasized to the Stuttgart Congress, in stating that the number of owners was increasing he did not mean to justify the present system. What was decisive for socialism was not the concentration of wealth but the productivity of labour. If the increase in the number of owners acted as a brake on productive forces, it was not conducive to socialism; but the increase must be recognized as a fact, whatever its social significance.

In the same way, the predictions of class polarization were erroneous. On the contrary, social stratification was increasingly complex as technology and the organization of society produced a more numerous middle class. It was therefore hopeless and utopian to expect socialism as a result of capital squeezing out the intermediate class. As the class of technicians and functionaries was increasing rapidly, so the ratio of the proletariat to the total population tended to fall. Nor was rural property tending to concentrate in fewer hands.

The prospects of socialism did not depend on a major crisis bringing about the collapse of capitalism. Such crises were less and less probable, as capitalism grew more capable of adapting itself to market difficulties. The belief of many socialists that crises were due to under-consumption by the masses was incorrect and was contrary to the views of Marx and Engels. Sismondi had put forward this idea, and Rodbertus after him; but Marx himself had pointed out that crises usually occur at a time when wages are going up. Volume III of *Capital*, however, described crises as the result of a conflict between the purchasing power of the masses and the urge of capitalism to improve and increase the forces of production. But the development of world trade had vastly increased the power of capital to react to local crises by mobilizing credit at short notice. Foreign markets were growing intensively rather than extensively, and there was no reason to foresee an absolute end to this increase. Rosa Luxemburg held that Marx's theory related to future crises of decline, whereas hitherto crises had been those of growth; but if this were so it would follow that Marx's theory of crises had a different meaning than he himself ascribed to it, and also that it was a mere speculative deduction unproved by evidence. As it was, the elaborate system of credit, cartels, and protective duties that helped to maintain exploitation was also an effective guard against crises and nullified the hope of an economic cataclysm.

According to Marx there were two main conditions of socialism: a high degree of socialization of the productive process under capitalism, and the political power of the proletariat. The first of these conditions, Bernstein argued, was far from being fulfilled. As to the second, it should be made clear whether the party expected to gain power through democratic electoral institutions or by revolutionary force. The basic trends of social development were not favourable to hopes of revolution. Contrary to prediction, social functions were becoming more differentiated, both generally and amid the working class. The theory that the workers' condition under capitalism was hopeless and could not undergo any real improvement had also been refuted. Marx had not been quite consistent here: he recognized the existence of tendencies that might limit exploitation and improve the wage-earner's lot, but as often as not he ignored them because they were inconsistent with his *a priori* theories. At the present time there was certainly no ground to expect class antagonisms to become more acute owing to increasing exploitation and poverty. But again, the prospects of socialism did not depend on this expectation: they depended on the increasing social productivity of labour as a result of general progress, and on the moral and intellectual maturity of the working class. Socialism was a gradual process of increasing socialization with the aid of democratic institutions and the strength of the organized proletariat. Democracy was not merely a weapon in the political struggle but an end in itself, the form in which socialism was to become a reality. It was not an automatic solution to all social problems, but a powerful and necessary instrument of progress. Since the social democratic movement had taken its stand on parliamentary ground, phrases about the 'dictatorship of the proletariat' were meaningless. Nor could there be any question of the working class building socialism by using force against the rest of society; on the contrary, the socialists should try to interest the petty bourgeoisie and peasants in their programme. The right course was to take advantage of the growing influence of social democracy on state institutions in order to reform the organization of the economy, remove obstacles to co-operative production, secure the right of trade organizations to control production, and establish safeguards against monopoly and guarantees of employment. If these things were achieved it would not matter that production was partly socialized and partly not. Private enterprises would socialize themselves by degrees, but a single wholesale conversion to public ownership would involve waste and terror on a large scale. This did not mean, Bernstein insisted, that the revolution was 'forbidden': revolutions were spontaneous, elemental processes and no one could stop them. But a policy of reform made no difference in this respect. The important thing was to recognize that the party was in fact working towards the socialist transformation of society through democratic and economic reforms, and it should have the courage to show itself in its true colours. Bebel, for instance, denied the charge that the party intended to use political violence; Kautsky had drawn up a reformist agrarian programme, and in the Reichstag the party had called for the establishment of arbitral courts. It was not the case, anyway, that threats of force and strikes were the most effective mode of action: the British workers had gained the vote not in the revolutionary days of Chartism but by allying themselves with the radical section of the bourgeoisie.

Bernstein summed up his attitude in a formula which became famous as the target of orthodox attack: 'What is generally called the ultimate goal of socialism is nothing to me; the movement is everything.' In his letter to the Stuttgart Congress he explained this as follows: the party at the present time should not rely on a great cataclysm but on the general extension of the workers' political rights and their participation in economic and administrative bodies; the conquest of power and the socialization of property are not ends, but means. In his principal work, however, he explains himself somewhat differently. Marx, he says, wrote that the working class has no ready-made Utopia to be introduced by a decree; it has no arbitrarily fashioned ideals; it knows that its emancipation will require long struggles and many historical processes, altering circumstances as well as people; we must bring into action the elements of the new society that have already developed under capitalism. To hold fast to traditional Utopias is injurious to social progress, as it distracts attention from the practicable reforms for which we should be fighting.

As can be seen, the formula 'the goal is nothing, the movement everything' is not clear in itself, and it distorts the idea of Marx's on which it is based. In *The Civil War in France*, in *The German Ideology*, and in other writings Marx emphasized that scientific socialism did not set out to allure people with arbitrary models of a perfect society; its purpose was to ascertain existing economic and social tendencies in order to stimulate or activate the real forces by which society was changed. It was necessary to study 'natural' historical tendencies in embryo or, as he put it in 1843, to 'force these petrified relationships to dance by playing their own tune to them'. This attitude of Marx's was certainly opposed to all sentimental and moralizing Utopias, but not to the hope of a single violent revolution. It did not mean that socialists should limit their horizon to urgent or immediately attainable ends, but only that their aims, including the 'ultimate goal' and the hope of a political revolution, should be based on observation of real historical tendencies and not arbitrary imaginings of a perfect world. In particular Marx made clear the way in which capitalism, as he believed, was creating the 'premisses' for a new order, viz. the collectivization of productive processes, class polarization, and the revolutionary training of the proletariat by the very conditions of its existence. These premisses made socialism possible and even necessary, but no changes in capitalism had any socialist significance prior to the political victory of the proletariat.

Bernstein was thus not justified in invoking Marx's authority for his views, though there was some colour for them in the writings of Engels. The essential question was not whether to accept or reject revolutionary violence, but whether processes of socialization within the capitalist economy were 'already' part of the building of socialism. If socialism could be realized 'little by little' under capitalism, there was no reason why the transformation should not turn out, one day, to be complete. Thus there would no longer be an impassable gulf between the two systems. The movement towards socialism was not the prelude to a great expropriation but simply meant more collectivization, more democracy, equality, and welfare—a gradual trend with no predetermined limit and, by the same token, no 'ultimate goal'. When Bernstein said that the goal was nothing and the movement everything, he was not expressing a banal demand that the party should only set itself practicable tasks. He meant, first and foremost, that the 'ultimate goal' as understood in Marxist tradition—the economic liberation of the proletariat by its conquest of political power—had no definite content. The socialist movement was capable of fighting successfully for many changes which would mean the realization of more and more socialist values; if it were to live merely on the expectation of a once-and-for-all cataclysm, it would not be serving the interests of the proletariat.

Moreover, according to Bernstein, the SPD was already a reformist party in many of its political attitudes. The revolutionary formulas in its programme were inconsistent with its actual policy and could only act as a brake on the latter. It was not a question of the party changing its policy, but rather of understanding the policy it was in fact pursuing, and adapting traditional ideas to current realities.

Furthermore, Bernstein rejected the formula in *The Communist Manifesto* to the effect that the workers had no fatherland. This might have been true in the 1840s, when the proletariat had no political rights and took no part in public life, but it was an anachronism when the workers had asserted their rights as citizens and could affect their country's destiny. The present-day worker had a fatherland and had good reasons to defend it. In the same way, colonialism should not be condemned by socialists out of hand, without regard to circumstances and to the form in which it was exercised. Marx had written that human societies are not the owners but the usufructuaries of the land they inhabit, and are in duty bound to hand it on to posterity in an improved and not a wasted condition. Thus, Bernstein argued, the right to a particular territory did not depend on conquest but on the ability to make good economic use of it. Civilized peoples who could cultivate the land to advantage had a better right to it than savages, so long as they did not rule with brutality or to the detriment of the natives.

5. *The significance of revisionism*

Bernstein's writings provoked an unprecedented flood of attack from orthodox Marxists of all shades. Scarcely any important socialist writer failed to join in: Kautsky, Rosa Luxemburg, Plekhanov, Bebel, Labriola, Jaurès, Adler, Mehring, Parvus, Clara Zetkin—all felt it their obligation to give tongue, which in itself showed that Bernstein's views were not a casual aberration but the expression of a tendency genuinely rooted in the socialist movement.

The philosophical critique of Marx's views played a very small part in these polemics; Bernstein's own remarks in this field were trite and lacking in understanding. The aspect of his writings that aroused indignation was that which disputed the theory of the concentration of capital and argued that the existing order might be gradually reformed by an alliance between the proletariat and the peasants and petty bourgeoisie. Plekhanov objected that the abandonment of the Marxist premiss that the workers had no hope of improving their lot under capitalism meant that socialism was no longer a revolutionary doctrine but a programme of legislative reform. If Bernstein was right, said Kautsky, socialism had no *raison d'être*. Labriola argued that Bernstein had thrown in his lot with the liberal bourgeoisie, and Rosa Luxemburg pointed out that socialism would be unnecessary if the capitalist economy had powers of adaptation enabling it to avoid crises of overproduction. Criticisms of this kind were purely ideological and expressed no more than a well-grounded fear that if Bernstein was right, classic revolutionary Marxism would cease to exist. But most of the critics also maintained that Bernstein was arguing from false premisses. Kautsky, Bebel, and Rosa Luxemburg held to the traditional theory of concentration, and in so doing showed that this term could be interpreted in different ways. Bernstein had not disputed that capital mergers and combinations were taking place in such a way as to increase the number of big industrial enterprises and their share in production. But he denied that there was a tendency for capital to accumulate in the hands of fewer and fewer owners, while small capitalists were squeezed out. Rosa Luxemburg objected that the shareholding system meant the concentration and not the deconcentration of capital; this was true, but did not refute

Bernstein's argument. Apart from this, however, all the orthodox critics perceived that if the polarization of classes and the disappearance of the middle class were called in question, the whole of Marxist doctrine would collapse. The universal practice of issuing small shares was, they said, only the method used by capital to attract small savings, and had nothing to do with the class division of society. Even Jaurès questioned Bernstein's view that class divisions were becoming more fluid: in spite of all differentiations, he claimed, the basic division between haves and have-nots remained in force. Jaurès feared, moreover, that if Bernstein's views were adopted the socialist movement would lose its class character and dissolve into vague radicalism. On this account Jaurès broadly supported Kautsky, although his own views were closer to Bernstein's as regards the socialist significance of reforms and the right and duty of social democrats to ally themselves with non-socialists in the pursuit of short-term objectives.

Rosa Luxemburg formulated the crux of the dispute most clearly. If it is supposed that capitalism can be reformed either by gradually removing the consequences of anarchical production or by improving the workers' standard of life, then there is no point in working for a revolution. But such reform is impossible, for anarchy and crises are in the nature of capitalism, and the worker is exploited by virtue of the fact that he sells his labour-power. This state of things cannot be eliminated or improved without expropriating the capitalists, which can only be done by a revolutionary seizure of power. There is a qualitative difference between revolution and reforms of any kind.

The critics' views did not prevent revisionist ideas from becoming widespread among German social democrats, the majority of whom had in practice been reformists before Bernstein published his theories. True, there were many party and union leaders who were uninterested in theory or the revision of party doctrine: the latter was neither a help nor a hindrance in the everyday process of struggle, bargaining, and reform, and could be left as it stood for purposes of rhetoric. None the less, once the new formula was uttered they accepted it without resistance. The revolutionary idea was much more the property of the party intellectuals than of the working masses. In the first years of the dispute the future left wing did not clearly take shape within the party, and up to the war period it was represented only by a few theorists and publicists who had no organizational role or practical influence and did not form a permanent group among themselves. To the orthodox Marxists who provided the party with its organization and doctrine, like Bebel and Kautsky respectively, Bernstein's views were of course a challenge to the revolutionary faith which they professed with full sincerity: the party was in their eyes a true embodiment of its programme, both on the practical and on the theoretical side. If, however, they were able to obtain majority support for anti-revisionist formulas, it was not because the party was imbued with revolutionary spirit but because most of its members regarded the traditional slogans as harmless and of little practical consequence.

Lenin took the view, which is still treated as a dogma by the Communist movement, that revisionism came into being as an ideology reflecting the interests of the aristocracy of the working class, whom the bourgeoisie permitted to enjoy the 'left-overs' of their feast of prosperity. This would suggest that only a small privileged part of the German working class lent a willing ear to reformist doctrine, while the great majority were fervent revolutionaries. But in fact, what was later called by its opponents 'practical' revisionism was chiefly found among the trade unions, the most immediately class-based organization of the proletariat; moreover, the unions at that time did not yet possess the elaborate bureaucracy which was later made the scapegoat for opportunism and revisionism. In any case, if Lenin's explanation were true it would be highly unfortunate for Marxist doctrine. Since the 'aristocracy of the working class' are wage-earners like their fellow workers, and differ from them only in earning more, it would appear that a higher standard of living turns workers from revolutionaries into reformists; but, according to traditional Marxism, poverty is not the source of the class struggle and the revolutionary consciousness, and a short-term improvement in the workers' lot has no significant effect on their innate revolutionism.

When Bernstein was writing, the German working class had behind it a long period of increasing real wages and the successful struggle for welfare measures and a shorter working day. It also had a powerful political organization, whose influence was steadily increasing. The Reichstag, it is true, did not carry much weight, and Prussia had not introduced universal suffrage, but elections, political mobilization, and the comparison of forces encouraged hopes of a successful struggle for republicanism and even of seizing power. The actual experience of the German working class by no means supported the theory that its position was essentially hopeless and could not be reformed under capitalism. In Russia, too, a revisionist tendency made its appearance when the social democrats were no longer a handful of intellectuals and a genuine workers' movement had begun to take shape. The history of revisionism does not suggest that the working class is naturally revolutionary because it is forced to sell its labour-power and is incurably alienated in consequence. Thus it was not only in the doctrinal field that revisionism called into question the traditional belief in the revolutionary mission of the proletariat: the belief was challenged, perhaps more effectively still, by the success of revisionism as a social phenomenon, which robbed socialism of the glamorous prospect of a 'final battle' for universal liberation. Instead of a new Fourteenth of July bringing human 'prehistory' to an apocalyptic close and ushering in the new era, the reformists offered a programme of laborious, gradual, and unspectacular improvement.

Thus was created the ideological foundation of a new social democracy, the further development of which had very little to do with the history of Marxist doctrine. Although this form of socialism derives genetically from Marxism, in part at least, its origin soon became unimportant. The new doctrine was a compromise between liberalism and Marxian socialism, or a socialist variant of liberalism. It was applied to situations other than those envisaged by classical Marxism, and appealed to different psychological motivations. The increasing dominance of revisionism in German social democracy spelt the end of Marxism as socialists had understood it before the First World War. The centre of gravity was soon to be transferred eastward, where revolutionary doctrine was embodied in new dynamic forms.

CHAPTER V

Jean Jaurès: Marxism as a Soteriology

1. Jaurès as a conciliator

As a theoretician, Jaurès counts for little among orthodox Marxists. He is of course generally recognized as one of the key figures of French socialism, but his views are regarded as a 'synthesis' (by his admirers) or a 'conflation' or 'patchwork' (by the more orthodox) of a variety of sources, especially French ones, among which Marxism occupied no more than a position of equality. Certainly he never treated Marxism as a self-sufficient and all-embracing system from which the interpretation of all social phenomena could be deduced, still less as a metaphysical key to the universe, explaining its every feature and providing moral and practical guidance as to how it should be changed. On the contrary, Jaurès made conscious efforts to combine the most varied philosophical and political traditions into a single vision of the world, believing as he did in the essential unity of intellectual and moral trends that presented themselves in apparent diversity at different stages of history. He was by nature a universal conciliator, and was aware of this fact. His political and philosophical opponents accused him of glossing over social and doctrinal differences, obscuring contrasts, being all things to all men, blunting the edge of the class struggle by a naïvely moralizing attitude, and so on. From the orthodox point of view, a writer and politician who invoked the authority of Proudhon and Blanqui, Michelet and Saint-Simon, Kant and Fichte, Lassalle and Comte, Rousseau and Kropotkin, instead of treating them all as enemies or naïve 'predecessors', was obviously not to be ranked as a Marxist, which in orthodox eyes is an all-or-nothing position. But if we do not approach the matter from a dogmatic standpoint, our judgement as to whether Jaurès was a Marxist will depend on which of Marx's thoughts, and which interpretation of them, we regard as containing the essence of his doctrine; and on this point there is no agreed conclusion, even among those who claim to have remained faithful to the spirit and letter of Marxism.

Unlike the most typical Marxists of his own day, Jaurès never believed that the idea of socialism could be fully objectivized as a scientific theory similar to that of evolution, or actually as an extension of the latter. Nor was Marxism, in his view, a theory of social development and nothing more: it was an impassioned moral appeal, a new and more perfect expression of man's eternal thirst for justice, unity, and brotherly love. Jaurès's ambition was not to intensify but to assuage conflicts, antagonisms, and enmity of every kind: the fundamental ideas of Marxism, he believed, did not signify a breach of historical continuity but appealed to the deepest moral instincts of mankind. Since men basically shared the same feelings, desires, and habits of thought, and since socialism to Jaurès was above all a moral concept, he naturally addressed his appeals and explanations to all social classes, the bourgeoisie included. This was not because he imagined that all social problems could be solved by philanthropy or the goodwill of the privileged classes, or that socialism could be achieved by a moral transformation alone instead of by pressure and fighting, but because he believed that all human beings possessed common values that were not those of any specific class. If they took those values seriously and drew practical conclusions from them, they would be bound to see that socialism offered the only chance of their fulfilment. Socialists, therefore, should take advantage of any support they might find outside the working class, among people whose moral instincts prompted them to support the socialist cause.

Socialism, to Jaurès, was essentially a question of morals and human values, an ideal to which mankind had more or less consciously aspired throughout the ages. Consequently he was repelled by an interpretation of it in terms of a break with man's spiritual and cultural heritage. Spiritual values, he believed, were continuous and grew stronger as history progressed. In the coming synthesis all human values and achievements would turn out to be part of the same culture, even though they were rooted historically in conflict and hatred. Trends that appeared contrary or irrelevant to one another would one day blend into a harmonious unity. Nothing, therefore, that the human spirit had ever created should be despised or overlooked. This vision of an ultimate synthesis is the most characteristic feature of Jaurès's thought. In his more enthusiastic moments he may be called the Pangloss of socialism, believing in the final unity of science and religion, idealism and materialism, national and class values, the individual and society, spirit and matter, man and nature. Even before the final synthesis it was possible to combine revolution and evolution, the political struggle and moral education—to work on man's feelings as well as his intellect, and to appeal to proletarian interests as well as to universal human values.

Moreover, the unity of human progress was not only a matter of the final synthesis but could be seen already in the gradual prevalence of the idea which was to find its fulfilment in socialism. Progress up to the present time consisted not only in technological change but in the embodiment of basic values in increasingly perfect forms, though their ultimate perfection of course lay in the future. Jaurès shared with Marx the belief that human affairs would one day be harmonized in a socialist world, and that past history and present conflicts were meaningful only in relation to this prospect. But he differed from Marx in his view of the continuity and cumulative character of the whole of past history, as opposed to the Hegelian belief that progress is realized by its 'bad aspect'. Jaurès believed in the steady upward progress of humanity, supported by an increasing accumulation of spiritual and social values, and not in a descent into the abyss, to be followed by a sudden, apocalyptic renascence.

2. *Biographical outline*

Jaurès's political career belongs wholly to the period of the Second International, and his death occurred at the moment of its dissolution. Born in 1859 at Castres in the South of France, he attended the *lycée* there and subsequently the École Normale in Paris. In 1881 he was third on the list of *agrégés*; the candidate with the highest marks had a career of no special distinction, while the runner-up was Henri Bergson. In the same year Jaurès became a teacher of philosophy in the *lycée* at Albi, and two years later he was made a lecturer at Toulouse University. In 1885 he was elected to the Chamber as a republican deputy, in opposi-

tion to the monarchist and clerical parties. Partly as a result of
his political activities he became attracted to socialist ideas,
which he regarded from the start as the legitimate development
of the ideals of the Revolution. In 1889 he lost his seat to a
conservative candidate and returned to Toulouse, where he
spent the next two years working on his doctoral theses. The first
of these, entitled *De la réalité du monde sensible* (published 1891,
second edition 1902) was a philosophical discourse in the strict
sense and expressed his basic metaphysical views, which are
important for the understanding of his public life. The second
thesis was in Latin: *De primis socialismi germanici lineamentis apud
Lutherum, Kant, Fichte et Hegel* (1891; a French translation, *Les
Origines du socialisme allemand*, was published in 1892 in the *Revue
socialiste*). This is more directly related to Jaurès's socialist views,
giving his interpretation of the philosophical sources that inspired the social theories of Marx and Lassalle. At this period
he also wrote socialist articles, chiefly in the *Dépêche de Toulouse*.
When re-elected to the Chamber in 1893 he was a socialist not
only in the sense of upholding the principles of a socialist order,
but in believing that the future of those principles depended on
action by the working class. During the next five years he became
an acknowledged leader of the socialist group in parliament,
and until 1914 his life was an integral part of French history.
In the main issues of the time—the Dreyfus case and the Millerand affair, questions of war and peace, Morocco and the
French colonial empire, the role and significance of the
International—Jaurès's attitude was always important and
sometimes decisive. Generally his views can be traced to philosophical principles which he appears to have had constantly in
mind. If he was whole-heartedly involved in the Dreyfus case,
without regard to considerations of tactics, it was because he
held, unlike Guesde, that the socialist movement should be the
mouthpiece of any cause in which human rights were at stake,
no matter who the victim was or to what class or group he
belonged: for socialism was responsible for all human values, not
only 'after the revolution' but here and now. When, after much
hesitation and to the indignation of the whole socialist left wing,
he supported Millerand's action in joining Waldeck-Rousseau's
government, it was because of his view that advantage should
be taken of every means of influencing existing forms of public

life: if co-operation with class enemies seemed likely to pay off in a particular case, it should not be rejected on grounds of strategic exclusivism. His socialist opponents retorted that he was abandoning the class viewpoint and was prepared to accept the shadiest allies for the sake of some immediate gain; he was, they claimed, a reformist and an opportunist. Jaurès was not a reformist, however, in the sense of abandoning the 'ultimate goal' or limiting his sights to the short-term, partial interests of the working class. On the contrary, he insisted at every turn on the basic principles and objectives of socialism. However, unlike the revolutionary syndicalists and the extreme Left of the International, but in agreement with most of the centre group, he regarded reforms not merely as a preparation for the final conflict but as an improvement of the workers' lot here and now. He did not consider that the proletariat embodied the whole virtue of society, since human values could not be the monopoly of a single class, even though that class might enjoy the historical privilege' of bringing them to a state of complete fulfilment. A policy of conciliation, compromise, and piecemeal agreements did not, as he saw it, signify opportunism or lack of principle but was an expression of faith in the power of the socialist ideal. The opponents of socialism were bound to recognize that in many matters it had right on its side, and in this way it could enlist support outside its natural home in the working class.

Both Jaurès and Guesde lost their seats in the election of 1898, when the Dreyfus agitation was at its height. Re-elected in 1902, Jaurés spoke frequently in parliament and at meetings and wrote innumerable pamphlets and articles on current politics and problems of socialism. He no longer had time to produce large single works, and most of the volumes he published at this period were collections of short pieces. They include *Les Preuves* (1898, on the Dreyfus case); *Études socialistes* (1901, second edition 1902: mainly theoretical); *Action socialiste* (1897); and *L'Organisation socialiste de France. L'Armée nouvelle* (no date). In addition he edited, and partly wrote, a *Histoire socialiste de la Révolution française*, published in instalments from 1879 to 1900; Jaurès's contributions were republished separately by A. Mathiez in 1922–4. Many articles scattered through various periodicals— *Revue socialiste*, *Mouvement socialiste*, *Humanité*, *Petite République*, *Matin*, *Revue de Paris*—have not yet been collected and repub-

lished. An edition of Jaurès's works by M. Bonnafous appeared
in nine volumes from 1931 onwards, but was not completed.

Jaurès's last years were overshadowed by the approach of
war, which aroused anxiety throughout the European socialist
movement. He was shot dead by a nationalist fanatic in a Paris
café on 31 July 1914, the last day of the nineteenth century. He
was certainly one of the liveliest and most versatile minds in the
socialist movement, interested in all aspects of public life and
culture. Although frequently attacked both by socialists and by
others, according to most accounts he aroused friendly feelings
in all those whom he met personally.

3. *The metaphysics of universal unity*

Unlike most socialist leaders except Lassalle, Jaurès was also a
philosopher in the professional sense of the word. His thesis *De la
réalité du monde sensible* shows no trace of Marxist influence but
is inspired by neo-Kantian ideas and particularly by Jules
Lachelier. This does not mean that it is irrelevant to his activity
as a writer and politician: on the contrary, it serves as a
metaphysical background to the latter, but at the same time it
illustrates the unorthodoxy of his view of Marxism. It was not
Marxist studies that led him to socialism, but moral motivations
that he shared long before he had heard of Marxism. Marxism
to him was not a philosophy or a metaphysic, but the theoretical
expression of the socialist movement; and he was never a Marxist
in the sense of expecting the doctrine to provide a key to all human
problems. His philosophical *magnum opus*, couched in the diffuse
rhetorical style of the École Normale, is an attempt to reconcile
almost every conflicting metaphysical standpoint and to show
that all of them are basically right, but each is incomplete in the
light of his universal theory of Being. It expresses a kind of evolutionary pantheism which, however, does not sacrifice individual
Being to the Absolute but defends the rights of subjectivity amid
the general trend of the universe towards final unity. When
Jaurès tackles the classic problem of the 'primacy' between sense
and intellect in the act of perception, he adopts a kind of
popular Kantianism: as sensual qualities present themselves in
permanent associations the mind is constrained to regard objects
as substances, and the idea of substance is present in every mind,
including the minds of those philosophers who declare there is

no such thing. Certainly the mind would not have evolved the idea of the substantial unity of objects if this were not suggested to it by sensual perception, but the latter could not of itself give rise to the idea of substance, which is due to the operation of the intellect. In this sense 'the real' and 'the intelligible' are one and the same.

However, Jaurès goes beyond this purely epistemological standpoint and develops a positive metaphysic over and above the Kantian critique. The mind does not create the organization of the universe, but neither does it simply reflect that organization as a result of perception. The perception of the order that pervades all Being is possible only because the mind is itself a part of that order, a product and a co-author of it. The different forms and levels of universal organization combine in a single purposeful whole: the astral system, chemical compounds, the organic world, and the world of mankind are all part of a rational evolution towards divine harmony and unity. At the highest level of Being, thought and reality are the same; the mind coalesces with the universe. This ultimate unity is a condition of the meaning of every particle of reality, and it also determines that meaning. There is no such thing as 'chance', which term only signifies the mind's perplexity in the face of events that spring from multiple causes. But to explain the meaning of existence it is not sufficient to reject the idea of chance, nor even (and here Jaurès parts company with Lachelier) to accept the view that all change is for a purpose. There must also be a category of 'progress' to which all events contribute after their fashion, and this is not contained in the idea of purpose as such. Progress implies a distinction between potentiality and actuality. The reality of each particular event is then determined not merely by its cause or even its purpose in relation to other events, but also by the part it plays in the progressive realization of the Absolute, the rational movement towards final harmony. Reality *is* the Absolute as it lives and develops. Human reason perceives the meaning of evolution and thus helps to cause it; so does the act of understanding in which sense is revealed. Thus, strictly speaking, there is no 'primacy' of truth or reason as opposed to Being, for in the last resort they are one and the same: Being affirms itself by taking on intellectual form.

Examining in turn the various elementary forms of the mental and physical world, Jaurès tries to show the meaningfulness of all that we experience with the mind and senses, but always from an eschatological point of view. For instance, he puts the question why there are three dimensions, and replies that this is so that the postulate of freedom can be realized in the physical world. If there were only one dimension, change could only take the form of movement forwards or backwards, and from the teleological point of view this would mean a simple increase or decrease of the distance to the ultimate goal, i.e. slavish virtue or absolute wickedness. Freedom, however, requires the possibility of a departure from the straight path in the direction 'most opposed' to it, i.e. at right angles to the original line. Moreover, freedom also requires that there be an infinite number of lines at right angles to the original one, i.e. that there be three dimensions. 'These three are both necessary and sufficient, expressing in the order of spatial extension the infinite freedom of infinite activity'. (*De la réalité du monde sensible*, p. 32.)

The starting-point of Jaurès's metaphysical system is self-identical Being (not, he emphasizes, the idea of Being), i.e. Being as understood by Parmenides and Hegel. All forms of partial existence are related to Being in a manner that is not specifically defined, but in which there is no place for a distinction between real and apparent existence: everything that seems to be an appearance or illusion exists in its own way, more particularly human subjectivity. Even dreams are not mere illusion: they are perceived, and therefore have a reality of their own. Consciousness does not reduce Being to an illusion, nor is it itself an illusion or a mere fleeting manifestation of Being. On the contrary, it can—as Descartes observed—arrive at the fact of Being by merely contemplating itself, and in so doing it shows that its own existence is not merely a fact but a necessity. Impressions are no less real, though they are real in a different way, than the physical movements that are their 'objective' counterpart. The evolution of Being comprises everything, gives it a meaning and in some sense justifies it. It tends towards perfect unity, but not so as to destroy the wealth of diversity in which Being is manifested. That unity is God, of whom it may be said that he is above the world but also, in a sense, that he *is* the world: he is the self in every self, the truth in every truth, the consciousness in every consciousness. The human mind needs God and finds him in spite of the sophists, just as it needs justice and finds it in spite of the sceptics. Faith is not a sign of weakness or ignorance; on the contrary, those who have no faith or do not feel the need for it are mediocrities.

Jaurès's thesis does not appear to have been influenced by Hegel, though in some respects it shows Hegelian tendencies: in particular the idea that the act by which Being is apprehended must be regarded as itself a *Moment* or aspect of the development of Being. In other words, thought does not turn Being into an illusion, nor is it merely a passive reflection of it, but, by understanding the evolution of Being, it acts as a necessary co-author and sharer in that evolution. Jaurès, when he wrote his principal thesis, does not seem to have known the *Phenomenology of Mind*; in his second dissertation he mentions Hegel's philosophy, but only in regard to the state. The general idea of the fundamental unity of all Being seems to have taken shape in his mind under the influence of Spinoza and the French neo-Kantians. But his evolutionary conception of the Absolute, which so strikingly recalls the pantheism of the Christian neo-Platonists, was probably worked out independently rather than borrowed from tradition. Today it also brings to mind the cosmology and cosmogony of Teilhard de Chardin. The importance of Jaurès's metaphysical pantheism does not lie in the field of Marxist theory, on which it had no influence whatever, but in the fact that it led him to embrace socialism and that he never departed from it in later years. On many occasions, in more or less popular writings, he returned to the ideas expressed in his doctoral thesis. In an article in the *Dépêche de Toulouse* of 15 October 1890, at the time of the thesis itself, he summed up his social and religious hopes in a vision of the triumph of socialism and of universal concord, joy, and human dignity. In that day

men will understand the profound meaning of life, whose secret aim is the harmony of all minds and forces and of every individual freedom. They will understand history better and will love it more, for it will be their own history, as they will be the heirs of the whole human race. And they will understand the universe better too: for as they behold the triumph of mind and spirit in humanity, they will soon realize that the universe out of which humanity is born cannot be fundamentally brutal and blind, that there is soul and spirit everywhere, that the universe itself is nothing but an obscure, infinite yearning and progress towards harmony, beauty, freedom and goodness.

In a speech in the Chamber in favour of secular education, on 11 February 1895, Jaurès declared that he understood the new generation which sought to reconcile naturalism and idealism with the aid of Spinoza and Hegel, for he himself could not accept the doctrine that the explanation of the universe lay in matter, 'cette suprême inconnue'. Nor could he regard the great religions as the result of mere calculation or deceit: although exploited for class purposes they had their roots in human nature and were, so to speak, an appeal to the future which might be heard some day. In *Socialisme et liberté* (*Socialism and Freedom*, 1898) he returned to the same ideas. The future order would be a supreme affirmation of the rights of the individual, and would differ from Christianity in that it would not conceive of God as a transcendental ruler over mankind. But human minds would not be content with mere negation. Many socialists were tending towards idealistic monism, regarding the world as an integrated progress of man and nature towards final harmony. Socialism would unite men with one another, and all men with the universe.

The advent of socialism will be like a great religious revelation. Will it not be a miraculous event when men and women who have grown up in the brutal obscurity of our planet attain justice and wisdom; when man by natural evolution rises above nature, that is to say above violence and conflict; when warring forces and instincts blend into a harmony of wills? And how can we forbear to ask ourselves whether there is not, at the root of all this, a secret of unity and kindliness that gives meaning to the world? ... A revolution of justice and goodness, carried out by that part of nature which we now call mankind, will be, as it were, a challenge and a signal to nature itself. Why should not the whole creation strive to free itself from inertia and confusion, since in the form of humanity it will already have achieved consciousness, enlightenment and peace? Thus, from the height of its triumph, humanity will proclaim words of hope to reach the very depths of nature, and will give ear to the voice of universal longing and expectation that will answer its cry. (*Œuvres*, ed. Bonnafous (9 vols., 1931–9), vi, 96–8.)

Similar thoughts are expressed in a lecture *L'Art et le socialisme* (1900) and in other writings. In Jaurès's view socialism is part of the universal trend towards harmony which gives a meaning to all the struggles and sufferings of which history is full. This, as he himself acknowledged, is a religious viewpoint, though pantheistic rather than Christian. It is as though Jaurès in his intellectual development unconsciously retraced the long road from neo-Platonic pantheism to Marxian soteriology: not only the step from Hegel to Marx, which was all Marx himself regarded as important, but the preceding stages as well. Marx in his early writings speaks, it is true, of a restoration of unity between man and nature, but in a different sense. Nature, to him, has no significance prior to that of mankind. It is not man who in his spiritual development reveals the spirituality of nature, its latent aspirations or unconscious goodness and wisdom; rather, by exercising his own wisdom man confers a human significance on nature. If the spirit is the work of nature, it does not therefore constitute a manifestation of nature as spirit. In the same way socialism is not the product of feeling, least of all an unconscious feeling by which the development of the universe is inspired and permeated. Marx could never have said that the revolution would take place 'in the name of justice and goodness', for these were not part of history and had no share in determining its meaning. Jaurès's belief in a purposeful harmony of the universe is of course foreign to Marxism, although it was the cause of Jaurès becoming a Marxist. Holding this belief, he considered that in the last resort there was no conflict between scientific knowledge of the world and the religious faith of pantheism. His attitude to religion was not that of Saint-Simon's followers, who in effect accepted the basic doctrine of Christianity. But Jaurès believed, it would seem, that historical soteriology was of no value except as part of a universal soteriology of Being. Like most pantheists he believed in universal salvation and the ultimate reconcilability of all things, i.e. the non-reality of evil.

4. *The directing forces of history*

As in general metaphysics, so in the philosophy of history Jaurès sought to reconcile two apparently opposite concepts: those of historical idealism and Marxism. In the preface to the *Socialist History of the Revolution* he argued that while history has economic 'foundations', economic forces act on human beings who impart to history the variety of their passions and ideas, living not only on a social but on a cosmic plane. Certainly the evolution of ideas depends in some measure on that of economic forms, but that dependence does not explain everything. Marx himself had believed that humanity in future times would be able to determine the course of its own development: this was not yet so, but even today superior souls were able to rise to freedom, and the dignity of the spirit played an increasingly important part in history. Arguing thus, Jaurès declared that his interpretation of history was 'materialist with Marx and mystical with Michelet'. As the historian of France and especially of the Revolution, Michelet was an important figure to Jaurès in that he emphasized the role of collective inspiration in bringing about great events.

In his critical writings Jaurès often takes a similar line to many of his Marxist contemporaries. For instance, he opposes the interpretation of historical materialism according to which every detail of history can be fully explained by the development of technology causing changes in the system of ownership, production, and exchange, and hence in class-relationships and the whole ideological superstructure. In a lecture of February 1900 on 'Bernstein and the evolution of socialist method' he states that particular branches of human spiritual activity have their own logic and are in some degree independent of economic processes. In *Socialism and Freedom* he writes: 'Just as a weaver, although bound by the shape of his loom, is able to weave fabrics of varying design and colour, so history, with the same equipment of economic forces, can fashion human destiny in various ways. The economic form conditions all human activities, but that is not to say they can be deduced from it.' In many other passages he makes clear, however, that he is concerned with more than Engels's 'relative independence of the superstructure'. He also holds that human history must be understood as a process of the steadily increasing prevalence of ideal values and their influence on events. There is no place for this idea in Marx's historiosophy, even as diluted by Engels. In the preface to a book by Benoît Malon, Jaurès observes that in spite of all conflicts human beings have an instinct of mutual sympathy that expresses itself in religion and philosophy and, most fully of all, in the working-class movement. In a lecture of December 1894 on the idealistic and materialistic views of history he says that historical development arises from the conflict between man and the use that is made of him, and that this development will come to an end when man is used according to what he is. 'Humanity thus realizes itself in economic forms that conflict less and less with its own idea. And in human history there is not only necessary evolution, but also an ideal sense and a purposeful direction.' Through all the moral changes due to the pressure of economic forces, humanity preserves an unchanging impulse and an undying hope of rediscovering itself. There is no conflict between materialism and historical idealism: history is affected by mechanical laws, but it also reflects a moral urge and an ideal law. Recalling Marx's critique of Bentham, Jaurès observes that Marxism itself would be meaningless if it were a mere description of indifferent historical 'necessities', and not also an affirmation of the human values enshrined in socialism. It would be contrary to common sense to suppose that the socialist idea could assert itself automatically, without the aid of human faith and enthusiasm. Capitalism, it is true, prepares the way for socialist forms of life and draws the lines of the future state, but we cannot confer the stamp of natural necessity on historical evolution. Socialism would not exist without the forces set in motion by capitalism in the form of technology, labour organization, and property; but it would also not exist if it were not for the conscious will of humanity, athirst for freedom and justice and inspired by the energy to transform the opportunities offered by capitalism into reality.

In discussing the problem of 'socialism as historical necessity' and 'socialism as a value' Jaurès does not resort to the typical categories of 'ethical socialism', i.e. he does not put the question 'Assuming that we know socialism to be the inevitable result of historical laws, how does it follow that we must approve its values?' Unlike the neo-Kantians he rejects the dualism of 'what is' and 'what ought to be', claiming to have overcome this by his pantheistic theory of development. Since the universe develops in accordance with ideal laws determined 'in the last resort' by a future harmony, and since goodness, beauty, and love are not immanent in human history but are part of the creative surge of nature itself, while humanity brings to its fullness the divine potentiality of Being, it follows that the apprehension by man of

his future destiny is not a purely intellectual act, to be com-
plemented by a subsequent act of moral approbation. The end to
which mankind has aspired more or less consciously throughout
history, and to which it still aspires, is not an arbitrary creation
of the mind: it is the articulation of the aspirations of universal
Being. Men are part of nature not only as organisms but as
creatures endowed with mind, feeling, and desires; once they
are aware of their own unity with the cosmos, their self-
understanding is at the same time an acceptance of nature and
of its necessities, which must be benevolent in their effect. There
is no contradiction between the indifferent course of nature,
subject to mechanical laws, and the rules of morality which must
derive from sources other than theoretical knowledge; hence
there is no longer any duality or separation between that which
is and that which ought to be.

Marx too rejected the Kantian dualism, but not for the same
reasons as Jaurès. Marx believed that in the last phase of 'prehistory', in which the proletarian movement paved the way for
a general revolution, the duality of necessity and freedom would
disappear, as what was historically necessary would be carried
out by free revolutionary activity. He believed that in this way
he had overcome the Kantian dualism, but he did not thereby
do away with the problem whether what was historically
necessary was also good. The question why this should be so
cannot in fact be answered, or even asked, within the framework
of Marx's views, because the fact (if such it is) that what is
necessary is also good in this case is a contingent one: the
historical necessity of socialism is not based on the proposition
that it is good for mankind, nor can its value be deduced from
its quasi-natural inevitability. The two aspects are logically and
historically distinct, and each is accidental with respect to the
other. There is no 'law' which lays down that man must achieve
liberation or unity with himself and nature; historical necessity
does not assure us *a priori* that man is not bound to endure slavery,
poverty, and unhappiness for ever. The fact that men desire to
free themselves from these things does not prove that they will
succeed, for history does not depend on human wishes. Hence,
although the changes scheduled to take place in the last phase
are due to revolutionary will and not to anonymous 'laws', the
efficacy of that will derives from objective circumstances and

not from the fact that it stands for justice and freedom. In this sense it can be said that the ultimate beneficence of historical necessity is a matter of chance: it happens to be the case that the laws of history favour the accomplishment of what human beings regard, or will regard, as satisfying their desires, and that this same end will, independently of their wishes, in fact constitute the fulfilment of human nature. Jaurès is concerned to avoid this element of contingency, because his vision of universal harmony leaves no room for a necessity which is devoid of purpose or neutral as between good and evil: in his view, intelligence and the invincible force of goodness are constantly shaping the course of the entire universe. There is no stage of evolution at which the universe is a blind force that men can only exploit or curb for their own ends. In short, Jaurès believes that universal Being desires the same ends as humanity does, and that this is so not by chance but because of man's place in the order of being and the fact that his desires and aspirations are the articulation of what the universe as a whole desires and aspires to.

5. Socialism and the republic

It is easy to see how closely Jaurès's political reactions are linked with his philosophy. Believing as he did in the over-all unity of history and the march of progress in all spheres of human life, he also held that the liberated society of the future would not be a radical negation of existing forms but a continuation and development of values that were already burgeoning. Thus he constantly reiterated, in one form or another, the view that socialism was the full realization of principles that were already discernible in history and especially in the 1789 Revolution. The Declaration of the Rights of Man and the Constitution of 1793 contained in essence all the ideas of socialism, which only had to be developed to their proper conclusion: in particular, freedom, equality, and justice must be extended from the political field to that of ownership and the system of production, and this was the proper meaning of socialism. The individual freedom guaranteed by the Revolution did not apply to economic affairs, and privileges of ownership remained although political privilege had been swept away. In justice, every human being had an equal right to the enjoyment of all the resources accumulated by humanity since the beginning of time. As Marx had contended, under socialism accumulated labour should serve to enrich workers' lives, whereas under private ownership living labour only went to increase the accumulation of labour in the form of capital. The aim of socialism was to subordinate the achievements of the past to life in the present. As Jaurès wrote in an article on 'Socialism and Life' (7 September 1901), 'Life does not cancel the past, but makes use of it. The revolution is a conquest, not a new rupture.' But the logic of the Declaration of the Rights of Man was a dead letter until the proletariat came on the political scene, and thus the plans of Saint-Simon and Fourier had come to nothing. Since 1848 it was clear that the socialist order could not be created merely by dreams of justice but only by the organized working class putting an end to the contradiction between the political sovereignty of the people and its economic enslavement. The 'political republic' must be turned into a 'social republic' by the extension of democracy to the whole of economic life.

The frequency with which Jaurès insisted that socialism was a continuation and not a negation of the republican idea was partly due to his anxiety to refute the anti-socialist argument that 'collectivism' was a denial of individual freedom, but partly also to the fact that, in France at least, socialists themselves were by no means unanimous on the point. The idea of socialism as the 'direct opposite' of the existing order suggested that socialists wanted to destroy the bourgeois republic with its democratic institutions, or to replace the rule of bankers and capitalists by that of bureaucrats in charge of nationalized industry—a fear expressed in many quarters at this time, not least by the anarchists. Hence Jaurès insisted that individual human values were the sole criterion of the values of social institutions. 'Socialists relate the value of every institution to the human individual. It is he who, by asserting his will to freedom and development, confers strength and vitality on institutions and ideas. The individual is the measure of all things: the fatherland, the family, property, humanity, God himself. This is the logic of revolutionary thought. This is what socialism means' (*Socialism and Freedom*). The collectivization of property would be a travesty of socialism if it meant that the political authorities were put in charge of the economy as well. 'If the politicians and administrators who already control the nation's diplomacy and armed forces were also given authority over the whole labour force, and if they could appoint managers at all levels in the same way as they now appoint army officers, this would confer on a handful of men such power as Asian despots never dreamt of—for they controlled only the surface of public life and not the economy of their countries' (*Socialist Organization*). Socialists did not propose to strengthen the state as an instrument of coercion but, on the contrary, to place state institutions and production once more under the control of associated individuals. The abolition of classes meant the abolition of those private interests that fought for control of the administrative machine, and hence an end to its corruption and oppressive function. Everyone would be, in the same sense, a worker for the public good: there would be no separate caste or group of administrators tyrannizing over the public. Freedom to work and enjoy the fruits of one's labour, freedom of speech and the printed word, freedom of assembly, of the arts and sciences—all this could be guaranteed incomparably better by socialism than by a system where these freedoms were curtailed by the privileges of private ownership. There was no reason to fear that people would be reluctant to do unpleasant or laborious work: rates of pay could take account of the nature of the job, and anyhow there might be people who felt a vocation to be dustmen. Nor should it be feared that producers would be deprived of initiative or that workers would lack incentive to increase and improve production, for it was easy to devise rewards for productivity and invention. In any case production would not be wholly centralized: there would be increased scope for corporations covering different branches of production, and for municipal and regional bodies. Representative institutions, both on a national scale and on the basis of smaller geographical or industrial units, would ensure that the people as a whole were able to supervise the entire economy. Freedom would not be curtailed but greatly extended when the basic social functions of production and distribution were placed under public control. The state would remain in charge of public services which required to be administered from the centre, but it would be a state of a different kind. Instead of private owners, as now, using the state's social functions for their own ends, the state would act for the benefit of society as a whole and would, as socialists had always maintained, cease to exercise political authority over individuals. It was not the purpose of socialism to impose on the public any particular idea of happiness, but to create conditions in which everyone could pursue his own happiness as he saw fit.

Socialism preserved and maintained all the values that mankind had created over the centuries, and had no intention of sacrificing anything that would increase man's dignity, freedom, and energy or further the quest for harmony. In particular, contrary to what was often asserted, it did not seek to diminish the idea of nationality, to deprive people of a fatherland or of patriotic feelings. The famous remark on this subject in *The Communist Manifesto* was no more than a *boutade*. Now that the proletariat enjoyed universal suffrage and education and had become a political power, it was absurd and insulting to suggest that it did not form part of the existing state and nation or that it must 'remain nothing until it became everything'—so Jaurès declared in Chapter X of *L'Armée nouvelle*. It was indeed counter-revolutionary to assert that the proletariat did not belong to the *patrie*, for it meant denying the value of the day-to-day struggle and of partial gains, without which there could be no final liberation. Since the Revolution the national and the democratic idea had been inseparable. The unity of a nation was not a matter of landownership, as some pretended, but the natural, almost physical longing of human beings to live in a community larger than the family; the whole of mankind was too large a unit to satisfy that need. Socialism was not out to destroy patriotism but to enlarge it. Abstract internationalism, ignoring national differences, was a chimera: mankind could only achieve unity by the federation of free nations. It was natural, therefore, that socialists defended the right of every nation to independence. The international character of the workers' movement in no way conflicted with patriotism or the desire to defend one's country against threats and aggression. The nation was not the primary object of socialism, which was concerned above all with individual freedom, but it was nevertheless an essential form of life without which socialism would wither away. It was impossible to imagine social liberation in conditions of national enslavement, or a socialist movement that did not operate on the national plane before it became international. Chauvinism, wars, aggression, and hatred were not part of the national idea

but were a contradiction of it. Socialism presupposed France
and the French Republic, as it presupposed every other human
value.

As socialism thus laid claim to everything of value that the
human race had ever produced, it may be said that in Jaurès's
mind all such values were, consciously or otherwise, a contribution to socialism. He did not perhaps assert this in so many words,
but he seems concerned to persuade everyone that they are
'really' socialists at heart and that if they attack socialism it is
because they have not thought out their own ideas properly.
Republicans, anarchists, Christians, intellectuals, patriots—all
would be socialists if they reflected sufficiently on the best way of
preserving the values that they hold most dear. In the past as
well as in the present, Jaurès is constantly discovering more or less
conscious socialist tendencies, hampered by ignorance or inconsistency. In the French Revolution he finds them among
Babouvists, Girondists, and Jacobins. In his thesis on the origins
of German socialism he detects the germ of socialist ideas at every
point in the history of German idealism, beginning with Luther.
The idea of Christian equality paved the way for that of civic
equality; fighting against the tyranny of Rome, Luther taught
his countrymen to fight tyranny of every kind. The Lutheran
notion of freedom as circumscribed by the divine law is part of
the critique of false freedom in the economic sphere. Kant and
Fichte, too, contributed to socialism by reconciling the freedom
of the individual with the authority of the state and its right
to control economic affairs. Even Kant's idea that property is a
precondition of citizenship was consistent with socialism in the
sense that wage-labourers who own nothing are not full citizens.
Fichte's *geschlossener Handelsstaat* embodied a kind of moral
socialism, for it involved the social regulation of production in
the common interest of its citizens. Hegelian philosophy was
another source of socialism, especially when it distinguished
abstract freedom, which was no more than individual caprice,
from freedom governed by reason and universal law. Perfect
freedom was not, as the liberals claimed, freedom short of injur-
ing others: its true definition implied that freedom of the
individual, instead of separating people, involved universal
aspirations. Hegel came close to socialism when he defended the
organic unity of a society in which individual values are

preserved and subjected to the law of reason. Finally, Lassalle and Marx resolved the contradiction between the moral and historical interpretations of socialism, reconciling Fichte and Hegel and—especially in Lassalle's case—discovering eternal justice in the dialectical movement of the world.

Socialism could not become a live movement until there was an active, self-conscious working class to uphold its values. But, as Marx had shown, socialism was in the interest of all mankind and not only of the workers. It was even in the interest of today's exploiters—sick men refusing to be cured, who were victims of the system despite their privileges. When communism arrived the children of today's bourgeoisie would not only see in it the negation of what their fathers had done: they would also realize that the bourgeois themselves, by their bold and energetic improvement of technology, had unconsciously prepared for the liberation that would bring their endeavours into harmony with those of the revolutionary proletariat.

Since every human being was an *anima naturaliter socialista*, it was right and necessary for socialists to appeal to human values of all kinds and not only those peculiar to the present situation of the proletariat. The revolution could not, without self-contradiction, be the work of a minority or the result of a *coup d'état*, even if this were technically possible. The changes involved by socialism would be far more profound than those of the bourgeois revolution, and they could not be brought about without the unequivocal support of a large majority of the population. General elections revealed the true strength of different groups in society and made a successful *coup* less and less likely. But in any case socialism required the whole-hearted co-operation of society, for it was not enough to overthrow the old order and then allow economic life to be governed by the free play of individual forces: the new organizational forms must be planned in advance and must embrace the whole system of production and distribution. Thus the revolution must be preceded by moral changes that would arouse the socialist consciousness and inspire enthusiasm for the values of the new order.

The socialists therefore must seek support among other classes, especially the farmers and petty bourgeoisie. Jaurès recalled that in Liebknecht's view the working class should be taken to include all those who lived wholly or mainly by the work of their hands, i.e. the peasantry and the petty bourgeoisie as well as the industrial proletariat. Moreover, Liebknecht maintained, the socialist party should be more interested in whether its members professed socialist ideas than in whether they were wage-earners. If the movement were based exclusively on the industrial proletariat it could not become a majority or achieve its aims. It must be a movement of the whole people other than the nobility, clergy, and upper bourgeoisie, who together formed only a small percentage of society. Jaurès thought on similar lines: socialism, by its universality, would attract almost the whole people, and the socialist revolution, unlike the bourgeois one, could therefore be accomplished without violence, bloodshed, or civil war. Co-operation with the bourgeoisie and bourgeois parties on particular issues was possible and desirable not only on tactical grounds but because the spirit of co-operation was the guiding principle of socialism. 'We want a revolution,' said Jaurès in a lecture on Bernstein's views,

but we do not want everlasting hatred. If, for the sake of some great cause—trade unions, co-operatives, art or justice, even bourgeois justice —we can get the bourgeoisie to march with us, how strong we shall feel when we can say to them: 'What a joy it is that those who were divided by hatred and mistrust can join forces even in a temporary fashion, for a single day—and how much more sublime and lasting will be our joy at the final encounter of all mankind!' ... What I wish, what we wish is that the socialist party should be the geometrical locus of all great causes and all great ideas. This does not mean that we are abandoning the fight for social revolution: on the contrary, we are arming ourselves in strength, dignity and pride so that the hour of revolution may strike all the sooner. (*Bernstein et l'évolution de la méthode socialiste*, 10 February 1900; *Œuvres*, vi. 139–40.)

This was the theoretical basis of Jaurès's activity in regard to the Dreyfus case, and also his attitude to the controversy over 'ministerialism'. Many French socialists of the *ouvriériste* persuasion took the view that the *Affaire* was a quarrel among bourgeois, with a member of the military caste as its protagonist, and was therefore no concern of the socialist movement. Guesde did not share this view and took a similar line to Jaurès at the outset, but he afterwards came to think that the party should not commit itself to the defence of a single individual in the opposing camp, as its proper task was to stand up for the whole oppressed working class: the bourgeois intrigues of which Dreyfus was a victim were not a good reason for abandoning the class struggle. The opposing arguments of Guesde and Jaurès were subsequently published in the pamphlet *Deux méthodes* (1900). Guesde's position was summed up in the contention that 'the proletariat should be guided solely by its own class egoism, since its interests are identical with the ultimate, universal interests of the whole human race'; 'there has been and can be no change in society until capitalist ownership is abolished'; 'we do not believe in negotiations: the class struggle excludes agreements between classes'; 'the revolution is only possible if you remain yourselves, a class against a class—a class that has never known, and is determined to avoid, the divisions that exist in the world of capital'.

Jaurès, on the contrary, held that the universal character of the proletariat's struggle was not something that only came into play after the revolution, but that it must manifest itself here and now, in all matters, in order that the revolution might come about. The proletariat, as an oppressed class, was already the mouthpiece of universal justice and the ally of all who had justice on their side, even if they were not its allies on other issues. It must therefore join forces in the present case with those sections of the bourgeoisie who stood for progress against reaction. It must defend the secular state against clericalism, even though this was the cause of the bourgeois radicals as well as its own; it must defend the republic against monarchists, and the cause of justice even when the victim was a member of the opposing camp.

A similar issue was raised in a more doubtful form by the Millerand affair. The latter's opponents maintained that his action in joining a bourgeois government was a deception of the working class, as it suggested that the proletariat already shared in political power; moreover, the socialist movement would be compromised if one of its leaders shared responsibility for the acts of a bourgeois regime which he could not prevent and which were bound to be in the interest of the exploiting classes. Jaurès replied that Millerand's act in joining the government would certainly not induce the latter to change its course basically, but it nevertheless bore witness to the strength of the socialist movement, and the latter's struggle against militarism and the reaction was aided by temporary alliances with the more progressive elements of the bourgeoisie.

The controversy brought to light two fundamentally different approaches to the idea of the political independence of the proletariat, and it also revealed the ambiguity of this idea in the context of the parliamentary activity of the socialist movement. There was a strong tradition, for which it was easy to find support in Marx's writings, in favour of treating the proletariat as a foreign enclave in bourgeois society—a class for which there could be no 'partial' liberation but which was destined to over-throw the entire political establishment and could therefore not ally itself with any of the other, hostile classes. But this exclusivism could not be consistently maintained in a situation in which socialist parties took part in parliamentary life and secured improvements in the condition of the working class by legislative means. Every improvement of this kind was to some extent an 'improvement of capitalism', and if Guesde consistently believed in his own principle that such improvements should be left to the capitalists, he ought not to involve the socialist party in parliamentary life or the struggle for immediate economic and legislative gains. The revolutionary syndicalists were more consistent in this respect, but by the same token they had no hope of influencing conditions in France. In any case, once the principle of attempting to 'reform capitalism' had been accepted it was impossible to draw an exact dividing line between tactical co-operation with other parties and an 'opportunist' policy of grafting socialism on to the existing order.

Jaurès was far from holding that the political independence of the proletariat was of no consequence. Arguing in general support of Kautsky against Bernstein, he accused the latter of submerging the proletariat among the other classes on the ground that both the working class and the bourgeoisie were far from being homogeneous. This was fallacious, Jaurès claimed, as there was a clear distinction between the haves and the have-nots. These two basic classes were radically opposed, but socialists need not be afraid of temporary alliances provided they kept in mind that their ultimate objective was not to improve the present system but to transform it. Socialism was unthinkable except as an achievement of the working class, and the hopes of such men as Fourier, Louis Blanc, and Owen could only be idle dreams. But—and this perhaps is the kernel of the dispute between Jaurès and the 'exclusivists'—the working class was building elements of socialism within the capitalist system. Jaurès seems to have had no doubt that the final transformation of society could only come about by revolution, but he did not understand this as entailing an act of violence or civil war. By 'revolution' he meant simply the radical transformation of the property-owning system in a socialist sense. The proposition that socialism can only come about by revolution thus becomes a tautology; Jaurès failed to notice this, and dismissed the question as to what form the revolution would take as a barren speculation relating to the unforeseeable future. But on this argument the revolution might take the form of a gradual evolutionary change from capitalism to socialism, although Jaurès seems to have denied this possibility. In his view socialism was taking shape within capitalism in many ways, thanks in particular to the workers' growing historical sense and power of self-organization, but also to democratic reforms in the working-class interest: universal education, labour laws, improved living standards, the secularization of public life, and the effect of unions and co-operatives in curbing exploitation. The 'ultimate goal' of socialism was distinct from these reforms, but the latter were more than a mere process of training for the decisive battle: they constituted the objective foundations of a socialist society, and it was not clear therefore why they should not in course of time lead, in a continuous and gradual progress, to the achievement of the goal.

6. *Jaurès's Marxism*

Jaurès did not consider himself a revisionist, although he often emphasized his debt to French socialist sources independent of Marxism. He defended against Bernstein the idea of the political independence of the proletariat, and he upheld the Marxian dialectic as a theory of natural evolution whereby one social formation engenders another as the result of its internal contradictions. A belief in this natural movement of history was necessary to an oppressed class, giving it faith in the success of its efforts. Jaurès accepted the Marxian theory of exploitation as the appropriation of the unremunerated part of the working man's labour, and the Marxian theory of value as a piece of

'social metaphysics' though not as a theory of prices. The idea
that socialism is the cause of all humanity and not of the working
class alone, but that it is the latter's mission to bring socialism
about, is of course one of the traditional pillars of Marxist
doctrine. It is also consistent with this idea to hold—though
perhaps no one did so as emphatically as Jaurès—that the value
of socialism resides ultimately in its effect on the spiritual
development of every human individual.

What essentially divides Jaurès from Marxism is his belief in
continuous and universal progress. Apart from the pantheist
metaphysic which treats historical progress as part of a universal
soteriology of Being, the progress in which Jaurès puts his trust
applies to all periods of history and every aspect of civilization.
The future salvation and absolute unity of the world are not, as
he foresees them, the result of a violent historical break but of
a gradual improvement in every sphere, especially that of
political and legal institutions. Marx, it is true, did not limit
progress to technological change, but expected that the
victorious proletariat would take over from bourgeois society its
scientific and, in part at least, its artistic achievements. He also
believed that past history was a preparation for socialism,
especially in the technique and organization of labour. But he did
not believe in a gradual and irreversible build-up of socialism
through the ages, with social and legal ideas and institutions
steadily approximating to the perfection that would supervene
after a final upheaval. This, however, is precisely what Jaurès
seems to have believed in, justifying in this way his policy of
contracting alliances on all hands, his appeals to all social classes,
and his role of a universal conciliator. Jaurès did not accept the
Marxian vision of progress using evil as a necessary instrument,
and the Hegelian tragedy of history was quite alien to him. His
philosophy of history, as we have seen, combined in a coherent
whole the notion of socialism as the salvation of the world with
that of socialism as the result of an immanent historical trend,
whereas in Marx's theory these two were contingent with regard
to each other. But Jaurès's consistency is achieved at the cost of
a prophetic optimism which enables him to believe that the
future world of universal unity will absorb the whole of past
history, and that it will one day be seen that no human labour
has been in vain, no effort of the spirit has spent itself against

the indifference of nature. His socialism and his metaphysic of salvation sprang from his love of the world and of his fellow men. If this last statement is an appraisal it relates to Jaurès as a human being, but not to the analytical coolness of his mind.

CHAPTER VI

Paul Lafargue: a Hedonist Marxism

LAFARGUE is certainly one of the principal *scriptores minores* of the Marxist canon. By the orthodox of the present day he is treated with the respect due to a minor authority. As the co-founder, with Guesde, of the French socialist party, as a polemicist against anarchists, Christians, and Jaurès, as a propagandist of Marxism and finally as Marx's friend and son-in-law, he fully merits a place in the second rank of the Marxist pantheon. True, his Marxism was highly simplified and it is hard to find anything in his writings that could be called a 'development' of the doctrine. But of all French Marxist writers he was closest to German orthodoxy, and in his day this was the touchstone of doctrinal purity.

Paul Lafargue (1842–1911) was a planter's son from Cuba: his father was partly negro, and he had Indian blood on his mother's side. When he was a boy the family came to France, where he was educated. He studied medicine at Paris, but was expelled from the University for socialist activities, after which he went to London and took his degree in 1868; in the same year he married Marx's daughter Laura. Returning to France at the end of 1868, he took up journalism and practised as a doctor. He was a member of the Commune and, after its defeat, fled to Spain, where he was active in the small socialist party led by Pablo Iglesias. At the end of 1872 he returned to London, where he stayed for ten years. He made his living as a photographer, wrote articles and pamphlets and helped Marx and Guesde to draw up the French party programme. After the amnesty for the *Communards* he returned to France in the spring of 1882, worked as a civil servant, and was an active propagandist of Marxism: he wrote extensively, gave lectures in the provinces, and assisted Guesde as party leader. In 1891 he was elected to the Chamber. He and Laura committed suicide, not from despair but in order to escape the onset of senile decay.

As a writer and theorist Lafargue was a gifted and versatile dilettante, one of many examples in the history of Marxism. His articles and pamphlets popularized a certain style which, like that of Plekhanov, contributed to diluting the intellectual values of Marxism. He wrote on almost every branch of social science: philosophy, history, ethnology, linguistics, religion, economics, and literary criticism. He was not an expert on any of these subjects, but knew something about all of them at second hand. Like most Marxists he believed that as Marx had provided a universal key it could be used by anyone to unlock the secrets of all sciences, however little particular knowledge he might possess. He also believed that he was contributing to the triumph of Marxism by discovering elements in non-Marxist works that seemed to confirm the truth of historical materialism by relating political and literary phenomena or social customs to this or that mode of economic production. He did not realize that it is easy to point to such relationships in large number but that they do not prove Marx's general theory, any more than a theory of genetics can be established by accumulating instances of the likeness between parents and their children.

In short, it cannot be said that Lafargue enlarged or improved upon Marxist doctrine in any way. None the less he is of some importance in the history of Marxism, both because he did more than anyone else to make it known in France and because his writings, simplified as they are, brought into prominence an aspect of Marxism that is less evident in writers of a more serious stamp. He was one of the first to criticize literature in a Marxist spirit, and his amusingly malicious pamphlet on Victor Hugo is still quite readable.

There is as yet no complete edition of Lafargue's writings. His most important works are *Le Déterminisme économique: la méthode historique de Karl Marx* (1907), a popular pamphlet *Le Droit à la paresse* (1883; translated as *The Right to be Lazy*, 1907), *Le Programme du parti ouvrier* (written jointly with Guesde, 1883), and a discussion with Jaurès on historical materialism (1895).

Lafargue's philosophical works do not go beyond popular sensationalism and the materialism of the Enlightenment. He lays great stress on the derivation of all abstract ideas from sensual perception, using the arguments of Locke, Diderot, and

Condillac. He maintained that the Platonist idea that abstracts can be intuited independently of perception was not only false but socially reactionary, as it regarded man as something more than a physical being and thus opened the way to religious mystification. This was why the bourgeoisie, having fought Christianity under the banner of materialism and sensationalism, had dropped its old iconoclasm as soon as it achieved power, turning to an alliance with the Church and reinstating the Platonic-Christian belief in supersensual cognition. Such had been the evolution of Maine de Biran and Cabanis; while the whole Romantic movement, from Chateaubriand onwards, was nothing but an attempt to reconcile the bourgeoisie with Catholicism. The bourgeoisie needed the fiction of eternal truths and supersensual knowledge in order to consecrate and per-petuate the social order that served its ends. Meanwhile the materialism of the Enlightenment was taken over by the proletariat, as a weapon against the ascetic morality preached by the Church in order to maintain class divisions and exploitation. Lafargue's materialism is expressed in crude formulas similar to those of de La Mettrie, Cabanis, or Moleschott, i.e. to what Marxist tradition stigmatizes as 'vulgar materialism'. He says, for instance, that 'the brain is an organ for thinking as the stomach is for digesting' (*Recherches sur l'origine et l'évolution des idées de justice, du bien ...*), or that 'the brain transforms impressions into ideas as a dynamo transforms motion into electricity' (dis-cussion with Jaurès). The epistemological problem of the independent function of abstraction is not touched on in his writings. The only valid objection, in his opinion, to the views of the eighteenth-century sensationalists is that the brain, thanks to the inheritance of acquired experience, has a 'disposition' to assimilate abstract ideas and is therefore not a mere *tabula rasa*. An argument he frequently advances in favour of sensationalism is that etymology shows that terms denoting abstract ideas such as justice, goodness, and the other virtues, as well as the idea of number and all other universals, are all derived from the names of empirical objects or qualities apprehended by the senses.

In his philosophical argumentation Lafargue is closer to Feuerbach than to Marx—a late Feuerbach, freed from any 'en-cumbrance' of Hegelianism. Idealistic philosophy and the history of religion are nothing to him but a system of delusions and an instrument of class division. Unlike Marx, he sees no cognitive value in the history of idealism; as for the age-long controversy between sense and spirit, beginning with the opposition between Zeno the Stoic and Plato, it is simply the history of truth versus error. Religion is the projection of human passions, *mores*, and social conditions into a world of supernatural beings. The idea that a soul inhabits the body arises from primitive attempts to explain the nature of dreams: the existence of dream-figures led men to imagine supernatural beings and deities and to conjecture that the soul was immortal. The belief in an incorporeal soul was characteristic of matriarchal society and disappeared as the patriarchal system prevailed, but revived as the latter declined, thus preparing the way for Christianity. Elsewhere, in his commentary on the party programme, Larfargue explains religion as being due to fear of the unbridled forces of nature: it is the reaction of primitive man, still half an animal, to his own helplessness in the face of elemental powers. As men succeed in extending their power over nature, so religion declines; it will disappear completely when the socialist revolution enables man fully to control the conditions of his own existence.

In his treatment of 'economic determinism' Lafargue again simplifies Marxism out of all recognition. He understands by historical materialism, firstly, that there is in social development no pre-existing purpose or intention: everything, including human behaviour, is the effect of natural, ineluctable causality. Free will is a delusion: men's acts are wholly determined by their natural circumstances or those they have created for themselves. In the man-made environment changes occur most frequently in the mode of production (which Lafargue appears to identify with productive forces, or rather the whole productive apparatus). These changes inevitably bring about corresponding changes in social institutions and ideologies; if the latter are not completely identical in different societies at the same level of technology, it is because of differences in the natural environment. In general, however, Lafargue agrees with Vico, who observed that all human societies go through the same phases of development. Matriarchate, patriarchate, slave-owning, feudalism, capitalism—all human communities pass through

these stages on the way to communism, and the last is as necessary as its predecessors.

The starting-point of social development is primitive communist equality, in which the ideas of justice and property are
unknown, as are moral restrictions of all kinds. Along with other
stereotypes of the Enlightenment Lafargue to same extent
revived the myth of the noble and contented savage, which was
unusual among Marxists of his day, though traces of it can be
found in Engels. In almost all respects, he maintained—in
physical development, happiness, and purity of soul—primitive
men were on a far higher level than those of today. 'It has been
proved that men and women in communities felt neither jealousy
nor parental affection: they lived polygamously, the woman
having as many husbands as she pleased and the man as many
wives as he could; travellers tell us that all these people lived in
a state of greater contentment and fellowship than do the
members of sad, selfish monogamous families.' So Lafargue
declares in the discussion with Jaurès, while in *The Right to be
Lazy* he writes: 'Consider the noble savage whom the missionaries
of trade and the traders in religion have not yet depraved by
Christianity, syphilis and the dogma of labour, and then look at
our wretched servants of the machine ... The physical beauty
and the noble bearing of members of primitive tribes, as yet un-
corrupted by what Pöppig calls the "poisonous breath of civilization", arouses the admiration and amazement of European
observers.' Similarly, Le Play remarks that 'The tendency of the
Bashkir people to indolence, the habit of reflection and the inactivity of nomadic life ... have endowed them with a subtlety
of mind and judgement and a distinction of manner such as is
seldom met with on the same social level in more developed
civilizations.'

Lafargue, like most of his predecessors, held up the idyllic
picture of primitive man in order to criticize industrial civilization rather than actually to start a 'back to nature' movement.
Nevertheless, not a few of the Arcadian clichés are present in his
depiction of the future Communist paradise. The perfect society
is not to be an embodiment of the idea of justice, but one in which
that idea has no meaning, since it is bound up with private
property and the regulation of property relationships. In
primitive communism social life was subject to the instinct of

revenge, which is rooted in biology. This lawless instinct was then transformed into a socially regulated system of retribution; but, as this was insufficient to settle all private accounts, the institution of private property was created so that individual claims and rights could be satisfied without recourse to blows. This is how the idea of justice first arose. Its original purpose was to sanction existing social equality, but under the system of private property it began to sanctify privilege and thus became anti-human.

As will be seen, Lafargue in effect reproduces Hobbes's theory of the social contract in the belief that he is offering a Marxist view of the rise of civilization; but, unlike Hobbes, he believes that the socialization of property to which capitalism is leading will restore mankind to a blessed state of innocence free from laws, claims, and obligations. This is perhaps especially clear in his controversy with Jaurès. The latter argued that in the interpretation of history materialism and idealism can and must be reconciled: for, on the one hand, human ideals can only be realized by economic changes, while, on the other, men need ideals in order to recognize historical necessity as beneficial. Rational ideas are known to us only as embodied in the world; equally, whatever happens in the world is the embodiment of a rational idea. The life of the mind reflects economic phenomena, but at the same time economic change is in part due to moral forces present in the mind: the desire for unity, beauty, and justice act as *idées-forces* throughout the course of history. In short, we must acknowledge both the theory that evolution is causally determined and the idea that gives it meaning and sees in it the embodiment of values. Whether as a means of understanding historical change or as a theory describing it, idealism is not a rival to Marxian materialism but a complement to it.

Lafargue's reply brings out clearly the irreconcilable conflict between two fundamentally different ways of thinking (or even mentalities), the naturalistic and the moralistic. There is, he declares, no inherent purpose in historical evolution and no aspiration towards ideals as an efficient cause, for evolution is not a specifically human phenomenon. The human species came into existence not by any conscious intention but because men developed hands. All abstract ideas, and in particular moral values and the idea of justice, derive from sensual perceptions interpreted in accordance with dominant economic conditions. 'The ideas of justice, based on the notions of "mine" and "thine", that cloud the minds of civilized human beings will vanish like a dream when private property gives way to common property.' (*Recherches sur l'origine ...*) The true, living ideal is not justice but peace and happiness, in a society in which everything belongs to all men. This is a modern version of the paradisal conditions of primitive communism, but only now will these aspirations become a reflection and counterpart of the actual course of economic change.

Lafargue's picture of the new order is most clearly drawn in *The Right to be Lazy*. Men will be happy under communism because they will not have to work. In the past they have been taken in by bourgeois and clerical propaganda telling them that work is meritorious in itself; but in fact work is a curse, and so is the love of work. 'All individual and collective woes are due to man's passion for work ... For the proletariat to realize its own strength it must shake off the prejudices of Christian, economic and free-thinking morality. It must rediscover its natural instincts and proclaim that the right to idleness is a thousand times more sacred and noble than the rights of man devised by the metaphysical lawyers of the bourgeois revolution. It must firmly refuse to work more than three hours a day, and spend the rest of the twenty-four in repose and revelry.' Modern technology makes it possible to reduce labour to a minimum while satisfying all human needs; under communism there will be no need for international trade, as 'Europeans will consume their goods at home instead of exporting them to the ends of the earth, and therefore sailors, dockers and transport workers will be able to lead a life of leisure ... The working class, like the bourgeoisie before it, will have to curb its taste for asceticism and develop its aptitude for consumption. Instead of the workers getting, at best, a small bit of tough meat every day, they will eat large juicy steaks. Instead of inferior wine mixed with water they will drink bumpers of fine claret and burgundy; water will be the drink of animals.'

In this way Lafargue, unlike Marx, envisages communism from the angle of consumption only. Marx, it is true, regarded the progressive shortening of the working day as a basic feature of the coming society, but he was thinking of men having to do less necessary work and enjoying more time for free creative activity. Communism in his eyes was not primarily an opportunity for carefree consumption but for self-fulfilment in action. For Lafargue it was more like the Abbaye de Thélème, as he suggests in his introduction to the French party programme: 'Rabelais was a far-sighted man. He foresaw the communist society of the future, in which we shall produce more than we need and all will be able to consume as much as they like.' Communism was a matter of liberating man's natural instincts from the inhibitions of a civilization based on private property. It was a true return to nature, to a life of natural inclination free from the trammels of morality.

We may see from this how naïve and trivial was Lafargue's interpretation of historical materialism, the Marxian theory of knowledge, and socialism itself. His writings, however, present one possible version of the simplified naturalism which quite commonly passed for Marxism in his day. Assuming that man's being is determined by inclinations due to his biological make-up, and that human history had tended to distort these rather than gratify them, it was reasonable enough to believe that social liberation would take the form of a liberation of natural instincts: this was likewise the principle of Fourier's socialism. The unique and specific character of human existence which played so large a part in Marx's theory was ignored in schemes like these: it was indeed hard to maintain on the basis that man was a product of evolutionary laws governing the whole of nature. This assumption, however, was not peculiar to Lafargue but was current coin among post-Darwinian Marxists. In his naïve optimism and his consumption-oriented doctrine of communism, Lafargue expressed in simplified terms a possible variant of naturalist philosophy. His ideas were a popularized blend of eighteenth-century sensationalism and the myth of the noble savage, of post-Darwinian evolutionism and Marxism—the latter serving rather to buttress eighteenth-century ideals than to correct them. It is in this that the originality of his Marxism consists, if indeed he is to be regarded as a Marxist at all.

CHAPTER VII

Georges Sorel: a Jansenist Marxism

1. The place of Sorel

How far do Sorel's writings belong to the history of Marxism? He was not a member of any political movement that claimed spiritual descent from Marx, and, although he took part in all the great polemics of his day, he did so from the outside as it were, so that the guardians of orthodox Marxism were not much concerned to refute his views. He kept aloof from political and party quarrels, and wrote no treatises on historical materialism. He did not consider himself an orthodox Marxist, and criticized both the master and his disciples as he thought fit to do so. He remains vaguely associated with Italian Fascism, as Mussolini and other ideologists for a time acknowledged him as a prophet of the movement. From the viewpoint of Marxism he may be considered an accidental oddity: at the outset of his literary career he had nothing in common with it, and his name hardly figures in the later development of the doctrine.

At the time of his main writings, however, Sorel not only considered himself a Marxist but believed that he could extract the core of Marx's philosophy—the class war and the independence of the proletariat—and oppose Marx himself to the whole body of contemporary orthodoxy, whether reformist or revolutionary. His unfulfilled ambition was to be the Luther of the Marxist movement, which he saw as corrupted by the struggle for power and privilege, as Rome had appeared to the German reformer in the guise of the Whore of Babylon. He dreamt of a Marxism that would be morally and doctrinally pure; his own version, though it drew on a great variety of sources, was not a patchwork but an extremely coherent whole. He undoubtedly influenced the first ideologists of Italian Communism, such as Antonio Gramsci, and also Angelo Tosca and Palmiro Togliatti.

However, Sorel differed from his Marxist contemporaries not

merely by interpreting Marx in his own way, nor even by sometimes criticizing him, since this happened even to such fanatics of orthodoxy as Rosa Luxemburg. The main point of difference was that all the orthodox regarded Marxism as scientifically true in the same sense as, for instance, evolution or the quantum theory, whereas for Sorel it was true in a pragmatic sense, as the ideological expression of a movement to liberate and rejuvenate the human race. That it was true meant that it was the one irreplaceable instrument that history had put into the hands of the proletariat, though there was no guarantee that the proletariat would make successful use of it. Marxism was the truth of its own age in the same sense as early Christianity had been—the hope of a fresh dawn for mankind, not a 'scientific' account of history, a means of accurate prognosis, or a reliable source of information about the universe. At the present stage of history it was the instrument best calculated to put into effect the supreme values of humanity; but these values, in their substance and origin, owed nothing to Marxism. Hence Sorel was free to change his mind about Marxism without changing his mind about values. He could be a Marxist or a nationalist and still remain faithful to the ideal in respect of which Marxism was only an instrument forged by history at a particular moment. From this point of view, even when most fervently devoted to Marxian philosophy he was not a Marxist in the same sense as Kautsky or Labriola—not because he construed the doctrine differently, but because he took a different view of its historical significance and was not afraid to interpret Marx in the light of quite other authorities such as Proudhon or Tocqueville, Bergson or Nietzsche. He was one of the few who tried to adapt Marxism to the philosophical style of the neo-romantic era, i.e. to interpret it in a pragmatic and activist sense, with emphasis on psychological factors and respect for the independent role of tradition, in a spirit radically opposed to positivism and rationalism.

Sorel's thoughts on social problems are dominated by the idea of greatness, dignity, heroism, and authenticity, and he treats the revolution, the proletariat, and the class war as historical instances of these supreme values. Radicalism and intransigence are in his eyes valuable for their own sakes, irrespective of object. He seems to approve everything in history that proceeds from strong authentic impulses, disinterested fervour, lofty aspirations, and generous hopes. He respects the ardour of religious faith but despises religion when it appears in the form of scholasticism or politics or is tainted by calculation or a spirit of rationalism and appeasement. He is an enthusiast for the workers' movement as a revolt in the name of a great revivifying myth, but he scorns parliamentary manœuvres and the feebleness of half-hearted reformism. He rejects the tradition of anticlericalism as a bridge between socialists and petty-bourgeoisie radicals, but also as a hangover of eighteenth-century rationalism with its optimistic faith in steady, inevitable progress. He opposes nationalism as a device for depriving the proletariat of its absolute separateness; but when estranged from the syndicalists, he turns towards nationalist radicalism with the same hope that made him a Marxist, namely that of recreating the world in its pristine image. In all struggles he is more interested in the heroism of the contendants than in who wins or who is in the right. The conquering spirit of the proletariat excites him more than the vision of socialism. When he joins the proletarian movement it is not for the sake of improving the lot of the oppressed, but because the surge of historic events promises a rebirth of greatness. He stands for the complete spiritual separation of the proletariat from the bourgeoisie and all its works.

Different as Sorel's intellectual sources are, they form a coherent pattern in his work. His Jansenist upbringing no doubt gave him a dislike of any optimistic faith in the natural goodness of mankind, an easy triumph of good over evil, or the attainment of great ends at small cost. From the same source came his contempt for Jesuitical tactics of conciliation, his general intransigence, the all-or-nothing rejection of compromise, and the belief in a sharp distinction between the elect and the rest of the world. In opposition to the doctrine of automatic progress he was attached to the tradition of radical Christianity, i.e. the Christianity of the martyrs.

His technical education and work as an engineer instilled into him a cult of expertise and efficiency, a dislike of dilettantism and empty rhetoric, a conviction that it was production and not exchange that mattered, and an admiration for capitalism in its early, ruthless, expansionist forms, before it was contaminated by philanthropy and the spirit of compromise.

From Marx he learnt to believe that the revolution that would restore society was to be carried out by the proletariat—a clearly differentiated class of direct producers, obliged to sell their labour-power and embodying the hope of a total revolution that would liberate mankind. The basic tenets of Sorel's Marxism are class war, contempt for utopianism, a literal belief in the abolition of the state, and the expectation of a total revolution carried out by the proletariat alone, in isolation from the rest of society.

Giambattista Vico contributed the notion of *ricorso*, the cyclical return of mankind to its own forgotten sources. The proletarian revolution was to be a 'reversion' of this kind, a rediscovery of the primal values rooted in tribal morality.

Another influence was Proudhon, from whom Sorel learnt to regard socialism as primarily a moral question, that of breeding a new type of man (the producer ethic), and to consider the proletariat as a kind of race apart, called on to divide the world between itself and all the rest. The importance Sorel attaches to family and sexual morality in social life is due to Proudhon, as is the habit of characterizing socialism in terms of justice and dignity rather than welfare.

Bergson was the chief philosophical exponent of the style of thought that dominates the work of Sorel: the opposition between 'global' intuitive perception and analytical thought, which in Sorel takes the particular form of opposing 'myth' to 'Utopia'. Bergson also provided Sorel with the conceptual means of contrasting scientific determinism, combined with a belief in the predictability of social processes, with the idea of unforeseeable spontaneity. In addition Sorel derived from Bergson a conviction of the inexpressibility of the concrete, which enabled him to protect his idea of the 'myth' against rational argument.

The influence of Nietzsche is clearly felt in Sorel's cult of greatness, his hatred of mediocrity, and of party huckstering in political life.

The great exponents of liberal conservatism—Tocqueville, Taine, Renan—exercised a strong influence on Sorel in his early period, and to some extent in his Marxist phase as well. From them he learnt to approach politics soberly, to perceive the corruption of democratic institutions and the interests that underlay humanistic rhetoric. From these authors too he imbibed an understanding of early Christianity, the Revolution, and the *ancien régime*.

From these various sources of inspiration Sorel created an ideological whole which shattered traditional agglomerations of values and combined ideas in a different way from any of his predecessors. It was as a Marxist that he stood up for values traditionally associated with the Right: the dignity of marriage and of the family, tribal solidarity, honour and tradition, customary law and the sanctity of religious experience. As a writer he paid little attention to coherence and structure and was more of an apostle than a controversialist. His thoughts appeared to develop without a plan, gropingly as it were, but always in accordance with certain ruling tendencies and values. His works make laborious reading, not because they are obscure but because they lack literary unity. Sometimes he begins by stating a problem and then plunges into digressions, long quotations, aggressive polemics, and violent challenges, in the course of which he seems to forget the point at issue. As a writer he stood far above the orthodox Marxists, but he had insufficient command over his talent. His polemical ardour and lack of logical discipline make it especially hard to summarize his thought, but some recurrent themes can be clearly identified. Brzozowski, himself a writer of a similar kind, thought this spontaneity and lack of preconceived system a great merit in Sorel. The latter's style is reminiscent of Bergson's 'creative evolution', developing in obedience to a governing tendency but without a predetermined goal.

The easiest way to present, or re-present, Sorel's thought in a systematic fashion is to list in parallel columns the ideas and values which he opposed or criticized and those which he advocated. This produces a result on the following lines:

utopianism	Marxist historical realism
epistemological rationalism	Bergsonian intuition and thinking in terms of 'wholes'
sociological rationalism	respect for tradition
determinism	spontaneity
happiness	dignity and greatness
political socialism	syndicalism
dilettantism	professionalism

cult of the French Revolution	cult of early Christianity
reform	revolution
belief in progress	voluntarism, individual responsibility
inter-class alliances	separateness of the proletariat
politics and power	production and the organization of production
optimism	pessimism
intellectuals and politicians	the proletariat
political parties	working-class syndicates
political revolution	general strike
Utopia	myth
democracy	freedom
consumer morality	producer morality
scholastic religion	the religion of mystics and martyrs
decadence	*ricorso*, a return to the sources
social sciences	the activist myth
the state	an association of producers

This set of antitheses may seem strange to anyone acquainted with the stereotypes and conceptual associations of classical Marxism, but Sorel's positive values, taken together, define his polemical attitude with great clarity. He was opposed to contemporary socialist politicians, the leaders of the International, who in his eyes were a mere band of self-seekers out to enjoy the fleshpots of office once they had wrested them from the bourgeoisie. Jaurès, in particular, he pilloried in almost all his writings as a symbol of petty-bourgeois socialism seeking to win over the bourgeoisie in order to appease the proletariat, to destroy the idea of the class struggle, and to introduce a new system of privilege on the basis of a spurious unity.

2. *Biographical outline*

Georges Sorel was born of bourgeois parents at Cherbourg in 1847. He studied at the École polytechnique and became an engineer in the Département des ponts et chaussées, where he worked until 1892. His first writings were published shortly before he retired: *Le Procès de Socrate* (1889), *Contribution à l'étude profane de la Bible* (1889), *La Ruine du monde antique* (1888). In about 1893 he became interested in Marx and afterwards in an anti-political syndicalist movement based in part on Proudhonist and anarchist traditions, its chief organizer being Fernand Pelloutier. In 1898 Sorel published *L'Avenir socialiste des syndicats*, later reissued as part of *Matériaux d'une théorie du prolétariat* (third edition 1919): this was the first attempt at a theoretical analysis of the experience of the syndicalist movement developing independently of the socialist parties and even in opposition to them. In the 1890s Sorel wrote for *L'Ère nouvelle* and *Devenir social*, where in 1895–6 he published studies of Durkheim and Vico. Active in the defence of Dreyfus, he was disillusioned to find that the socialist *Dreyfusards* exploited the *Affaire* for purely party ends. Bernstein's work to some extent led him to criticize orthodox Marxism, but his own objections soon developed along quite different lines. (Although basically opposed to reformism he continued to admire and respect Bernstein, and agreed wholeheartedly with his contention that the policy of the German socialists had nothing to do with their revolutionary programme.) As time went on he became increasingly severe in his criticism of the socialist party, parliamentary democracy, and what he called 'political socialism' as opposed to syndicalism. His chief Marxist writings are: *Réflexions sur la violence* (*Reflections on Violence*, 1908 and later, enlarged editions), *Les Illusions du progrès* (1908), *Matériaux d'une théorie du prolétariat* (1908: essays dating from 1898 onwards), and *La Décomposition du marxisme* (1908). The first two of these originally appeared in serial form in *Le Mouvement socialiste*, edited by Hubert Lagardelle. The fourth edition of *Réflexions sur la violence* (1919) contains an appendix with an enthusiastic defence of Lenin and the Bolshevik revolution. (Lenin himself took no interest in Sorel, whom he mentions only once and in a disparaging tone.)

In the course of time Sorel lost faith in French syndicalism, but he hoped for a while that a similar movement might win the day in Italy. He had close contacts with that country, having contributed to Italian socialist periodicals from 1898 onwards: he wrote articles on Vico and Lombroso, and his own books, translated into Italian, were praised by Croce and Pareto and attacked by Labriola. In 1910, however, deciding that syndicalism was irretrievably corrupted by reformist trends, he switched to support of radical nationalist movements in France and Italy and for a time co-operated with the Action Française; he also influenced the national-syndicalist groups in Italy which helped to provide the basis of Fascism. He welcomed the first beginnings of the latter movement in 1912 and reiterated his sympathy in 1919, seeing in Fascism the promise of a social rebirth inspired by nationalist mythology. For the same reason he hailed the Bolshevik revolution as a retreat from Westernism to the true spirit of Muscovy. The Fascists, after they came to power, paid lip-service to Sorel as their spiritual patron, but the real trend of their movement was to assert the brutal authority of dictatorial government, which Sorel abominated. On the other hand the first Italian Communist periodical, *Ordine Nuovo*, edited by Gramsci at Turin from 1919 onwards, regarded Sorel as an ideologist of the proletariat.

Sorel died in 1922 at Boulogne-sur-Seine, where he had lived for some years. Since the end of the 1920s his ideas have had no effective influence on any branch of the socialist movement or on the Communist International.

3. Rationalism versus history. Utopia and myth. Criticism of the Enlightenment

The 'rationalism' to which Sorel was opposed was not a particular philosophical statement but an intellectual attitude which drew its strength from Cartesianism, flourished in the eighteenth-century *salons*, and, in his opinion, had a pernicious effect on the contemporary interpretation of Marxism. Rationalism, thus understood, consists of creating simplified, abstract patterns of thought and making them do duty for the real, complex world. Examples of such patterns are theories of human nature which regard man as an assemblage of permanent, general characteristics and types of behaviour, regardless of the historical circumstances which in practice affect human actions. By reducing society to the speculative universal of 'man', rationalists are able to conjecture at will as to the nature of the perfect community and to construct utopian models of the future, free from conflict, contingency, and rival aspirations. Engels was not exempt from this way of thinking, for he too 'reduces the world to a single human being'. Rationalists also believe that all actions are governed by rational motives, and they thus blind themselves to the real-life complexity of psychological differences, the importance of tradition and custom, and the role played in social development by biological (particularly sexual) and many other factors. They regard the French Revolution, for instance, as the triumph of an idea over historical reality, oblivious of the many actual forces, especially those rooted in the plebeian levels of society, which combined to overthrow the old regime. Rationalism is a simplified, schematic mode of thought based on a legalistic form of reasoning which reduces human beings to the status of juridical units. The history of communist Utopias is full of rationalist preconceptions, and that is why they have never seriously competed with existing forms of government. As Pascal pointed out, rationalism is not, as the Cartesians would have us believe, a synonym of scientific thinking. Cartesianism was successful and popular because it turned science into a drawing-room topic. Like the Scholastics, Descartes set up between man and reality ingeniously devised intellectual machines which prevented man from using his mind to any purpose. He provided the uninstructed laity with a simple formula for discoursing on scientific subjects in the belief that the 'natural light' enables everyone, however amateur, to pass judgement on everything. The Enlightenment writers adopted the same style: for Condorcet as for Fontenelle the object was not to instruct men how to be farmers or manufacturers, but merely *salon* philosophers. The dominant ideology of the eighteenth century was that of men in the service of the monarchy, with the philosopher playing the role of court jester: '*causeurs*, satyrists, panegyrists, clowns in the pay of a degenerate aristocracy'—to quote Sorel's summing-up. To justify the moral depravity of the *salons* Diderot taught that the only instincts in nature were those of self-preservation and generation, and in Sorel's day Darwinism was interpreted in the same sense. The *Encyclopédie* contributed nothing to the development of science, but was a mere farrago of dilettantism for the purposes of polite conversation. The communist fantasies of Enlightenment authors were no threat to anyone. It was dangerous to criticize inhuman conditions in the mines, but the monarchy and its hangers-on had no objection to abstract praise of communism, republican virtues, and the natural law, or to those who disparaged tradition in the name of some paradisal Utopia.

Utopian literature from Plato onwards was, Sorel argued, a typical and sterile product of rationalist delusion. 'Since the Renaissance, Utopias have become a literary genre which, by simplifying economic, political and psychological questions to the extreme, has had a deplorable effect on the intellectual formation of revolutionaries' (*Matériaux* ... third edn., p. 26). Utopias are sterile because they postulate an abstract human individual uninfluenced by history, religion, inherited custom, or any national, biological, or psychological traits, and they create an imaginary state made up of such beings; they are also harmful, since their authors appeal to the prudence, enlightenment, or philanthropy of the privileged classes and weaken the proletariat's understanding of the class struggle. Marxism is closer to the Manchester school of bourgeois economics than to the utopian writers, for it is a realistic look at society torn by the class struggle, which can neither be avoided nor mitigated. Marx's occasional lapses into utopian naïvety, as in the *Critique of the Gotha Programme*, are contrary to the true spirit of Marxism, which does not appeal to a universal sense of justice or attempt to compress society into a logical schema, but takes account of the forces that have actually affected history in all their complexity. Thanks to Marxism, socialism has parted company with utopian ideas. It no longer seeks to be a 'scientific' blueprint for a future society, or to compete with the bourgeoisie in theorizing on the organization of production: its purpose is to provide the ideology of a radical class war.

Instead of constructing abstract plans for a perfect society, our task is to discover how social institutions have come into being spontaneously in the course of history, and to interpret them in the light of all the psychological and economic circumstances. This was done by Savigny when, in opposition to the rationalist doctrine of a social contract, he expounded the notion of law arising in the form of local custom, gradually accumulating and adapting itself to new conditions in the course of history. The utopians were ready with draft constitutions for the whole of mankind because they took little heed of actual history; Marxism offered an analysis of history as it really was, not as it appeared in a rationalist schema.

In *Reflections on Violence* Sorel devotes special attention to those aspects of social life that offer most resistance to rationalization and form, as it were, a core of mystery, yet have more effect on social development than all the rest. In the field of morality the clear, rational element comprises relationships of reciprocity analogous to commercial exchanges, while sexual life, by contrast, remains opaque and difficult to reduce to simple formulas. In legislation the most easily rationalized measures are those relating to debts and contracts; the most refractory are those concerning the family, which affects the whole of social life. In economics, trade is a lucid area but production, which is the final determinant, is obscurely embedded in local and historical traditions. The rationalists come to grief whenever they try to reduce to simple legal formulas aspects of life which belong to the 'dark areas' of experience and whose qualitative differences are the result of historical contingency. True history is more like a work of art than a pellucid logical construction.

The contrast between the rationalistic and the historical mentality is very similar to that between optimism and pessimism, in the special sense in which Sorel uses these terms. Among the optimists he includes Socrates, the Jesuits, the *philosophes*, the ideologists of the French Revolution, the utopians, believers in progress, socialist politicians, and Jaurès; among pessimists the early Christians, Protestants, Jansenists, and Marxists. Optimists believe that the evil in the world is due to inadequate legislation, a lack of enlightenment and of human feeling. They are convinced that legal reform will soon bring about the earthly paradise, but in practice their delusions and ignorance of social reality lead them to adopt policies of terror like those of the Revolution. Pessimists, on the other hand, do not believe in any all-embracing theory or infallible method of introducing order into the universe: they are conscious that human projects operate within narrow limits set by the weight of tradition, human weakness, and the imperfection of our knowledge. Aware of the interrelation of all aspects of life, they regard social conditions as forming an indivisible whole that cannot be reformed piecemeal, but must either be left alone or destroyed in a catastrophic explosion. In ancient Greece pessimism was the philosophy of warlike mountain tribes—poor, proud, uncompromising, and wedded to tradition—while optimism was that of prosperous city traders. The early Christians were pessimists; believing that no human effort could reform the world, they withdrew into themselves and impassively awaited the Second Coming. Protestantism began as an attempt to revive Christian pessimism, but later it fell under the spell of Renaissance humanism and adopted the latter's values. The pessimism of true Marxism lies in the fact that it does not believe in any automatic law of progress, in the possibility of gradual reform, or in the attainability of general happiness by a simple process of imposing on society some arbitrary construction of the mind. Marxism is an apocalyptic challenge to the proletarian consciousness, not in the name of some utopian programme but in that of an apocalyptic 'myth'.

A myth, in Sorel's sense, is not a kind of Utopia but the very opposite: not the description of a perfect future society, but the call to a decisive battle. Its value is not cognitive in the ordinary sense; it is not a scientific prediction, but a force inspiring and organizing the militant consciousness of a self-contained group. The myth of the proletariat is the general strike. Only by means of a myth can a fighting group maintain its solidarity, heroism, and the spirit of self-sacrifice. It is a state of mind that expects and prepares for the violent destruction of the existing order at a single blow, but has no ready-made paradise to set up against it. Unlike utopias, a myth is primarily negative, regarding the present world as a coherent whole that can only be destroyed root and branch: it represents a spirit of total opposition and cannot be criticized as though it were a plan of reform or a blueprint for the future. It must be wholly accepted or wholly rejected, and its devotees are impervious to any doubt that may be cast on its effectiveness. Utopians and social scientists imagine that they can foresee and plan the future, but the myth is an act of creation, not of prediction. The myth of a general strike embodies the whole idea of socialism and the self-consciousness of the proletariat, which radically severs its connection with the present society and seeks no help or allies of any kind.

These results could not be produced in any very certain manner by the use of ordinary language; use must be made of a body of images which, by intuition alone, and before any considered analyses are made, is capable of evoking as an undivided whole the mass of sentiments which correspond to the different manifestations of the war undertaken by socialism against modern society. The syndicalists solve this problem perfectly, by concentrating the whole of socialism in the drama of the general strike; there is thus no longer any place for the reconciliation of contraries in professorial gibberish [*la conciliation des contraires dans le galimatias par les savants officiels*]. (*Reflections on Violence*, Ch. IV)

The myth is not a matter of thinking about the future or planning it: it lives in the present, which it also helps to form. 'The myth must be judged as a means of acting on the present; any attempt to discuss how far it can be materially applied to the course of history is devoid of sense. It is the myth in its entirety which is alone important: its parts are only of interest in so far as they bring out the main idea.' (Ibid.)

As will be seen, while Sorel criticizes the rationalism of Descartes or the Enlightenment he does not expressly oppose to it an irrationalist point of view: he regards rationalist delusions as simply a mark of historical dilettantism, the mentality which prefers elegant speculation to complex reality. But when he contrasts social planning with the mythopoeic act he is no longer opposing historical reason to *a priori* abstractions, but upholding the claims of sentiment against analytical reasoning in general. The myth is an indivisible, inexpressible whole that can only be grasped in a single act of intuitive perception as described by Bergson. Acceptance of the myth is not an intellectual act, but an expression of readiness for destructive action. The myth is proof against argument, discussion, or compromise. It is anti-intellectual in a more radical sense than we find in Bergson, who did not condemn analytical reason as a source of decadence but merely defined the limits of its usefulness as an instrument for technical manipulation in describing physical or social reality. In Bergson's view rational and analytical thought on social problems was far from valueless, though it could not take account of historical breaches of continuity due to spontaneous creativity. For Sorel, however, belief in the myth was to be a complete substitute for sociological knowledge, and all practical acts must be subordinate to the expectation of an undefined, indescribable apocalypse. By thus setting up a mythology immune to rational criticism Sorel gave advance endorsement to political movements founded on 'instinct': from this point of view the Fascists were right to claim him for their own, whereas his connection with Marxism must be regarded as accidental.

4. 'Ricorsi.' The separation of classes and the discontinuity of culture

Although Sorel's myth is a negation of the present in the name of a future catastrophe, it also has some roots in the past, though not in the manner of religious myths. It purports to be a revival of what formerly was, a rejuvenation of the world by stripping it of the accumulated layers of civilization. This is what Vico called a *ricorso*, when a people reverts to its primitive state and all its works are creative, instinctive, and poetic, as in early Christianity or the decline of the Middle Ages. Revolutionary syndicalism is to bring about a universal rebirth of this kind, based on the proletariat as a self-contained enclave within an alien society.

Sorel laid especial emphasis on the separateness of the proletariat, but in a different sense from that of orthodox Marxism. When the leaders of the Second International spoke of the independence of the proletariat they had in mind the political distinctness, the independence of the workers' parties, the movement developing according to its own interests and pursuing its own goals. Neither Kautsky, Rosa Luxemburg, nor even Lenin and Trotsky ruled out tactical alliances with non-proletarian parties in particular circumstances, nor did they advocate a break with existing civilization: on the contrary, it was taken for granted that this included human values that socialism was capable of assimilating and to which it was indeed the sole rightful heir. To Sorel, on the other hand, the point at issue was not the political separateness of the workers' party, since he was opposed to parties as such and regarded them as a badge of bourgeois society. The party expressed, naturally and inevitably, the subjection of the proletariat to professional politicians. Not only could it not assist in liberating the proletariat but it was bound to frustrate its liberation, at best replacing the former tyranny by that of party officials, parliamentary orators, and journalists' clubs. The proletariat's hope lay not in parties, or in trade unions striving to improve conditions for the time being, but in revolutionary syndicates—expressly non-political, indifferent to parliamentary tactics, refusing to play the bourgeois game, devoting all their efforts to forming the consciousness and solidarity of the working class against the day when society would be totally transformed.

The syndicalist movement (or anarcho-syndicalist, as it is usually called) developed in France in the 1890s, in Italy and Spain a little later; in Germany it did not prevail to any extent. In keeping with the Proudhonist tradition it rejected any kind of political activity or participation in bourgeois institutions, and subordinated the economic struggle of the proletariat to the coming revolution, which would not replace existing political institutions by new ones of the same kind, but by loosely federated producers' associations governed exclusively by workers. Marx stigmatized this as a petty-bourgeois Utopia, arguing that workers' self-government could not in itself put an end to competition and anarchy in production, and that if Proudhon's ideal were realized it would bring back all the horrors of capitalist accumulation. To Sorel, however, syndicalism offered the only hope of a genuine victory of the proletariat. He did not join the movement, believing that' middle-class intellectuals could only do harm as members of workers' organizations, but he provided it with an ideology from outside.

The business of the syndicalist movement, then, was to imbue the workers with a sense of alienation from bourgeois society, to break with bourgeois morality and modes of thought, to have nothing to do with party and parliamentary intrigue, and to defend proletarian purity against ideologists and rhetoricians. The proletariat would never free itself if it tried to ape the bourgeoisie: its first rule must be to 'preserve its exclusively working-class character by keeping out intellectuals, whose leadership would bring about the re-establishment of hierarchies and create divisions among the workers' (*Matériaux*, p. 132). It is not only a question of organizational purity, however, but still more of spiritual purity. 'My friends and I are never tired of urging the workers to avoid being drawn into the rut of bourgeois science and philosophy. There will be a great change in the world when the proletariat discovers, as did the bourgeoisie after the Revolution, that it is capable of thinking in a manner appropriate to its own mode of life' (*Illusions*, p. 135). The new proletarian culture will be founded on labour, and 'will afford no cause to regret the disappearance of bourgeois culture. The war that the proletariat is called on to wage against its masters is, we know, calculated to arouse in it a sense of sublimity that today's bourgeoisie completely lacks ... We must make every effort to ensure that the rising class is not poisoned by bourgeois ideas, and for that reason we cannot do enough to free the people from the shackles of eighteenth-century literature' (ibid., pp. 285–6). The new philosophy is 'one of arms and not of heads' (*Décomposition du marxisme*, p. 60), its purpose being to convince the working class that its whole future lies in the class struggle. It is a philosophy that comes into being spontaneously: the revolutionary syndicalist movement is created by men who know little of Marxism, but it expresses the truest need of the class of producers. Without it the proletariat would be exposed to the same fate as the ancient Germans who, after conquering Rome, felt ashamed of their barbarism and succumbed to the decadent culture of the rhetoricians, or the men of the Reformation who let themselves be corrupted by the values of humanism. The proletariat, engaged in the class war, must firmly understand that all other classes without exception are opposed to its liberation. The society of the future will inherit capitalist technology, but there will be no place in it for the spiritual culture of capitalism. Any ideological or political battle, however justified in other ways, will do the workers more harm than good if it involves their co-operating with bourgeois radicals—for instance, in combating the Church and clericalism, not to speak of defending patriotic causes—since it will weaken the sense of class separateness and foster the dangerous illusion that the proletariat can effectively join forces with liberals to bring about social change. The revolution will be 'an absolute separation between two historical eras' (*Reflections*, Ch. IV), and the proletariat, which is to carry it out, must have no moral scruples *vis-à-vis* other classes. 'People who have devoted their lives to a cause which they identify with the regeneration of the world could not hesitate to make use of any weapon which might serve to develop to a greater degree the spirit of the class war' (ibid., Ch. VI.)

5. *Moral revolution and historical necessity*

This does not mean, however, that the proletariat is, or can be, indifferent to morality. On the contrary, the basic purpose of the revolution and of the preparatory period is to effect a moral transformation of the working class that will restore its dignity, pride, independence, and sense of mission and exclusivity. Although his best-known work is largely an apologia for violence, Sorel regards violence as being morally right only in so far as it plays a part in the moral education of its users. It is a military and not a police type of violence that he has in mind, devoid of cruelty and certainly not motivated by envy of the wealthier classes, which would be immoral and degrading to the proletariat. Far from seeking to replace the present form of government by one equally authoritarian, the object of proletarian violence is to do away with government altogether. Morally commendable violence is evinced, he argues, in spontaneous acts of popular justice by Norwegian mountain-dwellers, in lynch-law or the Corsican vendetta. It is the advocates of *political* revolution, such as the socialists who wish to supplant the privileged minority of today, who are liable, as the Revolution showed, to adopt inquisitorial methods of cruelty and terror as a cure for political or economic difficulties. In this absurd and hopeless course the Jacobins were encouraged by Rousseau's doctrine of the social contract, since they regarded themselves as the embodiment of the 'general will' and therefore entitled to do whatever they chose. Being morally unprepared to rule, the best thing they could think of was to imitate the *ancien régime*. The same kind of despotism would result if power were placed in the hands of Jaurès and others like him, who use humanistic rhetoric to imbue the proletariat with a bourgeois desire to see its party in power, instead of preparing it to smash the machinery of public authority.

For these reasons syndicalism is against democracy, which encourages the proletariat to take part in bourgeois institutions, especially parliament, and is a source of demoralization, corruption, and the undermining of class solidarity.

The general strike, which is the proper aim of the proletarian struggle, is thus to be distinguished from political revolution. In this conception of Sorel's the conventional opposition between an economic and a political strike does not apply. The general strike is not an economic one in the sense of an attempt to improve the situation of the working class in capitalist conditions, but it is also the contrary of a political revolution. The purpose of the latter is to attain power, and it is subject to all the laws of a fight for power, including tactical alliances, but it does not premise the division of society into only two camps. Besides the syndicates it presupposes other organizations, committees, or parties with programmes and ready-made forms for the future: it must be planned, and can therefore be criticized in detail. Moreover, a political revolution is not based on the Marxian doctrine of class division but on an anti-Marxist opposition between rich and poor; it appeals to base instincts of envy and vindictiveness, instead of the sublime heroism of popular champions. A general strike means the destruction of the existing order without any idea of setting up a new authority: its purpose is to restore control of production to free men who have no need of masters. It is a single, indivisible action, not to be broken down into stages or conceived as a strategic plan. The definition of socialism in terms of a general strike 'means that politicians' revolutions have had their day; the proletariat refuses to have new hierarchies set up over it. Our formula has nothing to say concerning the rights of man, absolute justice, political constitutions and parliaments: it rejects not only bourgeois capitalistic government, but any hierarchy that at all resembles that of the bourgeoisie' (*Matériaux*, pp. 59–60). Syndicalism cares nothing for doctrines or 'scientific' preparation: 'it proceeds as circumstances dictate, regardless of dogma, not fearing to commit its forces in ways that prudent men deplore. A sight calculated to discourage those noble minds who believe in the supremacy of science in modern times, who expect the revolution to be brought about by a mighty effort of thought, who imagine that the world has been ruled by pure reason since it was freed from clerical obscurantism.' But 'all experience has shown that revolution does not possess the secret of the future: it acts in the same way as capitalism, rushing to occupy every outlet that presents itself' (ibid., p. 64).

Revolutionary syndicalism is thus equally opposed to utopianism and to the Blanquist doctrine that a group of conspirators claiming a mandate from the proletariat may take advantage of circumstances to seize power and then transform society by means of force and repression. Blanquism or Jacobinism stands for a revolution of the poor against the rich, not a Marxian revolution carried out by producers alone. The latter is by no means aimed at a party dictatorship: Bernstein is right when he says that the assumption of power by the social democrats would not make the people sovereign, but merely dependent on professional politicians and newspaper owners. Until such time as the workers have a strong economic organization and attain a high standard of moral independence, the dictatorship of the proletariat can only mean the dictatorship of party orators and men of letters.

Again, the syndicalist revolution cannot be simply the result of the economic decadence of capitalism. Revolutions that take place when the old regime is in a state of impotence and collapse do not lead to improvement, but petrify the state of decay. The syndicalist revolution requires capitalism to be expansive—to suffocate by its own energy, not to die of inanition. It is not, therefore, in the workers' interest to weaken capitalism by forcing legislative concessions and reforms: it is best for them that capitalists should be overcome by a ruthless, predatory spirit of expansion, like the American conquistadors of capitalism. This is the way to foster the sense of absolute class division, the solidarity of the oppressed, inflexible heroism, the grandeur and dignity of a historical mission—everything that socialist politicians sacrifice when they cheat the exploiters into making petty concessions and in so doing demoralize the working class.

Nor should we be deluded by 'so-called scientific socialism' into thinking that victory is assured by historical necessity. As Bergson showed, history proceeds by unforeseeable acts of creation. The illusions of determinism are due to the exaggerated hopes aroused by the progress of natural science in the nineteenth century: the utopians naïvely imagined that the future course of society could be plotted like the movements of heavenly bodies. But, as Bergson's theory of personality and evolution makes clear, the future is constantly taking a fresh start as the result of freely creative action. The revolutionary movement is directed towards the future, but it foresees it only in terms of its own spontaneous action, guided by a single, indivisible, unanalysable idea—the sublime myth of a total transformation of the world in a final, apocalyptic battle. Such was the inspiration of early Christianity, which refused to compromise with the world or to regard itself as part of society, withdrawing instead into the myth of the Parousia. But the Church's later history shows how, defying the predictions of the wise, it periodically renewed itself in bursts of vigorous expansion, as initiated by the great reformers and founders of new monastic orders. The syndicalist movement is likewise a spontaneous process of renewal which may regenerate the working class, corrupted by politicians and legislation, and in due time bring salvation to all mankind.

The purpose of the new revolution is not to bring prosperity and abundance, or to make life easy. Sorel makes fun of Destrée and Vandervelde, who imagine the future socialist state as a Land of Cockaigne or a place where the inhabitants may do as they please, as in the Abbaye de Thélème. The mainspring of the revolutionary movement is not poverty but class antagonism, and the workers' cause is not that of the poor who want to take away the property of the rich, but that of direct producers who wish to be the organizers of production. The principal values of socialism are those of morality and not of well-being, and it may be noticed that the poorest members of the proletariat are the least, not the most, revolutionary-minded. A just society must, as Proudhon put it, acknowledge the 'law of poverty'; a frugal life is an honest and happy one. Proudhon saw the future society as a loose federation of agricultural and industrial associations, with public life based on communal and provincial units, freedom of the Press and of assembly, and no standing armies. Sorel despised all planning for the future and vouchsafed no details of the 'perfect society', but as an exponent of Proudhon he no doubt imagined it on similar lines. In *L'Avenir socialiste des syndicats* he says that society will be 'organized according to the plan of production', and that the object of socialism is to 'apply the workshop system to public life' (*Matériaux*, p. 70), so that all social issues will present themselves in terms of production units.

From the moral and organizational points of view Sorel's ideal seems to have been one of isolated mountain clans or Swiss communes practising direct democracy, more or less self-sufficient in production, and not involved in commercial exchanges on such a scale as to affect their customs and traditions. The morality of the proletariat was a morality of producers as opposed to merchants; modern democracy was still modelled on the stock exchange, whereas the democracy of the future would be analogous to co-operative manufacture.

These comparisons are not devoid of foundation. The history of democratic ideas and institutions is certainly related to the history of trade, and the whole Mediterranean culture arose and developed in terms of ports and commercial towns. Trading encourages habits of compromise, negotiation and bargaining as well as deceit and hypocrisy, rhetoric and demagogy, prudence and competition, love of wealth and comfort, rationalism and disregard for tradition, shrewd calculation and prediction, and the ideal of success. The subordination of production to exchange-value, which according to Marx is the essence of capitalism, is a natural culmination of these trends. The society in which 'everything is for sale', and in which family, tribal, and local links, irreducible to exchange relationships, count for nothing, was attacked by all the Romantics including Marx in his young days. Sorel, like Nietzsche, was a sworn enemy of this type of society and to that extent an heir of the Romantics, but the upshot of his criticism was very different from Marx's. He was attracted by the picture of untamed warrior clans fighting for survival rather than wealth or comfort, valiant but not cruel, proud in spite of their poverty, devoted to their tribal customs and their freedom, ready to fight to the death against foreign rule. The main purpose of socialism, in Sorel's mind, was to revive this type of morality as opposed to that of commercial society. 'Socialism is a moral issue in that it provides a new way of judging all human acts, or, in Nietzsche's famous phrase, a revaluation of all values' (*Matériaux*, p. 170, quoting from his own preface to the French translation of a work by Saverio Merlino). The new morality takes shape in the working class under capitalist conditions, and is in fact a prior condition of revolution and of economic change: here Sorel agrees with Vandervelde, who says that a victory of the workers without a radical moral transformation would plunge the world into a state of suffering, cruelty, and injustice as bad as the present, if not worse. The chief points at which the new morality comes into play are the family, war, and production, and in all these spheres it means an increase of dignity, solidarity, heroism, generosity, and personal responsibility. Sorel attaches especial importance to sexual restraint and family virtues, the weakening of which he regards as a natural reinforcement of bourgeois society. 'The world will become a juster place only in so far as it becomes more chaste—I believe there is nothing more certain than this' (ibid., p. 199). The ideal to which he looks up is that of the Homeric heroes as seen by Nietzsche.

6. *Marxism, anarchism, Fascism*

As we have already observed, the interrelation of values and ideas in Sorel's work is quite different from that of the orthodox Marxists or any critic of Marxism. In this respect he stands unique. His attacks on reformism are sometimes very like those of the orthodox social-democratic Left, but his criticism of Marxist orthodoxy has much in common with that of the anarchists. He attacks anarchism from a Marxist standpoint, yet on some points he criticizes Marx from the angle of Bakunin or Proudhon. The usual classifications of socialist thought at this period do not apply to him.

Like Marx, Sorel regarded socialism not merely as a better form of social organization but as a complete transformation of every aspect of life, morality, thought, and philosophy: not a mere set of reforms, but a reinterpretation of human existence. The socialists of his time did not, in his opinion, take a serious interest in human nature and the final aim of life. They adopted the shallow metaphysics of the eighteenth-century free-thinkers and failed to realize the importance of evil in Marx's historiosophy; their rationalistic optimism prevented them from matching the Church in understanding men, but it was necessary for socialism to offer all the values that the Church did if it was to prevail. Sorel, following Gustave Le Bon, did not hesitate to ascribe to socialism a religious and charismatic character: in this he differs from Marx's views, at all events in *Capital*.

Marxism, to Sorel, was above all the poetry of the Great Apocalypse which he identified with social revolution. He combated reformism not because it was ineffectual—on the contrary, he knew it to be effective—but because it was prosaic and unheroic. He believed in the class basis of socialism and the unique role of the producers as agents of the revolution. The proletariat, as a militant sect, must guard above all things its independence of existing society. Sorel dreamt of a free society, i.e. an association of producers with no bosses over them, its basic values deriving from the fact that it was devoted to material production; Marx, on the other hand, thought the great achievement of socialism would be the conquest of leisure, enabling people to devote themselves to creative work as the labour hours necessary for material production were progressively shortened. Marx put his faith in technology, which he thought would liberate mankind from the cares of material existence; Sorel, on the contrary, regarded productive activity as the source of all human dignity, and the desire to be free from such cares was, to him, no better than bourgeois hedonism. Marx was a rationalist inasmuch as he believed in scientific socialism, i.e. that a rational analysis of the capitalist economy would show that it was bound to be replaced by a collective system; he also believed in the continuity of civilization. Sorel regarded the idea of the historical necessity of socialism as a survival of the Hegelian *Weltgeist*; he accepted Bergson's theory of spontaneity and advocated a complete break in cultural continuity, yet at the same time he wished to preserve the traditions of the family and tribal solidarity. His arbitrary treatment of Marxist doctrine may be seen in the definition, which he ascribes to Marx, of a class as 'a collectivity of families united by traditions, interests and political views, and possessing a degree of solidarity such that they may be regarded as forming a single personality, a being endowed with reason and acting accordingly' (*Matériaux*, p. 184).

Sorel did not profess to be an anarchist: the anarchists of his day were not well defined from a class point of view, but tended to enlist support among the lumpenproletariat and the *déclassé* intelligentsia. A movement led by lawyers, journalists, and students clearly had nothing to do with revolutionary syndicalism as Sorel understood it, and he was also repelled by the anarchist groups of Bakuninist persuasion who combined conspiratorial methods with authoritarian principles. At the same time, he shared with the anarchists their basic premiss of the need to do away with all state institutions and their refusal to take part in parliamentary life or to support 'political socialism'. From Bakunin's time onward it was a constant feature of anarchist propaganda, emphasized, for example, by Machajski, that 'political' or 'party' socialism was only the prelude to a new tyranny, and that the 'dictatorship of the proletariat' as a form of state organization meant subjecting the workers to the despotism of professional politicians. Sorel also agreed with those anarchists who insisted on a 'moral revolution' as an integral part of the social revolution. 'Social democracy is cruelly punished today for having fought so hard against the anarchists, who tried to bring about a revolution of minds and hearts' (*Matériaux*, p. 380, commenting on a letter from Proudhon to Michelet). The nationalization of means of production was valueless in itself as far as liberating the workers was concerned, for it merely increased the power of politicians over producers.

It may appear strange that a writer who so fiercely attacked the idea of patriotism, state institutions, and party organization should have been recognized as an ideologist of the budding Fascist movement and should have supplied arguments to the functionaries and apologists of a brutal nationalist tyranny—the more so as, unlike Nietzsche, Sorel accepted the basic doctrines of Marxism. Yet his link with Fascism is a real one, though clearly it was impossible to judge the first intimations of Italian Fascism in 1912 with the eyes of those who witnessed the Second World War. Everything in Sorel's work that related to the revolution and the free post-revolutionary society belongs, it is true, to the realm of 'myth', which in principle admits of no discussion or explanation. Fascism drew its strength from the sense of desperation and desire for absolute change, the disillusionment with democracy and disbelief in the possibility of reform, the obscure need for some radical break with the existing scheme of things. Sorel's appeals were well adapted to the spiritual conditions out of which Fascism was bred. He did not set up to be the planner of a new order, but the herald of catastrophe. He called for a break in the continuity of civilization in the name of a better culture, a return to the popular sources of legislation and morality; in so doing he unconsciously showed that an attack on the whole of an existing culture is in effect an invitation to barbarism unless it is based on already existing values and a clear knowledge of what the new order is supposed to comprise. Sorel aims many shrewd blows at the naïvety of the rationalists; but if an attack on rationalism is not clearly distinguished from an attack on reason, if it appeals to a *philosophie des bras* which is not so very different from a philosophy of the mailed fist, then it becomes a rebellion against the mind and a plea for violence pure and simple. Sorel's advocacy of violence related, in his mind, to the warlike variety as opposed to that of a *gendarmerie*; but the distinction is a fine one, based on literary stereotypes and the idealization of Grecian or Viking heroes. A morality that regards violence in itself as a source of heroism and greatness is very near to being an instrument of despotism. The same is true of Sorel's criticism of parliamentary democracy: there was much truth in it, but the same could be said of Hitler's writings on the subject. The criticism of pervading corruption, abuses, cant, petty squabbling, and the competition for jobs masquerading as a conflict of ideas—all these have been denounced by anarchists, communists, and Fascists in very similar terms. But a criticism of democracy that wraps itself in 'myth' and advances no tangible alternative, merely the absence or the negation of democracy, can be nothing but an apologia for tyranny, at any rate when it descends from the realm of literature into practical politics.

As a professed Marxist who supplied inspiration to Fascism, Sorel is important in that the destiny of his idea reveals the convergence of extreme forms of leftist and rightist radicalism. If leftist radical phraseology confines itself to attacking bourgeois democracy without offering a better democracy in its place, if it merely opposes rationalism without setting up new cultural values, if it advocates violence unhampered by moral restrictions, then its programme is merely that of a new despotism and is essentially the same as that of the radical Right. If, as in Sorel's doctrine, the ultimate catastrophe is represented as an object in itself, or even as the supreme object, irrespective of the consequences it may produce, then the proletariat's role is, first and foremost, that of the expected agent of cataclysmic change. Since it failed to play this part, Sorel could without inconsistency turn to nationalism as a more promising embodiment of the cause, which in his eyes was still 'total revolution' and not the nation as such. Thus his passionate defence of Lenin and the Bolsheviks was highly ambiguous. He admired the Russian Revolution as a dramatic apocalypse, a death-blow to intellectuals, a triumph of willpower over alleged economic necessity, and an assertion of native Muscovite traditions over Western ones. 'The sanguinary object-lesson in Russia will prove to all workers that there is a contradiction between democracy and the mission of the proletariat. The idea of a government of producers will not perish; the cry "Death to intellectuals", for which the Bolsheviks are so much abused, may in the end be taken up by workers the world over. Only a blind man could fail to see that the Russian revolution is the dawn of a new era' (*Matériaux*, postscript to Preface of 1919 edn.). In the 1919 appendix to *Reflections on Violence* we read:

When the time comes to evaluate present-day events with historical impartiality, it will be recognized that Bolshevism owed a great part of its power to the fact that the masses regarded it as a protest against an oligarchy whose greatest concern had been not to appear Russian; at the end of the year 1917, the former spokesman of the Black Hundred said that the Bolsheviks had 'proven that they were more Russian than the rebels Kaledin, Roussky etc., who betrayed the Tsar and the country' (*Journal de Genève*, 20 December 1917) ... One may speak as a historian of the process of revolutionary repression in Russia only by keeping in mind the Moscovite character of Bolshevism ... the national traditions provided the Red Guards with innumerable precedents, which they believed they had the right to imitate in order to defend the Revolution ... If we are grateful to the Roman soldiers for having replaced abortive, strayed or impotent civilizations by a civilization whose pupils we are still in law, literature and monuments, how grateful will not the future have to be to the Russian soldiers of socialism!

Sorel knew little of Leninist doctrine: he admired Lenin as a prophet of the Apocalypse, and Mussolini for the same reason. He was ready to support anything that seemed heroic and promised to destroy the hated system of democracy, party strife, compromise, negotiation, and calculation. He was not interested in the petty question of human welfare, but in discovering the circumstances most propitious to an outburst of energy. The penetrating critic of rationalism ended as a worshipper of the great Moloch into whose jaws the blind, fanatic, jubilant mob advanced, in a warlike frenzy, to its own destruction.

CHAPTER VIII

Antonio Labriola: an Attempt at an Open Orthodoxy

1. Labriola's style

ANTONIO LABRIOLA played a similar role in Italy to that of Plekhanov in Russia and of Lafargue in France: he was the first in his country to expound Marxism as a system, and had an important influence on the form in which it was accepted there. When Labriola became a Marxist he already had behind him a long career as an academic philosopher. Although chiefly influenced in his formative years by Hegel and Herbart, he was strongly attached to the Italian tradition and imparted its peculiar features to his version of Marxism. It was also of importance that he was never a party activist, but only a publicist and theoretician.

Owing to the fragmentation of Italy before 1870 and its relative economic backwardness, the workers' movement took shape much later there than in the rest of Western Europe. Socialist ideas and slogans figured for some time as part of general radical ideologies which also expressed what Marxists were wont to regard as typical aspirations of the 'progressive' bourgeoisie. Confronted by the powerful opposition of the Church and clericalism, socialists and bourgeois radicals found themselves 'on the same side of the barricade' for much longer than in other countries, and were more conscious of the values they had in common. The division of Italy into a conservative-Catholic and a progressive camp remained fundamental even after the socialist movement became an organized political force on its own account. By virtue, therefore, of historical circumstances and of his own life-story, Labriola remained strongly attached to the radical Italian tradition in politics and philosophy, with its cult of such figures as Garibaldi and Giordano Bruno.

Labriola's philosophical style is also typically Italian in both its attractive and its less acceptable features. In the homeland of Thomas Aquinas, more perhaps than in any other country, secular philosophy from the sixteenth century onwards broke radically with scholastic modes of thought and logical skills. Outside the powerful but sterile domain of late scholasticism there was a distaste for schemes and systems and a preference for 'global' thinking as opposed to analysis: a predilection for discursive essays, and a strong emphasis on the didactic and rhetorical aspects of philosophical writing. All these tendencies can be found in Labriola's works. The boundaries between epistemology, psychology, ethics, and pedagogy are fluid, and he is clearly not concerned to make philosophy a separate, self-contained preserve of professional thinkers. The distrust of specialization within the domain of humanism, which even today makes itself felt in Italian culture and the Italian university system, was enhanced in the nineteenth century by the Hegelian tendency to think in global terms and relate every specific problem to some large, panoramic vision of history. This tendency allied itself in Italy with Renaissance-style universalism and the attitude of the *eroici furiosi* for whom the basic problems of existence were at stake in every particular question.

The literary style and global thinking of Italian philosophers, their dislike of rigid classification, specialization, and hierarchies of ideas, may help to explain the success in Italy of the historicist, anti-positivist version of Marxism which was championed by Labriola and upheld in the next generation by Gramsci. The attraction of this form of Marxism, as opposed to the scientistic and positivistic approach, was not so much that it raised the study of social problems to the dignity of natural science, but that it enabled all aspects of material and spiritual culture to be interpreted as expressions or manifestations of a single universal process or a particular historical epoch. This propensity to relate social phenomena to great historical 'totalities' was not specifically Marxist, but in combination with other principles it could be presented as a natural part of historical materialism. At the same time it fitted in with the relativist tendencies that seem to be a distinctive mark of Italian philosophy.

Such generalizations, of course, are highly simplified. Positivism and scientism duly made their appearance in Italy, and with Enrico Ferri we encounter a positivist, Darwinist, scientistic version of Marxism. In Italy, although nowhere else, there was a period during which positivism and Hegelianism were united rather than divided as regards their effect on society: both represented lay, radical, rationalist thought as against clerical reaction, and were on the same side of the cultural divide which ran through the nation. None the less, from the present-day viewpoint at least it would seem that the most fertile sources of Italian intellectual life derive from the tradition of historicism rather than scientism.

It was particularly hard for Italians, whether Marxist or not, to believe in a theory of uninterrupted historical progress, since the whole history of their country in modern times went to prove the contrary. After the three centuries of regression and stagnation which followed the Counter-Reformation, the whole radical intelligentsia was imbued with a sense of the country's economic and cultural backwardness. The hopes aroused by the Risorgimento were not such as to encourage the conviction that progress was an inevitable consequence of 'historical laws', and Italian philosophers, including Marxists, tended to be more sensitive to the variety, dramatic complexity, and unexpectedness of the historical process. From this viewpoint also, Labriola instilled into Italian Marxism a sceptical attitude towards comprehensive explanations of universal history.

2. *Biographical note*

Antonio Labriola (1843–1904) was born at Cassino, the son of a teacher. He was brought up on the ideals of 'Young Italy' (the secret society founded by Mazzini) and dreamt from his youth of the independence and unification of his country. He entered the University of Naples in 1861 and was influenced by Hegelianism, the chief exponents of which in Italy were Bertrando Spaventa and Augusto Vera. In an essay afterwards published by Croce, Labriola criticized Zeller and the neo-Kantians and argued that Kant's doctrine was finally superseded by Hegelianism. After graduating he became a schoolteacher at Naples, where he lived until 1874. His first philosophical work during this period was an analysis of the theory of affections in Spinoza (1865). In 1869 he wrote a more elaborate work on Socratic philosophy, which won a prize in a competition

organized by the Naples Academy of Moral and Political
Sciences. He continued his studies and became erudite in
philosophy, history, and ethnography; he was also interested in
Herbart's associationist psychology, which he adopted to a large
extent, and in the works of Vico, which influenced him all his
life. In the early 1870s he took up political journalism in a liberal
and anticlerical vein. In 1873 he published *Moral Liberty* and
Morality and Religion, which show a departure from the Hegelian
viewpoint though they are in no way specifically Marxist. In
the following year he was appointed to a professorial chair in
Rome, where he spent the rest of his life teaching, writing, and
joining in all the important controversies of the day.

His conversion to Marxism was not sudden but gradual. In
1889 he wrote in a lecture *On Socialism* that he had criticized
liberalism from 1873 onwards and had embraced a 'new intellectual faith' in 1879, based especially on his studies of the preceding three years. His essay *On the Idea of Freedom* (1887) shows
no clearly Marxist tendency, but his writings of the 1890s reflect
the viewpoint of a definite 'school'. *On Socialism* is an explicit
political declaration in which he criticizes bourgeois democracy
and defends internationalist socialism, the cause of the world
proletariat. His best-known Marxist work is *Essays on the
Materialist Conception of History*, containing a general account of
historical materialism and a discussion of *The Communist Manifesto*: this was published in 1896, and to the second edition in
1902 he added a polemical article against Masaryk's book on the
foundations of Marxism. The work was soon translated into
French and became a classic of European Marxist literature.
Labriola intended to write a fourth section based on his lectures
of 1900–1 and giving a general account of the nineteenth
century. He did not live to complete this, but the parts he had
written were published by his great pupil Benedetto Croce in
1906 in a collection of Labriola's unpublished or little-known
works entitled *Various Writings on Philosophy and Politics*, while
the remaining notes were published in 1925 by Luigi dal Pane,
who subsequently wrote a monograph on Labriola. The latter's
Marxist philosophy is also set out in a collection of letters to
Sorel, published in 1897 under the title *Talking of Socialism and
Philosophy*. It is noteworthy that of the many articles Labriola
published in the last fifteen years of his life, some clearly stress his

Marxist position (critique of Bernstein and of Millerand, article on the difference between socialism and radicalism), while others could equally well have been written by a radical rationalist (lecture on the freedom of science, speech commemorating Giordano Bruno). In this respect too Labriola differs from the orthodox German Marxists, who proclaimed their allegiance in everything they wrote.

3. Early writings

Labriola's essay on Spinoza's theory of affections is of no special importance, being merely a summary for school purposes of the relevant part of the *Ethics*. It is worth noting that he emphasizes the moral background of Spinoza's metaphysics and the latter's general naturalistic viewpoint, while adding that the significance of Spinoza's doctrine lies in the fact that he denies the metaphysical basis of value-judgements and derives the noblest human impulses from egoism as the sole creative force; he is also concerned to validate the category of freedom within the limits of a deterministic view of the universe.

The essay on Socrates, a much more important work, is an erudite and in part polemical dissertation on the theme, borrowed from Hegel and Zeller, that the key to Socrates' thought is to be found in Xenophon and not in Plato, and that we must resist the temptation to ascribe Plato's metaphysics to the elder philosopher. Labriola regards Socrates as a pedagogue first and foremost, and interprets his personality in terms of the internal contradictions of Athenian culture. He is not concerned with finding out Socrates' implicit metaphysical views, but with describing those that were consciously articulated in his mind. In Labriola's opinion, Socrates' activity is to be understood as an attempt to resolve the conflict between traditional conservatism and the scepticism and relativism produced by the variety and richness of Athenian culture. The humanism and relativism of the sophists was a symptom of the break-up of traditional communities, while Socrates' endeavour was to discover absolute norms of morality independent of human beings. He was not fully aware how far his own investigations transcended traditional values, but in fact he was looking for a new interpretation of the world that would afford support against the sophists. Socrates' belief in the chronic inadequacy of human knowledge was necessary in order to justify his search for absolute cognitive and moral norms independent of the arbitrary decisions of individuals. This search was evinced particularly in his revaluation of the concept of deity, which made him—following Aeschylus, Pindar, and Sophocles—the herald of a new religious consciousness, turning by degrees from the traditions of the old mythology towards monotheism. But the functions of the Socratic deity were exclusively moral: it was to be the repository of absolute values, proof against relativism and subjectivism. In the same way Socrates' logical investigations and his endeavours to elucidate concepts were not born of disinterested curiosity but were inspired by the same pedagogical purpose: hence his contempt for natural science. He had himself no metaphysical intentions and was purely pragmatic; nevertheless, he provided a basis for Plato's theory of ideas and metaphysic of the Good.

Labriola's views on Socrates illustrate his indebtedness to Hegel for the belief, which became part of his Marxist faith, that philosophical ideas are the expression of changing historical needs, arising from the internal contradictions of a particular phase of civilization. The influence of Hegel is also visible, besides that of Kant and Herbart, in Labriola's treatise on moral freedom. This is an obscure work as regards both argument and conclusions, which indeed is generally the case with philosophical treatments of this subject. However, it is clear that Labriola regards the question concerning free will (*liberum arbitrium*) as wrongly framed, and that in Hegelian fashion he seeks to replace the question of freedom in the sense of indifference by that of freedom conceived as the conformity between choice and conscience. He tries in this way to distinguish between determinism and fatalism, but does not get beyond vague general formulas. He regards as self-evident Kant's rule which makes moral judgements entirely independent of utilitarian factors and of the evaluation of the results of human actions. The imperative of obligation is implied in moral freedom, which realizes itself in acts of conscious obedience to that imperative. However, as the human will is the result of many social and psychological factors, it is assailed by conflicting spiritual aspirations, and its freedom does not consist in a potential ability to determine itself as it pleases, but in an actual choice conforming to an absolute norm. Unlike animals, whose actions are determined merely by the strength of habit or of this or that desire, man is free in the sense that he possesses a moral consciousness enabling him to resist natural impulses. The fact, and not the mere abstract possibility, of such self-determination entitles us to call him free. Labriola expressly protests against the 'naturalization' of the human conscience and the idea that it consists of a mere collection of instincts that are 'ultimately' attributable to animal needs. Like Herbart, however, he rejects the idea of the soul as a metaphysical entity or of separate spiritual powers, but is content to analyse the motivations that constitute an expression or a denial of freedom according as they do or do not conform to the individual's awareness of the moral imperative. There is, strictly speaking, no contradiction between the principle of causality and moral freedom, provided we regard human acts, in Leibnizian fashion, as self-determined (as opposed to external, mechanical, or 'natural' determination), or, following Schopenhauer, as causality 'seen from the inside'. It is easy to see in this way that freedom can and must be the purpose of an education that inculcates a moral consciousness and assimilates it to habit. To treat freedom as an innate quality of the soul is not only misleading but pernicious in practice, as it dispenses with the obligation to educate men to freedom: such education is the supreme purpose of the state, which in its ideal form is, above all, a pedagogical institution.

The essay on *Morality and Religion* shows clearly the influence of Kant and to a lesser extent that of Hegel. Its main points are three. First, 'practical judgements' are not derivable from theoretical ones and cannot be based either on psychological premisses (the content of an empirical moral consciousness) or on utilitarian grounds, but must be *a priori*; morality is founded on those practical judgements which run most contrary to instinctive desires. The multiplicity of moral opinions is an empirical fact and does not invalidate the contention that there is only one morality *par excellence*. Second, moral values belong exclusively to the good will, regarded as autonomous in all respects including its relation to the hypothetical will of God: moral imperatives based on the will of God are not truly moral, since they imply the submission of one will to another. Third, morality is wholly independent of religious faith. Religion is a universal and inseparable part of the spiritual life, and rationalists who criticize a particular historical form of it are missing the point when they attack religion in general. The purpose of religion is 'to compensate with a different form of idealism the discordance between our ethical demands and the natural world in which we live'. It can and does reinforce moral values and the moral consciousness, but it contributes nothing to the content of ethical norms, which must be derived from sources independent of any revelation or mythology. Religious faith has its own field of activity, and can coexist freely with other forms of spiritual life provided the division of functions is respected; the educational system should not be opposed to religious feelings, but should on the contrary encourage them. But the natural sense of goodness, independent of religious and metaphysical opinions, is a sufficient basis for morality. This sense is not the product of knowledge either, since value-judgements are radically different from cognitive acts, and moral norms are not to be derived from scientific observation. The moral consciousness involves ideals that are in a sense contrary to the natural course of things; their validity does not depend on empirical factors, though they vary in specific content according to social and psychological circumstances.

In retrospect it can be said that Labriola's attraction to Marxism and socialism was a natural outcome of his intellectual background and that, both in philosophy and in politics, it represented a strengthening and specialization of already existing tendencies. Philosophically he was most influenced from this point of view by two very different teachers, Hegel and Herbart. From the former he learnt to think in terms of great historical concepts and to interpret cultural values as manifestations of the eras to which they belonged: to adopt a relativistic viewpoint and to regard ideas as historical instruments rather than the subjective embodiment of ideal patterns. Hegel also taught Labriola to accept the category of progress while regarding the historical process as a tragic spectacle. Herbart, by contrast, inspired him with a distrust of metaphysics and speculative philosophy, and with a belief in empirical psychology as necessary to the interpretation of civilization. From the political point of view Labriola's socialism stemmed from his radical anticlerical outlook and identification with the people's cause. Even in his

Marxist days, however, his anticlericalism was combined with an understanding and a certain sympathy for religious sentiment, though not for the Church as an institution or a political instrument.

4. *Philosophy of history*

Apart from his role as a propagandist, can Labriola be regarded as an independent theoretician or the author of a specific variant of Marxism? It might be said by an ill-disposed reader of his works that their chief difference from contemporary orthodoxy lay in the vague and elusive manner in which he expressed his views. But if we read with closer attention and more goodwill we may come to the conclusion that the generality of his style is not due merely to a preference for rhetoric over precision of thought, but to a distrust of cut-and-dried formulas and a conviction that Marxism is not a 'final', self-sufficient rationalization and schematization of history, but rather a collection of pointers to the understanding of human affairs; these must be imprecise if they are not to degenerate into a dogmatic contempt for the variety of forces at work in history, and thus to reduce complicated social processes to a handful of bloodless 'universal' categories. The individuality of Labriola's Marxism does not consist so much in any combination of theses to be found in his work, as in the elasticity and openness of general formulas which enable Marxism to be enriched by ideas from other sources. It is easier, perhaps, to characterize his philosophy by those elements of hard-core orthodoxy that are absent from it. Contrary to Togliatti's claim, Labriola did not seek to make Marxism an integrated, self-contained system, but wished to preserve a certain degree of imprecision so as to prevent the doctrine from ossifying into self-satisfaction and an imagined mastery over universal knowledge. He took seriously the description of scientific socialism as a 'critical' theory—not in the sense that it attacked other doctrines, for the most obscurantist sect may do this, and the more obscurantist it is, the more violent the attack —but in the sense that it regarded no truths as everlasting, recognized that all established principles were provisional, and was ready to drop or modify its own ideas if experience should so dictate.

It is characteristic of Labriola that he approached Marxism

from a historical and not a sociological point of view. In his eyes it was not a matter of discovering general, permanent relationships between artificially distinguished aspects of social life, but of describing a single, unique, actual historical process, having regard to the whole variety of forces at work in it. As he wrote in his lectures of 1902–3,

History is always concerned with the heterogeneous—with nations conquering other nations, classes oppressing other classes, priests ruling the laity and layfolk getting the better of priests. All these are sociological facts, but they do not fit into sociological schemata: they can only be understood empirically, and this is the whole difficulty of historical investigation. The abstractions of sociology give us no clue as to why, in the general process of the development of the bourgeois classes, it was only in France that the events occurred which we call the Great Revolution.

Labriola was thus very far from believing that the notion of 'class' enables us to interpret the whole of past history and to foretell the future. He accepted the Marxist position that individuals do not choose their social links at will, and he opposed the rationalist delusion that social phenomena can be reconstructed on the basis of deliberate behaviour of individuals. The social bond is not the result of anyone's intention. 'Society is given *a priori*, since we know nothing of man as a *ferus primaevus*. The original datum is society as a whole: classes and individuals appear as elements in that whole and as determined by it.' (*Da un secolo all'altro*, VI.) But it is one thing to recognize the objectivity of the social bond and another to claim that it can be reduced to a mere relationship of classes. Schemes of history which represent it as a uniform, continuous, self-contained process are criticized by Labriola on four main grounds: the independence of the national principle, the irreducibility of religious sentiment, the discontinuity of progress, and the unpredictability of the future.

Nationality signifies to Labriola not only a social reality *sui generis* but also a value *sui generis*, irreducible to other ties and values. As he wrote to Sorel (14 May 1897),

Languages are not accidental variants of some universal Volapük but, on the contrary, are much more than purely external methods of denoting and communicating thoughts and feelings. They determine the conditions and limits of our internal life, which for this and many other reasons expresses itself in national forms and not in merely accidental ones. If there are 'internationalists' who are unaware of this they can only be called amorphous and woolly-minded—like those who derive their knowledge not from old apocalyptic sources but from Bakunin, the master of appearances, who even wanted equalization of the sexes.

In his lectures of 1903 Labriola used Hegel's division of nations into those historically passive and historically active, but did not seek to justify this in specifically Marxist terms. The category of nationhood is not, with him, merely a feature of tactical reasoning (though of course he defended self-determination, especially for Italy and Poland), but stands for an independent historical reality; in this he differs from the majority of Marxists.

As to religion, while he was less explicit during his Marxist period than in *Morality and Religion*, it is clear that he regarded religious sentiments (as distinct from theological systems and church institutions) as something other than the self-delusion of primitive minds, or a deception practised upon mankind, or the result of a transitory class situation. In a lecture on popular education (1888) he advocated non-religious schools but emphasized that he did not want to introduce anti-religious elements. 'It is an historical misfortune that we have in our country the Pope, a spiritual leader claiming territorial power; but let us not add to this the misfortune that would result from turning tens of thousands of teachers into anti-Popes.' The problem in any case was not a purely political one. Essentially there was no opposition between religion and other forms of culture. 'Culture is no enemy to any sincere, healthy manifestation of the spirit, and it is certainly no barrier to deep religious feelings. These have nothing to do with theological systems imposed by the orthodox, or with priestly rule: indeed, I will go further and say that all forms of priesthood which elevate it into a caste and a system of privilege are a denial of those feelings.' Similarly, in the lecture *On Socialism* he declares that socialists are the truest disciples of Jesus and the only Christians of the present age. These are not mere rhetorical flourishes, as may be seen from Labriola's notes for the lectures that were to form the last part of his *magnum opus* on historical materialism. Here we read:

Is religion a permanent fact or simply an invention, an aberration and a deceit? Certainly it is a need. Were the nineteenth-century rationalists therefore mistaken? Yes. It is not true, then, that the last century was an age of science? This is only partially the case. Is it then impossible to suppress religion? The fact that it is sometimes suppressed proves a certain thesis but does not define its limits. Is it the case, then, that man can never become master of the natural and historical world by virtue of his own intellect, moral autonomy and aesthetic sensibility? Yes and no.

These remarks are not clear enough to serve as the basis of an explicit theory of religion. They indicate, however, that Labriola never accepted the conventional Marxist view that religion is a historically explicable self-delusion and an instrument of mystification for class purposes, and is destined to die out as class antagonisms fade away and minds become more enlightened. Labriola distinguished clericalism and theological rationalizations of faith from the religious sense itself, and seemed to regard the latter as a permanent form of spiritual culture. This in itself suffices to create doubts as to whether he should be reckoned as a member of the Marxist camp by the criteria of his time. True, in a letter to Sorel of 2 July 1897 he says that the men of the future 'will probably give up any transcendent explanation of the practical problems of daily life, since *primus in orbe deos fecit timor*'. But this does not conflict with the remarks quoted above, since he did not regard the religious sense as offering 'explanations' of any kind: it was not for religion, he thought, to compete with science or to usurp its role in any way.

As regards the idea of progress, Labriola considers it necessary to the understanding of history but emphasizes that its role is a normative one. He repeatedly rejects the prejudice that history is a tale of continuous progress, in particular if this means that it is free from regression or that all civilizations have to go through the same stages of development. In *Problems of the Philosophy of History* (1887) he observes that faith in progress was a superstition that took the place of theology and was encouraged by Hegel's monistic philosophy of history: this, however, became a Procrustean bed for the historical sciences concerned with forms of social life such as law, language, and art. There was in fact no unity of history or constant trend for the better.

The original centres of civilization are many in number and cannot be reduced by any sleight of hand: that is, the sources of civilized life cannot be brought to an identity of form or of origin. Civilizations, linked by particular relationships, develop in accordance with their own traditions and by the interchange of values: we must therefore recognize that primary factors have a modifying effect on secondary influences ... The consideration of so many separate and independent series of events, so many factors that resist simplification, so many unintended coincidences ... makes it seem highly improbable, in fact no better than a delusion, to suppose that there is at the root of everything a real unity, a permanent subject of experience, constituting the essential meaning of every kind of impulse and activity from the earliest times to the present.

In short, there is no over-all 'meaning' of history, no rationalization of its actual course. 'The observation of human affairs obliges us to recognize that there is both progress and regression: many nations have been destroyed, many enterprises have failed and much human effort has been expended in vain.' The idea of progress enables us to say that some things have improved—for example, slavery has been abolished, men are equal before the law—but it is not a universal law of history, and indeed there are no such laws.

People have sought to extend to the whole human race the schema, worked out in France, of the transition from a serf economy to an economy of subjects and then of wage-earners; but anyone using this sacred formula will understand nothing, for instance, about fourteenth-century England. And what about the brave Norwegians, who were never serfs or subjects? How is it that in Germany beyond the Elbe, serfdom arose and developed *after* the Reformation, or that the European bourgeoisie instituted slavery afresh in America? (*Da un secolo all'altro*, IV)

Labriola in his Marxist phase believed more strongly than ever that the category of progress is not inherent in events but is a way of interpreting them—it provides us with an evaluating perspective, but does not emerge from the facts themselves.

This is particularly important when we are considering the future as well as the past. Labriola believed that there was good ground for expecting the advent of socialism, but he also believed that the future was undecided. A remark in his last work is directed not only against Hegel but against the commonest interpretations of Marxism: 'The wisest and most telling objection to all systems of the philosophy of history is that put forward by Wundt, namely that we do not know where history ends. that is, if I understand him rightly, we never see history as a completed whole' (ibid. I). And, further on: 'Socialism is an active reality so long as it is the manifestation and war-cry of an actual struggle; but when it starts to regard prophesies of the future as a measure and criterion of the present, it becomes no more than a Utopia' (ibid. III).

Since Labriola disputes the continuity, unity, and regularity of the historical process, it clearly may be asked in what sense he accepts the Marxist philosophy of history. He professes to be a historical materialist, but he gives an elastic sense to this concept and to the relationship between the base and the superstructure. According to him, the essence of historical materialism is contained in two statements. First, men have created political and legal institutions 'in proportion to the prevailing economic structure'. Second, religious and moral ideas 'always correspond to particular social conditions'; this statement he describes as 'more hypothetical', and he draws from it the unexpected inference that 'the history of religion and ethics is psychology in the broad sense of the term' (lectures of 1902). In his principal work he states that history 'is based' on technical development, that ideas 'do not fall from heaven', that moral ideas 'in the last resort' correspond to economic conditions, and so on. Such loose formulations as these were to be found in Marxist literature, but by the end of the century they were no longer specifically Marxist except for Engels's reference to determination 'in the last resort', the meaning of which has never been elucidated. Labriola's work on historical materialism is largely a critique of what he considered vulgar interpretations of Marxism as a theory of the 'preponderance' or 'dominance' of the 'economic factor' in history. The historical process, he argues, develops 'organically', and the so-called 'factors' therein are conventional abstractions and not social realities. They are necessary to the historian as conceptual instruments and to delimit the sphere of his investigation, but they should not be hypostatized into separate historical forces as a prelude to assigning one of them causal priority over all the rest. Historical events cannot be 'translated' into economic terms, although 'in the last resort' they may be explained by economic structures and these structures may, in the long run, give rise to 'corresponding' political and legal institutions.

In general, it must be acknowledged that Labriola did not

help to dispel the obscurity of the general tenets of historical materialism, though he tried to give them as undogmatic a sense as possible. Like Engels, he believed in the interrelation of all fields of human activity, and the independent force of the crystallized tradition of institutions and ideologies. It is not clear, however, what boundaries he assigns to determination by 'economic structures' and how far historical materialism, thus understood, differs from the contention, which was already a commonplace by the late nineteenth century, that both institutions and ideas are affected by the relations of production.

Another characteristic feature of Labriola's ideas—thought here again he expresses himself in generalities—is his opposition to the naturalist interpretation of history. In his view, to say that human history is a continuation of natural history is so abstract as to be meaningless. History is concerned with the artificial environment which men have created and which reacts upon them. Social ties, it is true, are formed independently of human intentions, but human beings develop both actively and passively, determining historical conditions and being determined by them.

Observations in this sense ('Man is both the subject and object of history', etc.) are too indefinite, however, to serve as the basis of an investigatory method. The Marxists who use them generally refer to them as a 'dialectic', as though this term denoted no more than common-sense, all-purpose formulas such as 'not only ... but also', 'both ... and', 'on the one hand ... on the other', and so forth. Historical materialism in such watered-down terms may provide a contrast to the type of history, such as St. Augustine's, which relates everything to designs of Providence; but it does not constitute a specific method over and beyond what every historian is prepared to recognize.

As to the meaning of socialism, Labriola does not seem to go beyond the views commonly formulated by socialists in his day. It denotes the collective ownership of means of production, the right to work, the abolition of competition, the principle 'to each according to his deserts'. It does not mean abandoning any of the achievements of modern times as regards political emancipation and the rights of the individual. Socialists do not set out to abolish freedom and equality before the law, but to enrich them by destroying the bondage and inequality that result from privilege and private ownership. The general tendency of socialism is to decentralize power and economic institutions, not to centralize them. The state will disappear with the class struggle; socialism will remove contingency from human life. While endorsing all this, Labriola avoids committing himself to the 'historical necessity' of socialism. He writes that capitalism 'prepares the way' for a socialist society, that socialist ideas are not a moral condemnation of capitalist exploitation but the recognition of a historical tendency, and that socialism 'is not a subjective critique of things, but the discovery of a self-criticism inherent in them'. All this, however, does not add up to a belief in the inevitability of a socialist future. Labriola also did not hold that socialism could only come about by a violent revolution, but hoped that the new social forms could be grafted by degrees on to the 'common stock of liberal institutions' (lectures of 1902), a view close to Bernstein's 'evolutionism'. True, he opposed revisionism in a letter to Hubert Lagardelle published in *Le Mouvement socialiste*, but the grounds of his objection are not clear, except that he accuses Bernstein of writing about everything at once and of being the spokesman of those who abandon socialism in disappointment because changes do not come soon enough. In the same way Labriola's polemics against writers such as Masaryk, Croce, and Sorel, who claimed that Marxism was breaking down, are very general in character and are rather a proclamation of loyalty to the Marxist camp than an objective contribution to its defence.

One of the reasons which, on his own showing, inclined Labriola towards Marxism was his dislike of metaphysical speculations and the *esprit de système*; he also emphasized the role of positivism in providing the basis for a philosophy that 'does not anticipate reality, but is contained in it' (letter to Sorel, 24 May 1897). The theme that philosophy is the self-revelation of reality rather than the intellectual pursuit of a hidden essence recurs frequently in Labriola's writings, where it is linked to the special position of Marxism as a philosophy of praxis. Labriola uses this term in a different sense from most of the orthodox, who were content with Engels's remarks on the practical role of human activity as a means of checking the validity of knowledge and identifying the scientific problems that required solution. 'The process of praxis comprehends nature or the historical evolution of man, but in speaking of praxis from the integral point of view we imply the overcoming of the opposition between theory and practice as it is vulgarly conceived' (Labriola to Sorel, 10 May 1897). Historical materialism 'takes as its point of departure praxis, i.e. the development of effectuality, and, as it is a theory of labouring mankind, it treats science itself as labour' (ibid., 28 May 1897). These remarks too are somewhat disconnected and reflect a tendency of mind rather than a clear-cut theory. It may, however, be said in very general terms that Labriola conceives of human intellectual activity, whether philosophy or science, as an aspect of practical life and not as the quest for a 'truth' waiting to be discovered: his historicism thus apparently admits of no cognitive values other than pragmatic ones, from the point of view of society and history as opposed to the individual. In other words, he appears to think that human thought is part of a historical process, and not a description of the world that can lay claim to 'objective' accuracy independent of time and circumstances. Historicism of this type dispenses with the notion of transcendental truth and ascribes a functional character to all human knowledge. If this was Labriola's view, he was in agreement with the young Marx and not with Engels's positivism. For, if praxis signifies the whole of man's part in history, the value of intellectual production as an aspect of that whole is to be measured by the mind's ability to 'express' changing historical situations, and not by the correspondence between some 'objective' universe and the description of it. This line of reasoning was later followed by Gramsci, probably under Labriola's influence.

Labriola's critique of agnosticism is on similar lines. He does not adopt the naïve attitude of Engels, who argued that when we learn something we did not know before, the 'thing in itself' becomes a 'thing for us'; but he considered agnosticism to be not so much false as meaningless. His view was that the category of the Unknowable is one that our minds simply cannot frame, so that any agnostic formula involves a concept to which no meaning can be attached. 'We can only think about what is given in experience, taking that term in its widest sense': thus he wrote to Sorel on 24 May 1897, and in the next letter he expressed his view more fully. 'Everything that is knowable can be known and will be known "at infinity", and anything that is not knowable does not concern us in the realm of knowledge ... It is mere fantasy to suppose that our minds can apprehend, as existing *in actu*, an absolute difference between what is knowable and unknowable in itself.' Hence the absurdity of Herbert Spencer, who spoke of the Unknowable as the limit of the knowable, and in so doing implied that something could be known about it. This criticism is in harmony with Labriola's functional and historical view of knowledge and his treatment of cognition not as unlocking the secrets of Being 'in itself' but as an articulation of the practical behaviour of human societies. From this point of view there can certainly be no such category as that of the Unknowable. Labriola, however, did not attempt, as he should on his own premisses, to discover the social and historical significance of agnosticism: he merely stigmatized it as 'cowardly resignation', while not accepting the crude explanation that it was a symptom of the decline of bourgeois civilization.

Despite his dislike of metaphysics and his radical 'humanization' and historicization of knowledge, Labriola did not advance any theory of the 'demise of philosophy'. In his view the conformity of philosophy with science was an ideal result that could hardly be expected in the foreseeable future; meanwhile philosophical reflection had its own purpose, namely to anticipate problems not yet taken up by science or, as Herbart observed, to build general concepts that imparted unity to the results of experience.

In spite of the imprecision of his writings, Labriola played an important part in the history of Marxism. His was probably the first attempt to reconstruct Marxism as a philosophy of historical praxis, treating this as a concept in terms of which all aspects of human life should be interpreted, including intellectual activity and its product. He was thus opposed to the scientistic ideology that dominated Marxism in his day. The doctrine outlined in his works was revived in the twentieth century by Gramsci and Lukács among others, inspired by the publication of Marx's early writings. This version gave new life to the idea of humanism as an epistemological standpoint, treating human history as the boundary of attainable knowledge and re-stressing the relativistic aspect of Marxist doctrine.

CHAPTER IX

Ludwik Krzywicki: Marxism as an Instrument of Sociology

MARXIST theoreticians may be divided into two broad intellectual categories. The first consists of those whose interest centres on Marxism itself, and who study the problems of philosophy, history, economics, or sociology for the purpose of demonstrating the correctness of Marxism. They are, as it were, professional Marxists, concerned to vindicate the doctrine in every branch of human thought. They may interpret it in different ways, but each of them is determined to prove that his interpretation is closest to the spirit of Marxism conceived as a pre-existing whole. They are imbued with 'orthodoxy' in the sense that, whatever they are engaged in, they never forget that the purpose of all their endeavours is to defend and exalt the doctrine of which they are custodians. They generally regard Marxism as self-sufficient and embracing every need, and they seldom refer to any other philosophy except to criticize it (apart, of course, from the pre-Marxist writers who have been canonized as 'sources'). At the time we are concerned with, the outstanding representatives of this type were Plekhanov, Lafargue, Lenin, and Rosa Luxemburg.

The second category comprises sociologists, philosophers, or historians who make use of Marxist conclusions as an aid to solving the problems of their respective disciplines. Marxism is to them a means, not an end: they are not interested in proving it right, but in understanding social phenomena. They are not regarded as orthodox by writers of the former class, who treat them with suspicion or disdain, realizing that they cannot be counted on to support the cause at any given moment. They do not assume that Marxism implicitly contains the answers to all important questions and that one has only to look properly in order to find them; they are indifferent to doctrinal purity and are prepared to use the work of Marxists and non-Marxists alike.

Ludwik Krzywicki was one of the outstanding members of this second category. His numerous works are almost entirely in Polish, except for a few Russian translations and minor contributions in other languages, and he therefore had no direct influence on the main stream of European Marxism. In Poland, however, he had a strong intellectual and moral influence on two or three generations of the intelligentsia, and played the chief part in familiarizing social and human scientists with Marxist concepts.

Krzywicki belonged to the last generation in which it was possible for a highly gifted and industrious person to master almost the whole of contemporary knowledge on social problems. Accordingly, he covered an extremely wide field as an investigator, teacher, and publicist. The subjects of his works include Slav archaeology, demography and statistics, fairy-tales and folklore, primitive societies, modern literature, the details of political and economic life in many countries of the world, questions of the family, religion, and education, the psychology of artists, parapsychology, agriculture, and foreign exchange problems. His chief interest, however, was social anthropology, the beliefs and customs of primitive peoples and the psychology of communities. He paid much attention to phenomena of social pathology, in which he hoped to discern causes and effects that were less evident in normal conditions: cases of mass delusion, moral infection, collective hallucination, panic, massacre, ecstasy, religious and political crazes, the psychology of martyrs, sadists, and cannibals. His literary style, apart from some youthful articles, is descriptive and not aggressive, but is permeated by an ideological approach: a sense of solidarity with the downtrodden, revulsion against capitalist society in which everything was for sale, disgust with urban civilization, and the dream of a society bound together by goodwill after the fashion of primitive communism. He did not engage in party activities, however, and only belonged for a brief period to the political socialist movement.

1. Biographical note

Ludwik Krzywicki (1859–1941) was born at Płock in Russian Poland: like most of the Polish intelligentsia of his generation, he belonged to a family of impoverished gentry (*szlachta*). He grew up under the shadow of repression following the 1863 insurrection: police terror, enforced Russification of the educational system, and a general atmosphere of impotent discontent. The landowning classes were falling into economic and cultural decline; industry, however, was on the up grade. Politically and culturally, Russian Poland did not begin to revive until the late 1870s. Meanwhile, as a result of the growth of industry and the defeat of hopes for early political liberation, there came into being the slogan of 'organic work'; Poland's national life was to be rebuilt by means of education, industrial activity, technical skills and rationalist attitudes in place of romanticism, rebellion, and conspiracy. The philosophical basis of this outlook was Western evolutionary positivism as expounded by Spencer, Darwin, and Taine. Krzywicki, as a young publicist, made it the first object of his attack, while at the same period young student groups began to seek new ideologies inspired by either nationalism or socialism.

In 1878 Krzywicki entered the University of Warsaw, where he studied mathematics. While still at school he had come into contact with socialist ideas, chiefly in a Saint-Simonist form; at the University he read *Capital* and was convinced by its arguments. Together with Stanisław Krusiński (1857–86) and Bronisław Białobłocki (1861–88), both of whom studied in Russia, he founded the first Marxist group in Poland and introduced its ideas to the reading public; neither he nor his fellow students, however, were orthodox Marxists in the strict sense. Białobłocki published essays on aesthetics and the theory of literature under the general influence of Chernyshevsky, while Krusiński's background was mainly positivist and scientistic. Both died too young to exert any real influence on Marxist thought. They and Krzywicki were in loose touch with the first Polish socialist party, known as the Proletariat. This was an underground body, founded in 1881 by Ludwik Waryński and others; it was broken up by the authorities and its leaders were hanged in 1885, the first of a long line of martyrs for Marxist socialism. (Socialist ideas had been current in Polish intellectual life for the past half-century, especially among the *émigrés* who fled from Poland after the insurrection of 1830.)

Krzywicki began his career as a publicist in 1883 with articles criticizing Herbert Spencer and his Polish followers. In the same year he was expelled from the University for taking part in a political demonstration. He emigrated to Leipzig, where he prepared for publication a Polish translation of Volume I of *Capital* by the Krzywicki–Krusiński group; this appeared in parts between 1884 and 1890. After studying anthropology, sociology, and political economy at Leipzig Krzywicki went to Switzerland (where he met German and Russian socialist *émigrés*, including Kautsky and Bernstein) and, at the beginning of 1885, to Paris. During this period he published in Polish *émigré* journals several articles in a revolutionary Marxist vein. In 1885 he returned to Poland, but to avoid arrest stayed for the first year in Galicia (under Austrian rule). He moved to Płock towards the end of 1886 and settled in Warsaw in the middle of 1888, writing extensively and taking part in numerous educational activities, legal and underground. Clandestine socialist organizations were just beginning to re-form in Poland: Krzywicki was closely connected with the Union of Polish Workers, founded in 1889, which concentrated on the economic struggle. When the workers' movement crystallized into two mutually hostile camps, the PPS and the SDKPiL, Krzywicki became a member of neither, though he contributed to PPS journals from time to time. Between 1890 and 1910 his political writing became distinctly milder in tone as his mind moved in the direction of evolutionary socialism. At this time he also wrote his most important theoretical works on historical materialism, published in 1923 as *Sociological Studies*, and several books on ethnography and anthropology: *Peoples. An Outline of Ethnic Anthropology* (1893); *A course of Systematic Anthropology. Physical Races* (1897); *Psychic Races* (1902); *The Wisdom of Primitive Peoples* (1907); 'The Sociology of Herbert Spencer' (in *Przegląd filozoficzny*, 1904). His articles on literary subjects and on urban civilization were collected in a volume *In the Abyss* (1909).

Except for visits to Berlin and the U.S.A. in 1892–3 Krzywicki remained in Warsaw until the First World War, becoming an acknowledged authority on scientific and social questions. After the war he taught at Warsaw University and elsewhere and was Director of the Institute of Social Economy, which studied conditions in Poland for the purpose of working out economic guidelines and which, in 1922, produced under Krzywicki's editorship the first serious studies of economic and social life in Soviet Russia. During the post-war years he completely abandoned the idea of revolution and, like many European socialists, regarded the Soviet regime as an attempt to violate economic laws. He remained a socialist to the end, however, while believing that socialist ideals could be realized gradually by the rationalization and democratization of the capitalist economy. He also continued to believe in the validity of the principal Marxist criteria for the study of social conditions. He died in Warsaw during the German occupation.

2. *Critique of the biological theory of society*

Krzywicki's writings in the 1880s did much to spread the knowledge of Marxism in Poland, but they did not contribute a great deal to theory and for the most part followed the standard version of historical materialism. They are largely polemical in tone. In his critique of Spencer and social Darwinism Krzywicki argued that the evolutionists, constructing models of society after the pattern of a living organism, were in effect propagating the ideology of class solidarity, endeavouring to put an end to the class struggle, and closing their eyes to the dissolution of traditional bonds in a society rent by contradictions and competition. He also joined issue with the social-Darwinist ideas invoked by ideologists of the Manchester school. Competition and the social conflict could not be treated as a particular case of the biological struggle for survival of the fittest: they were caused not by biological circumstances, but by the anarchy of production, which was a phase of social development and not an eternal law of nature. Nor was it true that the fittest survived in present conditions: what ensured survival was, as a rule, not ability but privilege. Krzywicki attacked the biological view of society on other occasions also, for example in reply to Gobineau's racialist philosophy of history and anthropological concept of the nation, and Lombroso's theory of criminality. The so-called 'spirit of a race' was not, Krzywicki held, a biological category but the legacy of historical conditions. Racialism could not account for changes in social institutions, or the fact that they differed in societies that were racially akin, or were similar in societies of different race; but all these things could be explained if social institutions and ideologies were seen as dependent on changes in the method of production and exchange. As for nations, Krzywicki agreed with Kautsky that they were not anthropological entities, but cultural and therefore historical ones. The national idea in Europe was mainly the creation of the commercial class, for whom a centralized nation-state provided an advantageous legal framework: true, ethnic unity had preceded the growth of national markets, but the latter had stimulated it into awareness of itself.

In the same way, Krzywicki held, the fashionable theories of Lombroso were vitiated by being based on a class approach instead of a scientific one: the Italian physician held that crime was due to heredity or innate anthropological traits, whereas it was in fact due to social conditions, poverty, and ignorance.

The anarchist ideology too was based on erroneous biological theories. It was a mistake to hold that anarchism differed from socialism as to means but agreed with it as to the purpose of the struggle. The anarchists believed in a permanent conflict between the individual and society, and saw history as a process in which human beings were constantly subjugated by institutions. They therefore refused to take part in a struggle that involved using political and parliamentary institutions, preferring to employ all their efforts to paralyse the existing state machine in the hope that men's benevolent instincts would then suffice to do away with social bondage and privileges. Proclaiming the slogan 'The worse, the better', they regarded all means as legitimate, including wholesale pillage, and welcomed to their ranks the lumpenproletariat and other *déclassé* elements. The socialists, by contrast, regarded social development not in terms of pathology but as a necessary evolution, and they expected the liberation of the individual to be brought about not by kindly instincts or eternal moral precepts, but by human beings exercising collective authority over the powers of nature. Anarchism, in their view, was a sterile revolt by pre-capitalist forms of production, ruined by the progressive concentration of capital.

3. Prospects of socialism

Krzywicki's attack was directed, finally, against all solidaristic doctrines and movements—whether attempts at a Christian pseudo-socialism, combating capitalism in the name of feudal institutions and seeking a solution of social problems in a system of tutelage over the workers, or democratic ideologies which glossed over the class system by the undifferentiated concept of the 'people'. What such democrats called the 'people' consisted of several strata whose interests by no means always coincided: workers, rich peasants, small tradesmen, craftsmen, etc. Only in backward Poland was it possible for such a vague form of democracy to survive: in the more developed countries the various strata had separated and were at odds with one another. Only capitalists and the working class really stood for progress in the sphere of production, while the other classes, especially the peasantry, represented bygone forms that were doomed to destruction by the development of modern industry.

In all these arguments Krzywicki's viewpoint is that of classical Marxism. He stands for the independence of the proletariat as the only class that can liberate society on the basis of technical progress and not of hopeless attempts to revive a pre-capitalist system. He confidently expects the middle classes to disappear as the concentration of capital increases. He accepts the basic principles of historical materialism and especially the view that historical development takes place when spontaneous technical progress comes into conflict with the politico-legal system and calls forth ideas which lead to the alteration of that system. In all societies, from the most barbarous onwards, the distribution of goods, and hence the class division, depends on the mode of production. Economic conditions 'account for' the genesis of ideologies or 'are the basis' of political institutions; moral and political ideas arise in response to social needs as the necessary forms in which men envisage their own interests and are capable of uniting to defend them. Ideas are not only a powerful agent of social development but a necessary condition of institutional change; however, they are secondary in the sense that they come into being as an articulation of previously unconscious interests, and can only become instruments of social cohesion if the necessary material conditions of such cohesion are already present, namely the community of certain interests and the divergence of others. Ideas that are not thus rooted in social needs are condemned to impotence, and this applies to all utopias and dreams of a perfect society. But ideas that organize and bring into the light of consciousness men's existing conditions and needs are necessary for the destruction of any social order that has become a brake on technical progress and thus an enemy of the class which stands for such progress.

The socialist revolution does not figure largely in Krzywicki's early works, even those published out of reach of the Tsarist censorship. It is clear, however, that on this point too he shared the view of orthodox European Marxists, namely that at a certain stage of development the contradiction between technical progress and the system of private property would lead to the revolutionary overthrow of capitalism. The crisis could not be brought about artificially but must be the result of the spontaneous maturing of capitalism; the business of socialists was to organize the class-consciousness of the proletariat and take control of the revolutionary process at the right moment. However, even in his early period Krzywicki does not appear to have believed in the inevitability of progress or of socialism itself. In an article entitled 'An Outline of Social Evolution', which appeared in *Głos* in 1887, he wrote that new productive forces did not always succeed in breaking up old societies, as witness India, where the caste system had proved stronger than other factors and condemned the country to centuries of stagnation. In his preface to the Polish translation of Kautsky's book on the *Economic Doctrines of Karl Marx* he stated that the new order that would result from the evolution of capitalism and the polarization of classes might be the work of either the proletariat or the bourgeoisie. In the former case there would be collective ownership of the means of production; in the latter, private ownership and wage-labour would remain but be subordinated to the state organization. In later articles he repeated this view more than once. His ideal was a socialist society with industrial democracy as its chief feature; he thought it possible, however, that capitalism would succeed in curing the anarchy of production and competition by transforming the whole of production into a state monopoly. This would mean a kind of state capitalism more or less similar to that envisaged by Rodbertus or Brentano: the workers would enjoy social security and economic planning would be introduced, but the basic features of socialism would be missing, namely the abolition of wage-labour and the control of production by the entire working class.

In his discussion of early society Krzywicki shows special sympathy towards primitive communism, which he considered to be the most democratic system known to history. Lafargue, who shared this view, was not an ethnologist by profession; but Krzywicki's scientific interest was no doubt reinforced by the vision of a community of equals, united in mutual respect and eschewing slave labour. His investigations were based on the theories of Lewis H. Morgan, whose classic work Krzywicki translated into Polish. The study of primitive societies, which he continued throughout his life, led him in course of time to conclusions that were hard to reconcile with historical materialism, or at any rate limited its scope.

4. Mind and production. Tradition and change

Krzywicki regarded himself as an adherent of the materialist interpretation of history. However, when we look at his best-known expositions of the theory we are struck by the extent of the reservations with which he accepts the rules of Marxist historiosophy.

In the first place, he regarded historical materialism as completely independent of any specific philosophical viewpoint, materialistic or other. To emphasize this point he referred to historical 'materialism' with the second word in quotation marks, indicating that he regarded it as conventional and misleading. He seldom dealt with epistemological or metaphysical problems, but from certain articles ('The Economy Principle in Philosophy', 1886; 'Qui pro Quo' in *Widnokręgi* (*Horizons*), 1914), it is clear that, like many in his time, he took a phenomenalist view, close to that of the empiriocritics and certain Kantists. He states that we apprehend the world in our own human fashion, making distinctions and categories that are instruments of prediction but not objective realities: we create 'objects' out of impressions, distinguish 'force' from 'matter' and impose 'laws' on nature after the manner of human legislation. There are in fact no natural laws independent of human perception, but within the limits of that perception we can express the relations between phenomena in cause-and-effect terms that admit of prediction: all this is to be understood as independent of metaphysical assumptions, particularly 'materialistic' ones. The whole evolution of the world is originally a construction of the mind, and the reason we project it on to reality is that in present-day society men are

the servants and not the masters of the machines they have
created.

. The 'secondary' nature of mental phenomena thus has nothing
to do with any metaphysical opposition between spirit and
matter, but is a sociological fact signifying that material needs
exist before they are consciously articulated.

The question arises, however, within what limits we are justified in accepting the dependence of mental phenomena on
'material' conditions of life. Krzywicki does not refer here to
the Marxist opposition between base and superstructure, but he
illustrates by various examples, some classic and others less so,
the way in which technical changes give rise to new needs that
cannot be satisfied within the existing legal order. The new
problems arise spontaneously but can only be solved by conscious
activity, with the aid of an ideology that plays an indispensable
part in organizing social forces hemmed in by the political
system of the day. Throughout history there have been arbitrary
Utopias or ideals unrelated to any real economic tendencies:
these are mere 'chips and shavings' of the historical process.
The seminal ideas of history do not operate by any immanent
power of their own but because they express the as yet unconscious aspirations of new sections of society for whom the old
conditions have become a strait-jacket. In this way Krzywicki
accounts on classical lines for such principles as personal freedom
and equality before the law, the condemnation of theft, the right
to lend at interest, and the cult of knowledge—all resulting from
the development of trade and the increased importance of the
bourgeoisie in Western Europe. He cites the case of Thomas
Münzer, who dreamt of an egalitarian evangelistic community
but, when it came to practical reforms, could propose no more
than changes that were feasible because they reflected the
interests of the merchant class. .

This does not mean, however, that ideological phenomena can
do no more than 'express' existing needs and organize forces that
are already present in society. Historical materialism explains
the genesis of ideas, or rather of those ideas that have had an
effect on history. But the idea, once come to maturity, has a
life of its own and may call forth new social forces in countries
where material conditions have not developed to the point of
generating them independently. As a striking example of social

evolution being thus hastened by ideas imported from outside, Krzywicki quotes the adoption of Roman civil law by European countries in the late Middle Ages. This system of law belonged to a society in which commerce was well established, and it was therefore suited to late medieval society, where the commercial economy was rapidly gaining ground. But the adoption of Roman law itself did a great deal to accelerate the 'material' process that was then beginning. 'But for the monuments of Roman law the development of Europe might have taken place some centuries later and followed a different course' ('Movements of Ideas', 1897, in *Sociological Studies*, p. 47). Thus a legal doctrine or any other ideology, while 'secondary' at the time of its origin, might subsequently, in other circumstances, become a 'primary', creative force—not a mere barometer of change, but a cause of it. In the same way, the socialist ideology in Russia was not the result of the ripening of social conditions there; it was imported from the West and itself contributed to the ripening process, though this fact in turn caused it to assume a different and more 'subjectivist' form.

Another important factor which debars us from assuming a simple correspondence between material and spiritual forms of social life is the independent force of tradition. Institutions, customs, and beliefs that begin as rational attempts to solve the problems of social life generally remain in being and petrify after the circumstances that justified them have changed. Survivals of this kind accumulate through the ages, each generation adding someting to the pile, and the total result, which Krzywicki calls the 'historical substratum', is a powerful curb on all human activity. Men are bound by outdated forms long after they could, materially speaking, be jettisoned. The metal axe continues for a long time to be made in the less efficient shape of the stone hatchet; stone buildings and tombs are made to imitate wooden ones; as Morgan pointed out, the names of family relationships in primitive languages reflect a pattern that has ceased to exist in the society in question. New social forces rebel against the weight of tradition, opposing the law of nature to that of history and norms of rationality to inherited standards, but the past continues to impede all our actions and hold up social progress. The final result of any historical process is not what it would be if 'objective conditions' were the sole determinant: it is affected in a marked degree by traditions, made up of customs, beliefs, institutions, local variations of temperament or what is called the 'spirit of a race', which in turn results from the long-term effects of environment on human nature. In consequence, the actual development of society is varied in the extreme and it is hard to discern a uniform schema of evolution. Krzywicki's studies of primitive societies led him to conclude that there was no universal law and that, for example, serfdom was not a necessary stage in all cases. In his later years he reached the unexpected conclusion that conscious human intentions have a greater effect on social processes in primitive societies than in civilized ones, because the former are less encumbered by accumulated material institutions and social ties are therefore less rigid. This observation is in accordance with Krzywicki's frequent criticism of industrial society, in which human personality is almost completely subdued to 'reified' ties and impersonal forms of co-operation, and creativity is stifled by the money-power. This degeneration was especially visible in the big cities, where individuality was drowned in a sea of mediocrity. Like Engels and many other nineteenth-century socialists, Krzywicki thought that one of the chief effects of the new order would be to deurbanize mankind and allow city-dwellers to get 'back to nature'. He did not define socialism in metaphysical terms, but he hoped that human labour and creativity would cease to depend on commercial conditions and that human relations would again be spontaneous and direct. His criticism of contemporary literature was based on the same opposition between personal and anonymous social ties: modernism in art seemed to him a typical product of big-city culture, a rebellion against the omnipotence of exchange-value and the degradation of human beings to the status of machines. It was a fruitless revolt, however, for its only answer to utilitarian culture was to take refuge from the world in a subjective attitude of *soi-disant* independence.

There may be discerned in Krzywicki's writings a tension between two recurrent themes. On the one hand, he makes much use of the category of 'progress', i.e. the extension of man's mastery over natural forces; but, on the other, he emphasizes that as this mastery increases human relations become more and more degraded and impersonal, the mind comes to depend on things, and there is less and less room for individual creativity. No doubt he hoped, like Marx, that the socialization of production would make it possible to reconcile man's dominion over nature with the claims of his personal life, and effect a synthesis of the two. But he did not develop this subject, and his attraction towards primitive peoples and rural life (though elsewhere he insists on its poverty) seems to betray regret for the lost innocence of the 'natural' life.

Another factor which to some extent limits the historical primacy of productive forces is that 'natural selection' in the psychological field continues to operate after the conditions which made it appropriate have ceased to exist. Historical circumstances throw up, for instance, such specific psychological types as the Girondists and the Jacobins, and the results of this selection may in their turn have a significant effect on history. Biological selection, too, may be important in this way. One instance is cannibalism, which Krzywicki, following Krafft-Ebing, considers to be, as a rule, a pathological form of sexual libido rather than the effect of superstition or shortage of food; whatever its causes, it appears that natural selection produces whole pathological peoples imbued with a cannibalistic urge.

Comparing Krzywicki's statements on the importance of various forces in the historical process, we find that the role of productive forces and relations of production in determining change is hedged in with so many restrictions that it is hard to accommodate his views to the canons of Marxism in his day. No particular process or event can in practice be explained simply by the development of productive forces or the conflict between them and political conditions, since there is always a whole series of other factors at work: demography, geography, psychology, tradition (this above all), and ideas from outside the given society. For the same reason there can be no historical schema to fit all societies, and no such thing as historical necessity. What then is left of the idea that the historical process depends on technical change? Krzywicki does not invoke any such vague formula as Engels's reference to determination 'in the last resort'. His view is probably best expressed as follows. All actual social processes are the result of a large variety of causes including technical progress; the special feature of the latter is that, in 'historical' societies at all events, changes take place sooner in this field than in others, so that technical change is the most rapid agent of change in general. There is as yet no mention of 'primacy', but this can be affirmed in the sense that some, though by no means all, important features of political and legal institutions are brought about by human needs arising from progress in the field of production. As to the 'secondary' character of the ideological product, this is not to be taken as meaning that *all* social, religious, or philosophical ideas have come into existence in order to meet material needs (since many utopias, for instance, serve no such purpose), or that the social importance of an idea is necessarily proportionate to the strength of such needs (for ideas themselves may stimulate social processes in the 'material' order). All that is meant by calling ideas or doctrines 'secondary' seems to be that those which show the greatest effectiveness in harnessing human passions, desires and energies owe their strength to pre-existing 'material' ties in which human beings are involved irrespective of their will or intention. This, of course, is a very much diluted version of historical materialism. No doubt it enabled Krzywicki to criticize biological theories of history, or those of Tarde or especially Le Bon, who attributed the basic social processes to the human instinct of mimicry. But what remains of Marxism in Krzywicki's theory is little more than what thinkers of every shade were soon taking for granted. Since every process that takes place is the result of various causes and since there is no quantitative measure of the relative importance of those singled out by Marxism, the contention that they are the 'main' or 'most decisive' factor is meaningless. Since 'accidental' facts (i.e. those not due to a 'material' cause) like the adoption of Roman law can affect human destiny for centuries, the importance of 'material' determinants can only be predicated in the most general terms. The technical level of a society and the pattern of material interests can only have a vague bearing on its history: the course and outcome of social conflict and even the ultimate effect of 'objective conditions' are not predetermined by historical laws but belong to the realm of contingency. Historical materialism in this form is not a theory of history or a self-sufficient method of investigation: it is a very general reminder that we should as far as possible look beyond political institutions and ideologies to discern factors and interests arising out of production methods, while not expecting that the latter will provide a complete explanation of the former or enable us to predict their evolution. It is also a reminder that historical processes do not depend on the arbitrary decisions of individuals, that not every plan for reforming the world has any hope of success, that not all ideas take root, and that the social effectiveness of an idea does not depend on its authorship, value, or accuracy. But these propositions too, thanks to the arguments of Marx and his followers, were soon to become generally accepted and were no longer even regarded as specifically Marxist.

Krzywicki's role in the dissemination of Marxist theory is thus an ambiguous one. He did much to introduce Marxist ideas and methods into Polish intellectual life, but the flexibility and eclecticism of his approach was one of the reasons why Polish Marxism failed to take on orthodox forms and tended to dissolve into a general rationalist or historicist trend. In this sense Krzywicki—like Labriola in Italy, though for slightly different reasons—was perhaps, from the Marxist point of view, not so much a battering-ram as a Trojan horse.

CHAPTER X

Kazimierz Kelles-Krauz: a Polish Brand of Orthodoxy

KAZIMIERZ KELLES-KRAUZ was the chief theoretician and ideologist of the main stream of the Polish socialist movement, i.e. the PPS. Among the Polish Marxists who played an important part in formulating and disseminating the doctrine he also stood closest to the German orthodoxy of his day, though he deviated from it on some major points. Throughout his short adult life he was a party propagandist and advocate of Marxism in a form acceptable to those left-wing socialists who also strongly supported the cause of Polish independence.

Kazimierz Kelles-Krauz (1872–1905) was born at Szczebrze-szyn in the south-eastern part of Russian Poland. While attending the *gimnazjum* at Radom he joined one of the many socialist groups that were being formed among young people in the eighties. Expelled from school and refused entry to Warsaw University, he went to study in Paris in 1892 and there worked for the Association of Polish Socialists Abroad. He published theoretical and political articles in French, German, and *émigré* Polish periodicals defending Marxism against critics of various kinds, including nationalists in the PPS, revisionists, and Rosa Luxemburg. He died of tuberculosis in Vienna. The most important of his many writings are: 'The Law of Revolutionary Retrospection as a Consequence of Economic Materialism' (in *Ateneum*, 1897); *The Class Character of Our Programme* (1894); 'The So-Called Crisis of Marxism' (in *Przegląd filozoficzny*, 1900); and the posthumous works *Economic Materialism* (1908, with a preface by Ludwik Krzywicki) and *Some Basic Principles of the Development of Art* (1905).

Like many Marxist theoreticians of his time Kelles-Krauz took the view that Marxism does not claim to decide philosophical or epistemological questions in the traditional sense but merely asserts its own phenomenalist standpoint, so that historical materialism has only the name in common with materialism considered as a 'substantialist' theory in contrast to a spiritualist one. He agreed with Labriola that Marxism was concerned with the relations between social consciousness and the external world, both regarded as phenomena, and not between 'mind' and 'matter'. The cognitive process was of interest to Marxism only as a social and historical phenomenon, not as a means of getting at 'things in themselves'. Accordingly, Marxism must accept that any given state of knowledge was meaningful only in relation to the whole of a given civilization, and that its truth consisted in its historical function; this meant, however, that the principle of relativism applied to Marxism itself. With reference to the slogan of a 'return to Kant', Kelles-Krauz wrote:

We should in any case understand this idea somewhat differently: what we would wish to do is to translate the critical standpoint into social terms. We would recall that any society or group, and, what concerns us most, the class to which an individual belongs, imprints a certain stamp on his consciousness, imposing on it *a priori* a certain conception of society and the world, from which he can no more free himself than he can see things otherwise than through his own retina. It follows that the proletariat too must have its own class-conditioned apperception and that its philosophy, like that of all previous classes, is essentially relative and transient: it will cease to be true, or to appear true, when— but not before—the new social apperception of the future classless society takes the place of that resulting from the class struggle. The philosophy of that future society, while deriving from Marxism, must in the nature of things be different and in some ways at least contrary to Marxism as we know it today, but what exactly it will be we cannot tell (*Economic Materialism*, p. 34).

Kelles-Krauz did not believe, therefore, in any privileged historical situation in which the class viewpoint of the proletariat coincides with a universally scientific or 'objective' viewpoint: in his recognition of the *a priori* principle in history and social affairs he is perhaps closer to Simmel than to Marxism. Within the limits of this relativism he supported the Marxist interpretation of history, while complementing it with observations of his own.

Historical materialism was, in his view, essentially a monistic theory, i.e. it asserted that a single form of human activity, namely the production of the necessities of life and of tools, was sufficient to account for the origin of all other aspects of life: the division of labour, the class structure, the distribution of goods, and all features of the superstructure. Following Cunow and Tugan-Baranovsky, he criticized Engels for holding that, besides material production, the propagation of the species and the forms of family life were a fundamental aspect of human activity that helped to determine social processes. In arguing thus Engels had abandoned the monistic standpoint which was the greatest achievement of Marxism. His mistake had been to confuse the natural process of human reproduction with the socially conditioned forms of the family: the former, being purely physiological, was unchanging and therefore could not explain social evolution, while the latter were dependent on economic conditions. In the same way Kautsky had departed from the monistic standpoint when he maintained that economic conditions could only account for the genesis of the common features of an epoch, but not for particular circumstances or the behaviour of individuals.

It would seem that Kelles-Krauz advocated a highly rigorous interpretation of Marxist 'monism', but in fact he is not consistent on this crucial point. He says that human life is governed by three main factors—the biological characteristics of the species, the natural environment, and social conditions—but that historical changes are the result of technical changes. 'Ethics, law, politics, religion, art, science, philosophy—all these are utilitarian in their origin and essence, and therefore they cannot conflict with the mode of production but must be adapted to it' (*Economic Materialism*, p. 10). But we find in history a tendency for needs to become autonomous. Certain forms of activity, especially intellectual and artistic life, which were originally the instruments of more basic needs, acquire a life of their own: the superstructure reacts on the base and becomes partially independent of it. It is none the less true that forms of social life, deprived of their economic basis, are bound to die out in time, but they generally survive the economic conditions that have brought them about.

All these considerations are consistent with the Marxist stereotypes of the period. Kelles-Krauz, like other Marxists, did not ask how far it made sense to speak of a 'monistic' interpretation of history while at the same time accepting the common-sense view that changes in art, science, philosophy, or religion depend on other factors besides changes in the relations of production—especially the logic of their own internal development and the operation of 'autonomized' needs in respect of each. His thought probably was that all forms of social life can be explained genetically in terms of the relations of production, but he did not see that it is misleading to use the term 'monism' in such a restricted sense.

Comparing the philosophy of Comte to Marxism, Kelles-Krauz says that the two agree in explaining human individuals as the result of many social influences, but also in ascribing a spiritual nature to all social phenomena: from the Marxist point of view, therefore, it is all the same whether we refer the superstructure to the base or 'express' new economic phenomena by new phenomena in the domain of the superstructure. If this is so, it is hard to see in what sense the 'primacy' of relations of production *vis-à-vis* the superstructure can be maintained.

One of the phenomena that are hard to explain on the basis of Marxist schemata is Marxism itself. How is it that the proletarian ideology could come into being and influence large numbers of workers at a time when there was no basis for it in the relations of production? Unlike the capitalist economy, which had a strong basis within the politico-legal framework of feudalism, socialism does not arise spontaneously under capitalism, but is only a dream of the future. Kelles-Krauz explains this paradox by what he calls, rather pretentiously, the law of 'revolutionary retrospection', whereby 'the ideals that any reform movement seeks to substitute for existing social norms are always similar to the norms of a more or less distant past'. It is of course true enough, though it was known before Kelles-Krauz and hardly deserves to be called a 'law', that new ideologies generally seek support in tradition and present themselves as the revival of modes of thought that have existed at some former time. Such reversions, or *ricorsi* in Vico's language, can be observed throughout the ideological history of the European bourgeoisie, one example being the adoption of a Roman disguise—first republican, then imperial—by revolutionary France. As to the proletariat, the object of its 'retrospect' is primitive communism. Thus, according to Kelles-Krauz, human development proceeds in a spiral fashion by the constant revival of old forms which bear an affinity to new ideas. This explains, among other things, the fact that reactionary ideologies closely resemble those which look towards the future, since both, though for different reasons, criticize the *status quo* in the light of values derived from the past. In France, for instance, the defenders of the medieval guild system join with the syndicalists to attack the liberals. In the same way, ideas that were to form the basis of Marxism—anti-individualism, belief in the regularity of social life, the historical sense as opposed to naïve rationalist utopias—could all be found in the writings of conservatives like Vico, or the French counter-revolutionaries such as de Maistre, Bonald, and Ballanche. Socialism is a reversion to pre-classical antiquity, and this is why the development of Marxism has been so strongly influenced by the investigators of primitive societies —Morgan, Taylor, and Bachofen.

Kelles-Krauz believed that his 'law' could be explained in Marxist terms, but he does not seem to have realized that it limited the application of historical materialism by recalling the importance of autonomous tradition in social development. While upholding the view that Marxism was a 'monistic' philosophy, in his replies to critics he emphasized, like other Marxist writers of his day, that it was a mistake to interpret historical materialism as denying that the superstructure had any effect on the evolution of the base. Like his fellow Marxists he ignored the question how the relative independence of the spiritual life, and of the institutions of the superstructure, could be reconciled with a belief in the 'ultimate cause' of human history, and what limits it imposed on the general formulas of historical materialism.

The same ambiguity may be seen in Kelles-Krauz's arguments on the social significance of art, a subject to which he devoted much attention. On the one hand, art may be explained genetically by utilitarian considerations, whether related to biology (the rudiments of artistic activity can be seen in animals) or to production (rhythm as an aid to work). The development of art is related to conditions of production, for it adapts itself to political or religious aims which in turn depend on class-interests: thus, for instance, the Doric and Ionic styles respectively express the simplicity of patriarchal conditions and the aspirations of a rising class of craftsmen. On the other hand, art itself has played an important part in social change since the very beginning, first as a means of socialization and later as a form for the organization of political and religious needs. In the end it becomes autonomous to such a degree, and aesthetic needs assert themselves so strongly, that the dependence of art on the mode of production, though it never quite ceases, is much reduced. Elsewhere Kelles-Krauz inclines to the opinion that independent aesthetic needs exist from the earliest stage of social life, and even among animals. These various opinions do not form a coherent whole. On this and other subjects Kelles-Krauz was one of the many who, in a praiseworthy attempt to overcome the schematic one-sidedness and 'reductionism' of primitive versions of Marxism, ended by unconsciously reducing historical materialism to the trivial statement that the various aspects of social life to some extent depend, and to some extent do not depend, on methods of production and the conflict of class-interests.

He regarded himself, however, as a Marxist in the full sense of the term, defending the doctrine against such eminent critics as Croce, Sombart, Masaryk, and Kareyev. He opposed the German revisionists but thought the resolutions of the Dresden Congress, condemning revisionism, were ambiguous. The Congress rejected any concession or adaptation to the existing order of society, but, Kelles-Krauz argued, any reformist activity could be described as 'adapting' to capitalism. The Italian socialist party had adopted a better and clearer standpoint at its congress at Imola: the party was reformist because revolutionary, and revolutionary because reformist. In other words, Kelles-Krauz agreed with most socialist theoreticians of the time that the purpose of reforms was to prepare the way for revolution: he did not enter into the complex problems raised by the attempt to combine a revolutionary and a reformist point of view. He combated the revisionism of Eduard David on the agri-cultural question, sharing the orthodox view that a collectivized economy was better for the land as well as for industry. He also fought against Rosa Luxemburg and the SDKPiL for their opposition to Polish independence, holding that national and social liberation constituted a single aim for the Polish socialist movement. The latter, however, must preserve its class character and not allow the bourgeoisie to exploit it for the purpose of achieving political independence only. Independence was a condition of the social liberation of the proletariat; free Poland was for the proletariat, not the other way about. Rosa Luxemburg was wrong in contending that as Poland was economically integrated with the Russian empire, the revival of an independent Poland would be contrary to objective economic trends. Capitalism developed best in national states, and the bourgeoisie therefore had an interest in Polish independence, while the proletariat would be in a much better position to fight if it were not subjected to national as well as social oppression. Socialists, however, must prevent the proletariat from being used merely for the overthrow of the Tsardom, in such a way that its class identity was obscured.

Kelles-Krauz did not live long enough to write any important books, but, in addition to his role as a popularizer of Marxism, a polemist, and an ideologist of Polish left-wing socialism, he helped to inspire what may be called the conservative side of Marxism. His 'law of revolutionary retrospection' is not a law and is merely commonplace in its general formulation, as is his notion of socialism as a 'spiral regression' to primitive society. But his more detailed observations on tradition as an autonomous force in history, and on the anti-rationalist historicism of the great conservatives as an important source of Marxism, helped to establish a somewhat different view of Marxism than that of Kautskyan orthodoxy. Kelles-Krauz's version sought to take into account not only history as the realization of 'laws' but also history as contingency: that is, he generally kept in view the fact that the present and future of human societies depend not only on the laws of evolution and on what had to happen according to the doctrine, but also on what simply happened. As to his phenomenalist outlook and interpretation of Marxism as a social theory that did not attempt to solve epistemological or metaphysical problems, Kelles-Krauz was not alone in holding these views: they were shared by many Marxists of his time, especially in the Austrian school. But in this respect too he helped to present a different picture that that offered by Plekhanov, Kautsky, or Lafargue. It is worth noting that during the period of the Second International the idea of Marxism as a form of philosophical materialism scarcely existed in Poland.

CHAPTER XI

Stanisław Brzozowski: Marxism as Historical Subjectivism

THE work of Stanisław Brzozowski is scarcely known outside his own country, yet the intellectual history of twentieth-century Poland cannot be understood without reference to the bizarre and disparate effects of his dynamic writings and personality. A philosopher, critic, and novelist who died of consumption before he was thirty-three and whose activity covered a span of barely ten years, he remains a controversial and painful subject as regards both the value of his work, concerning which opinions are fiercely divided, and the more mysterious elements of his life-story, which are still a puzzle to historians. A provocative writer who was regarded for a time as a prophet of the youthful intelli-gentsia in revolt against both positivism and Romanticism, he found himself at odds with all the political forces of his day—conservatives, socialists, and national democrats. His style is violent and appears to be constantly at boiling-point: whatever the object of his attention, he seems to be capable only of fervent admiration or unqualified contempt. Some critics thought the explosiveness of his manner was a mask for dilettantism, a want of originality or the power to discipline his mind and digest his thoughts—the more so as he changed his opinions with dizzying swiftness, evidently as the result of hasty writing, wide but super-ficial reading, and self-identification with the latest philosopher or writer who came within his ken. More attentive readers, how-ever, detected a certain logic in all these changes, and an imprint of personality which gave an individual stamp to all his borrow-ings from the intellectual store of West European, German, Russian, and Polish thinkers. In passing on the ideas of others he paraphrased them and tinged them with his own style to such an extent that they sometimes appeared unrecognizable: this was the case with Kant and Spencer, Hegel and Marx, Avenarius and Nietzsche, Proudhon and Sorel, Bergson and Newman, Dostoevsky, Loisy, and many others. The ambiguity and variability of Brzozowski's influence extended beyond the grave.

Young people of the Left were brought up on his novels and other writings (*The Flames*, a story of the heroic conspirators of the Narodnaya Volya, was required reading for each generation of revolutionaries), yet before and during the Second World War he was successfully claimed as a prophet by the radical nationalist camp. In this respect Brzozowski resembled Sorel, who in fact influenced him greatly.

Was he a Marxist, and if so, to what extent? He wrote of himself that he had never been orthodox and that when he joined the Marxists it was in the capacity of a dissident. He believed, however, that the 'philosophy of labour' which he professed in 1906–9 was a development of Marx's ideas, and he contrasted Marxism as it had figured in his life with the evolutionism of the orthodox and, above all, the whole tradition stemming from Engels. He was one of the first to contrast Marx and Engels as minds of a completely opposite stamp. Marxism, it may be said, was only one phase in his highly complicated intellectual history, but it was the phase of his maximum intellectual independence and influence on Polish culture. Marxism cannot be treated as the main line of his biography but only as a section of it, unintelligible without some reference to the remainder. His most important work from the standpoint of the history of Marxism is *Ideas*.

It is almost impossible to summarize Brzozowski's views without distortion. He believed that philosophy was not merely a process of reflecting on life but an enhancement of it, and that the meaning of philosophy was determined by its social effectiveness. Hence to describe the content of his writings irrespective of their personal and social genesis and function is to turn them into something they were meant not to be, namely an abstract doctrine. On the other hand, a philosopher who believes that philosophizing is an entirely immanent part of history has no right to complain that his ideas are 'distorted' by critics: for if meaning is always created and not extracted from something ready-made, there can be no question of 'distortion' when he proclaims his vision of the world or when others comment upon it.

Brzozowski's thought may be defined negatively in relation to certain intellectual positions which he opposed. In the first group of these are positivism, evolutionism, naturalism, and the theory of progress, all of which purport to interpret human life and make it intelligible as a function or extension of a natural process. Secondly, he opposed the Romantic tradition which contrasts the independent 'interior' of man with nature, alien to him and governed by its own laws. Brzozowski was, it is true, the most active exponent in Poland of modernist or 'neo-Romantic' thought, but he would have nothing to do with that aspect of it which he regarded as a continuation of the 'bad side' of Romanticism, i.e. the view that art should be completely free and unfettered by any consciousness of its social functions. He was equally opposed to the positivist, utilitarian approach and to the doctrine of 'art for art's sake'. He wished to preserve a place for artistic creation which was not determined by the laws of 'progress' and did not owe its significance to other than human powers, yet at the same time did not represent a breach of historical continuity or claim to be exempt from social responsibility.

1. Biographical note

Stanisław Brzozowski (1878–1911), the son of minor gentry, was born in the village of Maziarnia in south-eastern Poland. After a high school education he entered the Science Faculty of Warsaw University in 1896, but was expelled a year later for helping to organize a patriotic demonstration of students. Arrested in autumn 1898 for underground educational activities, he was released a few weeks later but kept under police supervision. Next year he contracted tuberculosis, and from then till 1905 he lived partly in Warsaw and partly at the nearby resort of Otwock. From 1901 he was extremely active as a writer of books and articles on subjects of popular philosophy, novels, plays, literary criticism, and drama reviews. In the first few years he published pamphlets on the philosophy of Taine, essays on Amiel, Śniadecki, Kremer, Avenarius, and Żeromski, and polemics against Sienkiewicz and Miriam-Przesmycki. At the beginning of 1905 he went to Zakopane in the Tatras and spent a year in Galicia, giving lectures at Zakopane and Cracow. At this time he wrote a pamphlet (published in 1924) on the phil-

osophy of Polish Romanticism, essays on Norwid and Dostoevsky, and a course of logic. At the beginning of 1906 he went
for a cure to Nervi near Genoa, then to Lausanne, Germany,
and Lwów (Lemberg); during that year he published several
articles and a book, *The Modern Polish Novel*. He returned to
Nervi at the beginning of 1907 and then spent six months at
Florence. While in Italy he wrote a study of Nietzsche and an
essay on historical materialism; he met Gorky and Lunacharsky
and published two books, *Culture and Life* and *Modern Polish
Literary Criticism*. He also took up the intensive study of Marxism and read the works of Sorel.

The following year was that of the 'Brzozowski affair', which
beclouded the philosopher's last years and shook the Polish intelligentsia to its foundations. In April 1908 a former Okhrana
agent named Mikhail Bakay gave to Vladimir Burtsev, a Russian *émigré* in Paris and the editor of a socialist journal, a list of
informers for the Okhrana which included Brzozowski's name.
The heinous charge was repeated in *Czerwony Sztandar*, the organ
of the SDKPiL, and both the socialist and the National Democratic (right-wing) Press unleashed a campaign against the 'spy'.
Brzozowski at once denied the charge and demanded that
it be investigated by a 'citizens' court' representing all the
socialist parties. After much preparation the court was constituted: it met at Cracow in February and again in March 1909,
but Brzozowski was struck down by illness before the next
session. The only witness against him was Bakay, who gave confused evidence. The court passed no sentence; controversy raged
meanwhile, with many eminent writers defending Brzozowski
against the charge of treason. After his death the matter was re-
opened many times with inconclusive results. Feliks Kon, a
Polish communist and a member of the Cracow court, investigated the Okhrana archives after the October Revolution and
found no evidence that Brzozowski had been a traitor. The
general opinion today is that either there was a confusion of
identity (both his Christian name and surname are very common in Poland) or the charge was a 'plant' by the Russian police.
In any case, it had a catastrophic effect on Brzozowski's personal
fortunes and those of his writings. (During the affair it came to
light that Yevno Azev, the leader of a terrorist organization of
the Russian Social Revolutionaries, was an Okhrana agent; his

name had also been on Bakay's list, but the ins and outs of this matter are not clear either.)

Despite persecution, poverty, and illness Brzozowski did not cease to work. In 1908 he published *The Flames*, in 1909 *The Legend of Young Poland*, perhaps his best-known work of philosophical criticism, and in 1910 the volume of essays *Ideas*, a summing-up of his philosophical reflections. He died in Florence. Many of his writings appeared posthumously, including memoirs written in the last months of his life, an unfinished novel, and an essay on Newman prefaced to a Polish translation of the *Grammar of Assent*.

2. *Philosophical development*

Like most of his contemporaries, Brzozowski was infected for a time by the positivist outlook of Darwin and Spencer. Soon, however, he not only abandoned evolutionism, determinism, and 'scientific' optimism, but made them the chief target of his attack. For his own part he adopted an individualist philosophy of 'action' which dispensed with objective criteria of cognitive, aesthetic, and moral values, relating them exclusively to the self-assertion of the individual in his uniqueness, and sought to preserve the idea of creativity as a challenge to all forms of naturalist determinism. He articulated this philosophy with the aid of the same sources as most of his contemporaries drew upon—Fichte, Nietzsche, Avenarius—and also of traditional Polish Romanticism, in which the cult of 'action' afforded an ideological compensation for the country's enslavement.

At this time Brzozowski's chief masters were Avenarius and Nietzsche. The former was one of those who had drawn unexpected, and in Brzozowski's view tragic, conclusions from evolutionist positivism. The Darwinists interpreted the whole of civilization and all intellectual activity as a weapon in the struggle of the human race for survival. This view facilitated, if it did not necessitate, a pragmatic attitude towards knowledge: since cognition, and its results preserved and codified in the form of science, were 'nothing but' the response of the species to its natural environment, the notion of truth, like that of goodness or beauty, ceased to have any transcendental meaning; things were valuable in the cognitive, aesthetic, or moral sense in so far as they helped to prolong and strengthen the life of the species. In the same way no scientific opinions, including the theory of evolution itself, could be regarded as 'true' in the everyday sense: they were merely organs of 'life', which in itself is neither good nor bad, true nor false, but simply exists through time. Yet this argument was based on a biological theory which claimed to be 'true' in the transcendental sense of everyday usage. The whole structure of 'scientific philosophy' turned out to be a vicious circle.

Empiriocritical philosophy did not overcome these difficulties, and Brzozowski, who for a time attached great weight to this philosophy, took the view that any theory of knowledge was bound to involve a vicious circle, as the general rules of its evaluation could not be formulated without prior assumptions. He accepted the empiriocritical negation of the concept of truth, while believing that it entailed the once-and-for-all abandonment of any claim to discover 'objective' values in the rationalist sense of the term. In Avenarius's view the predicate 'true', like 'good' or 'beautiful', did not denote a quality found in experience but merely a certain interpretation given by men to their perceptions and thoughts: truth was a 'character', not an 'element'. The epistemological question as to the nature of truth, regarded as an attribute of human judgements irrespective of the biological function of those judgements or the circumstances in which they were formed, was not a question that could be meaningfully put. There were no valid questions outside the sphere of empirical description, and no such thing as 'reason' considered and designed to form a picture of the world as it is 'in itself'. The task of philosophy was not to investigate the attributes of Being, but to generalize the data of experience while taking care not to endow its abstractions with any but a purely instrumental significance. It was for man to systematize experience in scientific form, not as the passive recipient of pre-existing reality but as its active organizer.

Brzozowski held at this time that we are obliged to accept these conclusions and abandon any claim to discover the 'truth'. What we regard as valuable is not so because it gives us a true picture of the world but because it is useful to us in the fight with nature, and the question why it is useful is the fruit of an addiction to metaphysics and has no real meaning. The world as we know it is our own creation, cut to our measure. We cannot intelligibly put questions about any other world or invent, as Spencer did, a category of the Unknowable, for the existence of such a category implies, absurdly, that we have knowledge of what we cannot know.

However, Brzozowski's biological relativism at this time was conceived in terms of the individual and not the species, and was thus ultimately closer to Nietzsche than to Avenarius. All that is true, good, or beautiful is referred not to the interests of the community but to the irreducible subjectivity of each human being. It is each one's business to create the world for himself, and he is entitled to apply the term 'good' or 'true' to whatever he regards as favourable to his own development. In science, art, and morality there are no universal criteria, only that of the individual who designs his own world in an act of unfettered creation.

In this phase Brzozowski's thought did not go beyond the stereotypes of neo-romanticism, except for the dramatic rhetoric in which he clothed them. In 1906–7, however, without apparently quite realizing the extent of the change, he moved away from the solipsistic theory of value and the Nietzschean slogan of creativity, towards an anthropocentric viewpoint which he called the 'philosophy of labour', and in which he was most influenced by Marx, Sorel, and Bergson.

Although he never expressly unfolded the reasons for this change, they may be tentatively reconstructed by comparing his early views on the Romantic philosophy with his later criticism of it. It would seem that he perceived the contradiction between his own critique of modernist art, which proclaimed its independence of society and thereby rejected social responsibility, and, on the other hand, a philosophy which postulated the freedom of the individual to create a world for himself as his own will or caprice dictated. If creativeness is defined by the lack of any connection with existing culture or responsibility for it, and if the mind proclaims itself as creative in so far as it breaks off continuity with the universe, then we are back to the Romantic vision that opposed the 'internal' and spiritual, to which alone it attached importance, to the indifferent world of objectivized nature and civilization, the realm of natural or sociological determinism. A philosophy based on this assumption is not a

creation forming part of the world, but a flight from its imperatives. If, as Nietzsche contended, the existing world has no
meaning for us, then the freedom of the creative subject is mere
contingency, an irresponsible refusal to inquire what social conditions make creativity possible, how far and in what circumstances we can be masters of our fate.

The ontology of culture which Brzozowski adumbrated at
this stage was opposed both to evolutionist positivism and to
Romanticism: these appeared diametrically opposed to each
other but, in his opinion, shared a common base. Both believed
that external reality does not have a meaning of its own but is
subject to its own laws, irrespective of mankind: to the positivists
it was something to be manipulated for technical purposes, to
the Romantics it was an insensible world of necessity possessing
no interest for us. But in either case the idea of man as a creative
being could not be saved: in the former because creativity was
only an adaptation to the demands of the natural environment
and was determined by the general laws of 'progress' in the same
way as changes in that environment, in the latter because
creativity was not supposed to apply itself to the external world
but to reject it in favour of the illusory autarky of a human
monad. The 'philosophy of labour' transcended both the evolutionist faith in progress and the Romantic cult of the self-
sufficient ego: it regarded the world as existing only by virtue of
the significance conferred on it by collective human effort, and
it sought in this way to preserve the dignity of man as the
initiator of the world, as unconditionally responsible for himself
and for external reality—as a collective Absolute, to whom no
ready-made laws afford a promise of triumph over destiny. This
is a kind of Marxist version of Kantianism: nature as we know it
and can meaningfully speak of it proves to be the creation of
man, but its human coefficient derives from labour and not from
transcendental conditions of experience.

The philosophy of labour was not the end of Brzozowski's
spiritual evolution. The last years of his life were largely filled
with religious speculations and a growing interest in Catholicism as presented by Newman and the modernists. To be sure,
Brzozowski had never been a 'progressive freethinker' or a militant atheist in the old-fashioned positivist or Marxist style. He
never set out to 'fight religious superstition', as he took seriously

all forms of the spiritual life and saw in Catholicism an important and fruitful source of cultural values. In a certain undefined sense he regarded himself as a religious man: shortly before his death he wrote in a letter that he had never lost faith in the immortality of the soul. But for a long time Catholicism was to him only a historical creation, a concentration of values and a seed-bed of philosophical, artistic, and literary production: he interpreted it in an immanent fashion, within the limits of self-contained human history. He did not believe at any time that cultural values could be wholly detached from their historical roots, the form and manner in which they had come to be, or that everything of value in Christianity could be simply taken over, without its Christian integument, into secular civilization. But in his last years his thoughts took a different turn; he was attracted by Christianity not only as an important cultural factor and a transmitter of values, but also as a means of intercourse with the supernatural. One can hardly speak of an outright conversion, nor can the nature of the change be exactly determined from the notes and letters dating from the last months of Brzozowski's life. It would seem, however, that there was no breach of continuity with his previous ideas but that he was still preoccupied, as he had been all his life, with the question: How can man give an absolute meaning to that which he himself creates? He appears to have decided that this absolute meaning, on which depends also man's faith in his own absolute dignity, can only come from the belief that our endeavours are capable of reaching the divine, timeless foundations of all being. Any realistic metaphysic of Christianity, or attempt at rationalizing faith, was alien to his mind. If he died as a Catholic it was the continuation of his philosophical pilgrimage, not a break with what had gone before.

3. *The philosophy of labour*

Looking more closely at the variant of Marxism outlined by Brzozowski, we see first of all that it is based on opposition to the then dominant evolutionist version popularized by Engels and Kautsky. In Brzozowski's view all the Marxist writings of his day, except those of Labriola and Sorel, were a successful attempt to distract attention from the essential problems that Marx had raised. 'There was not a single concept, vision or method which, in the transfer from Marx's mind to Engel's, did not become completely different, and indeed diametrically opposite as far as the philosophical nature of concepts is concerned' (*Ideas*, p. 264). Engels shared with the positivists a belief in the natural evolution of the world, of which human history was one aspect: history could be explained by the laws of nature, and there was an objective law of progress, independent of human will, which ensured that man would sooner or later attain a blessed state on earth. This positivist optimism, said Brzozowski, was not only a gratuitous invention but was degrading to man, as it signified that he was not the real master of his fate but was being steered by the 'law of progress' towards an earthly paradise which had a sort of quasi-existence already: it robbed man of the sense that he was the active subject of his own destiny, and of the will to be so. Engels's theory thus maintained the essential alienness of man *vis-à-vis* the world, just as all the conservative metaphysics of the positivists had done. 'To Marx the victory of the working class was necessary because he had convinced himself that he knew how to create and construct that victory, that he was laying its foundations and taking part in the work of achievement. To Engels the whole of this construction, including Marx's will animating it from the inside, was a matter of knowledge, a cognitive complex that maintained itself in his mind because it satisfied his demands, covered all the facts known to him and had an answer to every objection. The workers' victory was a necessity because it took shape in his mind as a logical inference from what he knew ... We are back at the same stage as though Marx had never existed' (ibid., pp. 348–9). 'To Engels it sufficed to feel that he represented, logically and intellectually, a form of life that was worthy of victory and power. He saw the world as a theatre of errors out of which there would finally emerge, necessarily and by the nature of things, that error which dominated his own mind' (p. 384). 'Basically he regards human beings as insignificant creatures, whose function is to be happy and free and not cause any logical perturbation in Engels's mind ... He loved the working class because it furnished him with a necessary argument; apart from this he had no spiritual attachment except to Marx' (p. 389).

Marx by contrast, according to Brzozowski, had no doctrine

that made it possible to predict historical events on the basis of ascertained 'natural' laws, valid alike for human affairs and for inanimate nature. This does not mean, however—and the point is worth stressing—that Brzozowski opposed the 'determinism' of Engels to the 'voluntarism' of Marx. He ascribed to Marx, not a voluntarist doctrine as the negation of determinism, but a philosophy that conceived itself as historical praxis. That is to say, Marxism was not a theory about praxis but was a form of social activity comprehending both history and itself as a historical factor, or, to put it otherwise, contemplating the historical process from the inside. In this way Brzozowski's interpretation is more radical than the collective subjectivism of the Russian empiriocritical Marxists: he not only regards the world as a meaning created by the collective effort of human beings, but relativizes his own meaning in the same manner. Brzozowski was perhaps the first who, anticipating Lukács and Gramsci, rejected the dispute among Marxists between determinists and followers of Kant. Both sides in this dispute regarded Marxism as a sociological attempt to ascertain social laws; but to Brzozowski the sense of Marxism consisted not in what it described or predicted, but in what it brought about.

Brzozowski had not much ground for taking this view, except the *Theses on Feuerback*: he relied more on intuition than on Marx's writings. He believed firmly, however, that he had rediscovered the basic philosophical impulse which Marx himself had, as it were, forgotten when he came to concentrate on the problem of attaining power.

The first target of attack by the philosophy of praxis as thus understood was the idea of a 'ready-made world' subject to laws of its own which mankind was capable of ascertaining in so far as it could exploit them for its own use. Such a world was an intellectualist delusion, a means of evading responsibility for the fate of humanity. What we know as nature, he argues, is not being-in-itself but is, at each particular stage of our knowledge, the degree of the power we exercise over Being. He expresses this idea in different variants in several places. 'From the point of view of the critique of knowledge, nature in the scientific sense of the term is the power achieved by human technical ability over the outside world' (*Ideas*, p. 7). 'Nature, as an idea, is experience envisaged in categories created by our real power

over the surrounding universe ... Nature, as an idea, is experience envisaged as the work of man, the world as a possible object
of technical activity' (p. 119). 'Man does not acquaint himself
with a ready-made world, but first unconsciously creates various
forms of activity and later becomes aware of them' (p. 154). 'The
reality encountered by human thought is nothing but human
activity and human life. What lies beyond humanity is something against which only human labour can assert itself ... Man
has no resources other than himself and that which he deliberately creates. Science is the awareness, the plan and method of
our activity and there are no boundaries to it, as human life and
labour endure and develop' (p. 164).

In other words, man's contact with reality is primarily active
contact, i.e. labour: all the rest, including the perception and
understanding of the world, is secondary. We know the world,
from the beginning and at every successive stage, as that upon
which our labour is directed, as a focus of resistance and effort.
This practical dialogue with our environment is the absolute,
intransgressible reality. There is no way of passing beyond it to
discover the 'real' face of Being, nor can the external world,
unaffected by us, come within the range of our conscious perception and create a subjective image there; nor is there any
pure self-knowledge in which we arrive at an unclouded, substantive ego that is perfectly transparent to itself. The world,
Brzozowski maintains, is 'coextensive with labour'. In the same
way we cannot, in our intellectual activity, separate perception
from evaluation: for there is no perception or theoretical reflection that does not have a human, partial, evaluative slant,
working within the horizon which is bounded from the outset by
man's practical need to control the world. Labour is an
'Absolute' for human beings in the sense that no theoretical
reflection can go beyond the realities created by labour and
organized according to its requirements. In the most general
sense Kant is right: objects conform to our concepts, because the
very presence of an object presupposes a human faculty of
organizing experience. But this faculty does not consist in a set
of *a priori* forms, nor is it due to any transcendental rationality:
it is simply the practical ability to transform the environment
in accordance with our needs.

Humanity, therefore, cannot itself be explained. We cannot

interpret man by referring his origin, existence, and perceptions to pre-human conditions (such as a body without consciousness, or the history of species), since these conditions can only be known to us within the practical perspective brought about by the totality of human efforts to maintain life and enhance its quality. We know things as the counterpart of our practical activity, and our own selves in the same state of interlocking tension. Neither the self nor the object is at any time 'given' in the form of a separate 'image': both are inescapably relativized *vis-à-vis* each other, and this interrelation is the final, unanalysable basis of all our knowledge of the history of men and nature and the laws of the universe.

This, in Brzozowski's view, is not simply another attempt to solve epistemological questions, but involves a radically new conception of our relation to the world. To believe that we find a 'ready-made world' obeying its own laws and waiting for us to observe or exploit it is to accept, as it were, the consolidated' results of human activity ('dead labour', in Marxian terms) as an inescapable necessity, and thereby to accept that human labour must be enslaved for ever. To believe that man is, in a radical sense, the creator of the universe is to accept responsibility for the future, rejecting the domination of the results of past labour over the world that our own efforts are bringing to birth. The whole of the past—the necessities of cause and effect as we know them, the world organized into objects by a particular system of connections—is nothing but 'dead labour', a deposit created by past human activity. 'What we know as reality is no more than the result of past history. When we say, then, that reality imposes certain bounds on our historical activity, we should say that past history or reality as it is, or the ideas occasioned by that reality, set absolute limits to our thinking ... For any philosophy of history, or metaphysics of being, or theory of knowledge that purports to abstract from history, is only possible on the basis of labour that has not recognized itself as the sole human activity that has consequences in the realm of being' (*Ideas*, p. 131).

It is easy to see that if we take the view that there is nothing which is not immanent in human history the dispute between materialism and idealism falls to the ground, since both are based on a false assumption. 'Both these opinions regard the content of the mind as constituting the essence of the universe. Idealism tells us how the world is created by what is in our minds, while materialism accepts the result and tries to forget the "process". Bergson, quite rightly, points out that evolutionism *à la* Spencer is essentially the same thing as evolutionism *à la* Fichte' (ibid., pp. 202–3). 'History is the creator of what we call our minds and nature: it is the ground on which we stand and which prevents us from falling into the abyss; we are from it, and only through it have we any contact with what is not human' (p. 207).

All the attributes that ignorant conservatism, with its eyes fixed on the past, would have us regard as features of a ready-made world are, from the point of view of the philosophy of labour, secretions of human effort, and this radically alters their significance. This applies in particular to the notion of time, which is neither a 'natural' frame within which events occur, nor a relationship between them independent of ourselves. We create the category of time in order to make ourselves aware of the possibility of controlling our own destiny, by opposing the human effort crystallized in past history to the energy which is free to project itself as it chooses: the past is what we have already done, the future is the open realm of our hopes and intentions. To the conservative way of thinking which dominates the evolutionist version of Marxism, time is not a reality: the future, in some mysterious way, already exists and is determined; human happiness and contentment are already inscribed on some future part of the unwinding scroll of progress. But this optimistic philosophy is a self-delusion and a flight from reality in the eyes of those who have learnt from Bergson that the future does not exist in any form and that only duration is real, i.e. nothing is real that has not appeared in actual duration. It is absurd, Brzozowski says, to attribute to Marx a belief in time as something that only actualizes eternal 'laws' and thus entrusts human fate to higher powers of which men are the compliant instruments. 'Teach me to feel myself the tree, And not the withered leaf'—the quotation from Meredith prefaced to Brzozowski's *Ideas* is central to his understanding of Marxism. To him it was above all a way in which men could comprehend the dependence of all forms of culture, including science and nature itself, on labour conceived as an original datum, not analysable into independent elements; and at the same time it signified the acceptance by men of responsibility for their own collective lot.

The understanding of culture must therefore be both genetic and functional. There are no transcendental or pre-existing rules determining the value of what men produce in the way of knowledge, religious myths, works of art, or systems of philosophy. Forms of civilization cannot be discussed without a knowledge of their origin. The question of truth, again, is not that of a connection, independent of ourselves, between the content of certain ideas and a self-existing object: truth is whatever strengthens society and aids it in the fight for survival. This, of course, is close to the pragmatist approach; but Brzozowski differs from James, whose philosophy he knew, in that he does not derive the meaning and truth of the products of culture and knowledge from particular situations or individual needs, but always relates them to the community. Only the whole labouring people can impart the dignity of 'truth' to anything they produce, in so far as it proves able to survive in their world and serves to further its development. In the same way Brzozowski, in accordance with his argument, refuses to accept the category of 'use' or 'life-value' in relation to pre-cultural, biological needs or instincts: for as humanity cannot be defined, or its origin explained, in terms of pre-human factors, so it cannot be treated as a complex of instincts or animal needs to which consciousness is superadded at a later stage. Needs and the demands of 'life' are historical, human categories, and the pragmatic significance of civilization relates to man as the creator of himself, not as a creature who grafts cultural institutions on to his animal existence. However, Brzozowski shares with pragmatism the fundamental conviction that the same value-criterion applies to scientific knowledge as to art, morals, social systems, religious sentiments and institutions: viz. their utility to humanity as the master of its own destiny.

This view does away with the traditional dichotomies of rationalism, positivism, and free thought as between religion and science, fact and value, art and knowledge, cognition and creation. If 'life' is the sole touchstone of value, no branch of culture can claim supremacy over another or set up universal criteria, but all deserve equally to be judged as instruments of the human struggle to survive and create a more abundant life; they are good if they enhance energy, and bad if they dissipate it in backward-looking delusions.

Since humanity is its own final basis and there is nothing beyond it to which we can appeal, it is no good looking for any guarantee in the shape of historical necessity or a pre-established order. 'The present state of humanity is the profoundest meta-physical work of man; it is reality *par excellence*. Our towns, factories, wars, arts and sciences are not a dream behind which something more profound waits to liberate us: they are absolute reality, irreducible to anything else' (*Ideas*, p. 215). 'There is no such thing as relations "to the world", "to nature", "to logic"; there are only intra-historical, intra-social relations between different efforts, tensions and directions of the will. What we call the world is a certain property of the human will: we take it for the world because we do not so much create it as find it' (p. 443). But what we find is brittle and uncertain: we can and do preserve ourselves daily by fresh efforts: nothing is truly ours, no satisfaction is permanent, no gain is everlasting. The meaning and value accumulated by centuries of human effort has to be maintained by an effort constantly renewed. The human condition is not a steady progress towards final satisfaction, happiness, or the enjoyment of benefits acquired once and for all: it is an unceasing struggle, the result of which is not and never will be certain. All we can hope to do in that struggle is to preserve our own dignity. We have no 'calling' other than what we actually decide our 'calling' to be.

If there is no criterion of truth and value outside 'life' itself, rationalism stands revealed as a conservative illusion. For, in Brzozowski's view, rationalism is the belief that actual forms of culture can be evaluated by criteria independent of the cultural process and can be explained by factors that are not the work of man. But such criteria and explanations do not in fact exist. There is no such thing as pure thought or pure aesthetic sensi-bility which can then be applied to real life. 'Social existence is not the application of thought and perception, but is itself the reality which creates the faculty and the content of perception. Each and every mental phenomenon is only a phase in the history of a particular social group, and the life of the group is its essential content' (*Ideas*, p. 419). Once again, the meaning and cognitive value of any product of culture can only be judged by its origin and functions and not by extra-historical criteria. Moreover, if the organic crystallization of a culture can be expressed in rational form, this signifies that it has already lost its creative force and belongs to the lifeless accumulation of the past. Live cultural tendencies can never be confined in perfectly rational and convincing forms. Rationalism is the attitude of those who wish to entrench themselves in ready-made positions and persuade others that these positions cannot be questioned. But thought and artistic creation, in their formative stages, are characterized by lack of self-confidence and by the imperfect logic of its forms.

4. Socialism, the proletariat, and the nation

The philosophy of labour is, in Brzozowski's view, a kind of metaphysic of socialism and a motivation, or rationalization, of his adherence to it. He was not an active party worker at any time, partly because he disapproved of socialist particularism and current versions of Marxism, but also because he believed, especially in his last years, that all political forms that derived organically from the life of a nation were in some way necessary to it, and none of them could claim a monopoly of the truth. He declared himself to be a socialist in the sense of holding that the workers would conquer if they could show that the mass of free labour could outweigh that which was possible with enslaved labour. This highly vague form of socialism was expressly neutral with regard to current ideas of the nature of the future order. He believed that as the whole of civilization must be interpreted as the self-organization of the working community, and as it was only from the point of view of labour that men could understand the meaning of their own efforts, it was from the class of direct producers that humanity must learn to understand itself and be imbued with the necessary hope and confidence to govern its own destiny. In this general sense Brzozowski believed in the special mission of the proletariat, and his Prometheanism on its behalf was expressed in formulas close to the syndicalism of Sorel. 'The class separatism of the proletariat is the only way to bring about a moral atmosphere among mankind, to rediscover the meaning of the word "humanity". The proletariat's increasing class consciousness is the one great, metaphysically genuine spiritual reality of our time. This is the point at which man's tragic dilemma is decided. We do not demand justice—no one knows what it is—nor do we promise or look for happiness: mankind never will be happy. Suffering has its absolute values which we do not want to lose. But we believe that man must exist because he has loved and valued his existence—because he creates himself as that reality whose existence he desires, as his own absolute meaning and as the purpose of the world' (*Ideas*, p. 222).

Socialism is thus expressed not in terms of welfare, security, and contentment, but of human dignity. The struggle for dignity is a struggle for 'free labour', defined as the opposite of labour 'controlled from above', or as a state in which the labourer, while at work, is not subject to any higher authority. Like Sorel, Brzozowski did not go beyond this general formulation, which is, of course, in accordance with Marxist tradition as far as it goes. He was not interested in the question of the seizure of political power by the proletariat, or of economic organization. What was needed was for the 'mind and will of the working class' to rise to a level at which the workers were in full control of the vital processes of society based on the productivity of labour. Political and economic changes that did not lead to the spiritual transformation of the workers, or increase their readiness and ability to take control of the productive process, were of no account. From this point of view Brzozowski, like Sorel and the anarcho-syndicalists, distinguished the socialism of the intelligentsia from that of the proletariat. The intelligentsia was merely a consuming class that produced nothing; but, as its activity took place in the mental sphere, it was naturally inclined to believe that forms of life are produced by consciousness and not the other way round. What the intelligentsia called socialism was only an attempt to secure for itself a dominant place in society, using the workers as an instrument to maintain its privileges. The hegemony of intellectuals in the socialist movement was a result of the spiritual immaturity of the proletariat. Brzozowski dreamt of a mass struggle of the proletariat, not led by the intellectuals but fully capable of fighting for itself.

No historical law guaranteed the success of socialism. If 'free labour' showed itself to be more productive, socialism would be possible; if not, not. The productivity of labour was to be the final criterion of social progress, but not—and this is a particular feature of Brzozowski's thought—because increased productivity would make possible an increase of consumption. The advance of technology and increased productivity meant the growth of man's power over his environment: this was to Brzozowski an end in itself, not simply the means to a more comfortable life. His whole conception of socialism was heroic and adventurous: man's conquest of nature needed no material gain to justify it; production was not a means to consumption, but to the maintenance of man's position as the independent lord of creation. The proletariat, in his eyes, was a collective warrior with the traits of a Nietzschean hero, the idealized embodiment of humanity as a metaphysical entity. Human ideals and values made sense and were historically momentous in so far as they helped man to wrestle with refractory nature, but that wrestling itself was in the last resort justified on spiritual grounds, as a self-assertion of the will.

To critics brought up on Marxist orthodoxy, this Prometheanism with its metaphysical and prophetic tone appeared highly suspect. Faced with the popularity of Brzozowski's writings amongst left-wing youth, Polish communist intellectuals attached importance to destroying his influence and, in effect, wrote him off as an ideologist of the Right. Andrzej Stawar, for instance, declared that the undifferentiated cult of labour belonged to the ideology of class solidarity. This was an exaggeration in that Brzozowski strongly emphasized the separate cultural identity of the proletariat and its special role in social development. It was true, however, that unlike the Marxists he defined the proletariat by the fact that it performed physical labour, and not by its place in the scheme of production or, especially, the sale of its labour as a commodity. In general, Brzozowski did not pay attention to the class division of society and the social conditions of production. In the last resort we cannot say exactly what he meant by the proletariat, 'free labour', or socialism. He used these terms as metaphysical categories to aid in the description of man as the conqueror of nature: labour, and the struggle itself, were their own reward. 'By means of labour the ideal becomes a fact. Labour is the divine element in which nature—for labour is a fact of nature— becomes the body of an ideal. Labour is the fruit of the will, the basis of its domination over the world' (letter to Salomea Perl-mutter, March 1906). In this sense the reproach that Brzozowski levelled against the socialist parties—that they treated the pro-letariat as a means to the conquest of power by intellectuals who were professional politicians—can, *mutatis mutandis*, be directed against himself: to him the proletariat was the instrument of a Promethean ideal derived from metaphysical reflection and not from observation of the actual tendency of the workers' movement. He was not concerned with what the workers actually wanted, but with what they must become in order that the conquistador's vision of human destiny might be fulfilled.

Another point of contention with Polish Marxists was Brzozowski's attitude to the national question. As time went on the ideas of 'nation' and 'fatherland' became more prominent in his writing, as did the role of traditional culture. Moreover, he used biological metaphors which, vague as they were, became increasingly suspect when radical-nationalist movements of a more or less Fascist type began to use similar metaphors in defence of national values. On such grounds Paweł Hoffman, another orthodox communist, denounced Brzozowski as a fore-runner of Fascism.

Brzozowski gave no thought to the tensions that might arise from an attempt to reconcile the national and the class points of view in social philosophy. It seemed clear to him that his loyalty to the workers' cause in no way conflicted with his belief in Poland as a source of national and cultural values; on this subject he wrote:

People have been at pains to show that the workers' movement can be, and is, a national movement. I do not know that their efforts were necessary. Poland is the field of action of the motive forces in Polish life and the resources which sustain it. To argue that the workers' movement can be independent of the nation's life and destiny is to say that it does not matter what range of forces and means of action it has at its disposal. As long as the Polish community is deprived of its rights, so long will our working class be an amorphous body of degraded paupers—not occupying the fourth rank in the social order, but the fifth, sixth or even lower. What is the issue here? To renounce one's national existence is to give up hope of influencing human reality: it means destroying one's own soul, for the soul lives and acts only through the nation. The so-called question of nationality does not arise, for it is the same as to ask whether we wish to lose our human dignity.

There are no opinions, interests or values that can dispense us from loyalty to this supreme value. A man without a country is a soul without substance—he is lukewarm, dangerous and harmful. For the human soul is the result of a long collective struggle, a long process of creation, and all its significance is due to the length of time that has gone into making it. The older our soul is, the more creative it will be. That is why the workers must consciously arouse themselves to love their country and remember its history. (*Ideas*, p. 225)

If this argument had simply meant that the liberation of the working class could not take place in conditions of national oppression, it would have been commonplace enough and would have been endorsed by Polish socialists in general. But it is clear that Brzozowski meant more than this, and in his discussion of Sorel and Bergson he developed his thought more fully. His point was that there could be no approach to culture except through national tradition, and 'culture' here included all forms of knowledge. Our relationship to the world is such that we perceive everything not only in terms of human history but also of national history, and we delude ourselves if we think we can step outside this. Summarizing Sorel's views, with which he evidently agrees, Brzozowski writes:

The idea of knowledge as the contemplation of some reality above or beyond human life is a fiction: in no circumstances can thought be independent of the community in which it comes to birth, or express anything but a certain sum of human activity ... Metaphysics came into being as a surrogate for patriotism, as its destruction; today the mother-country comes into its own again ... We cannot communicate with anyone except through the nation: there is no road to life except through that body-spirit by which we are sustained and exalted ... Knowledge is international only inasmuch as it affects the conditions of life of every nation; it cannot be attained by any shallow mind, or by anyone who has not been involved in the stern and tragic aspects of the life of his own people ... Poland, our language and our soul are not accidental figures of inanimate, uncaring nature: they are a great reality in their own right, a fundamental aspect of being, and will remain so as long as there are Poles on this earth. There are things that are even older and more profound than nations, but man as such can only know himself through the nation, for there are no non-national, international organs of spiritual life. (*Ideas*, pp. 248–51)

This passage clearly goes far beyond what would have been

accepted by even the least orthodox of Marxists, suggesting as it does that even science, not to speak of other forms of culture, depends on the national tradition as a necessary medium. To Brzozowski these thoughts were simply an expression of his belief in the value of the nation as a continuous, irreducible reality in which all its members participated. It is hard to deny, however, that his views gave a handle to nationalist radicalism with all its dangerous consequences. The attempts of extreme Rightists to claim him for their own cannot be dismissed as simply mistaken, and it is not easy to acquit him of all blame for this. On the other hand, none of the Marxists was able, either in theory or in practical politics, to resolve the conflict between the internationalism of the workers' movement and the intrinsic value of the national community, except by arbitrarily denying the latter as Rosa Luxemburg did. Nor did any of them apparently suspect that history might have thrown up social forms which were not necessarily reducible to a single pattern.

5. *Brzozowski's Marxism*

There is no need to demonstrate that Brzozowski's ideas of the proletariat and of socialism were very different from Marx's. Moreover, he was certainly wide of the mark in interpreting Marx's intention as follows: 'Nobody can understand Marx's thought who does not feel that he identifies himself with certain constructions of his own such as "productive forces", the "concentration of capitalism", etc. These cognitive concepts are really myths that Marx uses in the first place to represent to himself the trend and content of his own will; he then endeavours to impose this will on others, to build it up and sustain it in them' (*Ideas*, pp. 347–8).

However, irrespective of the later reception of Brzozowski's ideas and the many arbitrary features in his interpretation of Marxism, it can be said that he was the first to attempt to divert Marxist thought from the channel in which it had been flowing without arousing any misgiving, and to impel it in the direction that was afterwards followed in different ways by Gramsci and Lukács. Both the evolutionists and the Kantians accepted as axiomatic that Marxism was an account of the social reality of capitalism and its future, as 'objective' as any other scientific theory. Almost all were likewise agreed that Marxism was based on a kind of common-sense realistic metaphysic and that it interpreted human existence and perception in the way generally assumed in evolutionist theories. Brzozowski, arguing from a shaky factual basis, challenged both these axioms and proposed an interpretation of his own which is remarkably close to the philosophic outlook of Marx's early writings that have since come to light. He contended that Marxism could not in principle treat the social process as 'natural' reality independent of the act of perceiving it. The understanding of the world was itself a factor in changing it, and therefore the determinist explanation of social phenomena, as usually understood, could not be maintained. From the Marxist point of view the social universe and the knowledge of that universe were one and the same, and therefore the course of history could not be 'predicted' like the weather.

In addition, Brzozowski argued, Marxism was incompatible with the idea of a world that preceded and produced human reality and was then able to imprint its own image, together with that of human existence, upon human minds. Man perceived the world from a human angle and could not impartially observe himself as a part of it, for this would mean casting off his human skin and his whole dependence on history. There was no knowledge independent of the human situation in which it was acquired, and we could not even so much as form a concept of the world 'in itself'. The subjection of our perceptions to historical and social conditions was irrevocable, and we must reconcile ourselves to this as to an absolute reality.

However, Brzozowski's religious 'conversion' threw doubt on the possibility of consistently maintaining this strictly anthropocentric viewpoint. It was not, as we have mentioned, a conversion in the usual sense, or a commonplace effect of mental stress in a man close to death. In a letter of 2 May 1910 to Witold Klinger he wrote that he felt no need for revelation, as Catholicism satisfied him intellectually. However, in another letter to Klinger on 19 April 1911, a few days before his death, he wrote: 'My Catholicism includes many important aspects of my Marxism, not to speak of Darwinism, Nietzscheanism and all the other "isms".' Brzozowski did not leave a detailed account of the last phase of his philosophical evolution, but if we regard his conversion as a part of this and not merely a psychological phenomenon, we may perhaps explain the background to it as follows.

The leitmotiv of Brzozowski's thought was the desire to safeguard the absolute value of humanity and endow it with absolute meaning. He expressed this desire first in the Fichtean–Nietzschean category of creativeness and 'action', which appeared to provide a basis for asserting the absolute independence of the creative individual spirit. He abandoned this viewpoint after coming to the conclusion that creativeness was self-contradictory if it did not spring from a sense of obligation towards existing tradition and the centres of social energy that have arisen in the course of history. To defend the subjective, lyrical autarky of the personal 'interior' as an absolute value meant abandoning the world to the indifferent laws of nature: creativity would no longer signify making one's mark on the world, but running away from it. The answer to this was the Marxist vision of man as a collective creator, asserting his own absolute significance in and through his struggle with the external world, and treating the whole of reality as a factor in his own situation. The meaning of the universe was referred wholly to human existence, which took on the role of Atlas and would not, indeed could not, know or perceive anything unrelated to its own self-regarding determination to endure as a species.

It turned out, however, that even this point of view did not suffice to vindicate the absolute meaning of human existence, simply because it was a meaning arbitrarily asserted by a being who could regard himself as absolute only in his manner of envisaging the world and not in Being itself. Since man is condemned to fight for mastery over nature and affirms his dignity in conflict with the non-human world, so that his existence is neither necessary nor independent, his ascription to himself of an absolute position in the scale of values may appear to be no more than a caprice, and may be cancelled by irrational forces if ever they should prove stronger. Faith in the absolute meaning of human existence can only be preserved if it is based on the non-contingent existence of God. Radical anthropocentrism is impossible and self-contradictory because it implies that human existence is at the same time both contingent and absolute.

This hypothetical reconstruction may indicate the road which led Brzozowski from activistic narcissism, via the collective solipsism of Marxist doctrine, to the Church as a historical organism through which humanity is in touch with unconditional Being and is able, in the only possible way, to maintain its own unconditional significance.

CHAPTER XII

Austro-Marxists, Kantians in the Marxist Movement, Ethical Socialism

1. The concept of Austro-Marxism

THE term 'Austro-Marxism' was coined in 1914 by the American socialist Louis Boudin and has become generally accepted; it was also used by members of the school itself. The Austro-Marxists are distinguished by certain common tendencies and particular interests; they were not, however, a 'school' in the scholastic or rabbinic sense of a group of scholars acknowledging or professing a set of tenets by which they can be identified.

The chief theoreticians of Austrian social democracy—Max Adler, Otto Bauer, Rudolf Hilferding, Karl Renner, Friedrich Adler—all considered themselves Marxists in the full sense of the term, but they did not regard Marxism as a closed, self-contained system. In the preface to the first volume of *Marx-Studien* (1904) the editors, Max Adler and Hilferding, declared that they were faithful to the spirit of Marx's work but were not necessarily concerned with fidelity to the letter. This does not, of course, mean much in itself, as such statements were common even among the most dogmatic and pious Marxists ('Marxism is not dogma', 'We must creatively develop the Marxian heritage', and so on). The degree of flexibility of the various schools of thought must be measured not by professions of this kind but by how far they were put into practice, and in this respect the Austrians differed essentially from typical orthodox believers. Not only did they emphasize the links between Marxism and earlier thinkers—especially Kant—whom Marx had not authorized as 'sources', but they also saw no harm in using ideas, concepts, and questions that had come to the fore since Marx's time in non-Marxist philosophy and sociology, especially among the neo-Kantians. This, in their view, was not a betrayal of the doctrine but a corroboration and enrichment of it. They were anxious to show that Marxism and socialist ideas were an integral part of the European cultural tradition, and preferred to emphasize not the novelty of Marxism but its affinities and points of contact with various trends of European philosophy and social thought.

Another characteristic of the Austro-Marxists was their interest in re-examining the broad theoretical and epistemological foundations of Marxism, which Kantian criticism in particular had shown to be full of gaps and loose ends. While accepting the basic principles, including the theory of value, the class struggle, and historical materialism, they did not agree that Marxism logically presupposed a materialist philosophy or that its validity depended on the philosophical arguments of Engels, to which they objected as 'uncritical' in the Kantian sense. Their general attitude was a transcendentalist one, opposed to positivism and empiricism. They held that Marxism was a scientific theory in the fullest sense, but that this did not mean it had to conform to the criteria of knowledge advanced by the empiricists: these were arbitrary and could not provide science with an 'absolute' foundation, simply because they ignored the Kantian questions.

All Marxist theoreticians were obliged to answer, expressly or otherwise, the question whether Marxism was a scientific theory or an ideology of the proletariat. The orthodox replied without embarrassment that it was both, and that the class and the scientific viewpoints converged perfectly; but on reflection this simple answer gave rise to doubts. If Marxism was a scientific theory, then in order to recognize its truth it was sufficient to apply the generally accepted rules of scientific thought, without having first to adopt any political or class standpoint: Marxism, like the theory of evolution, would be accessible to one and all. It was generally added, as a rider to this, that although Marxism was scientifically true it was bound to be resisted by the possessing classes, as it prophesied their downfall. Nevertheless, its truth did not depend logically on any political attitude but on the correct application of rules of intellectual procedure. While it also served the interests of the proletariat, this fact added nothing to its intellectual content and could not logically strengthen the case for accepting it. If, on the other hand, Marxism was the 'ideology of the proletariat', then its acceptance was not merely a theoretical position but a political commitment, and one was impossible without the other. Those who took this view—Lenin in particular—continued to emphasize the scientific nature of Marxism, but they treated it as an instrument of political warfare and refused to admit even in theory that its development had an immanent logic that was independent of politics and might in some circumstances conflict with political expediency. In spreading the doctrine, those of Lenin's school appealed purely to class-interests and not to intellectual principles independent of class. The Austrian Marxists took a precisely opposite view, appealing to all rational minds and not only those who were interested in the theory by reason of their class position. In the field of ethics, similarly, they stressed the intellectual and moral universality of Marxism. To be a Marxian socialist it was sufficient to think aright and to respect humane values that were not those of any particular class but would be embodied most perfectly in socialism. Their attitude on this point resembled that of Jaurès, though they were much more rigid doctrinally. They regarded Marxism as the continuation of the 'natural' development of social knowledge, and socialism as the 'natural' interpretation of traditional human values in terms of present-day society.

Here again, it was accepted doctrine that Marxism was valid for all mankind, but this principle was differently interpreted in practice. Since socialists also agreed that the working class was the unreplaceable champion of human values, it was possible to treat the 'universality' of Marxism as an inessential flourish and bend all one's forces towards annihilating the political adversary. Contrariwise, it was possible to take the view of the Austrians and others who, while accepting the principle of the class struggle, believed that everyone who took seriously the ideals of liberty, equality, and fraternity must, to be consistent with himself, adopt a socialist attitude whatever his own class-interests.

To the Austrians universality was a major principle and not a mere piece of rhetoric. Consequently, when they wrote about the society of the future they had less to say about authority and institutional changes than about the free self-government of workers. They regarded the collectivization of property as an instrument of socialist change but not as the whole of socialism, which also involved socialization of the productive process itself and thus the control of all economic life by the society of producers. They believed that the Kantian rule of treating the individual always as an end and not a means was fully in accord with the principles of socialism, and that socialism would be a parody of itself if it did not have as its sole aim the free development of human persons in association.

At the same time the Austrians were opposed to Bernstein's revisionism and belonged in politics to the radical wing of European Marxism, or rather constituted a radical variant of their own, which included the idea of a democratic dictatorship of the proletariat and rejected that of the gradual building of socialist institutions within capitalist society. During and after the First World War the main theoreticians of Austro-Marxism went different ways in politics. Hilferding and Renner became social democrats in the present-day sense, while Max Adler and Bauer (and also Friedrich Adler) maintained their position on the radical socialist Left, identifying with neither social democracy nor with Leninist communism, but unsuccessfully attempting to mediate between them.

In addition to the monthly *Der Kampf* (from 1907) the Austrian Marxists published the volumes of *Marx-Studien*, already mentioned, which contained some of the most important theoretical works of Marxist literature: Adler's *Kausalität und Teleologie im Streite um die Wissenschaft* (1904) and *Die Staatsauffassung des Marxismus* (1922), Bauer's *Die Nationalitätenfrage und die Sozialdemokratie* (1907), Hilferding's controversy with Böhm-Bawerk on Marx's theory of value (1904), and Hilferding's *Finanzkapital* (1910).

2. *The revival of Kantianism*

Austro-Marxism should not be identified with Marxist neo-Kantism. Those of the Austrians who concerned themselves with epistemology and ethics—i.e. especially Max Adler, but also Bauer to some extent—may, it is true, be regarded as belonging to the Kantian-Marxist movement, but Austro-Marxism as such has other distinguishing marks besides a leaning towards Kant, and many Kantian Marxists cannot be regarded as members of the Austrian school.

The curious phenomenon of Marxist neo-Kantianism, or Marxism with Kantian overtones, is to be viewed not only within the history of Marxism but as an important part of the general revival of Kant's influence which began in the 1860s and led in the next few decades to an almost complete monopoly of Kantianism in German universities. Among the first leaders of this movement were Friedrich Albert Lange and Otto Liebmann. Before long, however, Kantianism divided into various trends and schools which differed both in their interests and in the interpretation of Kant's philosophy.

Kantianism was not merely a philosophical trend but, above all, a bid to rehabilitate philosophy as such against the scientistic outlook of the positivists. Positivism and German materialism were not so much philosophies as attempts at philosophical suicide. They asserted that the methods used by natural science were the only means of attaining reliable knowledge, and that therefore philosophy either had no *raison d'être* or could only consist of reflection on the results of science. Kantianism, on the other hand, offered an intellectual method within which philosophy was not only legitimate but indispensable, but was at the same time limited in its aspirations: it did not pretend to be a metaphysic and was not exposed to the reproach levelled against Hegel, Schelling, and their successors that their ideas were vague, futile *Schwärmerei*, an exercise of fancy untrammelled by logic. The Kantians taught that philosophy should concentrate on the critique of knowledge; natural science did not interpret itself, and there was nothing in it which guaranteed the validity of its results and methods; particular sciences were concerned with knowing the world, but they did not study the fact of cognition, which required special investigation to prove its validity.

Kantianism thus shared with scientism a general opposition to metaphysics, but did not hold with its nihilistic approach to philosophy as a whole. In the second place, it was particularly concerned with the theory of ethic values. The purely empiricist outlook seemed to lead naturally to a radical moral relativism: as science observes and generalizes 'facts' it knows the world of values only as a collection of social or psychological phenomena and has no means of forming value-judgements, any set of which is equally right or wrong so far as science is concerned. Here too Kantianism seemed to offer a protection against relativism: it promised to show that the realm of facts was indeed quite distinct from that of values (so far the Kantians agreed with the positivists), but that human reason is able to define at least the formal conditions that our ethical judgements must satisfy, so that we are not at the mercy of the arbitrary workings of human caprice.

The Kantians, then, were opposed to all-embracing ontological constructions but held, in opposition to scientism, that the critique of knowledge must logically precede all particular knowledge if the latter is to claim universal validity.

3. Ethical socialism

Kantianism in its original version was psychological rather than transcendental. That is to say, the *a priori* conditions of knowledge that Kant investigated passed simply for universal attributes of the human mind, which is so constructed that we cannot perceive objects without imposing on them the forms of time and space, causality, substantial unity, etc. This, however, does not do away with relativism but only shifts it to a higher level: for it means that science's picture of the world is universally valid in the sense that it conforms to the requirements of the species-structure of man, but not that it would be equally valid for any possible rational being.

Consequently, the next generation of Kantists, especially the Marburg school (Hermann Cohen and Paul Natorp), passed from the psychological interpretation to a transcendental one, arguing that Kant's *a priori* forms were not psychologically or zoologically contingent and not peculiar to the human species or any other, but were inherent in reason as such and were necessary conditions of any act of cognition. Moreover, reason could not function on the basis of empirical 'facts' as ready-made data. Philosophical criticism was based on science not, as the positivists claimed, in order to 'generalize' its results but in the sense that it investigated the epistemological conditions that made science possible. The Marburg school looked mainly to mathematics and theoretical physics to confirm its generally rationalist outlook. Everything in our knowledge that has universal validity derives from the pure activity of reason and not from contingent, empirical material. Pure reason is the foundation of natural science, and every intelligible idea of reality relates to reality as known. This does not mean that reality is relative *vis-à-vis* individuals or the human species, but that it is relative *vis-à-vis* pure, impersonal thought. Kant's 'thing in itself' is only a regulative concept, a kind of fiction serving to organize knowledge, or else it can be dropped altogether without philosophy suffering any loss.

However, the interest that the Marburg school aroused among certain German and Austrian Marxists was due less to its radical apriorism than to its attempt to found socialist ethics on Kant's theory of practical reason. Cohen and Natorp did not consider themselves Marxists, but they were socialists and believed that socialism could only be grounded in ethical idealism.

Cohen held that Kant had provided socialism with a moral foundation by showing, in the first place, that ethics could not be based on anthropology, for man's natural drives could not give rise to the idea of humanity and of the unique value of the individual. Humanity was not an anthropological but a moral concept: i.e. we cannot admit on the basis of purely natural inclinations that we are parts of a collectivity in which every individual has equal rights. Secondly, Kantian ethics were independent of religious dogma and faith in God: belief in the authority of divine commandments was the basis of a legal system, not a specifically moral one. Only man was a moral lawgiver, but his law could claim universal validity provided it was based on the equality of human beings as objects of moral behaviour. The Kantian ethic that commanded us to treat every human being as an end and not a means was the very essence of socialism, for it meant that the worker must not be treated as a commodity, and this was the basis of the doctrine of socialist liberation. The socialist idea of human brotherhood, in which all men were equal and were free—freedom being defined within legal order—was a logical deduction from Kantian doctrine.

Cohen was one of the originators of the idea of 'ethical socialism', which was adopted by most of those who sought to graft the Kantian tradition on to the Marxian theory of social development. Ethical socialism may be reduced to two main tenets. The first, and the more general, is that even if the Marxian philosophy of history is true and socialism is therefore inevitable, it does not follow that socialism must be accepted as a good. The inevitability of an event or a process does not mean that it is necessarily desirable or that we must support it. In order to accept socialism in addition to foreseeing it, we must have some value-judgements based on grounds other than historical materialism or any other theory of history. The Kantian ethic can provide such a ground, as it shows that the socialist order in which society has no aims other than the human person is a real value. The second principle of ethical socialism, though this was not stated by all its adherents, was that ethical precepts have universal validity, i.e. they apply to all individuals without exception, both as subjects and as objects of moral behaviour. From this it follows that socialism as an ethical postulate is unrelated to social class, and that every human being as such, regardless of class interests, can only preserve his humanity by recognizing the moral value of the socialist ideal. This of course did not mean, as the orthodox claimed, that ethical socialism denied the existence of the class struggle, or that its adherents believed that moral propaganda would suffice to bring about socialist changes. It meant, however, that they could and should advocate the ideals of socialism by appealing to universal human values and not only to working-class interests.

4. Kantianism in Marxism

As already stated, there were many neo-Kantists who considered themselves (unlike Cohen) to be Marxists as well as socialists, and who in one way or another reconciled historical materialism and scientific socialism with Kantian ethics or epistemology.

This curious symbiosis of Kantian and Marxian ideas may be accounted for by various circumstances. Marxism was less isolated from the rest of the world than it afterwards became, and it was natural that philosophical trends which gained in popularity outside socialist circles should affect Marxist thinking also. In the same way, half a century later, when Communist orthodoxy became diluted after the death of Stalin, attempts were made to infuse new life into the withering tree by drawing on external sources such as existentialism, phenomenology, structuralism, and even Christianity. However, the immanent logic of the doctrine might have led to the same result even without external influence. The principle that socialism is a universal value and not merely a class one led naturally to speculation as to how the two aspects could be combined. The particular interest of the working class was, on the face of it, easy to determine, but it was not obvious what the universal human interest was, and the canonical texts did not throw much light on this question. It seemed clear, however, that as Marxism admitted such a category as this universal interest it must also presuppose the idea of man in general, undifferentiated by class, since otherwise it made no sense to say that socialism would satisfy the aspirations of humanity. The workers, who were the historical standard-bearers of the universal cause, were supposed to fight exclusively for their own interests, which would coincide with those of humanity in some undetermined millennial future. But if the universal interest was to be an intelligible category it must exist here and now in the shape of a tangible reality and specific claims: humanity must, at the present moment, be a visible attribute of every human individual, and there must be moral precepts applying to everyone and not only to comrades in arms. This inference was a hard one for those fundamentalists of Marxism who, in the name of revolutionary purity and intransigence, demanded the complete separation of the socialist movement from 'bourgeois' culture.

The neo-Kantians, seeking formulas to express the universalist aspect of Marxism, seized upon and developed what had been something of a dead letter or an empty piece of rhetoric in the Marxist canon. But in so doing they came up against the question of the relationship between the universal and the class aspects of socialism, and were accused by the orthodox in general of advocating class solidarity, glossing over mortal antagonisms, and giving a handle to reformist tendencies. As a rule these attacks were couched in vague generalities, but there was some truth in the charge, unspecific as it was, that neo-Kantianism played into the hands of the reformist wing of social democracy. The neo-Kantians, however, at all events in the Austrian school, did not reject the idea of revolution: on more than one occasion they argued that Kant's own views were not opposed to revolution either logically or in a historical sense, and they adduced as evidence his attitude to the Revolution in France. In this they were right: it cannot be deduced from Kant's philosophy that it is illegitimate to overthrow an existing regime by force. But the Kantians, in conformity with their transcendentalist premisses, defined socialism in terms of morality rather than institutions, and their theory thus suggested strongly that the moral changes which the workers were capable of bringing about 'here and now' under capitalism would amount to the actual building of socialism. This was anathema to the orthodox, who believed that all the working class could do under capitalism was to prepare the way for revolution: socialism could not be built piecemeal, it was indivisible and consisted in taking over political power and expropriating the capitalists. The effect of defining socialism in moral terms was to blur the sharpness of the transaction from one era to another. To this extent neo-Kantianism, like Bernstein's revisionism, reflected an optimistic faith in 'socialism by degrees', though many or even most of the neo-Kantian Marxists did not express this in so many words.

The neo-Kantian movement was probably also rooted in German national pride. The socialist idea turned out to be the most genuine product of the German Enlightenment, and not only Kant but Lessing, Fichte, Herder, Goethe, and Schiller were often cited among its ancestors.

An outstanding and typical philosopher of the movement was Karl Vorländer (1860–1928), who wrote several works comparing and synthesizing the views of Kant and Marx (for example, *Kant und der Sozialismus*, 1900; *Kant und Marx*, 1911; *Kant, Fichte, Hegel und der Sozialismus*, 1920; *Marx, Engels und Lassalle als Philosophen*, 1921). His arguments may be summed up under three main heads.

In the first place Vorländer singled out the aspects of Kant's social philosophy which had been absorbed into the socialist idea, though they also applied to any form of radical democracy. Kant, for instance, opposed all hereditary privilege; he was against national oppression and standing armies and in favour of popular representation, the separation of Church and State, freedom under law, and a world political organization. He regarded revolution as legitimate if its aim was to secure freedom. He rejected the conservative idea that people should not

be given freedom until they were mature enough to use it
properly—as if they could ever learn to do so under a despotic
system of government.

So far Kant was no more than a radical democrat, but, in the
second place, Vorländer maintained that he had anticipated
Marx's theory of progress by means of contradictions. Nature
used antagonisms to bring about their resolution: the development of mankind was the result of the interplay of selfish impulses which, thanks to the mechanism of mutual limitation, led
to increasing socialization. Wars, in the same way, would
ultimately lead, in historical evolution, to the establishment of
lasting peace; conflicts of all kinds brought home to men the
necessity of a legal order within which political freedom could
flourish. At the same time Kant was a pessimist who believed
that evil was ineradicable and that, as he put it, nothing quite
straight could ever be made out of the crooked wood of which
man consisted. But this pessimism, which assumed that laws
would always be necessary, did not, in Vorländer's view, conflict
with Marxian historiosophy.

Most important, however, was the third group of arguments,
showing that Kant's moral philosophy not only could but must
be incorporated into scientific socialism. Vorländer recognized
that Kant's mode of thought was rationalist while that of Hegel
and Marx was historical, but he believed the two could be
combined. Hegel's historicism had played an important part in
the origin of Marxism, by providing a basis for the evolutionist
view of history. Thanks to Darwin and Spencer, however, the
theory of universal evolution now had better foundations in
biology and did not need the aid of Hegelian metaphysics.
What was harmful in the Hegelian tradition, on the other hand,
was the rejection of the distinction between *Sein* and *Sollen*,
what is and what ought to be. In Hegel's schema the notion of
'oughtness' appeared *post festum*, as an awareness of impotence.
Marx had followed Hegel in ignoring the distinction, but without it there was no basis for the idea of socialism. Thus the theory
of historical materialism was not thought through and lacked
epistemological or moral foundations. The criticism of Kant by
Marx and Engels was of minor importance, as they clearly did
not know much about him: Engels's attack on the concept of the
'thing in itself' proved his complete misunderstanding of the

problem. If Marx's theory was to form the consciousness of a social movement, it must represent socialism as an aim to be striven for: but Marxism failed to validate socialism as a goal. In general, the idea of progress involved evaluation, and there could be no theory of progress except from a teleological point of view. Kant's moral theory was thus a natural completion of Marxism. The categorical imperative laid down that desires and trends were morally good in so far as they could be included in a single order of ends. This of course was only a formal definition of the conditions that any moral precept must fulfil: concrete rules were by nature not categorical, but must vary according to historical circumstances. Marxism explained what actions were effective in achieving the aim which it shared with Kantianism, i.e. universal brotherhood and solidarity together with recognition of the irreducible value of every human individual. There was no contradiction here between Kant and Marx, and the Kantian moral doctrine could be introduced into Marxism without affecting any of the latter's basic premisses. (Vorländer, like most Marxists of his time, understood historical materialism in a loose sense: economic conditions 'defined' consciousness but did not 'produce' it; human volition played a part in history, and there was interaction between the base and the superstructure.) All that was required was for Marxism to enunciate its own latent value-judgements, without which it was ineffectual and unconvincing.

These or similar arguments were used by all the Kantian Marxists: Ludwig Woltmann, Conrad Schmidt, Franz Staudinger, and the Austrian school. Their main drift was always the same: the scientific interpretation of society and history tells us what is or what will be; no historical or economic analysis can tell us what ought to be, yet we must have a measure by which to judge present conditions and determine our aims. The rightness of socialism is not due to the fact that its causes can be explained or that the working class is appointed to bring it about; things are not admirable simply because they cannot be otherwise than they are—as Staudinger put it, a rotten apple can only be the way it is, but it is rotten for all that.

The Kantians opposed the Darwinian or biological interpretation of man as a being defined by the sum of his 'natural' needs. If he can be fully explained within the natural order, they argued, there was no basis for socialism: nature knows nothing of freedom, and we cannot infer from the natural world that man ought to be free. If, on the other hand (so Staudinger continued), freedom is a postulate which is necessarily inherent in the idea of man, then we must also postulate a social order ensuring the same degree of freedom to everyone. This was impossible with private ownership of the means of production, for then one individual could decide whether another was to live or starve. Hence socialism was the logical consequence of the demand that man should be able to realize his own nature, which was rational and therefore free.

The neo-Kantian Marxists differed as to how far Kant's moral philosophy could or should be embodied in socialist doctrine. Vorländer and Woltmann were Kantists in the full sense, holding that Marx's theory of society should be completed by the whole of Kant's moral and epistemological philosophy. Conrad Schmidt, however, believed that while Kant's distinction between the order of will and that of reason must be maintained, his formal imperative was not a sufficient ground for ethics, which must be based on the totality of social needs defined by changing historical conditions. If we consider what enables man to realize himself as a free, rational being we find that no moral precepts can have absolute value, for different courses of action favour the attainment of the 'ultimate goal' in different circumstances. The Kantian ethic states that a moral duty must be performed simply because it is a duty and for no other reason; but to a socialist the only good consists in man and whatever is to man's advantage, and moral duty can only be defined by social needs. This viewpoint is already one of ethical utilitarianism, and departs fundamentally from Kantian doctrine.

The question of the relationship between Kant and socialism was debated for many years in all the German-language organs of social democracy (*Die Neue Zeit, Sozialistische Monatshefte, Vorwärts, Der Kampf*). In 1904 the centenary of Kant's death was commemorated by the entire working-class Press of Germany and Austria. The orthodox, particularly Kautsky, Mehring, and Plekhanov, saw in the glorification of Kant a drastic breach with Marxist tradition. Mehring and Kautsky accepted the view that a descriptive judgement was to be distinguished from an evaluative one, but they did not see why this should oblige Marxists to seek support in Kantian philosophy. Kant's social desiderata, they argued, could perfectly well be met within the framework of bourgeois democracy and were in no way specifically socialist. The fact that the socialist movement had its own ethical basis was clear enough, but gave no support to Kantian arguments: ethics in whatever form were defined by historical circumstances and were not subject to unchanging rules. The ideals of the working class were explained by history, and it could be shown that they were not merely utopian but were in line with the general course of social development. This was all men needed to know: in particular, Marxists had no need of Kant's unhistorical imperative or the absurd assumption of free will.

As we saw in discussing Kautsky's polemics, it did not occur to orthodox Marxists to put the question: given that certain ideals and values arise in society as the 'natural' product of interests, what motives other than interest can lead the individual to accept them? What ground have we for saying that the socialist ideal, besides being a product of the class situation of the proletariat, is also worthy of support? If, as Marx held, socialism is not only the cause of the working class in particular, but the fulfilment of humanity and the promised flowering of all specifically human potentialities, how can we manage without universal human values? How can we consistently refuse to believe that our moral postulates include non-historical factors that are not transient but belong to the permanent, unchanging idea of humanity? But, on the other hand, is it not contrary to the spirit of Marx's teaching and to his own words to maintain that any values are universal and do not depend on history for their validity?

This dispute, as already stated was insoluble in the ideological context in which it took place. The Kantians had on their side the traditional distinction between the order of facts and that of values, which the orthodox accepted without drawing from it the proper logical conclusions. They for their part could quote Marx's derisive remarks about non-historical values, and they were rightly apprehensive of the social consequences of a doctrine that involved moral standards and judgements independent of class and in effect suggested that the fight for socialism should be based on universal values rather than class interests. The Kantians admitted that Marx had refused to distinguish between facts and values, *Sein* and *Sollen*, but they regarded this as a survival of Hegelianism which could be jettisoned without harm to the essence of his doctrine. They did not realize that the absence of this distinction is fundamental to Marxism and that in consequence the whole argument on both sides was being conducted in non-Marxist terms (historical determinism versus moralism). A few Marxists felt obscurely that the issues were wrongly formulated from the Marxist point of view, but none of them was able to clear the matter up. This was done many years later by Lukács, who pointed out that according to Marx (1) the working class comprehends social phenomena only in the very act of revolutionizing the world; (2) in general, knowledge of society is the self-knowledge of a society; and (3) therefore the understanding of the world and its transformation are not contrasted with each other (as in the relationship between natural science and its technological application) but are one and the same act, while the distinction between understanding and evaluation is a secondary abstraction that distorts the original unity.

5. The Austro-Marxists: biographical information

Max Adler (1873–1937), a lawyer by profession, spent his life in Vienna, where in addition to practising as a barrister he wrote learned works and engaged in party activity. He was not a leader of the organizing type and did not stand for Parliament before the war, though he was a deputy for a short time after it. His fellow socialists regarded him as a 'theoretician' in a somewhat pejorative sense, a scholar weaving a skein of argument for the intellectual pleasure of doing so. However, apart from his voluminous writings he was one of the main founders of party education in Austria, and with Renner and Hilferding set up a workers' school in Vienna, at which he taught. His books and articles deal with all the vital problems of socialism in his day, but his main concern was to consolidate the philosophical basis of Marxism, which he believed had been much neglected in socialist literature. His philosophical works, written in a heavy and complicated style, revert again and again to certain themes, in particular the 'social *a priori*' and the transcendental basis of the social sciences. These matters are discussed in his first book *Kausalität und Teleologie im Streite um die Wissenschaft* (1904) and recur in *Marxistische Probleme* (1913), *Das Soziologische in Kants Erkenntniskritik* (1924), *Lehrbuch der materialistischen Geschichts-auffassung*, Part I (1930), and the last of his works published during his lifetime, *Das Rätsel der Gesellschaft* (1936). Other permanent topics of his writing are state organization and demo-cracy (*Demokratie und Rätesystem*, 1919; *Die Staatsauffassung des Marxismus*, 1922; *Politische und soziale Demokratie*, 1926), and the subject of religion is touched on incidentally in may of his works. The orthodox accused him of compromising with religion; Bauer wrote in a memoir that Adler could never reconcile himself to the idea that the human spirit was mortal, and that he sought in the Kantian theory of time and space justification for the belief in a timeless existence of the mind.

Throughout his life Max Adler belonged to the left wing of social democracy. During the war, unlike Viktor Adler, he remained a member of the minority group which condemned the opportunism of the 'social patriots'. His attitude to the October Revolution was similar to that of Rosa Luxemburg: he denounced Bolshevik despotism but believed in the value of the soviets and thought that in altered circumstances the system in Russia would prove capable of democratic change.

Otto Bauer (1881–1938) was more of a political leader than Max Adler, but also made his name as an eminent theoretician. Born in Vienna, the son of bourgeois Jewish parents, he became a socialist at an early age and was soon one of the party's chief theorists and publicists. His first and also his most im-portant theoretical work, *Die Nationalitätenfrage und die Sozial-demokratie* (1907), is the best treatise on nationality problems to be found in Marxist literature and one of the most significant products of Marxist theory in general. After the 1907 elections Bauer became secretary to the parliamentary socialist party; at the same time he taught at the workers' college and wrote for the party Press, especially *Der Kampf* and the *Arbeiterzeitung*. Called up at the outbreak of war, he served as a lieutenant for a few months and was then captured by the Russians. During his imprisonment, which lasted until the February Revolution, he wrote the philosophical work *Das Weltbild des Kapitalismus*, which was published in 1924. Returning to Austria in September 1917 he joined the anti-war wing of the party and, in expectation of the collapse of the monarchy, defended against Renner the principle of national self-determination. After the break-up he was for a short time Foreign Minister of Austria, but resigned when it became clear that there was no hope of the Anschluss with Germany. He was more hostile to the Bolshevik revolution than Adler, holding that the attempt to establish socialism in a semi-feudal country was virtually bound to lead, as in fact it did, to the despotism of a small minority, i.e. the political apparatus, over the proletariat and the rest of society (*Bolschevismus oder Sozialdemokratie?*, 1920). Subsequently he reverted more than once to Russian questions, denouncing Stalinist terror, the annihilation of culture, and universal mutual spying as a system of government. In his last years, however, as the Fascist threat increased, he became less intransigent towards the Soviet Union. Even when most critical he had emphasized that he hoped to see democratic changes in Russia as the economic situation improved.

When the socialist movement broke in two after the First World War, Bauer did not identify with the reformist branch of social democracy but was one of those who sought to carry on the tradition of the socialist Left as established at the Zimmerwald Conference. The Austrian party was the main initiator of the short-lived organization known as the International Working Union of Socialist Parties, or more familiarly the 'Two-and-a-Half International'. This body, composed of a number of European socialist parties or groups, was founded at Vienna in February 1921 in the hope of mediating between social democrats and communists. Its secretary was Friedrich Adler, and among its leaders were Georg Ledebour (Germany) and Jean Longuet (France). Within two years it became clear that there was no hope of a reconciliation with the communists, and the Vienna Union was reabsorbed into the main social democratic organization.

Until 1934, when the counter-revolution took place in Austria, Bauer continued to be a popular and respected party leader and theorist. He believed that the socialists could in time achieve power without violence or civil war, and he tried to win over the peasants to socialism. In 1923 he published *Die österreichische Revolution*, a study of the fall of the Dual Monarchy. Unlike Renner, he did not believe that the socialists could, by taking part in coalition governments, bring about proletarian rule 'by degrees'. He had no wish, therefore, to share power with the Christian Social party, nor did the latter evince any desire for collaboration; when Bauer proposed to Dollfuss (Chancellor from 1932) a coalition against the Fascist threat, he met with a refusal. In 1933 the Austrian parliament was dissolved and the government's provocative actions drove the workers into a general strike: the short civil war which followed ended in the triumph of reaction and the suppression of the socialist party. Bauer fled to Czechoslovakia and, with a group of *émigrés*, endeavoured to save what was left of Austrian socialism by founding a new party. In May 1938 he moved to Paris, where he died soon after.

Karl Renner (1870–1950) came from a peasant family and, like Adler and Bauer, studied law in Vienna. He wrote works on the theory of the state and law and the national question: *Staat und Nation* (1899, under the pseudonym Synoptikus), *Der Kampf der österreichischen Nationen um den Staat* (1902, under the pseudonym Rudolf Springer), *Grundlagen und Entwicklungsziele der österreichisch-ungarischen Monarchie* (1904). In party politics he was, from the outset, closer than Bauer to the German revisionists. He emphasized that the working class should value partial gains and aim at playing an increasing part in governing the state, not at violent revolution. More of a parliamentarist than a party leader, he was in turn Chancellor, Minister of Home Affairs, and Minister of Foreign Affairs of the first Austrian Republic, and sat in Parliament until 1934. He survived Austrian Fascism, the Anschluss, and the War in political inactivity, and in 1945 became the first Chancellor of the post-war Republic; in the same year he was raised to the office of President, which he occupied until his death.

Rudolf Hilferding (1877–1943), a doctor by profession, was perhaps the most eminent Marxist writer on political economy during the period of the Second International. In 1904 he published in *Marx-Studien* his defence of Marx's theory of value (*Böhm-Bawerks Marx-Kritik*), and in 1910 the classic *Das Finanzkapital*, a general theory of the world economy in the imperialist era. From 1906 he lived in Germany, where he taught in the party school at Berlin and edited the journal *Vorwärts*. During the war he belonged to the anti-war group of socialists (the USPD), and with the rest of this group he rejoined the SPD after

1918. He was German Finance Minister in 1923 and 1928, and a member of the Reichstag. On Hitler's accession to power he emigrated and lived in Switzerland and France. Caught by the Nazi police during the Second World War, he died in the concentration camp at Buchenwald or, according to other sources, committed suicide in a Paris prison.

Strictly speaking, the term 'Austro-Marxism' denotes a group whose activities belong to the years 1904–14, but all its chief members were also active throughout the interwar period. Their works are today largely forgotten, though particular texts are revived from time to time; some historical studies have been devoted to this variety of Marxism, which has perhaps made more original contributions to the history of the doctrine than any other.

6. *Adler: the transcendental foundation of the social sciences*

Adler, as we have said, endeavoured to apply Kantian transcendentalism to the theoretical reconstruction of historical materialism. In his first work he set out in a condensed form the theory which he maintained throughout his life, amending or supplementing it from time to time. He began by criticizing the neo-Kantians of the Baden school, i.e. Rickert and Windelband, and also Stammler, Dilthey, and Münsterberg. The point on which he joined issue with them was their view concerning the special methodology of the humanistic sciences (*Geisteswissenschaften*) and in particular the legitimacy and necessity of a teleological viewpoint in regard to them. (The term *Geisteswissenschaften* was used by Dilthey; Rickert spoke of *Kulturwissenschaften*, Windelband of 'idiographic' sciences, and Stammler of social sciences). The argument of the new school of thought was that natural science endeavours to reduce its object to what is universal in it, i.e. science is concerned with a particular phenomenon only as the exemplification of a timeless universal law. In this way physical science explains phenomena by reducing them to abstractions. The study of human affairs, on the other hand, is concerned with unique and unrepeatable phenomena, historical events and individuals, values and purposes. Its task is not to explain its object, but to understand it in terms of the motives and experiences of the human beings concerned.

Human science is concerned with man as a *stellungnehmendes Wesen*, a being who adopts a certain attitude to events, and the human world cannot be described without reference to this motivational coefficient. Natural science, it is true, also studies man as an experiencing subject, but this naturalistic psychology is concerned with recurrent phenomena and regular associations, and is therefore no part of human science. There are laws of psychology, but a 'historical law' is a contradiction in terms. Moreover, according to Windelband and Rickert, the teleological viewpoint applies to natural science too, though in a restricted sense. All knowledge involves the adoption and rejection of judgements, and these activities are related to truth-values as a supreme objective. Cognition as a form of purposive human behaviour is concerned with values, and to recognize truth as a value is to recognize it as an object of general obligation: when I acknowledge a judgement I imply that it is everyone else's duty to acknowledge it too. No investigation in the field of natural science can arrive at this cognitive obligation, and the 'necessity' which truth imposes is not one of causation but of duty. The value of truth does not derive from science but is a precondition of it: it must therefore flow from an obligation founded in a consciousness transcending the individual. It is not the case that judgements are true because they tell us what reality is 'truly' like: on the contrary, we recognize as real that which ought to be acknowledged in judgements: truth is a value, and reality is relative to truth. The object of knowledge is constituted in a transcendental obligation. Again, it makes no sense to suppose that we know reality as it is in itself by means of representations, for we can only compare representations with one another and not with an object known in some other way. Existence is not an object of representation but is only the predicate of an existential judgement. It cannot therefore be said that our knowledge is directed towards Being, but only that the rules of thought furnish us with criteria for asserting or denying the existence of things. 'The being of objects is founded in obligation' (Rickert).

Adler's attack was directed against these arguments. He conceded that truth could not consist in conformity to an object 'given' independently of its constitution in the cognitive act, for we can know nothing of objects in this sense. 'That this world which is common to us all does not derive its objective form from the fact that "realities", unhappily unknown, are all about us and impart themselves in the form of "qualities", but that what we come firmly up against is nothing but our own mind, i.e. the invariable rule by which representations in it are associated —this is a thought which appears almost monstrous at first, but which finally becomes self-evident and allows us to repose in tranquillity' (*Kausalität und Teleologie*, p. 286). Adler also accepts the Kantian view that an object is a unity of representational associations and that space, time, and our own behaviour in the world are only possible thanks to forms of apperception. He regards this as perfectly consistent with Marx's doctrine, which is not one of naïve realism and has little but the name in common with materialism. But he disputes other points of the neo-Kantian theory of knowledge, in particular that the laws of thought can be regarded as moral commands or that the distinction between truth and falsehood, and not merely between the affirmation and denial of judgements, is rooted in obligation.

It seemed clear to Adler that Marx's doctrine had nothing to do with materialism as a metaphysical system: misunderstandings on this point were due to the misleading term 'historical materialism' and also to the fact that Marx felt a certain affinity with eighteenth-century materialism—not because he shared its view of the world, but because he saw it as an ally against barren idealistic speculation. Materialism had no foundation either in Marxism or in the natural sciences, which were ontologically neutral and had themselves demolished the unintelligible abstraction called 'matter'. The term 'historical materialism' had also encouraged the mistaken idea that Marx regarded economic development as a kind of soulless 'matter', of which human minds and wills and civilization were the mere passive 'reflection'. This led to the false criticism that Marxism ignored the individual and regarded social development as an autonomous process independent of human beings (Lorenz Stein), or that it treated economics as the only 'real' phenomenon and consciousness as an unnecessary duplication of it (Stammler). These, said Adler, were absurd charges, and none of the most orthodox Marxists, such as Cunow, Kautsky, and Mehring, had understood historical materialism in this manner. Marxism was a theory—the first scientific theory—of social phenomena, which it studied from the viewpoint of causal connections while fully realizing that in the world of man these connections are effected by purposive action and by the agency of human intentions, aims, and values. As a theory of this kind, based on experience, Marxism was neither logically nor historically bound up with any particular ontology, such as materialism, but was ontologically neutral like any other science. As to the basic epistemological question of the relation between experience and thought, Marx and Kant converged. The Kantian *a priori* categories were the components of experience that gave it universal validity. If the principles of the association of representations were not contained in experience itself, science would be impossible: this was Kant's view, and it was also Marx's. His criticism of political economy was a 'critique' in the Kantian sense, i.e. a search for instruments of cognition that would enable human knowledge to claim universal validity. This could be seen in Marx's 'Introduction' (the Introduction to *Grundrisse*, published in *Die Neue Zeit*), where he showed how the concrete could be reconstructed out of abstract notions, while emphasizing that this was not, as in Hegel, a description of how the concrete actually arose but only of how it came to be grasped in cognition. The concrete whole with which science was concerned was the product of thought, a conceptual creation and not the content of perception. Did Marx not say in Volume III of *Capital* that science would be unnecessary if the form of a phenomenon coincided with the 'essence'? Clearly the social sciences as Marx conceived them had their own *a priori* categories, the existence of which confirmed the Kantian critique. Marx himself did not observe this analogy, which showed that it was grounded in logic and was not a matter of intellectual borrowing.

Such, then, is the first sense of the 'social *a priori*'. In social investigation human thought presupposes synthesizing forms that are involved in the process of experience but do not derive from it: on the contrary, it is only through them that experience can have universal validity.

But this, Adler continues, does not mean that these formal *a priori* conditions of experience have the character of an obligation, as Rickert and Windelband maintain. Admittedly human acts, including cognitive ones, are purposive in their nature, and we strive after truth as a value. But the fact that truth presents itself to us as an object to be attained does not mean that the aspect of purpose is contained in the concept or definition of truth. If we regard something as true we ascribe to it universal validity, not merely validity for ourselves, and we expect others to acknowledge it; but this does not mean that its truth depends logically on this requirement of ours or on our affirmation of it. Experience may compel me to acknowledge certain judgements; but this is a logical compulsion, not a moral duty, for the latter would imply that I can perform it or not as I choose, whereas I cannot reject a judgement that my senses force upon me. The teleological view of the neo-Kantists rests on a confusion between the veracity that belongs to knowledge, and the desire for truth as an aspect of purposive behaviour: the former of these is in fact quite independent of the latter.

Adler thus adheres to the traditional concept of truth, which, while not presupposing any metaphysic of the world 'in itself', implies that cognitive acts do not constitute truth but ascertain it.

The fact, however, that in addition to 'contingent' truths (in Leibniz's sense: i.e. those that we can imagine not being so, like all empirical truths) we also have knowledge of the 'necessary' truths of mathematics and logic, indicates that the mind to which this necessity appears must also be something necessary and not a mere contingent datum. And indeed, if we consider the matter, we find that it is impossible to conceive such a thing as 'the absence of consciousness'. It is erroneous to say that we know of a past in which there was no consciousness in the world, for the past devoid of consciousness cannot present itself except to consciousness. A conscious being cannot know what 'unconsciousness' is: the absence of consciousness cannot be a content of consciousness. This, however, is an intellectual necessity, not an ontological one: it does not mean that consciousness as a thing or substance is necessary, but that the content of all our knowledge necessarily includes consciousness.

Again, this necessary consciousness is not the empirical self or contingent subjectivity: it is consciousness in general, the transcendental unity of apperception. Contrary to the system of Hegel or Fichte, transcendental consciousness is not a metaphysical entity, an autonomous Being or 'spirit'. It is known to us only through the individual consciousness, as being that which enables the individual empirical consciousness to ascribe universality to its own content. Consciousness in general belongs to the ego, but is not personal: the ego is not the possessor of consciousness in general, but the form in which it manifests itself.

The theory of 'consciousness in general' points to the second sense of the 'social *a priori*'. When we discover in our own consciousness a claim to universality and the satisfaction of that claim, we discover at the same time the social character of our own ego. We find that the existence of other people, and therefore the social tie, does not require to be deduced from perception but is directly 'given' in the very manner in which our cognitive acts are performed. All empirical subjectivity is 'socialized' in its every act, and is able to perceive this without going outside itself: there is therefore no problem of solipsism, and no need to postulate a 'social fact' as something secondary to the immediate data of experience. Society is directly evident to the ego thanks to the latter's own transcendental components.

Thus the Marxian concept of man as a social being is seen to be best founded in the category of transcendental consciousness, which shows that socialization is not merely a historical fact but is in an integral part of the constitution of consciousness, an attribute of every individual *qua* human. The content of my ego presupposes the community of mankind—a fact already perceived, though not theoretically demonstrated, by Comte, who regarded individuality as a fiction and society as the only reality. Marx did not formulate his thoughts in this way, but he too believed that the content of every individual consciousness was necessarily socialized; language itself, in which that content is expressed, is of course a social inheritance. Kant's theory supplies this idea with an epistemological basis. There is a profound analogy between Kant's refutation of the apparent substantiality of the self, and Marx's critique of commodity fetishism and rejection of the 'reified' appearances of social phenomena. The life of a society is not secondary to that of the individuals composing it, but is a network of relationships comprehending those individuals. Man is a social being in his very essence, and not simply because he associates with others for reasons of instinct or calculation. Just as, in Marx's analysis, the apparent objectivity of commodities resolves itself into social relations, so the appearances of personal consciousness resolve themselves into a general consciousness (*das Bewusstsein überhaupt*) linking individuals with one another. Whether we know it or not, in communication with others we relate our thoughts to transcendental consciousness. A reality which cannot be directly perceived, but is accessible to critical analysis, is manifested in the relations between human beings, just as value is manifested in exchange-value.

To quote Adler once more:

Truth in respect of content (*die inhaltliche Wahrheit*) not only presupposes logically the intellectual compulsion of the individual consciousness in the sense explained above, but would also be unthinkable as a historico-social product, if it were not that the peculiar nature of human thought whereby it is both a separate, individual consciousness and also a manifestation of consciousness in general constitutes the transcendental ground which alone makes possible the interaction and co-operation of human beings in the process of bringing about the knowledge of truth. For it is only thus that what is intellectually necessary becomes universally valid, so that there is a community of human existence (*Verbundenheit menschlichen Wesens*) to which every empirical individual consciousness can be related, in its intercourse with others, as to a unity comprising them all. If, on the other hand, the individual in his concrete historical reality is regarded as something altogether prior to social life, there is no possible way in which he can achieve such a union with his fellow-man as to consider him as a subject and not an object. It is a complete misunderstanding—and indeed atrocious metaphysics, since it is essentially a revival of the notorious dogma that everything can come out of nothing—to suppose that the unity of the social tie can come about as the result of human beings living in communities, in such a way as to be the mere sum or integration of those individuals. In order to grasp the fundamental significance of the concept of 'consciousness in general', and also to bring out the specific novelty of Marx's basic idea of the socialization (*Vergesellschaftung*) of the individual, it cannot be sufficiently emphasized that the true problem of society does not originate in the association (*Verbundenheit*) of a number of human beings, but simply and solely in the individual consciousness.' (*Kausalität und Teleologie*, p. 380)

This passage indicates, in somewhat involved language, the two basic concepts denoted by the term 'social *a priori*'. In the first place, knowledge cannot lay claim to universal, objective validity unless we accept the category of transcendental consciousness, providing every individual consciousness with a repertoire of 'necessary forms' for the organization of experience. Secondly, the social tie can only be understood if we regard it as grounded in the existence of the individual, not merely created as the answer to empirical needs. Each individual, as it were, bears the whole of humanity in his own self-consciousness. Transcendental consciousness thus performs a double function: it explains the unity of human beings and the tie between them, and thus the concept of 'man in society', and it shows how knowledge can be a general possession and a matter of obligation, not merely a collection of relative, contingent perceptions by a multiplicity of minds. On both these points Kant (at all events in the Marburg interpretation) and Marx (as interpreted by Adler) are at one. Transcendental consciousness, it should be added, is not a separate, substantive entity but is that part of each individual consciousness which has an impersonal character.

The universal validity of the moral law can be accounted for in a similar way: it too could not exist if it were not rooted in the 'general consciousness'.

It would seem that in Adler's view relations between people are logically prior to people themselves: this can be regarded as a particular exemplification of the general idea of the Marburg school which, in contrast to the common-sense or 'substantialist' view, regarded things as the product of relations and not the other way about.

All this, however, does not constitute an argument for the view that the social as opposed to the physical sciences should be based on teleology and not on causality. According to Adler the study of social phenomena is based on cause and effect like any other, even though the possibility of social relations and the 'form of social life' itself are presupposed before we can begin to study anything and cannot themselves be causally explained. But the primacy of 'consciousness in general' applies to physical science also: nature as an object of study is only possible on account of the formal regularities of thought. In the case of social phenomena it is clear enough that what happens involves human action, purposes, and values, but this is a form of causality, not a denial of it. We cannot distinguish nature from civilization on the ground that one is concerned with causes and the other with aims, or that the study of the latter is teleological, or that the first has to do with abstract laws and the second with unique occurrences. In both cases our study is objective, concerned with cause and effect and with discovering general rules; in both, the object is constituted by *a priori* conditions of knowledge. The only difference is that in humanistic studies we treat connections and events as consciously experienced, though they are causally conditioned as well.

As long as we are concerned only with what is simply given by the operation of consciousness in general, there comes into view a huge realm of existence that is given simply as natural existence (*Natur-dasein*); and conscious beings are part of this in so far as they are merely considered as parts of nature. But when we turn our minds to the question how this natural world is given, how it is conceived, judged, worked upon and made use of, and how in all these respects it is possible for so many individuals, acting quite independently of one another, to achieve agreement and mutual understanding even in their most hostile acts, then, in addition to the bare natural fact that exists only for each particular act of knowledge and is therefore isolated from all others, we become aware of that other great fact of the unique, thorough-going community and unity (*der eigenartigen durchgängigen Ver-bundenheit und Ineinssetzung*) of human beings that know and act upon their knowledge. (*Kausalität und Teleologie*, p. 427)

Adler's theory is not as clear as could be desired, but its general trend is plain enough. Since the transcendental consciousness is not a 'spirit' in the sense of an impersonal, self-existing substance, but exists only in the individual consciousness in such a way as to make it essentially identical with every other, it might seem that it amounts to no more than the collectivity of judgements comprising the whole of 'necessary knowledge', i.e. synthetic *a priori* judgements in the Kantian sense. If so, however, the question 'How does our knowledge acquire the character of necessity?' (apart from that of analytical judgements) has been formulated but not answered. If we reply that this necessity derives from the transcendental consciousness, and if this consciousness is in fact nothing but a collection or repository of necessary judgements, then we have not answered any question at all.

But this criticism of Adler's argument does not apply only to him. He is right in holding, like all transcendentalists, that the universal validity of our knowledge, its certainty irrespective of contingent historical and biological facts, cannot be demonstrated empirically: as both Kant and Husserl maintain, there can be no experimental epistemology. It follows that in the realm of empirical knowledge we are condemned not only to uncertainty but also to the impossibility of finding out how much of our knowledge is valid and how much depends on accidents of the human condition. The Marburg neo-Kantians were aware of this, and they saw that the psychological interpretation of Kant is no cure for the relativity of knowledge. But if so, it does not follow that we have any other means of overcoming this relativism. We must also take it that rationalism cannot justify the claim of knowledge to objectivity and must be content with hypothetical and unverifiable theories of transcendental consciousness that only appear to provide a refuge from scepticism and relativism, by introducing an arbitrary *deus ex machina* of epistemology.

Adler's ascription of transcendentalism to Marx is also highly questionable. True, the idea of 'socialized man' implied for Marx that the human individual as such was, as it were, a 'carrier' of social Being and only knew himself through society. But this does not imply any view as to how the socialization comes about. There is no ground for saying that according to Marx it cannot be explained historically but only by some kind of transcendental consciousness. As for the *a priori* conditions of our knowledge of society, it is true that Marx drew a distinction, which he never explained precisely, between the essence of a thing and a phenomenon; he also says that social processes cannot be theoretically reconstructed by accumulating single observations, but only by using conceptual instruments that precede observations. Marx does not explain, however, where these instruments are to come from or how their use is to be justified. To imagine that they are something in the nature of Kantian categories is quite arbitrary and is not an interpretation of Marx, but an introduction of quite different ingredients into his theory. Nor is there any analogy between Marx's analysis of commodity fetishism and Kant's critique of the substantive ego. Marx reduces the relations between commodities to relations between people, but this does not mean he thought that human beings were secondary to their own social ties. Individuals under capitalism were, in point of fact, dissolved amid the anonymous forces of communal life, but this was a criticism of capitalism and not something that had to endure for ever. Socialism, according to Marx, meant a return to individuality and the conscious treatment of one's own powers as belonging to society; but the object of this was to overcome the anonymous character of individual life resulting from alienation, i.e. from social processes escaping the control of 'real individuals'. Thus the critique of commodity fetishism had the opposite meaning to what Adler supposed.

Moreover, Adler's interpretation of the purposive character of social phenomena, and his critique of the neo-Kantians, are so expressed that it is not clear in what respect he disagrees with the purely naturalist interpretation of society, against which he is constantly protesting. If his argument is that social phenomena are subject to universal determinism in the same way as all others, while their peculiar character lies in the fact that they are experienced and that they present themselves as purposive actions, then these are propositions with which the most unbending 'mechanist' would agree. No one could deny that men experience the events they take part in or that their actions are governed by various motives, desires, and values. The radical determinist merely claims that this makes no difference to the fact that these motives, desires, and experiences are conditioned just as inevitably as all other events. Adler seems to accept this view, and consequently his statement that causality in human affairs operates 'through' the purposive actions of human beings does not differ from out-and-out 'mechanism'.

7. Adler's critique of materialism and the dialectic

It is clear that from the point of view of Engels's schema Adler counts as an 'idealist', at least in the sense in which Kant is so described. (The object of cognition is constituted in and by the act of cognition; transcendental consciousness is prior to any 'nature' that we can talk about intelligibly; the category of 'matter' is an absurdity.)

In all his philosophical writings Adler repeated the same thought: Marx's theory is a scientific reconstruction of social phenomena, and is ontologically neutral (or, as he calls it, 'positivist') in the same way as any other science. It is not based on any materialist metaphysic, which in any case is an untenable doctrine. Adler criticizes materialist philosophy at length in his *Lehrbuch der materialistischen Geschichtsauffassung*, where he argues on similar lines to Fichte. It is impossible to derive consciousness from 'physical motion', since physical motion is only given to us as the content of consciousness. Philosophy cannot take as its starting-point the question of the primacy of mind or nature, since Kant has taught us that reason cannot pronounce upon the world until it has examined its own right to do so. Our starting-point must be the 'critical' question of the possibility and validity of cognition. But, if we put this question without metaphysical prejudice, we see that any concept of reality that we can meaningfully create relates to reality constructed in conceptual forms: from no fact of experience can we deduce anything like the 'thing in itself'. In this sense it can be said that everything *is* consciousness, which does not mean that it is the content of the empirical self: on the contrary, the cognitive acts of the self are directed towards a reality that is common to all men, since the self participates in transcendental consciousness and is merely a form of the latter's activity. Here Adler joins issue with the materialism of Lenin, who seeks to refute idealism by arguing that the world existed before men and hence before the appearance of consciousness, and that consciousness is a function of the brain, which is a physical object. These, Adler retorts, are naïve and uncritical arguments. The existence of the world 'before' consciousness is given only in the form of a certain content of consciousness, and in the same way the brain is not known to us as the producer of our consciousness, but only indirectly through consciousness itself. The theory of 'reflection' is a trivial *petitio principii*. It first defines impressions as a reflection of the world, and then argues that since this is so, there must be a world to be reflected; but we cannot define impressions in this way without assuming some previous knowledge of the world.

Adler's argument is basically a repetition of the traditional themes of German idealism, and introduces no new features. It can be expressed as follows: if the world were 'given' in consciousness as a world that is completely independent of consciousness and does not presuppose it, it would be both given and not given. It is therefore a self-contradictory concept, or a concept that pretends not to be one.

It would seem that Adler, following the Marburg interpretation, rejects the category of the 'thing in itself' as superfluous and meaningless. To say that consciousness contains 'everything' is in his eyes (though he does not expressly say so) a tautology: whatever we know about the world, we know as an object of our knowledge. From this point of view, which is that of Fichte rather than Kant, the critical position amounts to maintaining that the world is a correlative to judgements about the world, which in their totality are termed consciousness-in-general. Adler expressly rejects as meaningless the question as to the origin of that which is contained in consciousness, for consciousness in fact comprises 'everything'.

Adler's transcendentalism, however, is not fully consistent. On the one hand, like Cohen and Natorp, he regards the transcendental consciousness as an autonomous world of 'truth' to which reality is relativized: a world which has no need of empirical human beings in order to exist, or rather to be 'valid'—for existence is only the predicate of an existential judgement, and consciousness-in-general is not a kind of Platonic realm of ideas, while its ontological status cannot even be an object of questioning. But, on the other hand, Adler frequently uses the concept of 'species-consciousness', which he identifies with transcendental consciousness. This, however, involves the existence of mankind as a differentiated species, and cannot lay claim to absolute validity. Thus Adler oscillates between anthropological relativism and transcendentalism in the true sense. The former viewpoint suffices when he is concerned, as he most often is, to show, or rather to state, that the community of mankind and the unity of the species have an epistemological basis, since all human beings share in the same impersonal form of the spirit. But it does not suffice when he also seeks to maintain that we are entitled, within certain limits anyway, to ascribe to our knowledge universal and absolute validity: this requires a world of necessary truths, the necessity of which does not depend on the empirical activity of the human mind. These, however, are two completely different purposes: to justify the humanistic faith in the unity of mankind, and to vindicate the claims of human knowledge to certainty. Adler's concept of transcendental consciousness is used to serve both purposes, which at times leads to confusion. This also gives rise to the double sense of the concept of the 'social *a priori*', which we have already mentioned and which Adler never clearly distinguished. On the one hand, this *a priori* is a collection of non-empirical categories, applicable in a particular way to the description of social phenomena; on the other hand, it is that part of the content of every individual consciousness in which the latter discovers itself as a member of the human species with the power of communicating with its fellows.

This confusion also affects Adler's interpretation of Marx. Marxism is a theory which offers a basis for belief in the perfect unity of human beings (which is what socialism is about) and also a method of discovering universally valid truths about social phenomena. There is, of course, no conflict between these aspects of Marxism, but it is often not clear which of them Adler is talking about.

Adler deserves a special place in the history of Marxism because, among other things, he was one of the few who tried to reinstate the dialectic in the Hegelian sense of an unceasing interplay between Being and thought about Being, instead of contenting themselves with the Engels–Plekhanov method of accumulating examples to show that in this or that sphere of reality 'quantitative changes lead to qualitative ones', or 'development is the result of a conflict of opposites'. However, Adler's exposition of the dialectic was highly abstract and unrelated to the actual problems of the social sciences. *Marxistische Probleme*, the work in which he dealt especially with dialectical questions, did nothing to bring about a return of Marxism to Hegelian sources.

According to Adler, dialectical thought is its own object. In the dialectical movement every concept is understood in relation to its opposite—not by the ordinary comparison of one content with another, but by reason of the tendency of each towards self-cancellation. Our thought never embraces the whole of Being, but singles out particular aspects or qualities; consciousness, however, is aware of its own limitations and strives to overcome them by relating its own content to the concrete whole (*Totalität*), which is itself inexpressible. The mind is thus in a state of constant tension and must at once transcend every result that it achieves, aiming at the unattainable goal of a self-identity which would also mean identity with its object. But the law of the mind is not that of things: reality can be called dialectic only as the mind conceives it and not as it is 'in itself'. It is not clear, however, how Adler can make this distinction, since in his view the only reality we have contact with is that of thought. Later he apparently abandoned the critique of the 'dialectic of nature', having concluded that nature, being comprehended by thought, is no less 'dialectic' than thought itself.

8. Adler: consciousness and social being

Adler, as we saw, regarded himself as a true adherent of the Marxian philosophy of history, but he rejected the term 'historical materialism' as based on a misunderstanding and as merely polemical in intent. He repeats all the current defences of Marxism against the charge that it 'takes no account' of human activity as a whole, that it regards social development as independent of human beings, etc. He emphasizes that the causal explanation of social phenomena is not in conflict with the existence of the human will. He overlooks, however, that the question is not whether men's acts are motivated but whether they are unequivocally determined by circumstances, while the objection that Marxism regards history as independent of human beings is aimed at historical determinism and not at the absurd idea that men and women behave no differently from stones. Like nearly all Marxists he fails to put the question clearly at this point, repeating merely that Marxism is not 'fatalistic', since it recognizes human initiative, and at the same time that science must regard all social processes as causally determined. This is a very weak explanation, for if human initiative in history is determined by circumstances it is only one of the many forms of universal causality, and the objection that men are 'only instruments' of an anonymous process has not been met; while if is not so determined, it is impossible to maintain the determinist position and belief in 'historical laws'.

However, Adler's specific contribution does not consist in general, unanalytical remarks about 'men making history'. His interpretation of historical materialism is distinguished by the attempt to call in question the whole traditional distinction between 'material' and 'spiritual' factors in the historical process. The general error of Marxists was, in his view, to oppose inanimate 'productive forces' and 'relations of production' to the spiritual 'superstructure', when it was clear that relations of production represented a system of conscious human behaviour and were thus no less spiritual than the superstructure itself. In the same way productive forces, if regarded not as lifeless objects but as elements in the social process, presupposed human consciousness on the part of the makers and users of tools. There were no factors in social life that were simply 'inanimate matter' and changed or developed of their own accord. Technique and economic phenomena were as much manifestations of the spirit as was ideology. Marx did not regard the superstructure as a passive reflection of 'objective' conditions, nor did he deny the autonomy of its features such as law, science, and religion. Consciousness was determined by 'social', not 'material', being, and 'social' implied 'spiritual'. What were called 'economic conditions' were spiritual phenomena at the lowest level of a particular phase of social development, i.e. those that were directly connected with the production and reproduction of human existence.

It is not clear exactly what is left of historical materialism after this interpretation. It would seem that in Adler's system the distinction, in social phenomena, between 'forms of consciousness' and 'objective' processes ceases to have any meaning, and so therefore does the basic idea of the materialist interpretation of history. Adler insists, however, that Marx's conception was that in the last resort the human spirit is the driving force of history. 'If we remember Marx's words: "With me the ideal is nothing else than the material world reflected by the human mind and translated into forms of thought" (*bei mir ist das Ideelle nichts andres als das im Menschenkopf umgesetzte und übersetzte Materielle*), we cannot fail to see that there is no economic causality that does not also take place inside the human head' (*Die Staatsauffassung des Marxismus*, p. 163). This, however, is extremely far-fetched, and distorts Marx's ideas out of recognition: what he meant was not that all economic phenomena take place in the human mind, but that what takes place in the mind can be explained economically.

9. What is and what ought to be

In questions relating to ethics and their philosophical basis Adler repeats in his own fashion arguments that were the common property of all neo-Kantists, and from this point of view criticizes Kautsky's naturalism. If all historical processes are determined independently of the human will, then there is no place for ethics. It is meaningless to say that I 'ought' to do this or that, if everything I do is dictated by circumstances beyond my control. Nature knows neither good nor evil, and no empirical observation will enable us to find such a distinction in it. Hence Marxism as a theory of social phenomena is morally neutral. However, as beings endowed with mind and will we cannot avoid asking the questions 'What ought we to do?' and 'What is good?', and we are not helped to answer these by knowing what is regarded as right or good. Socialism cannot be considered as merely the result of the 'natural' development of phenomena, since if this is the case it does not follow that we ought to help in bringing it about, or regard it as an aim or ideal. Moral judgements cannot be derived from statements about biological or historical facts: they can only be based on recognizing the human will as a faculty of self-determination which is not a form of natural energy and which creates the principles of obligation autonomously—i.e. without regard to external considerations, whether of biology, religion, or utilitarianism.

In *Marxistische Probleme* and other works written before 1914 Adler treated ethical questions from a typically neo-Kantian standpoint. However, in an article of 1922 on the relation of Marxism to classic German philosophy he criticized the Kantists who held that socialism must be justified ethically as well as historically—a position that Adler himself had maintained until recently. His criticism, however, is extremely tenuous. He states that according to Marx socialism is based on purely empirical observation of the historical chain of causes and effects, and that its historical inevitability 'coincides' with its moral value. This coincidence is reflected in the concept of 'socialized man', who is impelled by social conditions to bring about what he regards as moral. Curiously, Adler fails to observe that this argument overlooks the Kantians' main objection, which he himself often used against Kautsky, viz.: how does 'socialized man' decide what is good or bad, and how does he find ethical grounds for his decision?

Bauer approached ethical questions on similar lines. In an article of 1905 entitled 'Marxismus und Ethik' he considers the problem of an unemployed worker who is offered pay in return for acting as a strike-breaker, and to whom it has to be explained that this is a wrong thing to do. The workman recognizes that his interests coincide generally with those of the proletariat as a whole, but he points out that in this particular case there is a conflict and he does not see why he should sacrifice his own interests for the sake of class solidarity. There is, says Bauer, no scientific answer to this question, for science does not pronounce moral judgements. The difference between Marxism and Hegelian idealism is precisely that the former does not identify 'natural' necessity with an obligation of the spirit, for it does not treat nature as a manifestation of the Idea. In the same way moral questions cannot be answered in terms of natural necessity: there must be special principles to guarantee the validity of value-judgements. Kant formulated such a principle in the shape of the formal categorical imperative, which does not tell us directly what we ought to do but provides a criterion for judging whether any particular moral rule is good or bad. Kant's ethical doctrine does not conflict with Marxism, but adds to it a moral foundation that is essential to all human beings. On the basis of the Kantian imperative we can prove that a proletarian who shows solidarity in fighting for the interests of his class is not in the same moral position as a strike-breaker; it would be impossible to show this, however, if morality had no more than a utilitarian basis. If I seek to find out not only which of the warring classes is historically most likely to win, but also which I should fight for, Marx's doctrine does not in itself tell me the answer. The orthodox are wrong in claiming that Kant's moral philosophy leads to class solidarity inasmuch as it formulates universal rules, unconnected with class-interest. On the contrary, it makes possible a moral distinction between bourgeois and proletarian interests and shows that we should opt for the latter because the particular interest of the proletariat stands for that of all humanity; if it did not, we should have no reason to take its side. The fact that the proletariat's cause is that of all mankind is known to us from Marx's analysis, and Kantian ethics cannot take the place of the historical and economic knowledge that we need in order to take moral decisions; but, on the other hand, such knowledge is not in itself capable of justifying a decision.

Bauer appears in the course of time to have altered his attitude to Kant and neo-Kantianism. In *Das Weltbild des Kapitalismus* and in an article of 1937 on Adler he treats neo-Kantianism as an expression of philosophical reaction, analogous to the political attitude of the bourgeoisie in Bismarck's time. The defeat of liberalism was also the end of bourgeois materialism in Germany, and its philosophical counterparts were neo-Kantianism and empiriocriticism. The bourgeois intelligentsia sought to induce the proletariat to ally itself with the liberals, and their ideologists therefore underlined the merits and value of Marx's work, while interpreting it so as to eliminate the revolutionary content and reduce socialism to a moral postulate and nothing more. Bauer thus criticizes Kantianism from the very standpoint which he had condemned in orthodox Marxists, without meeting the objections that he himself formerly advanced.

10. *The state, democracy, and dictatorship*

The Austro-Marxists were more agreed on philosophical questions than they were as regards the function of the state and the objectives of the political struggle of the proletariat. Renner's views on this subject, in particular, were close to Bernstein's and to those prevalent in German social democracy as a whole, owing in part to the Lassalle tradition. As Renner argued especially in his wartime and later articles, the evolution of capitalism towards imperialism had led to changes in the function of the state which gave the working class the opportunity to use the existing state machine to bring about socialist changes. Marx, in considering the state, had had in mind liberal capitalism, where the state organization refrains from interfering in production and trade. Imperialism had changed all this; the state itself had become a powerful instrument for the concentration of capital, and as a result capital had ceased to be cosmopolitan and become much more 'national'. State intervention was extending to more and more areas of economic life, and this process was irreversible. The bourgeoisie was obliged in its own interest to increase the application of centralized control to industry, banking, and commerce, while working-class pressure had obliged the state to provide more social benefits and services. Thanks to class organizations the labour market was dominated by the collective action of the workers, who had it in their power to extract many concessions from capital, not only in short-term wage increases but in the form of permanent welfare institutions. It could not therefore be said that in capitalist society the state could never function in the interest of the proletariat. Experience had proved the contrary, and it was to be expected that private property would take on a more and more public character and that the working class would have increasing influence over its institutions. Thus it was no longer the case that the workers had an interest in weakening and destroying the state: on the contrary, they could use it as a lever to bring about socialist changes, and they ought to make it as strong and efficient as possible. This analysis led naturally to a general advocacy of the reformist path to socialism: Renner believed that a socialist society would develop as the workers gained more control over state institutions and as the proletariat succeeded more and more in obliging capital to perform public functions.

Bauer and Adler, however, were less optimistic. Bauer, it is true, agreed that it could not be said that the state was always an organ of the bourgeoisie and was completely subordinated to its interests; this, he pointed out, was contrary to many of Marx's own observations, for example about periods of joint control by the aristocracy and the bourgeoisie, or the state at a given moment becoming an autonomous force owing to an equilibrium in the class struggle. Marxism, he argued, did not exclude the possibility that the proletariat and the bourgeoisie might share the state power, though this would not diminish the antagonism between them: this was what happened in Austria after the fall of the monarchy. But where bourgeois property was threatened, the bourgeoisie preferred to hand over political power to dictators if by so doing it could preserve its economic privileges: witness the example of Fascism. Bauer, it appears, did not believe that the proletariat had to 'destroy the machinery of the state' before it could seize power, but he also did not believe that socialism could develop organically out of the existing state by the extraction of successive concessions from the bourgeoisie.

Adler's position on these questions was closest to the traditional doctrine of the revolutionary Marxists. His views on the state were summed up in *Die Staatsauffassung des Marxismus*, the starting-point of which is a critique of Hans Kelsen's *Sozialismus und Staat* (1920). Kelsen had attacked Marxism as an anarchist Utopia, arguing that the abolition of the state was an impracticable ideal: law must always be the organization of coercion *vis-à-vis* individuals, but it need not be for the purpose of maintaining economic exploitation. To suppose that legal coercion could ever be abolished was to imagine a moral transformation of humanity that there was absolutely no reason to expect. There was no choice between the state and a stateless society, but there was one between democracy and dictatorship.

Adler, on the basis of classical Marxist theory, combated these arguments at all points. The state, he contended, performed other functions than those of class oppression, but they were not essential or characteristic ones. The state was the historical form of human society that characterized all periods dominated by class antagonisms. More precisely, in communities that had not yet developed a class division, the state and society were the same: it was only later that the state became separate from society and an instrument of the interests of the privileged classes.

A particular form of the state, Adler goes on, is political democracy with its parliamentary institutions, universal suffrage, and civil liberties. Not only is political democracy not opposed to class dictatorship, but it presupposes it. The bourgeois state is a dictatorship of the bourgeoisie, and political democracy is the way in which that dictatorship is organized. Political democracy cannot create economic equality or cure social antagonisms. It is based on the will of the majority, a principle which presupposes conflicting interests.

The opposite of political democracy is social democracy—this distinction can also be found in anarchist literature, which Adler endorses to some extent, observing that socialists agree with anarchists as to the ultimate aim while differing as to the means of achieving it. Social or 'true' democracy (Adler, with his transcendentalist point of view, held that there was an 'objectively true' concept of democracy in tune with human nature) is the same thing as socialism. It presupposes the unity of society at least in the sense that when it prevails, the basic conflicts of interest due to class divisions will cease to exist. In this sense it signifies the abolition of the state. The state as a class organization will cease to exist, for there will be no more particular interests; various forms of organization that are necessary to social life will remain, but there will no longer be a bureaucracy alienated from society. The state will be built up from below, starting with small assemblies on a local or production basis. In general, the present centralizing tendency is a transitory one: the organization of the future will be a federation or an assemblage of corporations linked only by their common aims and interests.

The dictatorship of the proletariat is a necessary stage on the road towards a society of this kind, but it is not the same thing as social democracy. On the contrary, like the dictatorship of the bourgeoisie at the present time, it presupposes political democracy and majority rule. The dictatorship of the proletariat is a transitional form in which society has not yet attained the desired unity but is torn by particular interests, so that it requires political organizations, i.e. parties, to represent those interests, and the state to mediate between them. Parties, too, are a transitional institution and must disappear together with class divisions.

The transition from the present form of political democracy to a democratic dictatorship of the proletariat must take the form of a revolution, but Adler stresses that it need not be a violent one. Whether or not it can be effected by peaceful means and without violation of legality is a secondary point, and we cannot be certain exactly how events will develop. Adler, however, is against reformism in the sense of a belief that socialism can be achieved by gradual, organic change. The difference between capitalism and socialism is 'qualitative': one cannot simply ripen into the other. Socialists support reforms and fight for them, but they are always conscious that reforms are not a partial realization of socialism, but only a means of preparing for revolution.

In all this Adler is very close to German orthodox Marxism,

and he shares with it the firm belief that socialism involves the removal of all conflicts of interest. Socialist freedom requires no institutions to ensure majority rule, for it is a 'true' freedom based on the 'principle of universalism': as in Rousseau's ideal society, it is not the will of the majority that counts, but the general will. Adler does not explain how the 'general will' can express itself without representative institutions, which, we are given to understand, will be superfluous. He merely states that socialists do believe, in spite of Kelsen, that human beings can change for the better: once class conflicts are done away with, socialist education will bring out the natural feeling of solidarity that will ensure harmony without compulsion.

Adler holds, in fact, that socialism is not only the ideal of a harmonious society, guaranteed by historical necessity, but also the reconciliation of empirical community life with the requirements of 'human nature', the transcendental unity of mankind which cannot find expression as long as class divisions breed inequality and injustice. He agrees not only with Rousseau but also with Fichte in believing that it is possible to restore to man his authentic essence, to make him once more what he really *is*—not merely what he would like to be, or must be by virtue of the 'laws of history'. Adler's philosophy thus postulates —this time in agreement with Marx but not with the orthodox of the Second International—a particular kind of reality that, though it is not empirically perceivable, already exists in some way, and is, as it were, the entelechy or 'truth' of humanity: the totality of the imperative demands of human nature, impelling the course of events towards a reconciliation of human essence with human historical existence. Adler's whole thought is centred on these two strictly correlated ideas: the unity of humanity as the transcendental constitution of consciousness, and the unity of humanity as an actual state of affairs which is the objective of the socialist movement.

Adler concedes, it is true, that the community of the future will not put an end to all tension, nor will it dry up the sources of development. Since, however, there will be general solidarity and freedom from material cares, we can expect that people will devote themselves with more fervour to the problems of art, metaphysics, and religion: this may give rise to fresh conflicts, but they will not be such as to disturb the basic solidarity of mankind. Here too Adler was in agreement with the general Marxist stereotypes: he believed in the absolute salvation of humanity and in a perfect harmony grounded in the moral consciousness of all members of society.

Adler dismisses the objection put forward by sociologists—Max Weber and especially Robert Michels—that any democracy, simply because it is a representative system, tends to evolve a bureaucracy which in time becomes an independent force, the master of the electorate instead of its servant. Michels in his classical work *Zur Soziologie des Parteiwesens in der modernen Demokratie* (1914) concluded from a detailed analysis of the functioning of political parties, and especially the social democrats, that the emergence and autonomization of a political apparatus is an inevitable result of the democratic process within a party: consequently, he argued, democracy is bound to fall into an internal contradiction, or, in other words, perfect democracy is a theoretical impossibility. In the pursuit of its objectives the party creates a political machine which is virtually irremovable and can nearly always impose its will on the electors without violating the system of representation, while at the same time creating and furthering its own professional or factional interests. It can be expected that in future the oligarchic tendencies in democratic bodies will encounter more opposition from the masses than they to today; but such tendencies cannot be prevented from existing and recurring at all times, for they are rooted in the very nature of social organization.

Adler does not accept this 'law of oligarchy'. Under political democracy, he agrees, it is inevitable that autonomized 'apparatuses' will come into being, both in political parties and in the state: no party, not even the workers', is exempt from this danger. But under social democracy it can be averted, by education and by decentralizing the state. Hence Adler especially values workers' councils as institutions of direct control by producers over economic processes, and for the same reason he sharply criticizes Lenin and the Soviet state. The Bolsheviks, he says, have not established a dictatorship of the proletariat, but a party dictatorship over the proletariat and the whole of society—the terrorist rule of a minority, and a far cry from the predictions of Marx, to whom the dictatorship of the proletariat meant the rule of the entire working class in conditions of political democracy. Adler thus attacks the Bolsheviks from a position similar to that of Rosa Luxemburg, and at the same time criticizes Kautsky for wrongly opposing democracy to dictatorship.

Like the German centrists, Adler failed to provide an exact definition of the term 'revolution'. He agreed with Marx that the revolution must smash the existing state machine, but he also believed that it might, though not necessarily, be effected by legal and parliamentary means, without violation of the constitution. He did not make clear how these statements were to be reconciled. Like nearly all Marxists he was also vague in his description of the future socialist order. He saw no difficulty in arguing that on the one hand society would be linked by a unity of interests and aims and that production must therefore be centrally planned, while on the other hand socialism implied the maximum degree of decentralization and federalism. In these matters all Marxists were content with general formulas, declaring that they were not utopians and were not disposed to predict the details of socialist organization. They ignored, or answered in generalities, the objections of the anarchists, who showed more discernment in this particular sphere.

11. The future of religion

While the Austro-Marxists were in general agreement with German orthodoxy on questions of the state, revolution, and democracy, both Adler and Bauer expressly differed from it as to the interpretation of religious faith. The orthodox, following Marx and Engels, regarded religion as the outcome of specific social conditions, oppression, ignorance, and 'false consciousness'. They advocated religious tolerance in state and party, but they were convinced that as exploitation and oppression were done away with and public enlightenment increased, religious beliefs were bound to die a natural death. As to the content of such beliefs, their incompatibility with the 'scientific outlook' seemed too obvious to need discussing.

Adler did not accept these stereotypes, inherited by Marxism from the rationalists of the Enlightenment; he did not believe that men could ever do without religion, or that it was desirable that they should. In this respect too he was influenced by Kant, though he did not accept his view in every detail.

In Adler's opinion the evolutionist assertion that religious beliefs had gown up as a result of nature-worship was arbitrary and improbable, for there was no reason why concepts that bore no relation to experience should arise on a purely empirical basis. Religion was not a misinterpretation of experience, but resulted from the insoluble conflict between the natural and the moral order. Man was unable to resolve the contrast between his awareness of himself as a free, rational, purposive being and, on the other hand, the necessities of nature which restricted his freedom and spiritual expansion, brought upon him suffering and death, and created an impassable gulf between morality and happiness. No theoretical reflection and no empirical knowledge could reconcile these two orders of existence or provide a picture of the world as a synthetic whole (*Totalität*). This could only be done by religion, which, thanks to the idea of the divine Absolute, gave a universal meaning to the world of nature and the world of spirit, including scientific inquiry. This did not mean, however, that the idea of the Absolute could be inferred from empirical data or rational reflection. Religious concepts had a practical, not a theoretical, significance, which again did not mean that they were delusions but that they were arrived at by a practical route. Religion that purported to replace scientific knowledge was superfluous and was rightly criticized. The existing forms of religion were historical in character, but contained an unchanging nucleus which might one day be seen in its pure form as a 'rational religion' (*Vernunftreligion*)—not in the sense that its truth was proved by reason, but in the sense that it derived from man's practical attempts to define himself as a rational being, and not from any external revelation. Religion realized for the first time the primacy of practical reason, for it effected a synthesis between man as a part of nature and man as a moral and practical being, and conferred a meaning on human personality, to which nature is indifferent. God, as the absolute synthesis of Being, is not an object of theoretical proof but is the postulate of practical reason in the Kantian sense: not merely something we desire, for our desires may be illusions, but something required by our existence as free, morally oriented subjects. Genuine religion is thus 'subjective' in the sense that its proper meaning is related to human personality and cannot be based on an external revelation; but it is not subjective in the sense that it is an arbitrary caprice or an illusory compensation.

Adler's thoughts on religion, expressed, for example, in *Das Soziologische in Kants Erkenntniskritik* (1924), are based, it will be seen, on the opposition of 'nature' and 'spirit'; it is not clear how this is to be reconciled with the transcendentalist position which holds that everything is relative to the universal consciousness, and which thus leaves no room for nature conceived as in-different and independent of consciousness. It would appear that Adler, on the one hand, wished to assert the perfect unity of the human species and evolved for this purpose his concept of transcendental consciousness, while on the other hand, realizing that this concept failed to allow for the unreplaceable value of the human individual, he sought to rescue the latter by means of the divine Absolute. He seems thus to have felt that a purely anthropocentric or even purely transcendentalist position was unsustainable, as it took no account of personal subjectivity. In this respect his hesitations are reminiscent of Brzozowski, except that Adler maintained his absolute transcendentalism to the end instead of trying to synthesize it with his *Vernunftreligion* and so repair the incoherence of his philosophy.

Otto Bauer did not go so far as Adler in the philosophical interpretation of religion, but he too diverged from the Marxist stereotypes. He believed that historical materialism did not imply any specific *Weltanschauung* or answer to the problem of religion or philosophical materialism. A world outlook could be interpreted as a function of class-interests: thus Calvinism was specially adapted to the needs of the bourgeoisie in the early stages of capitalism, while Darwinian materialism 'reflected' the laws of capitalist competition. The modern bourgeoisie was returning to religion, seeking in it a defence against threats to the social order. But church institutions, the clergy and their theological systems must be distinguished from the religious feeling which afforded consolation to the humiliated and oppressed. The socialist party should not profess or advocate an anti-religious outlook: it was fighting for clear political aims, not for the existence or non-existence of God. Nor should it be expected that the need for religion would die out in a socialist society. Men had a permanent need to seek for the hidden meaning of the world, and this could not be stifled. The expec-tation was rather that when religion was freed from social entanglements, that aspect of it would come to light which did not depend on passing circumstances but on the nature of the human spirit itself (*Sozialdemokratie, Religion und Kirche*, 1927). Unlike Adler, however, Bauer did not avow any religious convictions of his own, even in an abstract philosophical form.

12. Bauer: the theory of the nation

Bauer's book on the question of nationality is seldom read nowadays, as may be seen from the fact that references to it in various encyclopedic works are generally incorrect. Yet it is the most important Marxist study in this field, and is based on a shrewd historical analysis.

Bauer criticizes a number of existing theories of the nation. Firstly, those of the spiritual type, which define it as the embodiment of a mysterious 'national soul', and secondly, materialist racial theories after the manner of Gobineau, based on the concept of a no less mysterious biological substance inherited by the national community: both these are metaphysical and therefore unscientific interpretations. Thirdly, voluntarist theories like that of Renan, which define a nation by the will to form a state: these are mistaken, because they imply that a people which is content to remain within a multinational state—like a large proportion of the Czechs—does not qualify as a 'nation'. Fourthly, empirical definitions which define a nation by enumerating various separate features such as language, territory, origin, customs, law, religion: these are unsatisfactory, because the individual features are not essential and play a different part at different times in forming the national life, so that by listing them we have not grasped the essence of the phenomenon.

What then is a nation? We can answer this question by taking the existing, clearly recognizable national units and examining the historical conditions that have given rise to them. Bauer does this with especial reference to the German nation, and arrives at the following conclusions.

The primary determinant of a nation is national character: this, however, itself requires explanation, and alters in the course of history. The factors that create and stabilize it are both natural and cultural. The physical community is defined not only by the existence of common forbears, but to a greater extent by the fact that conditions of life lead to a differentiated selection of physical types in accordance with the Darwinian law: certain characteristics are conducive to the survival of maritime peoples, others of hunters, etc. The inheritance of selected qualities is not contrary to historical materialism, but supplements it. As a result of shared conditions of life and natural selection there comes into being a cultural community which is, as it were, a piece of crystallized history. 'The nation is never anything but a community of destiny. This community, however, becomes effective on the one hand through the natural inheritance of qualities bred by the common destiny of the nation, and on the other by the transmission of a cultural patrimony the nature of which is determined by the nation's fate' (*Die Nationalitätenfrage*, p. 21). The existence of a national character does not consist merely in the fact that the individuals forming the nation are in some ways alike, but in the fact that historical forces have made them so.

In history up to the present time the national community has taken two forms. The first is the tribal link, which dissolves and is modified with ease; the second is the nation embodying a class society, especially since the beginnings of capitalism. The community of the early Germanic tribes and that of the medieval empire based on the ethos of chivalry differ from that created by specifically capitalist economic and cultural ties. Commodity production and trade, the improvement of communications, national literature, the post, newspapers, universal education and military service, democracy, the franchise, and finally the working-class movement—all these have successively contributed to uniting the isolated German peoples into a nation conscious of its unity. Even today, however, though less so than in the Middle Ages, participation in the national culture is reserved to the ruling classes. Peasants and workers are the backbone of the nation, but are culturally inactive. It is the business of the socialist movement to fight for the participation of all classes in the national culture.

Hence Bauer draws the inference, which is natural to his argument but contrary to the received Marxist opinion, that socialism not only does not obliterate national differences but reinforces and develops them by bringing culture to the masses and making the national idea the property of everyone. 'Socialism makes the nation autonomous, so that its fate is determined by its own will, and this means that in a socialist society nations will be increasingly differentiated, their qualities more sharply defined and their characters more distinct from one another' (*Die Nationalitätenfrage*, p. 92). Clearly, if the nation is (as Bauer finally describes it) 'a collectivity of human beings united by community of destiny in a community of character' (p. 118), then the more the people shares in deciding its own fate, the more evident and significant national characteristics will become. Socialism does not level out national differences, but enhances to an extreme degree the importance of the national principle in history.

This does not mean, however, that it intensifies national hatred or oppression. On the contrary, national hatred is a distorted form of class hatred, and national oppression is a function of social oppression. Hence the working class, fighting against all oppression, fights national oppression too, and in bringing about a socialist society it destroys the conditions that might revive national enmity and conflicts of national interest. The existence of many nations and national characters is part of the cultural wealth of mankind, and there is no reason to seek to diminish their number. In the preface to the second edition of his book (1922) Bauer refers to Duhem, who detected national peculiarities even in such a 'universal' field as physics: the British are more concerned with constructing easily visualized mechanical models regardless of theoretical consistency, while the French are more interested in uniformity of theory. Bauer relates this state of affairs to the different development of absolute monarchy in the two countries.

There is, then, no harm in the fact that the socialist movement itself is differentiated according to nationality, and it would be fatal to impose a uniform pattern on everyone. There is no conflict between proletarian internationalism and national variety. Members of the proletariat are linked together by a similarity of destiny, but not by a common destiny in the same sense as a nation. By destroying the conservative tradition and enabling every nation to decide its own affairs, socialism opens up entirely new prospects of the development of national consciousness and culture. The liberal bourgeoisie supported the right of nations to self-determination because the nations that were awakening and throwing off the yoke of absolutism provided it with new markets. The imperialist bourgeoisie, on the other hand, endeavours to subjugate undeveloped countries. The working class sometimes profits by imperialist policy, but the adverse consequences far outweigh the good, and in any case the racial and imperialist ideology is profoundly alien to socialism. 'When the capitalist class aims at creating a large multinational state under the dominion of a single nation, the working class takes up the old bourgeois idea of a free national state' (*Die Nationalitätenfrage*, p. 455).

Socialism, therefore, is on the side of national self-determination; but does this mean that the working class in multinational states should fight under the banner of separate statehood for each nation? This was a key question for the Austrian social democrats. Bauer used the same arguments as Rosa Luxemburg, though he was far from sharing her nihilist attitude to the national question. The fight for separate statehood was harmful to socialism because it linked the workers with the bourgeoisie. The right course was to work within the framework of existing states, demanding freedom for all nations to organize their spiritual and cultural life. 'A constitution that gives each nation the ability to develop its own culture, and that compels no nation to reconquer and reassert this right again and again in a fight for political power; a constitution that does not base the power of any nation on the rule of a minority over the majority—this is what the proletariat demands in the field of national policy ... Each nation should govern itself and be free to meet its own cultural needs from its own resources: the state should confine itself to watching over those interests that are common to all its nations and are neutral as between them. In this way national autonomy and self-determination is necessarily the constitutional objective of the working class of all nations in the multinational state' (ibid., pp. 277–8).

Bauer considered, therefore, that in Austrian conditions the best course was to fight for complete national autonomy for all ethnic groups in the Monarchy, for the maximum enlargement of the powers of national institutions, and the maximum limitation of the functions of the state. In agreement with Renner, he contended that the national principle should not be based on territory. There were in Austria-Hungary many areas of mixed language and many linguistic enclaves, while migration to the towns and various economic factors caused incessant changes in the territorial basis of nationality. Consequently the personal principle should prevail, i.e. every citizen should choose his own national status. Each nation would set up its own organization and possess funds for the development of national culture, schooling in its own language, and institutions of all kinds. National self-governing bodies should be the foundation of the whole authority of the state. Generally speaking, a separate state for each nation would no doubt present some advantages, but granted complete freedom of national life, the interests of large states would prevail. Bauer was of course aware of the difference between the position of those peoples who lived wholly within the confines of the Monarchy, such as the Czechs, Hungarians, and Croats, and those who were divided by international frontiers, like the Poles, Ruthenes, Germans, and Serbs. He foresaw the possibility of an armed rising by the Poles in pursuit of national unity, but he thought this depended on events in Russia. If the revolution succeeded there, the Poles and other nations of the Russian empire would gain their autonomy and Austria-Hungary would have to accept a similar solution. If the revolution failed, the Poles might rise against the partitioning powers and bring about the dismemberment of the Monarchy. But the working class should not base its hopes on an imperialist war and the collapse of Austria-Hungary, for this would mean the victory of reaction in Russia and Germany. The struggle should be carried on on the basis of the existing state.

Bauer change his mind, however, during the Balkan War, as he came to the conclusion that the Monarchy was bound to collapse owing to the strong pressure of the Slav nations for independence. During the war of 1914–18 he proclaimed the right of every nation to form a state of its own.

To sum up: Bauer shared the opinion of all Marxists that national oppression was a function of class oppression. He did not agree with them, however, that national differences would disappear in a socialist society, and he thought it a good thing that they should continue to exist. Unlike Lenin and Rosa Luxemburg, but like the Polish socialists of the PPS, he ascribed intrinsic value to the national community and thought this value should be defended. The Leninists, especially Stalin in 1913, attacked him on the ground that he did not come out firmly for the right of each nation to break away from the Monarchy, but confined his aim to self-determination in the form of cultural autonomy. But there was no essential theoretical difference between them. Bauer maintained that the working class should not fight under the banner of national separatism, and so did Lenin. Lenin, however, regarded national oppression as a destructive force of which the party should take advantage to overthrow the existing order. Bauer, who did not touch on this idea, was concerned to do away with national oppression, not to exploit it for party ends. He believed that in conditions of complete freedom and autonomy the problem of state separatism would cease to exist. There remained, of course, the question of the partitioned nations, especially Poland. Bauer did not take a clear line on this in his book, at any rate less so than Lenin, who endorsed the view that it would be a shameful farce if the Polish proletariat were to fight for the resurrection of the Polish state. Later, however, Bauer recognized not only Poland's right to independence but also, in contrast to Lenin's view, the real need for such independence. In the last resort the difference between him and Lenin was that to Lenin the national question was a tactical one of exploiting anti-Russian resentment, while national oppression would automatically disappear under socialism, whereas Bauer regarded nations as valuable in themselves and enriching human culture by their differences.

Renner, from this point of view, was much more of an Austro-Hungarian patriot. He also advocated cultural autonomy, but to the last opposed the idea that the socialist party should rest its hopes on the dissolution of the Monarchy. However, both he and Bauer emphasized that political democracy was a prerequisite to the solution of national conflicts, and that national oppression could not be done away with in conditions of despotism.

13. *Hilferding: the controversy on the theory of value*

Hilferding's controversy with Böhm-Bawerk epitomizes the whole range of problems connected with the Marxian theory of value and discussed during the period of the Second International. Eugen Böhm-Bawerk, the chief exponent of the 'psychological school' of economics, criticized Volume I of *Capital* in his *Geschichte und Kritik der Kapitalzinstheorien* (1884) and, after the publication of Volume III, produced a further criticism entitled *Zum Abschluss des Marxschen Systems* (1896: English translation, *Karl Marx and the Close of his System*, 1898). Hilferding believed that bourgeois political economy was no longer capable of forming integrated theories, but that the psychological school was an exception and was therefore worth noticing. Accordingly, in *Böhm-Bawerks Marx-Kritik* (*Marx-Studien*, vol. i, 1904) he summed up the Austrian economist's arguments against Marx and combated them from the orthodox standpoint.

According to Böhm-Bawerk, Marx had furnished no empirical or psychological grounds for his theory that labour constitutes value. Like Aristotle, he argued that as objects were exchanged they must possess some comparable, commensurate feature, and he arbitrarily assumed that this must consist in the labour input. In so doing Marx had made several errors. Firstly, he took into account only the products of labour; but the products of nature, such as land, were also exchanged, and accounted for quite a large part of the sum of transactions. Secondly, Marx entirely disregarded use-value, which was illegitimate since, as he himself emphasized, use-value was a condition of exchange-value. Thirdly, Marx assumed that apart from use-value an object consists of nothing but crystallized labour. But this ignores its scarceness in relation to demand, the fact that it is an object of need, the fact that it is or is not a natural product: why then should only one of its properties be the basis of value?

Moreover, Böhm-Bawerk continues, the category of value in Marx's sense is useless because it cannot be measured quantitatively apart from price, and one reason for this is that complex labour cannot, as Marx would have it, be reduced to a multiple of simple labour: forms of labour differ in quality and cannot be expressed in units of labour-time. The proposition that value governs the terms of exchange thus cannot be empirically verified and affords no explanation of true economic processes.

In addition, Volume III of *Capital* contradicts Volume I, for in considering the origin of the average rate of profit Marx states that prices as a rule do not correspond to values, and that actual exchanges always take place at a rate different from the proportionate input of socially necessary labour. Admittedly, Marx also says that these deviations are made up for on the global scale, i.e. that the sum total of all prices is equal to that of all values; but this is a tautology if we cannot define the relative values of any particular commodities. Since the concept of value does not explain the actual price relationship, it cannot serve any purpose in economic analysis.

In his rebuttal of this argument Hilferding tries to show that Böhm-Bawerk failed to understand Marx's theory of value and that his objections are either misconceived or do not lessen its utility.

As to the ignoring of use-value, Hilferding says that in the act of exchange use-value does not exist for the seller, so it would be hard for him to take it as the basis of price. According to Marx, as long as there is no commodity production and exchange is a casual and inessential phenomenon, objects are exchanged according to the will of their possessors, but in the course of time exchange-value becomes independent of use-value. Why then is labour the determinant of value? To this question Hilferding replies that objects acquire exchange-value only as commodities, i.e. when they are quantitatively confronted with others on the market: the possessors take part in the act of exchange not as human individuals but as embodiments of the over-all relations of production. The subject of economics is only the social aspect of commodities, i.e. their exchange-value, although the object itself is a 'unity' of exchange-value and use-value. The commodity expresses social relations, and hence the labour contained in it takes on a social character as necessary labour. In the exchange context people are not people in the psychological sense, and commodities are not objects defined by their qualities. But Marx endeavours to find the link between factors of production, and this link appears in the exchange process in a mystified form, as a link between things and not people. The commodity is defined quantitatively as the sum of the labour contained in it, and 'in the last resort' social changes can be reduced to the law of value. A theory which takes as its starting-point use-value, human needs, and the utility of objects seeks to explain social processes on the basis of the individual relation between the person and the thing; but it fails of its purpose, as it cannot on this basis discover any objective social measure or apprehend the real course of social development, which cannot be deduced from the relationship between an individual who wants something and the object that satisfies his want. In Marx's theory, by contrast, the principle of value 'causally dominates' the whole life of society. Within the total framework of social relations, things that are not commodities, such as land, may take on the character of commodities: man's control over natural forces enables him to obtain an exceptional amount of surplus value, and this privilege is expressed as the price of land. As for the attributes of commodities other than value, which Böhm-Bawerk mentions, they afford no basis for quantitative comparison.

As regards the reduction of labour to a common measure, Marx does indeed maintain that complex labour is a multiple of average simple labour, i.e. that involved in the expenditure of labour-power such as every human being on the average possesses. Different kinds of work depend on the degree of complexity, and the quantitative proportion between them is determined by the social process itself. Certainly there is no absolute measure by which complex labour could be reduced to simple labour independently of the market; but there is no need of this, for the purpose of economics is not to account for specific price-relations but to discover 'the laws of the social development of capitalism'. Absolute prices as they are given in experience are the starting-point of this investigation, but what it is concerned with are the laws of change, to which absolute prices are irrelevant: the important thing to note is that a change in the productivity of labour alters the relation between prices. Simple labour enters into complex labour in many ways, for example as labour expended in training complex labour-power, and so in the end complex labour can be conceived as the sum of simple labour. Böhm-Bawerk confuses the theoretical and the practical measurement of value: the latter is not possible, but the former is, and the only true measurer is the whole of society and the laws of competition that govern it. The idea that it is possible in practice to measure the value of particular commodities led to the utopian notion of a 'labour currency'; Marxism, however, is not concerned with fixing prices but with observing social laws.

Nor is it true, Hilferding continues, that Marx's theory of

average profit refutes the theory of value. In Volume I of *Capital* he discusses equivalent exchange, but he does not say that actual exchange takes place at the rate determined by the proportionate input of socially necessary labour, and he is careful to point out that prices diverge from values. These divergences do not invalidate the law of value, but only 'modify' it. Economic theory is concerned to find out whether price-changes conform to a general tendency that can be expressed as a 'law': it is not concerned with the value of particular products. Marx's statement that the sum total of prices equals the sum total of values is not an empty one, for it enables us to conclude that all profit comes from production and not from circulation, and that the total volume of profit is identical with the total volume of surplus value. The argument that it is not only value that determines price is not a refutation of Marx, for Marx holds that when prices are given, their subsequent movement depends on the productivity of labour.

A careful reading of this controversy leads to the conclusion that Hilferding did not really answer Böhm-Bawerk's objections but was content to repeat the relevant arguments from *Capital*, so that his refutation is not convincing. Böhm-Bawerk's main arguments are three: (1) value in Marx's sense cannot be measured quantitatively, partly (but not solely) because there is no way of reducing different kinds of labour to a common measure; (2) prices depend on many factors, not only value, and we cannot ascertain the quantitative importance of value in relation to the others; (3) therefore the statement that value governs the movement of prices and social relations is both arbitrary (because it is not clear on what ground we are asked to believe that value is determined by labour-time) and scientifically useless, for it does not help us to explain the movement of prices, still less to foresee it. Hilferding accepts the first two points but denies that they affect Marx's theory, since it does not purport to explain actual terms of exchange but only to discover the general laws of change, and these are subordinate to the law of value.

We need only repeat here the remarks we have already made in discussing *Capital*. In the empirical sciences we generally define a law as a statement that in such and such particular conditions, such and such phenomena always occur. Clearly the statement that the value of a commodity is equal to the amount of socially necessary labour put into it is not a law but a definition of value. It could be proved that it was not an arbitrary definition if we were able to show that this particular attribute of commodities does govern actual price-changes; this latter proposition could then be called a law. But here is the real difficulty: price-changes depend on several factors—the average rate of profit, the supply–demand ratio, value, etc.—and we cannot ascertain their quantitative distribution. Hilferding evades the point by means of the formula 'in the last resort', which is familiar from historical materialism. Economic changes are determined in the last resort by the value of commodities; but what does this mean, if we accept that actual price-changes are *not* determined only by value? Hilferding only says that, other things being equal, changes in the productivity of labour produce price-changes: the producer who uses a technique more efficient than the average will make a higher profit. This is of course true, but it can be established independently of the so-called law of value and is generally known without the benefit of that law: the concept of value does no more to explain it than does the concept of production costs. If the cost of producing an article is lower because of improved technique, the producer stands to make a bigger profit. Price-changes resulting from changes in productivity can be explained without the aid of the concept of value. Value figures in these arguments as a *qualitas occulta* and is accounted for in the same fashion. Since we know it quantitatively only through prices, to say that 'as there are prices, there must be value' is no better than to say, like the character in Molière, that as we know by experience that opium puts people to sleep, we can deduce that it has soporific qualities. All phenomena connected with the movement of prices can be just as well explained without reference to value. That inefficient producers are driven out of business by larger, more efficient ones is well known and obvious, and is amply explained by the movement of prices: it is arbitrary to say that it is explained by the 'law of value', for this does not enable us to foresee price movements any better than we could without it. Hence the law of value is not a scientific statement that can be empirically verified or refuted.

The position is similar as regards the reduction of complex

labour to units of simple labour. Hilferding's statement that this process takes place of its own accord in the movement of market prices, but that it cannot and need not be quantitatively expressed, means simply that price-changes are the empirical phenomenon and are not explained by the proportion between different kinds of labour. Hence the principle of reduction has no meaning that enables us to foresee or explain anything. As for the statement that value can be measured theoretically but not practically, its meaning is very obscure: it is hard to see what can be meant by saying that any magnitude cannot be measured in practice but only in theory.

The assertion that in days when there was hardly any commodity production the terms of exchange depended on the 'will' of individuals, but that afterwards they became subject to the law of value, is contrary to Engels's statement in the preface to Volume III of *Capital* that in primitive times goods were exchanged according to value, whereas the developed commodity economy introduced other factors regulating prices.

But the law of value has in fact another sense, as Hilferding explains. In economic theory as Marx understands it we are not concerned with actual terms of exchange but with the origin of profit. This theory does not explain the actual history of capitalism, but tells us that profit comes entirely from the workman's unremunerated labour, that capital does not create value, and that the only source of value is 'productive' labour (the definition of which, as we know, arouses numerous doubts). Since the 'real producers', i.e. the workers, have no power over the values they create, while all these values (including the value of labour-power) are exchanged according to the impersonal laws of the market, the 'law of value' as Marx conceives it is an economic description of the process of the universal alienation of capitalist society. It is an ideological, not a scientific category, and cannot be verified empirically. As a category of this kind it is of course significant and of importance to the doctrine; but it serves different purposes than the political economy which seeks to ascertain actual price movements, predict changes in the economic climate, and give practical advice for the conduct of economic affairs. Marx's theory of value is intended to be of practical importance too, but in quite a different sense. Its purpose is not to describe the quantitative relations between phenomena so that we can more easily influence events, but to unmask the anti-human character of a society in which production is entirely geared to the multiplying of exchange-value; to lay bare the 'alienation' of social life, and to throw light on the contradiction between man's requirements and his empirical existence. A theory of this kind is not so much an explanation as an ideological appeal, and must be understood as such. The controversy between Marxists and critics of the theory of value is thus insoluble, as the latter expect from a general economic theory something that Marx's doctrine is unable to provide.

Hilferding believes, it is true, that it is possible to deduce from the labour theory of value a 'law of changes' in capitalist society which would demonstrate the inevitability of socialism. He does not explain, however, how this is to be done. Marx believed in the necessity of socialism, but he did not indicate what features of the capitalist economy meant that socialism was certain to come about. It is not sufficient to say that capitalism suffers from an anarchical production system, undergoes periodical crises, and arouses the working class to revolt. All this does not prove that an economy of this kind which has existed, with whatever destructive consequences, for a considerable time cannot go on existing indefinitely: Marx ought to have shown that at a given moment the system is bound to break down, but the theory of value does not help to establish this conclusion.

14. *Hilferding: the theory of imperialism*

Hilferding's *Finanzkapital* gives the impression of a plan to rewrite almost the whole of Marx's *Capital* so as to adapt it to altered economic conditions. He expounds Marx's theory of currency, credit, interest rates, and crises, but the most important part of his work is concerned with changes in the world economy since Marx's death: these changes are connected with the concentration of capital, but they are of a 'qualitative' nature and cannot be represented as a simple continuation of earlier processes.

The argument starts from the theory of value and the theory of the average rate of profit. Value in the strict sense, i.e. crystallized labour-time, cannot be expressed directly but is manifested in exchange as the quantitative ratio between prices. The fact that production is geared to profit means that exchange does not conform to the principle of 'equal pay for equal work' but to that of 'equal profit for equal capital': sale is effected at production prices, not according to value. The impossibility of directly expressing the value of commodities points up the utopian character of such doctrines as Rodbertus's socialism, in which society fixes the standard amount of labour-time for each product as a basis of exchange.

The dominance of profit as a motive in production leads naturally to the concentration of capital and to technical progress: the latter expresses itself economically in the constantly increasing proportion of constant capital in the organic composition of capital, and also in a change within constant capital itself: fixed capital increases faster than circulation capital. This means that the transfer of already invested capital is increasingly difficult: circulation capital can be transferred at will from one branch of production to another, but fixed capital is linked to the production process. It would thus be extremely hard for an average rate of profit to emerge if there did not exist, in the form of joint-stock companies and banks, the means of mobilizing capital on a large scale. The interests of banks, however, differ in some ways from those of individual capitalists. Competition which drives some firms out of business is not advantageous to the banks, though it is to the surviving firms. The banks therefore aim to prevent competition among their customers, and at the same time they are interested in a high rate of profit. In other words, the banks tend to create industrial monopolies.

One result of monopoly production is a change in the function of trade. In the period of the primary accumulation of capital trade plays a decisive role: it is the starting-point of the development of capitalism, and in the first phase, thanks to the credit system, it makes production dependent on itself. In a developed capitalist economy this dependence ceases, and production and trade are separate. Then, as capital becomes concentrated, trade loses its autonomy or even becomes superfluous as a distinct branch of economic life. Commercial capital thus decreases, and its share of profit is taken over by industrial capital. The merchant becomes increasingly the agent of syndicates and cartels.

The concentration of capital leads to the concentration of banks; but, reciprocally, the greater amount of capital is at the banks' disposal, the more they are able to bring about in their own interest the concentration of industrial capital. There is thus what would today be called a positive feedback. The banks accumulate the reserve capital of the capitalists and a large part of the cash resources of the non-producing classes: consequently the amount of capital available to industry is considerably greater than the total of industrial capital. This is advantageous to industry, but makes it highly dependent on bank capital. 'The bank capital, or capital in the form of money, which is thus in reality transformed into industrial capital, we call finance capital' (*Finanzkapital*, iii, 14).

Discussing the prospects of the cartellization of industry, Hilferding puts the question whether there is any impassable limit to this process, and answers that there is not. One can imagine the whole of capitalist production in the form of a universal cartel consciously regulating all productive processes. In such circumstances prices would be fixed conventionally and this would turn into a calculation which divided the total output between the cartel magnates and the rest of society. Money would cease to play a part in production, and the anarchy of the market would be done away with. Society would still be divided into antagonistic classes, but it would have a planned economy. Hilferding does not say that matters are bound to develop in this way, but that such is the tendency of the concentration of capital. In later years he came to regard this prospect as highly probable; he did not deduce that there was no hope for socialism, but he inclined to the view that socialism, by means of peaceful expropriation, could take over the machinery of capitalist planning almost ready-made.

However, as long as the process of concentration did not attain this hypothetical absolute form, crises were inevitable in the capitalist economy: production must go through cyclic stages of prosperity and depression. The possibility of crises was inherent in the very conditions of commodity production: the division of commodities into commodity and money, and the development of credit, meant that there could be a situation of insolvency due to marketing difficulties, and insolvency at any one point led to a natural chain reaction, for sales were the precondition of repro-duction. Moreover, the urge to increase profit, which was the sole motive force of production, contained an inbuilt contradiction, as it also endeavoured to limit the consumption of the working class. This did not mean that crises were solely due to the low level of consumption by the workers and that, as Rodbertus's followers hoped, they could be cured simply by raising wages. An economic crisis, Hilferding explains, is a disturbance of circulation, but of a specifically capitalist kind, so that the laws of circulation as such do not account for it. Every industrial cycle begins with such accidental circumstances as the opening of new markets and new branches of production, important technical improvements, or the growth of population. These factors cause a rise in demand which spreads to other branches of production that are in some way or other dependent on the initial ones. The period of capital turnover is shortened, i.e. the amount that the businessman must invest decreases in relation to the production capital employed. But the conditions that favour technical progress at the same time produce a fall in the rate of profit and lengthen the period of capital turnover. At a certain stage, expanding production meets with insufficient demand and has to seek fresh markets. Meanwhile capital naturally flows into branches where the organic composition is at its highest, and thus the investments in those branches are larger than in others, where the rate of profit is lower. The resulting disproportion interferes with the whole process of commodity circulation: crises as a rule are most severe in the branches of production that are most technically advanced. This leads to a chain reaction of falling prices and profits. In addition, during boom periods prices and wages rise, but prices increase more rapidly than goods, for this is the condition of increased profit. Hence consumption cannot keep pace with production, and at a given moment the system breaks down. At that moment, owing to the huge demand for bank credit during the boom, the banks are unable to even out the disproportion by granting credits. There is an acute demand for ready money, but producers can obtain it only by realizing the cash value of their own products. Everyone wants to sell at once, with the result that nobody buys: prices collapse while huge stocks accumulate, and the upshot is bankruptcy and unemployment on a large scale.

Owing to the interdependence of capitalist agencies, crises in one country affect others by way of import restrictions, and depressions tend increasingly to be worldwide. The least vulnerable concerns are those with the largest amount of capital, for they can cut production drastically without going bankrupt. Hence crises are themselves a cause of the concentration of capital, for they tend to eliminate small producers and leave the giants holding the field.

The reign of finance capital also leads to a change in the function of the state and to the decline of bourgeois-liberal ideology. The size of the area in which finance capital can operate freely becomes of even greater importance. Finance capital requires a strong state which can protect it from foreign competition and, by political and military means, facilitate the export of capital. Imperialism is the natural result of the concentration of capital and the fight to maintain and raise the profit level. The ideal situation, of course, is one in which the metropolis gains political domination over new markets and territories providing a cheaper labour force: hence finance capital supports imperialist policy and the spread of capitalist production throughout the world. The ideological weapons of the liberal bourgeoisie are out of date. The ideals of free trade, peace, equality, and humanitarianism are replaced by doctrines sanctioning the expansion of finance capital: racism, nationalism, the ideal of state power, and the worship of force.

These developments have an important effect on the class composition of society. The old and sometimes mortal conflicts between the upper and lower bourgeoisie, between town and country or bourgeois and landowners, are less and less in evidence. Hilferding shows how the magnates of capital, as they gain control over the whole economic activity of the middle classes, create such a unity of interests that society tends more and more towards a class polarization between the workers and all the rest. The petty bourgeoisie has no longer any prospects beyond what large-scale capital allows it, and is forced to identify its interests with those of the cartels; it is also the class most receptive to imperialism and racism, to ideas of power and political expansion. Technical progress tends to reduce the working-class population, first relatively and later absolutely, while administrators, technicians, and production managers are required more and more. At the present time these classes are clearly dependent on capital, not only in the economic field but in that of ideas, and provide support for reactionary political movements. But their position is vulnerable: the demand for their talents is less than the supply, and there is already a tendency to streamline managerial techniques so as to limit or decrease their numbers. In course of time we may expect members of this class to throw in their lot with the proletariat, as they come to realize that their position and interests as salary-earners are essentially similar to those of the working class.

The reign of finance capital does not diminish class antagonism but intensifies it to the highest degree, while at the same time weeding out the class structure, so to speak, by eliminating intermediate political forces and arraying against each other the hostile forces of a financial oligarchy and the proletariat. The latter's economic organizations, fighting for better terms for the sale of labour-power, naturally evolve political organizations which go beyond the framework of bourgeois society. The coalescence of the state machine with finance capital is so obvious that the least conscious of the proletariat are aware of the antagonism between themselves and the whole existing system. The proletariat cannot, of course, oppose to imperialism the reactionary and senseless cry of a return to free trade and a liberal economy. At the same time, realizing as it does the inevitable tendency of the present system, the proletariat cannot support it even though its ultimate result is to bring about a proletarian victory. The proletariat's answer to imperialism can only be socialism. Imperialism and the reign of finance oligarchy greatly facilitate the political struggle and advance the prospects of socialism, not only by causing wars and political catastrophes that help to revolutionize the consciousness of the proletariat, but still more because they bring about the socialization of production to the utmost extent possible under capitalism. Finance capital has separated the management of production from ownership and created huge capital accumulations subject to unified control. Hence the expropriation of the financial oligarchy by the state, once the proletariat has gained power, is a comparatively easy task. The state need not and should not expropriate all medium-sized and small enterprises, which, in any case, are at the present time completely dependent on the magnates of finance. Finance capital has already performed most of the expropriation. The state has only to take over the big banks and industrial firms in order to control production; if it is a working-class state it will use its economic power in the public interest and not to increase private profit. A single wholesale expropriation would be economically superfluous and politically dangerous.

At the end of his work Hilferding formulates the 'historical law' that 'In social formations based on class antagonisms, great social changes take place only when the ruling class has achieved the maximum concentration of its forces' (*Finanzkapital*, v. 25). This stage, he predicts, will soon be reached by bourgeois society, which will thus create the economic conditions for the dictatorship of the proletariat.

Hilferding's work had a greater influence on the development of Marxism than any other product of the Austrian school. It was in fact the most comprehensive attempt at a scientific analysis, from the Marxist point of view, of post-Marxian trends in the world economy. Hilferding was one of the first to point out the importance of the separation between capitalist ownership and production management, and to point out the increasingly significant role of managers and technicians. He also gave a lucid summary of the economic and political consequences of the new era of the concentration of capital.

His work is written from the standpoint of 'classical' Marxism, i.e. on the basis that concentration will lead finally to the polarization of classes and that the industrial proletariat is the battering-ram which will destroy the world of capital. He did not, however, draw the same conclusions from this analysis as Lenin subsequently did. Hilferding regarded capitalism as a worldwide system that would be destroyed owing to the exacerbation of class antagonism between the bourgeoisie and the proletariat. Lenin, from the same global point of view, concluded that the contradictions of imperialism would lead to its breaking down not at the points where economic evolution had gone furthest but at those where there was the greatest concentration and complexity of social conflicts. Other, non-proletarian demands—in particular those of the nationalities and the peasantry—must be present to constitute a reservoir of tension, and revolution was most probable where claims and dissensions were most numerous, rather than at the principal centres of finance capital. Hilferding believed in a proletarian revolution in the Marxian sense, as did Rosa Luxemburg, Pannekoek, and the whole of West European left-wing socialism; Lenin believed in a political revolution led by the party, supported by the proletariat but requiring in addition the impetus of other claims which it purported to represent and which it harnessed to its cause.

CHAPTER XIII

The Beginnings of Russian Marxism

1. Intellectual movements during the reign of Nicholas I

HISTORICAL determinism and the peasant question: these two headings sum up the history of the radical intellectual movement in nineteenth-century Russia, both in its pre-Marxist phases and in at least the first phase of the evolution of Marxism. The two questions were by no means independent of each other: the issue was whether and how far the theory of 'historical necessity' was reliable in general, and in particular what light it threw on the future of Russia—an overwhelmingly peasant country with a rudimentary industrial proletariat, governed by an autocracy and suffering, even after the 1861 reform, from many of the evils of feudalism.

The peculiarities of Russian Marxism are generally attributed to the special political and economic circumstances of the Empire, the effect of patterns created by pre-Marxist revolutionary movements, and the country's philosophical and religious tradition. There is no doubt much truth in these explanations, though they do not suffice to account for the spread of Russian Marxism in its Leninist form in other parts of the world after the October Revolution.

In considering the special character of Russian history emphasis has been laid not so much on political despotism as such but rather on its 'Oriental' nature: i.e. the far-reaching independence of the state and its bureaucracy *vis-à-vis* civil society, and its dominance over every social class including the most privileged. The Marxist thesis that state institutions in a class society are 'nothing but' organs of the privileged classes is harder to apply to Russia than to West European societies. In the nineteenth century some Russian historians, such as B. N. Chicherin, expressed the view, which is still held by some today, that the Russian state, far from being the outcome of previously existing class antagonisms, itself, as it were, created social classes from above. The Russian Marxists did not accept the theory of the autonomous nature of the Russian state in such an extreme form, but Plekhanov and Trotsky, for instance, agreed that the independence of the state apparatus in Russia was incomparably greater than elsewhere in Europe. Plekhanov in his historical analyses laid special emphasis on the 'Asiatic' features of the Russian autocracy: hence the importance he attached to decentralization in political programmes. Berdyayev wrote that Russia was a victim of the hugeness of her territory: the needs of defence and imperial expansion had led to the growth of a bureaucratic-military apparatus of coercion which constantly thwarted the short-term interests of the possessing classes and, from the time of Ivan the Terrible onwards, had consolidated itself while brutally suppressing their aspirations. All major economic changes in Russian history have been effected from above by means of state power: this is true of Peter the Great's time, of the reforms of Alexander II, and of industrialization and collectivization under Stalin. The essential feature of what is today called totalitarianism—namely the principle that the whole life of society, especially economic and cultural activity, must not only be supervised by the state but must be absolutely subordinated to its needs—has been characteristic of Russia for centuries: it could not, of course, always be put into practice so effectively, but it was and is the constant basis of the activity of the state apparatus. It follows from this principle that the state is the only legitimate source of any social initiative, and that any organization or crystallization of social life that is not imposed by the state is contrary to its needs and interests. It also follows that the citizen is the property of the state, and that all his acts are either directed by the state or are a challenge to its authority. Russian despotism created a society in which there was scarcely any middle term between servility and rebellion, between total identification with the existing order and absolute denial of it. Hence it was only late in the day and with great difficulty that Russia assimilated the idea of freedom which had taken shape in Western Europe through centuries of struggle between kings and barons, the nobility and the bourgeoisie—freedom which is defined by law and presupposes a legal order of society. In Russia social conditions were such that freedom was conceived only as anarchy, as the absence of law, since law presented itself in scarcely any other form than as the arbitrary will of a despotic ruler. Between absolutism and disorderly peasant revolt it was difficult in the extreme to evolve an idea of freedom sanctioned and limited by law: revolutionary movements naturally slid into the idea of a new form of totalitarianism (Pestel, Tkachov) or towards the anarchist vision of a society free from all laws and political institutions. Extremism and maximalism, which are often singled out as characteristics of Russian culture, may be regarded as due to the history of a country which never produced a strong middle class and whose stability always depended on the strength and efficiency of a centralized bureaucracy and only to a very small degree on the organic crystallization of interest-groups—a country in which to think about social reforms in a natural manner was to think of revolution, and there was no clear-cut dividing line between literary criticism and assassination.

The weakness of the towns and the minor role played by commerce for centuries impeded the growth of an independent intellectual culture. The emancipation of intellectuals, the cultivation of logical faculties, the power to reason and debate, and the love of abstract analysis—all these are features of urban culture and are linked with commercial prosperity. The assertion of Moscow's supremacy and the destruction of Novgorod prevented the development of urban civilization, and the Orthodox religion helped to isolate Russia from the West. Russian Caesaro-Papism meant not only that the Eastern Church was the servant of Tsarist despotism, but also that the rulers claimed dominion over their subjects' souls: the Church was subordinated to the Tsardom in such a way as to give the latter unlimited authority over individual consciences, and the natural consequence was a system of state police supervision of citizens' thoughts. The rivalry between secular and ecclesiastical power which did so much to develop Western civilization was virtually absent in Russia: the Church identified itself with the state and allowed the latter to reign supreme in intellectual life. At the same time, Russia as a political organism was endowed with the Church's religious messianism. After the fall of Byzantium the Orthodox Church evolved the idea of Moscow as the 'Third Rome', the successor, appointed for all eternity, to the capital of Christendom that had been conquered by the Turks. Moscow as the centre of Orthodoxy and Moscow as the capital of the Tsars were one and the same: Orthodox messianism became indistinguishable from Russian messianism, and the Tsar was not only a political autocrat but the guardian of religious truth.

This, of course, is a simplified picture which does not apply equally to all periods of Russian history, but it helps to explain certain features of revolutionary Marxism in Russia.

It was natural in these circumstances that religious and philosophical thought in Russia did not develop on the same lines as in Western Europe. Russia did not go through a scholastic phase or develop the powers of logic and analysis, the classification and definition of concepts, the marshalling of arguments and counter-arguments, that were the legacy of medieval Christian philosophy in the West. On the other hand, Russia also had no part in Renaissance civilization and was not convulsed by the spirit of scepticism and relativism which left such deep marks on European culture. Both these deficiencies are glaringly evident in Russian philosophical thought from its beginnings in the Enlightenment period. Its exponents are literary men and intellectual amateurs, intrigued by social or religious questions but incapable of systematizing their thoughts, of analysing concepts with laborious care or appraising the logical value of arguments. The philosophical writings of the greatest Russian thinkers are often fascinating from the rhetorical and literary points of view, full of passion and authentic feeling and free from 'scholasticism' in the pejorative sense: Russians did not ask what philosophy was for, they all knew its purpose. But as a rule their works are devoid of logical rigour, ill-constructed and inconsistent, shapeless, lacking in sequence and methodical subdivision. At the same time we are struck by the absence of scepticism and relativism. There is plenty of scoffing but very little irony: a frenzy of denunciation, but little power of detachment; even the humour expresses rage and despair rather than merriment. The brilliance of the nineteenth-century Russian novel no doubt proceeds from the same causes as do the defects of Russian philosophy. Academic philosophy of the Western type did not really exist in Russia until the last quarter of the century, and had produced no works of the first rank when it was swept away by the Revolution.

It is noteworthy that the Russian philosophy which leads in a direct line to Russian Marxism has as its starting-point questions and alternatives similar to those that prompted Marx's early thinking and took the form of reflections on Hegel's philosophy of history. These discussions go back to the dark and forbidding era of Nicholas I. The young Vissarion Belinsky and the young Bakunin begin their philosophizing from the same celebrated phrase about the identity of the real and the rational which inspired and organized the critique of the Young Hegelians. Belinsky, who knew Hegel at second hand in a dilettante fashion, believed he had discovered the rationality of history even in its barbaric and despotic manifestations. It was possible, he thought, to come to terms with cruel reality if one grasped the insignificance of all that was individual, contingent, and subjective, and the greatness of historical Reason, craftily mocking at the desires and hopes of human beings. In articles written in 1839 Belinsky expounded his philosophy of reconciliation, or rather submission to the majesty of 'universality' embodied in an Asiatic satrapy. But within two years he had broken completely with this Hegelian, or rather pseudo-Hegelian, historiosophic masochism and had come to believe in the merit of the human individual as the sole intrinsic value, which must not be sacrificed to the Moloch of the historical *universale*. After his conversion to socialism and then to naturalism *à la* Feuerbach, Belinsky remained in the Russian tradition as the type of a mind oscillating between desperate fatalism and moralistic revolt, between the 'rationality' of the uncaring progress of the *Weltgeist* and the irrationality of the sentient individual, between 'objectivism' and sentimentalism.

The most important issue in Russian intellectual life under Nicholas I was that between Slavophils and Westernizers. Slavophilism was a Russian variant of Romantic philosophy in its opposition to the Enlightenment, rationalism, liberalism, and cosmopolitanism. The Slavophils (Ivan Kireyevsky, Alexey Khomyakov, Konstantin Aksakov, Yury Samarin) were in search of a philosophy to legitimize the Russian autocracy and the Eastern Church's claim to be the sole depositary of Christian truth. They idealized pre-Petrine Russia, especially the Russia of the first Romanovs, in which they discerned principles that could protect the nation from the pernicious imitation of Western liberalism and make it the spiritual leader of the world. For this purpose they elaborated the doctrine of 'community' (*sobornost*'), the spiritual unity of society based on devotion to eternal truths and opposed to the mechanical, purely legal bond of interest that prevailed in Western Europe. The essence of the Russian spirit was freedom conceived as a result of the love of God, not the negative and unspiritual freedom of the liberals. Another essential feature was the integral development of the individual, in which human reason does not rely on its power of abstract thought but harmonizes its activity with living faith as the source of all spiritual values. This faith does not exist in the Roman Church, which maintains only the hierarchical unity of law, or in Protestant bodies, which have sacrificed the ideal of unity to a subjective love of freedom. In contrast to the West, whose intellectual culture and theology are based on confidence in the abstract power of logic, while its social organization takes for granted the antagonism of individual and class-interests, restrained only by the repressive force of law, the Russian spirit is that of a free organic union based on voluntary submission to divine truth and the unity of secular and religious authority.

The Westernizers did not have such a clearly defined social philosophy as the Slavophils. Westernism was the general name for the policy of 'Europeanizing' Russia: it went with the cult of natural science, an attachment to liberal principles, hatred of Tsarist despotism, and the conviction that only by taking the 'Western road' could Russia emerge from her backwardness and cultural stagnation. Although both the Slavophils and the Westernizers had roots in Russian tradition, symbolized respectively by Moscow and St. Petersburg, it is noteworthy that almost all the adherents of both schools were students of German philosophy and often defined their position with the aid of Hegelian categories. It might seem that in Nicholas I's time the conservatives had little enough reason to fear that Russia would be engulfed in a tide of liberalism. Nevertheless, despite the country's political and economic stagnation, Western ideas were beginning to seep through and find acceptance among the young, as witness the Petrashevsky discussion group. In the time of Alexander II and Alexander III, however, 'pure' versions of

Slavophilism and Westernism became less important compared with trends which incorporated features of both in different ways and in varying proportions, as did all the variants of populism.

2. Herzen

Aleksandr Ivanovich Herzen (1812–70) was the first important advocate of a 'third solution', leaving room for Russia's own, non-capitalist way to social liberation and also for the values of Western liberalism. In his cult of science and hostility to religion and the autocracy he was sharply opposed to the Slavophil tradition, but his critique of capitalism was essentially in accordance with it.

As a schoolboy Herzen vowed hostility to Russian despotism, and he remained faithful to that vow. He settled in the West in 1847, and from 1855 published a periodical entitled *Polyarnaya Zvezda* (*The Pole Star*) and afterwards *Kolokol* (*The Bell*), which played a major part in animating the radical movement among' the Russian intelligentsia. Like most intellectuals of his generation he went through a Hegelian phase, in which he attacked conservative interpretations of the 'rationality of the real' and upheld the dialectic as the principle of permanent negation and criticism of the existing order. He wrote some philosophical essays which, while they contain nothing original, played some part in propagating naturalist and anti-religious attitudes in Russia. His main influence, however, consisted in his critique of capitalism and hope of a specifically Russian road to socialism based on the traditional peasant community, the *mir* or *obshchina*.

Herzen was opposed to capitalism and Western civilization not because it bred poverty and exploitation but because it degraded people by the exclusive cult of material values: the universal ideal of prosperity crippled the personality, society became spiritually barren and was sunk in general mediocrity. As a rich member of the gentry, free from material cares and living in the comfort of Western capitals while he denounced the philosophy of wealth, Herzen was a suspect figure to some radicals, but he won much popularity with his appeal to a tradition that would enable Russia to achieve social justice while spurning capitalist values. He believed that the human personality was a supreme and intrinsic value, and that the purpose of social institutions was to enable it to develop and enrich itself spiritually in every way. Western civilization had the opposite effect, by standardizing all values and allowing the universal spirit of competition to destroy the spontaneous solidarity of all human beings. This was an attack on capitalism from the standpoint of aristocracy rather than socialism. However, Herzen had the people's cause at heart and was anxious not merely to preserve the values created by the privileged classes, but to extend them to everybody. The common ownership of land by the *mir* seemed to him to hold out the prospect of a new social order which would unite justice and equality with the voluntary solidarity of individuals, abolishing despotism but not replacing it by universal egoism and money-grubbing. In this way Herzen began a discussion that was to dominate Russian thinking for the next three decades: the question of Russia's road to socialism by way of the village commune.

Herzen has been invoked as a pioneer by populists, liberals, and Marxists. To the Marxists he was not only a denouncer of the autocracy but also a standard-bearer of the cult of science, an enemy to religion and the Orthodox Church and a philosopher who could, without much exaggeration, be called a materialist. Despite his hatred for despotism, however, it is hard to call him an ideologist of revolution: he certainly was not one in the sense in which the next generation spoke of revolution, when it seemed hopeless to put any faith in a reform of the existing system. Herzen did not get on with the revolutionaries of the 1860s: he disliked their primitivism and contempt for the non-utilitarian values of art and education, their dogmatism, intolerance, and cult of a revolutionary apocalypse, which they seemed to desire for its own sake and to which they were prepared to sacrifice all existing values. A certain conservatism in Herzen's thought made him aware of the danger of the fanatic belief in progress that regards living generations as far less important than those still to come.

Although Herzen thought that Russia's situation was historically privileged and that she could build a just society thanks to the tradition of the village commune (which he mistakenly believed to be a survival of primitive communism), he did not link this with any nationalist messianism or with the idea of Moscow as the future Mecca of humanity. He was a Russian patriot, but not a chauvinist: in 1863 he offended a large part of public opinion by defending the cause of the insurgent Poles. This was one reason, though not the only one, why his star began to fade during the 1860s.

The death of Nicholas I and the defeat in the Crimea ushered in an era of reforms which either caused fresh intellectual divisions or made it necessary for old ones to be reformulated. With the abolition of serfdom and the grant of land to the peasants in 1861, followed by reforms in the judicial system, the army, and local government, the question of Russia's future under capitalism ceased to be purely speculative and took on practical significance. Intensive industrialization was still some thirty years away; the peasantry was encumbered with many remnants of serfdom, and economic questions were almost purely agricultural in scope; but it was nevertheless clear to all that a period of 'modernization' had begun and that it was time to think about its possibilities and dangers.

3. Chernyshevsky

The writings of Nikolay Gavrilovich Chernyshevsky (1828–89) were much more important to the radical intelligentsia of the sixties than those of Herzen. Chernyshevsky was another of the chief inspirers of populism, though he is not generally termed a populist in the strict sense. He also looked to the village commune for Russia's social regeneration, but he was more of a Westernizer than Herzen: he adopted in full the naturalist philosophy of Feuerbach and presented it to the public in a work entitled *The Anthropological Principle in Philosophy* (1860). He was a consistent exponent of Enlightenment-type utilitarianism on a materialist basis. He believed that all human motives come down in the last resort to a calculation of pleasures and pains and that egoism is the sole driving force of human behaviour. This, however, did not mean that there could not be co-operation and solidarity, or acts of the kind described as self-sacrifice or disinterested aid: all such acts could perfectly well be interpreted as instances of the universal desire for pleasure and profit.

All these are traditional motifs, familiar from the history of utilitarian doctrine. From the same source Chernyshevsky derived his belief in rational egoism, i.e. the organization of communal life in such a way that all individual egoisms are satisfied in a general harmony. The conflict of egoisms is due to faulty social institutions and lack of education. Chernyshevsky accepted the basic values of liberalism: he desired the 'European-ization' of Russia, the overthrow of the autocracy, political freedom, universal education, and the emancipation of the peasants. He also believed, however, that Russia could enjoy industrial progress and liberalism without extinguishing the communist flame that burnt on in the *obshchina*, and that the horrors of capitalist development could be avoided.

As disappointment ensued after the reform of 1861, Cherny-shevsky laid increasing emphasis on revolutionary hopes. As time went on he lost interest in the village commune and devoted more attention in his writings to political developments and the need to overthrow the Tsardom by force. He was arrested in 1862 and sentenced to hard labour after two years' imprisonment. While in prison he wrote his celebrated novel *What is to be Done?*, which became the catechism of Russian revolutionary youth. It is a work of small literary value, didactic, boring, and pedantic, but all the more faithful to Chernyshevsky's doctrine that art, like science, had no intrinsic value but was to be judged by its immediate social utility. The novel succeeded in its purpose of instilling into revolutionary youth a spirit of asceticism, serious-ness, devotion to the people's cause, and contempt for the moral conventions of their elders. It did much to popularize the moral 'style' of radical circles, marked by doctrinairism, fanaticism, sincerity and self-sacrifice, the cult of science, and the lack of a sense of humour. Lenin respected and admired Chernyshevsky all his life as the teacher who had introduced him to revolutionary ideology, and we may say that Lenin was an ideal specimen of the type which Chernyshevsky portrayed and which was not uncommon among the revolutionaries: an intellectual so exclusively devoted to the cause that any discussion which cannot be made to serve the revolution is no better than idle chatter, and values that cannot be put to use in the same way are merely food for aesthetes and dilettanti. Conversion to the revolutionary faith made it natural for many of the Russian intelligentsia, shocked and humiliated by poverty, ignorance, and oppression, to abandon all values that were peculiar to the privileged classes. Given the gigantic task of raising Russia out of her backwardness and barbarism, the cult of spiritual, aesthetic, or intellectual values that was so strong in Herzen's case seemed a betrayal of the revolutionary mission. Utilitarianism and materialism were, so to speak, the natural expression of this attitude. The connection can be seen in Chernyshevsky and also in two writers who died young but were extremely popular in the 1860s: N. A. Dobrolyubov (1836–61) and D. I. Pisarev (1840–68). To the latter is attributed the remark that a pair of boots is worth more than all the works of Shakespeare.

Materialism—and this term can be applied to Chernyshevsky without reservation—thus had a clear political sense in Russia in the second half of the century. It of course involved hostility to the Church and religion, and thereby served in the fight against autocracy; at the same time, by seeming to justify a utilitarian philosophy of life, it was a negation of the culture and habits of the educated classes. Its votaries were able to brand all disinterested artistic and intellectual pursuits as idle amusements of the aristocracy, and to apply to all human thoughts and actions the key question: 'Whom does it profit?' In and after the sixties, as elsewhere in Europe, materialism was reinforced by the popularity of Darwinism. For the radicals, however, Darwinism was a two-edged sword. On the one hand, it gave opponents of religion scientific ground for saying that all human affairs could be explained in purely biological categories; on the other, especially as interpreted by Spencer, it suggested that human history and society could be explained in terms of natural selection, the struggle for existence, and the survival of the fittest. This latter consequence (as it was thought to be) of Darwinism was unwelcome to the revolutionaries on two grounds. In the first place, it might imply that the struggle for existence was an eternal law of nature, which put a stop to dreams of a perfectly harmonious future society. Secondly, if universally applied it introduced a kind of biological fatalism which condemned to sterility any individual efforts or moral endeavours. Whatever men may do, according to social Darwinism those who remain in possession of the field will finally be those who show most power of adaptation—not those whose sufferings are today most acute, or whose cause appears morally just. In this way scientism, utilitarianism, and materialism, which the revolutionaries adopted as weapons in the political struggle, appeared to show that the struggle had no purpose. Hence Chernyshevsky took from Darwinism the theory of the origin and mutation of species, but not the theory of natural selection; while later sociologists of the populist camp endeavoured to limit the Darwinian theory in various ways so as to avoid having to draw unwelcome conclusions.

4. Populism and the first reception of Marxism

The radical movement which developed in Russia after 1861 bore the general title of populism (*narodnichestvo*). Historians differ as to the exact meaning and applicability of this term. In an article of 1898 entitled 'What heritage have we abandoned?' Lenin defined populism as consisting of three factors. In the first place, the populists (*narodniki*) considered capitalism in Russia a retrograde phenomenon and wished to halt its development. Secondly, they regarded the peasantry and especially the *obshchina* as a self-contained institution in the sense that it could not be analysed in terms of social class: they thus ignored class differences among the peasantry. Thirdly, they did not perceive the link between the intelligentsia and political institutions on the one hand and the class interests of Russian society on the other, and they thus imagined that the intelligentsia could be an independent force capable of imparting to history whatever course it chose. This account of populism, it will be seen, contains no reference to political strategy or policy *vis-à-vis* the autocracy. Those whom the Marxists combated under the name of populists in fact included both reformists and revolutionaries; some relied on terrorism, others on propaganda; they differed in their view of historical determinism, their attachment to the Slavophil or Westernizing tradition, and their attitude to Marxism. Most of the populist theoreticians were acquainted with Marxism and accepted some of its features, though none of them except Danielson styled himself a Marxist. The aspects of populism singled out by Lenin were those on which debate actually centred in the 1890s. He also characterized it from the point of view of class origin, as an ideology of small propertyowners who wished to free Russian life from feudal constraint, but were frightened by the advance of capitalism which threatened to destroy their economic position. In the same article Lenin contrasted the populist tradition with that of the 'Enlightenment' writers of the sixties, such as Skaldin, who opposed all remnants of servitude and demanded political freedom, self-government, education, and the Europeanization of Russia: these writers represented the ideology of capitalist progress in a more or less pure form and did not realize the contradictions and antagonisms that the triumph of capitalism was bound to bring with it. Unlike the liberals of this stamp, the populists stood for a romantic Utopia: they realized what catastrophic results capitalism would bring, but they hoped to avert them by impossible dreams of a return to pre-capitalist forms of production and the preservation of the *obshchina* as the germ of the socialist future. The populists' merit, according to Lenin, was that they were the first to pose the question of the economic contradictions of capitalism in Russia, though they had no answer to offer except the reactionary idea of a golden age. From this point of view Lenin compared them to Sismondi, who, like them, represented the ideological interests of small owners threatened by the advance of capitalism. Like them, too, Sismondi denounced the poverty, exploitation, and anarchy of capitalist production, but had nothing to set against it except a return to craftsmanship and petty trading.

The view is held, for example by Richard Pipes, that populism in the sense defined by Lenin in this article never existed as a single intellectual or political movement. According to this view populism properly denotes a tendency which arose in the early 1870s and was based on the Bakuninist idea that it was not for the intelligentsia to impose socialism or any other doctrine on the people, but to support whole-heartedly the latter's wishes and aspirations and work for the revolution on the lines the people desired. This, it is argued, was a clearly anti-intellectual trend, involving no theory of socialism or attitude to the development of Russian capitalism, and was in fact the negation of political activity. The Marxists, and particularly Struve, are responsible for coining the term 'populism' to denote the opponents of capitalism and glorifiers of the peasant commune, but in this sense it was a political weapon and did not correspond to a historical reality. Other scholars, such as F. Venturi, A. Walicki, and Soviet historians, while not disputing that the populist ideology took many forms, use the term in the broad sense given to it by Marxist literature in the belief that it expresses the essence of the ideological controversy of the last quarter of the century in Russia, though in particular cases we may be in doubt as to whether this or that writer belongs to the populist camp.

The question is not of the first importance as far as the history of Marxist doctrine is concerned, but it is necessary to take note of the development of populism for two reasons. In the first place, populism in a broad sense was the first intellectual movement in Russia to be infiltrated by Marxism. Secondly, Marxism in Russia largely took shape through the controversy with populism and was for a long time dominated by the 'peasant question' and polemics with agrarian socialism. This accounts for certain features of the version of Marxism that finally prevailed in Russia, namely Leninism, and also for the fact that this version has since been particularly influential in parts of the world where the peasant question still dominates other social problems.

Populism in this broad sense developed around 1870 and was, in its different varieties, the chief form of social radicalism in the seventies and eighties: in the latter decade, however, orthodox Marxism made its appearance and created a new polemical situation.

The populists of varying shades were all agreed in identifying themselves with the cause of the Russian 'people', and devoted all their efforts to its emancipation. They differed, however, as to whether this meant emancipation by the people's own efforts, or whether there would have to be a revolution prepared and led by a conspiratorial organization. They agreed in believing that capitalism in Russia could only be a source of social degradation, and in hoping that the country could manage without it; but they differed in their general views of historical progress and determinism. They were united in despising political reforms and attaching no importance to liberal and constitutional slogans. These views determined the basic attitude of the populists towards Marx's theories. They were glad to invoke his authority, but did so in a highly selective manner. They naturally welcomed his emphasis on the destructive effects of capitalist accumulation—exploitation, poverty, and spiritual degradation—and the anti-human consequences of the division of labour in its advanced form. They also gave a favourable reception to those parts of his theory which served to denounce 'formal' democracy, political liberties, and the whole liberal superstructure of capitalism and free competition. On the other hand, they rejected his view that capitalism was a tremendous historical advance and that the liberation of the working people must be preceded by the technological and social development that capitalism brought with it: in short, they rejected the Marxian-Hegelian theory of progress by contradiction, together with any suggestion that all countries had to go through the same historical evolution and endure the rigour and injustice of capitalist accumulation before they could embark on a socialist revolution. There were, of course, disputes among them as to the true meaning and degree of applicability of Marx's theory of capitalism, especially in the light of Russian conditions: the statements of Marx and Engels themselves on this point, taken together, were by no means unequivocal.

The three writers who did most to influence radical thinking in Russia in the 1870s were P. L. Lavrov, N. K. Mikhailovsky, and P. N. Tkachov. Pyotr Lavrov (1823–1900) aroused the intelligentsia to a sense of guilt *vis-à-vis* the people and an urge to expiate their privileges. His *Historical Letters*, published in the late sixties, and the periodical *Vperyod* (*Forward*), which appeared in Zurich in 1873–6 (he had fled from Russia in 1870), called on young members of the intelligentsia to work among the people and fan the flame of revolution. Under the combined influence of Lavrov and Bakunin there took place in 1872–4 the celebrated movement in which hundreds of young people went into the villages with the object of educating the peasants for socialism or, in the case of the Bakuninists, bringing their revolutionary instincts to the fore. The result of the pilgrimage was highly disappointing. No new Pugachovs and Stenka Razins made their appearance, nor did the peasants reveal a latent enthusiasm for socialism; they were more likely to denounce the agitators to the police than to heed their appeals. This did much to weaken Bakunin's influence, but it did not undermine the activity of Lavrov's followers, though they were obliged to change tactics.

Lavrov held that the intelligentsia could and must be the fount of revolutionary consciousness, but he did not believe that the Russian peasant was revolutionary and socialist by nature. His belief in the mission of the intelligentsia was of a moral and not a determinist character. He did not contend that there was any historical law which made it certain that Russia would adopt socialism; but he believed this could be brought about by an enlightened élite identifying itself morally with the people's cause. He demanded from the young intelligentsia self-sacrifice and a spirit of battle: their success would depend on the firmness of the people's will, not on ineluctable historical laws. Together with Mikhailovsky, Lavrov represented a viewpoint which was later called, in Russia, 'subjective sociology': viz. that social processes, unlike natural ones, are partly determined by subjective desires and ideals which animate people because they are thought to be right, not necessarily because they are expected to triumph. Our view that something is morally right cannot depend on whether we think it inevitable; and, as history is influenced by the fact that many people regard their own position as morally right, there is no reason to think that any universal laws, indifferent to human desires and ideals, are bound to impel the historical process in any particular direction. Lavrov shared the faith in the village commune as a possible nucleus of socialism in Russia, but he did not glorify the country's technical and economic backwardness; he thought the dissemination of socialist ideals among the toiling masses would lead to a revolution after which all problems of economic development could be solved. As to the struggle for a constitution and political freedom, it could only be a source of confusion and a waste of revolutionary energy. The basic elements of Lavrov's ideology— the denial of historical determinism and of the inevitability of capitalism in Russia, faith in the intelligentsia as the standard-bearer of socialism, the creative role of ideals in history, the village commune as the nucleus of socialism, indifference to the political struggle for 'liberalization'—these together form a stereotype which was to be the chief target of Marxist attack. Among pre-Marxist writers Lavrov contributed especially to awakening the revolutionary and socialist consciousness of the Russian intelligentsia. His attacks on religion as the fruit of ignorance, on law as the instrument of coercion by the privileged classes, on property as the result of theft, his emphasis on moral qualities and moral motivation among revolutionaries, his call for revolutionary asceticism and enlightenment for the people—all this went to form the radical ethos which prevailed in Russia for a long time and to a considerable extent inspired the social democratic intelligentsia.

N. K. Mikhailovsky (1842–1904) occupied a much more important place than Lavrov in the Marxists' anti-populist polemics. He was active as a writer for a longer period and was more influential, as he lived in Russia and wrote in the legal press, and, unlike Lavrov, he was not a revolutionary.

Mikhailovsky sought to integrate the peasant question in Russia into a social philosophy based on personalist and moralistic principles. In his books and articles in *Otechestvennye zapiski* (*Annals of the Fatherland*) and, in the 1890s, in his own periodical *Russkoye bogatstvo* (*Russia's Wealth*), he concentrated on analysing the social effects of capitalist economy and showing, with the aid of 'subjective sociology', that it was not historically necessary for Russia to tread the dolorous path of proletarianization and the class struggle. There were no inexorable laws of history independent of human ideals. In reasoning about society the question to ask was 'What is desirable?' and not 'What is necessary?': social processes were the work of people and depended, in part at least, on what people believed to be good. Social thought should be framed in normative categories, for values that were generally accepted were, for that very reason, a real social force. In general, no idea of progress could be formed without evaluative premises: it was not a question of pursuing the unrealizable ideals of a sociology free from value-judgements, but of examining critically the values underlying current theories of progress, viz. those of the positivists and Marxists.

Mikhailovsky's criticism was thus levelled at both Spencer and the Marxists. Spencer believed that progress was based on the unlimited differentiation of all forms of life, so that the development of the division of labour in society was progress *par excellence*. But this, said Mikhailovsky, was the reverse of the truth. If we start from the point of view of the good of the individual—and individuals are the only social reality—we see that the division of labour leads to spiritual degradation and destroys the possibility of the all-round development of the individual. This was also Marx's view. The object of life was not to develop one-sided aptitudes and increase production for its own sake, but to further the harmonious and many-sided development of personality. From this point of view the capitalist economy which favoured specialization for the sake of increased productivity was not an instance of progress but a cultural calamity. Capitalism signified pauperization of the spirit as well as the body: it broke the ties of solidarity and atomized society, universalizing the spirit of competition and struggle. Russia, however, had preserved in the village commune a form of social and productive organization which could bar the way to capitalism. The *obshchina* was based on simple, not complex, co-operation, and left the way open for all-round personal development: its members held their property in common and lived in a state of solidarity, not competition. In its present form it was not ideal, but the task was to remove the external obstacles that impeded its development and not to encourage disruptive factors in the name of abstract 'progress'. The Marxists, with their faith in the inevitability of capitalism in Russia, were in effect proclaiming a gospel of inactivity and capitulation, accepting the prospect that the great majority of the workers would be condemned to proletarianization, exploitation, and spiritual death. In acclaiming capitalism as progressive they were using a concept of progress in which the abstract idea of the common good was quite independent of the good of the individuals who made up society. But in reality all human values were personal values. There was no general good or perfect society that could be set up against the benefit of human individuals—for it is they and not society who feel and think, suffer and desire. The domination of impersonal values, even such as Justice or Science, over real individuals is contrary to anything that can properly be called progress.

Not without reason, the Marxists regarded Mikhailovsky as a Romantic critic of capitalism. In his attacks on it we recognize themes from Romantic literature, the utopian socialists, Rousseau and the anarchists, Saint-Simon and his followers, Stirner and Herzen. These attacks coincided on essential points with Marx's social philosophy (the pernicious consequences of the division of labour, the replacement of solidarity by competition, etc.), but the difference was that according to Marx humanity, to attain salvation, must first descend into the inferno of capitalism: the tyranny of money and machines over live human beings would end by destroying itself and enabling men to recapture their lost values. The question was, however, whether this applied to each country separately, or whether the fact that capitalism in some parts of the world had created the pre-conditions of socialism might not make it possible for others to avoid going through the full cycle. Marx himself had considered this point, and his well-known remarks on Russia afforded support in one important respect to the populists, who duly made use of them. In 1874 Engels, in controversy with Tkachov, expressed himself strongly against the idea that the socialist revolution could take place in a country without a proletariat, like Russia. He agreed, however, that the village commune might provide a nucleus of socialism if it survived until there was a proletarian revolution in the West: in other words there could only be a 'Russian road to socialism' if socialism first triumphed in its natural habitat, the highly industrialized countries. This idea is repeated in the preface by Marx and Engels to the Russian edition of *The Communist Manifesto* (1882): if a Russian revolution were to give the signal for the proletarian revolution in Western Europe, the village commune might be the nucleus of socialist changes. The populists were especially pleased with a letter which Marx wrote in 1877 to the editor of *Otechestvennye zapiski*: the letter was not sent, and was published in Russia only in 1886. In it Marx says clearly that the schemata of *Capital* apply to Western Europe and do not claim universal validity (though it must be observed here that there is no hint of this limitation in *Capital* itself). Therefore, Marx goes on, there is no necessary reason why Russia should follow in the footsteps of the West; but she will be obliged to do so if she continues on the course of 1861, for she will then lose her chance of separate, non-capitalist development. Marx expresses the same idea even more emphatically in a letter of March 1881 to Vera Zasulich and in his preparatory notes for this letter. (Neither Vera Zasulich nor Plekhanov thought fit to publish the letter, as they evidently feared it would give valuable ammunition to the populists: it came to light only after the Revolution.) Here he repeats that the argument of *Capital* does not in any way pre-judge the question of the *obshchina*, but adds that, having examined the matter, he believes that the latter can be a source of social regeneration if it is not destroyed by external pressure. Russia, thanks to its backwardness, is privileged socially as well as technologically. Just as it can adopt Western techniques in a ready-made, developed form without going through all the stages that have been necessary in the West, and was able to set up a banking and credit system that took centuries to establish in Western countries, so in the field of social evolution Russia can avoid the horrors of capitalism and develop the village commune into a universal productive system. Marx does not, of course, predict that this will necessarily be so, but repeats that Russia still has open to it the possibility of non-capitalist development. Altogether it may be said that on this crucial issue in Russian polemics at the time, Marx was much less of a Marxist than his Russian disciples. The latter, however, showed in the 1890s that the issue had become pointless, as by then no power could arrest the development of capitalism and the decline of the *obshchina*. Engels at this time reverted to his previous opinion and, in letters of 1892 and 1893 to Danielson, acknowledged that the *obshchina* was a lost cause. However, in a letter of 1885 to Vera Zasulich he supported the populist conspirators in another way by stating that Russia was in an exceptional situation in which a handful of people could, if they chose, bring about a revolution.

On this last point Engels was in agreement with Tkachov and his adherents. Pyotr Tkachov (1844–85) took part in underground activities from his early youth and was imprisoned more than once. From 1873 he lived abroad and became the chief ideologist of those populists who founded their hopes on a revolution brought about by terrorist conspiracy. Tkachov came to the conclusion, later formulated by Marx, that if Russia embarked on a capitalist course nothing could prevent its further development along this line, and the country would have to go through the same martyrdom as the West. But there was still time to avert this, for capitalism had not yet taken hold in Russia. The opportunity must therefore be seized to carry out a revolution at once and avoid the capitalist cycle of development. It was no good counting on the people's innate revolutionary instincts. The revolution could only be the work of a conscious, well-organized minority, an underground party with strict discipline and centralized command. The object of the revolution was the 'happiness of all', in particular the abolition of inequality and the destruction of élite cultures. Here

Tkachov repeats themes from the totalitarian Utopias of the eighteenth century: the perfect society will suppress any possibility of exceptional individuals arising and will create equal conditions of life and education for all its members; a centralized authority of the enlightened *avant-garde* will plan every aspect of public life. Tkachov does not explain how the principle of equality can prevail in a society where the majority is subjected to the absolute, unfettered dictatorship of the revolutionaries, or how he reconciles hatred for élitism with the assumption of power by a revolutionary élite. His communism is of a homespun kind and displays no theoretical insight. But he is responsible, more than anyone else in Russia, for the idea of a centralized and disciplined party as the main organ of revolution. Historians have often emphasized his role as a precursor of Lenin on this point. The clandestine populist association founded in 1876 and known as Zemlya i Volya (Land and Liberty) owed its organizational ideas to Tkachov although it did not take over his social ideology. Lenin, while showing the greatest contempt for the populists especially in their later stages, had a high respect for the organizational traditions of the underground populist movement.

In the eyes of Marxist critics all the ideologists of populism were 'subjectivists', for they believed that the future of Russia could be decisively shaped by moral ideals spread by an enlightened élite (Mikhailovsky), socialist education of the people under the guidance of the intelligentsia (Lavrov), or the revolutionary will of an organized party (Tkachov). There remained, however, the question that Mikhailovsky put to the Marxists: if the scientific and completely unsubjective attitude consists in accepting what is said to be inevitable, i.e. whatever actually happens, how do the Marxists justify their own revolutionary activity? This question came to the fore later on, especially in the argument between the orthodox and the 'legal Marxists'. The populists, as it were, repeated in Russian terms the dilemma which had challenged Marx as a young man, between historical fatalism and a moralist Utopia. How can one justify theoretically and consistently the attitude of a revolutionary who desires to weigh up social phenomena in their practical, cause-and-effect relationships, not measuring them by arbitrary moral criteria, yet who does not wish to be a mere spectator or chronicler of events but believes that he can affect them by his own actions?

It should be noted that the populist doctrine in general, and the glorification of the village commune in particular, were not confined to moralists in search of a social ideal. The defence of the commune and the idea of bypassing capitalism in Russia also had purely economic foundations, as expounded, for example, by the populists Vorontsov and Danielson. These men were not political revolutionaries but, on the contrary, endeavoured to persuade the government that for the sake of economic and social progress it should cease to promote capitalist reforms and work for industrialization on different lines. They claimed to judge between the rural commune and capitalism from the standpoint of economic efficiency, while also pointing out the social consequences of each.

V. P. Vorontsov (1847–1918), in articles written in the seventies and published in book form in 1882, argued that capitalism in Russia was not only undesirable but impossible, at all events in a developed form. Russia could not follow the same path as the West, partly because its access to foreign markets was barred by stronger competitors, and also because it could not count on a home market large enough to permit the expansion of capitalist production. The development of capitalism so far was due less to natural conditions than to government protectionism—a policy that was ruinous and incapable of attaining its own aims, though it might well succeed in proletarianizing the peasantry. The home market could not expand sufficiently because capitalism, by destroying village crafts, was depriving the peasants of income with which to buy industrial products. The post-emancipation years had shown that land was passing into peasant hands on a large scale instead of its ownership being concentrated. Vorontsov was not an opponent of industrialization or a worshipper of primitive technology, but he believed that if the government went on fostering capitalism Russia would suffer from all the evils of the system without enjoying its benefits. The government should nationalize those branches of industry which required large-scale investment and should entrust small-scale industrial production to workers' co-operatives; at the same time it should remove the fiscal burdens and encumbrances which were breaking up the village commune, and should allow agriculture to develop freely on traditional lines. Vorontsov thus advocated a kind of state socialism under the aegis of the Tsarist government. The Marxists of course mocked this proposal, but, as R. Pipes observes, it is not very different from the principles of Lenin's New Economic Policy.

N. F. Danielson, the translator of *Capital* (1872) and a Marxist by conviction, also held that capitalism in Russia was bound to meet insuperable obstacles: it was in no position to conquer foreign markets, and was destroying its own home market by proletarianizing the peasants and bringing about mass unemployment. Russia's social needs could be met only by a 'popular' system in which the means of production belonged to the producers. Instead of being destroyed, the village commune should be made to adopt modern techniques and thus become the foundation of a socialist society.

The populist economists cared as little, or even less, about political freedoms and constitutions as most other members of the populist camp; but they set the whole of radical opinion against them by offering a programme of reforms whereby Russia might find salvation under the Tsar's auspices. In so doing, however, they raised new problems with which Marxist literature had to come to grips. In the nineties the question of markets was one of those most discussed in Marxist circles. In order to confute the populists it was necessary to prove that Russian capitalism was in a position to create a market sufficient for its own development. This problem was studied by all the chief Marxist writers, including Struve, Tugan-Baranovsky, Plekhanov, Lenin, and Bulgakov.

Almost immediately on its inception in the mid-seventies Zemlya i Volya was faced with the decision whether to concentrate on the political struggle or on socialist propaganda. The former meant in practice fighting for constitutional liberties and for the liberalization of Russia on Western lines; but the populists' dilemma was that this seemed incompatible with their socialist ideals. If Russia were to adopt a liberal and parliamentary system the prospect of socialism would recede to an indefinite future, for it was hard to foresee a time when socialism would triumph on the basis of popular representation. The adherents of the traditional populist ideology therefore preferred a policy of revolutionary propaganda and education, while opposing both the idea of an alliance with the liberals (who were few and far between at this time) and an attempt to take over power by revolutionary force. Before long, in 1879, the organization split into two groups. The advocates of the political struggle formed the People's Will party (Narodnaya Volya) with a programme of terrorist action, while its adversaries formed a group named Black Repartition (Chorny Peredel) to carry on propaganda for the sharing-out of large estates among the peasantry. Unlike the abstract ideals of socialism, this was calculated to appeal to the rural population, and the members of this group were thus faithful to the populist tradition of concentrating on issues understood by the people. Narodnaya Volya, a small organization of fanatically brave and devoted terrorists, bequeathed the legend of A. I. Zhelyabov and Sofya Perovskaya, who organized the assassination of Alexander II. It did not produce any theoretical works of importance; its chief propagandist was Lyov Tikhomirov (1852–1923), who subsequently recanted his revolutionary views and became an arch-reactionary and monarchist. Zhelyabov and Perovskaya were hanged after the Tsar's murder on 1 March 1881; Zhelyabov declared in court that he was fighting for justice in Christ's name, and before his execution he kissed the cross.

While the members of Narodnaya Volya held that the main revolutionary task was to fight against the state, whose destruction would remove every hindrance to social liberation, the non-political adherents of Black Repartition opposed the Blanquist idea of seizing power without the participation of the masses. The repressions which followed the Tsar's murder effectively destroyed the populist underground in both its forms. While the heroes of Narodnaya Volya became a revolutionary legend, the Black Repartition movement produced the first outstanding ideologist of Russian Marxism in the person of G. V. Plekhanov.

XIV

Plekhanov and the Codification of Marxism

PLEKHANOV ranks with Kautsky in the importance of his role in the history of Marxism and the dissemination of Marxist doctrine. He is generally, and rightly, called the father of Marxism in Russia. Many populists had read Marx and been influenced by him, but Plekhanov was the first Russian to adopt Marxism as an integral, self-sufficient world-view, embracing all philosophical questions and social theories and providing complete guidance for political activity. Without exception, all Russian Marxists of Lenin's generation were Plekhanov's pupils and acknowledged the fact. In addition, his writings were influential far beyond Russia. He was not an original theoretician, nor did he intend to be: he sought to remain faithful to the doctrine as he understood it, and to defend it against all comers. He was an accomplished writer with a wide knowledge of history, world literature, and social thought, though he was less well acquainted with pure philosophy. He was also an excellent popularizer and publicist. His mind was of a strongly dogmatic cast, and he was attracted to all-embracing schemata. He did more, perhaps, than anyone to reduce Marxism to a catechetical form: he wrote the first works which can be called manuals of Marxism and which were in fact used as such. His major role in Russian history is the more remarkable as he spent the whole of his Marxist life in emigration, keeping in touch with Russian affairs through periodicals and conversations with friends, and wrote of the mission of the Russian proletariat though he had no contact with actual workers. Nevertheless, he was the true instigator of the Marxist movement in Russia, and consequently also of Russian social democracy.

1. The origins of Marxist orthodoxy in Russia

George Valentinovich Plekhanov (1856–1918), the son of a

landowner, was born at Gudalovka in the Central Russian province of Tambov. He attended the cadet school at Voronezh and in 1873 was enrolled at the Constantine Military Academy in St. Petersburg. However, he abandoned the military career after a few months and in 1874 entered the Mining Institute. Losing interest in his studies there, he was expelled after two years. During this period he imbibed the works of Chernyshevsky and other radical writers and met a number of revolutionaries, two of whom—Pavel Akselrod and Lyov Deutsch—were to be his closest collaborators and friends. At this time they were populists of the Bakunin persuasion. Plekhanov was a founder member of Zemlya i Volya and in 1876 was co-organizer and chief speaker at a demonstration in St. Petersburg against political persecution in Russia. He fled to Berlin to escape arrest, and returned in the middle of 1877 to embark on the career of a professional revolutionary. He worked for a time at Saratov organizing revolutionary groups and anti-Tsarist propaganda and composing Bakuninist manifestos and appeals. At this time he shared the populist contempt for political action to secure liberal and constitutional reforms, but he also opposed individual acts of terror as being ineffective and out of tune with the cult of the people. He was in this sense a 'classic' populist, and when the split came in 1879 he declared against the terrorists and became leader of the Black Repartition group, which concentrated on propaganda among the people in the belief that only a mass movement of peasants and workers could bring freedom to Russia. However, this activity was carried on only by a handful of conspirators and was soon stopped by police repression. The group still had a semblance of existence at the beginning of 1880, but early in that year its chief members—Plekhanov, Deutsch, and Vera Zasulich—were obliged to flee abroad.

Plekhanov, who was not to see Russia again until 1917, settled in Geneva. During his first two years there he was converted to Marxism, which does not mean that he was ignorant of it previously: like many other populists he was acquainted with Marxist doctrine and accepted many of its principles. From the articles he wrote as a populist we may infer that he subscribed to historical materialism and did not hold with 'subjective sociology', but considered that the general dependence of political and ideological systems on the economic base was compatible with the idea that Russia, owing to its special historical circumstances, might be able to avoid the Western path of development. In accordance with Bakunin's social philosophy, he argued in Marxist terms against the idea of a political struggle for the liberalization of Russia: as social development ultimately depended on the economic base, the aim should be a social and not a political revolution—not changes in the superstructure, but a transformation of the country's economic system. Plekhanov's conversion to Marxism was not a matter of coming to believe in the primacy of economic conditions as opposed to 'ideas', or in materialism as opposed to religion (he had lost his religious faith in early youth): it consisted in the adoption of three basic conclusions in regard to Russian conditions which were at variance with populist ideology. These were, first, that socialism must be preceded by a political revolution of a liberal-democratic kind; second, that Russia must go through a capitalist phase before she could be ready for a socialist transformation; and third, that that transformation must be carried through by the industrial proletariat and not by the 'people' in general, still less the peasantry. In short, Plekhanov's acceptance of Marxism represented a change in his idea of political strategy rather than a radical alteration of *Weltanschauung*.

Having embraced Marxism, Plekhanov remained faithful to it all his life. To some extent he altered his stand on particular questions affecting the tactics of social democracy in Russia (though he scarcely seemed aware that he had done so), but he derived from Marxism the intellectual satisfaction of a system that leaves practically nothing to contingency, making it possible to believe in the iron regularity of history and 'in principle' to foresee all future events. Having once attained confidence in the all-embracing system Plekhanov remained of the same mind on all theoretical questions, repeating the same truths again and again and, at most, supplementing them with fresh examples or applying them to new problems.

In Geneva, where he was beset with money troubles (he received help from Lavrov, and afterwards lived chiefly from his writings and occasional lectures), Plekhanov tried for a time to continue his populist activities: he published two numbers of a journal and made contact with what was left of the organization in Russia. His efforts came to nothing, however, both because the organization was so weak and because its members soon underwent a change of opinion in the direction of social democracy.

Having decided that the fight for democratic freedoms was the most urgent need in Russia, that it was by no means a matter of indifference what political system the exploited classes lived under, and that a change from absolutism to bourgeois democracy did not simply mean, as the populists contended, exchanging one exploiter for another, Plekhanov had to grapple with the question of the relationship of the workers' movement to the bourgeoisie. In his populist days he had maintained that the fight for political liberties was the affair of the bourgeois, and that if the revolutionary movement took any effective part in it it would merely be pulling the chestnuts out of the fire for its own exploiters. Having now decided that the fight for democracy was essential to the prospects of socialism, Plekhanov had to consider how it was possible to justify the alliance in this fight of two basically hostile classes, the bourgeoisie and the proletariat. This problem was the main object of his attention for the next few years.

In 1883 a small band of *émigré* converts to Marxism formed the Labour Emancipation Group—the first Russian social-democratic organization in the West European sense. It never became a political party, and in effect consisted only of its founders: Plekhanov, Deutsch, Vera Zasulich, and Akselrod, who had joined them in exile; yet in the first two years of its existence it created the ideological foundations of Russian social democracy. This was due principally to two works by Plekhanov, *Socialism and the Political Struggle* (1883) and *Our Differences* (1885), which marked the beginning of the breach between populism and the socialist revolutionary movement in Russia. The populists were wrong, said Plekhanov, to blame the Marxists on the ground that, as they held socialism to be a product of the evolution of capitalism, they must in Russia be allies of the bourgeoisie: the laws of history could not be bent by adjurations or the purest of revolutionary motives. The first task was to find out in what direction Russia was being impelled by inexorable economic necessity. Now it was clear that the village commune was doomed to disappear and could not form the basis of a socialist organization. Socialism in Russia, as in the West, could only be brought about by the contradictions of the capitalist economy which must soon overspread the country. Since the reforms of Alexander II Russia had embarked on capitalism and a money economy, and this could not be altered by dreams of a 'leap' from primitive, natural economy to communism. The capitalist differentiation of the peasantry had begun and was bound to continue, condemning millions to expropriation and proletarianization: land would be concentrated in the hands of a dwindling number of owners who would improve cultivation with modern techniques. Industry and transport were inevitably transforming Russia into a capitalist country subject to the normal laws of accumulation. Society was bound to be divided between the bourgeoisie and a growing army of the proletariat, and Russia's future would be decided by the struggle between them.

The development of Russian capitalism, however, was hampered by numerous survivals of feudalism and by the political autocracy. The bourgeoisie was interested in the Europeanization of Russia and the replacement of absolutism by liberal institutions. Russia's first need was not a socialist revolution but a bourgeois political one to sweep away the obstacles that the state superstructure opposed to the free expansion of capitalism. Despite populist dreams this revolution could not coincide with the socialist one, which presupposed an advanced state of industrial development and a well-organized, class-conscious proletariat. Russia must go through a capitalist era, which could not be avoided and ought to be welcomed. A bourgeois revolution was in the highest interest of the Russian proletariat, which needed a period of political freedom to organize itself and develop its strength for the socialist revolution of the future.

Hence the bourgeoisie and the proletariat, though basically antagonistic, had a common interest in seeking democratic changes in Russia. But—and this is especially important for Marxist strategy—although the next revolution would be a bourgeois one, it did not follow that it must be carried out by the bourgeoisie or even under its leadership. The weak and cowardly Russian bourgeoisie would not be equal to the task, and the bourgeois revolution could only take place under the leadership of the proletariat. This argument was attacked with especial vigour by the populists, who demanded to know why the proletariat should fight in order to give a clear field to its oppressors. But, said Plekhanov, this is a wrong way of putting the question. The proletariat has an interest in political freedoms and the abolition of the autocracy, as this is the precondition of its own victory. Moreover—and this is the second basic feature of social democratic strategy—in the struggle against absolutism the proletariat must not be a mere instrument in the hands of the bourgeoisie but an independent force, conscious of its own interests and how far they concide with those of the capitalists, and also conscious that in proportion as capitalism succeeds in its objectives, the basic antagonism of the proletariat and the bourgeoisie will become more and more evident.

Daily experience, however, does not enable the workers themselves to develop a socialist consciousness and become fully aware of their position as a class. It is the task of the enlightened intelligentsia to act as their spiritual and political guide and open their eyes to the coming struggle. The proletariat must learn the lesson of bourgeois revolutions in the West, where, for lack of class-consciousness and organization, the workers shed blood in revolutionary upheavals which in the end profited only the bourgeoisie. The Russian proletariat can avoid this if it is imbued with socialist consciousness by an organized social-democratic movement; it cannot be helped, however, that after a bourgeois revolution the working class will not be the masters but will be in opposition to the system they have fought to establish. Basically Russia must follow the same development as the West, but there is reason to expect that on account of her very backwardness, capitalism will flourish and decay more rapidly than in Western Europe. By adopting advanced technology, learning from the experience of other countries, and possessing a ready-made theoretical basis, Russia may be able to shorten the cycle of development, but cannot bypass it altogether. Between the bourgeois and the socialist revolution there must be a period of capitalist exploitation. The social democratic movement should profit from the mistakes and defeats of the Western proletariat so as to avoid falling into the same errors and accelerate the course of events.

In the light of these predictions and recommendations, the whole populist ideology is revealed as a reactionary Utopia. The populists want Russia to enjoy the benefits of industrial development without its consequences in the form of rural proletarianization, the concentration of landownership, and the decline of the village commune. They also want socialism without its social preconditions, i.e. the class struggle between the proletariat and the bourgeoisie and the advanced technological, political, and social development that goes with capitalist society. These are self-contradictory demands and are contrary to the scientific, deterministic interpretation of social phenomena, which shows that the links between different aspects of social life and successive phases of development are matters of objective necessity, independent of human will.

Even if we suppose that a handful of revolutionaries by some chance or other seized power by a *coup d'état*, they could not introduce a socialist system because Russian capitalism is insufficiently developed. The result—so Plekhanov writes prophetically in *Our Differences*—would be 'a political abortion after the manner of the ancient Chinese or Persian empires—a renewal of Tsarist despotism on a communist basis'.

In both the works mentioned above Plekhanov showed himself to be an extreme Westernizer, as he remained throughout his life. Thanks to them Russian social democracy adopted an ideology of a basically 'European' type, reflecting the conviction that the schemata of Western development described by Marx were equally applicable to Russia. They laid the foundation of a strategy for Russian socialists which concentrated on political revolution of a liberal type. The programme included two paradoxical elements: that the proletariat should be the driving force of a bourgeois revolution, and that it was for the non-proletarian intelligentsia to instil socialist consciousness into the working class. The first of these propositions was not in conflict with Marx's doctrine, but it left open the question that was to confront socialists: if there has to be an alliance with other classes in a bourgeois revolution, should the proletariat's ally be the bourgeoisie (as might seem natural), or rather the peasantry or part of it? Twenty years later this question helped to split the Russian social democrats into two camps. As to the second premiss, it is debatable how far it is consistent with Marxist schemata; but this controversy too did not break out until later.

2. Dialectical and historical materialism

Thanks to their faith in the immutable laws of social development Plekhanov and his group were able to maintain their
courage and hope during the long years when the revolutionary
movement in Russia died out almost completely, and reaction
appeared triumphant. The eighties were a time of discourage-
ment and political retrogression. At this time Plekhanov gained
the reputation of being the chief spokesman of Russian Marxism;
his writings filtered through in small quantities only, but they did
reach the few people who, in the nineties, were to lay the
foundations of the social democratic movement in Russia itself.
In 1889 Plekhanov was expelled from Switzerland as the result
of an accidental explosion caused by a group of Russian terrorists
with whom he had nothing to do; he moved to France, but was
expelled again in 1894 for attacking the French government in
a speech at the congress of the International in Zurich. He then
went to London, but was allowed shortly afterwards to return to
Geneva. At the end of 1894 he published legally in Russia, under
the pseudonym Beltov, a book originally entitled *In Defence
of Materialism*, but renamed (in order to get past the censor)
*A Contribution to the Question of the Development of the Monistic View
of History*. This innocuous-sounding work established Plekhanov's position as the supreme authority in Russia on matters
of Marxist doctrine, and was for years the main source from
which the faithful imbibed their knowledge of its philosophical
foundations. It contains almost everything that Plekhanov later
repeated in his many works on philosophical and sociological
questions. In addition to criticizing 'subjective sociology', chiefly
in the writings of Mikhailovsky and Kareyev, and the populist
Utopia of Russia's 'separate road', the work is a systematic
exposition of Marxism and its theoretical sources, considered
from the point of view of their merit in preparing the way for
the materialist interpretation of history, and their idealistic
'errors' and 'inconsistencies'. In this field Plekhanov partly
created, and partly followed Engels in popularizing, a large
number of stereotypes which became part of the current coin
of Marxism.

According to Plekhanov the basic categories and intellectual trends of Marxism were derived from the following sources, purged of their errors and contradictions.

Firstly, eighteenth-century materialism, especially the French materialism of Holbach and Helvétius. This had the merit that it explained spiritual phenomena by material ones; it discerned the source of all knowledge in sense-perception, and understood that human ideas and feelings are created by social environment. It fell into a vicious circle, however, in attributing changes in the environment to the influence of ideas. Moreover, it did not attain to an evolutionary view of history; it erred by 'fatalism' and had no knowledge of dialectical method.

Secondly, classical German philosophy, especially Hegel. In this and other works by Plekhanov, the picture of Hegel is mainly taken from Engels: it is much over-simplified and seems to be based on fragmentary and cursory reading. The dialectic is presented as a method of inquiry which considers all phenomena from the point of view of their development and interdependence, and in every form of life seeks to find the germ of that form's destruction and transformation into its opposite: it seeks everywhere to discover forces and attributes beyond those which appear at first glance. Development according to the 'triadic' schema is not, however, essential to Hegel's doctrine. The dialectic also discerns qualitative leaps in nature and society, arising from the accumulation of quantitative changes. In this way Plekhanov, like Engels, treats the dialectic as a method which can be abstracted from Hegelian philosophy, detached from idealist metaphysics, and applied to a materialist world-view. Hegel's other great merit is to have seen that human history is subject to laws independent of the will of the individual; however, in his eyes the necessity of history is of a spiritual nature and thus 'ultimately' coincides with freedom. Marxism transforms this idealistic world-view by showing that the necessities of history are rooted in material conditions of life, and that freedom consists of understanding the laws of history and taking advantage of them in order to act effectively.

Thirdly, utopian socialism. The utopians sought means of reforming society, but instead of studying inevitable consequences and laws of development they posed questions of a normative kind, asking what is good or desirable from the point of view of the requirements of human nature. By so doing they condemned themselves to sterility, for goodwill is powerless by itself to effect social changes.

Fourthly, the French historians of the restoration period. Guizot, Thierry, and Mignet had done much to interpret historical processes as struggles due to the differing material interests of social classes, and in this respect they paved the way for Marxism. But they remained bound to the idealist philosophy of history, ascribing social conflicts and forms of property, in the last resort, to unaltering human nature—whereas the latter postulate clearly cannot explain changing historical forms.

The defects of all these theories were finally cured by Marx's philosophy, which Plekhanov compares in importance to the Copernican revolution or to Darwinism. Like Copernicus, Marx laid the foundations of social science by introducing the idea of necessity, which is the basis of all scientific thinking, into the study of social phenomena. (In Hegel's philosophy of history, necessity was only a logical category. Plekhanov does not explain, however, in what sense Copernicus originated the theory of necessity in natural science.) But the comparison with Darwin is more significant. As Darwin explained the evolution of forms of life by the adaptation of species to changes in the environment (this is Plekhanov's idea of the essence of Darwinism), so Marx showed that human history can be explained by man's relations with external nature and especially his growing control over it by means of tools. Marx's historical monism is based on the premiss that 'in the last resort' all historical changes are due to the development of tools, the ability to make which determines the character of the human species and the social bond of co-operation. The objection that technical change itself depends on human intellectual effort is invalid, for intellectual progress is in turn the result of technical progress: in this way cause and effect are constantly interchanging. At any given moment of history the level of productive forces determines the intellectual level of society, including technical inventions which make production more efficient still. Man is constantly being changed by external circumstances, and thus there is no such thing as unchanging human nature.

At a particular level of productive forces there come into being relations of production which in turn are the basis of political institutions, social psychology, and ideological forms. However, there is at all times a reciprocal influence: political institutions affect economic life; the economy and psychology of a society are two aspects of one and the same process, the 'production of life' or the struggle for existence, and both depend on the level of technology. Psychological attitudes adapt themselves to economic conditions, but 'on the other hand' the conflict of technology with relations of production produces changes in human psychology which precede economic changes. Thus Marxism cannot be reproached with one-sidedness, for it takes account of the whole multiplicity of mutual reactions in society.

Economic conditions are also the source of ideological creations, including science, philosophy, and art. True, one form of art may influence another, but the notion of 'influence' in itself explains nothing: different peoples can only influence one another artistically if their social conditions are similar.

History cannot be explained by the special role of outstanding geniuses. On the contrary, it is history that explains them: a genius is one who grasps the meaning of incipient social relations sooner than other people, and expresses in a more perfect way the tendency of a particular social class.

Since the necessity that governs the world is universal, freedom from the Marxist point of view—as in the philosphy of Spinoza or Hegel—is not a matter of enjoying a kind of margin within which causality does not operate, but of being able to control nature by understanding its laws. The measure of this control increases throughout history, and we have reached the point where it is possible to envisage 'the final triumph of mind over necessity, of reason over the blindness of law': this will be because men have learnt to govern social processes, over which they formerly had no power. (Plekhanov does not explain how mind can 'triumph' in this way if its activity is ruled by iron necessity, so that man's power over nature is determined by nature itself independently of human beings.)

Similar ideas to these are repeated in Plekhanov's many subsequent articles, books, and lectures, some of which have become classics of Marxist instruction even outside Russia: for example, *Fundamental Problems of Marxism* (1908), *The Role of the Individual in History* (1898), and *Contributions to the History of Materialism* (1896). All his theoretical writings are to some extent polemics against those whom, at any particular moment, he regarded as most dangerous to the integrality and consistency of Marxist doctrine. This means that his adversaries were either close to Marxism or were desirous of reforming or revising it 'from within': after the populists came the German revisionists, then the neo-Kantians and the Russian school of empiriocriticism.

Unlike most West European Marxists, who saw no logical connection between Marxism as a theory of social development and any particular view of epistemological or metaphysical questions (Kautsky, too, came to believe in course of time that there was no such connection), Plekhanov insisted that Marxism was a complete and integral body of theory embracing all the main questions of philosophy. 'Dialectical materialism'—Plekhanov was apparently the first to use this term to denote the whole of Marxist philosophy—could not be separated from 'historical materialism', which was the application of the same principles and rules of thought to the investigation of social phenomena. This insistence on the integrality of Marxism was inherited from Plekhanov by Lenin, and became part of the ideology of the Soviet state. It is based on the premiss that social democracy cannot be neutral in any philosophical question, and that it possesses a comprehensive world-view which cannot be partially adopted without deforming each of its parts. Marxist philosophy as expounded by Plekhanov was a repetition, without attempt at further analysis, of Engels's formulas, generally in an exaggerated version. Materialism rests on the assertion which Marxism adopted from Feuerbach, that Being or matter is 'self-based', while all thought is a product of Being. However, dialectical materialism differs from Feuerbach in stating that the human subject is not merely passively aware of objects, but comes to know the world in the process of acting upon it. This does not mean, says Plekhanov, that men form or help to form the objects they become aware of, but only that the cognition of objects 'in themselves' takes place chiefly as a result of labour and not of contemplation. Materialism is an irrefutable theory confirmed by science, and all its modern critics—Croce, Schmidt, Bernstein—are only repeating arguments that were long ago demolished by Feuerbach. The dialectic is the theory of the development of the world with its interconnections, contradictions, and qualitative 'leaps', and these are demonstrated by modern science, for instance De Vries's theory of mutations (Plekhanov does not explain how biological mutations are prepared for by an accumulation of 'quantitative changes'). Qualitative changes are seen in the transformation of water into ice or steam, of a chrysalis into a butterfly, or again in arithmetic, as after the digit 9 we make a 'leap' into double figures. Plekhanov is full of such naïveties, and one of them is the idea that 'dialectical contradictions' are incompatible with formal logic: this recalls the contention of the Eleatic philosophers that motion is self-contradictory, as a moving body both is and is not in a given place. As rest is a particular case of motion, formal logic is a particular case of dialectical logic and 'applies' to reality treated as unchanging. A political revolution is an example of a qualitative leap; dialectical contradictions include the class struggle, etc.

All these arguments, which were to become part of the canon of dialectical materialism in Russia, are evidence of the shallowness of Plekhanov's philosophical education and the oversimplicity of his thought. In questions of historical materialism he shows better powers of analysis and knowledge of the subject. Here too, however, he is concerned above all to preserve his monistic faith in 'productive forces' as the all-sufficient motive power of history. However, following Engels, he takes issue with the statement that Marxism explains all historical processes in terms of a 'single factor', since, he contends, all 'factors' are only methodological abstractions: there is in reality one single historical process, and this is determined 'in the last resort' by technical progress. The phrase 'in the last resort', Plekhanov explains, means that in a given society we can distinguish 'intermediate stages' through which productive forces determine various features of social life—economic conditions, the political system, psychology, and ideology. In addition there is always the factor of interaction: the superstructure is determined by the base but afterwards reacts upon it; the base is constituted by the requirements of productive forces but itself affects those forces, and so on.

These ideas do not fit into a coherent whole. Like other Marxists of his time, Plekhanov cannot explain how the belief in productive forces as the ultimate cause of events is to be reconciled with the theory of interaction. If the 'higher stages' can initiate changes in the lower, it is not clear what becomes of historical 'monism' or how it can be said that the lower stages condition the higher 'in the last resort'; if changes cannot be so initiated, what is the meaning of 'interaction'? Again, it is not clear how it can be said that, for example, political institutions, ideologies, and property relations are 'only abstractions' used for purposes of argument, while at the same time making a substantive distinction between 'stages' and asserting, in addition, that everything depends on changes in the forces of production, as though for some reason these were not 'factors' like the others. In *Fundamental Problems of Marxism* Plekhanov adds for good measure that productive forces are determined by geographical conditions, so it would seem that, contrary to what is said elsewhere, these last are the real and ultimate cause of history. It is clear that Plekhanov, like many Marxists, wishes to maintain his belief in a single principle accounting for the whole of history, but not to part company with common sense which tells us that events are due in general to a variety of concurrent causes. Hence the numerous reservations which are meant to attenuate the rigour of the 'monistic' explanation, but in fact destroy it, as the vague expression 'in the last resort' finally loses its meaning when we also speak of 'interaction'. We are in fact thrown back on the common-sense view that important events are due to a multiplicity of forces whose relative strength cannot be calculated, including of course the level of technology in a society, its class structure and political system. But there is nothing specifically Marxist in this formulation, and therefore it is not one that can be uttered by true believers.

Plekhanov, like Kautsky, is also convinced that social processes can be studied in the same completely objective way as natural phenomena, human history being subject to universal laws of change—evolution, contradiction, qualitative leaps—in the same way as geological formations. He replies in this sense to Stammler's criticism that Marxists ignore the teleological character of human behaviour, and that when they urge mankind to co-operate with what they claim to be inevitable progress, it is as though they were to demand support for an eclipse of the sun which is bound to take place anyway without human aid. This criticism is groundless, Plekhanov says, because Marxists recognize that among the circumstances necessary to certain social processes are the purposive actions of human beings, their feelings, passions, and desires; they maintain, however, that such feelings and desires are necessarily determined by productive forces and the social conditions which these create. Plekhanov, however, seems to miss the point of Stammler's objection, as Kautsky did in the case of Bauer. It is one thing to reflect on past history, in which human feelings, purposes, and passions appear simply as psychological and social factors helping to shape the course of events; it is another to consider one's own share in processes whose future results one believes to be determined by irresistible historical forces. If an individual is considering what purpose to aim at or why he should take part in a given social movement, the statement that his aims, whatever they may be, are irrevocably determined by productive forces does not help him to make up his mind, any more than the statement that certain results of the historical process are inevitable. Plekhanov says that if I join a movement' that I regard as historically necessary and certain to prevail, I am treating my own action as an indispensable link in that necessary process. But this is no answer to Stammler; for the belief that a movement is going to win is not in itself an argument for joining it, except to someone who wants to be on the winning side at all costs. This viewpoint, i.e. that of the long-sighted opportunist, is of course a possible one, but it is not the one Plekhanov is concerned with, and it does not answer the question what moral grounds exist for joining a movement that is certain to succeed. If there are no such grounds there is no reason why I should join it, and if there are, they must derive from some other source than the 'laws of history'. This was the neo-Kantist objection, which Plekhanov failed to understand. He regarded himself as a necessary link in the process of socialist change, implying that it could not take place without him: this may have been true in his case, but it conflicts with his own principles as to the historical role of the individual, and it still does not explain why he, or anyone else, should have taken upon themselves to be the necessary link.

To sum up the characteristics of Plekhanov's theoretical writing we may say that it is marked by an absolute conviction of historical necessity; the denial of any basic distinction between the study of nature and that of society; the belief that historical materialism is an 'application' of the rules of dialetical materialism, and an insistence on treating these two fields as part of a unique, indivisible whole; strong emphasis on the integrality of Marxism as the social democratic world-view, and the belief that social democracy as such must have a philosophical doctrine of its own; strong emphasis, also, on the importance of the philosophical tradition in the genesis of Marxism.

Plekhanov was one of the principal founders of that style of Marxist writing which Lenin adopted in a still cruder form and which recalls the polemics of religious sects. Having decided, on his conversion to Marxism, that it supplied the answers to all problems of philosophy and social development, Plekhanov never afterwards wrote as a man seeking for the solution of a theoretical problem, but as an adept defending an established doctrine. He uses any argument that comes to hand, the object being not to follow the discussion wherever it leads, but to knock the adversary down. He derides opponents who invoke any scientific authority (for Marxism bows to no authority outside itself), but he himself quotes any authority that may serve his turn, irrespective of whether he knows anything of the field in question, so that he constantly falls into factual error. He piles up examples to confirm the 'laws of dialectic' or of historical materialism without realizing the extent of the gap between a collection of mostly trivial instances (water turning to steam, biological mutations, etc.) and the general principle they are supposed to illustrate, for example that all processes consist of an accumulation of quantitative changes culminating in a qualitative leap. He does not observe that while it is easy to find examples, for instance, of particular cultural features which are due to the technical level of a society, or ideological ones which are due to class conflict, it is no less easy to find examples the other way round, for example technical development which is due to political institutions or political institutions due to ideological tradition. Such examples, however, do not prove any general theory of historiosophy beyond vague assertions that 'on the one hand' such and such circumstances account for such and such others, while 'on the other hand' the process may be reversed.

3. Marxist aesthetics

Much space is devoted in Plekhanov's writings and lectures to the discussion of art from the viewpoint of historical materialism: he was a pioneer in this field, along with Mehring and Lafargue. He was more at home in the history of art than in philosophy, and was able to support his argument with examples from diverse periods. Here too, however, there is a wide gap between his frequently accurate observation of the dependence of artistic activity on technical conditions and social conflict, and his general thesis that 'The artistic life of civilized nations is no less subject to necessity than that of primitive peoples. The only difference is that among civilized nations art no longer *directly* depends on technique and the means of production' (*Unaddressed Letters*, 1899–1900, i). He uses the accounts of various ethnographers to show that in primitive society art is connected with work either in the sense of imitating it (as in group dances, which, he says, serve to reproduce the 'pleasure' of working), or by aiding it (for example, musical rhythm), or again by association with such values as wealth or physical fitness, wherein the symbols that arouse such association come to be regarded as beautiful. In class societies, on the other hand, the dependence of art on productive forces is indirect, as art 'expresses' the ideals, feelings, and thoughts of this or that class. Eighteenth-century French comedy expressed popular discontent with the existing order, classical tragedy the ideals of the court and aristocracy, and so on. Plekhanov fails to notice that such observations as these are not specifically Marxist. The effect of class-interests and social changes on literary genres or styles of painting was known to many non-Marxist historians and critics, including some that Plekhanov himself quotes, such as Guizot, Taine, and Brunetière. What is essentially Marxist is not the recognition of such influences but the claim that they account for the whole of artistic creation, and that there is a necessary link between the state of class-relations in a given society and its artistic output. If this were taken seriously we should have to suppose that a keen enough mind could deduce the whole of a country's art and literature from its economic situation, i.e. that one could write the works of Shakespeare if one knew enough about the economy of Elizabethan England. Plekhanov, of course, does not say anything so absurd, but he fails to see that it would be a natural consequence of his theory. He is constantly endeavouring to show that artistic activity is wholly accounted for by class values and that the merits of a work of art should be judged by its content, which is also expressible in non-artistic language; at the same time, he wishes to preserve the distinction between ideological content and artistic presentation. Here again we are saved by the magic formula: 'in the last resort the value of a work of art is determined by the specific gravity of its subject-matter' (*Art and Social Life*, 1912). To know the genesis of a work of art, then, is to know the criteria of its artistic merit: these are not absolute, for everything changes, but they are objective, i.e. we can state with certainty what is or is not beautiful in the conditions of its time. The work is to be judged by the correspondence between its 'idea' and its 'form': the more closely they coincide, the more successful it is. But to be able to judge this we should have to know, independently of the actual work of art, what 'forms' are best suited to express the given idea; and Plekhanov does not suggest how we can acquire such knowledge. Nor is this all. It is not sufficient, we are told, for the form to correspond to the idea: for the work to be beautiful, the idea must be a 'true' one. We see here to what extent Plekhanov, partly of his own accord and partly under Chernyshevsky's influence, evolved the basic premisses of what was to be called 'socialist realism'. Not that Plekhanov's own preferences were based on such criteria, or that he ascribed artistic merit to all works that 'expressed' ideas he believed in and to no others: on the contrary, his tastes were those of most educated people in his time, including a detestation of new trends in painting. But his theory laid the foundation for measuring artistic value by political utility.

Plekhanov believed that the slogan 'art for art's sake', and the idea that the main purpose of a work of art was to produce artistic values as an end in themselves, was itself the necessary product of a certain kind of social situation, that in which the creative artist feels isolated from society. This, he considered, was the state of affairs at the turn of the century. Impressionism and Cubism were a sign of bourgeois decadence: the former was superficial and did not look beyond the 'outer shell' of phenomena, the latter was 'nonsense raised to the third power'.

The same applied to symbolist literature in Russia and abroad, for example Merezhkovsky, Zinaida Gippius, and Przybyszewski. In a typical passage Plekhanov wrote: 'Let us suppose the artist wants to paint a "Woman in a blue dress". If what he paints is like his subject, we call it a good picture. If, however, all we see on the canvas is a few stereometric figures tinted here and there, in a more or less primitive fashion, with layers of more or less diluted blue paint, we may call it a painting of whatever we like, but not a good picture.' (Ibid.)

There is of course nothing surprising in such naïvety: we know that after a certain age people cannot appreciate new artistic forms that are too unlike the ones they knew in youth, and reject them as extravagant and unnatural. But Plekhanov does not regard such judgements as mere expressions of his own taste, but as the inevitable logical consequence of the Marxist theory of society, and therefore as 'scientific' statements. From this point of view the influence of his writing, which virtually established the canons of Soviet aesthetic taste, was deplorable, even though he believed firmly in creative freedom for the artist and knew how barren art was when executed under compulsion, to please political masters or to present the world as it should be instead of as it is (cf. his criticism of Gorky's *The Mother*).

4. *The struggle against revisionism*

As the result of rapid industrialization and the great famine of 1891–2 the nineties witnessed a revival of political activity in Russia; Marxism and social democratic ideology became the subject of widespread public debate. This was to some extent a triumph for Plekhanov as the chief exponent of the doctrine; but the larger or smaller social democratic groups that came into existence in the cities produced new leaders and theorists who, while respecting Plekhanov as a teacher, were not prepared blindly to follow his advice in politics. He for his part did not bear opposition gladly and claimed absolute authority in all matters of doctrine and also of socialist policy in Russia. This state of affairs led to painful tension on some occasions, the best known of which was Lenin's disappointment at his meeting with the master in 1900.

In the late 1890s much of Plekhanov's energy was taken up by the controversy with Bernstein and the neo-Kantians. He was the

first to launch a frontal attack on Bernstein and was, with Rosa
Luxemburg, the most intransigent critic of revisionism: none of
the Germans equalled in virulence these two *émigrés* from
Eastern Europe. Unlike Rosa Luxemburg, however, he directed
his attack at the philosophical bases of revisionism, which, again
unlike most critics, he treated as a point of contention of the
first order. Kantianism he regarded as an attempt to instil
bourgeois mentality among social democrats: it taught, in the
first place, that men could not know things 'in themselves', and
it thus left room for religious faith, which had always been
a means of spiritual enslavement of the oppressed classes.
Secondly, the Kantists, in accordance with the theory of infinite
progress, regarded socialism as an ideal which could be
approached by degrees but never actually reached. They thus
created a philosophical basis for reformism and opportunism,
abandoning socialism as a practicable aim and revolution as
the means to it. At the same time Plekhanov attacked the
analyses of changes in capitalist society which Bernstein used
to justify his departure from revolutionary Marxism. Even if the
middle classes represented a growing proportion of the population as a whole, and the workers' lot was actually improving
in absolute terms, this did not weaken the Marxist theory of
intensifying class antagonism. Real wages might go up, but
social inequalities still increased (the relative impoverishment of
the proletariat). If the trade union mentality was spreading
among the workers, this was not due to the class situation but
to opportunistic leaders. In this matter Plekhanov argued on the
same lines as Rosa Luxemburg and Lenin. The doctrine teaches
that the working class is, by the nature of things, a revolutionary
class; if shallow empiricism does not appear to bear this out, it
cannot be due to any change in the workers' class situation but
only to the machinations of renegades among the union and
party leaders.

Plekhanov's other prinicipal target was Russian 'economism',
which he regarded as a variant of Bernsteinian revisionism.
Some of its advocates still paid lip-service, at least, to the 'final
aim' of social democracy, but, in accordance with the classic
tradition of populism, their approach to the workers was confined
to immediate practical issues such as economic claims, to the
neglect of political work, the struggle for constitutional freedoms,

and the cultivation of a socialist consciousness among the proletariat. The 'economists' distrusted the idea of intellectuals leading the working-class movement: they believed that the latter should be composed of workers and not merely be working-class in name and ideology, and they held this to be the intention of Marx himself, who maintained that the proletariat could only be liberated by its own efforts. The 'economist' viewpoint was represented among the *émigrés* by S. N. Prokopovich and his wife E. D. Kuskova, but in Russia itself it enjoyed for a time a certain predominance over orthodox social democracy: it was expressed chiefly in the pages of the underground journal *Rabochaya Mysl'* (*Workers' Thought*), from 1897.

Plekhanov attacked the economists with similar arguments to those he had used against populism. Only socialism as a final aim gave meaning to the struggle for reforms and particular economic gains by the proletariat. A campaign which confined itself to these partial aims and could not, therefore, become a country-wide proletarian movement was not a fight for social democracy, and to regard it as a true workers' movement was to abandon Marxism. What Marxism required in Russian conditions was to fight for democratic freedoms that would provide a framework for the final battle, and to subordinate economic demands to the political struggle for socialism. If the 'economists' claimed that they represented the true consciousness of the Russian working class, then, as in the case of German reformism, it was their own fault that that consciousness was not evolving in a socialist direction.

Plekhanov thus stood for uncompromising orthodoxy against revisionism and economism. For some years he and Lenin were political allies; but the dispute over the editorship of *Iskra*, while it had much to do initially with Plekhanov's personal claim to supremacy among the social democrat *émigrés*, was also due to the fact that he thought Lenin over-conciliatory towards the economists and 'legal Marxists'. In the argument over the party programme drafted in 1902 there were no essential differences between the two men: Lenin wished to make Plekhanov's draft more precise and less abstract, but he did not object to its basic premises. At the Brussels–London Congress in the summer of 1903, at which the party split into Bolsheviks and Mensheviks, Plekhanov took Lenin's side as regards centralized forms of organization and also in the celebrated dispute over paragraph 1 of the Rules, which, as proposed by Lenin, defined a party member as one who personally participated in the work of a party organization—the object being to create a party of 'professional revolutionaries'. At the same Congress, in reply to a delegate who raised the question of the absolute value of democratic principles, Plekhanov made his celebrated speech declaring that the cause of the revolution was the supreme law for revolutionaries, and that if it should require the abandonment of any democratic principle, such as universal suffrage, it would be criminal to hesitate.

5. *The conflict with Leninism*

Plekhanov was thus a Bolshevik—but only for a short time, after which he allied himself once more with Akselrod, Martov, and others whom he had criticized at the Congress. Before long he was attacking Bolshevism and Lenin's idea of the party, accusing the Bolsheviks of ultracentralism and of aiming at absolute power and a party dictatorship over the proletariat. In numerous polemics he argued that Lenin's conception of the party, which made it completely independent of the spontaneous consciousness of the proletariat, meant that the role of the working class would be usurped by a party of intellectual professional revolutionaries: this party would become the sole source of political initiative, which was grossly at variance with Marx's theory of the class struggle. It was equally contrary to Marxism and to historical experience when Lenin declared that the working class could not attain to socialist consciousness by itself. This showed a lack of confidence in the workers and was idealistic to boot, as it implied that the class-consciousness of the proletariat was not the result of its living conditions ('being determines consciousness'), but must be the work of intellectuals.

Plekhanov's anti-Bolshevism, founded on classical Marxist schemata, grew more and more violent as time went on. Just as he had brought the same charges against the 'economists' as previously against the classical populists, namely that they showed excessive respect for spontaneity and neglected political activity, so now he attacked the Bolsheviks on the grounds for which he had condemned the terrorist branch of the populist movement. He accused them of Blanquism, Jacobinism, 'voluntarism', aiming to force social development by conspiratorial means and to bring about a revolution not by the operation of natural laws but at the behest of a handful of plotters. He maintained his own strategic viewpoint that the proletariat should co-operate with the bourgeoisie for democratic aims, and even the Revolution of 1905 did not alter his conviction, though he realized how uncertain such an alliance would be. Lenin, on the other hand, envisaged a bourgeois revolution followed immediately by a democratic-revolutionary dictatorship of the proletariat and peasantry. Plekhanov for his part did not regard the peasantry as a useful political ally. He seems to have thought that the proletariat could carry on the fight against the bourgeoisie and overtly aim at its destruction, while at the same time joining forces with it to overthrow the autocracy. This view rested on his dogmatic, anti-populist belief that the phases of development in Russia would be basically the same as in the West. His doctrinaire attitude and his hesitations considerably weakened his position as a social democratic leader after 1905. He continued to stand closer to the Mensheviks than to the Bolsheviks, while occasionally attempting, without success, to bridge the gulf between them.

Plekhanov held that the Bolsheviks had departed from Marxism in the philosophical sphere also. He regarded the attempts to introduce empiriocriticism into Marxist philosophy as a typical symptom of the basic Bolshevist attitude. The Bolsheviks despised or ignored the 'objective laws' of social development and believed in a revolution brought about by organization and strength of will: it was natural therefore that they should be attracted by a subjectivist philosophy which regarded the human mind as the 'active organizer' of the universe. This was indeed true of the empiriocritical philosophers in the Bolshevik camp, but it was far from meeting with Lenin's approval. The fight against empiriocriticism was the last occasion on which Lenin and Plekhanov found themselves in alliance.

Plekhanov spent the years after 1905 chiefly in writing on historical, philosophical, and aesthetic questions. He also began preparatory work on a long *History of Russian Social Thought*, of which he was only to complete three volumes.

During the period from 1905 to 1914 Plekhanov's attitude to

basic questions was close to that of the central group of the International. When war broke out he adopted a 'national' position like most members of that group, switching at once from anti-war slogans and proletarian internationalism to the defence of Russia's cause and that of the Entente. This of course did not mean that he had given up Marxism: as the Central Powers had attacked Russia the war was a defensive one, and support for it was in accordance with the resolutions of the International. Moreover, the defeat of Germany was in the interest of international socialism, as it would advance the revolutionary movement in both Germany and Russia. The rest of Plekhanov's patriotic activity—his call to national unity and a suspension of the class struggle—could be justified on the same grounds. In the result, he found himself on the extreme right wing of the social democratic movement.

The collapse of the autocracy, which had been awaited for decades, came in February 1917. Plekhanov returned to Russia at the end of March. He was received with enthusiasm, but it soon became clear that as a theoretician who had spent nearly forty years abroad he was unable to find his bearings in the new situation. His view was that, Tsarism having been swept away by a bourgeois revolution, there should now 'naturally' be a long period of constitutional and parliamentary rule; at the same time the war with Germany should be fought through to victory. In this he stood closer to the Provisional Government than to any socialist group. He continued, as a Marxist, to combat the idea of a socialist revolution in the near future: socialism could not be victorious in an economically backward country with a huge preponderance of peasants. He regarded the events of October as a deplorable error by the Bolsheviks, which might ruin all the achievements of the February Revolution. He died in a Finnish sanatorium on 30 May 1918, embittered and unreconciled to a situation which he himself had done a great deal to bring about, but which did not fit into his theoretical schemata.

S. H. Baron, the author of a basic work on Plekhanov, observes that his struggle against revisionism did much to facilitate the rise of Leninism, but that his subsequent opposition to Leninism brought him to a position close to the revisionists. The same author considers that the root cause of Plekhanov's political defeats was his unshakeable faith in the applicability of the West European pattern of development to Russia. He considered the Bolsheviks to be Bakuninists rather than Marxists: in this he was certainly right to some extent, on the basis of what Western Europe regarded as Marxist orthodoxy. But even though he correctly foresaw what would happen to a revolution carried out on Leninist principles, nevertheless the fact that it could succeed at all was inexplicable in terms of his social philosophy.

Soviet Russia, as was to be expected, condemns Plekhanov for his later political attitude but, following Lenin, applauds him as a Marxist theoretician. A complete edition of his writings was published shortly after his death; separate works have since appeared, dealing with philosophy but not politics (except for the early anti-populist treatises). In view of his controversy with the Bolsheviks he could not, of course, be ranked as a 'classic of Marxism' in terms of Soviet state ideology. None the less he remains one of the chief begetters of that ideology, which, under the name of Marxism-Leninism, in time succeeded—with the aid of the party, state, and police—in supplanting and destroying the Marxist idea.

XV

Marxism in Russia Before the Rise of Bolshevism

In the 1890s Marxism became a subject of public debate in Russia and was an essential and influential part of the country's intellectual life. At this time, however, it was chiefly a movement of the intelligentsia. Contrary to the position in Western Europe, Marxism and socialism existed in Russia before there was a working-class movement. The reference here is to Marxism as a doctrine which defines itself as the mature consciousness of the working class and which is based on the Marxian analysis and critique of capitalist conditions, regarding capitalism as an essential phase of social progress and an independent workers' movement as the precondition of a socialist transformation. As already mentioned, Marxism had considerable influence on populist thinkers, but they made use of it chiefly to denounce the effects of capitalism, while hoping that Russia might avoid these by choosing a road of her own. Marxism as a social democratic ideology took shape, during the first ten years or so, largely in opposition to populism. The main subject of Marxist literature was the development of capitalism in Russia, and its main theme was that it was a utopian dream to seek to prevent it. The prospects of socialism depended on the working-class movement which would develop as the capitalist economy expanded, and which could fight effectively only in conditions of political freedom: the first objective for social democrats, therefore, was to carry out a democratic revolution and overthrow the autocracy.

It soon became clear, however, that when Marxism was no longer defined simply by opposition to populism, its application to the future of capitalism in Russia could be judged in different ways. To some of the intelligentsia Marxism was in effect a substitute for a liberal ideology, which the country did not otherwise possess. Those who thought in this way emphasized the need to introduce democratic freedoms, which they regarded as an end in themselves and not simply a means of developing the socialist movement. Interpreting Marx as they did, they expected a long period of capitalist conditions and regarded socialism either as a distant prospect with little practical meaning at the present time, or as a regulative moral norm. This was the attitude of the group whom their opponents later called 'legal Marxists', and who from the beginning advocated ideas similar in many respects to German revisionism. Most of them eventually abandoned Marxism and became liberal ideologists. The social democrats, on the other hand, linked the struggle for democracy with the coming fight for socialism by an organized movement of the proletariat.

The fact that Leninism eventually prevailed may suggest that pre-revolutionary Marxism in Russia should be studied entirely in relation to its Leninist variant. But the quarter-century was one of many-sided discussion in the fields of politics, philosophy, and social doctrine, and produced many variants of Marxism, some of which are more interesting than Lenin's from the theoretical point of view. At the same time it is hard to say that the perspective created by later events, and by what we know today of the historical consequences of Russian Marxism, is a false one. In describing a historical process we cannot really do so 'from the inside', i.e. treating each event in turn as if we knew no more of its effects than people did at the time. It is true to a certain extent that the history we write is that of the 'victors'. We can only judge the importance of events, including intellectual events, by their consequences, and every historical account must be based on a selection of what is most important. It is therefore legitimate to treat Leninism as the mainstream of twentieth-century Marxism, although when we compare Lenin's works with those of his Marxist opponents we often find the latter a good deal richer in theoretical content.

One of the events that animated ideological discussion and helped to crystallize the Marxist movement in Russia was the disastrous famine of 1891–2. Populist economists regarded it as a confirmation of their views and a proof of the horrors of capitalism, while the Marxists disputed this analysis. It was not only a question of economic causes, however, but of the whole range of social problems connected with Russia's future. Study groups of Marxists and Marxist sympathizers began to be formed in the ensuing years, chiefly among students. From these there soon emerged leaders who laid the foundations of Russian social democracy: Lenin, Struve, Potresov, Martov.

1. Lenin: early journalistic writings

If the greatness of historical figures is measured by the consequences that can be ascribed to their acts, Lenin must certainly rank as the greatest man of the twentieth century. The October Revolution was of course, like all revolutions, the result of many chances and coincidences; in particular it was made possible by the February Revolution and the resulting breakdown of the Tsarist government machine. Yet hardly anyone, even Trotsky, has called in question that Lenin's presence and activity, in forming the Bolshevik party and at the time of the Revolution itself, was an indispensable condition of its outbreak and success. It is also beyond dispute that Lenin decisively influenced the character of the Soviet state as a historical formation of a completely new kind.

The subject of the present work is the history of Marxist doctrine and not of the socialist or communist movement; but in Lenin's case more than in any other it becomes clear that there is a certain artificiality in this distinction. From the outset of his political activity Lenin devoted himself, with extraordinary consistency and resolution, to a single cause and a single task. He was wholly absorbed in working for revolution in Russia, and all his theoretical works were subordinated to this end. Lenin was never a theorist in the sense of approaching questions in a spirit of intellectual curiosity and the disinterested quest for a solution. All questions, even epistemological ones, were potential instruments of the revolution, and all answers were political acts.

There is some controversy as to Lenin's intellectual and political development up to the time when he laid the foundations of Bolshevism. However, except for Soviet official hagiography most historians agree that as a young man he was strongly influenced by the tradition of populism in its terrorist form; that afterwards, until about 1899, he was a 'Westernizing' Marxist like Plekhanov; and that it was only in 1899–1902 that he worked out his own variant of Marxism, in which the populist tradition was again partly in evidence.

Vladimir Ilyich Ulyanov (he wrote under the pseudonym 'Lenin' from the end of 1901 onwards) was born on 22 April 1870 (10 April, Old Style) at Simbirsk, now Ulyanovsk. His father, Ilya Nikolayevich Ulyanov, was the provincial school inspector, a senior and well-paid member of the Tsarist bureaucracy: he seems to have been a loyal and conservative official. The children received a religious but unbigoted upbringing. The elder son Alexander, born in 1866, studied at St. Petersburg University and belonged to a clandestine group, inspired by Narodnaya Volya and claiming to be a terrorist branch of that organization, which plotted to assassinate the Tsar. The amateur conspiracy was discovered, and in May 1887 Alexander Ulyanov was hanged. Vladimir at this time was taking his final school examinations. His brother's death naturally aroused in him a sense of hatred for the authorities and an interest in the revolutionary cause. That autumn he entered the University of Kazan, whence he was expelled three months later for taking part in a demonstration against new regulations limiting the autonomy of universities and the freedom of students. He moved to his mother's estate at the village of Kokushkino and spent much time reading, particularly the works of Chernyshevsky, which impressed him greatly. In 1888 the family took a house in Kazan, but the brother of the would-be regicide was not allowed to resume his university studies. During his first and his second stay in Kazan Lenin was connected with local groups which sought to keep alive the Narodnaya Volya tradition. He had similar contacts in Samara, where he spent the next three years. Thanks to his mother's efforts he was allowed to become an extra-mural student at St. Petersburg University; he passed all the examinations in the course of a year, graduated at the end of 1891, and spent the next eighteen months or so in a lawyer's office at Samara. In the years around 1890 he read Marx and Plekhanov and became converted to Marxism as a doctrine that explained the mechanism of the capitalist economy and provided a theory of revolution, not brought about by terrorist conspiracy but by the expansion of capitalism and the developing class-consciousness of the proletariat.

In September 1893 Lenin moved to St. Petersburg and began his political apprenticeship in the industrial and intellectual capital of Russia. During the next two years he made his name in socialist circles as an expert on Marxism and became acquainted with many of his subsequent collaborators and opponents—Struve, Martov, Krzhizhanovsky, and Potresov. He also met Nadezhda Krupskaya, whom he was to marry in 1899 and who thereafter shared in all his literary and political activity. Martov (by his real name Yuly Osipovich Tsederbaum) was born at Constantinople in 1873, the son of well-to-do Jewish parents. He was brought up in Odessa and enrolled at St. Petersburg University in 1891, but was expelled for taking part in socialist discussion groups. He was arrested and spent some months in prison, after which he lived at Vilna. There he gained experience of propaganda among the workers, and on his return to St. Petersburg in 1895 he was able to help the socialist intelligentsia to make contact with the real proletariat. He urged that the social democrats, instead of expounding theory to the workers, should concentrate on immediate practical conflicts, especially the observance of factory legislation. This would soon awaken a spirit of solidarity among the workers and convince them that the state was on the side of the exploiters and that particular disputes were only instances of the antagonism between the workers and the system as a whole. The social democratic groups in St. Petersburg accordingly went to work among the proletariat on these lines.

The earliest of Lenin's writings date from 1893–5 and are chiefly aimed against the economic doctrines of the populists. The first, a review of a book by V. Y. Postnikov on *Peasant Farming in South Russia*, was rejected by the periodical to which it was sent. Postnikov's book spoke of the progress of capitalism in Russian agriculture and the differentiation of peasant incomes, and in this way furnished arguments against the populist ideology. In the same year Lenin also wrote an unpublished report for a discussion group on the market question. Here he joined issue with the populist economists for stating that capitalism was unable to create a home market in Russia as it was undermining its own position by proletarianizing the peasants and curtailing their purchasing power. Lenin argued that impoverishment and proletarianization did not prevent the market from increasing. The proletarianized peasants were obliged to sell their labour-power, and in this way created a market, while capitalism, as it developed, also created a market for means of production.

In 1894 Lenin wrote a dissertation of some length attacking the social philosophy of populism and particularly the views of Mikhailovsky and Krivenko. This work, entitled *What the 'Friends of the People' are and How they Fight the Social Democrats*, was hectographed and distributed to social democratic groups; its middle section has not been preserved. In it Lenin combats the 'subjective' and moralistic viewpoint of populist writers and contrasts it with Marxism as a scientific, determinist doctrine which does not ask any questions about what 'ought' to be but considers all social processes, including the phenomena of consciousness, as 'natural' events determined by the relations of production. 'Marx treats the social movement as a process of natural history, governed by laws not only independent of human will, consciousness and intentions, but, on the contrary, determining the will, consciousness and intentions of men ... If the conscious element plays so subordinate a part in the history of civilization, it is self-evident that a critique whose subject is civilization can least of all take as its basis any form of, or any result of, consciousness' (*Collected Works*, vol. 1, p. 166). There is no conflict between determinism, which rejects the 'stupid fable of free will', and the possibility of evaluating human acts or the role of the individual in history. All history consists of the acts of individuals; the question is in what conditions individual acts can be effective. Moreover, 'Everybody knows that scientific socialism never painted any prospects for the future as such: it confined itself to analysing the present bourgeois regime, to studying the trends of development of the capitalist social organization, and that is all' (ibid., p. 184).

On this point Lenin takes the same view as Plekhanov and the orthodox Germans: Marxism is a determinist interpretation of history which, by observing the present state of society, predicts how it will develop independently of human wishes, opinions, or values. Marxism can thus answer the question as to which human aspirations are in accordance with 'objective' trends and which are condemned to remain idle dreams. Like other orthodox Marxists, Lenin does not reply to the objection of the subjectivists and neo-Kantians that to know which of our actions are likely to succeed is not the same as having a reason for them: whence is this reason to be derived? By speaking of 'progress' we tacitly introduce a value-judgement, implying that the social process is not only necessary but deserves support; but this cannot follow from any mere descriptive analysis.

Lenin nevertheless uses the concept of progress, without explaining how it relates to a determinist historiosophy. He declares that capitalism is progressive as compared with Russian autocracy, and this clearly does not simply mean that the country is heading for a capitalist economy. However—and this is of fundamental importance in Lenin's eyes—capitalism in Russia and the future democratic changes associated with it are 'progressive' not in themselves but because they will facilitate the struggle of the working class to overthrow capitalism. He emphasizes that Marxists must call themselves social democrats and never forget the importance of 'democratism' and the struggle against feudalism, absolutism, and the Tsarist bureaucracy, since these must be overthrown before the bourgeoisie can be dealt with.

That is why it is the direct duty of the working class to fight side by side with radical democracy against absolutism and the reactionary social estates and institutions—a duty which the Social-Democrats must impress upon the workers, while not for a moment ceasing also to impress upon them that the struggle against all these institutions is necessary only as a means of facilitating the struggle against the bourgeoisie, that the worker needs the achievement of the general democratic demands only to clear the road to victory over the working people's chief enemy, over an institution that is purely democratic by nature, *capital* ... (*Collected Works*, vol. 1, p. 291)

Lenin repeats this admonition several times, and its purport is clear. Democracy is not an end in itself; political freedom is mainly for the benefit of the bourgeoisie, but the working class has an interest in it as it will facilitate the struggle for socialism. This view presages an early breach between the social democrats and the 'legal Marxists', who regarded political freedoms as valuable in themselves and not merely weapons in the fight for the 'next stage' of history. Lenin from the beginning envisaged the struggle against absolutism in the context of the future victory of socialism, and only from this point of view did he take seriously anti-Tsarist activity or alliances with democratic forces. To measure the 'progressiveness' of social institutions it was not enough to compare different formations based on class antagonism: everything must be related to the final aim of socialism. On this point Lenin's eschatology is fully in accordance with Marx's ideas. Democratic institutions, and the political and cultural freedoms that go with the capitalist economy, are not values in themselves: their sense is entirely determined within the capitalist order.

Lenin agreed with Plekhanov at this time in holding that capitalism was bound to prevail in Russia. The populists, in his view, were involved in a contradiction on this point. They wished to do away with feudal survivals and yet preserve social institutions that could only exist by virtue of those survivals: to abolish the remaining restrictions of serfdom and feudal servitude, yet to avert the inevitable consequences of this process in the shape of the expropriation and class differentiation of the peasantry. They were reactionaries inasmuch as they wished to preserve institutions that progress condemned to be swept away, such as the attachment of the peasant to the soil.

The work quoted above clearly formulates the basic practical task to which Lenin devoted the rest of his career: the organization of a socialist workers' party thanks to which the proletariat would not be a mere instrument of the bourgeoisie in the struggle against absolutism, but would be an independent body aware of its antagonism to capital as well as to the Tsardom. In forming the workers' party the intelligentsia would play only a subsidiary part: 'the role of the "intelligentsia" is to make special leaders from among the intelligentsia unnecessary' (ibid., p. 298). The proletariat was not only to form an independent movement but to lead the fight against absolutism. This last point is only indicated in general terms, but it figures in later writings as the key to Lenins's tactics.

In 1893–4, then, Lenin made his appearance on the political and intellectual scene of St. Petersburg as a Marxist in the classical Plekhanov sense. All the main elements of the social democratic outlook can be found in these early works: the assertion that historical inevitability is central to Marxism and that the latter has no room for evaluative elements; that the cause of capitalism has irrevocably prevailed in Russia; and that the task of social democracy is to help the workers organize an independent political movement which will lead all democratic forces in the fight against absolutism and thus clear the field for the future victory over capitalism.

The year 1895 is of especial importance both in Lenin's biography and in the history of Russian socialism. It is the date of Lenin's first journey abroad, his arrest, the creation of a social democratic organization in St. Petersburg, the first contacts between the social democratic intelligentsia and the workers, and Lenin's first conflict with Peter Struve and with what was later called 'legal Marxism'.

2. *Struve and 'legal Marxism'*

The term 'legal Marxism' is applied to the writings of a group of Russian philosophers and economists who advanced Marxist ideas in the 1890s but who, almost from the beginning, took up an increasingly critical attitude towards essential features of orthodoxy, both in political economy and in the social field. None of the 'legal Marxists' were orthodox in the way that Plekhanov or Lenin was, and after 1900 they embraced political liberalism and, for the most part, Christian philosophy. In the nineties, however, they dominated the field of Marxist journalism in Russia. Their main differences from orthodoxy may be summed up in a few points. While accepting the principles of historical materialism, they held that it had no logical connection with philosophical materialism and was compatible with a spiritualist philosophy, or with positivism or Kantianism. They regarded Marxism as a scientific explanation of historical processes, but agreed with the neo-Kantians that it did not account for moral principles and that these must be derived from another source. They regarded political freedoms and democratic institutions as valuable in themselves, and were interested in the possibilities of political and economic reform under capitalism, not only from the point of view of the 'ultimate aim' but from that of the immediate interest of the workers, peasants, and intelligentsia and of cultural development. Marxism, to them, was rather a theory of society than a practical weapon: they were more interested in its cognitive value than its political function. They criticized Marx's theory of value, of the falling rate of profit, and the concentration of capital in agriculture. In some respects they anticipated German revisionism, and in others they endorsed its criticisms. They did much to popularize

Marxism among the intelligentsia, but also to undermine its influence. They are regarded as the Russian counterpart of the revisionists, but the analogy is only partially valid. By the end of the century the legal Marxists were among the protagonists of the ideological struggle for liberal reforms: they existed as a group until Russian socialism and liberalism finally parted company.

The most eminent of the legal Marxists was Pyotr (Peter) Berngardovich Struve (1870–1944). Other members of the group were Nikolay Aleksandrovich Berdyayev (1874–1948), Mikhail Ivanovich Tugan-Baranovsky (1865–1919), Sergey Nikolaye-vich Bulgakov (1871–1944), and Semyon Ludwigovich Frank (1877–1944). The term 'legal Marxism' was mainly used, in a pejorative sense, by Lenin and others of the orthodox camp. As pointed out by R. Kindersley in the principal monograph on the subject, the term did not refer so much to the fact that they published books or articles that were allowed by the censorship (for so did Lenin), but rather to their 'legal' status as individuals, i.e. that they lived under their own names and did not as a rule carry on underground activity. The orthodox used the term, however, to suggest that the group regarded legal reformist activity as the only way to achieve social change in Russia.

Struve, whose father was governor of the province of Perm, entered St. Petersburg University in 1899 and studied first zoology, then law. He was a typical intellectual as opposed to a political figure, and became a Marxist for theoretical rather than political reasons. As a student he had a reputation for wide reading and expert knowledge of Western philosophy and sociology. Marxism attracted him by its scientific, unsentimental approach to social questions, its thoroughgoing determinism and the light it threw on social prospects in Russia. From his youth Struve was attracted by liberal ideas, and—as R. Pipes points out in his monograph—from the beginning he treated liberalism as an end and socialism as a means, whereas to orthodox Marxists it was the other way round. A convinced Westernizer, he saw Russia's future in terms of 'Europeanization' and believed that the working class would be the chief agent in this process. In 1890–1 he was the leader of a group which discussed social and philosophical questions. He was influenced at an early stage by neo-Kantian literature, and this was reinforced by a year spent at the University of Graz in 1891. Like all Marxists of his generation he began his writing career by attacking the populists on the peasant question and that of capitalism in Russia. In reviews and articles in 1892–3 he argued that class differentiation in the countryside and the development of a commodity economy were not only inevitable but salutary, and that capitalism had put an end to dreams of a barter economy and the maintenance of the village commune. In the autumn of 1894 his book *Critical Remarks on the Subject of Russia's Economic Development* was published in St. Petersburg. This was a Marxist work in the sense that Struve declared himself to be a historical materialist and criticized 'subjective sociology' from that point of view, renewing his attacks on populist economic theory and vain attempts to reverse the course of history; but in some important respects the book foreshadowed his future position as a revisionist. In the first place, he rejected the common Marxist view that the state is 'nothing but' an instrument of class oppression. On the contrary, it performed many necessary functions that were not tied to any particular class-interest: this was so under any social system, and would be the case when capitalism was superseded. Secondly, and more importantly, Struve was in favour of evolutionary socialism, developing out of the capitalist system by a process of gradual and continuous change; he thus also rejected the theory of the inevitable impoverishment of the working class. The book is not only a critique of the populist Utopia but also a hymn of praise to capitalism, not only because it contains the seeds of its own destruction and replacement by higher things, but because it represents enormous progress in every sphere: the productivity of labour, economic rationalization, political and cultural freedoms, and the socialization of life. The book ends with a sentence that became famous as the target of populist attacks: 'Let us admit our lack of culture and be schooled by capitalism.' The populists accused Struve of glorifying capitalism and of being a bourgeois ideologist; but he considered himself a Marxist and a social democrat, and for some years he and Lenin treated their differences of opinion as divergences within the social democratic movement. If the term 'legal Marxism' is intended to denote a clearly separate movement, aware of its separateness, this is to some extent a projection into the past of Lenin's attitude after he had broken with Struve. On the other hand, it is reasonable enough to regard the legal Marxists as forming a single group, since they showed certain common trends from the beginning, although for some years the differences between revolutionists and revisionists were less important than their joint opposition to populism.

In autumn 1895 Struve went to Switzerland, where he met Plekhanov, and then to Berlin, where he studied for some months. In the following year he and Potresov were sent to the congress of the International in London by a social democratic organization formed largely on the initiative of Martov and Lenin and named (after they had both been arrested) the League for the Liberation of the Working Class. Struve's contacts with the Fabians encouraged him to place his hopes in socialism evolving out of capitalism. At the beginning of 1897 he and Tugan-Baranovsky took over *Novoye Slovo*, a periodical previously published by liberal populists. Until its suppression nearly a year later this became the principal organ of Russian Marxism, publishing articles by Plekhanov, Lenin, Martov, and other leaders, and also a discussion between Struve and Bulgakov on Stammler's new book concerning historical materialism. Struve endeavoured to reconcile historical materialism with freedom on the lines of Kant's distinction between the empirical and the noumenal world, though he seems to confuse this distinction with that between physical and psychological reality. He declares that all ideals and evaluative experiences can be causally explained by social circumstances; however, since they present themselves psychologically as independent of such conditions and as possessing a reality of their own, this psychological reality cannot be described in entirely the same language as the world of phenomena, and we must therefore assume that there is some kind of independence as between historical conditions and human ideals. This reasoning is clumsy and unconvincing, but it shows the tension in Struve's mind between historical materialism and the desire to safeguard certain non-historical and non-relative values. Before long he resolved this tension by abandoning Marxism altogether.

In March 1898 a number of social democratic groups sent delegates to a meeting at Minsk which was intended to be the founding congress of the Russian Social Democratic Workers' party. It did not bring about the desired integration, and nearly all the participants, who were few in number, were arrested immediately after the meeting. However, it left behind it not only the name (and the numeration of party Congresses up to the present time, this being regarded as No. 1) but also a manifesto drafted by Struve, though he was not present at the Congress itself. This stated that the immediate task of the working class was to achieve political freedoms; that in view of the weakness and cowardice of the bourgeoisie it was for the proletariat to overthrow the autocracy; but that the proletariat must continue to fight against the bourgeoisie for its own class aims and must preserve its separate identity as a class. All this was in accordance with Plekhanov's doctrine. However, the drafting of this programme for the nascent party was Struve's last act as a social democrat. Bernstein's book and articles confirmed his doubts as to the Marxist doctrine of revolution, though he rightly did not think much of Bernstein's criticism from the philosophical point of view. Before long he put forward similar conclusions with better arguments of his own. In 'Die Marxsche Theorie der sozialen Entwicklung' ('Marx's Theory of Social Development'), published in 1899 in *Archiv für soziale Gesetzgebung und Statistik*, he attacked the notion of social revolution as contradictory and formulated his general objections to Marx's theory of society, though he continued to treat that theory with respect and even to call himself a Marxist.

Struve argued that Marx's theory of the pauperization and degredation of the working class had in its time been based on well-ascertained data. Apart from the fact, however, that later developments had shown that these did not necessarily represent a permanent trend, Marx in any case had failed to notice that if his theory were right on this point the outlook for socialism would be hopeless: for it could not be expected that a class condemned to increasing degradation of mind and body would be able to bring about the greatest revolution in history, including not only economic changes but the efflorescence of art and civilization. There was no reason to maintain that social antagonisms, especially the opposition between producers and the relations of production, must go on becoming more and more acute. On the contrary, the theory of the intensification of social contradictions and the universal collapse of capitalism conflicted with the other premisses of historical materialism. It was wrong to think of the economy and the legal superstructure as two independent ontological realities, standing in a relationship of cause and effect or, as Stammler would have it, of content and form. Both these supposed entities were hypostases, intellectual creations and not real phenomena. What was real was the constant pressure of economic facts on legal ones, and a process of constant adaptation. Marx himself had admitted that the process of socialization went on uninterruptedly in a capitalist economy, but he assumed without proof that this must be accompanied by a steady increase in the 'capitalist' character of the legal system, so that the gap between the two abstract entities was bound to get wider. In reality the opposite was the case: socialist development took place within capitalist society in both the economic and the legal sphere, and the inevitable disharmony of these two became less and less acute as time went on. 'In a real society there is neither absolute antagonism nor absolute harmony between the economy and the law, but they constantly collide yet partially adapt to each other.' If the notion of a social revolution means anything it can only mean the slow process of social change which at some moment may, but need not, be accompanied by a political revolution; the process of socialist change takes place not by the continual increase of tension but by its gradual elimination. This view is in accordance with historical materialism, whereas the idea of a violent social revolution is contrary to it. The continuity of change is an epistemological condition of the intelligibility of the concept of change, whereas the idea of capitalism and socialism being opposed to each other in all respects and separated by an abrupt hiatus is quite unintelligible. As to the political revolution establishing a dictatorship of the proletariat, such a dictatorship becomes less likely or desirable, not more, as the proletariat grows in strength: for as the strength and social importance of the working class increase, so does the socialist element in the system of society.

This, it will be seen, is a repetition, on the empirical side, of Bernstein's argument to the effect that social reform under capitalism is itself the building of socialism. The 'epistemological' point, on the other hand, is decidedly far-fetched. Marx said that socialist conditions are prepared within the capitalist system by the growth of co-operation and concentration of the technological process of production, and he predicted that a political revolution, i.e. the seizure of power by the organized proletariat, was the necessary condition of a change in economic relations and especially the socialization of means of production. However this doctrine may be criticized, it does not appear to contain any logical inconsistency. The basic practical content of the social revolution was to be the violent expropriation of the capitalists, and it is hard to see why this should be logically impossible.

Struve's connection with the social democrats lasted for a year or two longer, but in 1901 it ceased in a welter of accusations and intrigue. For some time after Lenin and Martov returned from exile in Siberia they conducted involved negotiations with Struve with the object of collaborating on periodicals, existing or projected, but it was clear that the breach between them was too wide. Struve criticized, one after the other, various crucial points of social democratic ideology and Marxist philosophy, and in the end rejected them all. In 1899, following Böhm-Bawerk and the Russian 'economists', he criticized Marx's theory of value, stating that Marx had tried to combine in one concept two entirely different phenomena, the social fact of exploitation and the economic fact of exchange. If, as argued in Volume III of *Capital*, industry creates the average rate of profit, this simply means that economic realities do not correspond to the concept of value as defined by labour, for value is ultimately determined as a function of production costs; while value as in Volume I of *Capital* remains a purely metaphysical entity, of no use to political economy.

The estrangement was completed by Struve's philosophical criticism. True, he had never professed dialectical materialism after the fashion of Engels or Plekhanov: his views were those of a 'scienticist' and positivist, but his general determinist and empiricist outlook was in accordance with the way of thinking prevalent among Marxists. In 1900, however, he wrote a long introduction to Berdyayev's *Subjectivism and Individualism in Social Philosophy* (published in 1901) in which he expressly abandoned positivism for a Kantian transcendentalism on a religious basis. As values cannot be derived from experience, he argued, we must either fall into extreme relativism or accept that they have an ontological foundation and are not simply due to arbitrary, subjective decisions. The absoluteness of values implies the reality of the Absolute and the non-empirical: a substantive soul endowed with freedom, and a supreme Being. On this basis we can recognize the absolute value of personality, which is the foundation of liberal social philosophy. Liberalism in Struve's sense is above all a nominalist conception, rejecting the idea that any suprapersonal collective entity such as society or the state can claim to encroach upon the inalienable rights of the individual, his freedom and urge towards unlimited self-perfection.

Struve left Russia at the end of 1901 and in the following year settled in Stuttgart, where he edited the journal *Osvobozhdenie* (*Liberation*): this was not the organ of any political party, but was closely linked with the liberal movement that was taking shape in Russia, and was devoted to unmasking and combating the autocracy. From this time on Struve's activity as a writer and politician has no connection with the history of Marxism except that he was constantly under fire from the social democrats.

Of the other legal Marxist writers, Berdyayev had least in common with Marxism. As a student he belonged to social democratic groups, was arrested, and exiled for three years to Vologda, as were Bogdanov and Lunacharsky for the same reason. However, from the beginning of his career as a writer he stood much further from Marxism than did Struve. In the book referred to above he accepted the premisses of historical materialism and the idea of the class struggle, but with reservations that were incompatible with even the loosest conception of Marxism. He believed that there must be an ontological repository of unchanging moral and logical values, and that historical circumstances, in particular the class struggle, govern the rules of cognition and obligation only in the sense that in each phase of history a different class is the exponent of those rules. Hence, while accepting the positivist argument that obligation cannot be deduced from empirical data, he endeavoured from the outset to base moral absolutism on other grounds. Of the former legal Marxists Berdyayev became the best known to the Western public, but this was after his expulsion from Soviet Russia and on account of his works attacking Communism and preaching a kind of Christian existentialism, based on faith in the absolute value of personality.

Tugan-Baranowsky, Bulgakov, and S. L. Frank were known in the 1890s chiefly as economists, the first-named being professionally the most qualified in this field. They were concerned to a large extent with the key question of markets and whether Russian capitalism was—as the populists denied—capable of creating a home market sufficient for its expansion. Tugan-Baranovsky argued that the viability and development of capitalism did not depend on the level of consumption, as the market for means of production expanded faster than that for consumption goods. Since, under capitalism, production and accumulation were ends in themselves, capitalism was in a position to create its own conditions of compound reproduction and was not absolutely dependent on popular consumption. In that case, however, as Rosa Luxemburg had pointed out, capitalism could apparently keep going indefinitely and there was no economic reason to prophesy its overthrow. Tugan-Baranovsky worked out a theory of crises to supplement Marx's arguments, but he did not in fact believe that capitalism would collapse as a result of its crises or of the imbalance between production and the market. In this he was not at variance with Lenin, who likewise did not hold that capitalism was certain to collapse owing to the difficulty of finding outlets.

The economic revisionism of the legal Marxists centred on Marx's theory of value. Their attack had no special political effects, but it struck at what the orthodox regarded as the keystone of the doctrine. Since value in Marx's sense was unmeasurable and did not in fact define the terms of exchange, so that there was no logical transition from value to price, it followed, according to Bulgakov, that value must be regarded purely as a social category of no importance in studying price movements, but essential to the broad analysis of capitalism. In this way, like Sombart, Bulgakov sought to protect the theory of value by limiting its applicability. Frank, in *Marx's Theory of Value and its Significance* (1900), questioned the utility of Marx's concept if, as Marx himself intended, it was supposed to denote not exchange-value but an intrinsic property of goods, whether marketed or not. In the end the legal Marxists either rejected the category of value altogether, as being of no interest to economics in so far as it differed from price, or adopted the theory of marginal utility whereby value depends on the purchaser's sense of need, expressed as the price he will pay for the last (marginal) unit of a commodity that he is disposed to regard as useful.

The legal Marxists also attacked Marx's economic theory on other essential points. Tugan-Baranovsky declared that the theory of the diminishing rate of profit conflicted with other elements of the doctrine—the value of constant capital falls as the productivity of labour increases, so that the rate of profit may be constant although productivity is rising—and also that it was contrary to factual observation. Bulgakov, like the German revisionists, criticized the theory of concentration in agriculture.

In spite of all these criticisms Russian Marxism could be regarded as a single ideological camp, though with internal differentiations, as long as the Marxists held that the chief task of social democracy was to combat the populist idea of a separate, non-capitalist road for Russia. Before the end of the century, however, it was clear that the populist economic doctrine was losing ground in the sense that appeals to stop capitalism developing were ineffectual, while Marxists of all shades regarded the defence of the village commune as a hopeless cause. Thus, around 1900, what might have appeared secondary differences within Russian Marxism took on the aspect of a basic dispute, especially as they coincided in time with the debate over revisionism in Germany and the birth of a liberal movement in Russia. Marxism could no longer define itself simply as anti-populism. The relationship of social democracy to the bourgeoisie, the question of revolution, and the relation between the political and economic struggle of the working class became the paramount subjects of debate. In 1898–1900 three main trends may be discerned in Russian Marxism: revolutionary orthodoxy, revisionism or 'legal Marxism', and 'economism'. Before long, however, the legal Marxists went over to liberalism and ceased to count as revisionists. Bulgakov, Berdyayev, Frank, and Struve returned by different paths towards Christianity. They continued to play an important part in intellectual life as the contributors to three collections of essays, the first two of which —*Problems of Idealism* (1902) and *Landmarks* (1909)—are among the most significant events in the history of the Russian intelligentsia before the Revolution. The third, entitled *De Profundis*, was produced in 1918 but immediately confiscated, and was practically unknown for half a century: it depicted the revolutionary apocalypse as a national and cultural calamity.

It may seem strange that although revisionism made its appearance in Russia before there was an organized social democratic movement, it did not remain in existence for long, whereas it did so in Germany despite the opposition of an orthodox party establishment. However, German revisionism was the theoretical superstructure of a reformist struggle waged successfully for many years by an organized workers' movement. In Russia reformist ideas had a very fragile basis in political experience, and the idea of a wholesale and final revolution was deeply rooted in the minds of the radical intelligentsia. Moreover, while in Germany revisionism appeared from the beginning as a section of the social democratic movement existing alongside the liberals, in Russia it played for a time the part of the liberal movement with which it eventually merged, while the writers we have been considering regarded Marxism as a weapon against populist conservatism rather than a theory of global revolution. Marxism harmonized with the attitude of those who, having been inspired in their youth by the ideals of 'scientism', sought after a scientific interpretation of society as opposed to populist moralism; they also found in Marxism a promise of the triumph of capitalism and therefore of democratic and constitutional principles in Russia. Marxism proved that Russian absolutism was doomed by history, and this was probably more important to the legal Marxists than the prospect of socialism. When the Russian social democrats made it clear in the course of time that they regarded any alliance with liberalism as purely tactical, it became impossible to maintain a half-Marxist and half-liberal standpoint.

There is another important fact to be noted in the history of Russian revisionism. Because Marxism and social democracy made their appearance in Russia independently of a workers' movement and were at the outset purely intellectual in character, Marxism took on a much more dogmatic and fanatical form than in the West, where it had constantly to adjust to the realities of labour politics. In Russia, where 'revolution' had been a word to conjure with for decades and where there was every reason to mistrust the prospects of reform, the tiny group of revolutionaries were naturally doctrinaire in the extreme, the more so as their convictions were of purely moral and intellectual origin and were not due to their being members of an oppressed class. In the resulting atmosphere theoretical problems were debated in terms of loyalty and treachery rather than simple truth and falsehood, and tactical questions were unvaryingly and solely related to the 'ultimate end'. Despite ideological differences the Russian socialists shared the mentality of populist conspirators rather than that of West European social democrats. It is significant that as soon as a Russian workers' movement came into existence there also appeared, though not for long, a variant of German revisionism in the shape of 'economism', i.e., roughly speaking, a trade-unionist doctrine of non-political efforts to improve the workers' lot.

3. *Lenin's polemics in 1895–1901*

Up to 1899 Lenin was mainly absorbed by the controversy with populism, but the critique of legal Marxism, and later especially of economism, already figured prominently in his works. In 1895 his first printed article appeared in a miscellany published by Potresov, under the title *The Economic Content of Narodism [Populism] and the Criticism of it in Mr. Struve's Book*. This was an analysis of Struve's work on *Russia's Economic Development*: while critical in parts, it did not accuse Struve of treason and anti-Marxism but rather urged him to conform more strictly to the orthodox position. Apart from attacking the populists, Lenin's work contains some general theoretical remarks, and he reiterates his view of the progressiveness of capitalism: 'Yes, the Marxists do consider large-scale capitalism progressive—not, of course, because it replaces 'independence' [sc. of the peasantry] by dependence, but because it creates conditions for abolishing dependence' (*Works*, vol. 1, pp. 379–80). Criticizing Struve for opposing the idea of reform to that of the breakdown of capitalism, Lenin argues that one is a means to the other. His main criticism of Struve is that he is an 'objectivist'. He agrees with Sombart, whom Struve quotes, that 'in Marxism itself there is not a grain of ethics from beginning to end', since (as Lenin adds) 'theoretically, it subordinates the "ethical standpoint" to the "principle of causality"; in the practice it reduces it to the class struggle' (ibid., p. 421). He also agrees that scientific socialism rejects philosophy altogether: 'From the standpoint of Marx and Engels philosophy has no right to a separate, independent existence, and its material is divided among the various branches of positive science' (p. 418). In short, he understands the 'scientific' character of Marxism in the same way as Plekhanov and most of the orthodox Germans: Marxism is a non-evaluative, non-philosophical theory of social phenomena. Thus far Lenin is in agreement with Struve. But this formulation may suggest that Marxism confines itself to describing historical necessities and of itself offers no practical counsel, except of course as to the efficacy of certain actions. This was the difficulty of those who found it necessary to supplement the Marxist doctrine with a normative ethic derived from elsewhere, generally from Kant. Struve at this time had not gone so far, but confined himself to observing that Marxism was 'objective', i.e. descriptive only. To Lenin, however, this was unacceptable. An objectivist, in his view, was one who speaks only of the necessities involved by a particular social formation, and, by limiting himself to these, runs the risk of becoming an apologist for them simply as necessities. A materialist, on the other hand, does not so limit himself but goes on to explain what class forces are involved. 'Materialism includes partisanship, so to speak, and enjoins the direct and open adoption of the standpoint of a definite social group in any assessment of events' (ibid., p. 401).

From the theoretical point of view this is clumsy and unconvincing: for it is clear that to analyse 'historical necessities' in the light of the class structure of a society is not to go beyond a purely 'objective' description, and it is not explained why materialism as such should oblige us to anything or imply any active commitment. It is evident, however, that Lenin wished to avoid the dilemma propounded by the neo-Kantians: either Marxism describes the social process without telling us what human individuals should do about it, or it must be supplemented by normative ideas. Lenin, though he was unable to express his thought clearly, was endeavouring to bring out the essential point which was first elucidated by Lukács: Marxism does away with the dichotomy between facts and values, for it is identical with the self-knowledge of the working class; that class comprehends the social process in the very act of revolutionizing the world, so that in this one privileged case the under-standing and the making of history appear as a single act. Lenin consistently ignored the neo-Kantian criticism and, being unable to examine the question properly, confined himself to summary statements like those quoted. He perceived vaguely, however, that it is the characteristic feature of Marxism that it is neither purely descriptive nor purely normative, nor a combination of descriptive and normative judgements, but claims to be at once a movement and an act of understanding—the self-awareness of the proletariat in the act of struggle. Knowledge of the world, in other words, is an aspect of changing it: theory and its practical application are one.

In 1895 Lenin went abroad for the first time and met in Geneva the founding fathers of Russian Marxism, Plekhanov and Akselrod. The meeting was successful, though the *émigrés* had trouble convincing Lenin of the necessity of an alliance with the liberal bourgeoisie. Soon after returning to Russia he was arrested: police measures had been intensified owing to a wave of strikes in St. Petersburg, which the social democrats had done much to instigate. He remained in prison for a year and a half, writing appeals and pamphlets, and was then sentenced to three years' exile at Shushenskoye in the Krasnoyarsk area of Siberia, where he continued to study and write intensively. While in prison he drafted a programme calling on the social democratic party to fight for democratic freedoms and social legislation. The programme does not envisage the conquest of state power by the working class, but only a share in the making of laws. The party is to help the workers develop class-consciousness and to point out the objectives of the struggle; it must also explain to the workers that while they should support the bourgeoisie in the fight for political freedom, this is only a temporary alliance. In the summer of 1897 Lenin published in *Novoye Slovo* a fresh attack on the populists entitled 'A Characterization of Economic Romanticism', in which he compared their doctrine with that of Sismondi, the champion of small producers threatened by the expansion of capitalism. Sismondi might succeed in revealing the dire consequences of capitalist accumulation, but he had nothing to set against it except a romantic, sentimental nostalgia for the pre-capitalist era. Like the populists he was no better than a reactionary, for he dreamt of returning to the past instead of seeing that the solution to the contradictions and injustices of capitalism lay in allowing it to develop to the full. Lenin also reverted to the question of the home market, anticipating to some extent the problems later raised by Rosa Luxemburg. It was not true that capitalism was prevented from realizing surplus value by reason of the collapse of small owners and the resulting contraction of the market: productive consumption offered capitalist production a wide field of expansion.

While in exile Lenin wrote a pamphlet on *The Tasks of the Russian Social Democrats*, published in 1898 in Geneva, which defined the party's general strategy in regard to 'alliances' with other social forces. Social democrats were to support all moves against the autocracy and to denounce all forms of oppression, whichever social groups were its victims. They should support protests against national, religious, social, and class oppression, aiding the bourgeoisie against the 'reactionary strivings of the petty bourgeoisie', and the latter in their democratic demands upon the Tsarist bureaucracy. The party, however, was not to consider itself a champion of the interests that it supported. Although it aided the persecuted sectarians, it had no concern for their religious aspirations. To support, in fact, meant simply to exploit. Social democracy was, in Lenin's view, the only force that was engaged consistently and unreservedly against the autocracy: all others were irresolute or half-hearted. The party could and must act as a centre for all the social energies which would one day bring absolutism to the ground, but at the same time it must have exclusively in view the interests of the proletariat as a separate class. 'The social democrats render this support in order to expedite the fall of the common enemy, but expect nothing for themselves from these temporary allies, and concede nothing to them' (*Works*, vol. 2, p. 334). 'Support for the democratic demands of the petty bourgeoisie certainly does not mean support of the petty bourgeoisie: on the contrary, it is precisely the development which political liberty will make possible in Russia that will, with particular force, lead to the destruction of small economy under the blows of capital' (*A Draft Programme of Our Party*, 1899; *Works*, vol. 4, p. 243). In a letter to Potresov, written from exile and dated 26 January 1899, Lenin says: 'to free all *fortschrittliche Strömungen* [progressive trends] from the rubbish of Narodism and agrarianism and to utilize all of them in this purified form. In my opinion 'utilize' is a much more exact and suitable word than *Unterstützung und Bundesgenossenschaft* [support and alliance]. The latter indicates the equality of these *Bundesgenossen* [allies], whereas they must (in this I fully agree with you) follow in the wake, sometimes even "with gnashing of teeth"; they have absolutely not grown so far as to reach equality and will never grow to reach it, owing to their cowardice, disunity etc.' (*Works*, vol. 34, p. 30).

It is thus clear that Lenin from the outset regarded all political alliances as meaning simply the utilization of other groups for social democratic ends. Social democracy must rally around itself all forces that can in any way contribute to the break-up of the existing system, in the full awareness that that break-up is ultimately intended to destroy its 'allies' as well. From this point of view Lenin's attitude, and subsequently that of the whole Leninist movement, is identical whether it be a question of the bourgeoisie against absolutism, peasants against land-owners, religious sects aspiring to freedom, nationalities oppressed by Great Russian imperialism, or democratic institutions themselves. There is of course no mention of 'utilizing' the working class, for all these strategic rules are designed to enable that class, which is the *raison d'être* of the struggle, to attain its 'final aim'. Nevertheless, it soon became clear that as far as basic strategy was concerned the working class too, in Lenin's concept, was rather an instrument than a substantive agent.

While in exile Lenin also wrote a treatise on *The Development of Capitalism in Russia* (*Works*, vol. 3), which was published in 1899. This is his *magnum opus* against the populists, full of statistics and detailed analysis of the trends in agriculture and industry. It argues that Russian agriculture is in a state of commodity economy and shows all the signs of capitalist change: class differentiation, competition, and proletarianization on a large scale. In industry, Lenin depicts the process of concentration and the formation of a single country-wide market, sweeping away medieval forms of production and exchange.

While controversy with the populists played a diminishing role in intellectual life, unorthodox ideas were making their appearance among social democrats and were causing Lenin anxiety. He was roused to fury, as he himself states, by an article of Bulgakov's attacking Kautsky's recent analysis of the agrarian question. He was also disturbed by the growing popularity of Bernstein and the influence of neo-Kantianism, of which Struve and Bulgakov were to some extent the Russian spokesmen. He even began, as he wrote to Potresov on 27 June 1899, to study philosophy: he read Holbach and Hélvetius, and intended to apply himself to Kant. But he attached less importance to purely philosophical disputes at this time than subsequently. Meanwhile, besides theoretical revisionism the younger social democrats had taken up 'economism': Lenin reacted violently to the first signs of this movement, which attacked the very foundations of social democracy as he conceived it. In summer 1899, on receiving the document known as the 'Credo', drawn up by Kuskova and Prokopowicz and setting out the 'economist' programme, Lenin wrote a sharp protest which was endorsed by sixteen other exiles, and was published next year at Geneva by the local organization of social democrats.

The 'Credo' called in question the desirability of a separate political workers' party in Russia, which its authors regarded as an artificial application of Western experience to quite different conditions. The workers' movement, they argued, should always aim at the point of least resistance: in the West it was much easier to carry on a political than an economic struggle, but in Russia it was the reverse. Marxists should therefore concentrate on helping the workers' economic struggle and should back up the liberal opposition, which would presumably be directed by non-socialist democratic forces. Lenin regarded this as a prescription for political suicide, and in reply set out principles that were generally accepted by the orthodox. The workers' movement must have its own political aims and an independent party to pursue them; it must organize opposition elements of every kind, while never forfeiting its independence or running the risk of becoming an instrument of bourgeois parties.

Russian 'economism' was, as it were, a revival of 'classic' (non-political, non-terrorist) populism, with the working class substituted for the peasantry. It maintained that intellectual leaders should concentrate on the most obvious and easily understood aspirations of the workers, viz. their economic aims, leaving it to the liberals to fight for freedom and themselves playing only an auxiliary role in the political battle. Economism was not revisionism as this term is used of Bernstein and his supporters, who had no intention of persuading the workers to abandon the political and parliamentary struggle; but it corresponded to the trade-unionist tendency which was strongly rooted in German social democracy and which was allied for a considerable period with the theoretical revisionists.

Lenin's alarm at this new deviation was well founded, for it dominated social democracy in Russia for about two years and won over a majority of the *émigrés*, leading to a split among their ranks. After 1900 the 'economists' declined in importance, but it was nevertheless largely in answer to them that Lenin wrote *What is to be Done?*, in which he laid the ideological foundations of Bolshevism.

Lenin's Siberian exile ended at the beginning of 1900, and in July of that year he went abroad for the purpose of organizing Russian social democrats into a united movement. The first step to be taken, as he had long believed, was to found a periodical which would act as a link between scattered groups and make it possible to create a real party. Such a periodical would of course have to be printed abroad and smuggled into Russia. The name chosen for it was *Iskra* (*The Spark*).

The process of launching the paper was beset by quarrels that need not be gone into here. Lenin's meeting with Plekhanov was a disaster. In a posthumously published note on his encounter with the Geneva veterans he speaks bitterly of the older man's arrogance, though he (Lenin) had approached him with respect and admiration. Evidently Plekhanov was jealous of his authority among the Russian social democrats and vented his pride and intolerance on the young disciple. As Lenin put it, and as he was to remember for the future, 'An enamoured youth receives from the object of his love a bitter lesson—to regard all persons "without sentiment", to keep a stone in one's sling' (*Works*, vol. 4, p. 342).

In spite of these troubles the first number of *Iskra* was published in December 1900. It was printed successively in Leipzig, Munich, London, and Geneva, and had as its contributors the intellectual cream of Russian Marxism—Lenin, Plekhanov, Martov, Akselrod, Potresov, and Vera Zasulich.

The years 1901–3 marked a new stage in the development of Russian Marxism and Russian social democracy. During this time the foundations were laid of the Leninist variant of Marxism, the novelty and specific character of which were visible only by degrees. Up to now Lenin's ideological statements had been no different from those of Plekhanov or the Western orthodox Marxists, apart from the strong emphasis he laid on certain elements of the doctrine. Among these was the principle, which he repeated at every opportunity, that only the final aim —the conquest of political power by the proletariat—endows current actions with any meaning, and that social democrats may conclude any alliance and support any cause if by so doing they will bring the ultimate aim any closer. All other movements and social classes, human beings and ideologies, must be treated as subservient to the 'final revolution'.

XVI

The Rise of Leninism

1. The controversy over Leninism

The character of Leninism as a variant of Marxist doctrine has long been a subject of dispute. The question is, in particular, whether Leninism is a 'revisionist' ideology in relation to the Marxist tradition, or, on the contrary, a faithful application of the general principles of Marxism to a new political situation. The political bearing of this controversy is obvious. Stalinist orthodoxy, which on this point is still in force within the Communist movement, naturally takes the second view. Stalin maintained that Lenin added nothing to the inherited doctrine and took nothing away from it, but applied its principles unerringly, not only to Russian conditions but, most important, to the entire world situation. On this view Leninism is not a specifically Russian application of Marxism or one limited to Russian conditions, but a universally valid system of strategy and tactics for the 'new era' of social development, viz. that of imperialism and proletarian revolutions. Some Bolsheviks, on the other hand, regarded Leninism as more particularly an instrument of the Russian revolution, while non-Leninist Marxists argued that Lenin had been false to Marx's doctrine on many essential points.

The question, thus ideologically formulated, is in practice insoluble, like all such questions in the history of political movements or religious sects which have a strong inbuilt need of fidelity to their sources. It is natural and inevitable that the generations which come after the founders of the movement are confronted by questions and practical decisions that are not expressly foreseen in the existing canon, and that they interpret the canon in such a way as to justify their acts. In this respect the history of Marxism resembles that of Christianity. The result is generally to produce compromises of various kinds between doctrine and the demands of practice. New lines of division and conflicting political formations take shape under the immediate pressure of events, and each of them can find the support it requires in tradition, which is never perfectly integrated and consistent. Bernstein was indeed a revisionist in the sense that he openly rejected certain features of Marxist social philosophy and did not profess to be an inflexible custodian of the Marxian heritage on all points. Lenin, on the other hand, endeavoured to present all his acts and theories as the only possible or correct application of an existing ideology. He was not, however, a doctrinaire in the sense of preferring fidelity to Marx's text to the practical efficacy of the movement which he led. On the contrary, he had immense practical sense and the ability to subordinate all questions, whether of theory or tactics, to the single purpose of revolution in Russia and in the world. All questions of general theory had, in his view, already been settled by Marxism, and it was only necessary to draw intelligently on this body of doctrine to find the right solution for particular circumstances. In this he not only regarded himself as a faithful executor of the Marxist testament, but believed that he was conforming to the practice and tactics of European social democracy as exemplified more particularly in the German party. Up to 1914 he regarded German social democracy as a pattern and Kautsky as the greatest living authority on theoretical questions: he relied on him not only in theoretical matters but also on tactical Russian questions about which he himself knew a good deal more, such as the boycott of the Second Duma. In 1905 he wrote, in *Two Tactics of Social-Democracy in the Democratic Revolution*:

When and where did I ever claim to have created any sort of special trend in international social-democracy, *not identical* [Lenin's italics] with the trend of Bebel and Kautsky? When and where have there been brought to light differences between me, on the one hand, and Bebel and Kautsky on the other—differences even slightly approximating in gravity to the differences between Bebel and Kautsky, for instance, at Breslau on the agrarian question? (*Works*, vol. 9, p. 66 n.)

The question whether Lenin was a 'revisionist' cannot be decided simply by comparing his writings with those of Marx or posing the unanswerable question as to what Marx would have done or said in this or that situation. Clearly Marx's theory is incomplete or ambiguous in many places, and could be 'applied' in many contradictory ways without manifestly infringing its principles. Nevertheless, the question of the continuity between Marxism and Leninism is not wholly without significance. It can best be considered, however, not in terms of 'fidelity' but rather by examining the general trend of Lenin's attempts, in the theoretical field, to 'apply' or supplement the Marxist heritage.

To Lenin, as we have said, all theoretical questions were merely instruments of a single aim, the revolution; and the meaning of all human affairs, ideas, institutions, and values resided exclusively in their bearing on the class struggle. It is not hard to find support for this attitude in the writings of Marx and Engels, who in many theoretical passages emphasized the transience and class-relatedness of all aspects of life in a class society. None the less, their specific analyses were generally more differentiated and less simplified than such 'reductionist' formulas might seem to imply. Both Marx and Engels had a considerably wider horizon of interest than that suggested by the question 'Is this good or bad for the revolution?'; to Lenin, on the other hand, this was the all-sufficient criterion as to whether a matter was important at all and, if so, how it should be decided. Marx and Engels had a sense of the continuity of civilization, and did not consider that all human values, including science, art, morals, and social institutions, were 'nothing but' instruments of class interests. Nevertheless, the general formulas in which they expressed their historical materialism lent themselves well enough to the use Lenin made of them. To Lenin philosophical questions had no meaning in themselves but were merely weapons in the political struggle: so were art and literature, law and institutions, democratic values and religious ideas. On this point he not only cannot be reproached with deviating from Marxism, but it can rather be said that he applied the principles of historical materialism more thoroughly than Marx. If law, for instance, is 'nothing but' a weapon in the class struggle, it naturally follows that there is no essential difference between the rule of law and an arbitrary dictatorship. If political freedoms are 'nothing but' an instrument used by the bourgeoisie in its own class-interest, it is perfectly fair to argue that communists need not feel obliged to uphold these values when they come to power. As science, philosophy, and art are only organs of the class struggle, it can be seen that there is no 'qualitative' difference between writing a philosophical treatise and using fire-arms—the two are merely different weapons for different occasions and should be regarded in this light, whether used by friend or foe. These aspects of Lenin's doctrine became drastically evident after the Bolsheviks seized power, but they are expressed in his writings from the earliest years. Lenin often held the advantage in discussions with Marxists of other shades of opinion because of the devastating simplicity and consistency with which he applied the principles they had in common. When his adversaries were able to point out that he was in conflict with something Marx had actually said—for example, that 'dictatorship' did not signify a despotism unfettered by law—they were proving Marx's own inconsistency rather than Lenin's unorthodoxy.

None the less, on one or two essential points the innovations that Lenin introduced into the Russian revolutionary movement suggested considerable doubt as to his fidelity to Marxist tradition. In the first place, Lenin at an early stage advocated an alliance between the proletariat and the peasantry as the basic strategy for the 'bourgeois revolution', while his opponents contended that an alliance with the bourgeoisie would be more in accordance with the doctrine in this case. Secondly, Lenin was the first to see the national question as a powerful reservoir of energy that social democrats could and should use to further their cause, instead of merely an awkward hindrance. Thirdly, he formulated his own organizational rules and his own version of the attitude the party should adopt towards a spontaneous outbreak by the workers. On all these points he was criticized not only by reformists and Mensheviks but also by such a pillar of orthodoxy as Rosa Luxemburg. On all of them, too, his doctrine turned out to be exceedingly practical, and it can safely be said that on all three points his policy was necessary to the success of the Bolshevik revolution.

2. *The party and the workers' movement. Consciousness and spontaneity*

The basic principles of Leninism as a separate political entity were formulated in 1901–3. These years saw the creation in Russia of the chief political groups which, while constantly at odds with one another, carried on the struggle against the Tsardom until the October Revolution: viz. the Bolshevik and Menshevik wings of social democracy, the social revolutionaries (S.R.s), and the constitutional democrats ('Kadets').

The principal organ in which Lenin's ideas gradually took visible shape was *Iskra*. Up to the Second Party Congress in 1903 the differences between Lenin and the rest of the editorial board were not of great consequence, and it was he who in fact gave the paper its tone: he edited it first in Munich and then in London, where he moved in the spring of 1902. *Iskra* was intended not only to combat revisionism and economism in Russian social democracy but to act as a link between groups which, despite the formal existence of the party, were still disunited as regards both ideology and organization: as Lenin put it, 'A newspaper is not only a collective propagandist and a collective agitator, it is also a collective organizer' ('Where to Begin', in *Works*, vol. 5, p. 22). *Iskra* in fact played a decisive part in preparations for the Congress, which, when it assembled, united the Russian social democrats into a single party and immediately split the party into two warring groups.

On the key question of the party's role Lenin laid the foundations of Bolshevik ideology in his conflict with economism, which he regarded as highly dangerous even though its influence was waning. The economists interpreted historical materialism as a theory of the primacy of the proletariat's economic struggle as compared with political aims (which, in the immediate future at any rate, were mainly the business of the Russian bourgeoisie), and they identified the working-class movement with a 'movement of workers' in the sense of a spontaneous struggle by the workers as a body. The emphasized the strictly class character of their own programme and attacked the *Iskra* group for touting after the intelligentsia and liberals, for exaggerating the importance of theory and ideology, and for giving too much weight to the common antagonism of all classes to the autocracy. Economism was a kind of Russian Proudhonism, or *ouvriérisme* as it was called. According to its adherents social democracy should be the organ, rather than the leader, of a true workers' movement.

In several articles and particularly in *What is to be Done?* (1902)

Lenin attacked the economists for denying the party's role as a vanguard, and expressed in general terms his view on the importance of theory in the social democratic movement. The vital question for the prospect of revolution was, he argued, the theoretical consciousness of the revolutionary movement, and this could in no way be evolved by a spontaneous movement of workers. 'There cannot be a revolutionary movement without a revolutionary theory': this was even truer in Russia than elsewhere, since social democracy was in its infancy and since the task confronting the Russian proletariat was no less than to overthrow the bastion of European and Asiatic reaction. This meant that it was destined to be the vanguard of the world proletariat, and it could not perform this role without a proper equipment of theory. The economists spoke of the importance of 'objective' economic circumstances in social development, regarding political consciousness as an automatic consequence of economic factors and therefore denying it the right to initiate and activate social processes. But the fact that economic interests were decisive did not mean that the workers' economic struggle could itself assure them final victory, since the basic class interests of the proletariat could only be satisfied by a political revolution and a proletarian dictatorship. The workers, left to themselves, were not capable of attaining to consciousness of the fundamental opposition between their class as a whole and the existing social system.

We have said that there could not have been social-democratic consciousness among the workers. It would have had to be brought to them from without. The history of all countries shows that the working class, exclusively by its own effort, is able to develop only trade-union consciousness, i.e. the conviction that it is necessary to combine in unions, fight the employers, and strive to compel the government to pass necessary labour legislation etc. The theory of socialism, however, grew out of the philosophic, historical and economic theories elaborated by educated representatives of the propertied classes, by intellectuals.' (*Works*, vol. 5, p. 375).

This was so in the West ('Marx and Engels themselves belonged to the bourgeois intelligentsia') and so it would be in Russia. Lenin appealed on this point to Kautsky, who wrote that the class struggle of the proletariat could not in itself create socialist consciousness: the class struggle and socialism were separate phenomena, and it was the task of social democracy to instil socialist consciousness into a spontaneous movement.

If the party regarded itself as merely the organ or servant of a spontaneous workers' movement, it could never be the instrument of a socialist revolution. It must be the vanguard and organizer, the leader and ideologist without which the workers could not advance beyond the horizon of bourgeois society or undermine its foundations. Here, however, Lenin adds a remark of decisive importance.

Since there can be no question of an independent ideology formulated by the working masses themselves in the process of their movement, the only choice is—either bourgeois or socialist ideology. There is no middle course—for mankind has not created a 'third' ideology, and in a society torn by class antagonisms there can never be a non-class or an above-class ideology ... But the spontaneous development of the working-class movement leads to its subordination to bourgeois ideology ... trade-unionism means the ideological enslavement of the workers by the bourgeoisie. Hence our task, the task of social-democracy, is *to combat spontaneity*. (*Works*, vol. 5, p. 384)

The doctrine of 'bowing to spontaneity', or *khvostizm* ('tailism'), is the chief target of Lenin's attack on the economists— Martynov, Kuskova, and others. The workers may fight to sell their labour-power on better terms, but the task of social democracy is to fight for the abolition of wage-labour altogether. The antagonism between the working class and the whole capitalist economic system can only be grasped by scientific thought, and until it is grasped there can be no general political struggle against the bourgeois system.

This fact, Lenin continues, leads to certain inferences as regards the relation between the working class and the party. In the economist view the revolutionary organization is no more or less than the organization of workers. But to be effective an organization of workers must be broadly based and as open as possible in its methods, and must have a trade-union character. The party cannot identify itself with a movement such as this, and there is no party in the world that is identical with the trade unions. On the contrary, 'the organization of the revolutionaries must consist first and foremost of people who make revolutionary activity their profession ... In view of this common characteristic of the members of such an organization, all distinctions as between workers and intellectuals ... must be effaced' (ibid., p. 452). Such a party of professional revolutionaries must not only gain the confidence of the working class and take over the spontaneous movement, but must make itself the centre of all forms of protest against social oppression, concentrating all the energies directed against the autocracy regardless of their origin or what class-interests they represent. The fact that social democracy is the party of the proletariat does not mean that it should be indifferent to the oppression and exploitation of other groups, even of the privileged classes. Since the democratic revolution, although bourgeois in content, is to be led by the proletariat, it is the latter's duty to rally all the forces that aim to overthrow the autocracy. The party must organize a general campaign of exposure; it must support bourgeois demands for political freedom, combat the persecution of religious sectarians, denounce the brutal treatment of students and intellectuals, support peasant claims, make itself felt in every sphere of public life, and unite the separate currents of indignation and protest into a single powerful stream which will sweep away the Tsarist order.

To cope with these requirements the party must be composed chiefly of professional revolutionaries—men and women who regard themselves, and are to be regarded, not as workers or intellectuals but simply as revolutionaries, and who devote their whole time to party activity. The party must be a small, centralized, disciplined organization on the lines of Zemlya i Volya in the seventies: in conspiratorial conditions it is impossible to apply democratic principles within the party, though it is natural to do so in overt organizations.

Lenin's idea of the party was much criticized as despotic, and some historians today believe that it contained in embryo the whole hierarchical, totalitarian structure in which the socialist system was subsequently embodied. It should be considered, however, in what respects his idea differed from those generally accepted at the time. He was accused of élitism and of desiring to substitute a revolutionary organization for the working class; it was even maintained that his doctrine represented the particular interests of the intelligentsia or of intellectuals, and that he wished to see political power entirely in their hands and not in those of the proletariat.

As regards the alleged élitism of treating the party as a vanguard, it should be noted that Lenin's position was no different from that generally accepted among socialists. The idea of a vanguard figures in *The Communist Manifesto*, whose authors describe the communists as the most conscious part of the proletariat, with no interests other than those of the class as a whole. The view that the workers' movement could not of itself evolve a revolutionary socialist consciousness, but must receive it from the educated intelligentsia, is one that Lenin shared with Kautsky, Viktor Adler, and most of the social democratic leaders, who stressed their difference from the syndicalists on this point. Basically the thought expressed by Lenin is indeed a truism, since clearly no workman could have written *Capital* or the *Anti-Dühring*, or even *What is to be Done?* No one could dispute that the theoretical foundations of socialism must be laid by intellectuals and not by factory workers, and if this was all that was meant by the 'instilling of consciousness from outside', there was nothing to argue about. The proposition that the workers' party was something different from the whole working class was also generally accepted, and it cannot be shown that Marx identified the party with the proletariat, though it is true he never defined exactly what the party was. What was new in Lenin's thought was not the idea of the party as a vanguard, leading the working class and imbuing it with socialist consciousness. The novelty consisted, in the first place, in his statement that the spontaneous working-class movement must have a bourgeois consciousness, since it could not develop a socialist one, and no other kind existed. This does not follow from any of Kautsky's arguments quoted by Lenin, nor from any of the premisses of Marxism. According to Lenin every social movement has a definite class character. Since a spontaneous workers' movement is incapable of a socialist consciousness, i.e. a proletarian one in the proper theoretical and historical sense of the term, it follows, curious as it may seem, that the workers' movement is a bourgeois movement unless it is subordinated to the socialist party. This is supplemented by a second inference: the working-class movement in the true sense of the term, i.e. a political revolutionary movement, is defined not by being a movement of workers but by possessing the right ideology, i.e. the Marxist one, which is 'proletarian' by definition. In other words, the class composition of a revolutionary party has no significance in determining its class character. Lenin consistently maintained this view, holding for instance that the British Labour Party was a bourgeois party although its members were working men, whereas a tiny group with no roots in the working class was entitled, so long as it professed the Marxist ideology, to declare itself the sole representative of the proletariat and the sole embodiment of proletarian consciousness. This is what Leninist parties have done ever since, including those which had not even minimal support among actual workers.

This does not mean, of course, that Lenin was indifferent to the composition of his own party or that he intended to build up a revolutionary organization consisting solely of intellectuals. On the contrary, he frequently insisted that there should be as high a proportion of workers in the party as possible, and he treated the intelligentsia with supreme contempt. The term 'intellectual' was a pejorative one in his vocabulary and was regularly used to signify 'irresolute, unreliable, undisciplined, consumed with individualism, capricious, up in the clouds', and so forth. (The party workers whom he most trusted were of working-class origin, such as Stalin and Malinovsky; the latter, as it turned out, was an Okhrana agent and rendered his masters invaluable service as one of Lenin's closest collaborators, made free of all the party's secrets.) There can be no question of Lenin having intended to 'substitute' intellectuals for workers, or having regarded them as the embodiment of socialist consciousness simply because they were intellectuals. That embodiment was the *party*, a body of a special kind in which, as we have seen, the distinction between intellectuals and workers was to disappear. The intellectual ceased to be an intellectual, and the workman to be a workman: both were components of a strictly centralized, disciplined revolutionary organization.

Thus, according to Lenin, the party with its 'correct' theoretical consciousness embodies the proletarian consciousness irrespective of what the real, empirical proletariat may think about itself or about the party. The party knows what is in the 'historical' interest of the proletariat and what the latter's authentic consciousness ought to be at any particular moment, although its empirical consciousness will generally be found lagging behind. The party represents that consciousness not because the proletariat agrees that it should, but because the party knows the laws of social development and understands the historical mission of the working class according to Marxist theory. In this schema the empirical consciousness of the working class appears as an obstacle, an immature state to be overcome, and never as a source of inspiration. The party is completely independent of the actual working class, except in so far as it requires its support in practice. In this sense Lenin's doctrine of party hegemony certainly means that in politics the working class can and must be 'replaced'—not by intellectuals, however, but by the party. The party cannot act effectively without proletarian support, but it is for the party alone to take political initiatives and to decide what the proletariat's aims shall be. The proletariat is incapable of formulating its own class aims, and if it tries to do so they will be bourgeois aims confined within the limits of capitalism.

It will thus be seen that it was not 'élitism', or the theory of socialist consciousness being introduced from outside into a spontaneous workers' movement, which made Lenin's party into the centralized, dogmatic, unthinking yet highly effective machine that it became, especially after the Revolution. The theoretical source, or rather justification, of that machine was Lenin's conviction that the party, by virtue of its scientific knowledge of society, is the one legitimate source of political initiative. This later became the principle of the Soviet state, where the same ideology serves to justify the party's monopoly of initiative in all fields of social life, its position as the sole fount of knowledge concerning society and therefore the sole proprietor of that society. It would of course be hard to maintain that the whole system of the totalitarian state was preformed, let alone consciously intended, in Lenin's doctrine as expressed in 1902; but the evolution of his party before and after the seizure of power confirms to some extent the Marxist or rather Hegelian belief in a 'logical order of things' embodied, although imperfectly, in the historical order. Lenin's premisses require us to believe that the interests and aims of a social class, the proletariat, can and indeed must be determined without that class having a say in the matter. The same, moreover, is true of the whole of society once it is ruled by that class and therefore presumably shares in its aims: once again the tasks, purposes, and ideology of the whole body are governed by the party's initiative and under its control. Lenin's idea of party hegemony developed naturally into that of the party's 'leading role' in a socialist society—i.e. into a despotism based on the principle that the party always knows better than the community itself what are the latter's interests, needs, and even desires: the people themselves may be too backward to understand these, but the party can divine them thanks to its scientific knowledge. In this way the notion of 'scientific socialism', opposed on the one hand to utopianism and on the other to a spontaneous workers' movement, became the ideological basis of a party dictatorship over the working class and the whole of society.

Lenin never abandoned his theory of the party. At the Second Congress he admitted that he had exaggerated slightly in *What is to be Done?*, but he did not say in what respect. 'We all know now that the "economists" bent the stick one way. To straighten matters out somebody had to bend it back the other way, and that is what I have done. I am convinced that Russian social-democracy will always vigorously straighten out whatever has been twisted by opportunism of any kind, and that therefore our stick will always be the straightest and the fittest' (speech on the party programme, 4 August 1902; *Works*, vol. 6, p. 491).

A further distinction must be made in considering how far *What is to be Done?* embodies the theory of the monolithic party. At this time and afterwards Lenin took it for granted that different views would be expressed within the party and that particular groups would be formed. He thought this natural but unhealthy, since in principle only one group could be in possession of the truth at a given time. 'Those who are really convinced that they have made progress in science would not demand freedom for the new views to continue side by side with the old, but the substitution of the new views for the old' (*Works*, vol. 5, p. 355). 'The much-vaunted freedom of criticism does not imply substitution of one theory for another, but freedom from all integral and pondered theory; it implies eclecticism and lack of principle' (ibid., p. 369). There can be no doubt that Lenin always regarded fractionalism and differences on essential points as a sign of disease or weakness in the party, though it was many years before he stated that all such manifestations should be cured by radical means, either by an immediate split or by expulsion from the party; only after the Revolution was there a formal ban on fractionalism. Even before the Revolution, however, Lenin did not hesitate to break with his colleagues over important matters. Believing as he did that all differences of view, not only on questions of major principle and strategy but also in matters of organization, in the last resort 'reflected' class antagonisms, he naturally regarded his opponents in the party as 'carriers' of some kind of bourgeois deviation or as symptoms of bourgeois pressure on the proletariat. As to the fact that he himself at all times represented the true and best-understood interests of the proletariat, Lenin never had the slightest doubt.

The theory of the party expounded in *What is to be Done?* was supplemented in Lenin's organizational proposals for the Second Congress, which met at Brussels after long preparation on 30 July 1903; it was afterwards transferred to London, where it sat until 23 August. Lenin attended from Geneva, where he had been living since the spring. The first and acutest point of difference concerned the celebrated paragraph 1 of the party Rules: Lenin wished membership to be confined to those who participated actively in one or other of the party organizations, whereas Martov proposed a looser formula admitting all who 'worked under the guidance and direction' of a party organization. This apparently trifling dispute led to a near split and to the formation of two groups which, as soon became clear, were divided not only on organizational matters but on many others. Lenin's formula, backed by Plekhanov, was rejected by a small majority. During the rest of the Congress, however, Lenin's supporters gained a slight predominance owing to the walk-out of two groups, the Bund (General Jewish Workers' Alliance) and the 'economists' representing the periodical *Rabocheye Delo*. The small majority which Lenin's group thus gained in the election to the Central Committee and the Party Council led to the coining of the famous terms 'Bolshevik' and 'Menshevik', after the Russian words for 'majority' and 'minority'. Their origin was thus fortuitous, but Lenin and his followers seized on the appellation 'Bolshevik' and clung to it for decades, suggesting as it did that throughout the party's later vicissitudes the Bolsheviks were the true majority group. Many who were unfamiliar with the history of the Congress, on the other hand, took the word to mean 'maximalist': the Bolsheviks themselves never suggested this interpretation.

The dispute over the membership clause in fact reflected two opposite ideas of party organization, about which Lenin had much to say at the Congress and in subsequent articles. In his opinion the effect of the 'loose' formula put forward by Martov, Akselrod, and Akimov was to allow any professor or schoolboy who might help the party, or any worker who came out on strike, to call himself a member. This would mean that the party lost all cohesion, discipline, and control over its own ranks; it would become a mass organization, built from below and not from above—a collection of autonomous units, unfit for centralized action. Lenin's idea was the exact opposite: strictly defined conditions of membership, rigid discipline, absolute control of the party authorities over its organizations, a clear dividing line between the party and the working class. The Mensheviks accused Lenin of adopting a bureaucratic attitude towards party life, of contempt for the working class, of dictatorial ambitions, and of wishing to subordinate the whole party to a handful of leaders. Lenin for his part wrote after the Congress (in *One Step Forward, Two Steps Back*, 1904; *Works*, vol. 7, p. 405 n.): 'Comrade Martov's fundamental idea—self-enrolment in the Party— was this same false "democracy", this idea of building the Party from the bottom upward. My idea, on the other hand, was "bureaucratic" in the sense that the Party was to be built from the top downwards, from the Party Congress to the individual Party organizations.'

Lenin had rightly perceived the fundamental importance of the dispute at the outset, and later on several occasions he compared it to the quarrel of the Jacobins and the Girondists. This was an apter parallel than the dispute between Bernstein's followers and German orthodoxy, for the Mensheviks' position was very close to the centre of German social democracy: they stood for a less centralized and 'military' organization and believed that the party should be a working-class one not only in name and ideology, but by including as many workers as possible and not being merely a staff of professsional revolution-aries. They thought the party should allow considerable autonomy to individual organizations and not deal with them exclusively by way of command. They accused Lenin of distrusting the working class, though they themselves accepted the doctrine of consciousness having to be instilled from outside it. It soon became clear that the Menshevik wing tended to adopt different solutions in other matters also: the dispute over a single paragraph of the Rules had in fact divided the party into two camps which, instinctively as it were, reacted differently to strategic and tactical issues. In every case the Mensheviks gravitated towards an alliance with the liberals, while Lenin proclaimed the peasant revolution and a revolutionary alliance with the peasants. The Mensheviks attached importance to legal forms of action and, when this became possible, to fighting by parliamentary means; Lenin for a long time opposed the idea of social democrats participating in the Duma, and subsequently treated it purely as a propaganda platform, putting no faith in any reforms it might enact. The Mensheviks emphasized trade-union activity and the intrinsic value of any improvements the working class might secure by legislation or by strike action; to Lenin, all such activity was valuable only in so far as it helped to prepare for the final conflict. The Mensheviks regarded democratic freedoms as valuable in themselves, while to Lenin they were only weapons that might serve the party in particular circumstances. On this last point Lenin quotes with approval a characteristic remark made at the congress by Posadovsky: 'Should we subordinate our future policy to certain fundamental democratic principles and attribute absolute value to them, or should all democratic principles be exclusively subordinated to the interests of our Party? I am decidedly in favour of the latter' (*Works*, vol. 7, p. 227). Plekhanov also supported this view, which illustrates how, at the very outset, the 'interest of the party' was exalted above all other considerations including the immediate interests of the class that the party was supposed to represent. Other writings by Lenin leave no doubt that he ascribed no value to 'freedom' as such, although his appeals and pamphlets are full of references to the 'fight for freedom'. 'They who serve the cause of freedom in general without serving the specific cause of proletarian utilization of this freedom, the cause of turning this freedom to account in the proletarian struggle for socialism, are, in the final analysis, plainly and simply fighters for the interests of the bourgeoisie' ('A New Revolutionary Workers' Association', article in *Proletary* (*The Proletariat*), June 1905; *Works*, vol. 8, p. 502).

In this way Lenin laid the foundation of what was to become the Communist Party—a party distinguished by ideological unity, efficiency, a hierarchic and centralized structure, and the conviction that it represents the interests of the proletariat whatever the proletariat itself may think: a party which deems its own interest to be automatically that of the working class and of universal progress, because it possesses the 'scientific knowledge' that entitles it to ignore, except for tactical purposes, the actual wishes and aspirations of the people it has appointed itself to represent.

The Mensheviks, like Rosa Luxemburg, regularly accused Lenin of Blanquism, plotting to destroy the existing order by a *coup d'état*, embracing the conspiratorial ideology of Tkachov, and striving for power regardless of 'objective' conditions. Lenin replied that his theory had nothing to do with Blanquism, that he wished to build up a party with real proletarian support and had no thought of a revolution carried out by a handful of conspirators. The Mensheviks claimed that he had an anti-Marxist faith in the decisive role of 'subjective factors', i.e. of revolutionary will-power. Historical materialism taught that revolutionary consciousness could not be artificially created by the party's efforts but depended on the ripening of social conditions. To attempt to provoke a revolution instead of waiting for economic events to bring about a revolutionary situation was to violate the laws of social development.

This criticism, though exaggerated, was not without foundation. Lenin, of course, was not a 'Blanquist' in the sense of envisaging a *coup d'état* which a small group of conspirators, properly prepared, could carry out at any moment. He realized that revolutions were elemental occurrences that could not be planned or produced at will. His view was that a revolution in Russia was inevitable, and that when it broke out the party must be prepared to direct it, to ride the wave of history and to seize power, sharing it initially with representatives of the revolutionary peasantry. He was not planning to cause a revolution, but to foster the growth of revolutionary consciousness and eventually take control of the mass movement. If the party was the 'subjective factor' in the revolutionary process—

and this is how both Lenin and his opponents understood the matter—he was indeed of the opinion that the spontaneous uprising of the working class would come to nothing unless the party was there to give it shape and direction. This was an obvious corollary of the party's role as the only possible vehicle of socialist consciousness. The proletariat itself could not evolve that consciousness, and therefore the will to revolution could not be brought about simply by economic events but must be deliberately organized. The 'economists', the Mensheviks, and the left-wing German social democrats, all of whom expected economic laws to bring about a socialist revolution automatically, were following a disastrous policy, for this would never happen. It was no good appealing to Marx in the matter (according to Lenin, Rosa Luxemburg 'vulgarized and prostituted' Marx's doctrine). Marx did not say that socialist or any other consciousness arose automatically from social conditions, but only that conditions made its development possible. For the possibility to become a reality, the revolutionary idea and will must be present in the form of an organized party.

There is no certain answer as to which side in the dispute was interpreting Marx more accurately. Marx believed that social conditions gave rise to the consciousness which would in time transform those conditions, but that to be effective it must first take on an explicit and articulate form. Many texts of his can be quoted in support of the view that consciousness is 'nothing but' the reflection of an actual situation, and this appears to justify the *attentisme* of the orthodox view. But, on the other hand, Marx regarded his own writing as the expression or explicitation of a latent consciousness: in the first text in which he refers to the historic mission of the proletariat, he says: 'We must force these petrified relationships to dance by playing their own tune to them.' Somebody must play the tune —the 'relationships' cannot do so of their own accord. If the principle that 'social being determines consciousness' applies only to past history, in which social consciousness invariably took on 'mystified' forms, and ceases to be valid when the proletariat comes on the scene, then the doctrine that a vanguard is necessary to arouse consciousness is in accordance with Marx's teaching. The problem is then merely to identify the criteria by which we determine that conditions have ripened to the point at which the arousal is possible. Marxism gave no indication as to what these criteria were. Lenin often stated that the proletariat was (sc. 'in the nature of things') the revolutionary class; this, however, did not mean that it would of itself develop a revolutionary consciousness, but only that it was capable of receiving it from the party. While Lenin, therefore, was not a 'Blanquist', he did believe that the party alone could and must be the initiator and source of revolutionary consciousness. The 'subjective factor' was not only a necessary condition of the advance to socialism (as all Marxists accepted, including the Mensheviks), but was the real creator of revolutionary consciousness, though it could not start a revolution without help from the proletariat. Although Marx himself never put the matter in these terms, there is insufficient ground for holding that Lenin's opinion on the point was a 'distortion' of Marxism.

3. The question of nationality

The Second Congress also provided the occasion for taking a stand on the national question, which was a basic element in the politics of the Tsarist empire. The matter was raised by the Bund, whose claim to be recognized as the sole representative of the Jewish working population was rejected by a majority including Lenin. Like many others, including Kautsky and Struve, Lenin thought the Jews could not be considered a nationality, as they lacked a common language and a territorial base; but he also objected to the Bund proposal on grounds of principle, as it implied the creation of a federal party based on national criteria. In Lenin's view differences of origin, education, and occupation ought to be of no account in the party, and this was still more true of nationality. Centralization was to do away with all differences between party members, each of whom was to be the embodiment of the purest party spirit and nothing else.

The problem engaged Lenin's attention more and more as the subject peoples of the empire manifested their separatism in nationalist movements. He wished the party to denounce national oppression and use the question as a lever, among others, to unseat the autocracy. There is no doubt that Lenin hated Great Russian chauvinism and did his best to extirpate it within the party. At the end of 1901, apropos of the violation of Finland's modest autonomy by the Tsarist government, he wrote: 'We are still slaves to such a degree that we are employed to reduce other peoples to slavery. We still tolerate a government that suppresses every aspiration towards liberty in Russia with the ferocity of an executioner, and that furthermore employs Russian troops for the purpose of violently infringing the liberties of others' (*Iskra*, 20 November 1901; *Works*, vol. 5, p. 310).

There was no dispute among social democrats on the question of national oppression; but by no means all of them accepted the principle of self-determination, i.e. the right of each nationality to a separate political existence. The Austrian Marxists stood for national autonomy within the Dual Monarchy: each ethnic group was to have complete freedom of language, culture, education, publication, etc., but political independence was not expressly mentioned. Renner, Bauer, and their colleagues were incessantly troubled by national conflicts within the party: the Austro-Hungarian proletariat belonged to a dozen or more national groups, mostly not in clear-cut areas but jumbled up geographically, so that political separatism raised an inextricable problem of frontiers. As far as Russia was concerned, Lenin thought that cultural autonomy would not suffice and that self-determination would be no use unless it included the right to form separate states. He expressed this view on several occasions, and encouraged Stalin to do so in a pamphlet on the national question in 1913. The right of self-determination was the subject of a long dispute with SDKPiL, which on this account remained outside the Russian Social Democratic Workers' party for some time. Lenin's most determined adversary, as already mentioned, was Rosa Luxemburg, whose position on the matter, apart from the special circumstances of Poland, was stronger in terms of fidelity to Marx. In Lenin's view all peoples were equally entitled to self-determination, and, unlike the founders of scientific socialism, he made no distinction between 'historical' and 'unhistorical' nations.

However, in theory at all events the dispute was not so violent as it might appear. Lenin acknowledged the right of self-determination, but from the beginning he made certain reservations: these account for the fact that within a short time after the Revolution, although Lenin's formulas remained unchanged, the 'right' in question became no more than an empty flourish, as indeed it was bound to do.

The first restriction was that although the party upheld the right to self-determination it did not commit itself to supporting all separatist aims: in many, indeed most, cases it found itself on the opposite side to the separatists. There was no contradiction in this, Lenin argued: the party might demand the legalization of divorce, but it did not follow that it wanted all married couples to split up.

We, the party of the proletariat, must always and unconditionally oppose any attempt to influence national self-determination from without by violence or injustice. While at all times performing this negative duty of ours (to fight and protest against violence), we on our part concern ourselves with the self-determination of the *proletariat* in each nationality rather than the self-determination of peoples or nations ... As to support of the demand for national autonomy, it is by no means a permanent and binding part of the programme of the proletariat. This support may become necessary for it only in isolated and exceptional cases. ('On the Manifesto of the Armenian Social-Democrats', *Iskra*, 1 February 1903; *Works*, vol. 6, p. 329)

The second restriction followed from the general principle that the party is interested in the self-determination of the proletariat and not of the people as a whole. Attacking the Polish Socialist party, Lenin wrote that in demanding Poland's independence unconditionally this party 'proves how weak in theoretical background and political activity is its link with the class struggle of the proletariat. But it is to the interests of this struggle that we must subordinate the demand for national self-determination ... A Marxist can recognize the demand for national independence only conditionally' ('The National Question in our Programme', *Iskra*, 15 July 1903; *Works*, vol. 6, p. 456). The Polish question was crucial in these discussions for three reasons. First, Poland was the largest of the subjected nations of Europe; second, it was divided among three great Continental powers; and third, according to Marx, Polish independence would strike a decisive blow against reaction in the shape of the Tsarist autocracy and the other partitioning powers, Germany and Austria-Hungary. Rosa Luxemburg and Lenin both believed, however, that Marx's view on this point, if it had ever been valid, was out of date. Rosa Luxemburg ruled out the restoration of Polish independence as contrary to the economic tendencies of the Tsarist empire; in any case she regarded self-determination as a bourgeois invention designed to hoodwink the proletariat with the pretence of ideals common to a whole nation. Lenin was less firm on this point, though he rejected the idea that Polish social democrats should go for independence as an aim in itself irrespective of the party's interest. He quoted with full approval some remarks made by Mehring in 1902: 'Had the Polish proletariat desired to inscribe on its banner the restoration of a Polish class state, which the ruling classes themselves do not want to hear of, it would be playing an historical farce ... If, on the other hand, this reactionary Utopia seeks to win over to proletarian agitation those sections of the intelligentsia and of the petty bourgeoisie which still respond in some measure to national agitation, then that Utopia is doubly untenable as an outgrowth of the unworthy opportunism which sacrifices the long-term interests of the working class to the cheap and paltry successes of the moment.' At the same time Lenin goes on to say: 'No doubt the restoration of Poland prior to the fall of capitalism is highly improbably, but it cannot be asserted that it is absolutely impossible ... And Russian social-democracy does not in the least intend to tie its own hands' (ibid., pp. 459–60).

Lenin's position is thus clear, and it is hard to see how he can ever have been represented, as he notoriously was, as a champion of political independence for all peoples. He was a convinced opponent of national oppression and proclaimed the right of self-determination, but always with the reservation that it was only in exceptional circumstances that social democracy could support political separatism. Self-determination was at all times absolutely subordinate to the party's interests, and if the latter conflicted with the national aspirations of any people, the latter were of no account. This reservation in effect nullified the right of self-determination and turned it into a purely tactical weapon. The party would always try to utilize national aspirations in the struggle for power, but the 'interest of the proletariat' could never be subordinated to the desires of a whole people. As Lenin wrote soon after the Revolution in his *Theses on the Treaty of Brest-Litovsk*, 'No Marxist, without renouncing the principles of Marxism and of socialism generally, can deny that the interests of socialism are higher than the interests of the right of nations to self-determination' (*Works*, vol. 26, p. 449). Since, however, the interest of the proletariat is by definition identical with the interest of the party, and its true aspirations can only be uttered through the party's mouth, it is clear that if the party comes to power it will be alone competent to decide questions of independence and separatism. This was inscribed in the party's programme in 1919, which stated that the level of historical development of each nation must decide the question as to who expresses its real will in the matter of independence. Since, as the party ideology also lays down, the 'will of the nation' is always expressed in the will of its foremost class, i.e. the proletariat, while the latter's will is expressed in that of a centralized party representing the whole multinational state, it is clear that a particular nation has no power to determine its own destiny. All this is fully in accord with Lenin's Marxism and his interpretation of the right to self-determination. Once the 'interest of the proletariat' is embodied in the interest of a proletarian state, there can be no doubt that the interest and power of that state are superior to all national aspirations. The invasion and armed suppression, on one occasion after another, of nations seeking to be free was quite consistent with Lenin's views. His objections to the brutal methods applied in Georgia by Ordzhonikidze, Stalin, and Dzerzhinsky may have been due to a desire on his part to use as little cruelty as possible, but they did not affect the right of the 'proletarian state' to subjugate its neighbour: he saw nothing wrong in the fact that the Georgian people, with a social democratic government established by legal elections, was the object of an armed incursion by the Red Army. In the same way, the recognition of Poland's independence did not prevent Lenin, as soon as the Polish–Soviet war broke out, from forming the nucleus of a Soviet government for Poland—though it is true he believed, with almost incredible blindness, that the Polish proletariat would greet the invading Soviet troops as its liberators.

In short, on the presumption that the interest of the proletariat is the only absolute value and is identical with the interest of the party, which has proclaimed itself the vehicle of the 'true' consciousness of the proletariat, the principle of national self-determination can be no more than a tactical weapon. Lenin was well aware of this, which is not to say that the principle was an unimportant part of his doctrine. On the contrary, his discovery of national aspirations as a powerful source of energy which the party could and should use in the fight for power was one of the most important features of his policy and did much to ensure its success, in opposition to the orthodox view that the Marxist theory of the class struggle made it unnecessary to pay specific attention to national problems. Lenin, however, was not only 'right' in the sense that his theory paid off: it was also in accordance with Marxism. Since the 'interest of the proletariat' is the supreme value, there can be no objection to exploiting national quarrels and aspirations in order to promote that interest, nor to the later policy of the Soviet state in supporting such aspirations in conquered and colonial territories in order to weaken the capitalist powers. On the other hand, Engels's distinction between 'historical' and 'unhistorical' nations, and Lenin's between the nationalism of great nations and that of small ones, do not seem to follow from the basic doctrine and may be regarded as bypaths, related to particular historical circumstances.

The principle of national self-determination in its 'pure' form, i.e. as an absolute right valid in all circumstances, is clearly contrary to Marxism, and from this point of view Rosa Luxemburg's position was easy to defend: the class division is paramount and is international, and there can be no national interests that are worth fighting for. But in the light of Lenin's far-reaching reservations, which reduced the principle to one of mere tactics, it is impossible to maintain that his defence of it was contrary to established doctrine. In other words, the dispute between him and Rosa Luxemburg on this issue was one of tactics and not of principle. National differences and national culture had no intrinsic value in Lenin's eyes but were, as he often repeated, essentially political weapons of the bourgeoisie. As he wrote in 1908, 'The proletariat cannot be indifferent to the political, social and cultural conditions of its struggle; consequently it cannot be indifferent to the destinies of its country. But the destinies of the country interest it only to the extent that they affect its class struggle, and not in virtue of some bourgeois "patriotism", quite indecent on the lips of a social democrat' (*Works*, vol. 15, p. 195). 'We do not support "national culture" but international culture, which includes only part of each national culture—only the consistently democratic and socialist content of each national culture ... We are against national culture as one of the slogans of bourgeois nationalism. We are in favour of the international culture of a fully democratic and socialist proletariat' (ibid., vol. 19, p. 116). 'The right to self-determination is an exception to our general premise of centralization. This exception is absolutely necessary in view of reactionary Great-Russian nationalism; and any rejection of this exception is opportunism (as in the case of Rosa Luxemburg); it means foolishly playing into the hands of reactionary Great-Russian nationalism' (ibid., p. 501).

Lenin frequently expressed himself on these lines before and during the War; he quoted with emphasis the famous saying that the working man has no fatherland, and believed it quite literally. At the same time he was the only important social democratic leader who proclaimed the unrestricted right to self-determination and expressly applied it to the oppressed peoples of the Tsarist empire. At the end of 1914 he wrote a short article 'On the National Pride of the Great Russians' (*Works*, vol. 21), which was one of the texts most frequently reprinted and quoted as Russian communism came to be more and more permeated with chauvinism. Unlike all Lenin's other articles, in which he denounces and derides every form of 'patriotism' (always in quotation marks), he declares on this occasion that Russian revolutionaries love their language and country; that they are proud of their revolutionary traditions and for this reason desire the defeat of the Tsardom in every war, as the least harmful outcome for the working population; and that the interest of the Great Russians is in accordance with that of the Russian proletariat and of all others. This is the only text of its kind in Lenin's works, and diverges from the remainder in so far as it seems to regard national culture as valuable in itself and worth defending. In the light of Lenin's doctrine as a whole it gives the impression of an attempt, by watering down his views, to rebut the charge of treason that was levelled against the Bolsheviks at the time and to show that their policy deserved support on 'patriotic' grounds as well. Certainly it is hard to see how the defence of Great Russian national pride can be reconciled with the statement that 'the place of those who advocate the slogan of national culture is among the nationalist petty bourgeois, not among the Marxists' ('Critical Remarks on the National Question', *Works*, vol. 21, p. 25). However, the article of December 1914 is not at variance either with the principle of self-determination or with the restrictions Lenin imposed upon it.

4. The proletariat and the bourgeoisie in the democratic revolution. Trotsky and the 'permanent revolution'

All social democrats were agreed that Russia was on the eve of a bourgeois revolution which would sweep away the autocracy, establish democratic freedoms, give the land to the peasants, and abolish the relics of serfdom and personal dependence. But this left undecided several important questions, which to some extent involved the theoretical foundations of Marxist doctrine.

The idea that the proletariat would lead the coming revolution, as the Russian bourgeoisie was too weak and cowardly to do so, came from Plekhanov and was more or less common property among the social democrats, who from the beginning joined issue on this point with the populists and later the 'economists'. However, the Mensheviks did not adhere to this opinion consistently, but inferred from the bourgeois character of the revolution that the proletariat's natural allies in overthrowing the autocracy were the bourgeoisie and the liberal parties, and that after the revolution these latter would be in power and the social democrats would be in opposition.

On this point Lenin at an early stage declared for quite different tactics. The fact that the revolution would pave the way for capitalism in Russia did not mean that the bourgeoisie would hold political power after it, or that the social democrats ought to ally themselves with the liberals to bring it about. Lenin was guided in this not only by his inveterate hatred of the liberals, but mainly by his conviction that the peasant problem was the decisive element: this led him to condemn the adoption in Russia of any schema based on the experience of democratic revolution in the West. Unlike the orthodox Marxists he perceived the huge revolutionary potential that lay in the peasants' unfulfilled demands, and he urged the party to exploit this even though, from the traditional point of view, it might seem to involve a 'reactionary' programme of backing smallholders.

(According to 'classic' patterns the concentration of property would speed the advance towards socialism, and the break-up of estates was therefore 'reactionary'.) Lenin, with his sharply practical, opportunist, undoctrinaire outlook, was less interested in Marxian 'correctness' and mainly, or exclusively, concerned with the political efficacy of the proposed tactics. 'Generally speaking,' he wrote,

It is reactionary to support small property because such support is directed against large-scale capitalist economy, and consequently retards social development and obscures and glosses over the class struggle. In this case, however, we want to support small property not against capitalism but against serf-ownership ... There are two sides to all things in the world. In the West, the peasant proprietor has already played his part in the democratic movement, and is now defending his position of privilege as compared with the proletariat. In Russia, the peasant proprietor is as yet on the eve of a decisive and nation-wide democratic movement with which he cannot but sympathize ... In a historic moment like the present, it is our direct duty to support the peasants.

Our principal immediate aim is to clear the way for the free development of the class struggle in the countryside, the class struggle of the proletariat, which is directed towards attainment of the ultimate aim of the international Social-Democratic movement, the conquest of political power by the proletariat and the laying of the foundations of a socialist society. ('The Agrarian Programme of Russian Social-Democracy', in *Zarya*, August 1902; *Works*, vol. 6, pp. 134, 148)

Lenin thus accepted the general notion of an 'alliance with the bourgeoisie', but immediately and fundamentally qualified it: not the liberal bourgeoisie which was prepared to come to terms with the monarchy, but the revolutionary, republican 'bourgeoisie', i.e. the peasants. This was the chief bone of contention between him and the Mensheviks, more important than the question of the party Rules; it was also the main theme of Lenin's *Two Tactics*, written after the Third Congress in 1905.

But it was a question not only of alliance during the revolution, but of power thereafter. Lenin proclaimed the slogan of rule by the proletariat and peasantry in the bourgeois society that the revolution was to establish. This society, he believed, would permit the unrestrained development of the class struggle and the concentration of property, but political power would be exercised by the proletariat and peasantry through their respective parties. With this in view the social democrats must cultivate peasant support and prepare a suitable agrarian programme. This too became a subject of dispute: Lenin proposed to go for the nationalization of all the land, emphasizing that this was not a specifically socialist measure and that it would gain peasant support while not undermining bourgeois society. Most Bolsheviks, like the S.R.s, favoured confiscating the big estates and church lands without compensation, and then partitioning them. The Mensheviks were for 'municipalizing' the expropriated lands, i.e. handing them over to local authorities. In an appeal *To the Rural Poor* in 1903 Lenin wrote: 'The social-democrats will never take away the property of the small and middle farmers who do not hire labourers' (*Works*, vol. 6, p. 397); but in the same pamphlet he stated that after the socialist revolution all means of production, including land, would be held in common. It was not clear how the 'rural poor' were' expected to reconcile these two statements.

All social democrats regarded the distinction between the minimum and maximum programme as a matter of course, and all were concerned as to how social democracy would carry on the fight for the 'next stage' after the bourgeois revolution. None of them ventured to predict how long Russia's capitalist era would last. The Mensheviks, however, generally thought that it would take a whole historical epoch to assimilate Western democratic and parliamentary institutions, and that the transition to socialism was a remote prospect. Lenin, for his part, took seriously the principle, which was quite in the spirit of Marxism, that all tactics must be geared to the future socialist upheaval, and that the 'final aim' must be constantly kept in mind and govern all the party's acts. The question was: if the bourgeois revolution gave power to the people, i.e. the proletariat and peasantry, would they not inevitably seek to transform society in a socialist direction, so that the bourgeois revolution would grow into a socialist one? This problem came to the fore in the years just before the 1905 Revolution, and immediately after it in the writings of Parvus and Trotsky.

Leo Trotsky (Lyov Davidovich Bronstein) had made a name for himself in 1902–3 as a gifted exponent of Marxism in Russian *émigré* circles. Born in 1879 on 7 November (New Style) at Yanovka in the province of Kherson, the son of a Jewish farmer (of whom there were a few in the Ukraine), he went to school at Odessa and Nikolayev and became a Marxist at the age of 18. He studied mathematics for some months at Odessa University, but soon devoted himself to political work and was active in the South Russian Workers' Union, which although not purely social democratic was much influenced by Marxist ideas. He was arrested at the beginning of 1898, spent nearly two years in gaol, and was then sentenced to four years in Siberia. In prison and in exile he eagerly pursued his Marxist education, and in Siberia gave lectures and published articles in the legal Press. Escaping from banishment with a false passport in the name of Trotsky, under which he belongs to history, he joined Lenin in London in the autumn of 1902 and became a contributor to *Iskra*. At the Second Party Congress he was one of the majority which voted against Lenin's draft paragraph 1, on the ground that Lenin was trying to turn the party into a close circle of conspirators instead of a working-class organization. He remained for a time in the Menshevik camp, but broke with it before long as he disapproved of the trend towards an alliance with the liberals. In 1904 he published in Geneva a pamphlet entitled *Our Political Tasks*, which among other things attacked Lenin's conception of the party. He asserted that Lenin despised the people and the working class and was trying to substitute the party for the proletariat, which meant that in course of time the Central Committee would replace the party and a dictator would replace the Central Committee. This prophecy, which has been much quoted since, was based on the same premises as Rosa Luxemburg's criticism of Lenin: the idea of a centralized, hierarchic party of professional revolutionaries was contrary to the fundamental Marxist principle that the working class can only be liberated by its own efforts.

For many years Trotsky acted mainly as an independent social democratic publicist, identifying with neither wing of the party but using his influence in the direction of restoring unity. In Munich he became a friend of Parvus (A. L. Helfand), a Russian Jew who had settled in Germany and belonged to the left wing of the German social democrats, and who is regarded as the true forerunner or originator of the theory of permanent revolution. His view was that the democratic revolution in

Russia would bring to power a social democratic government which would of necessity endeavour to continue the revolutionary process towards socialism. Trotsky adopted this idea and expounded it in the light of the 1905 Revolution. Generalizing from that event, he stated that as the Russian bourgeoisie was so weak the coming revolution must be headed by the proletariat and therefore would not stop at the bourgeois stage. Russia's economic backwardness meant that the bourgeois revolution would be immediately followed by a socialist revolution. (This was similar to Marx's and Engels's forecast for Germany in 1848.) But, while in the 'first stage' the proletariat would be supported by the peasantry, in the socialist revolution it would have the mass of small owners against it. Being a minority in Russia, the proletariat would not be able to maintain itself in power unless aided by a socialist revolution in the West; but it was to be expected that the revolutionary process would spread promptly from Russia to Europe and to the rest of the world.

Trotsky's theory of 'permanent revolution' thus rested on the two propositions, which he frequently repeated in the coming years, that the bourgeois revolution in Russia would evolve continuously into a socialist one and that this would touch off a conflagration in the West. If it did not, the Russian revolution could not survive, as the proletariat would have to contend with overwhelming opposition from the peasant masses.

Until April 1917 Lenin did not believe that the first revolution would immediately develop into the second, and he contested Parvus's view that a social democratic government would come to power in the 'first stage'. Such a government could not last, he wrote in April 1905, because 'only a revolutionary dictatorship supported by the vast majority of the people can be at all durable ... The Russian proletariat, however, is at present a minority of the population in Russia' ('Social-Democracy and the Provisional Revolutionary Government', *Works*, vol. 8, p. 291). The social democrats should therefore reckon on sharing power with the peasantry, which in its entirety was interested in overthrowing the autocracy, but not on an immediate transition to socialism. On the other hand, Lenin wrote before the 1905 Revolution that the dictatorship of the proletariat must be a dictatorship against and over the entire class of peasant proprietors. This is clearly expressed in his *Notes* on Plekhanov's second draft of the party programme:

The concept of 'dictatorship' is incompatible with positive recognition of outside support for the proletariat. If we really knew positively that the petty bourgeoisie will support the proletariat in the accomplishment of its, the proletariat's, revolution it would be pointless to speak of a 'dictatorship', for we would then be fully guaranteed so overwhelming a majority that we could get on very well without a dictatorship ... The recognition of the necessity for the dictatorship of the proletariat is most closely and inseparably bound up with the thesis of the Communist Manifesto that the proletariat alone is a really revolutionary class.

The more 'indulgence' we show, in the practical part of our programme, towards the small producer (e.g. the peasant), the more 'strictly' must we treat these unreliable and double-faced social elements in the theoretical part of the programme, without sacrificing one iota of our standpoint. Now then, we say, if you adopt this standpoint of ours you can count on 'indulgence' of every kind, but if you don't, well then don't get angry with us! Under the dictatorship we shall say about you: there is no point in wasting words where the use of power is required. (*Works*, vol. 6, pp. 51, 53 n.)

In accordance with these views Lenin wrote in 'Revision of the Agrarian Programme' in 1906 that: 'The nearer the peasant uprising is to victory, the more likely is the peasant proprietor to turn against the proletariat, the more necessary is it for the proletariat to have its independent organization ... The rural proletariat must organize independently together with the town proletariat to fight for the complete socialist revolution' (*Works*, vol. 10, p. 191). The programme must therefore contain 'a precise definition of the next step the movement can and should take to consolidate the peasants' gains and to pass from the victory of democracy to the direct proletarian struggle for socialism' (ibid., p. 192). At the party's 'unity congress' in April 1906 Lenin clearly took the view that peasant resistance would defeat the revolution if there were not, as he was sure there would be, a proletarian uprising in the West.

The Russian revolution can achieve victory by its own efforts, but it cannot possibly hold and consolidate its gains by its own strength. It cannot do this unless there is a socialist revolution in the West. Without this condition restoration is inevitable, whether we have municipalization, or nationalization, or division of the land: for under each and every form of possession and property the small proprietor will always be a bulwark of restoration. After the complete victory of the democratic revolution the small proprietor will inevitably turn against the proletariat; and the sooner the common enemies of the proletariat and of the small proprietors, such as the capitalists, the landlords, the financial bourgeoisie and so forth are overthrown, the sooner will this happen. Our democratic republic has no other reserve than the socialist proletariat in the West. (*Works*, vol. 10, p. 280)

This shows clearly how far Stalin exaggerated when he spoke later of a 'basic antagonism' between Leninism and the theory of permanent revolution. Stalin maintained against Trotsky that, in the first place, this theory implied distrust of the peasants as a revolutionary force, suggesting that as a class they would be enemies of the proletariat in the socialist revolution. Secondly, Trotsky called in question the possibility of building socialism in one country and did not believe that the revolution could preserve its achievement in Russia without an upheaval in the West. On both points, according to Stalin, Lenin and Trotsky were totally opposed from the outset. But in fact Lenin held before 1917, and was by no means alone in doing so, that even a democratic revolution in Russia, let alone a socialist one, could not maintain itself without a socialist revolution in the West. Lenin stressed the need to organize the rural proletariat, i.e. the landless peasants, whose interests, he believed, coincided with those of the town workers and who would therefore support a socialist revolution; but he realized before 1917 that the entire peasantry would turn against the proletariat at the 'second stage'. Finally, Lenin thought that although the 'first stage' could not lead to a socialist government it would inaugurate the 'direct proletarian struggle for socialism'. The theory of permanent revolution was contrary to Lenin's views only in so far as it suggested that the 'first stage' would lead at once to rule by the proletariat or its party. It was only later, when Lenin based his tactics on the class struggle in the countryside and put forward the doctrine of a dictatorship of the proletariat and the rural poor, that he was compelled to oppose a policy based on the theory of an unbridgeable gulf between the proletariat and the peasantry as a whole.

The theory of the party, the national question, and the

relationship of the proletariat to the bourgeoisie and the peasantry—on these three points, even before the Revolution of 1905, Leninism took shape as a new formation within the socialist movement, although its novelty was not at first perceived by Lenin himself. Leninism envisaged a socialist movement allied with the peasantry but not with the urban bourgeoisie: the proletariat was to organize itself for a democratic revolution in a semi-feudal country, in the hope of first sharing democratic power with the peasantry and then initiating the struggle for socialism and a proletarian dictatorship against the bourgeoisie and the peasant proprietors. In all this the proletariat was to act under the leadership of the party—the true keeper of the proletariat's consciousness—which, while it sought the workers' support, considered itself 'proletarian' not by reason of that support but because of its 'scientific' understanding of society. It was to be a centralized, hierarchical party, built around a core of professional revolutionaries, and in its tactics and ideology independent of the 'empirical' proletariat. Its task was to exploit all elements and forms of opposition and to channel all the energies—whether national, social, religious, or intellectual— directed against the *ancien régime*, but to use them for its own purposes and not to identify with them. Thus it supported the liberal opposition to the Tsardom even though its own future intent was to destroy liberalism. It supported the peasants against the relics of feudalism, although its ultimate purpose was to deprive the peasants of the right to own land. It supported religious sectarians against Orthodox persecution, although it professed atheism and intended to do away with 'religious prejudices'. It supported national movements and aspirations to independence in so far as they helped to disrupt the Empire, although its own purpose was to abolish national states altogether. In short, it set out to make use of all destructive energies aimed against the present system, while intending eventually to destroy, as separate social forces, all the groups that embodied those energies. The party was to be a kind of universal machine, uniting social energies from every source into a single current. Leninism was the theory of that machine, which, aided by an extraordinary combination of circumstances, proved effective beyond all expectation and changed the history of the world.

XVII

Philosophy and Politics in the Bolshevik Movement

1. Factional struggles at the time of the 1905 Revolution

THE effects of the Second Congress were felt throughout the remaining life of the Russian social democratic movement. It became clear soon after the Congress that Lenin could not, as he had hoped, use the small majority he had gained in its latter stage to achieve control over the party. This was mainly because of Plekhanov's 'treachery'. The Congress had appointed an editorial board for the party journal: this body, which was at that time practically independent of the Central Committee and often more important in practice, consisted of Plekhanov, Lenin, and Martov, while the rest of the 'minority'—Akselrod, Vera Zasulich, and Potresov—were eliminated on a motion by Lenin. Martov, however, declined to function on the board as thus constituted, while Plekhanov broke with the Bolsheviks a few weeks later and, by the weight of his authority, succeeded in reconstituting the board with all four Menshevik members. This caused Lenin in his turn to resign; from then on *Iskra* became a Menshevik organ, and it was a year before the Bolsheviks were able to found one of their own.

The Congress was the occasion for an avalanche of articles, pamphlets, books, and leaflets in which the new-born factions exchanged insults and charges of disloyalty, intrigue, misappropriation of party funds, etc. Lenin's book *One Step Forward, Two Steps Back* was the most powerful piece of artillery fired in this campaign. It analysed all the important votes at the congress, defended the centralist idea of the party, and branded the Mensheviks as opportunists. In *Iskra*, on the other hand, articles by Plekhanov, Akselrod, and Martov accused the Bolsheviks of bureaucratic centralism, intolerance, Bonapartism, and plotting to subordinate genuine working-class interests to those of professional revolutionaries from the intelligentsia. Each side levelled the same charge against the other, that its policy was not a true expression of proletarian interests: but the charge missed its mark, as they meant different things by 'proletariat'. The Mensheviks had in mind an actual movement by actual workers, whom it was the party's role to assist to victory. To Lenin the actual, spontaneous workers' movement was by definition a bourgeois phenomenon, while the true proletarian movement was defined by the supremacy of proletarian ideology, that is to say of Marxism in its Leninist interpretation.

The Bolsheviks and Mensheviks continued to be, in theory, sections of a single party. The breach inevitably affected the party in Russia, but it was less evident there, as many leaders regarded the *émigré* squabbles as of little account, while working-class social democrats had hardly heard of them. The two factions jostled for influence in the underground organization and formed committees on every hand, while Lenin and his supporters pressed for a fresh congress to be held as soon as possible, to heal the split which was paralysing party action. Meanwhile Lenin created the organizational and ideological basis of the Bolshevik faction with the aid of new leaders and theorists such as Bogdanov, Lunacharski, Bonch-Bruyevich, Vorovsky, and others.

The 1905 Revolution came as a surprise to both factions, neither of which had anything to do with the first spontaneous outbreak. Of the *émigrés* who returned to Russia Trotsky, who did not belong to either group, played the most important part: he made his way to St. Petersburg at once, while Lenin and Martov did not return till November 1905, after the proclamation of an amnesty. The first stage of the revolution was linked with the formation, by the Petersburg workers, of trade unions that were in fact organized by the police, as if to confirm Lenin's warning of what would happen to the working class left to itself. The unions, however, which were under the patronage of Zubatov, chief of the Moscow Okhrana, got out of hand from the point of view of their organizers. Father Gapon, who took seriously his role as a leader of the working class, became a revolutionary as the result of 'Bloody Sunday' (9 January 1905), when the police fired on a crowd of peaceful demonstrators at the Winter Palace. This event touched off the crisis which was already coming to a head owing to defeats in the war with Japan, strikes in Poland, and peasant revolts.

In April 1905 Lenin summoned a Bolshevik congress in London which proclaimed itself to be a congress of the whole party and, for a time, set the seal on its division, passing anti-Menshevik resolutions and electing a purely Bolshevik Central Committee. However, as the Revolution progressed members of both factions in Russia co-operated with one another, and this helped towards a *rapprochement*. The spontaneous workers' movement created new bodies in the shape of workers' councils (Soviets). Bolsheviks inside Russia at first distrusted these as non-party organs which could not possess true revolutionary consciousness; Lenin, however, soon recognized them as the nucleus of workers' power in the future, and instructed his followers to join them and do their best to control them politically.

In October 1905 the Tsar issued a manifesto promising a constitution, civil liberty, freedom of speech and assembly, and an elected parliament, the Duma. All the social democratic groups and the S.R.s denounced these promises as fraudulent and boycotted the elections. In the last two months of 1905 the revolution reached its peak; the revolt of the Moscow workers was suppressed in December. Bloody repressions followed in all the revolutionary centres of Russia, Poland, and Latvia, while reactionary bands inspired mass terror and pogroms. For some time after large-scale revolts were put down, local outbreaks and acts of violence took place and were stamped out by the authorities. Despite this ebb of the revolutionary tide, Lenin at first hoped for an early renewal of the struggle; but he finally accepted the need to work within the reactionary system, and stood out for social democratic participation in the elections to the Third Duma in mid-1907. On that occasion (cf. below), he was opposed by a majority of his own group, but supported by the Mensheviks.

As a result of the Revolution, the social democratic party was formally reunited. At the Stockholm Congress in April 1906 —the Mensheviks had a considerable majority, but the old names were retained—organizational unity was restored in a form that lasted for the next six years, until Lenin brought about a final split in 1912. Ideological and tactical unity, however, were still lacking. The basic differences and mutual accusations continued, although for a time Lenin used less crude and insulting terms about the Mensheviks than previously. Each group interpreted the results of the Revolution as a confirmation of its own theories. Lenin argued that it was clear that the bourgeoisie (in this case the Kadets) was ready to come to terms with the Tsardom in return for trifling concessions and was more afraid of a popular revolution than of the autocracy. The Revolution had also shown, he contended, that the only force that could be counted on besides the proletariat was the peasantry, which at this stage was the natural ally of the social democrats. Some Mensheviks, on the other hand, thought the Revolution had failed because in its second phase the proletariat had been isolated by the excessive radicalism of its demands, which had alienated the bourgeoisie instead of turning it to account as an ally. Trotsky was led by the events of 1905 to formulate his theory of permanent revolution more precisely, arguing that a Russian revolution must at once evolve into a socialist phase and that it could touch off a socialist upheaval in the West.

Thus in the post-revolutionary period the old divisions remained and new problems confronted the two factions, who reacted according to their respective ideas. The Mensheviks were much more inclined to make use of the new parliamentary opportunities; Lenin's followers at first held out for a boycott, and when they finally agreed to be represented in the Duma they treated it as a sounding-board for revolutionary propaganda and not an instrument of social reform. The Mensheviks, though they took part in armed clashes during the Revolution, regarded an armed uprising as a last resort and were more interested in other forms of struggle, whereas to Lenin an uprising and the conquest of power by violence were the only possible way of achieving revolutionary aims. He was scandalized by Plekhanov's words 'We should not have taken up arms', and quoted them repeatedly to show what an opportunist the Mensheviks' ideological leader was. The Mensheviks favoured the most decentralized forms of government in the future republican state, and for this reason among others they proposed to make over confiscated lands to local government authorities, arguing that nationalization would mean strengthening the central power, which would be in the hands of the bourgeoisie. (The 'Asiatic' character of the Russian state was another reason why Plekhanov was in favour of decentralizing measures.) Lenin held to the plan for nationalization—i.e. not the confiscation of peasant land, or rural collectivization, but the transfer of 'absolute rent' to the state; in his view the post-revolutionary government would be one of the proletariat and peasantry, so the Menshevik argument had no force. Other Bolsheviks again, including the young Stalin, were for partitioning all the confiscated land: this was closest to what the peasants actually desired, and was finally inscribed in the programme. The Mensheviks, both in and outside the Duma, were inclined towards tactical alliances with the Kadets; Lenin denounced the Kadets as lackeys of the Tsardom and preferred to work with the peasants, represented after 1905 chiefly by the Labour Group (Trudoviki). The Mensheviks devised plans for a broad non-party organization of the proletariat in a general workers' congress, i.e. a nation-wide system of Soviets, whereas to Lenin this meant eliminating the party and replacing it, *horribile dictu*, by the proletariat. He also violently attacked Akselrod, Larin, and other advocates of the workers' congress, arguing that the Soviets were only of use for insurrectionary purposes. 'Soviets of workers' deputies and their unification are essential for the victory of the insurrection, but a victorious insurrection will inevitably create other kinds of organs' (from the symposium *Questions of Tactics*, Apr. 1907; *Works*, vol. 12, p. 332).

The next few years were filled with argument on these questions, especially the agrarian programme and relations with the Kadets. The Menshevik group was much more beset with doubts and was often irresolute in tactical matters, inclining to ascribe importance to legal institutions and broadly based proletarian organizations. Lenin wished the party to use every opportunity of legal activity, but to preserve its clandestine organization and to resist the blandishments of constitutionalism, parliamentarianism, and trade-unionism; all legal forms must be subordinate to the eventual aim of seizing power by force. At the same time Lenin was opposed to the S.R. policy of terrorism against individuals. He emphasized before 1905 that the party did not renounce terror as a matter of principle and that it was necessary in certain circumstances, but attacks on ministers and other public figures were premature and counter-productive, as they dissipated revolutionary forces and could not bring about any significant effect. In the latter part of the revolutionary period he crossed swords with the Mensheviks over 'expropriations', i.e. acts of armed robbery by terrorist groups for the purpose of replenishing party funds (Stalin in Transcaucasia was one of the chief organizers of this activity). The Mensheviks, and Trotsky, condemned this practice as unworthy and demoralizing, but Lenin defended it provided it was not exercised against individuals but against banks, trains, or state property. At the London Congress in the spring of 1907 'expropriations' were condemned by a Menshevik majority, against Lenin's opposition.

The party's ranks were much depleted by the period of reaction. After the 'unity congress' in September 1906 Lenin estimated its numbers at over 100,000. The delegates at the Congress represented about 13,000 Bolsheviks and 18,000 Mensheviks; the Bund re-joined, bringing in 33,000 Jewish workers; to these were added 26,000 Polish and Lithuanian social democrats and 14,000 Latvians, yet Trotsky in 1910 estimated the total at only 10,000. However, despite repressions, the post-revolutionary situation offered much wider opportunities for legal activity. At the beginning of 1907 Lenin moved to Finland, whence he re-emigrated at the end of the year. He proclaimed a boycott of the elections to the Second Duma, but not all social democrats obeyed, and 35 were elected. After about three months the Second Duma, like the first, was dissolved, whereupon Lenin abandoned the boycott policy and sanctioned his followers' participation in the Third Duma, not for the sake of social reform but to expose the delusions of parliamentarianism and to push the peasant delegates in a revolutionary direction. A few months previously, anyone who opposed the boycott showed, according to Lenin, that he had no conception of Marxism and was an arrant opportunist; now, anyone in favour of it was a self-confessed opportunist and ignoramus. Among the Bolsheviks there came into being a sub-group who criticized Lenin 'from the left', and whom he dubbed 'otzovists', i.e. 'recallists', for demanding the recall of the social democratic delegates from the Duma; while another group were nicknamed 'ultimatists' because they drafted an ultimatum to be addressed by the party to its deputies, mostly Mensheviks, on pain of recall if they did not obey. The distinction between the two sub-groups was not essential, but there was against Lenin a faction of revolutionary Bolsheviks who thought the party should have nothing to do with parliament but concentrate on direct preparation for the coming revolution. The most active member of this group, A. A. Bogdanov, had for years been Lenin's most faithful collaborator; he had played the main part in organizing Bolshevism inside Russia and can be regarded as the joint creator, with Lenin, of Bolshevism as a separate political movement. Among the other otzovists or ultimatists were several intellectuals—Lunacharsky, Pokrovsky, Menzhinsky—some of whom later reverted to Leninist orthodoxy.

The tactical controversy with the otzovists was intertwined in a curious fashion with a philosophical dispute which arose at this time in the social democratic camp and which drew from Lenin a treatise in defence of materialism, published in 1909. This dispute had a previous history which should be briefly described.

2. *New intellectual trends in Russia*

At the turn of the century the Russian intelligentsia showed a marked tendency to abandon positivism, scientism, and materialism, which had for so long been the dominant modes of thought. The same trend was seen throughout Europe, in philosophy and social thought as in poetry, painting, and drama. The typical free-thinking Russian intellectual of the last quarter of the century believed that science had the answers to all questions of social and individual life, that religion was a collection of superstitions maintained by ignorance and deceit, that the biologist's scalpel had annihilated God and the soul, that human history was irresistibly impelled by 'progress', and that it was the task of the intelligentsia to support progress against autocracy, religion, and oppression of all kinds. Historical optimism, rationalism, and the cult of science were the keynotes of evolutionary positivism *à la* Spencer, reinforced by the tradition of nineteenth-century materialism. Russian Marxism in its first stage duly gave pride of place to these positivistic elements of the inherited world-view. To be sure, the second half of the nineteenth century was not only the period of Chernyshevsky and Dobrolyubov, but also that of Dostoevsky and Solovyov. But the most dynamic and influential parts of the intelligentsia, and the great majority of the revolutionaries, whether populist or Marxist, accepted the rationalist and evolutionist catechism as a natural concomitant of their struggle against the Tsardom and the Church.

In the early 1900s, however, this outlook began to give place to a variety of intellectual attitudes in which it is hard to distinguish any common feature except that they rejected the scientistic, optimistic, and collectivist ideals of the previous century. In addition to academic philosophy in the style of Kant (A. I. Vvedensky) or Hegel (B. N. Chicherin), new works by non-academic philosophers struck a religious, personalist, and anti-scientistic note. Many Western philosophers were translated: not only Wundt and Windelband but also Nietzsche, Bergson, James, Avenarius, Mach, and even Husserl, together with Max Stirner, the prophet of egocentric anarchism. In poetry symbolism and 'decadence' flourished, and Russian literature was enriched by the names of Merezhkovsky, Zinaida Gippius, Blok, Bryusov, Bunin, Vyacheslav Ivanov, and Byely. Interest in religion, mysticism, oriental cults, and occultism was almost universal. Solovyov's religious philosophy experienced a revival. Pessimism, Satanism, apocalyptic prophecies, the search for mystic and metaphysical depths, love of the fantastic, eroticism, psychology and self-analysis—all these merged into a single modernistic culture. Merezhkovsky, with Berdyayev and Rozanov, brooded on the metaphysic of sex; N. Minsky extolled Nietzsche, wrote religious poems, and co-operated with the Bolsheviks. Ex-Marxists returned to the Christian faith of their ancestors; a generation which had identified an interest in religion with obscurantism and political reaction gave place to a generation which regarded 'scientific' atheism as a symbol of naïve, narrow-minded optimism.

In 1903 there appeared *Problems of Idealism*, a collection of essays many of whose authors had recently been Marxists, but which condemned Marxism and materialism for their moral nihilism, contempt of personality, determinism, and fanatical pursuit of social values regardless of the individuals who made up society; they also attacked Marxism for its uncritical worship of progress and sacrifice of the present to the future. No ethical system, Berdyayev claimed, could be based on a materialist world-view, since ethics presupposed the Kantian distinction between what is and what ought to be. Moral norms cannot be deduced from experience, and the experimental sciences are therefore useless to ethics. For these norms to be valid there must be an intelligible world in which they have their being, other than the world of experience, and their validity also presupposes the free, 'noumenal' nature of man. Moral consciousness thus postulates freedom, the existence of God, and the immortality of the soul. Positivism and utilitarianism cannot provide man with absolute criteria of value. Bulgakov attacked materialism and positivism on the ground that they failed to solve metaphysical puzzles, regarded the world and human existence as the work of chance, denied freedom, and offered no criteria of moral value. The world and man's presence in it were only intelligible in the light of faith in the divine harmony, and social commitment could be based on nothing but a sense of religious duty. Only when our acts are given meaning by their relation to divinity can we speak of true self-realization and the integration of personality, which is the supreme human value.

Most of the authors of *Problems of Idealism* were agreed in holding that the validity of legal or moral norms presupposes a non-empirical world and that self-realization must not be sacrificed to the demands of society, since personality is an intrinsic and absolute value. Novgorodtsev emphasized the need for law to be based on *a priori* norms of justice; Struve criticized the ideal of equality in the sense of universal levelling and the elimination of personal differences. Most of the writers, especially S. L. Frank, invoked Nietzsche to support their personalist views, scanning his philosophy for condemnation of moral utilitarianism, eudaemonism, slave-morality, and the sacrifice of personal creativity to the 'welfare of the masses'. Struve, Berdyayev, Frank, and Askoldov all in some degree endorsed Nietzsche's attacks on socialism as a philosophy of mediocrity and the values of the herd; all regarded socialist ideals as designed to stamp out personal values for the sake of Man as an abstraction. All were sceptical of historical laws and criteria of progress derived from empirical history without the benefit of *a priori* moral norms; and all saw in socialism the prospect of abstract 'collective' values tyrannizing over personality.

Problems of Idealism was an important event in Russian cultural history, not because its ideas were especially novel but because it was a concerted attack on all the intellectual and moral stereotypes which the progressive intelligentsia had derived from nineteenth-century evolutionism and utilitarianism, and because it criticized Marxism not from the populist point of view, still less that of conservative orthodoxy, but from that of the most up-to-date, neo-Kantian, or Nietzschean philosophy. The key concepts that were accepted by revolutionists of every shade, and the main historiosophical dogmas of the 'progressive' intellectuals, were challenged by men who until recently had, at least to some extent, regarded them as their own. Atheism, rationalism, evolutionism, the categories of progress and causality, and the premisses of 'collectivist' morality—all these, it was claimed, did not represent the victory of reason over superstition but were symptoms of intellectual poverty. The new critics brought into the light of day everything in Marxism and socialism that was contrary to freedom and personal values, all doctrinaire schemes that enslaved the present to the future and self-realization to collective ideals. At the same time, without being fully aware of it, they brought to light the conflict between the absolute value of the individual and his development, and the desire for social change—a conflict especially obvious when the individual was extolled on Nietzschean lines. The Marxists, who regarded *Problems of Idealism* as nothing but a manifestation of bourgeois liberalism, were quick to emphasize those elements of the new movement which could be regarded as glorifying egocentrism or the morality of the *Herrenmensch* who despises the sufferings and aspirations of the masses. Lyubov Akselrod, who at this time was, with Plekhanov, the most vigorous defender of traditional Marxist philosophy, published in *Zarya*, under the pseudonym 'Orthodox', an exhaustive criticism of the new ideas from this point of view. She was able, as Lenin generally was not, to summarize the opposing arguments in a sober, factual manner; her reply, however, consists mainly of repeating hallowed formulas and trying to show that the cult of personal values as preached by Berdyayev, Frank, and Bulgakov is a glorification of egoism and

a dissolvent of social obligation. Rehearsing the Marxist attack
on religion as an instrument of oppression and inequality, she
lays stress on the link between historical and philosophical
materialism: in this as in all other respects she was a disciple of
Plekhanov. The question was a live one in Marxist controversy:
Max Zetterbaum had recently published a series of articles in
Die Neue Zeit arguing that historical materialism did not involve
any particular ontological position and was compatible with
Kantian transcendentalism. This view, popular among German
and Austrian Marxists, was of course anathema to Plekhanov
and 'Orthodox'. The 'mechanistic outlook', as she writes
(accepting responsibility for this expression), is an integral
interpretation of the world which includes pre-human history
as well as that of mankind; there is room in it for a rational
concept of progress: what is historically progressive is whatever
tends towards the preservation of society and of individuals (she
does not attempt to unravel the complications of this formula).
There is no basic difference between the study of human history
and the natural sciences: social science is just as 'objective' and
just as much concerned with laws and repeatable phenomena as
physical science.

This summary and over-simplified reply was made easier by
the fact that the authors of the work criticized did not profess
to be Marxists and defended idealism under its own name. It
was harder to deal with those social democrats who were led
astray by the new heresy and tried to combine the Marxist
tradition with a socialist philosophy based on 'subjectivist'
trends, and in particular on the empiriocritical brand of
epistemology.

It is noteworthy that while attempts were also made in the
West (especially by Viktor Adler's son Friedrich) to graft
empiriocriticism on to Marxism, it is only in Russia that one
can speak of a whole school of philosophers of this way of
thinking, who exercised appreciable influence though only for a
short time. Unlike many Western 'revisionists', this school did
not contend that Marxism was philosophically neutral and could
be combined with any epistemological theory, but sought, on
the contrary, to adopt a philosophy in harmony with Marxist
social theory and revolutionary strategy. In the same way as
their orthodox critics, they endeavoured to create an integral

picture of the world in which a particular philosophical doctrine, and no other, would provide a basis for historical materialism and the theory of the revolution. In this respect they shared in the doctrinaire spirit which prevailed among Russian social democrats. What attracted them in empiriocritical philosophy was its scientistic and anti-metaphysical rigorism and its 'activistic' approach to epistemology. Both these characteristics seemed well in accord with the iconoclastic attitude of Marxism towards inherited philosophical 'systems', and with the revolutionary orientation of the Bolshevik wing of Russian social democracy.

3. Empiriocriticism

This term is associated with a fairly large number of philosophers and physicists, chiefly in Germany and Austria, among whom the most prominent names are those of Ernst Mach and Richard Avenarius. The two men worked independently of each other and their conclusions were not identical, but their thinking ran on similar lines although expressed in different terms.

The objective that Avenarius set himself was to demolish all philosophical concepts and explanations that turn the world into a mystery by postulating a difference between the phenomena we perceive and the 'true' reality which lies beneath or beyond them. Above all he sought to refute epistemological idealism, which derived from the distinction between 'mental impressions' and inaccessible 'things in themselves'. He also held that all agnostic doctrines were based on the same false distinction. If his ideas were fairly often interpreted, by Wundt among others, as a new variety of 'subjectivism' or even 'immanentism', this was due partly to a certain inconsistency in his argument and partly to the extreme complexity of his language, which bristles with neologisms and endeavours to make a clean sweep of all the traditional abstractions of philosophy.

The error which causes us to distinguish between the 'contents of the mind' and the thing itself, or between the subject's 'interior' and the object—this error, leading to all the aberrations of idealism and agnosticism, is due to an instinctive process which Avenarius calls 'introjection'. If we examine our perceptions without any philosophical prepossession, we do not find them mysterious. Philosophy, however, persists in telling us that our 'impression' or 'sensation', for example when we touch a stone, is something other than the thing itself (in this case the stone), and that the problem is how they are related to each other. If it were so we could never find the answer, for there is no way of comparing the likeness with the original and seeing whether they agree, whatever this may precisely mean. But the question is a false one. We do not have to do with the thing and the impression separately, and if we dichotomize the world in this way we condemn ourselves to barren speculation which can only result in our capitulating before the mystery of a world concealed by a veil of sensations, or embracing the idealist delusion that the world is nothing but a medley of 'mental states'. Introjection—i.e. the mental process by which, as it were, we 'take in' physical objects in the form of 'subjective' images or reflections—is due to a false, though historically inevitable, interpretation of our relations with the world. Since we rightly presume that other people's mental experience is similar to ours, and since we thus treat them as experiencing subjects and not as automata, we attribute to them a mental 'interior' similar to our own—a sort of container for their experiences, which we cannot ourselves directly perceive. Having thus dichotomized other people we do the same for ourselves, treating our own perceptions as mental states caused by outside stimuli but different from them. We thus divide the world into what is 'subjective' and what is 'objective', and then speculate on how the two are related. Hence, in due course, the distinction between the body and the immaterial soul, and all spiritualist and religious illusions. But the mistake of introjection can be avoided: I can recognize that another person is a cognizant subject like myself without making a distinction between his or my *for intérieur* and that which is external. Once we shake off the illusion that we have an 'inner consciousness' in which 'external objects' are mysteriously present—objects which exist independently of the fact that they are 'given', but which we cannot know in any other way—we are freed from all the traditional questions and categories of philosophy, the disputes between realism and spiritualism, and the insoluble problems inherent in the notions of substance, force, and causality.

However, the removal of the delusion does not solve the

question of the 'act of cognition', which in the ordinary sense implies a distinction between the knower and the known. This relationship must now be defined in terms free from the error of introjection. The critique of introjection is the negative aspect of Avenarius's thought; its positive counterpart is the idea of 'principal co-ordination'. The content of my experience includes things, other people, and also myself, for the self that I experience directly is present in the same way as a thing, i.e. as the known and not the knower: it is not a subjective 'interior' transforming things into copies of themselves. At the same time, the self is irremovably present in experience as a relatively permanent part of it, and 'principal co-ordination' is the name given to the permanent conjunction of the 'term' and 'counter-term' of experience, which are equipollent and combined in such a way that neither is 'prior' to the other. The 'central term' is each separate human being, and the counter-term, i.e. what was formerly called the object of experience, is numerically identical for any number of central terms. Different people, in other words, perceive the same object: the counter-term does not multiply itself to match the number of 'subjects', and this rules out epistemological idealism. By removing the possibility of idealism and solipsism we also eliminate the problem of the 'thing in itself' hiding behind phenomena: for this would imply a counter-term that is not a counter-term since it is not 'given', and would therefore be self-contradictory. 'Principal co-ordination' does not, Avenarius continues, affect the sense we ascribe to scientific knowledge: for when we address ourselves to any object we create a situation of 'co-ordination', i.e. we include that object in a cognitive combination. We may think, for instance, that we are asking what the world was like when there was no one to perceive it, but in fact we are adding an imaginary observer to the scene and asking what the world would have been like then. We cannot raise a question about any part of the universe without embracing it in our act of inquiry and thus making it a counter-term of experience. We may say, and this is probably what Avenarius intended, that the act of inquiry cannot be eliminated from the content of the question, and therefore the situation of questioning is an instance of 'principal co-ordination'. It is impossible to put a question concerning 'independent' being, for the very act of uttering it establishes a dependence. To ask about 'being-in-itself' is to ask how we can know the world without creating a cognitive situation, that is to say without knowing it. In this sense all the traditional questions of epistemology and metaphysics, as posed by Descartes, Locke, Kant, and their successors, are seen to be wrongly framed and meaningless.

If human cognitive activity is understood in this light, Avenarius claims, its true biological significance becomes plain. Cognition is a form of behaviour comprising the reactions of the body to stimuli which constantly disturb our biological equilibrium, and the reactions have no other purpose than to restore it. Cognition, being simply a biological reaction, is not concerned with 'truth' in any transcendental sense or with discovering 'how things really are'. The predicates 'true' and 'false' do not belong to components of experience: like 'pleasant' and 'painful', 'good' and 'bad', 'beautiful' and 'ugly', they are related to a particular interpretation of experience, they are 'characters' and not 'elements'. Human ideas about the world, whether philosophical doctrines or religious beliefs, are to be interpreted biologically and not in relation to 'truth': they can without exception be genetically understood as the response of individuals or communities to needs occasioned by changes in the environment. This does not mean that the content of my knowledge is not valid for all mankind. Some features of biological existence are universal, and so therefore are certain 'truths' enunciated by human beings; but this universality refers to the human species and not to any transcendental validity of knowledge. From the purely biological point of view cognition is of course possible, but not a theory of it which would entitle us to claim that our knowledge is true 'objectively', i.e. independently of the act of cognition.

Although it was Avenarius's object to free philosophy from the dualism of 'mind' and 'matter' by reducing all Being to experience in which the self and the object are present on equal terms, he was unable to avoid drawing conclusions that brought him under suspicion of 'subjectivism' or inconsistency. If the self is not a subject but is something known, and if the 'central term' is inseparable from any account of experience, in what does the act of knowing consist? It would appear to be an experience which is nobody's, a situation in which something is 'given' not to anyone in particular but in general, an act of perception without a percipient. If I say that 'I see' something or other, this statement comprises 'me' as a grammatical and epistemological subject and implies that 'I', as the cognizant subject, am not on a par with the other components of the perceptual field: otherwise it would be truer to say that something 'is perceived' than that 'I' perceive it. But Avenarius's explanation is not clear: how could the category of subject be banished from the account of experience, and what is the difference between the 'central term' of the empiriocritics and the 'subject' in the ordinary sense? If we hold to the view that the self is only a component of the perceptual field it is not clear why 'principal co-ordination' happens at all, i.e. why the self must be present in every act of experience.

It is in fact hard to reconcile the two fundamental categories of 'introjection' and 'principal co-ordination'. The critique of introjection is intended to do away with the 'subject' as a superfluous construction and with the distinction between 'subjective' and 'objective' Being. Experience is left as an ontologically neutral zone, whose relation to 'being-in-itself' cannot be meaningfully inquired into. Epistemological aspirations are relinquished, and science is left to deal with its problems as they are, without ontological interpretation. This is how Mach understood the matter. If, however, we also adopt the theory of 'principal co-ordination', the subject, under a different name, reappears as a separate category, whose inevitable presence in experience can only be understood on the supposition that it is the knower and not the known—yet Avenarius rejects this supposition. If we accept both parts of his interpretation, the result may easily lead us into an absurdity: the self, as a component of experience on the same footing as things, is for some unintelligible reason the condition of the appearance of all its other components. The inadmissibility of this is clear when Avenarius identifies the 'central term' of co-ordination with the human nervous system —so that the latter, a physical object, is the condition of the presence of all other physical objects. Avenarius does not, of course, state this absurd conclusion, but it is hard to see how it can be avoided if both his basic tenets are maintained.

A second fundamental difficulty, to which Natorp and especially Husserl drew attention, is that of the physiological interpretation of cognitive values combined with the recognition of scientific knowledge as true in the everyday sense. If, as Avenarius says, truth is not part of experience but is a secondary interpretation of it, the whole purpose of scientific knowledge is reduced to biological utility. On this purely pragmatic view, what is 'true' is that which it is advantageous to accept in given conditions: some 'truths' may be universally valid, but this only means that they are advantageous in all circumstances because of the unaltering features of human species-life. But at the same time Avenarius bases his biological interpretation of knowledge on observations of the physiology of perception: he accepts these as valid or 'true' in the everyday sense, and thus seems to fall into a *petitio principii*. Hence, Husserl argued, the whole idea of 'biological epistemology' is an impossibility: we cannot find the meaning of all experience on the basis of certain particular data of experience which we tacitly regard as 'true' in the ordinary sense.

Avenarius sought to explode all the traditional questions of philosophy by doing away with 'subjectivity' as a superfluous construction, without which these questions would not arise. But his doctrine of 'principal co-ordination' thwarts the attempt and introduces a major inconsistency into the whole theory. The real achievement of his critique, for which the theory of 'co-ordination' is unnecessary, is to show the insuperable difficulties of treating the content of perception as consisting of copies or images of objects that are independent of the perceptual situation. His intention was to restore to cognitive acts their 'natural' character, unblurred by philosophical speculation. In the 'natural' conception of the world there was, in his view, no dichotomy between mind and matter, and cognition was not a process of storing images of things into a mental container. The critique of introjection was not meant to be a discovery of something new but a return to the naïve, immediate view of the world, in which cognitive acts would recover their true biological meaning; it was also in accordance with the basic principle of intellectual economy. In Avenarius's view, as in that of Mach, the principle of economy was not a general law of physics, as in Maupertuis, but signified, as in Spencer's philosophy, that any living organism, including the human brain, acts so as to attain its object with the minimum output of energy. The whole history of human thought exemplified this: the capitalization of knowledge proceeded by increasingly far-reaching generalizations and increasingly efficient ways of recording and transmitting acquired information. All abstract ideas were instruments of this process: so were human speech and writing, the laws of science, and the methods of mathematics. Scientific laws did not purport to reflect any particular facts in their every detail, but to express recurrent aspects of phenomena that were of biological importance: they were short cuts which saved effort in the manipulation of things. Metaphysical categories like 'thing', 'substance', 'spirit', and 'matter' were by-products of the same activity. They were useful in so far as they denoted certain relatively permanent combinations of qualities in experience, but when petrified in language our imagination was apt to treat them as metaphysical entities. The task of science, in accordance with the principle of economy, was to purge experience of such superfluous constructions.

Mach's philosophy is not open to the same charge of inconsistency as that of Avenarius, since it contains no equivalent of the principle of co-ordination. Mach was an experimental physicist and a historian of physics: he had a stronger sense than Avenarius of the relativity of knowledge, and did not believe in a one-way process of 'purifying' experience so as to achieve a definitive, uniform scientific world-picture. He regarded science as a biological instrument of the human species, developing in accordance with the principle of economy, and equally provisional and relative at each successive stage. Like Avenarius he took a pragmatic view of cognition, whether precritical perception or scientific hypotheses. This conception of knowledge left no room for metaphysics. The world consisted of collections of various qualities, which showed varying degrees of permanence and changed in a more or less predictable manner. These qualities or 'elements', perceived without prepossession, had no ontological significance; they were in themselves neither mental nor material; considered in relation to the human body they were sensations, while in their interdependence they appeared as things. These, however, were secondary interpretations: experience itself did not require us to attribute any ontological status to colours, sounds, pressures, time, or space. The actual content of knowledge, including the laws of science, comprised nothing that was not in experience. The purpose of science was to select, classify, and record concisely the results of experience, in accordance with the biological needs of the human species, and to facilitate manipulation and prediction; 'truth' in the transcendental sense was a superfluous addition and introduced nothing of value. All knowledge was experiential in origin and content, except for those parts of mathematics that were purely tautological and gave no information about the world. On this point Mach was faithful to the Humean tradition: all knowledge consists of the description of experience and of analytical judgements; there is no 'necessity' in it except of a linguistic kind, there are no synthetic *a priori* judgements.

Mach's ideas were basically a new version of Humean positivism, intended to free the human mind of an encumbering load of concepts, questions, and distinctions that were not rooted in experience but owed their existence to the inertia of language. He was not a 'subjectivist', treating material qualities as mental states, but sought to outlaw questions of the relationship between mental images and things in themselves, as the concepts they implied were not part of experience and were the fruit of philosophical prejudice. The world as man perceived it was selected and organized in a certain way under the pressure of biological needs. Although its primary features were found in experience, and although science, properly conceived, could add nothing to them, it could arrange experience by means of abstract concepts and laws so that the whole universe appeared under the aspect of a certain order; this order, however, was the work of human selection and was, in this sense, of our own making.

If we try to identify the common intention of Avenarius, Mach, and the many philosophers and physicists who thought like them, we find it to consist in a form of scientism and positivism, closely related to modernistic European culture. In their opposition to metaphysical preconceptions, whether materialist or religious, the empiriocritics sought to return to a direct, spontaneous, unphilosophical outlook on the world: to restore to man his 'natural' status as a cognitive being, freed from the abstract constructions of philosophy and religion and from the jugglery of language. They also held that the order of the universe which knowledge displays to us is not a 'real' order to be passively apprehended but is a product of man's adaptive power. The return to 'nature' and the idea that man is responsible for the order of the external world are characteristic of the intellectual life of the time. The anti-metaphysical scientism of the empiriocritics, and their biological, pragmatic view of knowledge, attracted Marxists in search of a new and more thoroughgoing interpretation of the universe in accordance with the revolutionary spirit.

4. *Bogdanov and the Russian empiriocritics*

The principal Russian empiriocritics were the Bolsheviks Bogdanov, Lunacharsky, and Bazarov. There is, however, nothing specifically Bolshevik about their philosophy, although they themselves believed that their political and philosophical positions were closely connected. The same applies to the Mensheviks Yushkevich and Valentinov, and to the S.R. Viktor Chernov. All these were in search of a 'monistic' philosophy embracing the whole of experience and practical politics, but in a different way from that of Engels and Plekhanov, which seemed to them naïve, arbitrary, and unsupported by any analysis of the concepts they used.

The output of the Marxist empiriocritics is enormous and has not as yet been fully studied. Bogdanov was certainly the most important of them, both as a philosopher and as a politician. He was a doctor by profession but a man of varied learning, versed in psychology, philosophy, and economics, a novelist and one of the most active Bolshevik organizers and ideologists. In all his work he was obsessed with the monistic quest for a philosophy containing the key to every problem and explaining everything by a single principle.

Aleksandr Aleksandrovich Bogdanov (real name Malinovsky) was born at Tula in 1873. He studied natural science at Moscow, and medicine at Kharkov until 1899. He was a populist until 1896, when he became a social democrat together with Bazarov (Rudnev). In 1897 he published a popular Marxist handbook of economics, of which Lenin wrote a highly favourable review. This work presented a conspectus of all economic systems in a catechetic form and did much to create the conventional schemata of economic history which became part and parcel of Marxism-Leninism. In 1899, fascinated by the 'energism' of Wilhelm Ostwald, he published *Basic Elements of the Historical View of Nature*, which sought to construct a monistic world-view based on the concept of energy. In this work he displays the relativist tendency which he regarded as a corner-stone of Marxism: all truths are historical in the sense that they express man's biological and social situation; truth is a matter of practical applicability, not objective validity. He later took the view that energism was only a certain way of observing the world, but did not explain the 'stuff' it was made of and therefore could not satisfy the mind's monistic aspirations.

Arrested in Moscow in 1899 and sentenced to exile, Bogdanov lived in Kaluga and then Vologda until 1903. During this period he met Berdyayev, as well as Lunacharsky and other social democrat intellectuals. He was the inspirer and part-author of a collective work of 1904 entitled *An Outline of the Realist World-View*, and answer to *Problems of Idealism*; other contributors were Lunacharsky, Vladimir Fritche, Bazarov, and Suvorov. In 1904–6 Bogdanov published his three-volume *magnum opus*, *Empiriomonism*, an attempt to adapt the epistemology of Mach and Avenarius to historical materialism.

Bogdanov was a Bolshevik from 1903 onwards. Lenin, despite Bogdanov's heretical views on philosophy, maintained political ties with him for some years; he encouraged Lyubov Akselrod to write against empiriocriticism, but did not himself join the fray until the philosophical deviationists also opposed his policy towards the Duma. After the split in the social democratic party Bogdanov was Lenin's chief lieutenant in St. Petersburg; from 1906 he worked to rebuild the united organization there, and joined Lenin in Finland as one of the three Bolshevik members of the Central Committee. He opposed the participation of social democrats in the Duma elections, and was later an 'ultimatist'. The left-wing Bolsheviks who, with different degrees of firmness, rejected legal methods and pressed for the continuation of a directly revolutionary policy after 1907 were all more or less adherents of the empiriocritical philosophy. In 1909 Bogdanov and his friends were expelled from the Bolshevik Centre, and afterwards from the Central Committee. For a time the group published its own journal and, with financial help from Gorky— who, to Lenin's anxiety, sympathized with the unorthodox trend —founded a party school at Capri as a centre for the revival of revolutionary Bolshevism. The school functioned for some months in 1909, and again at Bologna in 1910–11. Besides Bogdanov its lecturers included Lunacharsky, Aleksinsky, Menzhinsky (a future head of the Ogpu), and occasionally Trotsky. Lenin was invited to give a lecture at the school, but declined. In 1911 Bogdanov's group disintegrated and he returned to Russia for good. He continued to pour out philosophical writings, seeking more and more generalized formulas in which to express his monistic views. Together with other deviationists he published two collective works: *Essays on the Philosophy of Marxism* (1908; Bogdanov, Bazarov, Berman, Lunacharsky, Yushkevich, Suvorov, and Helfand) and *Essays on the Philosophy of Collectivism* (1909; Bogdanov, Gorky, Lunacharsky, Bazarov). Among his own publications were *The Decline of Fetishism* (1910), which analysed 'fetishism' in general terms as a cognitive and social phenomenon; *The Philosophy of Living Experience* (1913), a popular account of empiriomonism; and *Tectology, a Universal Organizational Science* (1913; vol. ii, 1917). The last was an attempt to lay the basis of a universal science comprising philosophy, sociology, physics, and technology: it may be regarded as a forerunner of praxeology. In addition Bogdanov published manuals of economics that were much reprinted, and several dissertations on 'proletarian culture': he pursued this with vigour after the Revolution and was one of the chief ideologists of the institution known as 'Proletkult'.

During the war Bogdanov served at the front as an army doctor. He did not rejoin the party; in 1926 he was appointed director of the Haematological Institute in Moscow, and two years later he died as the result of a transfusion experiment on himself. Even this had its philosophical bearing: blood transfusion was, to him, a proof of the biological unity of mankind, and was thus linked with the 'collectivist' outlook.

An author who produced over fifty books and innumerable articles on all kinds of subjects could not be a philosopher of the first rank. He was also a bad writer: his principal work is diffuse, chaotic, vague, and repetitive. Nevertheless, he was the most influential expounder of 'proletarian philosophy', and for many years the whole Bolshevik party learnt economics from his books. As a philosopher he was superior to Lenin in all respects: erudition, knowledge of his subject, independence of thought, and skill in formulating problems. He also appears to have been an excellent organizer. He lacked, however, what Lenin possessed in full measure, the non-doctrinaire ability to change tactics in a new situation: like most ideologists, he was too consistent for his own good.

Bogdanov's 'empiriomonist' philosophy is based on three main ideas. All spiritual and mental activities are instruments of life in the biological and social senses; psychic and physical phenomena are alike from the ontic point of view; the life of the human race tends towards the integral harmony of all its manifestations. The first two ideas are found in Mach, but Bogdanov gives them a distinctive interpretation on the strength of which he calls his theory empiriomonism and not empirio-criticism. The third point is specifically connected with socialist doctrine.

According to Bogdanov, Mach's philosophy supports Marxism inasmuch as they both treat cognitive processes as instruments of man's fight for existence, and reject the possibility of ideas not derived from experience. The 'objectivity' of acts of cognition lies in the fact that they are valid for human societies and not only for the individual. This collective aspect distinguishes physical phenomena from 'subjective' ones. 'The objective character of the physical world consists in the fact that it exists not for me personally but for all, and has for everyone a definite meaning, the same, I believe, as it has for me' (*Empiriomonism*, i, 25). Nature is 'collectively organized experience'. Space, time, and causality are forms in which men co-ordinate their respective perceptions; but this co-ordination is not as yet complete. There are experiences, socially significant and with a social origin, which nevertheless conflict with other experiences. This is due to social antagonisms and the class division, which have the effect that human beings only understand one another within certain limits, while their discordant interests inevitably produce conflicting ideologies. In an individualistic society like ours each person's experience centres on himself, whereas in primitive communist societies the 'self' was merged in the community. In the society of the future it will be different again, when work is collectively organized and there will be no possibility of conflict between my own self and another's.

Work is genetically prior to all other forms of community life.

However, when the immediate expenditure of energy in the fight with nature is supplemented by organizational forms to increase the efficiency of labour, these call into being ideological instruments including all modes of communication: language, abstract knowledge, emotions, customs, moral norms, laws, and arts. 'The ideological process constitutes all that part of social life that lies outside technical processes, beyond the immediate struggle of social man with external nature' (ibid. iii, 45). Science is not an ideology, for it develops as an immediate organ of technology. Ultimately, however, all forms of collective spiritual life, whether ideological or scientific, are subservient to the struggle for existence and have no significance apart from their function in that struggle. This subordination of all forms of life to the requirements of technology and increased efficiency is not yet visible to all, on account of ideological delusions which keep alive countless metaphysical fetishes; but it is becoming visible to the proletariat, and in the future it will be common to all mankind. 'The technical value of products, replacing the fetish of exchange value, is the sum of the social energy of human labour crystallized in those products. The cognitive value of an idea is its power to increase the volume of social energy of labour, by planning and "organizing" the forms of men's activity and the instruments they use. The "moral" value of human behaviour consists in increasing the social energy of labour by harmoniously uniting and concentrating human activity and by organizing it in the direction of maximum solidarity' (ibid. 135–6).

This purely pragmatic (but, it should be added, socially pragmatic) interpretation, according to which knowledge and the life of the mind generally are an assemblage of instruments whose 'ultimate' purpose is to assist technical progress, leaves no room for the concept of truth in the traditional sense, i.e. the conformity of our judgements to independent reality. The 'natural' world, in Bogdanov's view, is the result of the social organization of experience, and 'truth' means utility in the struggle for existence. This attitude, he claims, is strictly scientific, as it sweeps away all the metaphysical fetishes that have deluded philosophers and common men over the centuries. Having reduced the universe to collective experience, and cognitive values to socially useful ones, we have no need of such categories as 'substance' or 'thing in itself', or such specifications as 'spirit', 'matter', 'time', 'cause', 'force', etc. Experience contains nothing that answers to these concepts, and they are not required for the practical handling of objects.

Bogdanov's critique of the 'thing in itself' as a superfluity which can be eliminated from Kantian philosophy is based on a misunderstanding. Bogdanov and Mach, from whom he took this interpretation, appear to think that in Kant's view there is behind every phenomenal object a mysterious 'thing in itself' to which we have no access: if it be removed, the phenomena remain as they were and nothing has been lost except a 'metaphysical' construction. This, however, is a parody of Kant's thinking. What he held was that the 'phenomenon' is the mode in which things appear, so that they are immediately accessible to us, but organized in *a priori* forms. If the 'thing in itself' were removed, the phenomenon would be removed also. In short, the concept of a 'phenomenon' must mean something quite different for Bogdanov and Mach than it does for Kant, but they do not explain this meaning.

Mach's merit, according to Bogdanov, was that he broke with the dualism of 'mind' and 'matter' and introduced instead the concept of 'experience', in which phenomena appear as mental (psychical) or physical according to whether we connect them with one another or relate them to our own bodes. But Mach did not completely eradicate the dualism, as he retained these two aspects and did not explain why they should be different. The answer offered by expiriomonism is that the 'stuff' of mental and physical phenomena is identical; there is no area of 'subjectivity' in the universe, only the discordance between individual and collective experience, which is due to social causes and which history will in time remove.

We come here to the obscurest part of Bogdanov's philosophy. He appears to be saying that our thoughts, feelings, perceptions, acts of will, etc. are made of the same material as water or stones, but that this material is in some sense 'ultimate' and therefore cannot be defined: encompassing everything, it cannot be explained in terms of anything specific. In this respect, of course, Bogdanov's concept of 'experience' is on a par with all fundamental categories in all monistic doctrines, including 'matter' as understood by the materialists. Apart from this there is only the general idea that man's being is entirely a part of nature, that our subjectivity is no different in kind from the rest of the universe. In this sense the doctrine is a 'materialist' one, i.e. it reduces man to the functions prescribed by his position in nature and regards him as wholly explicable within the natural order. But the matter becomes more complicated when Bogdanov tries to describe this identity in his nebulous theory of 'substitution'.

This theory involves a psychophysical parallelism, not on the basis that mental and physical phenomena are 'two aspects' of a single process—for this involves the error of 'introjection', as though the body was the receptacle of the mind—but in the sense that there is a functional link between them analogous to that, for example, between the visual and tactile qualities of a single body. This is not a monism of 'substance', but a 'monism of the type of organization in accordance with which experience is systematized, a monism of the method of cognition' (*Empirio-monism* i, 64). Within the field of uniform 'experience' there is no problem of transition from inanimate to organic nature, for the whole of nature is an assemblage of homogeneous elements, and it is only our abstract thinking that calls parts of it 'inanimate', whereas they too are parts of our own life. This does not signify, however, that they have a 'psychical' character (for that would mean that they were valid only for the individual), but that there is in them a substratum of which we know nothing specific but which is related to their 'physical' aspect in the same way as mental phenomena are related to physiological ones in human beings. In human life physiological processes are the 'reflection' of direct experiences, and not the other way about. 'Physiological life is the result of the collective harmonization of the "external perceptions" of a living organism, each of which is the reflection of a single complex of experiences in another organism (or in itself). In other words, physiological life is the reflection of direct life in the socially organized experience of living subjects' (ibid. 145). Physical nature itself is derivative in relation to direct complexes which differ in their degree of organization; we must suppose that the world we perceive is of like nature to our experience, for otherwise we could not imagine the one affecting the other; we must therefore accept a kind of panpsychism, but without the assumption of different substances. Within the totality of experience, lower forms of organization 'corresponding to' the inorganic world precede higher ones corresponding to the human mind, and in this sense the 'priority' of nature *vis-à-vis* human existence remains valid. The following passage, though somewhat lengthy, is the most concise summary of Bogdanov's epistemology:

'The mental' and 'the physical' as forms of experience do not correspond to the concepts of 'mind' and 'nature'. The latter have a metaphysical sense and relate to 'things in themselves'; but we, discarding metaphysical 'things in themselves' as empty fetishes, place in their stead 'empirical substitution'. This substitution, which originates in each man's recognition of the psyche of others, presupposes that the 'basis' of the phenomena of physical experience consists of direct complexes organized in different degrees, including 'psychic' complexes. In recognizing that the physiological processes of the higher nervous centres, as phenomena of physical experience, are, the reflection of psychic complexes which can also be 'substituted' for them, we also saw that all the physiological processes of life admit of the substitution of 'associative', i.e. psychic complexes; but in proportion as the physiological phenomenon is less complex and less highly organized, so also are the substitutes. We noted, further, that in the 'inorganic' world outside physiological life empirical substitution still takes place, but the 'direct complexes' that are to be substituted for inorganic phenomena have an organizational form that is not associative but of another, lower kind: they are not 'psychical' combinations but are less definite, less complex and at a lower level of organization, which in the lowest, limiting phase appears simply as a chaos of elements.

Thus it is among the direct complexes that we substitute for physical experience that we must seek analogies for 'nature' and 'mind' in order to establish their mutual relation. But the very formulation of this question suggests the answer: 'nature', that is to say the inorganic and the simplest organic complexes, is genetically prior, while 'mind', i.e. the higher organic and associative complexes, and particularly those which constitute experience, are genetically secondary.

Thus our viewpoint, although not 'materialist' in the narrow sense, belongs to the same category as 'materialist' systems: it is an ideology of 'productive forces', of the technical process.' (*Empiriomonism*, iii, 148–9)

The obscurity and ambiguity of this philosophy is due to the fact that Bogdanov, unlike Mach, does not simply deny the validity of the 'metaphysical question' but, having declared it to be meaningless, then proceeds to try and solve it, which he cannot do without contradiction. His starting-point is a kind of collective subjectivism: the world is a correlative to the human struggle for existence, and it is no use ascribing any other meaning to it or inquiring as to its independent nature. Things are crystallizations of human projections, governed by practical ends; they make their appearance only within the horizon that biology determines for the human race; they are components of collective experience, which figures as the one absolute point of reference. Within the framework of this relativization 'mental' phenomena differ from physical ones only inasmuch as the latter are valid collectively and the former only for individuals. Having said this, Bogdanov then presents physiological phenomena as the 'reflection' of mental processes, which does not make sense in terms of the previous distinction. He goes on to seek analogies in the field of inanimate nature and thus falls into a kind of panpsychism; he tells us that it is not really panpsychism, as it does not presuppose any 'substance', but he does not explain its true nature. As a result, we are unable to fathom the meaning he attaches to the 'priority' of experience in relation to the distinction of mental and physical phenomena. He uses the term 'mental' or 'psychical' in at least three senses, though he appears not to be aware of this: sometimes it means 'valid only for the individual', sometimes 'subjective' in the ordinary sense, and sometimes 'reflected in physiological processes'. This results in hopeless confusion, which there is little point in trying to remedy.

None the less, the main intention of Bogdanov's epistemology is clear: to do away with metaphysical 'fetishes', concepts without empirical correlates, and to preserve a strictly anthropocentric point of view in which the whole of reality is presented as the intentional correlate of human praxis. In this way he seeks to eliminate all 'substantial' entities, especially 'matter' and 'subject', and also 'time', 'space', 'causality', and 'force', as well as the concepts of 'truth' and 'objectivity' in the usual sense. The resulting picture, he claims, is strictly scientific, being free from metaphysics, and likewise humanistic, as it firmly relates all reality to human existence. In both respects this is in harmony with the intentions of Marxism, which is a scientistic, activistic, and socially pragmatic philosophy: it has no need of the category of individual subjectivity or truth in a transcendental sense, and relates the whole universe to human labour, thus making man the creator and organizer of the world. This, in Bogdanov's judgement, is true not of any form of Marxism but only of that embodied in the Bolshevik movement. He and the other Russian empiriocritics believed that their 'activist' epistemology was well attuned to the spirit of Bolshevism and to its general idea that the revolution would not break out of itself when economic conditions were ripe, but that it depended on the will-power of a group of organizers. Bogdanov, to whom 'organization' was an obsession, used the term with equal freedom in regard to party matters and the principles of epistemology.

Each of the Russian empiriocritics differed from the others in some respects. Some, like Valentinov, were strict Machists; others devised variant names for their ideas, such as Bogdanov's 'empiriomonism' and Yushkevich's 'empiriosymbolism'. However, they all agreed in emphasizing the anti-metaphysical, scientistic aspect of Marxism as opposed to the dualism of 'matter' and 'subject', and in envisaging the world in terms of human social praxis. The same viewpoint of collective subjectivism dictated their interpretation of Marx's *Theses on Feuerbach*.

5. The philosophy of the proletariat

Bogdanov endeavoured to apply his theory directly to the prospect of socialism as a system under which all minds would at last share the same picture of the world, and even the separateness of the individual ego would disapear.

The philosophical basis of 'proletarian culture' was as follows. All human cognitive activity is directed to one end, namely man's success in the fight with nature. One can of course distinguish 'scientific' activities, which are directly concerned with technical efficiency, from 'ideological' ones, which perform the same function indirectly through the forms of social organization. This is not a distinction according to epistemological criteria of truth or falsehood, but only relates to the way in which the activities in question increase the productivity of labour. In both cases the principle holds good that 'truth is the living, organizing form of experience; it guides our activity and gives us a foothold in the battle for life' (*Empiriomonism*, iii, p. viii).

In other words, the validity of the results of cognition does not consist in their being 'true' in the usual sense, but in the help they afford in the struggle for survival. We thus reach a position of extreme relativism: different 'truths' may be useful in different historical situations, and it is quite possible that any truth is valid only for a particular epoch or social class. Nor is there any epistemological reason to distinguish truth from emotions, values, or social institutions, all of which are equally to be judged according to how far they strengthen man in his fight with nature. At the same time, we can speak of the viewpoint of one class being 'superior' to another's, not as if it were 'true' in an absolute sense but because the social forces it represents are more conducive to technical progress.

According to Marx's theory, the division of labour led to the separation of organizational functions from executive ones, and in course of time to the division of classes. The managing class gradually ceased to perform any technical activity and became parasitic. Its ideology naturally mirrored this situation, evolving religious myths and idealist doctrines. Direct producers, on the other hand, are instinctively drawn to materialism: 'the technique of machine production, expressed in cognition, unfailingly produces a materialist outlook' (ibid. 129). The materialism of the 'progressive' bourgeoisie expressed their link with technical progress; but, being the outlook of a privileged class, it could not do without various metaphysical fetishes. The materialism of the proletariat, however, rejected metaphysics and took a purely scientific view of the world. The word 'materialism' was really a survival, and was appropriate to the new outlook only in the sense that it was anti-metaphysical and anti-idealist.

The proletariat, as the class destined to sweep away class antagonisms and restore to mankind the unity of labour, knowledge, and will, was the best embodiment of man's natural tendency to extend his power over nature. The proletariat was the standard-bearer of technical progress, which required the elimination of everything that opposed individuals to one another. In present-day society social antagonisms had reached their peak and it was almost impossible for the classes to come to terms or understand one another. 'The opposition of normative and cognitive ideologies is increasing and is dividing the classes into two societies that regard each other in the same way as they do the forces of external nature' (ibid. 138). In the society of the future, however, there would be a return to perfect unity. In the solidarity of close co-operation men would have no reason to oppose their ego to others', all individual experiences would be harmonized, there would be 'a single society with a single ideology' (ibid. 139). This ideology, it need hardly be said, would be that of empiriomonism, as the most radical thought-form eschewing the traditional fetishes of metaphysics.

No other Marxist, perhaps, carried the doctrine of the primacy of productive forces over ideology to such an extreme as Bogdanov; nor did any express so consistently the collectivist ideal and the hope that individuality would disappear in the perfect society. The Utopia of the absolute unity of society in all respects was, to Bogdanov, a natural consequence of his Marxist faith. As all forms of spiritual life are wholly determined by the division of classes, and indirectly by the technical level of society, and as technical progress was the sole criterion of 'truth' and required the elimination of class antagonisms, it was clear that socialism would abolish all differentiation between human beings, and that the subjective sense of difference would lose its *raison d'être* when it no longer had an economic basis in the conflict of individual interests. These conclusions of Bogdanov's, which are not to be found in Marx himself, are a link between the former's views and the totalitarian Utopias of the eighteenth century.

The same doctrinaire belief, inherited from Marxist tradition, in the ancillary function of culture and its absolute dependence on technology led Bogdanov to the theory of 'proletarian culture' (Proletkult) and the belief that it was the proletariat's mission to effect a clean break in cultural history. Since the classes were so estranged and hostile that they regarded one another as things and not people, they could not possibly have a common culture. The culture of the proletariat must borrow nothing from the tradition of the privileged classes but must make a Promethean effort to create *ex nihilo*, paying attention to its own needs and to nothing else whatever.

In a pamphlet entitled *Science and the Working Class* (1920) and in other writings Bogdanov proclaimed the slogan of 'proletarian science'. Marx, adopting the standpoint of the working class, had transformed economics; it was now time to recast all sciences in accordance with the proletarian world-view, not excluding, for example, mathematics and astronomy. Bogdanov did not explain what proletarian astronomy or integral calculus would be like, but he declared that if workers had difficulty in mastering the various sciences without long, specialized study it was chiefly because bourgeois scientists had erected artificial barriers of method and vocabulary so that the workers should not learn their secrets.

The theory and practice of Proletkult did not find favour with the Bolshevik leaders except Bukharin, who edited *Pravda* after the Revolution and supported Bogdanov's idea in its columns. Trotsky was against it, and Lenin criticized it sharply on several occasions. This was not so much because some of its advocates, including Bogdanov, had fallen into philosophical heresy, but because the idea seemed to Lenin an idle fantasy unconnected with the party's true objectives. In a country with a huge percentage of illiterates the need was to teach them reading, writing, and arithmetic (the ordinary kind, not a proletarian version) and give them an elementary idea of technology and organization, not to pull civilization up by the roots and start again from zero. In any case Lenin did not share the view of some Proletkult enthusiasts and their Futurist allies that the art and literature of past ages should be scrapped by the working class.

It was of course impossible for Proletkult to adhere consistently to the principle of a 'clean break', either in theory or, still more, in actual artistic production. None the less, Bogdanov and others had raised a question which is neither trivial nor absurd from the point of view of Marxist doctrine. Given that culture is 'nothing but' an instrument of class-interests —and Marx afforded much foundation for this view—and that proletarian interests are in all respects contrary to those of the bourgeoisie, at any rate 'at the stage of socialist revolution', how was it possible to defend the idea of cultural continuity or of a universal culture for all mankind? Did it not logically follow from Marxism that the proletariat, in the struggle for socialism, must not take over any part of the existing heritage? The theoreticians of Proletkult were, however, in an ambiguous position. In opposition to those who spoke of an 'art for all mankind' they quoted historical examples to show that different classes and periods had developed their own artistic forms; it was natural, therefore, that the proletariat should evolve an art of its own reflecting its struggle and its historical mission. But, at the same time, they accepted the notion that art was common to humanity, although every class and every period gave it different forms according to its own tastes and interests. In effect, therefore, they agreed that there was a continuing cultural heritage to be added to by each generation—a view in accordance with common sense, but not with the theory that art is purely a matter of class interests.

Before the October Revolution these disputes were of no great practical importance, but it was different when the Soviet state had to decide on its cultural policy and what it meant by 'proletarian culture'. Lunacharsky, Lenin's first Commissar for Education, had to solve practical problems in this field, and Proletkult became, especially from 1917 to 1921, a fairly large organization devoted to the cultivation of revolutionary art and science among the workers. Lunacharsky showed moderation and tolerance, especially in comparison with the doctrinaire attitude of the revolutionary *avant-garde*. His belief in the dependence of art on social class did not blind him to artistic values, although—like most Marxist theoreticians on art, at all events educated ones—he had difficulty in accommodating his 'bourgeois' tastes to his 'proletarian' ideology. Thus, although he hoped to see an upsurge of proletarian art in the future, and explained its absence in the present by such evident facts as the workers' lack of education, he never shared the fanaticism of the Proletkult extremists. He pursued a policy of repression— mild enough at this stage—towards bourgeois artists and writers, but he realized that art would wither and die under police control. The period of his authority—from 1917 to 1929—is regarded as the golden age of Soviet culture, though it did not seem so to those who were harassed even then for producing works with insufficient revolutionary spirit. The artistic merit of the twenties may have been exaggerated, but there is no comparison between them and, for instance, Zhdanov's dictator- ship over Soviet cultural life after the Second World War.

6. *The 'God-builders'*

Anatoly Vasilyevich Lunacharsky (1875–1933) is noted in the history of Russian Marxism not only for helping to spread the empiriocritical heresy and for his work as a literary critic and dramatist (not of the first rank) and art theoretician, but also for his plan, which especially infuriated Lenin, for a 'socialist religion'.

This plan, known as 'God-building' (*Bogostroitelstvo*), was a Marxist counterpart to the general increase of interest in religion after the 1905 Revolution, just as the empiriocriticism of the social democrats was a result of the permeation of the revolutionary intelligentsia by philosophic modernism. The movement is chiefly associated with the names of Lunacharsky and Gorky, and was a kind of reconstruction of the 'religion of humanity' expounded by Comte and especially Feuerbach.

Lunacharsky developed his idea of an anthropocentric Marxist religion in several articles and in a book entitled *Religion and Socialism* (1908, second volume 1911). G. L. Kline, an authority on the Russian religious tradition, observes that the God-builders adopted not only Feuerbach's deification of humanity but, perhaps in an even greater degree, Nietzsche's ideal of the superman.

The new religion was to be an answer not only to the 'God-seeking' movement (*Bogoiskatelstvo*) of Christian philosophers but also to the arid old-fashioned atheism of Plekhanov and the other orthodox Marxists, for whom the history of religion was summed up in the opposition between it and science. Lunacharsky and Gorky argued that historical religions were not a mere bundle of superstitions but were the expression, albeit ideologically false, of desires and feelings that socialism should take over and ennoble, not destroy. The new religion was purely immanent and had no need of belief in God, the supernatural world, or personal immortality, but it embraced all that was positive and creative in traditional faiths: the sense of community, man's yearning to transcend himself, a profound communion with the universe and the rest of mankind. Religion had always set out to reconcile men with their lives and give them a sense of the meaning of existence: this, and not metaphysical explanation, was its chief function. The old myths had collapsed, but men still sought to find a meaning in life; socialism opened up dazzling prospects and was able to inspire feelings of unity and enthusiasm that deserved to be called religious. Marx was not only a scholar, but equally a religious prophet. In socialist religion God was replaced by humanity, a superior creation in which the individual could find an object of love and worship: he could thus rise above his insignificant ego and experience the joy of sacrificing his own interest to the infinite increase of collective Being. Man's affective identification with humanity would liberate him from the fear of suffering and death, restore his dignity and spiritual strength, and enhance his creative abilities. The new faith was a premonition of the great harmony of the future: individual mortality was cancelled by collective immortality, and human actions thus acquired a meaning. The true creator of God was the proletariat, and its revolution was the fundamental act of God-building.

All this Promethean rhetoric and deification of humanity, with its stress on a future harmony as a surrogate of transcendence for the individual, was in effect a repetition of Feuerbach's philosophy, with anthropology considered as 'the secret' of theology. It added nothing to Marxist philosophy, and was merely an attempt to give emotional colour to 'scientific socialism'. As in Feuerbach, the words 'religion' and 'religious feeling' were used as mere ornaments and were unrelated to any actual religious tradition. 'God-building' was an attempt to assimilate the neo-Romantic vocabulary and to channel the religious inclinations of the intelligentsia, and religious emotion generally, into the service of socialism. Plekhanov and Lenin, however, condemned it as a dangerous flirtation with 'religious obscurantism', and after the Revolution Lunacharsky dropped the 'new style' and reverted to the traditional language of atheism. Thereafter 'God-building' had no discernible influence on Marxist ideology.

7. *Lenin's excursion into philosophy*

While the Russian empiriocritics mostly considered themselves Marxists, they did not conceal their contempt for the naïve and uncritical 'common-sense' philosophy of Engels and Plekhanov. In a letter of 25 February 1908 to Gorky Lenin described the history of the dispute with Bogdanov and his allies: he wrote that in 1903 Plekhanov had spoken to him of Bogdanov's errors but had not thought them particularly dangerous. During the 1905 Revolution he (Lenin) and Bogdanov had tacitly ruled out philosophy as a neutral field. In 1906, however, Lenin had read the third volume of *Empiriomonism* and been intensely irritated by it; he sent some lengthy critical remarks to Bogdanov which, however, have not survived. When *Essays on the Philosophy of Marxism* appeared in 1908, Lenin's exasperation knew no bounds.

Every article made me furiously indignant. No, no, this is not Marxism! Our empirio-critics, empirio-monists and empirio-symbolists are floundering in a bog. To try to persuade the reader that 'belief' in the reality of the external world is 'mysticism' (Bazarov); to confuse in the most disgraceful manner materialism with Kantianism (Bazarov and Bogdanov); to preach a variety of agnosticism (empirio-criticism) and idealism (empirio-monism); to teach the workers 'religious atheism' and 'worship' of the highest human potentials (Lunacharsky); to declare Engels's teaching on dialectics to be mysticism (Berman); to draw from the stinking well of some French 'positivists' or other, of agnostics or metaphysicians, the devil take them, with their 'symbolic theory of cognition' (Yushkevich)! No, really, it's too much. To be sure, we ordinary Marxists are not well up in philosophy, but why insult us by serving this stuff up to us as the philosophy of Marxism! (*Works*, vol. 13, p. 450)

Plekhanov, who had been directly attacked by the empirio-critics, was the first in the orthodox camp to cross swords with them in defence of Engels's traditional materialism; he denounced their philosophy as 'subjective idealism', treating the whole universe as the creation of the perceiving subject. When splits occurred in the party Plekhanov—with some reason, given the situation of the Bolshevik intelligentsia—associated in his attack the Bolshevism of his opponents with their idealist doctrine. He maintained that Russian empiriocriticism was a philosophic attempt to justify Bolshevik 'Blanquism', a policy which flouted Marxist theory by seeking to hasten social development by violent means instead of letting it happen naturally. Bolshevik voluntarism was of a piece with the voluntaristic epistemology which regarded knowledge as an act of subjective organization and not an account of things as they existed independently of the human mind. Empiriocriticism, Plekhanov claimed, was contrary to the realism and determinism of Marxist doctrine in the same way as Bolshevik policy was contrary to Marxist historical determinism.

In defending his realist position against the Machists Plekhanov went so far as to admit that human perceptions were not 'copies' of objects but were signs of hieroglyphics. Lenin was not slow to reproach him for this, describing it as an inadmissible concession to 'agnosticism'.

Lyubov Akselrod ('Orthodox') also took up the cudgels on Engels's behalf in an article against Bogdanov published in 1904, in which she said that Lenin had encouraged her to write it eighteen months earlier. Conscious (as she said) of her duty to the party, she argued that Mach and Bogdanov treated objects as collections of impressions, thus making mind the creator of nature, in direct opposition to Marxism. This subjective idealism, which defined society by its consciousness, would lead 'with remorseless consistency' to social conservatism. As Marx had shown, the dominant consciousness was that of the ruling class, and consequently 'subjectivism' meant perpetuating the existing society and giving up thoughts of the future as idle and utopian.

In *Philosophical Essays* (1906) Lyubov Akselrod attacked not only Bogdanov but also Berdyayev, Struve, the Kantians, and philosophic idealism in general. The book contains almost everything that Lenin later wrote in his rebuttal of empirio-criticism; it is more concise than Lenin, but equally crude in tenor. Two main arguments are advanced in support of the view that the external world is 'reflected' in our perceptions or 'corresponds' to them. In the first place, we distinguish true and false perceptions, delusions and 'correct' observations, and we could not do this if reality and our sensations were one and the same. Secondly, everyone knows that things are not in our heads, but outside them. Kant's philosophy was a compromise between materialism and idealism: he preserved the concept of an external world, but under pressure from theology and mysticism he described that world as unknowable. The compromise, however, will not work: our knowledge has its source either in consciousness or in matter, there is no third possibility. Matter cannot be defined, for it is 'primal fact', the 'essence of all things', the 'beginning and sole cause of all phenomena', the 'original substance', etc. Matter is 'given in experience' and can be known by sensual perception. Idealism asserts that there is no object without a subject, but science has shown that the earth existed before man, so consciousness must be the product of nature and not a condition of it. All our knowledge, including mathematical knowledge, comes from experience, which consists of the 'reflection' of external bodies in our minds. To claim, as Mach does, that the world is man's creation is to make science impossible, for science presupposes an external world as the object of its study. Idealism leads to reactionary conclusions in politics. Mach and Avenarius regard man as the measure of the universe, and 'this subjective theory is of great objective value: it is easy to prove by it that the poor are rich and the rich poor, as everything depends on subjective experience' (*Philosophical Essays*, p. 92). Subjective idealism also leads infallibly to solipsism, since if everything is in 'my' imagination there is no ground for belief in the existence of other subjects. This is the philosophy of primitive man: the savage believes, literally, in everything that comes into his head, confusing dreams with reality, false perceptions with true ones, and thought with actual being, in the same manner as Berkeley, Mach, Struve, and Bogdanov.

In the same work Lyubov Akselrod defends determinism against Stammler, who objected that it was inconsistent to believe both in historical determinism and in revolutionary will-power. On this point too she echoes Plekhanov's counter-argument: it is human beings who make history, but their acts and the effectiveness of their intentions depend on circumstances outside their control. There is no difference between natural and historical necessity or, therefore, between the methods of the natural and social sciences. Bourgeois ideologists claim that only the present is real: in so doing they express the fears of a class that history has doomed to destruction, but to Marxists the future is 'real' in that it can be foreseen in the light of historical laws.

It should be added that Lyubov Akselrod and Plekhanov both indicate that the term 'reflection' should not be taken literally. Sensations are not 'copies' of things in the same sense as mirror-images, but in the sense that their content depends on the objects that produce them.

Lenin evidently thought that Plekhanov and 'Orthodox' had not refuted empiriocriticism as thoroughly as it deserved, and he therefore entered the fray himself although conscious that his philosophical education was fairly rudimentary. He spent most of 1908 working on the subject, including several months in London, where he studied at the British Museum. The result was published in Moscow in 1909 in the form of a book entitled *Materialism and Empiriocriticism: Critical Comments on a Reactionary Philosophy*.

In attacking empiriocriticism Lenin was not especially concerned with the objections of various philosophers to the doctrine on grounds of internal consistency. His object was to show that it did not succeed in avoiding the 'basic problem of philosophy', that of the priority of mind over matter or vice versa, but was a piece of verbal jugglery concealing out-and-out Berkeleyan idealism, and was therefore calculated to uphold religious spiritualism and the interests of the exploiting classes.

Lenin's argument is based on the principle of 'partisanship' (*partiinost'*) in philosophy. He uses this term in two different senses. In the first place it means that there can be no middle position between materialism and idealism as Engels defined these, and that philosophers who claim to have transcended the opposition are merely disingenuous idealists. Moreover, all the main questions of philosophy are ancillary to this one. Whether the world is knowable, whether determinism holds true, what are the criteria of truth and the significance of time and space— all these questions are special instances or an extension of the 'basic problem': any answer given to them is either materialistic or idealistic in tendency, and the choice between the two cannot be avoided.

Secondly, 'partisanship' means to Lenin that philosophical theories are not neutral in the class struggle but are instruments of it. Every philosophy is in the service of some class-interest, and in a society torn by the class struggle this cannot be otherwise, whatever the intentions of the philosophers themselves. It is no more possible to be a non-party man in philosophy than in direct political action: 'non-partisans in philosophy are just as hopelessly thick-headed as they are in politics' (*Materialism and Empiriocriticism* v. 5; *Works*, vol. 14, p. 286). 'Non-partisanship in philosophy is only wretchedly masked servility to idealism and fideism' (vi. 5; ibid., p. 355). Only materialism can serve the interests of the working class, and idealist doctrines are instruments of the exploiters.

Lenin does not discuss the relations between these two meanings of 'partisanship', nor does he consider whether the association of philosophies and classes can be projected into the past: for example, did the materialist Hobbes and the plebeian Christian sectaries represent the ideology of the oppressed classes and of property-owners respectively? He confines himself to arguing that at the present time the basic social antagonism between the proletariat and the bourgeoisie corresponds to the division of philosophers into the materialist and the idealist camp. The connection of idealism with political reaction is most clearly shown by the fact, which Lenin regards as obvious, that all forms of idealism and, particularly, epistemological subjectivism are buttresses of religious faith, either in practice or as a matter of logical consistency. It was hard for Lenin to corroborate this charge against the empiriocritics, who on the basis of their own philosophy attacked all forms of religious faith; Berkeley, however, was an easier target, as he held that belief in the reality of matter, which his theory denied, was the chief support of atheism. Anyway, said Lenin, the disputes among idealists were of trifling importance: there was no basic difference between Berkeley, Hume, Fichte, the empiriocritics, and Christian theologians. The attacks of Catholic philosophers on subjective idealism were mere family quarrels; similarly, the empiriocritics' opposition to religion was a fraud intended to lull the vigilance of the proletariat and lead it by different paths in the same direction as religious mythology. 'The subtle epistemological crotchets of a man like Avenarius remain a professorial invention, an attempt to form a small philosophical sect "of his own"; but, as a matter of fact, in the general circumstances of the struggle of ideas and trends in modern society, the objective part played by these epistemological artifices is in every case the same, namely to clear the way for idealism and fideism, and to serve them faithfully' (vi. 4; ibid., p. 341).

It was easy to see, therefore, that the empiriocritics were deceiving their naïve readers when they claimed to construct a picture of the world in which the elements of experience were ontologically neutral, neither 'psychical' nor 'physical'.

Mach and Avenarius, who differed in nothing but their fraudulent terminology, and their brother-philosophers in Germany, Britain, and Russia purported to reduce the world to a collection of impressions, so that 'material reality' became merely the product of consciousness. If they had consistently followed out their theory they would have ended up in the absurdity of solipsism, regarding the whole world as the creation of an individual subject. If they did not state this conclusion it was because they desired to mislead the reader or feared to reveal the emptiness of their own doctrine. In any case they were lackeys of the clergy and unintelligible word-spinners, out to deceive the simple-minded and confuse the true philosophical issue, while the bourgeoisie took advantage of the people's bewilderment to maintain itself in power. 'Every one of us knows what is physical and what is mental, but none of us knows at present what that "third" is. Avenarius was merely covering up his tracks by this subterfuge, while *in fact* declaring that the self is the primary (central term) and nature (environment) the secondary (counter-term)' (iii. 1; ibid., p. 147).

But, Lenin continues, science enables us to refute this idealist nonsense. No educated person doubts that the earth existed before the appearance of mankind. But the idealist cannot admit this, for on his own premises he must hold that the earth and the whole physical world is a figment of the human mind. Contrary to the plain facts of science, he must argue that man came first and nature second. Moreover, we know that man thinks with his brain, which is a physical object; but the idealist cannot admit this either, since he regards all physical objects as the product of thought. It is clear, therefore, that idealism contradicts the most elementary scientific knowledge and is contrary to all progress, whether social or intellectual.

Having thus demolished idealism Lenin opposes to it the philosophy of the militant proletariat, i.e. dialectical materialism. A fundamental part of this is the theory of reflections or images, according to which sensations, abstract ideas, and all other aspects of human cognition are the reflection in our minds of actual qualities of the material world, which exists whether or not it is perceived by anyone. 'Matter is a philosophical category denoting the objective reality which is given to man by his sensations, and which is copied, reflected and photographed by our sensations while existing independently of them' (ii. 4; ibid., p. 130). As Lenin repeats again and again, it is literally a question of 'copying': our sensations are images of things, not merely effects or, as Plekhanov would have it, 'symbols'. 'Engels speaks neither of symbols nor of hieroglyphs, but of copies, photographs, images, mirror-reflections of things' (iv. 6; ibid., p. 232). Sensations are not a screen between us and the world but a link with it, a subjective imitation of it.

Dialectical materialism does not claim to solve the physical problems concerning the structure of matter, but that is not its business. It can accept all that physics tells us, 'for the sole property of matter with whose recognition philosophical materialism is bound up is the property of being an objective reality, of existing outside the mind' (v. 2; ibid., pp. 260–1).

On this last point Lenin is inconsistent, for he himself confidently answers various questions of physics: for example, he says that it is reactionary nonsense to claim that there can be more than three dimensions, and all forms of indeterminism are likewise nonsensical. As to matter being defined simply by its property of 'existing outside the mind', this was later a subject of dispute among Leninists, as it suggested that matter must be characterized by its relation to the experiencing subject, so that mind enters into the concept of matter as its correlative; in the same way Lenin uses 'objective' to mean 'independent of mind'. Elsewhere he says, following Lyubov Akselrod, that matter cannot be defined, as it is the broadest category of all and therefore cannot be expressed in particular terms; he does not attempt to reconcile this with the statement quoted above.

An essential part of the theory of reflection is the rejection of relativism and acceptance of the traditional idea of truth as conformity to reality. Truth, says Lenin, can be predicated of sensations, concepts, and judgements. We can say of any product of cognitive activity that it is true or false, i.e. a right or wrong 'reflection' of reality; that it presents the world as it is 'in itself', independent of our knowledge, or that it gives a distorted picture of the world. But the objectivity of truth does not conflict with its relativity, as Engels showed. The relativity of truth does not mean, as, for example, pragmatists argue, that the same judgement is true or false according to who pronounces it and in what circumstances, and what benefit accrues from assenting to it at the time. Science, as Engels pointed out, can never tell us with absolute certainty the limits within which its laws are valid, and consequently they are all liable to revision. This, however, does not change truth into falsehood or vice versa, but merely signifies that what was thought to be universally valid applies only in certain conditions. No truths are ultimately verified, and in that sense all are relative. All knowledge, too, is relative in the sense that we can never know all about the universe and that although our knowledge continues to expand it remains incomplete. But these reservations do not affect the concept of truth as conformity to reality. As Engels also said, the most effective criterion of truth, i.e. the best way to find out whether a judgement is true, is to put it to the test of practice. If we can apply to practical manipulations the discoveries we have made concerning natural relationships, the success of our actions will confirm that our judgements were the right ones, and failure will prove the opposite. The practical criterion can be applied equally in natural science and in social science, where our analysis of reality is confirmed if the political actions based on it are effective. This effectiveness is not 'utility' in the pragmatist sense: our knowledge is potentially useful because it is true, it is not true because it is useful. Marxist theory, in particular, has been signally confirmed by practice: the successes of the workers' movement based on it are the best proof of its validity.

Once we have recognized the objective nature of truth, the empiriocritical principle of 'economy of thought' is seen to be an idealist subterfuge, purporting to replace conformity with reality by an ill-defined criterion consisting in the economy of effort.

It is also clear that the empiriocritics' objections to Kant's philosophy are aimed 'from the right', i.e. from a more reactionary position than his. They challenge the distinction between the phenomenon and the noumenon, but they do so in order to show that the 'thing in itself' is superfluous, i.e. there is no reality independent of mind. Materialists, however, criticize Kant from the opposite point of view—not for recognizing that there is a world beyond phenomena, but for holding that we can know nothing about it. There is no difference, they contend, between the phenomenon and the thing in itself, inasmuch as there is no reality that cannot in principle be known; they condemn Kant's agnosticism, while recognizing the 'materialist element' in his idea of the reality of the world. From the materialist point of view reality may be divided into the known and the not yet known, but not into phenomena that can be known and 'things in themselves' that cannot.

As regards such categories as space, time, and causality, Lenin follows Engels's interpretation. Dialectical materialism does not regard causality as a functional dependence, but there is a true necessity in the relations between events. Practice is the best confirmation of the real necessity of the causal connection: whenever we observe a regular sequence of events and are able thereby to produce a desired consequence, we demonstrate that the cause-and-effect relation is not the work of our imagination but a real quality of the physical world. Such connections must, however, be understood dialectically: in cases where types of events and not merely single events are involved there is always a mutual interaction, though one element retains its primacy (not defined more closely) over the other. Time and space are neither the product of an organizing perceptual force, nor *a priori* forms of sensibility, nor antonomous entities independent of matter; they are objective qualities of physical being. Thus the relations of succession in time and arrangement in space are real properties of the world, but do not possess the status of independent metaphysical entities.

Lenin holds that dialectical materialism as expounded by him is not only an effective weapon in the practical sense but is also the only philosophy consistent with the present state of natural and social science. It is because the physicists themselves do not understand this that science is, or appears to be, in a crisis. 'Modern physics is in travail: it is giving birth to dialectical materialism' (v. 8; ibid., p. 313). Scientists must realize that dialectical materialism is the only way out of the trouble they have got into through ignorance of Marx and Engels. It will soon triumph even though some scientists oppose it, the reason for their attitude being that most of them are servants of the bourgeoisie, though they have achieved great things in specialized fields.

Lenin's book is of interest not for its own merits but for its influence on the development of philosophy in Russia. As philosophy it is crude and amateurish, based on vulgar 'common-sense' arguments eked out by quotations from Engels (only two sentences by Marx are quoted in the whole book) and unbridled abuse of Lenin's opponents. It shows complete failure to understand their point of view, and reluctance to make the effort to do so. It adds hardly anything to what is contained in the passages quoted from Engels and Plekhanov, the main difference being that Engels has a sense of humour and Lenin none. He makes up for it with cheap mockery and invective, decrying his adversaries as reactionary madmen and lackeys of the clergy. Engels's arguments are vulgarized and turned into cut-and-dried catechetical forms: sensations are 'copies' or 'mirror-reflections' of things, philosophical schools become 'parties', etc. The exasperation which pervades the book is typical of a primitive thinker who cannot understand how anyone of sound mind can seriously maintain (as Lenin supposes) that by the power of his own imagination he has created the earth, the stars, and the whole physical universe, or that the objects he is looking at are in his head when any child can see that they are not. In this respect Lenin's battle with idealism is similar to that of certain unsophisticated Christian apologists.

Lenin's attacks were answered by Bogdanov, Bazarov, and Yushkevich: the latter, in *Pillars of Philosophical Orthodoxy* (1910), attacked Plekhanov as a flat-footed ignoramus who had no more idea of philosophy than a gendarme. Both Plekhanov and Lenin, he declared, exemplified the decadence of Russian Marxism by their dogmatic self-assertion and inability to understand anyone's views but their own. Yushkevich was especially severe on Lenin's ignorance, his inability to write, and the coarseness of his language: he accused him of factual errors, of 'bringing the habits of the Black Hundred into Marxism', of not having read the books he quoted, etc. The definition of matter by its power to cause sensations was itself a capitulation to Machism—this applied to Plekhanov, and to Lenin who had copied from him. Neither Mach nor Berkeley had questioned the 'existence of the world': the question at issue was not its existence but the validity of categories like substance, matter, and spirit. The empiriocritics, said Yushkevich, had achieved a Copernican revolution by abolishing the dualism of mind and matter; they had changed nothing in man's natural relation to the world but, on the contrary, restored the spontaneous value of realism by freeing it from metaphysical fetishes. Lenin in fact confused epistemological realism with materialism (he repeats several times that materialism consists of recognizing 'objective material reality', 'independent of the subject'—but if so, nearly every Catholic philosopher is a materialist). The whole theory of 'reflection' was a repetition of the naïve pre-Democritean belief in images that detach themselves mysteriously from the object and strike upon one's eye or ear. No one can say what the 'similarity' is supposed to be between the 'thing in itself' and a purely subjective image of it, or how the copy can be compared with the original.

Materialism and Empiriocriticism had no particular influence before the Revolution or directly after it (though a second edition appeared in 1920). Later it was proclaimed by Stalin to be a fundamental epitome of Marxist philosophy, and for about fifteen years, together with a short work by Stalin himself, it was the chief source of philosophical learning in the Soviet Union. Slight as its value was, it represented one of the last points of contact between orthodox Leninist Marxism and European philosophy. In later decades there was virtually no contact, even in the form of polemics, between Leninism and non-Marxist thought. The official Soviet criticism of 'bourgeois philosophy' took for granted that the latter in its various forms was a repetition of the idealist nonsense of Mach and Avenarius, which had been annihilated by Lenin's refutation.

The importance of Lenin's book, however, must be seen in the political context. It does not appear that when writing it he had any intention of 'enriching', supplementing, or—Heaven forbid —reforming Marxism. He was not in search of answers to any philosophical questions, for all the important ones had been solved by Marx and Engels; in his preface he mocks at Lunacharsky for saying 'Perhaps we have gone astray, but we are seeking.' Lenin was not seeking. He believed firmly that the revolutionary movement must have a clear-cut, uniform *Weltanschauung*, and that any pluralism in this respect was a grave political danger. He also believed that idealism of any kind was a more or less disguised form of religion, which was invariably used by exploiters to delude and stupefy the masses.

8. Lenin and religion

Lenin regarded religion as a key issue in the party's ideological activity, since the adversary was a mass phenomenon and not merely a group of theoreticians like the empiriocritics. His own attitude towards it was absolutely clear as a matter of philosophy, but his tactics were relatively flexible and changeable.

Lenin was brought up in an unbigoted religious atmosphere; he lost his faith at the age of fifteen or sixteen, before he had any contact with Marxism. From then on he took atheism for granted as scientifically self-evident, and at no time argued the case for it on merits. The problems of religion, in his view, presented no substantive difficulties but were matters of education, politics, and propaganda. In 'Socialism and Religion' (1905; *Works*, vol. 10) and some later writings he argues that religious beliefs are an expression of the impotence of the oppressed and poverty-stricken masses, an imaginary compensation for their sufferings—'spiritual booze', as he puts it (p. 83), coarsening in his usual way the language of Marx and Engels. At the same time religion and the Churches were a means of keeping the masses humble and submissive, an 'ideological knout' to keep the exploiters in power and the masses in a state of misery. The Orthodox Church was a glaring example of the conjunction of spiritual and political oppression. Lenin also laid stress on the need to exploit the repressive attitude of the regime towards religious sectarians. The party programme spoke from the outset of religious tolerance, the right of the individual to profess any faith he chose, and also the right to carry on atheistic propaganda; Church and State were to be separated, and the public teaching of religion abolished. But, unlike many Western social democrats, Lenin emphasized that while socialists might regard religion as a private matter *vis-à-vis* the state, it was not private so far as the party was concerned. In present conditions the party must tolerate believers in its midst (atheism did not figure expressly in its programme), but it was committed to carrying on anti-religious propaganda and educating its members to be militant atheists. The party could not be philosophically neutral: it was materialistic, therefore atheistic and anti-clerical, and this world-outlook could not be a matter of political indifference. However, anti-religious propaganda must be linked with the class struggle and not treated as an end in itself in the spirit of 'bourgeois free thought'.

Whatever his tactical concessions, Lenin was on political grounds an implacable opponent of religious belief. Hence the violence of his attack on the empiriocritics, whose philosophy coincided in part with that of the 'God-builders'. The latter were only trying to add rhetorical and sentimental trimmings to Marxism, but in Lenin's eyes they were engaged in a perilous compromise with religion. In his main philosophical work, in letters to Gorky, and on other occasions he argued that religion stripped of its cruder superstitions and using the language of social progress was even more dangerous than the besotted Orthodox Church which brutally proclaimed its union with Tsarist despotism. Religion in a humanist disguise was all the better able to conceal its class content and delude the unwary. Thus, while Lenin was prepared to compromise with believers on tactical grounds, his mind was firmly made up on the question of substance and he refused to admit any suggestion that the party's world-view could leave any room whatsoever for religious faith.

Lenin's position in these matters was in accordance with the Russian free-thinking tradition. The link between the Orthodox Church and the Tsarist bureaucracy was manifest. When the Soviet government came to power, most, though not all, church-men were hostile to it. Owing to this and to the basic principles of Leninism, the fight against the Church soon took on wider dimensions than those indicated in the party's programmes. The government did not confine itself to expropriating Church estates and secularizing schools, measures which in any case were regarded as bourgeois reforms and not specifically socialist. The Church was in practice deprived of all public functions and prevented from teaching, publishing books and periodicals, and educating the clergy; monasteries and convents were for the most part dissolved. The treatment of religion as a private affair *vis-à-vis* the state could not apply in a one-party system in which party membership was, in the vast majority of cases, a precondition of state service. Persecution of the Church and the faithful varied in intensity according to political circumstances— it was much relaxed, for instance, during the war of 1941–5—

but the principle that the socialist state must strive in every way to eradicate 'religious prejudices' has remained in force and is wholly in accordance with Lenin's doctrine. The separation of Church and State is only workable when the state is ideologically neutral and does not, as such, profess any particular world-view. The Soviet state, regarding itself as the organ of the proletariat and atheism as an essential feature of the one and only proletarian ideology, can no more accept the principle of disestablishment than, say, the Vatican with its similarly built-in ideology. Lenin and the other Marxists always held that there was no difference in this respect between a proletarian and a bourgeois state, both of which were bound to support a philosophy that represented the interests of the ruling class. But for this very reason the separation of Church and State, which Lenin used as a battle-cry against the Tsardom, was contrary to his theory of the relations between ideology, classes, and the state and could not be maintained after the Bolsheviks seized power. On the other hand, the nature and scale of anti-religious measures was of course not prescribed by the doctrine and varied according to circumstances.

9. Lenin's dialectical Notebooks

Apart from occasional passages in articles and speeches, Lenin wrote nothing further on purely philosophical subjects. (His article of 1921 on 'The Significance of Militant Materialism' is in the nature of a propaganda directive; that of 1913 on 'The Three Sources and Three Component Parts of Marxism' is a popular exposition and has no claim to originality.) However, there appeared posthumously in the Soviet Union a volume entitled *Philosophical Notebooks* (*Works*, vol. 38) consisting of extracts made by Lenin from various works and manuals, chiefly in 1914–15, together with approving or exasperated comments and some philosophical observations of his own. In certain cases it is not clear whether the notes are summaries of what he has read or represent his own position. The book is of interest inasmuch as the principal notes are concerned with the dialectic and to some extent tone down the crude formulas of *Materialism and Empiriocriticism*. They show, in particular, the influence of Lenin's wartime reading of Hegel's *Logic* and *Lectures on the Philosophy of History*. These convinced him that the Hegelian dialectic was of great importance in the development of Marxism: he even wrote that *Capital* could not be understood without a thorough study of Hegel's *Logic*, and added with irreproachable consistency: 'So, after half a century, no Marxist has yet understood Marx.' This *boutade* should not be taken literally, for it is hard to believe that Lenin did not think he himself had understood Marx until 1915, but it shows to what extent he was fascinated by Hegel's speculation.

As the *Notebooks* show, Lenin was most interested by the question of 'universality' and 'individuality' in Hegel's logic and by the dialectic considered as a theory of the 'unity and conflict of opposites.' He sought to discover in Hegel's dialectic the themes which could be taken over and used by Marxism after the transposition to a materialist basis. As to the question of abstraction and the relation between direct perception and 'universal' knowledge, Lenin emphasized everything in Hegel that was opposed to Kant's doctrine (for example, that the 'thing in itself' was completely indefinite and was therefore nothing) and pointed out the autonomous cognitive function of abstract thinking: according to Lenin logic, dialectic, and the theory of knowledge were all the same thing. Whereas *Materialism and Empiriocriticism* concentrated on combating the subjective interpretation of sensations and seemed content to regard them as the source of all knowledge of the world, the *Notebooks* raise the question of abstractions that are contained in perception itself and introduce unending 'contradictions' into the cognitive process. Laws, and hence 'universality', are already contained in the particular phenomenon, and similarly the individual perception contains 'universal' elements, i.e. acts of abstraction. Nature is thus both concrete and abstract; things are what they are only in terms of conceptual knowledge, which apprehends them in their general regularity. The concrete cannot be grasped in its full concreteness by a particular act of perception. On the contrary, it reproduces itself only through an infinite number of concepts and general laws, so that it is never exhausted by cognition. Even the simplest phenomenon reveals the complexity of the world and the interdependence of all its components; but because all phenomena are thus interconnected, human knowledge is necessarily incomplete and fragmentary. In order to apprehend the concrete in all its particularity we should have to have absolute and universal knowledge of all the connections between phenomena. Every 'reflection' of the world suffers from internal contradictions which, as knowledge progresses, disappear and are replaced by new contradictions. The reflection is not 'dead' or 'inert', but by its fragmentary nature and contradictions gives rise to the increase of knowledge, which continues indefinitely but never reaches absolute finality. Thus truth manifests itself only as the process of the resolution of contradictions.

Since there is always a certain tension or 'contradiction' between the particular and the abstract components of knowledge, it is always possible in the cognitive process to absolutize the latter at the expense of the former, i.e. to think in idealist terms. Along with Lenin's emphasis on the 'universal' aspects of the 'reflection' (which is contrary to the description of it in his main philosophical work), this idea is a second important departure from the rough-and-ready interpretation of idealism as a fraud invented by the clergy and the bourgeoisie. Idealism, it now appears, has 'gnoseological sources': it is not just a mental aberration, but the absolutization or one-sided development of a real aspect of cognition. Lenin even remarks that wise idealism is closer to wise materialism than is foolish materialism.

The second important subject of the *Notebooks* is the 'conflict and unity of opposites'. The whole of the dialectic, Lenin claims, can be defined as the science of the unity of opposites. Among the sixteen 'elements of the dialectic' which he enumerates, the conflict of opposites appears in various forms as the main motif. Every single thing is the sum and unity of opposites, every property of things turns into its opposite; content 'conflicts' with form, features of lower stages of development are reproduced in higher ones by the 'negation of the negation', etc.

All these ideas are expressed in very brief and general terms and are therefore not suited to over-precise analysis. Lenin does not inquire how 'contradiction', a logical relationship, can be a property of objects themselves; nor does he explain how the introduction of abstractions into the content of perception fits into the theory of 'reflections'. It can be seen, however, that like Engels he regarded the dialectic as a universal method that could be expounded, irrespective of object, as a generalized 'logic of the world', and that he treated Hegel's logic as the raw material of a materialistic transformation. However, his remarks in general suggest an interpretation of Hegelianism that is less simplified than Engels's. The dialectic is not merely an assertion that 'everything changes', but an attempt to interpret human knowledge as a perpetual interplay between subject and object, in which the question of the 'absolute primacy' of either loses its sharpness.

The *Notebooks* were published mainly to serve the party in its critique of mechanistic materialism. While party philosophers used *Materialism and Empiriocriticism* to combat all doctrines suspected of idealism, they quoted the *Notebooks* to emphasize the difference between Marxism and mechanicism, especially in the campaign against Bukharin and his followers in the 1930s. There was of course no question of admitting that the two texts were in any way inconsistent with each other. Later, when the teaching of dialectical materialism in the Soviet Union departed from the schema laid down by Stalin, the *Notebooks* were used as the new basis and the sixteen 'elements' took the place of Stalin's 'four main features of the dialectic'. However, *Materialism and Empiriocriticism* is still revered as the philosophical foundation of Leninism, a status conferred on it by Stalin. It has had a deplorable effect in furnishing pretexts for the stifling of all independent philosophical thought and in establishing the party's dictatorship over science and culture in every sphere.

As Valentinov and others pointed out, the extreme obstinacy with which Lenin defended materialism was rooted not only in Marxism but in the tradition of the Russian materialists, especially Chernyshevsky, whose philosophy was a popularization of Feuerbach. Comment on these lines was also heard in the Soviet Union in the 1950s, but was condemned as it suggested that Leninism was a specifically Russian philosophy and not the infallible, universally valid continuation of Marxism.

Apart from the question of the influence of Russian sources, it is clear that Lenin's philosophy was closely linked with his political programme and the idea of a revolutionary party, and that he himself was fully aware of this. A party of professionals in which all theoretical questions were strictly subordinated to the struggle for power could not safely countenance philosophic pluralism or be neutral in ideological questions. For the sake of its own success it must possess a clearly defined doctrine or body of inexpugnable dogma, binding upon its members. Party discipline and cohesion demanded that any risk of laxity, vagueness, or pluralism in theoretical matters should be eliminated. That the ruling ideology must be strictly materialist was ensured by Marxist tradition and by the need to combat religious thought in all its forms as an obstacle to revolution, as well as to avoid an ontologically neutral philosophy. Lenin castigated, in friend and foe alike, any tendency to compromise even verbally with religion, or to side-step ontological questions on the ground that they were wrongly formulated or insoluble. Marxism, he believed, was a ready-made answer to all the major questions of philosophy and admitted of no doubts. Any attempt to shelve philosophical questions was a threat to the party's ideological unity. Thus his coarse, uncompromising materialism was not only the effect of a particular tradition but was part and parcel of his technique for action. The party must have the sole right to decide all ideological questions, and from this point of view Lenin well understood the danger that idealism presented to his political programme. The idea of totalitarian power, embracing every aspect of cultural life, was gradually taking shape in his mind and was eventually put into practice; it was well served by his philosophy, which was not concerned with investigating and solving problems but with imposing a dogmatic intellectual system on the socialist movement. In this way the fury of his philosophical attacks and lack of interest in others' arguments had their roots in his political doctrine.

Even for Leninists, however, *Materialism and Empiriocriticism* was ambiguous on two important points. Firstly, as already mentioned, Lenin held, unlike Engels and Plekhanov, that 'objectivity', i.e. independence of the subject, was the only attribute of matter that materialists as such were bound to recognize. This statement was evidently designed to free Marxist philosophy from any dependence on changing scientific theories, especially in physics: as 'matter' suffered no harm from any attributes that science might bestow or take away from it, science presented no danger to materialism. But this gain was achieved by emptying 'matter' of all content. If matter is defined simply by the fact of being something other than the perceiving subject, it is clear that this can equally be said of any 'substance' that is regarded as differing from the content of perception. 'Matter' becomes simply another term for 'everything', without implying any of the attributes—spatial, temporal, or dynamic—that we generally associate with 'materiality'. Secondly, this definition readmits the vague dualism that it purports to exclude. If everything 'outside' the subject is material, then either the subject itself is not material or we must extend the definition of matter to comprise subjective phenomena. The formula that 'matter is primary and mind secondary' appears to presuppose that mind and matter are different, and is thus contrary to materialist monism. Lenin's work does not answer these problems or deal with them consistently, and there is no point in trying to probe more closely: the obscurities of his text are not due so much to inherent philosophical difficulties as to Lenin's indolent and superficial approach and his contempt for all problems that could not be put to direct use in the struggle for power.

XVIII

The Fortunes of Leninism: from a Theory of the State to a State Ideology

1. The Bolsheviks and the War

THE years 1908–11 were a period of catastrophic decline and disintegration in the Russian social democratic movement. After the post-revolutionary repressions there was a temporary stabilization of the Tsarist regime, as civil liberties were considerably increased and attempts were made to base the weakened social structure on other foundations than the bureaucracy and the army. Stolypin, the Prime Minister, introduced reforms designed to create a strong class of peasantry with medium-sized holdings. These measures aroused the alarm of socialists, especially those of the Leninist persuasion, who realized that if the agrarian question could be solved under capitalism by means of reform, the revolutionary potential of the land-hungry masses would be irretrievably lost. In an article of 29 April 1908 entitled 'On the Beaten Track!' (*Works*, vol. 15, pp. 40 ff.) Lenin recognized that Stolypin's policy might succeed and might establish a 'Prussian road' of capitalist development in agriculture. If this happened, 'Marxists who are honest with themselves will straightforwardly and openly throw all "agrarian programmes" on the scrap-heap altogether, and will say to the masses: "The workers have done all they could to give Russia not a Junker but an American capitalism. The workers call you now to join in the social revolution of the proletariat, for after the solution of the agrarian question in the Stolypin spirit there can be no other revolution capable of making a serious change in the economic conditions of life of the peasant masses."

Stolypin's policy did not last long enough to bring about the hoped-for results, which might have completely altered the later course of events: Lenin wrote after 1917 that the Revolution could not have succeeded had the Bolsheviks not taken over the S.R. programme of confiscating the land and sharing it out to the peasants. Despite the assassination of Stolypin in 1911, for some years Russia was clearly moving in the direction of a bourgeois state with the rudiments of a constitutional monarchy. This development led to new divisions among the social democrats. In addition to the 'otzovists', i.e. those Bolsheviks who believed exclusively in illegal revolutionary action, Lenin at this time incessantly attacked the 'liquidators', a term more or less synonymous with the Mensheviks. He accused Martov, Potresov, Dan, and most of the other Menshevik leaders of wishing to liquidate the illegal party organization and replace it by a 'formless' legal assembly of workers, geared to a 'reformist' struggle within the existing order. The Mensheviks did not in fact wish to wind up the party's illegal activity, but they attached much more importance to peaceful methods and to the legal development of workers' organizations, hoping that when the autocracy was overthrown the social democrats would be in a similar position to their brothers in Western Europe. Meanwhile the old intra-party divisions continued to exist. The Mensheviks accepted the Austrian recipe for the national question ('ex-territorial autonomy'), while the Bolsheviks advocated self-determination including the right of secession. The Mensheviks maintained their links with the Bund and the Polish Socialists, both of which Lenin regarded as organs of bourgeois nationalism. However, Plekhanov, unlike most of the Menshevik leaders, was against the policy of the 'liquidators', and accordingly Lenin dropped his campaign of abuse and polemics against him and reverted to a kind of shaky alliance with the veteran of Russian socialism.

The various dissensions resulted in a new and final split in the party. In January 1912 the Bolshevik Conference at Prague declared itself to be a general party congress, elected its own Central Committee, and broke with the Mensheviks. Besides Lenin, Zinoviev, and Kamenev the Central Committee included Roman Malinovsky, the Okhrana agent, against whom Lenin was repeatedly warned by the Mensheviks: he called these warning 'the filthiest slander they could collect in the garbage heaps of the Black-Hundred newspapers' ('The Liquidators and

Malinovsky's Biography', May 1914; *Works*, vol. 20, p. 204).
Malinovsky was indeed an obedient executor of Lenin's orders,
as the Okhrana had instructed him to be, and he had no
ideological or political ambitions of his own. Shortly after the
Prague Conference Stalin was co-opted on to the Central
Committee at Lenin's instance, thus making his début in the field
of Russian social-democratic politics.

Lenin spent the last two years before the outbreak of war at
Cracow and the nearby resort of Poronin, whence it was easier
to maintain contact with the organization in Russia. The
Bolsheviks neglected no opportunity of legal action. From 1912
they published *Pravda* in St. Petersburg; the paper reappeared
after the February Revolution and has been the party daily ever
since. There were a few Bolshevik members of the Duma, who
co-operated with the Mensheviks until forbidden to do so by
Lenin.

The outbreak of war found Lenin at Poronin. Arrested by the
Austrian police, he was set free a few days later thanks to the
intervention of the PPS and the Vienna social democrats. He
then returned to Switzerland, where he remained until April
1917, fulminating against the 'opportunist traitors' who had
wrecked the International and working out directives for
revolutionary social democracy in the new situation. Lenin was
the first and only important leader of social democracy in Europe
to proclaim the slogan of revolutionary defeatism: the proletariat
in each country should endeavour to bring about the military
defeat of its own government so as to turn the imperialist war
into a civil war. Out of the ruins of the International, most
of whose leaders had gone over to the service of the imperialists,
there must be created a Communist International to direct the
revolutionary struggle of the proletariat.

These appeals might well have seemed idle dreams, as only
a handful of socialists were prepared to support them. Most
social democrats took the view that they should suspend the class
struggle and rally to the defence of their country. Among the
Russians who thought in this way was Plekhanov, who, while
continuing to profess himself a Marxist, whole-heartedly
accepted the patriotic viewpoint. This sharply put an end to the
truce between him and Lenin, and Plekhanov and Potresov were
once more decried as 'clowns' and lackeys of the reactionary

leader Purishkevich. Lenin took a similar view of all socialist leaders who based their attitude on the principle of national self-defence, such as Hyndman in Britain and Guesde and Hervé in France: naturally there were no 'aggressors' among the belligerent powers. By degrees, however, anti-war groups were formed in all countries, mostly by socialists who had formerly occupied a central position: Bernstein, Kautsky, and Ledebour in Germany, Ramsay MacDonald in Britain. Here too belonged most of the former Mensheviks, headed by Martov and Akselrod, and also Trotsky. For a time, despite their fundamental differences, Lenin's group sought to come to terms with these 'pacifists'. Owing principally to the efforts of Swiss and Italian socialists an international conference was held at Zimmerwald in September 1915 and adopted a compromise anti-war resolution. Zimmerwald was regarded for a while as the embryo of a new international movement, but after the Russian Revolution the divergences between the centre and the Zimmerwald Left proved stronger than the conflict between the pacifists and the 'social chauvinists', as the defenders of their country at any price were called. The Zimmerwald Left, consisting of seven out of the thirty-eight delegates, in addition to signing the general resolution issued one of their own, calling on socialists to resign from imperialist governments and found a new revolutionary International.

At an early stage Lenin attacked the anti-war, pacifist social democrats almost as fiercely as he did the 'social chauvinists'. His main objections were, firstly, that the centrists wanted peace through international arbitration and agreement, not by waging a revolutionary war against their own governments. This meant a return to the pre-war order and a quest for peace by 'bourgeois' methods. The centrists were evidently lackeys of the bourgeoisie, and they failed to see that the only way to stop imperialist war was by a revolution that would at least overthrow the three great continental empires. Secondly, the pacifists wanted 'peace without annexations or indemnities', by which they meant only to cancel wartime annexations, thus preserving the old empires with all their nationalist oppression. The revolutionary objective must be, however, to invalidate all annexations and secure the right of all peoples to self-determination and, if they so desired, to form their own national states. Lenin was on strong ground in condemning socialists who inveighed against annexation and oppression, but only when perpetrated by their national enemies. The Germans were full of indignation at the treatment of subject nationalities in Russia, but said nothing about conditions in the Reich and Austria-Hungary; Russian and French socialists demanded freedom for the subjects of the Central Powers, but kept quiet about those of the Tsar. Finally, although the pacifists condemned chauvinism in words they could not make up their minds to break with the opportunists once and for all, but dreamed of reuniting with them and resurrecting the corpse of the International. This point is especially important. As on the occasion of all previous disputes and splits within the party, Lenin showed equal ferocity against his opponents and against 'appeasers' in his own camp, who hesitated to break completely with the opposition and thus sacrificed their principles to a hankering for organizational unity. The centrists condemned Lenin's attitude as fanatical and sectarian, and it is true that on several occasions it appeared to have reduced him to the leadership of a helpless, isolated group. In the end, however, he was proved right inasmuch as no other tactics could have produced such a centralized, disciplined party as the Bolsheviks, and at the critical moment a more loosely organized party could not have mastered the situation and seized power.

During his last years outside Russia Lenin wrote what is perhaps the most generally known of his works: *Imperialism, the Highest Stage of Capitalism* (published at Petrograd, 1917). This pamphlet—the economic portions of which contain nothing that is not to be found in Lenin's main sources, Hobson and Hilferding —was intended to serve as a theoretical basis for the new tactics that were to dominate the revolutionary party. Stressing the worldwide character and uneven development of imperialism, Lenin laid the foundation for the tactics which were soon to become binding on Communist parties: the right course was to support any movement tending to overthrow the system at any point, for any reasons and in the interests of any class: liberation in colonial countries, national or peasant movements, bourgeois national uprisings against the big imperialists. This was a generalization of the tactics he had been preaching in Russia for years: to support all claims and all movements against the

Tsarist autocracy, so as to exploit their sources of energy and seize power at the critical moment. The victory of the Marxist party was the final aim, but it could not be achieved by the proletariat alone. Lenin soon came to the conclusion, in fact, that a revolution could not be carried out by the working class in its own name, without the support of other mass movements such as the nationalities or the peasants; in other words, a socialist revolution in the traditional Marxist sense was an impossibility. This discovery was the source of nearly all the successes of Leninism, and nearly all its failures.

The question of relations with the peasantry was at this time one of the main points of disagreement between Lenin and Trotsky. Up to the outbreak of war Trotsky lived chiefly in Vienna, where from 1908 onwards he edited his own journal *Pravda* (in 1912 he accused the Bolsheviks of stealing its title). He worked with the Mensheviks from time to time on various questions but did not join them, as he held different views of the coming revolution, prophesying that it would evolve into a socialist phase. He made repeated but unsuccessful efforts to restore party unity. From 1914 he belonged to the anti-war wing and joined Lenin in attacking 'social patriotism'; he also drafted the Zimmerwald Manifesto. Together with Martov he published a journal in Paris to which Lunacharsky and other leading social democratic intellectuals contributed. From the Second Congress until 1917, when he joined the Bolsheviks, he was the object of exceptional hostility on Lenin's part, whether or not they agreed on actual issues. Lenin described him, according to circumstances, as a noisy phrase-maker, a play-actor, an intriguer, a go-between, and a 'Yudushka' ('little Judas', a hypocritical character in Saltykov-Shchedrin's novel *The Golovlev Family*); he lost no opportunity of saying that Trotsky was a man without principle, dodging between one group and another and only caring that he should not be found out. In 1911 he wrote: 'It is impossible to argue with Trotsky on the merits of the issue, because Trotsky holds no views whatever. We can and should argue with confirmed liquidators and otzovists, but it is no use arguing with a man whose game is to hide the errors of both these trends; in his case the thing to do is to expose him as a diplomat of the smallest calibre' ('Trotsky's Diplomacy on a Certain Party Platform', 21 Dec. 1911; *Works*, vol. 17, p. 362).

In 1914 he repeated the same idea: 'Trotsky, however, has never had any "physiognomy" at all: the only thing he does have is a habit of changing sides, of skipping from the liberals to the Marxists and back again, of mouthing scraps of catchwords and bombastic parrot phrases' ('The Break-Up of the "August" Bloc', 15 Mar. 1914; *Works*, vol. 20, p. 160). As for 'Trotskyism' itself: 'From the Bolsheviks Trotsky's original theory has borrowed their call for a decisive proletarian revolutionary struggle and for the conquest of political power by the proletariat, while from the Mensheviks it has borrowed "repudiation" of the peasantry's role' ('On the Two Lines in the Revolution', 20 Nov. 1915; *Works*, vol. 21, p. 419).

Trotsky in fact shared Lenin's view that the party must be the guiding force in the revolutionary struggle and not an adjunct to the bourgeoisie. Like Lenin, he was against both liquidators and otzovists, and he foresaw, sooner than Lenin, the 'revolution in two stages'. However, he did not believe in the revolutionary potential of the peasantry, and he thought the proletariat would prevail in Russia thanks to a general European revolution.

2. *The Revolutions of 1917*

Although the various socialist groups lived in the expectation of a revolution, the outbreak in February 1917 took place without their aid and came as a surprise to all of them. Some weeks before, Trotsky had settled in the United States in the belief that he was leaving Europe for ever. Lenin, in January 1917, gave a lecture in Zurich on the 1905 Revolution which contained the words: 'We of the older generation may not live to see the decisive battles of this coming revolution' (*Works*, vol. 23, p. 253). If any party had anything directly to do with the February Revolution it was the Kadets (liberals) in concert with the Entente governments. Lenin himself observed that the capitalists of France and Britain as well as of Russia wished to prevent the Tsar concluding a separate peace with the German Emperor, and had therefore conspired to remove him from the throne. The conspiracy coincided with a revolt of the masses, made desperate by hunger, defeat, and economic chaos. The Romanov dynasty, which had stood for three hundred years, collapsed overnight, and it was clear that no serious elements in society had been prepared to defend it. For eight months, for the first and last time in its history, Russia enjoyed complete political freedom: not thanks to any legal order, but chiefly because no social force was in command of the situation. The Provisional Government established by the Duma shared uncertain authority with the Councils (Soviets) of Workers' and Soldiers' Deputies, formed in imitation of 1905, but neither was in proper control of the armed masses of the big cities. The Bolsheviks for the time being were a small minority in the Soviets, and all parties were completely confused as to the course the revolution was taking.

Lenin arrived in Petrograd in April: the Germans had given him a safe conduct, together with a few dozen repatriates of various political parties. His adversaries used the pretext to brand him as a German agent. Lenin accepted German aid not, of course, in order to help the Kaiser's war but in the hope that revolution would spread from Russia to the rest of Europe. In *Letters from Afar*, written just before he left Switzerland, he formulated his basic strategy. As the Russian revolution was a bourgeois one, the task of the proletariat was to unmask the deceit of the ruling classes, who could not give the people bread, peace, and freedom; the order of the day was to prepare the 'second stage' of the revolution, which would give power to the proletariat supported by the indigent, semi-proletarian part of the peasantry. These maxims were developed, immediately after his return to Russia, in the famous 'April Theses'. No support for the war or the Provisional Government; power for the proletariat and the poor peasants, replacement of the parliamentary republic by a republic of Soviets, abolition of the police, army, and bureaucracy, all officials to be elective and removable; confiscation of large estates, Soviet control over all social production and distribution, re-establishment of the International, and adoption by the party of the designation 'Communist'.

These slogans, with their clear demand for an immediate transition to the socialist phase of the revolution, were opposed not only by the Mensheviks, who saw them as a complete denial of the socialist tradition, but also by many Bolsheviks. Lenin's firmness, however, prevented all hesitation. At the same time he made it clear to his followers that the Provisional Government could not be overthrown at once, as it was supported by the Soviets. The Bolsheviks must first gain control of the Soviets and get a majority of the working masses on their side, convincing them that the imperialist war could only be ended by a dictatorship of the proletariat.

In July Lenin revoked the slogan 'All power to the Soviets', having decided that the Bolsheviks could not gain a majority in them for the time being, and that the dominant Mensheviks and S.R.s had gone over to the counter-revolution and become the servants of Tsarist generals. The peaceful road to revolution was thus closed. The revocation of the slogan took place after the Bolshevik show of force which, though Lenin strenuously denied this in later years, was probably a first attempt to seize power. Threatened with arrest, Lenin fled from Petrograd and went into hiding in Finland, directing the party's activity and at the same time writing *The State and Revolution*—an extraordinary semi-anarchist blueprint for a proletarian state in which power was to be directly exercised by the whole people in arms. The basic ideas of this programme were not only soon falsified by the course of the Bolshevik revolution, but were derided by Lenin himself as anarcho-syndicalist fantasies.

General Kornilov's unsuccessful putsch increased the general confusion and made things easier for the Bolsheviks. Lenin's policy was for the party to aid in the resistance to Kornilov but not to drift into supporting Kerensky's government. As he wrote in a letter to the Central Committee on 30 August, 'The development of this war alone can lead *us* to power, but we must speak of it as little as possible in our propaganda, remembering very well that even tomorrow events may put power into our hands, and then we shall not relinquish it' (*Works*, vol. 25, p. 289).

In September the Bolsheviks gained a majority in the Petrograd Soviet, and Trotsky became its chairman. In October a majority of the Central Committee voted for an armed rising; Zinoviev and Kamenev dissented, and made their attitude publicly known. The seizure of power in Petrograd was comparatively easy and bloodless. The Congress of Soviets which assembled on the following day, with a Bolshevik majority, passed a decree on the land question and a decree calling for peace without annexations or indemnities. A purely Bolshevik government was in power and, as Lenin had promised, it had no intention of letting go.

There can be no doubt that Lenin's insurrectionary policy and all his calculations were based on the firm expectation that the Russian Revolution would touch off a world revolution or at least a European one. This view was in fact shared by all the Bolsheviks: there was no question of 'socialism in one country' for the first few years after the Revolution. In a farewell letter to Swiss workers in 1917 Lenin wrote that in view of Russia's agrarian character and the mass of unsatisfied peasant aspirations, a Russian revolution 'might', by reason of its scale, be the prelude to a world socialist revolution. But this 'might' soon disappeared from Lenin's speeches and articles, and for the next few years they are full of confidence that proletarian rule in Western Europe is just round the corner. In September 1917 he wrote: 'The maturing and the inevitability of the world-wide socialist revolution is beyond doubt ... If the proletariat gains power it will have *every* chance of retaining it and of leading Russia until there is a victorious revolution in the West' ('The Russian Revolution and Civil War', *Works*, vol. 26, pp. 40–1). Almost on the eve of the October Revolution he wrote: 'Doubt is out of the question. We are on the threshold of a world proletarian revolution' ('The Crisis has Matured'; ibid., p. 77). After the Revolution he declared to the Third Congress of Soviets on 24 January 1918: 'Today we see that the socialist revolution is maturing by the hour in all countries of the world' (ibid., p. 471). In August 1918: 'We already see how frequent the sparks and explosions of the revolutionary conflagration in Western Europe have become, inspiring us with the assurance that the triumph of the world workers' revolution is not far off' (*Works*, vol. 28, p. 54). On 3 October 1918: 'The crisis in Germany has only begun. It will inevitably end in the transfer of political power to the German proletariat' (ibid., p. 101). On 3 November 1918: 'The time is near when the first day of the world revolution will be celebrated everywhere' (p. 131). On 6 March 1919, at the First Congress of the Third International: 'The victory of the proletarian revolution on a world scale is assured. The founding of an international Soviet republic is on the way' (p. 477). On 12 July 1919, at the party's Moscow Conference, he predicted that 'next July we shall welcome the victory of the world Soviet republic, and that victory will be full and irreversible' (*Works*, vol. 29, p. 493).

These prophecies were based not only on the observation of events, the 'rising tide of revolution' and the outbreaks in Bavaria, Hungary, and Estonia, but also on Lenin's conviction that the European war could only be stopped by overthrowing capitalism. In a speech on 3 July 1918 he said, as reported in *Pravda*, that 'the war was becoming hopeless. This hopelessness was an earnest that our socialist revolution had a very good chance of holding on until the world revolution broke out; and the guarantee of this was the war, which only the working masses could end' (ibid., vol. 27, p. 502). It is also beyond doubt that Lenin did not believe in the permanence of victory in one country. At the Third Congress of Soviets in January 1918 he said: 'The final victory of socialism in a single country is of course impossible' (ibid., vol. 26, p. 470). In an article on 12 March 1918: 'Salvation lies *only* along that road of world socialist revolution upon which we have set out' (ibid., vol. 27, p. 161). In a speech on 26 May 1918: 'We do not shut our eyes to the fact that in a single country, even if it were a much less backward country than Russia, even if we were living in better conditions that those prevailing after four years of unprecedented, painful, severe and ruinous war, we could not carry out the socialist revolution completely, solely by our own efforts' (ibid., p. 412). In a speech on 23 July 1918: 'Aware of the isolation of its revolution, the Russian proletariat clearly realizes that an essential condition and prime requisite for its victory is the united action of the workers of the whole world, or of several capitalistically advanced countries' (p. 545).

When these hopes were disappointed and it became clear that the European proletariat either did not wish to follow the Bolshevik example or would fail in its revolutionary attempts, and that the war could be brought to an end by other means than revolution, the party was confronted with the question of what to do with the power it had conquered. There was no question of giving up that power or, in practice, of sharing it with other socialist forces. (The short episode of the Left S.R.s was insignificant and did not deserve the description of 'participation in power'.) The dispute over 'socialism in one country' broke out after Lenin's death; Stalin in his fight with Trotsky completely falsified the background to the problem, but he was probably more faithful to Lenin's ideas than Trotsky. The point at issue was not whether socialism should or should not be built in a country that found itself in isolation for various historical reasons, but whether the building of socialism in Russia should be subordinated to the cause of world revolution or vice versa. This question was of decisive importance for the policy of the Soviet state, especially, but not only, its foreign policy and the fixing of goals for the Comintern. Trotsky could point to many statements by Lenin showing that he regarded the Russian Revolution as a prelude to world revolution, and Soviet Russia as the advance guard of the international proletariat. Naturally Lenin never disavowed anything he had said on the subject, and Stalin did not do so expressly either; instead, he misrepresented the argument as though it was a question of whether socialism could be built in one country, implying that Trotsky was abandoning the cause of socialism in Russia. As regards Lenin, it must be recognized that after the civil war his attention was almost wholly taken up by the problems of peaceful construction, and in his last years his policy was that of a head of state and not the leader of a world revolution. It is true that in a speech on 29 November 1920 he said: 'As soon as we are strong enough to overcome capitalism as a whole, we shall immediately seize it by the scruff of the neck' (*Works*, vol. 31, p. 441), and no doubt he really meant this; but when he wrote that 'Communism equals the Soviets plus electrification of the whole country' he clearly meant the electrification of Russia and not of Western Europe. His change of front was not accompanied by any express theoretical justification; Stalin's attempt to contrast Lenin's position with Trotsky's on this point was purely demagogic, as the question did not exist in Lenin's day in the form in which Stalin put it. Stalin, however, was not only more cautious than Trotsky in his estimate of the prospects of world revolution, but also interpreted more logically Lenin's dictum that Soviet Russia was the advance guard of the revolution: for if Soviet Russia is the world proletariat's most precious possession, clearly whatever is good for the Soviet state is good for the world proletariat. There could of course be a problem of what to do if the immediate interest of the Soviet state conflicted with the immediate interest of a revolutionary movement in another country. But in such cases Stalin's strategy of never sacrificing Soviet interests to the uncertain fortunes of a foreign revolution was in accordance with Leninist principles.

There is, indeed, no better proof that Lenin acted in this way than the history of the Treaty of Brest-Litovsk. This humiliating capitulation of the young republic to the Germans was forced through by Lenin despite the infuriated opposition of his own party and nearly the whole of Russia. To patriots outside the Bolshevik party it was a national disgrace; to Bolsheviks, a betrayal of the world revolution and a recantation of Lenin's frequent assurances before October 1917 that there could be no question of a separate peace with German imperialism. The treaty was a defeat, and Lenin never tried to pretend otherwise: he was not in the habit, as Stalin later was, of representing every setback as a brilliant triumph. Lenin was fully conscious of the dilemma: as he explained to the party, he must either save Bolshevik power by an ignominious peace, or wage a revolutionary war against Germany with every likelihood that Russia would be defeated and Bolshevik power destroyed. The lesson was a bitter one, as is shown by the frequency of his references to the treaty during the rest of his life. But his action in forcing the Central Committee to accept it despite the intial opposition of a large majority (with Bukharin as one of its main leaders) was the first clear instance of the policy later followed by Stalin: the interests of the Soviet state and Bolshevik power are paramount, and must never be put at risk for the sake of a problematical world revolution.

Almost immediately after the Revolution the question of the legitimacy of the new authority was unambiguously resolved in accordance with Leninist principles. The elections to the Constituent Assembly, preparations for which had been made before the Revolution, took place towards the end of November, and the Bolsheviks received about a quarter of the votes. This was the only instance in Russian history of an election held on a basis of equal, universal suffrage, and it took place when the popularity of the Bolsheviks was at its peak. The Assembly, when it met on 18 January 1918, was dispersed by armed sailors, and thus ended the history of Russian parliamentary democracy. Both before and after the dispersal of the Assembly Lenin repeatedly declared that to give it power signified a return to the rule of the bourgeoisie and the big landowners; in point of fact it had an S.R. majority, expressing the wishes of the peasant masses. In a speech on 14 December 1917 Lenin had said: 'We shall tell the people that their interests are superior to the interests of a democratic institution. We must not return to the old prejudices, which subordinate the interests of the people to formal democracy' (*Works*, vol. 26, p. 356). Again, on 26 December, he stated that: 'The slogan "All power to the Constituent Assembly!", which disregards the gains of the workers' and peasants' revolution ... has become in fact the slogan of the Cadets and Kaledinites and of their helpers ... Every direct or indirect attempt to consider the question of the Constituent Assembly from a formal, legal point of view, within the framework of ordinary bourgeois democracy and dis-regarding the class struggle and civil war, would be a betrayal of the proletariat's cause, and the adoption of the bourgeois standpoint' (pp. 381–2).

In saying this Lenin was only repeating his long-standing belief that it was none of the people's business to decide what its interests were. He had indeed no intention of 'returning to the old prejudices'; for a time, however, he believed that if a dictatorship had to be exercised against the peasantry, i.e. the bulk of the Russian people, it could still be a dictatorship supported by the great majority of the proletariat. This illusion too was dispelled before long. At the outset, however, the new state could count on support from a majority of the workers and peasants; otherwise it could not have survived the appalling hardships of the civil war, when, as Lenin freely admitted, the future of Soviet power more than once hung by a thread. The superhuman energy that the Bolshevik party displayed in those years, and the sacrifices it was able to elicit from the workers and peasants, saved Soviet power at the cost of economic ruin, immense human suffering, the loss of millions of lives, and the barbarization of society. In the last phase of the struggle the revolution encountered a further defeat in the Polish war, which finally destroyed the hope that the Soviet system could be transplanted to Europe at an early date.

As to the reasons for the success of the October Revolution, Lenin made no attempt to present the matter in traditional Marxist terms but referred to Russia's backwardness, the unsatis-fied peasant demands, and the war situation. On 23 April 1919 he wrote: 'It was easier for the Russians to begin the great proletarian revolution, but it will be more difficult for them to continue it and carry it to final victory, in the sense of the complete organization of a socialist society. It was easier for us to begin, firstly, because the unusual—for twentieth-century Europe—political backwardness of the Tsarist monarchy gave unusual strength to the revolutionary onslaught of the masses. Secondly, Russia's backwardness merged in a peculiar way the proletarian revolution against the bourgeoisie with the peasant revolution against the landowners' (*The Third International and its Place in History*; *Works*, vol. 29, p. 310). On 1 July 1921, at the Third Congress of the Comintern, he put the matter even more clearly: 'We were victorious in Russia, and with such ease, because we prepared for our revolution during the imperialist war. That was the first condition. Ten million workers and peasants in Russia were under arms, and our slogan was: an immediate peace at all costs. We were victorious because the vast mass of the peasants were revolutionarily disposed against the big landowners.' Secondly, 'We were victorious because we adopted the agrarian programme of the Socialist-Revolutionaries instead of our own, and put it into effect. Our victory lay in the fact that we carried out the Socialist-Revolutionary programme' (*Works*, vol. 32, pp. 473, 475).

Lenin had indeed realized for a long time that if the Russian communists had to wait, like the Western parties, for the 'contradiction between relations of production and productive forces' to mature to the requisite point, they could say good-bye to the hope of a proletarian revolution. He was fully aware that the course of events in Russia bore no relation to the traditional Marxist schemata, though he did not consider the theoretical problem in all its bearings. The massive strength of the Russian revolution lay not in the class conflict between workers and bourgeoisie but in the aspirations of the peasants, the wartime débâcle, and the longing for peace. It was a communist revolution in the sense that it transferred state power to the Communist Party, but not in the sense of confirming Marxist predictions as to the fate of capitalist society.

3. *The beginnings of socialist economy*

The economic history of Soviet Russia under Lenin is divided into two periods: that of 'War Communism' and, from the spring of 1921, the 'New Economic Policy' (N.E.P.). The term 'War Communism' was coined during the second period, and is misleading in that it suggests a temporary policy resulting from the civil war and the need to adopt extraordinary measures to feed the country in its state of economic ruin. History books not infrequently put the matter in this way and suggest, further, that the N.E.P. was planned in advance but could not be put into effect owing to the exceptional circumstances of the war: in other words, it was not a retreat and a confession of error, but a return to the previously chosen path from which the party had been temporarily forced to deviate.

In actual fact, both the course of events and Lenin's account of them make it clear that War Communism was thought of from the beginning as the economic system to be maintained until the 'complete victory of communism', while the N.E.P. was an admission of defeat. The key question in devastated Russia was of course the production of food, especially grain. War Communism consisted primarily of requisitioning from the peasants all food surpluses, or rather all foodstuffs that the local authorities or the requisitioning squads regarded as surplus. As it was impossible to calculate accurately the quantity of stocks and 'surpluses' on millions of small farms, the requisition system not only turned the peasant masses against the government and led to bribery and coercion on a vast scale, but ruined agricultural production and thus undermined the whole system of power. Lenin believed, however, that in a country of small farmers free trade in grain, as a principle rather than a temporary measure, was tantamount to the restoration of capitalism, and that those who proposed it in the name of economic recovery were no better than allies of Kolchak. In a speech on 19 May 1919 he referred to 'this historical epoch, when the struggle of the oppressed working people for the complete overthrow of capital *and the abolition of commodity production* [present author's italics] stands in the forefront' (*Works*, vol. 29, p. 352), and declared that free trade in grain was Kolchak's policy. On 30 July of that year, in a speech on the food situation, he re-emphasized the point stating that the question of free trade was decisive in the final battle with capitalism, and that 'there cannot be any concessions here, in this particular sphere', as free trade was the economic standby of Denikin and Kolchak. 'We know that one of the main sources of capitalism is freedom to trade in grain in the country, and it is this source that has been the ruin of all previous republics. Today the last, decisive battle against capitalism and against freedom to trade is being fought, and for us this is a truly basic battle between capitalism and socialism. If we win in this fight there will be no return to capitalism and the former system, no return to what has been in the past. Such a return will be impossible so long as there is a war against the bourgeoisie, against profiteering and against petty proprietorship' (ibid., pp. 525, 526). Similarly, in an article written but not published at this time, he wrote: 'Freedom to trade in grain is a return to capitalism, to the full power of the landowners and capitalists, to a savage struggle between people for profit, to the "free" enrichment of the few, to the poverty of the masses, to eternal bondage' (ibid., p. 570).

While, then, Lenin did not envisage an immediate transition to collective or state farming, he was in no doubt that rural production must from the outset be under direct state control and that free trade in commodities meant the ruin of socialism. His intention from the start was that agricultural production should be based on police coercion of the peasants and on the direct confiscation of produce in the form of quotas which were supposed (though this was impossible to work out in practice) to leave the peasants enough seed corn for the following year and a minimum on which to feed themselves.

The transition to N.E.P. was due to the catastrophic failure of this policy—a failure predicted by the Mensheviks and S.R.s, who for their pains had been denounced, imprisoned, and murdered as henchmen of the White Guards.

Lenin sounded the retreat at the party's Tenth Congress, in March 1921. He announced that small farming would have to go on for many years, and 'the unrestricted trade slogan will be inevitable ... It is apt to spread because it conforms to the economic conditions of the small producer's existence' (*Works*, vol. 32, p. 187). He acknowledged that in the nationalization of trade and industry the party had gone further than theoretical or practical considerations justified, and declared that 'we must satisfy the middle peasantry economically and go over to free exchange; otherwise it will be impossible—economically impossible—in view of the delay in the world revolution, to preserve the rule of the proletariat in Russia' (ibid., p. 225). As Lenin emphasized soon afterwards, the N.E.P. was meant as a serious long-term policy, consisting not only of replacing the appropriation of surpluses by a uniform grain tax, but of numerous other measures: wide concessions to foreign capital in Russia, aid to co-operatives, the leasing of state factories to private persons, relief to private traders and the distribution of state products through private merchants, greater independence and initiative for state enterprises as regards the use of financial and material resources, and the introduction of material incentives into production. 'Commodity exchange is brought to the fore as the principal lever of the New Economic Policy' (ibid., p. 433). Lenin made no secret of the fact that a disastrous error had been committed.

We expected—or perhaps it would be truer to say that we presumed without having given it adequate consideration—to be able to organize the state production and the state distribution of products on communist lines in a small-peasant country directly as ordered by the proletarian state. Experience has proved that we were wrong. It appears that a number of transitional stages were necessary—state capitalism and socialism—in order to *prepare*—to prepare by many years of effort—for the transition to communism. Not directly relying on enthusiasm, but aided by the enthusiasm engendered by the great revolution, and on the basis of personal interest, personal incentive and business principles, we must first set to work in this small-peasant country to build solid gangways to socialism by way of state capitalism. (*Pravda*, 18 Oct. 1921)

In attempting to go straight over to communism we, in the spring of 1921, sustained a more serious defeat on the economic front than any defeat inflicted upon us by Kolchak, Denikin or Pilsudski. This defeat was much more serious, significant and dangerous. It was expressed in the isolation of the higher administrators of our economic policy from the lower and their failure to produce that development of the productive forces which the programme of our Party regards as vital and urgent. The surplus-food appropriation system in the rural districts—this direct communist approach to the problem of urban development—hindered the growth of the productive forces and proved to be the main cause of the profound economic and political crisis that we experienced in the spring of 1921. (Address dated 17 Oct. 1921; *Works*, vol. 33, pp. 58, 63–4)

After the Brest treaty, the N.E.P. was a second major demonstration of Lenin's extraordinary ability to sacrifice doctrine to the retention of power. It excited less opposition in the party, as all could see that the country was on the brink of an abyss, but it was none the less a retreat towards capitalism— a case, as Lenin put it, of *reculer pour mieux sauter*. In the preceding years he had supposed that all important economic problems could be solved by police and military terror. This had been the Jacobins' policy; he believed that it had brought excellent results, but like them he found himself on the edge of a precipice, though he was able to draw back at the last moment. His economic directives during the period of War Communism were simple: they consisted of shooting, imprisonment, and intimidation. It turned out, however, that Marxist doctrine was quite right: economic life has its own laws, which cannot be set aside by terror; in time of famine and the breakdown of society, the execution of profiteers will not put an end to profiteering.

4. The dictatorship of the proletariat and the dictatorship of the party

The new situation, however, brought about other changes that were bound to arouse dissension in the party. All the pre-Revolutionary promises had suddenly became scraps of paper. Lenin had undertaken to abolish the standing army and the police, to equalize the pay of high officials and specialists on the one hand and skilled workers on the other; he had promised that the people in arms would exercise direct rule. Directly after the Revolution, and long before N.E.P., it was evident that these were utopian dreams. An army with a cadre of professional officers had to be organized at once on a basis of rank and strict discipline, like any other army. Trotsky revealed his genius as the chief organizer of the Red Army, and was the main architect of victory in the civil war. The methods used were drastic enough—hostages were taken and executed, deserters and those who harboured them were shot, as were soldiers for offences against discipline, etc. But such methods would not have been possible without a large, trustworthy force under arms: to keep an army together by intimidation and terror there must be enough people willing to apply that terror in a situation where counter-terror is also powerful. It was necessary, immediately after the Revolution, to establish a force of political police, which was efficiently created by Feliks Dzerzhinsky. It soon became clear that production could not be organized without privileges for specialists, and that it could not be based on intimidation alone: as early as April 1918 Lenin recognized, in 'The Immediate Tasks of the Soviet Government', that it was necessary to 'compromise' in this respect and to depart from the principles of the Paris Commune. Lenin also proclaimed from the beginning of the Revolution that it was important to learn from the bourgeoisie (Struve in his time had been branded as a renegade for saying the same thing). Those who thought socialism could be built without learning from the bourgeois—so Lenin told the Central Executive Committee on 29 April 1918—had the mentality of Central African natives (*Works*, vol. 27, p. 310). In his writings and speeches he devoted more and more attention to 'civilization' (*kultura*), i.e. the technical and administrative skills necessary to run industry and the state. He emphasized that communists must stop being arrogant, must admit their ignorance and learn these skills from the bourgeoisie. (Lenin was always highly distrustful of communists except for the purpose of political agitation and fighting: in 1913, when he heard that Gorky had consulted a Bolshevik doctor, he wrote at once urging him to find a real doctor and not a 'comrade', who was sure to be an ass). In May 1918 he bethought himself of a better model than the Paris Commune, namely Peter the Great. 'While the revolution in Germany is still slow in "coming forth", our task is to study the state capitalism of the Germans, to spare no effort in copying it and not shrink from adopting *dictatorial* methods to hasten the copying of it. Our task is to hasten this copying even more than Peter hastened the copying of Western culture by barbarian Russia, and we must not hesitate to use barbarous methods in fighting barbarism' ('"Left-Wing" Childishness and the Petty-Bourgeois Mentality', *Works*, vol. 27, p. 340). The principle of unity of control in industry was soon introduced, and dreams of the collective administration of factories were condemned as a syndicalist deviation.

Thus the new society was to be built by means of increasing technical and administrative knowledge on the one hand, and coercion and intimidation on the other. The N.E.P. brought no relaxation of political and police terror, nor was it intended to. The non-Bolshevik Press was closed down during the civil war, and was never again permitted to appear. The opposition socialist parties, the Mensheviks and S.R.s, were terrorized and liquidated. The autonomy of the universities was finally suppressed in 1921. Lenin constantly repeated that the 'so-called freedom of the Press' was a bourgeois deceit, like freedom of assembly and the right to form parties, since in a bourgeois society the common people had no printing presses and no rooms in which to assemble. Now that the Soviet system had given these facilities to the 'people', the latter obviously could not allow the bourgeoisie to use them for deceptive purposes; and as the Mensheviks and S.R.s had sunk to the position of bourgeois parties, they too must submit to the dictatorship of the proletariat. The closure of Menshevik newspapers in February 1919 was justified by Lenin on the ground that 'the Soviet Government, right at the time of the last, decisive and sharpest armed clash with the landlord and capitalist troops, cannot put up with people who are unwilling to endure great sacrifices alongside the workers and peasants fighting for their just cause' (*Works*, vol. 28, p. 447). At the Seventh Congress of Soviets in December 1919 he declared that when Martov accused the Bolsheviks of representing a minority of the working class he was speaking the language of the 'wild beasts of imperialism'—Clemenceau, Wilson, and Lloyd George. The logical conclusion was that 'we have to be on the alert and to realize that the Cheka is indispensable!' (*Works*, vol. 30, p. 239).

The dissolution of non-Bolshevik organizations and periodicals, the expulsion from Russia (this clement measure was still employed) of hundreds of the country's chief intellectuals, purges in all cultural institutions, the atmosphere of terror in every walk of life—all this had the unplanned but natural effect that social conflicts came to be reflected within the Bolshevik party itself; and this in turn led to the application within the party of the same principle of despotic rule as the party exercised over the rest of society. The civil war had brought economic ruin and general exhaustion, and the working class, drained of its strength, was unresponsive to appeals to show the same enthusiasm and self-sacrifice in the cause of peaceful construction as it had on the field of battle. That the Bolsheviks represented the whole working class had been an axiom since 1918; it was unverifiable, as no institutions existed for the purpose. The proletariat, however, began to display anger and discontent, most forcefully in the Kronstadt rising of March 1921, which was suppressed with heavy bloodshed. The sailors of Kronstadt, like the great majority of the working class, were in favour of Soviet power, but they did not identify it with the despotism of a single ruling party: they wanted rule by the Soviets as opposed to party rule. Within the party itself, proletarian discontent was reflected in the strong 'workers' opposition', represented in the Central Committee by Aleksandr Shlyapnikov, Aleksandra Kollontay, and others. This group wanted economic management to be entrusted to a general organization of workers, i.e. trade unions; they called for the equalization of pay, and protested against despotic methods of control within the party. In short, they wanted the kind of 'dictatorship of the proletariat' that Lenin had written about before the Revolution. They believed that democracy for the workers and democracy within the party could be safeguarded even when there was no democracy for anyone else. Lenin and Trotsky no longer entertained any such illusion. They branded the 'workers' opposition' as an anarcho-syndicalist deviation, and its spokesmen were eliminated from party work on various pretexts, though they were not imprisoned or shot.

The episode gave rise to a general debate on the place and function of trade unions in the Soviet system. Three years earlier, in March 1918, Lenin had inveighed against the Mensheviks for saying that 'in the interests of preserving and strengthening the class independence of the proletariat the trade unions should not become state organizations ... This view was and is either a bourgeois provocation of the crudest kind or an extreme misunderstanding, a slavish repetition of the slogans of yesterday ... The working class is becoming and has become the ruling class in the state. The trade unions are becoming and must become state organizations which have prime responsibility for the reorganization of all economic life on a socialist basis' (*Works*, vol. 27, p. 215). The idea of turning the trade unions into state organizations followed logically from the theory of the proletarian dictatorship. Since the proletariat was identified with state power, it was clearly nonsense to imagine that the workers would have to defend their interests against the state. Trotsky held to this view, but Lenin changed his mind on both points in the above-quoted passage. Having decided in 1920 that the Soviet state was suffering from bureaucratic distortion, he attacked Trotsky for holding the views he had himself recently advanced, and declared that it was the business of the trade unions to defend the workers' state but also to defend the workers against their own state, or rather its abuses. At the same time he was violently opposed to the idea that the unions should take over the state's function of managing the economy.

Meanwhile Lenin took steps to prevent opposition groups from arising in future within the party. Rules were adopted prohibiting the formation of intra-party factions, and empowering the Central Committee to expel from its midst members who had been elected at the party congress. In this way, by a natural progression, the dictatorship first exercised over society in the name of the working class, and then over the working class in the name of the party, was now applied to the party itself, creating the basis for a one-man tyranny.

Another theme which becomes more and more prominent in Lenin's last years is that, just mentioned, of 'bureaucratic distortion'. He complains more and more frequently that the state apparatus is expanding indefinitely without need and at the same time is incapable of getting anything done, that everything is muddle and red tape, that civil servants refer the most trifling questions to high party officials, and so on. It seems never to have occurred to Lenin that the root of these troubles lay in the fact that the whole system was based, as he constantly emphasized, on force and not on law. He demanded that people be imprisoned right and left for inefficiency, and then wondered why they were afraid to take decisions and referred them higher up whenever they could. He demanded vigilant supervision and exhaustive records, and yet was astonished at the amount of 'pen-pushing'. (His statement that 'socialism equals Soviet power plus electrification' is often quoted; less often his statement, just after the Revolution, that 'what socialism implies above all is keeping account of everything' (meeting of the Central Executive Committee, 17 November 1917; *Works*, vol. 26, p. 288).) He created a system in which, depending on the whim of a local party or police authority, any criticism might be regarded as counter-revolutionary and expose its author to imprisonment or death, and at the same time he urged the working people to be fearless in their criticism of the state apparatus. His diagnosis of the cancer of bureaucracy was a simple one: it was due to lack of education, 'culture' and administrative ability. There were two remedies, also simple: to imprison the inefficient, and to create new supervisory bodies of honest officials. He attached great importance to the Workers' and Peasants' Inspectorate (Rabkrin), headed by Stalin, which was appointed to supervise all branches of the administration and other supervisory bodies, and on the honesty of which, in his view, the success of the fight against bureaucracy ultimately depended. This body, besides adding to the burden of terror and issuing incompetent instructions in all directions, was used by Stalin, who became Secretary-General of the party in 1922, as a stick to beat his opponents and a weapon in intra-party struggles. This, of course, Lenin did not foresee. He had applied his 'final cure' to bureaucracy in the shape of an additional link in the bureaucratic chain which, as he well knew, was fastened upon the country irrevocably. The hierarchy grew and grew; it had powers of life and death over every citizen; it was at first directed by sincere communists, but in course of time absorbed a mass of careerists, parasites, and sycophants who, over the years, modelled the style of government in their own image.

The last two years of Lenin's life were overshadowed by physical infirmity due to sclerosis and a succession of strokes, despite which he continued fighting to the end. His famous 'Testament', consisting of notes written in December 1922 and January 1923 in preparation for the party congress, was concealed from the Soviet public for the next thirty-three years. The notes express his feeling of helplessness at the difficulties of the state and the approaching struggle for power in the party hierarchy. He criticizes Stalin for concentrating excessive power in his own hands and for being high-handed, capricious, and disloyal, and therefore unfit to remain in the office of secretary-general. Lenin also enumerates the faults of Trotsky, Pyatakov, Zinovyev, and Kamenev, and criticizes Bukharin for un-Marxist views. He blames Ordzhonikidze, Stalin, and Dzerzhinsky for Great Russian nationalism and the brutality of the methods used in the invasion of Georgia. He speaks of the need to 'provide the non-Russians with a real safeguard against the truly

Russian bully', and predicts that, given the 'apparatus which . . . we took over from tsarism and slightly anointed with Soviet oil', the promised freedom to secede from the Union 'will be a mere scrap of paper, unable to defend the non-Russians from the onslaught of that really Russian man, the Great-Russian chauvinist, in substance a rascal and a tyrant, such as the typical Russian bureaucrat is' (*Works*, vol. 36, pp. 605–6).

These appeals, warnings, and reproaches were of little practical importance. Lenin called for the protection of national minorities and the right of self-determination immediately after the Red Army, with his blessing, had invaded Georgia, with its democratically elected Menshevik government. He hoped to prevent factional strife by enlarging the Central Committee, as though its size could make any difference when he himself had virtually put an end to democracy within the party. He criticized all the main party leaders and called for Stalin's replacement, but who did he think should be the new secretary-general—Trotsky, with his 'excessive self-assurance', Bukharin, who was not a Marxist, Zinovyev or Kamenev, whose 'treason' in October 1917 was 'no accident', or Pyatakov, who could not be relied on in important political matters? Whatever Lenin's political intentions were, the 'Testament' today reads like a cry of despair.

Lenin died on 21 January 1924. (There is no evidence to support Trotsky's later suggestion that he was poisoned by Stalin.) The new state was to develop along the lines he had inculcated. His embalmed corpse, exhibited to this day in the mausoleum in Moscow, aptly symbolizes the new order which, he promised, was soon to embrace all mankind.

5. The theory of imperialism and of revolution

The Bolshevik theory of imperialism was the work of Lenin and Bukharin: the latter was the first to formulate the basis of a strategy of revolution for the new historical era. Lenin in his work on imperialism—based for the most part, as already mentioned, on J. A. Hobson's *Imperialism* (1902) and R. Hilferding's *Finanzkapital* (1910)—enumerates five principal features distinguishing imperialism from pre-monopolistic capitalism: (1) the concentration of production and capital, leading to the domination of the world economy by big monopolies; (2) the fusion of bank and industrial capital and the consequent rise of a financial oligarchy; (3) the specially important role of the export of capital; (4) the division of the world among monopolistic leagues of international capitalists; (5) the completion of the territorial partition of the world among the great imperialist powers. This situation does not relieve the contradictions of capitalism, but intensifies them to the utmost; the inequalities of development within the system and the fierceness of competition not only do not reduce the likelihood of wars but make them increasingly inevitable. The last point is stressed by Lenin in his attack on Kautsky, who had argued that it was possible to foresee the world economic system passing into a phase of 'ultra-imperialism' in which the great powers and the great international cartels would stabilize the partition of the world and thus eliminate the risk of war. Kautsky put this forward as a general hypothesis and not something that was bound to occur, but Lenin was scandalized by the idea of capitalism without wars, a state of affairs in which revolutions too would be much less likely. Kautsky's 'stupid fable' was anti-Marxist and a symptom of opportunism: imperialism could not exist without wars, for there was no other way of regulating and eliminating the inequalities of world development. Hence, in his article 'The Military Programme of the Proletarian Revolution' (1916), Lenin drew the conclusion that socialism could not triumph simultaneously in all countries: the revolutionary process would begin in one or several countries, and this would lead to further conflicts and wars.

The connection between the prospects of revolution and the uneven development of the world economy, which at the same time constituted a single system, was expounded by Bukharin in books written during the war and in the first years after the Revolution. Imperialism, he explained, sought to overcome the anarchy of production and to organize a rational economy, with the state as a supervisory and regulating force; but it was unable to eliminate contradictions and competition, and hence to avoid imperialist wars. The capitalist system as a whole was ripe for socialist revolution; however, this was much less likely to break out in places where technological development had reached its height and where the bourgeoisie, thanks to its fat profits, was able to bribe the workers with high wages and dissuade them from revolution, than where the concentration of contradictions was greatest, i.e. on the fringe of the capitalist world, in backward, colonial, or semi-colonial countries. Thanks to the combination of intensive exploitation, national oppression, and peasant movements, these countries were the weakest link where the chain of the world system could be broken by force. Social movements in underdeveloped countries could not lead to the immediate establishment of socialism, but they were the natural allies of the proletariat in the advanced countries, and could create transitional social forms in which the achievement of bourgeois democratic objectives would coincide with the gradual and peaceful development towards socialism, based on the combined forces of workers and peasants.

By 1916, however, Lenin had taken the argument a stage further. In 'The Discussion on Self-Determination Summed Up' he wrote:

To imagine that social revolution is *conceivable* without revolts by small nations in the colonies and in Europe, without revolutionary outbursts by a section of the petty bourgeoisie *with all its prejudices*, without a movement of the politically non-conscious proletarian and semi-proletarian masses against oppression by the landowners, the church and the monarchy, against national oppression, etc.—to imagine all this is to repudiate social revolution ... Whoever expects a 'pure' social revolution will *never* live to see it ... The socialist revolution in Europe *cannot be* anything other than an outburst of mass struggle on the part of all and sundry oppressed and discontented elements. Inevitably sections of the petty bourgeoisie and of the backward workers will participate in it—without such participation *mass* struggle is impossible, without it *no* revolution is possible—and just as inevitably will they bring into the movement their prejudices, their reactionary fantasies, their weaknesses and errors. But *objectively* they will attack *capital* (*Works*, vol. 22, pp. 355–6).

It is not clear whether Lenin was fully aware of the consequences of this theory or the extent to which it diverged from Marxist tradition. At all events, it laid down firmly that a socialist uprising could only take place when there were numerous unsatisfied claims and aspirations of the kind which Marxists assign to the 'bourgeois' phase of development, i.e. primarily those of the peasants and subject nationalities. This means that as capitalism approaches the situation, foreseen by Marx, in which society consists only of the bourgeoisie and the proletariat, a socialist revolution becomes less and less likely. Lenin's statement that unsatisfied peasant and national claims and the presence of 'survivals of feudalism' might assist the proletariat, reinforcing it with the energy of 'non-proletarian' demands, was of course not in conflict with the strategy of Marx and Engels, who adopted a similar position on various occasions, for example in their hopes for a proletarian revolution in Germany in 1848 or a Russian revolution in the seventies, or their view that the Irish question would strengthen the hand of the British working class. Marx and Engels, it is true, did not put forward any precise theory as to how such alliances would operate, nor was it clear how their hopes were to be theoretically reconciled with the general theory of socialist revolution. But the statement that a proletarian revolution could not happen at all without the reinforcement due to 'survivals of feudalism' was a novelty in Marxism and a complete departure from the traditional theory.

Lenin was no doubt right when he accused the leaders of the Second International of being revolutionary in words and reformist in action. He alone thought seriously of the seizure of power, and, what is more, he thought of nothing else. His position was clear: power must be seized wherever it was politically possible to do so. He did not indulge in theoretical calculations as to whether productive forces had matured to the point of a socialist uprising; his calculations were all concerned with the power situation. He himself could rightly be accused of being a determinist in words and a Realpolitiker in action. Sometimes, though not often, he repeated the determinist catechism ('Everything that takes place in history takes place of necessity. That is elementary.'—'The Russian Brand of Südekum', 1 Feb. 1915; *Works*, vol. 21, p. 120), but this determinism only served to convince himself and others that the communist cause was historically bound to triumph; it was not applied to any specific political acts. He even jettisoned the idea, which had been regarded as one of the rudiments of Marxism, that all countries must go through the capitalist stage of development. At the Second Congress of the Comintern on 26 July 1920 he declared that backward peoples might bypass the capitalist 'phase' and proceed direct to socialism, with the aid of the proletariat in the advanced countries and of Soviet power. (Without this, indeed, it would have been hard to justify the exercise of Soviet authority over dozens of primitive tribes and small nations who belonged to the Russian Empire.)

Lenin, then, was not interested in 'economic ripeness', but only in the existence of a revolutionary situation. In an article of 1915 on 'The Collapse of the Second International' he defined the main features of such a situation as follows: (1) It is usually insufficient for 'the lower classes not to want' to live in the old way; it is also necessary that 'the upper classes should be unable' to live in the old way—popular discontent is not enough, there must also be a disintegration of the apparatus of government. (2) 'The suffering and want of the oppressed classes have grown more acute than usual', and (3) 'As a consequence of the above causes there is a considerable increase in the activity of the masses, who ... are drawn ... themselves into independent historical action.' But 'not every revolutionary situation gives rise to a revolution; revolution arises only out of a situation in which the above-mentioned objective changes are accompanied by a subjective change, namely the ability of the revolutionary class to take revolutionary mass action strong enough to break or dislocate the old government' (*Works*, vol. 21, pp. 213–14).

It is easy to see that the conditions prescribed by Lenin are most likely to occur in time of war and particularly of military defeat. Hence his anger at suggestions that capitalism might avoid wars and thus preclude, in all probability, the chance of a revolutionary situation arising. Hence, likewise, his desire that revolutionists should aim at their country's own defeat in the imperialist war and thus turn it into a civil one.

The fact that Lenin was wholly preoccupied by the question of political power meant that he was the only social democratic leader who was completely free from any vestige of what he called 'bourgeois pacifism'—the hope of abolishing wars without the revolutionary abolition of capitalism, and, when war had broken out, the attempt to bring it to an end by methods of international law. A symptom of bourgeois pacifism was the use of the concept of aggression, regardless of the class character of the war. War should be seen in terms of classes and not of states —it was not the collision of two state organisms, but a product of class interests. Lenin frequently quoted Clausewitz's remark that 'War is simply the continuation of policy by other means', and on the strength of this dictum the Prussian general of Napoleonic times is credited with formulating 'the main thesis of dialectics with reference to wars' (ibid., p. 219). War was a manifestation of conflict due to class interests, and the difference between warlike and peaceful means of resolving these conflicts was purely technical and had no political significance; war was 'simply' a way of attaining ends that could at other times be attained without it, and had no particular moral or political quality independent of class interests. It did not matter who was the aggressor, there was in fact no difference between offensive and defensive wars; all that mattered were the class interests underlying the military operations. Lenin's statements on this subject are numerous and perfectly clear, though not often quoted by his present-day disciples. 'It is absurd to divide wars into defensive and aggressive' (speech on 14 Oct. 1914; *Works*, vol. 36, p. 297). 'It is not the defensive or offensive character of the war, but the interests of the class struggle of the proletariat, or—to put it better—the interests of the international movement of the proletariat that represent the sole criterion for considering and deciding the attitude of the social-democrats to any particular event in international relations' ('Bellicose Militarism and the Anti-Militarist Tactics of Social-Democracy', Aug. 1908; *Works*, vol. 15, p. 199). 'As if the question were: Who was the first to attack, and not What are the causes of the war? What are its aims? Which classes are waging it?' (open letter to Boris Souvarine, Dec. 1916; *Works*, vol. 23, p. 198). 'The character of the war (whether it is reactionary or revolutionary) does not depend on who the attacker was, or in whose country the "enemy" is stationed; it depends on *what class* is waging the war, and what politics this war is a continuation of' (*The Proletarian Revolution and the Renegade Kautsky*, 1918; *Works*, vol. 28, p. 286).

It thus appears not only that 'aggression' is a fraudulent bourgeois concept serving to conceal the class character of wars, but that the working class organized in its own state has every right to wage war on a capitalist state, since by definition it represents the interests of the oppressed and has justice on its side. Lenin does not shrink from this conclusion. 'For instance, if socialism is victorious in America or in Europe in 1920, and Japan and China, let us say, then move their Bismarcks against us—if only diplomatically at first—we certainly would be in favour of an offensive revolutionary war against them' ('The Collapse of the Second International'; *Works*, vol. 21, p. 221 n.). In a speech on 6 December 1920 Lenin declared that war was bound to break out soon between the U.S.A. and Japan and that, while the Soviet state could not 'support' either against the other, it should 'play one off' against the other and exploit the war in its own interest (*Works*, vol. 31, p. 443). At the Seventh Party Congress in March 1918 he proposed a resolution to the effect that 'the Congress will empower the Central Committee of the Party both to break all the peace treaties and to declare war on any imperialist power or the whole world when the Central Committee of the Party considers that the appropriate moment for this has come' (*Works*, vol. 27, p. 120). This, it is true, was drafted in the atmosphere of Brest-Litovsk, but it is general in application and is wholly in accordance with Lenin's doctrine. As the proletarian state is by definition in the right *vis-à-vis* capitalist states, and since the question of aggression is beside the point in judging a war, it is clearly the right and duty of the former state to attack the latter for the sake of the world revolution whenever occasion offers—all the more so as peaceful coexistence between capitalism and socialism was, in Lenin's opinion, impossible. In the speech on 6 December 1920, already quoted, he declared: 'I said that we had passed from war to peace, but that we had not forgotten that war will return. While capitalism and socialism live side by side, they cannot live in peace' (*Works*, vol. 31, p. 457).

Such were the simple ideological foundations of the foreign policy of the socialist state. The new state by definition represented the leading force in history; whether attacking or defending itself, it was acting in the name of progress. International law, arbitration, disarmament talks, the 'outlawing' of war—all these were deceptions as long as capitalism existed, and afterwards they would not be necessary, for wars were as impossible under socialism as they were inevitable under capitalism.

6. Socialism and the dictatorship of the proletariat

Although Lenin's whole activity was subordinated to the struggle for the 'ultimate aim', i.e. the building of a socialist society, he did not concern himself before the war with specifying what that society would be like. His writings contain scattered references to familiar socialist ideas such as the collectivization of property, the abolition of wage-labour and of the commodity economy, etc., but he does not go into details. He did, however, explain before the Revolution what he meant by the 'dictatorship of the proletariat', and the terms in which he did so remained unaltered throughout his career. In *The Victory of the Cadets and the Tasks of the Workers' Party* (1906) he expressed himself several times with emphasis: 'Dictatorship means unlimited power based on force, and not on law' (*Works*, vol. 10, p. 216). 'Authority—unlimited, outside the law, and based on force in the most direct sense of the word—is dictatorship' (ibid., p. 244). 'The scientific term "dictatorship" means nothing more nor less than authority untrammelled by any laws, absolutely unrestricted by any rules whatever, and based directly on violence. The term "dictatorship" has *no other meaning but this*—mark this well, Cadet gentlemen' (ibid., p. 246).

To make clear that his views had not changed, Lenin repeated the above statements in 1920. Dictatorship was the 'directest form of coercion', and the dictatorship of the proletariat was the exercise of force by the proletariat against the exploiters it had overthrown. As to how that force would be organized, Lenin gave the answers in his pamphlet *The State and Revolution*, directed against the leaders of the Second International. On the eve of the creation of the Third International (which he had in mind as early as 1915), and in the hope that revolution would soon break out all over Europe, Lenin thought it necessary to expound once again the Marxist theory of the state and of the changes that socialism would involve in the functioning of state institutions.

According to Marx and Engels, Lenin points out, the state is the result of irreconcilable class antagonisms, but not in the sense that it harmonizes them or arbitrates between them; on the contrary, the state as such has hitherto always been the instrument whereby the possessing classes have coerced the oppressed classes. Its institutions cannot be neutral in the class conflict, but are only the legal expression of the economic oppression of one class by another. Since the whole function of the bourgeois state is to perpetuate the exploitation of the working class, the institutions and organs of that state cannot be used to emancipate the workers. The suffrage in bourgeois states is not a means of relieving social tension, let alone of enabling the oppressed classes to gain power: it is merely a way of maintaining the authority of the bourgeoisie. The proletariat cannot free itself except by destroying the state apparatus; this is the main task of the revolution, and must be clearly distinguished from the 'withering away' of the state in accordance with Marxist theory. The bourgeois state must be smashed here and now; the withering away applies to the proletarian state after the revolution, i.e. at a future time when all political authority will be done away with.

Lenin refers particularly to Marx's article on the Paris Commune and his *Critique of the Gotha Programme*, and also to essays and letters by Engels. Reformism in the socialist movement and the idea of using the bourgeois state to serve the interests of the proletariat are, he declares, contrary to the basis of Marxism: they are delusions or deceitful manœuvres of opportunists who have renounced the revolution. The proletariat needs a state (this is where the anarchists go wrong), but it must be a state that tends to wither away and destroy itself. To overcome the resistance of the exploiters in the transitional period, the length of which cannot be foreseen, there must be a dictatorship of the proletariat which, unlike all previous forms of state, will be the dictatorship of the great majority of society over the remnants of the possessing classes. During this period the freedom of capitalists must be limited, while full democracy will be possible only when classes have been done away with altogether. During the transition the state will be able to function without difficulty, as the majority will have no trouble crushing the minority of exploiters and will have no need of a special police machine.

The experience of the Paris Commune serves to illustrate the general features of communist state organization. In such a state, the standing army will be disbanded and the people will be armed instead; all state officials will be elected and dismissed by the working people; the police as such will not be needed, as their functions, like those of the army, will be performed by the whole of the population that is capable of bearing arms. In addition, the organizational functions of the state will become so simple that they can be performed by anyone who knows how to read and write. No special skill will be required for the running of society in general, and there will therefore be no separate caste of officials; simple administration and accounting will be performed by all citizens in turn, at a wage equal to that of manual workers (Lenin lays great stress on this). Everyone will be in equal degree a servant of the state, paid on an equal basis and equally obliged to work. They will be alternately manual workers and officials, so that nobody will become a bureaucrat. Given the simplicity of administration, equality of pay, and the election and removability of public officers, there will be no risk of the formation of a parasitic caste of bureaucrats alienated from society. To begin with there must be political compulsion, but as the state withers away its functions will gradually lose their political character and become matters of pure administration. Orders will no longer be given from the top; necessary central planning will be combined with broad territorial autonomy. In 'Materials Relating to the Revision of the Party Programme', written in April–May 1917, Lenin spoke of 'public education to be administered by democratically elected organs of local self-government; the central government not to be allowed to interfere with the arrangement of the school curriculum, or with the selection of the teaching staffs; teachers to be elected directly by the population with the right of the latter to remove undesirable teachers', etc. (*Works*, vol. 24, p. 473).

The final objective is the complete abolition of the state and of all constraint; this will be possible as people get accustomed to the principles of voluntary coexistence and solidarity. Crimes and excesses are due to exploitation and poverty, and so will gradually disappear under socialism—this conviction of Lenin's was practically universal among socialists.

Lenin's Utopia, described in these terms while the European war was raging, may well seem astoundingly naïve to those who read it after fifty years of Soviet power; it had about as much to do with the state that was soon to come into existence as Thomas More's fantasies had with the England of Henry VIII. But it is a sterile exercise to point out the grotesque divergences between programmes and their 'fulfilment' half a century later. Lenin's Utopia is in general accord with Marx's ideas, but as compared with Lenin's own earlier writings, not to speak of the later ones, it presents one striking difference, viz. that it says nothing whatever about the party.

There is no reason to doubt that Lenin penned his fantasy in good faith; it should be recalled that when he did so he believed, wrongly, that there was about to be a world revolution. But he apparently did not perceive that the picture he drew was manifestly contrary to his own doctrine of revolution and of the party. The 'dictatorship of the majority' was supposed to be exercised through a political organization imbued with a scientific understanding of history; this qualification, which cuts across the idea of a 'transitional proletariat state', is not mentioned at all in *The State and Revolution*. At the time of writing the book Lenin evidently envisaged that the whole people, armed and liberated, would directly perform all functions of administration, economic management, the police, the army, the judiciary, etc. He also believed that restraints on freedom would apply only to the former privileged classes, while the workers and labouring peasants would be perfectly free to regulate their lives as they chose.

However, the nature of the system that developed after the Revolution was not merely the result of historical accidents connected with the civil war and the halting of the revolutionary movement outside Russia. The system, with all its despotic and totalitarian features (the distinction is important), was prefigured in its main lines by the Bolshevik doctrine as Lenin had worked it out over the years, though naturally the consequences were not fully realized or predicted.

The basic principle laid down by Lenin in different forms on many occasions since 1903 was that categories such as freedom and political equality were not intrinsic values but only instruments of the class struggle, and it was foolish to advocate them without considering what class interests they served. 'In practice the proletariat can retain its independence only by subordinating its struggle for all democratic demands, not excluding the demand for a republic, to its revolutionary struggle for the overthrow of the bourgeoisie' ('The Socialist Revolution and the Right of Nations to Self-Determination', Apr. 1916; *Works*, vol. 22, p. 149). Under the bourgeois system, the difference between a despotism and a democracy was only significant in so far as the latter facilitated the working-class struggle; it was a secondary difference, one of form only. 'Universal suffrage, a Constituent Assembly, a parliament are merely a form, a sort of promissory note, which does not change the real state of affairs' ('The State', lecture delivered on 11 July 1919; *Works*, vol. 29, p. 485). This is true *a fortiori* of the post-revolutionary state. Since the proletariat is in power, no consideration is important in itself except the maintenance of that power; all organizational questions are subordinate to the preservation of the dictatorship of the proletariat.

The dictatorship of the proletariat will—not provisionally, but permanently—abolish the parliamentary system and the separation of the legislative power from the executive. This is to be the main difference between the Soviet republic and a parliamentary regime. At the Seventh Congress of the Russian Communist Party (Bolshevik) in March 1918 Lenin presented a draft programme embodying this principle: 'Abolition of parliamentarism (as the separation of legislative from executive activity); union of legislative and executive state activity. Fusion of administration with legislation' (*Works*, vol. 27, p. 154). In other words, the rulers determine the laws by which they rule and are not controlled by anyone. But who are the rulers? In the same draft Lenin emphasizes that freedom and democracy are not intended to be for all, but for the labouring and exploited masses and for the sake of their liberation. At the outset of the Revolution Lenin hoped for support not only from the proletariat but from the working peasants as opposed to the kulaks; but it soon became clear that while the whole of the peasantry supported the Revolution against the big landowners, they were much less enthusiastic for the next phase. The party placed its hopes from the beginning on kindling the class struggle in the countryside, and tried to rouse the poor peasants and farm-labourers against the richer peasants, *inter alia* by the so-called 'Committees of the Poor'. The results were meagre, and it was clear that the common interest of the peasants as a class was generally stronger than the conflict between poor peasants and kulaks. Lenin soon began to speak for preference of 'neutralizing' the peasantry as a whole, and at the Tenth Party Conference in May 1921, on the eve of N.E.P., he declared: 'We tell the peasants frankly and honestly, without any deception: in order to hold the road to socialism, we are making a number of concessions to you, comrade peasants, but only within the stated limits and to the stated extent; and, of course, we ourselves shall be the judge of the limits and the extent' (*Works*, vol. 32, p. 419).

The first 'transitional' slogan, that of the dictatorship of the proletariat and the needy peasants, was never more than a delusion or a propaganda device. The party in due course openly admitted that the dictatorship of the proletariat was exercised over the whole peasantry, which thus had no say in deciding the matters that concerned it most, though it was still an obstacle that had to be taken into account. The situation was indeed obvious from the beginning: as the November elections showed, if the peasants had had a share in power the country would have been governed by the S.R.s, with the Bolshevik minority in opposition.

The proletariat thus shared its dictatorship with nobody. As to the question of the 'majority', this never troubled Lenin much. In an article 'Constitutional Illusions' (Aug. 1917; *Works*, vol. 25, p. 201) he wrote: 'in time of revolution it is not enough to ascertain the "will of the majority"—you must *prove to be stronger* at the decisive moment and at the decisive place; you must *win* ... We have seen innumerable examples of the better organized, more politically-conscious and better armed minority forcing its will upon the majority and defeating it.'

It was clear from the beginning, however, that the proletarian minority was to exercise power not in the manner described in *The State and Revolution*, but in accordance with the principle that the proletariat is 'represented' by the party. Lenin did not shrink from using the phrase 'dictatorship of the party'—this was at a time when the party still had to answer its critics and was sometimes cornered into frankness. In a speech on 31 July 1919 he declared: 'When we are reproached with having established a dictatorship of one party and, as you have heard, a united socialist front is proposed, we say, "Yes, it is a dictatorship of one party! That is what we stand for and we shall not shift from that position, because it is the party that has won, in the course of decades, the position of vanguard of the entire factory and industrial proletariat' (*Works*, vol. 29, p. 535). In a document on the trade unions in January 1922, after mentioning the 'contradictions' arising from the backwardness of the masses, he declared: 'The aforementioned contradictions will inevitably give rise to disputes, disagreements, friction, etc. A higher body is required with sufficient authority to settle these at once. This higher body is the Communist Party and the international federation of the Communist Parties of all countries —the Communist International' (*Works*, vol. 33, p. 193).

From the theoretical point of view the matter was elucidated by Lenin's famous pamphlet '*Left-Wing' Communism—an Infantile Disorder* (1920), from which it appeared that there was no problem at all.

The mere presentation of the question—'dictatorship of the party *or* dictatorship of the class; dictatorship (party) of the leaders, *or* dictatorship (party) of the masses?'—testifies to most incredibly and hopelessly muddled thinking … It is common knowledge that the masses are divided into classes … that as a rule and in most cases— at least in present-day civilized countries—classes are led by political parties; that political parties, as a general rule, are run by more or less stable groups composed of the most authoritative, influential and experienced members, who are elected to the most responsible positions, and are called leaders. All this is elementary. All this is clear and simple. Why replace this with some kind of rigmarole, some new Volapük?

The Russian Bolshevik … cannot help regarding all this talk about 'from above' *or* 'from below', about the dictatorship of leaders *or* the dictatorship of the masses, etc., as ridiculous and childish nonsense, something like discussing whether a man's left leg or right arm is of greater use to him. (*Works*, vol. 31, pp. 41, 49)

In thus ruling the issue out of court, Lenin implied that there was no problem about the relationship between a class and a party, or a party and its leaders, and that government by a handful of oligarchs can properly be called government by the class they claim to represent, although there is no institutional means of telling whether the class wants to have them as its representatives or not. Lenin's argument is so crude that it is difficult to believe he meant it seriously (in the above passage he was replying to the German Spartacists, who had criticized him on similar lines to Rosa Luxemburg); yet it harmonizes well enough with his general style of thought. Since nothing 'really' exists except class interests, any alleged problem concerning the independent interests of a governing group or apparatus is a false problem: apparatuses 'represent' classes, that is 'elementary' and everything else is 'childish nonsense'.

Lenin was quite consistent in such matters. According to *The State and Revolution* only an ignoramus or a crafty bourgeois could suggest that the workers are incapable of directly and collectively managing industry, the state, and the administration. Two years later, it turned out that only an ignoramus or a crafty bourgeois could suggest that the workers were capable of directly and collectively managing industry, the state, and the administration. Obviously industry requires single managers, and it is absurd to talk of 'collegiality'. 'Opinions on corporate management are all too frequently imbued with a spirit of sheer ignorance, a spirit of opposition to the specialists ... We must get [the trade unions] to regard this task in the spirit of the fight against the survivals of the celebrated democracy. All these outcries against appointees, all this old and dangerous rubbish which finds its way into various resolutions and conversations must be swept away' (speech to Ninth Congress of R.C.P. (B.), 29 Mar. 1920; *Works*, vol. 30, pp. 458–9). 'Does every worker know how to run the state? People working in the practical sphere know that this is not true ... We know that workers in touch with peasants are liable to fall for non-proletarian slogans. How many of the workers have been engaged in government? A few thousand throughout Russia and no more. If we say that it is not the Party but the trade unions that put up the candidates and administrate, it may sound very democratic and might help us to catch a few votes, but not for long. It will be fatal for the dictatorship of the proletariat' (speech to Congress of Miners, 23 Jan. 1921; *Works*, vol. 32, pp. 61–2). 'But the dictatorship of the proletariat cannot be exercised through an organization embracing the whole of that class ... It can be exercised only by a vanguard that has absorbed the revolutionary energy of the class' (speech on 'The Trade Unions, the Present Situation and Trotsky's Mistakes', 30 Dec. 1921; ibid., p. 21).

It thus appears, thanks to a peculiar dialectic, that a proletarian government would be the ruin of the dictatorship of the proletariat—a perfectly plausible conclusion, given Lenin's interpretation of the latter term. It also appears that 'true' democracy means the abolition of all institutions that have hitherto been regarded as democratic. On this last point Lenin's language was not quite consistent: at times he extolled Soviet power as the highest form of democracy, since it meant rule by the people, while at others he stigmatized democracy as a bourgeois invention. This led to amusing contradictions, as in his speech to the Third Congress of Soviets on 25 January 1918: 'Democracy is a form of bourgeois state championed by all traitors to genuine socialism, who now find themselves at the head of official socialism and who assert that democracy is contrary to the dictatorship of the proletariat. Until the revolution transcended the limits of the bourgeois system, we were for democracy; but as soon as we saw the first signs of socialism in the progress of the revolution we took a firm and resolute stand for the dictatorship of the proletariat' (*Works*, vol. 26, p. 473). In other words, traitors to socialism assert that democracy is the opposite of dictatorship, but we have abandoned democracy for dictatorship, which is its opposite. Such awkwardnesses indicate that Lenin was conscious of the daily erosion of what few democratic institutions remained, but wished from time to time to invoke the virtuous-sounding name of democracy.

Directly after the Revolution the traditional democratic freedoms which the Bolsheviks had insistently demanded until they came to power turned out to be weapons of the bourgeoisie. Lenin's writings confirm this repeatedly as far as freedom of the Press is concerned. '"Freedom of the press" in bourgeois society means freedom for the *rich* systematically, unremittingly, daily, in millions of copies, to deceive, corrupt and fool the exploited and oppressed mass of the people, the poor' ('How to Guarantee the Success of the Constituent Assembly', 28 Sept. 1917; *Works*, vol. 25, p. 376). As against this, 'freedom of the press means that all opinions of *all* citizens may be freely published' (ibid., p. 377). This was so on the eve of the Revolution, but a few days after it things were different. 'Earlier on we said that if we took power, we intended to close down the bourgeois newspapers. To tolerate the existence of these papers is to cease being a socialist' (speech to the Central Executive Committee, 17 Nov. 1917; *Works*, vol. 26, p. 285). Lenin promised—and kept his word—that 'we shall not allow ourselves to be deceived by such high-sounding slogans as freedom, equality and the will of the majority' (*Works*, vol. 29,

p. 351). 'At the present time, when things have reached the stage of overthrowing the rule of capital all over the world, or at all events in one country ... all those who in such a political situation talk about "freedom" in general, who in the name of this freedom oppose the dictatorship of the proletariat, are doing nothing more nor less than aiding and abetting the exploiters, for unless freedom promotes the emancipation of labour from the yoke of capital, it is a deception' (speech on 19 May 1919; *Works*, vol. 29, p. 352). The point was put most clearly and concisely at the Third Congress of the Comintern: 'Until the final issue is decided on the general scale, this awful state of war will continue. And we say "*A la guerre comme à la guerre*; we do not promise any freedom, or any democracy"' (5 July 1921; *Works*, vol. 32, p. 495). The whole question of representative institutions, civil rights, the rights of minorities (or of the majority), control over government, constitutional problems in general—all these are silenced by the maxim *à la guerre comme à la guerre*, and the war is to go on until communism triumphs the world over. In particular, and this is the heart of the matter, the whole idea of *law* as a system of social mediation ceases to exist. Since law is 'nothing but' the instrument whereby one class oppresses another, there is clearly no essential difference between the rule of law and rule by direct compulsion; all that matters is which class has the upper hand. In a letter to D.I. Kursky in May 1922 Lenin wrote: 'The courts must not ban terror ... but must formulate the motives underlying it, legalize it as a principle, plainly, without any make-believe or embellishment.' In an accompanying draft amendment to the Criminal Code he proposed the wording: 'Propaganda or agitation that objectively serves [variant: serves or is likely to serve] the interests of that section of the international bourgeoisie which refuses to recognize the rights of the communist system of ownership that is superseding capitalism, and is striving to overthrow that system by violence, either by means of foreign intervention or blockade, or by espionage, financing the press, and similar means, is an offence punishable by death, which, if mitigating circumstances are proved, may be commuted to deprivation of liberty, or deportation' (sc. from Russia: *vysylka za granitsu*) (*Works*, vol. 33, pp. 358–9). At the Eleventh Congress of the R.C.P.(B.) Lenin declared that the Mensheviks and S.R.s who maintained that the N.E.P. was a retreat towards capitalism and that this proved the bourgeois character of the revolution, would be shot for making such statements (ibid., pp. 282–3).

In this way Lenin laid the foundations of the legislation that distinguishes a totalitarian from a merely despotic system, the operative fact being not that it is severe but that it is spurious. A law may provide draconic penalties for small offences without being specifically totalitarian; what is characteristic of totalitarian law is the use of such formulas as Lenin's: people may be executed for expressing views that may 'objectively serve the interests of the bourgeoisie'. This means that the government can put to death anyone it chooses; there is no such thing as law; it is not that the criminal code is severe, but that it has no existence except in name.

As already mentioned, all this took place at a time when the party was not yet in full control and had sometimes to answer criticism. Paradoxically, the sharp and unambiguous formulas in which Lenin called for the use of terror and denied the possibility of democracy and freedom testified to the fact that freedom had not yet been completely eradicated. In the Stalin era, when there was no criticism from outside the party to contend with, the language of terror was replaced by that of democracy: especially in Stalin's later years, the Soviet system was presented as the supreme embodiment of popular rule and every kind of democratic freedom. In Lenin's day, however, the leaders had to answer socialist critics both in Russia and in the rest of Europe, who protested strongly at the idea that the dictatorship of the proletariat involved the destruction of democracy. Kautsky's onslaught on the Soviet system in his *Dictatorship of the Proletariat* (1918) drew a furious reply from Lenin: in *The Proletarian Revolution and the Renegade Kautsky* (1918) he repeated his attack on ignoramuses who talked of democracy irrespective of its class content, wilfully obscuring the fact that bourgeois democracy was for the bourgeoisie and proletarian democracy for the proletariat. Kautsky had argued that when Marx spoke of a 'dictatorship of the proletariat' he had in mind the class content of the regime and not its methods of government; democratic institutions, in Kautsky's view, were not only compatible with proletarian rule but were a condition of it. To Lenin all this was nonsense. Since the proletariat was governing, it must govern by force, and dictatorship was government by force and not by law.

7. *Trotsky on dictatorship*

Kautsky's next pamphlet, *Terrorism and Communism*, was answered by Trotsky in a work bearing the same title: an English translation appeared in 1921 as *The Defence of Terrorism*. This revealing work is in some ways even more emphatic than Lenin's utterances. Trotsky, who had foreseen in 1903 that Lenin's theory of the party would lead to a one-man tyranny, was completely converted to that theory by 1920. His pamphlet is noteworthy as containing the most general exposition, written when he was in power, of the theory of the state under a proletarian dictatorship, and also the most explicit account of what has come to be called the totalitarian system. True, the pamphlet was written during the civil war and the war with Poland (concerning which Trotsky says with remarkable naïvety: 'We hope for the victory, for we have every historical right to it'), but it clearly aspires to be a work of general theory; the many quotations from Trotsky's previous speeches show that he is not merely exaggerating his thesis in the heat of the moment. He presents the general principles of the dictatorship of the proletariat in the same way as Lenin. Bourgeois democracy is a cheat; serious issues in the class war are decided not by votes but by force; in time of revolution the right course is to fight for power and not wait foolishly for a 'majority'; to reject terror is to reject socialism (he who wills the end must will the means); parliamentary systems have had their day— they mainly reflected the interests of the intermediate classes, while in the revolutionary era it is only the proletariat and the bourgeoisie that count; talk of 'equality before the law', civil rights, etc. is, at the present day, nothing but metaphysical claptrap; it was right to disperse the Constituent Assembly, if only because the electoral system was overtaken by the rapid course of events, and the assembly did not represent the people's will; it was right to shoot hostages (*à la guerre comme à la guerre*); freedom of the Press could not be permitted, as it aided the class enemy and its allies, the Mensheviks and the S.R.s; it was idle to talk about 'truth' and who was right—this was not an academic debate, but a fight to the death; the rights of the individual were irrelevant nonsense, and 'as for us, we were never concerned with the Kantian-priestly and vegetarian-Quaker prattle about the "sacredness of human life"' (*The Defence of Terrorism*, p. 60). The Paris Commune had been defeated because of sentimental and humanitarian qualms; in a dictatorship of the proletariat the party must be the highest court of appeal and have the last word in all important matters; 'the revolutionary supremacy of the proletariat presupposes within the proletariat itself the political supremacy of a party, with a clear programme of action and a faultless internal discipline' (ibid., p. 100); 'the dictatorship of the Soviets became possible only by means of the dictatorship of the party' (p. 101).

Trotsky, however, answers questions that Lenin evaded or ignored. 'Where is your guarantee, certain wise men ask us, that it is just your party that expresses the interests of historical development? Destroying or driving underground the other parties, you have thereby prevented their political competition with you, and consequently you have deprived yourselves of the possibility of testing your line of action.' Trotsky replies: 'This idea is dictated by a purely liberal conception of the course of the revolution. In a period in which all antagonisms assume an open character, and the political struggle swiftly passes into a civil war, the ruling party has sufficient material standard by which to test its line of action, without the possible circulation of Menshevik papers. Noske crushes the Communists, but they grow. We have suppressed the Mensheviks and the S.R.s—and they have disappeared. This criterion is sufficient for us' (p. 101).

This is one of the most enlightening theoretical formulations of Bolshevism, from which it appears that the 'rightness' of a historical movement or a state is to be judged by whether its use of violence is successful. Noske did not succeed in crushing the German Communists, but Hitler did; it would thus follow from Trotsky's rule that Hitler 'expressed the interests of historical development'. Stalin liquidated the Trotskyists in Russia, and they disappeared—so evidently Stalin, and not Trotsky, stood for historical progress.

From the principle of government by a vanguard it followed, of course, that

the continuous 'independence' of the trade union movement, in the period of the proletarian revolution, is just as much an impossibility as the policy of coalition. The trade unions become the most important economic organs of the proletariat in power. Thereby they fall under the leadership of the Communist Party. Not only questions of principle in the trade union movement, but serious conflicts of organization within it are decided by the Central Committee of our party ... [The unions] are the organs of production of the Soviet State, and assume responsibility for its fortunes—not opposing themselves to it, but identifying themselves with it. The unions become the organizers of labour discipline. They demand from the workers intensive labour under the most difficult conditions (*The Defence of Terrorism*, p. 102).

The state is, of course, organized in the interest of the working masses; 'this, however, does not exclude the element of compulsion in all its forms, both the most gentle and the extremely severe' (ibid., p. 122). In the new society compulsion will not only not disappear but will play an essential part: 'The very principle of compulsory labour service is for the Communist quite unquestionable ... The only solution of economic difficulties that is correct *from the point of view both of principle and of practice* [present author's italics] is to treat the population of the whole country as the reservoir of the necessary labour-power ... The principle itself of compulsory labour service has just as *radically and permanently* [present author's italics] replaced the principle of free hiring as the socialization of the means of production has replaced capitalist property' (pp. 124–7). Labour must be militarized: 'we oppose ... capitalist slavery by socially regulated labour on the basis of an economic plan, obligatory for the whole people and consequently compulsory for each worker in the country ... The foundations of the militarization of labour are those forms of State compulsion without which the replacement of capitalist economy by the Socialist will for ever remain an empty sound ... No social organization exept the army has ever considered itself justified in subordinating citizens to itself in such a measure, and controlling them by its will on all sides to such a degree, as the State of the proletarian dictatorship considers itself justified in doing, and does' (pp. 129–30). 'We can have no way to Socialism except by the authoritative regulation of the economic forces and resources of the country, and the centralized distribution of labour-power in harmony with the general State plan. The Labour State considers itself empowered to send every worker to the place where his work is necessary' (p. 131). 'The young Socialist State requires trade unions, not for a struggle for better conditions of labour—that is the task of the social and State organization as a whole—but to organize the working class for the ends of production, to educate, discipline, distribute, group, retain certain categories and certain workers at their posts for fixed periods' (p. 132). To sum up, 'the road to Socialism lies through a period of the highest possible intensification of the principle of the State ... The State, before disappearing, assumes the form of the dictatorship of the proletariat, i.e. the most ruthless form of State, which embraces the life of the citizens authoritatively in every direction' (p. 157).

It would be difficult indeed to put the matter more plainly. The state of the proletarian dictatorship is depicted by Trotsky as a huge permanent concentration camp in which the government exercises absolute power over every aspect of the citizens' lives and in particular decides how much work they shall do, of what kind and in what places. Individuals are nothing but labour units. Compulsion is universal, and any organization that is not part of the state must be its enemy, thus the enemy of the proletariat. All this, of course, is in the name of an ideal realm of freedom, the advent of which is expected after an indefinite lapse of historical time. Trotsky, we may say, provided a perfect expression of socialist principles as understood by the Bolsheviks. It should be noted, however, that we are not told clearly what, from the Marxist point of view, is to replace the free hiring of labour—which, according to Marx, is a mark of slavery, as it means that a man has to sell his labour-power on the market, i.e. treat himself as a commodity and be so treated by society. If free hiring is abolished, the only ways of inducing people to work and produce wealth are physical compulsion or moral motivation (enthusiasm for work). The latter was of course much extolled by both Lenin and Trotsky, but they soon found that it was chimerical to rely on it as a permanent source of effort. Only compulsion was left—not capitalist compulsion based on the necessity to earn a living, but sheer physical force, the fear of imprisonment, physical injury, and death.

8. *Lenin as an ideologist of totalitarianism*

Lenin, who in important practical matters was much less doctrinaire than Trotsky, departed from his own principles on at least two points. In the first place, he recognized that the trade unions had a part to play not only in the execution of planned production but also in defending the workers against the state—although previously, with true Marxist logic, he had maintained, like Trotsky, that this meant the working class defending itself against itself, which was absurd. Secondly, he admitted that the state was suffering from 'bureaucratic distortion', though it was not clear how this could fit into his mental scheme: on the face of things, from the viewpoint of class interests, capitalist bureaucracy was an instrument of oppression and socialist bureaucracy of liberation. It does credit to his common sense that in both these matters he was able to sacrifice dogma to reality, but unfortunately he saw the light too late to do anything. In any case, for one word in favour of trade-union independence he uttered ten about the danger of syndicalism, and he had no cure for bureaucracy except more bureaucracy. Any illusion that the party itself could be an enclave of free speech and free criticism, suppressed in society at large, was doomed to early disappointment. Lenin himself, as we have seen, never regarded cliques or disputes within the party as a healthy sign. As early as 1910, at grips with the otzovists and the slogan of 'complete freedom of revolutionary and philosophical thought', he wrote: 'This slogan is thoroughly opportunist. In all countries this kind of slogan has been put forward in the socialist parties only by opportunists and in practice has meant nothing but "freedom" to corrupt the working class with bourgeois ideology. "Freedom of thought" (read: freedom of the press, speech and conscience) we demand from the *state* (not from a party) together with freedom of association' ('The *Vperyod* Faction', Sept. 1910; *Works*, vol. 16, p.270). This, of course, referred to the bourgeois state. Once the authority of the state was identified with that of the party, the rules applying to freedom of criticism must evidently be the same for both. The *Gleichschaltung* of the party took longer, but was equally inevitable: the matter was settled in principle at the Tenth Congress, in March 1921, by Lenin's attack on factionalism and 'the luxury of studying shades of opinion', and his statement that 'we must make it quite clear that we cannot have arguments about deviations and that we must put a stop to that' (*Works*, vol. 32, pp. 177–8). For some years after Lenin's death it was impossible completely to prevent the overt formation of groups and 'platforms' within the party, or rather the party apparatus; but before long genuine or imaginary 'deviations' were dealt with by the punitive arm of the state, and the ideal of unity was achieved by police methods.

If it can be said, however, that Lenin's doctrine and the style of thought that went with it laid the foundations of the totalitarian system, this is not on account of the principles invoked to justify the use of terror and the stifling of civil liberties. Once the civil war begins, extreme measures of terrorism are to be expected from both sides. The extinguishing of civil liberties in order to maintain and strengthen the regime does not amount to totalitarianism unless accompanied by the principle that every activity—economic, cultural, etc. —must be completely subordinated to the aims of the state; that not only are acts against the regime forbidden and ruthlessly punished, but no political actions are 'neutral' and the individual citizen has no right to do anything that is not part of the state's purposes; that he is the state's property and is treated by it as such. The Soviet system, which took over these principles from Tsarist Russia and brought them to a far greater degree of perfection, is in this respect also the work of Lenin.

Lenin never believed in the possibility of impartiality or neutrality in any sphere of life, including philosophy. Anyone who claimed to belong to no party, or declared himself neutral, was a secret enemy. Attacking the railwaymen's union shortly after the Revolution, on 1 December 1917, Lenin told the Congress of Soviets of Peasants' Deputies: 'At a time of revolutionary struggle, when every minute counts, when dissent and neutrality allow the enemy to put in his word, when he will certainly be heard, and when no haste is made to help the people in their struggle for their sacred rights, I cannot call such a stand neutrality; it is not neutrality; a revolutionary would call it incitement' (*Works*, vol. 26, pp. 329–30).

There were no 'neutrals' in politics, or anywhere else. What-ever question Lenin was concerned with at any time, all that interested him was whether it was good or bad for the revolution or, afterwards, for the Soviet government. His four short articles on Tolstoy, written in 1910–11 after the latter's death, are a typical example. His central theme is the existence of 'two aspects' in Tolstoy's work: the first reactionary and utopian (moral perfection, charity towards all, and non-resistance to evil), the second 'progressive' and critical (description of the oppression and misery of the peasants, the hypocrisy of the upper classes and the Church, etc.). The 'reactionary' aspect of Tolstoy's doctrine was emphasized by reactionaries, but the 'progressive' aspect might afford 'useful material' for the purpose of arousing the masses, although the political struggle was already much wider in scope than Tolstoy's criticism. Lenin's article of 1905, 'Party Organization and Party Literature', was used for decades, and is still used, to justify ideologically the enslavement of the written word in Russia. It has been argued that it refers only to political literature, but this is not so: it relates to every kind of writing. It contains the words: 'Down with non-partisan writers! Down with literary supermen! Literature must become part of the common cause of the proletariat, "a cog and a screw" of one single great Social-Democratic mechanism set in motion by the entire politically conscious vanguard of the entire working class' (*Works*, vol. 10, p. 45). For the benefit of 'hysterical intellectuals' who deplore this seemingly bureaucratic attitude, Lenin explains that there can be no mechanical levelling in the field of literature; there must be room for personal initiative, imagination, etc.; none the less, literary work must be part of the party's work and controlled by the party. This, of course, was written during the fight for 'bourgeois democracy', on the assumption that Russia would in due course enjoy freedom of speech but that literary members of the party would have to display party-mindedness in their writings; as in other cases, the obligation would become general when the party controlled the apparatus of state coercion.

Lenin's often-quoted speech to the Komsomol Congress on 2 October 1920 deals with ethical questions on similar lines. 'We say that our morality is entirely subordinated to the interests of the proletariat's class struggle ... Morality is what serves to destroy the old exploiting society and to unite all the working people around the proletariat, which is building up a new, a communist society ... To a Communist all morality lies in this united discipline and conscious mass struggle against the exploiters. We do not believe in an eternal morality, and we expose the falseness of all the fables about morality' (*Works*, vol. 31, pp. 291–4). It would be hard to interpret these words in any other sense than that everything which serves or injures the party's aims is morally good or bad respectively, and nothing else is morally good or bad. After the seizure of power, the maintenance and strengthening of Soviet rule becomes the sole criterion of morality as well as of all cultural values. No criteria can avail against any action that may seem conducive to the maintenance of power, and no values can be recognized on any other basis. All cultural questions thus become technical questions and must be judged by the one unvarying standard; the 'good of society' becomes completely alienated from the good of its individual members. It is bourgeois sentimentalism, for instance, to condemn aggression and annexation if it can be shown that they help to maintain Soviet power; it is illogical and hypocritical to condemn torture if it serves the ends of the power which, by definition, is devoted to the 'liberation of the working masses'. Utilitarian morality and utilitarian judgements of social and cultural phenomena transform the original basis of socialism into its opposite. All phenomena that arouse moral indignation if they occur in bourgeois society are turned to gold, as if by a Midas touch, if they serve the interests of the new power: the armed invasion of a foreign state is liberation, aggression is defence, tortures represent the people's noble rage against the exploiters. There is absolutely nothing in the worst excesses of the worst years of Stalinism that cannot be justified on Leninist principles, if only it can be shown that Soviet power was increased thereby. The essential difference between the 'Lenin era' and the 'Stalin era' is not that under Lenin there was freedom in the party and society and that under Stalin it was crushed, but that it was only in Stalin's day that the whole spiritual life of the peoples of the Soviet Union was submerged in a universal flood of mendacity. This was due, however, not only to Stalin's personality but also, if one may so put it, to the 'natural' development of the situation. When Lenin spoke of terror, bureaucracy, or an anti-Bolshevik rising by the peasants, he called these things by their names. Once the Stalinist dictatorship set in, the party (though attacked by its enemies) had no mistakes whatever to its discredit, the Soviet state was flawless, and the people's love for the government was unbounded. The change was natural in the sense that in a state where every vestige of institutional control over the government had been done away with, the latter's only justification was that, as a matter of foreordained principle, it embodied the interests and aspirations of the working people: this may be called an ideological form of legitimacy, distinct from the charisma which belongs to a hereditary monarchy or from a properly elected regime. The omnipotence of the Lie was not due to Stalin's wickedness, but was the only way of legitimizing a regime based on Leninist principles. The slogan constantly met with during Stalin's dictatorship, 'Stalin is the Lenin of our day', was thus entirely accurate.

9. Martov on the Bolshevik ideology

Together with Kautsky and Rosa Luxemburg, Martov was the third eminent critic of Bolshevik ideology and tactics in the years immediately after the Revolution. His *World Bolshevism* (1923, in Russian), a collection of articles written chiefly in 1918–19, is probably the most important attempt to criticize Leninism from the Menshevik standpoint, i.e. it represents a social democratic view similar to Kautsky's. Martov claimed that the assumption of power by the Bolsheviks in Russia had little in common with the proletarian revolution as traditionally understood by Marxists. The successes of Bolshevism were not due to the maturity of the working class, but to its disintegration and the demoralization of war. The pre-war working class, educated in socialism for years or decades by the parties, had been depraved by the years of slaughter and altered in character by the influx of the rural element, a process which had taken place in all the belligerent nations. The former authority of ideas had vanished; crude, simple maxims were the order of the day; actions were dictated by direct material needs and the belief that all social questions could be solved by force of arms. The socialist Left had been defeated in its attempt, at Zimmerwald, to save what remained of the proletarian movement. The fact that Marxism had disintegrated during the war into 'social patriotism' on the one hand and Bolshevik anarcho-Jacobinism on the other was only a confirmation of the Marxist theory that consciousness depends on social conditions. The ruling classes, by means of their armies, were perpetrating mass destruction, pillage, forced labour, etc. In the midst of this general regression, world Bolshevism had arisen on the ruins of the socialist movement. Contrasting the promises in Lenin's *The State and Revolution* with post-Revolutionary reality, Martov nevertheless takes the view that the true sense of Bolshevism does not lie in the restriction of democracy: Plekhanov's old idea that the revolution should for a time deprive the bourgeoisie of electoral rights could have been applied if there had existed other forms of institutional democracy. The ideology of Bolshevism is based on the principle that scientific socialism is true and must therefore be imposed on the masses who, deluded by the bourgeoisie, cannot understand their own interests; for this purpose it is necessary to destroy parliament, the free Press, and all representative institutions. This doctrine, Martov says, is in accordance with a certain strain in the tradition of utopian socialism: measures similar to those of the Bolsheviks figured in the programme of the Babouvists, Weitling, Cabet, or the Blanquists. They are, however, contrary to dialectical materialism. From the principle that the working class is spiritually dependent on the society in which it lives, the utopians drew the inference that society must be transformed by a handful of conspirators or an enlightened élite, with the labouring masses playing the role of a passive object. But the dialectic view, expressed, for example, in Marx's third *Thesis on Feuerbach*, is that there is a constant interaction between human consciousness and material conditions, and that as the working class struggles to alter these conditions it changes itself and achieves spiritual liberation. The dictatorship of a minority cannot educate either society or the dictators themselves. The proletariat can only take over the achievements of bourgeois society when it becomes capable of taking the initiative as a class, and it cannot do so in conditions of despotism, bureaucracy, and terror.

The Bolsheviks, Martov continues, are not entitled to appeal to Marx's formulas concerning the dictatorship of the proletariat and the destruction of the former state machine. Marx attacked the electoral law in the name of universal eligibility and popular sovereignty, not the despotism of a single party. He called for the abolition of the anti-democratic institutions of the democratic state—police, standing army, centralized bureaucracy—but not the abolition of democracy as such: the dictatorship of the proletariat meant to him not a form of government but a particular kind of society. The Leninists, on the other hand, proclaim the anarchist slogan of smashing the state machine and are seeking at the same time to rebuild it in the most despotic form possible.

The dispute between Lenin and Martov thus ended at the point where it had begun in 1903. When Martov spoke of working-class rule he meant what he said, whereas in Lenin's view the working class left to itself could only produce bourgeois ideology, and to give it real power would amount to restoring capitalism. As Lenin wrote quite rightly in August 1921: 'The slogan "more faith in the forces of the working class" is now being used, in fact, to increase the influence of the Mensheviks and anarchists, as was vividly proved and demonstrated by Kronstadt in the spring of 1921' ('New Times and Old Mistakes in a New Guise'; *Works*, vol. 33, p. 27). Martov wanted the state to take over all the democratic institutions of the past and increase their scope; Lenin's state was communist only inasmuch as the communists had a monopoly of power in it. Martov believed in cultural continuity; to Lenin, the only 'culture' that should be taken over from the bourgeoisie consisted of technical and administrative skills. However, Martov was mistaken when he accused the Bolsheviks of expressing in their ideology the hunger of the demoralized masses for material goods. This view was occasioned by the mass plundering which marked the first phase of the Revolution; but neither Lenin nor any other Bolshevik leader regarded plundering as an expression of communist doctrine. On the contrary, Lenin maintained that increased labour productivity was the hallmark of socialist superiority, and he relied mainly, if not wholly, on technical progress to bring about socialism. He wrote, for instance, that if scores of regional electric power-stations were constructed—which, however, would take at least ten years—even the most backward parts of Russia would pass straight to socialism without any intervening stage (*The Tax in Kind*, May 1921; *Works*, vol. 32, p. 350). It was in fact the Bolsheviks who established the idea that global production indices are the basic evidence for the success of socialism; although of course not in so many words, they sanctified the principle of production for its own sake, irrespective of whether it makes life better for the producers, i.e. the whole working community. This was an important aspect, though not the only one, of the cult of state power as the supreme value.

10. Lenin as a polemicist. Lenin's genius

The great bulk of Lenin's published work consists of attacks and polemics. The reader is invariably struck by the coarseness and aggressiveness of his style, which are unparalleled in the whole literature of socialism. His polemics are full of insults and humourless mockery (he had in fact no sense of humour at all). It makes no difference whether he is attacking the 'economists', the Mensheviks, the Kadets, Kautsky, Trotsky, or the 'workers' opposition': if his opponent is not a lackey of the bourgeoisie and the landowners he is a prostitute, a clown, a liar, a pettifogging rogue, and so on. This style of controversy was to become obligatory in Soviet writing on topics of the day, though in a stereotyped, bureaucratic form devoid of personal passion. If Lenin's opponent happens to say something he agrees with, the man is 'forced to admit' whatever it is; if a dispute breaks out in the enemy camp, one of its members has 'blurted out' the truth about another; if the author of a book or article does not mention something that Lenin thinks he ought to have mentioned, he has 'hushed it up'. His socialist adversary of the moment 'fails to understand the ABC of Marxism'; if, however, Lenin changes his mind on the point at issue, the one who 'fails to understand the ABC of Marxism' is he who maintains what Lenin was maintaining the day before. Everyone is constantly suspected of the worst intentions; anyone who differs from Lenin on the most trifling matter is a cheat, or at best a stupid child.

The purpose of this technique was not to satisfy any personal dislike, still less to arrive at the truth, but to achieve a practical object. Lenin himself confirmed this ('blurted it out', as he would have said of anyone else) on an occasion in 1907. On the eve of reunion with the Mensheviks the Central Committee had brought Lenin before a party tribunal for 'impermissible' attacks on them: he had said in a pamphlet, among other things, that the St. Petersburg Mensheviks had 'entered into negotiations with the Cadet Party for the purpose of selling workers' votes to the Cadets', and had 'bargained with the Cadets to smuggle (*protashchit'*) their man into the Duma, in spite of the workers, with the aid of the Cadets'. Lenin explained his action to the tribunal as follows. 'The wording [i.e. that just quoted] is calculated to evoke in the reader hatred, aversion and contempt for people who commit such deeds. Such wording is calculated not to convince, but to break up the ranks of the opponent; not to correct the mistake of the opponent, but to destroy him, to wipe his organization off the face of the earth. This wording is indeed of such a nature as to evoke the worst thoughts, the worst suspicions about the opponent, and indeed, as contrasted with the wording that convinces and corrects, it "carries confusion into the ranks of the proletariat" (*Works*, vol. 12, pp. 424–5). Lenin, however, is not expressing penitence for this. In his opinion it is right to incite to hatred instead of appealing to argument, unless the adversary is a member of the same party; and at the time of the remarks complained of, the Bolsheviks and Mensheviks were two separate parties on account of the split. He rebukes the Central Committee for 'remaining silent about the fact that at the time the pamphlet was written a united party did not exist in the organization from which it emanated (not formally, but in essence), and whose aims it served ... It is wrong to write about Party comrades in language that systematically spreads among the working masses hatred, aversion, contempt, etc. for those who hold other opinions. But *one may and one must write* in that strain about an organization that has seceded. Why must one? Because when a split has taken place it is one's duty *to wrest* the masses from the leadership of the seceding section' (ibid., p. 425). 'Are there any limits to a permissible struggle stemming from a split? No Party standards set limits to such a struggle, nor can there be such limits, for a split implies that the Party has ceased to exist' (p. 428). We may thank the Mensheviks for provoking Lenin to this avowal, which is confirmed by the activity of his whole life: no holds are barred, and all that counts is to achieve one's object.

Unlike Stalin, Lenin was never actuated by motives of personal revenge: he treated people—and this, it should be emphasized, included himself—exclusively as political tools and instruments of the historical process. This is one of the most salient features of his personality. If political calculation so required, he could pelt a man with mud one day and shake hands with him the next. He vilified Plekhanov after 1905, but ceased to do so at once when he found that Plekhanov was opposed to the liquidators and the empiriocritics and was, with the prestige of his name, a valuable ally. Up to 1917 he hurled anathemas at Trotsky, but all this was forgotten when Trotsky became a Bolshevik and proved to be a highly gifted leader and organizer. He denounced the treachery of Zinoviev and Kamenev in publicly opposing the plan for an armed uprising in October, but afterwards he allowed them to occupy high positions in the party and the Comintern. When someone had to be attacked, personal considerations went by the board. Lenin was capable of shelving disputes if he though it possible to agree on basic issues—for example, he overlooked Bogdanov's philo-sophical errors until the latter opposed him over the question of the party being represented in the Third Duma; but if the dispute concerned something he considered important at the time, he showed the adversary no mercy. He derided questions of personal loyalty in political quarrels. When the Mensheviks accused Malinovsky, one of the Bolshevik leaders, of being an Okhrana agent, Lenin rebutted these 'base slanders' with the utmost ferocity. After the February Revolution it came to light that they were true, whereupon Lenin attacked Rodzyanko, the president of the Duma. Rodzyanko, it appeared, had been informed of Malinovsky's role and had brought about his resignation from the Duma, but had not told the Bolsheviks (who at this time were covering Rodzyanko's party with abuse), on the ground, forsooth, that when he received the information from the Minister of the Interior he had given his word of honour not to reveal it. Lenin was full of pseudo-moral indignation at the fact that the Bolsheviks' enemies had abstained from helping them on the ridiculous pretext of 'honour'.

Another characteristic of Lenin's is that he often projected his hostility into the past in order to show that the opponent had always been a villain and a traitor. In 1906 he wrote that Struve had been a counter-revolutionary as early as 1894 ('The Victory of the Cadets and the Tasks of the Workers' Party'; *Works*, vol. 10, p. 265), although no one could have supposed this from

Lenin's arguments with Struve in 1895, when they were still collaborating. For years Lenin regarded Kautsky as a theorist of the highest authority, but after Kautsky took up a 'centrist' position during the war Lenin denounced him for having shown 'opportunism' in a pamphlet of 1902 (*The State and Revolution*; *Works*, vol. 25, p. 479) and claimed that he had not written as a Marxist since 1909 (preface to a pamphlet by Bukharin, Dec. 1915; *Works*, vol. 22, p. 106). Throughout 1914–18, in his attacks on the 'social chauvinists', Lenin invoked the Basle Manifesto of the Second International, which called on parties to have nothing to do with the imperialist war; but after the final breach with the Second International it appeared that the Manifesto was a deception by 'renegades' (*Notes of a Publicist*, 1922; *Works*, vol. 33, p. 206). For many years Lenin insisted that he did not stand for any separate trend within the socialist movement, but that he and the Bolsheviks held to the same principles as the social democrats of Europe, especially Germany. But in 1920, in '*Left-Wing' Communism—an Infantile Disorder*, it was revealed that Bolshevism as a brand of political thought had existed since 1903, which indeed was the case. Lenin's retroactive view of history was of course nothing in comparison to the systematic falsification of Stalin's day, when it had to be shown at all costs that the current assessment of individuals and political movements was equally valid for all past years. In this respect Lenin only made a modest beginning, and often adhered to a rational mode of thought: for instance, he maintained to the end that Plekhanov had rendered great services in popularizing Marxism and that his theoretical works should be reprinted, although Plekhanov at the time was wholly on the side of the 'social chauvinists'.

Since Lenin was interested only in the political effect of his writings, they are full of repetitions. He was not afraid to repeat the same ideas again and again: he had no stylistic ambitions, but was merely concerned with influencing the party or the workers. It is noteworthy that his style is at its coarsest in factional dispute and when he is addressing party activists, but that he speaks to the workers in much milder terms. Some of his works addressed to them are masterpieces of propaganda, such as the pamphlet *Political Parties in Russia and the Tasks of the Proletariat* (May 1917), which gives a concise and lucid account of the position of the respective parties on the main questions of the hour.

In theoretical debates, too, he was more concerned to over-whelm the adversary with words and abuse than to analyse arguments in detail. *Materialism and Empiriocriticism* is an out-standing example, but there are many others. In 1913 Struve published a book entitled *The Economy and Prices*, in which he argued that value in Marx's sense, independent of price, was a metaphysical and non-empirical category and was economically superfluous. (This was not a new idea but had been put forward by many critics from Konrad Schmidt onwards.) Lenin com-mented in these terms: 'How can one help calling this most "radical" method most flimsy? For thousands of years mankind has been aware of the operation of an objective law in the phenomenon of exchange, has been trying to understand it and express it with the utmost precision, has been testing its explanations by millions and billions of day-by-day observations of economic life; and suddenly a fashionable representative of a fashionable occupation—that of collecting quotations (I almost said collecting postage stamps)—comes along and "does away with all this": "worth is a phantom"' ('Socialism Demolished Again', Mar. 1914; *Works*, vol. 20, p. 200). Lenin proceeds to explain: 'Price is a manifestation of the law of value. Value is the law of price, i.e. the generalized expression of the phenomenon of price. To speak of "independence" here is a mockery of science' (ibid., p. 201). Then the summing-up: 'Expelling laws from science means, in fact, smuggling in the laws of religion.' And the judgement: 'Does Mr. Struve really think he can deceive his readers and disguise his obscurantism with such crude methods?' (ibid., pp. 202, 204). This is a typical example of Lenin's treatment of an adversary. Struve had said that value cannot be calculated independently of price; Lenin says that to speak of independence is a mockery of science. There is no attempt to meet the real argument, which is drowned in a welter of verbiage and abuse.

It should be repeated, however, that Lenin did not exempt himself from this purely technical, instrumental attitude towards people and affairs. He had no thought of personal gain; unlike Trotsky for instance, he was in no way a *poseur* and was not given to theatrical gestures. He regarded himself as an instrument of the revolution and was unshakably convinced that he was in the right—so convinced that he was not afraid to stand alone, or almost alone, against his political opponents; he resembled Luther in the steadfastness of his belief that God, or rather History, spoke through his lips. He rejected with scorn the reproach, made, for example, by Ledebour at Zimmerwald, that he was calling on the Russian workers to shed blood while himself remaining safely in a foreign country. Such objections were absurd from his point of view, since it was to the advantage of the revolution that he should operate from abroad; given Russian conditions there could not be a revolution without the emigration. In any case no one could accuse him of personal cowardice. He was capable of assuming the heaviest responsibility, and always took up a clear-cut attitude in any dispute. He was certainly right in reproaching the leaders of all other socialist groups with being afraid to seize power. The others found it safer to put their faith in historical laws; Lenin, who was not afraid, played for the highest stakes and won.

Why did he win? Certainly not because he correctly foresaw the course of events. His prophecies and estimates were often wrong, sometimes glaringly so. After the defeat of 1905 he believed for a long time that another upsurge was imminent; when he realized, however, that the tide of revolution had subsided and that there would have to be long years of work in reactionary conditions, he immediately drew all the inferences from the situation. When Wilson was elected President of the United States in 1912 he declared that the two-party system in America was bankrupt *vis-à-vis* the socialist movement. In 1913 he stated no less categorically that Irish nationalism was extinct in the working class. After 1917 he expected a European revolution any day, and thought he could run the Russian economy by means of terror. But all his misjudgements were in the direction of expecting the revolutionary movement to be stronger, and to manifest itself earlier, than it actually did. They were fortunate errors from his point of view, since it was only on the basis of false estimates that he decided on an armed insurrection in October 1917. His mistakes enabled him to exploit the possibilities of revolution to the full, and were thus the cause of his success. Lenin's genius was not that of foresight, but of concentrating at a given moment all the social energies that could be used to seize power, and subordinating all his efforts and those of his party to this one aim. Without Lenin's firmness of purpose, it is unthinkable that the Bolsheviks could have succeeded. But for him they would have prolonged the boycott of the Duma beyond the critical moment; they would not have ventured on an armed uprising to secure power for themselves alone; they would not have signed the Treaty of Brest-Litovsk, and they might not, at the last moment, have adopted the New Economic Policy. In critical situations Lenin committed violence on the party, and his cause prevailed as a result. World communism as we know it today is truly his work.

Neither Lenin nor the Bolsheviks 'made' the Revolution. Since the turn of the century it had been clear that the autocracy was in a precarious state, though no 'historical laws' prescribed the manner of its downfall. The February Revolution was due to the coincidence of many factors: the war, peasant demands, memories of 1905, the conspiracy of the liberals, support from the Entente, the radicalization of the working masses. As the revolutionary process developed, the slogan was that of Soviet power, and those who supported the October Revolution wanted power for the Soviets, not for the Bolshevik party. But 'Soviet power' was an anarchist Utopia, the dream of a society in which the mass of the people, most of it ignorant and illiterate, would in permanent mass rallies decide all economic, social, military, and administrative questions. It can hardly be said that Soviet power was even overthrown. The slogan 'the Soviets without the communists' was frequently used in popular anti-Bolshevik revolts, but it meant nothing in practice and the Bolsheviks knew this. They were able to enlist support for themselves *as a Soviet government*, and to canalize the energies of the Revolution at a time when they were the only party prepared to govern single-handed.

None the less, the actual revolutionary process was much more Soviet than specifically Bolshevik, and for some years the culture, mood, and habits of the new society reflected the fact that it originated in an explosion in which the Bolsheviks were the best-organized force but were by no means a majority of society. The Revolution was not a Bolshevik *coup d'état*, but a true revolution of the workers and peasants. The Bolsheviks alone were able to harness it for their own ends; their victory was at once a defeat for the Revolution and a defeat for communist ideas, even in their Bolshevik version. Lenin described the dangers ahead with admirable clarity at the Eleventh Party Congress in March 1922 (the last he attended). Speaking of the communists' weakness *vis-à-vis* the culture inherited from Tsarist times, he said:

If the conquering nation is more cultured than the vanquished nation, the former imposes its culture upon the latter; but if the opposite is the case, the vanquished nation imposes its culture upon the conqueror. Has not something like this happened in the capital of the RSFSR? Have the 4,700 Communists (nearly a whole army division, and all of them the very best) come under the influence of an alien culture? True, there may be the impression that the vanquished have a high level of culture. But that is not the case at all. Their culture is miserable, insignificant, but it is still at a higher level than ours. (*Works*, vol. 33, p. 288)

This is one of Lenin's most penetrating observations on the state he had created. The slogan 'learn from the bourgeoisie' was put into practice in a way that was both tragic and grotesque. With enormous labour and only partial success the Bolsheviks set about assimilating, as they are still doing, the technical achievements of the capitalist world. With no labour at all, they adopted swiftly and completely the methods of government and administration of the Tsarist chinovniks. The revolutionary dreams have survived only in the form of phraseological remnants decorating the regime's totalitarian imperalism.

SELECTIVE
BIBLIOGRAPHY

SECTION 1: THE SECOND INTERNATIONAL

BEER, MAX, *Fifty Years of International Socialism*, London 1937.

BRAUNTHAL, J., *Geschichte der Internationale*, 2 vols., Hanover, 1961–3.

COLE, G. D. H., *A History of Socialist Thought*, vol. iii: *The Second International*, London, 1956.

COMPERE-MOREL, A. C. A., *Encyclopédie socialiste, syndicale et coopérative de l'Internationale ouvrière*, 8 vols., Paris, 1912–13.

VAN DEN ESCH, PATRICIA, *La Deuxième Internationale*, Paris, 1957.

HAUPT, G., *La Deuxième Internationale, 1889–1914. Étude critique des sources, essais bibliographiques*, Paris–La Haye, 1964.

JOLL, JAMES, *The Second International*, London, 1955

SETTEMBRINI, D., *Socialismo e rivoluzione dopo Marx*, Naples, 1974.

SECTION 2: GERMAN ORTHODOXY

Kautsky: Works:

Karl Marx' ökonomische Lehren, Stuttgart, 1887.

Thomas More und seine Utopie, Stuttgart, 1888.

Die Klassengegensätze von 1789, Stuttgart, 1889.

Das Erfurter Programm in seinem grundsätzlichen Teil erläutert, Stuttgart, 1892, (many impressions; last edn. Hanover, 1964).

Die Vorläufer des neueren Sozialismus, Stuttgart, 1895.

Die Agrarfrage, Stuttgart, 1899.

Bernstein und das sozialdemokratische Programm. Eine Anti-Kritik, Stuttgart, 1899.

Ethik und materialistische Geschichtsauffassung. Ein Versuch, Stuttgart, 1906. (Eng. trans. Chicago, 1918).

Patriotismus und Sozialdemokratie, Leipzig, 1907.

Der Ursprung des Christentums, Stuttgart, 1908.

Der Weg zur Macht, Berlin, 1909.

Der politische Massenstreik, Berlin, 1914.

Demokratie oder Diktatur, Berlin, 1918.

Terrorismus und Kommunismus, Berlin, 1919.

Von der Demokratie zur Staatssklaverei, Berlin, 1921.

Die materialistische Geschichtsauffassung, Berlin, 1927.

On Kautsky:

BLUMENBERG, WERNER, *Karl Kautsky's literarisches Werk*, The Hague, 1960 (bibliography).

Ein Leben für den Sozialismus. Erinnerungen an Karl Kautsky, Hanover, 1954.

MATTHIAS, E., 'Kautsky und der Kautskyanismus', in *Marxismus-studien*, vol. ii, Tübingen, 1957.

WALDENBERG, MAREK, *Wzlot i upadek Karola Kautsky'ego (Kautsky's Rise and Decline)*, vols. i and ii, Cracow, 1972 (with a copious bibliography).

Mehring:

MEHRING, FRANZ, *Gesammelte Schriften*, ed. T. Hoehle, H. Koch, and J. Schleifstein, East Berlin, 1960 ff.

SCHLEIFSTEIN, J., *Franz Mehring. Sein marxistisches Schaffen 1891–1919*, East Berlin, 1959.

Cunow:

Die Marxsche Geschichts-, Gesellschafts- und Staatstheorie, vols. i and ii, Berlin, 1920–1.

Ursprung der Religion und des Gottesglaubens, Berlin, 1924.

SECTION 3: ROSA LUXEMBURG

Works:

Die industrielle Entwicklung Polens, Leipzig, 1898.

Sozialreform oder Revolution?, Leipzig, 1899.

Massenstreik, Partei und Gewerkschaften, Hamburg, 1906.

Die Akkumulation des Kapitals, Berlin, 1913 (Eng. trans. London, 1951).

(Junius) *Die Krise der Sozialdemokratie*, Zurich, 1916.

Die Akkumulation des Kapitals oder was die Epigonen aus der Marxschen Theorie gemacht haben. Eine Anti-Kritik, Leipzig, 1921.

Einführung in die Nationalökomomie, hrsg. von P. Levi, Berlin, 1925.

Die Russische Revolution. Eine kritische Würdiging, Aus dem Nachlass hrsg. und eingel. von Paul Levi, Berlin, 1932 (Eng. trans. Ann Arbor, 1961).

Politische Schriften, hrsg. und eingel. von Ossip K. Flechtheim, 3 vols., Frankfurt–Vienna, 1966–8.

In English:

Selected Political Writings, ed. R. Looker, London, 1972.

On Rosa Luxemburg:

CIOLKOSZ, ADAM, *Róża Luxemburg a rewolucja rosyjska (Rosa Luxemburg and the Russian Revolution)*, Paris, 1961.

FRÖHLICH, PAUL, *Rosa Luxemburg, Gedanke und Tat*, Paris, 1939 (Eng. trans. London, 1940).

KOWALIK, TADEUSZ, *Róża Luxemburg. Teoria akumulacji i imperializmu* (*Rosa Luxemburg. Theory of Accumulation and of Imperialism*), Warsaw, 1971.

NETTL, J. P., *Rosa Luxemburg*, vols. i and ii, London, 1966 (with a copious bibliography).

ROLAND-HOLST, HENRIETTE, *Rosa Luxemburg: ihr Leben und Wirken*, Zurich, 1937.

SECTION 4; BERNSTEIN AND REVISIONISM

Works:

Die Voraussetzungen des Sozialismus und die Aufgaben der Sozialdemokratie, Stuttgart, 1899 (many impressions; Eng. trans. by E. C. Harvey under title *Evolutionary Socialism*, London, 1909).

Zur Geschichte und Theorie des Sozialismus, Berlin, 1901.

Der politische Massenstreik und die politische Lage der Sozialdemokratie in Deutschland, Breslau, 1905.

Geschichte der Berliner Arbeiterbewegung, 3 vols., Berlin, 1907–10.

Sozialismus und Demokratie in der grossen englischen Revolution, 2nd edn., Stuttgart, 1908; last edn., Hanover, 1964.

Erinnerungen, Berlin, 1929.

On Bernstein:

ANGEL, PIERRE, *Edouard Bernstein et l'évolution du socialisme allemand*, Paris, 1961.

GAY, PETER, *The Dilemma of Democratic Socialism*, London, 1952.

MEYER, TH., *Bernsteins konstruktiver Sozialismus*, Berlin–Bonn, 1977 (with a copious bibliography).

SECTION 5: FRENCH MARXISTS

Jaurès

BLUM, L., *Jean Jaurès*, Paris, 1937.

CHALLAYE, F., *Jaurès*, Paris, 1936.

HAMPDEN, J., *Jean Jaurès*, 1943.

JAURÈS, J., *Œuvres*, ed. Max Bonnafous, Paris (incomplete; 9 vols. appeared 1931–9).

LEVY, LOUIS, *Anthologie de Jean Jaurès*, Paris, 1946.

RAPPAPORT, C., *Jean Jaurès, l'homme, le penseur, le socialiste*, Paris, 1915.

Lafargue:

LAFARGUE, PAUL, *Le Droit à la paresse*, Paris, 1883.

—— *Idéalisme et matérialisme dans la conception de l'Histoire*, Lille, 1901.

—— *Le Déterminisme économique de Karl Marx*, Paris, 1928 (1st edn., 1907).

—— *Critiques littéraires*, Paris, 1936.

VARLET, J., (ed.), *Paul Lafargue, théoricien du marxisme*, Paris, 1933 (an anthology).

STOLZE, G., *Paul Lafargue, théoricien, militant du socialisme*, Paris, 1937.

Sorel:

SOREL, GEORGES, *Les Illusion du progrès*, Paris, 1947 (1st edn., 1908).

—— —— *Réflexions sur la violence*, Paris, 1908 (Eng. trans. with an introduction by E. A. Shils, Glencoe, Ill., 1950

—— —— *La Décomposition du marxisme*, 1908 (2nd edn. Paris, 1910).

—— —— *Matériaux d'une théorie du prolétariat*, Paris, 3rd edn., 1919.

FREUND, M., *Georges Sorel. Der revolutionäre Konservatismus*, Frankfurt-on-Main, 1932.

GORIELY, G., *Le Pluralisme démocratique de Georges Sorel*, Paris, 1962.

HOROWITZ, I. L., *Radicalism and the Revolt against Reason*, London, 1961.

PIRON, G., *Georges Sorel*, 1927.

ROTH, J. J., 'The Roots of Italian Fascism: Sorel and Sorelismo', in, *Journal of Modern History*, vol. 39, Mar. 1967.

SECTION 6: LABRIOLA

LABRIOLA, ANTONIO, *Della coscienza morale* (*On Moral Consciousness*), Naples, 1873.

—— —— *La concezione materialista della storia* (*Materialist Concept of History*), 2nd edn., Bari, 1938.

—— —— *Scritii vari di filosofia e politica* (*Various Writings on Philosophy and Politics*), Bari, 1906.

—— —— *Opere* (*Works*), 3 vols. Milan, 1959.

DAL PANE, LUIGI, *Antonio Labriola. La vita e il pensiero* (*Antonio Labriola. Life and Thought*), Rome, 1935.

SECTION 7: POLISH MARXISTS

BRZOZOWSKI, STANISŁAW, *Kultura i Życie* (*Culture and Life*), Lemberg, 1907.

—— —— *Idee* (*Ideas*), Lemberg, 1910.

—— —— *Listy* (*Letters*), ed. M. Sroka, vols. i and ii, Cracow, 1970.

KELLES-KRAUZ, KAZIMIERZ, *Pisma Wybrane* (*Selected Writings*), vols. i and ii, Warsaw, 1962 (includes complete bibliography).

KOWALIK, TADEUSZ, *Krzywicki*, Warsaw, 1965.

KRZYWICKI, LUDWIK, *Dzieła* (*Works*), Warsaw, 1957 ff.

STAWAR, A., *O Brzozowskim i inne szkice* (*On Brzozowski and other Essays*), Warsaw, 1961.

SUCHODOLSKI, B., *Stanisław Brzozowski. Rozwój ideologii* (*Stanisław Brzozowski. Evolution of his Ideology*), Warsaw, 1933.

WALICKI, ANDRZEJ, *Stanisław Brzozowski—drogi myśli* (*Stanisław Brzozowski—The Paths of Thought*), Warsaw, 1977.

SECTION 8: AUSTRO-MARXISTS, KANTIANS IN MARXISM

Texts:

ADLER, MAX, *Kausalität und Teleologie im Streit um die Wissenschaft*, in *Marx-Studien*, vol. i, Vienna, 1904.
— — *Der Sozialismus und die Intellektuellen*, Vienna, 1910.
— — *Marxistische Probleme*, Stuttgart, 1913.
— — *Der soziologische Sinn der Lehre von Karl Marx*, Leipzig, 1914.
— — *Politik und Moral*, Leipzig, 1918.
— — *Demokratie und Rätesystem*, Vienna, 1919.
— — *Die Staatsauffassung des Marxismus*, Vienna, 1922 (last edn., Darmstadt, 1964).
— — *Das Soziologische in Kants Erkenntniskritik*, Vienna, 1924.
— — *Kant und der Marxismus. Gesammelte Aufsätze zur Erkenntniskritik und Theorie des Sozialen*, Berlin, 1925.
— — *Lehrbuch der materialistischen Geschichtsauffassung*, vol. i, Berlin, 1930; vol. ii, Vienna, 1969.
— — *Das Rätsel der Gesellschaft*, Vienna, 1936.
BAUER, OTTO, *Die Nationalitätenfrage und die Sozialdemokratie*, Vienna, 1907.
— — *Grosskapital und Militarismus*, Vienna, 1911.
— — *Nationalkampf oder Klassenkampf?*, Vienna, 1911.
— — *Bolschewismus oder Sozialdemokratie?*, Vienna, 1920.
— — *Das Weltbild des Kapitalismus*, Jena, 1924.
— — *Sozialdemokratie, Religion und Kirche*, Vienna, 1927.
— — *Eine Auswahl aus seinem Lebenswerk mit einem Lebensbild Otto Bauers*, ed. Julius Braunthal, Vienna, 1961.
COHEN, H., *Kants Begründung der Ethik*, Berlin, 1877.
— — *Ethik des reinen Willens*, Berlin, 1904.
HILFERDING, R., *Böhm-Bawerks Marx-Kritik*, in *Marx-Studien*, vol. i, Vienna, 1904.
— — *Das Finanzkapital*, Vienna, 1910.
RENNER, KARL, *Staat und Nation*, Vienna, 1899.
— — *Mehrarbeit und Mehrwert*, Vienna, 1902.
— — *Die soziale Funktion der Rechtsinstitute*, Vienna, 1904.
— — *Der deutsche Arbeiter und der Nationalismus*, Vienna, 1910.
— — *Staatswirtschaft, Weltwirtschaft und Sozialismus*, Berlin, 1929.
STAUDINGER, F., *Ethik und Politik*, Berlin, 1899.
— — *Kulturgrundlagen der Politik*, vols. i and ii, Jena, 1914.
VORLÄNDER, K., *Kant und der Sozialismus*, Berlin, 1900.
— — *Kant und Marx. Ein Beitrag zur Philosophie des Sozialismus*, Tübingen, 1911.
— — *Kant, Fichte, Hegel und der Sozialismus*, Berlin, 1920.
— — *Marx, Engels und Lassalle als Philosophen*, Berlin, 1921.

— — *Von Machiavelli bis Lenin*, Leipzig, 1926.

WOLTMANN, L., *System des moralischen Bewusstseins*, Düsseldorf, 1898.

— — *Der historische Materialismus*, Düsseldorf, 1900.

Austromarxismus, ed. H. J. Sandkühler und R. de la Vega, Frankfurt-Vienna, 1970 (an anthology).

Marxismus und Ethik, ed. R. de la Vega und H.-J. Sandkühler, Frankfurt, 1970 (an anthology).

Works on Austro-Marxism:

HEINTEL, PETER, *System und Ideologie. Der Austromarxismus im Spiegel der Philosophie Max Adlers*, Vienna–Munich, 1967.

KAUTSKY, BENEDIKT, *Geistige Strömungen im österreichischen Sozialismus*, Vienna, 1953.

LESLER, N., *Zwischen Reformismus und Bolschewismus. Der Austromarxismus als Theorie und Praxis*, Vienna–Frankfurt–Zurich, 1968.

STEINER, H., *Bibliographie zur Geschichte der österreichischen Arbeiterbewegung*, vols. i and ii, Vienna–Frankfurt–Zurich, 1967.

SECTION 9: RUSSIAN MARXISM

AKSELROD, L., *Filosofskie ocherki* (*Philosophical Essays*), St. Petersburg, 1906.

— — (Ortodoks), *O 'problemakh idealizma'* (*On 'Problems of Idealism'*) Odessa, 1905.

AKSELROD, P. B., *Istoricheskoe polozhenie i vzaimootnoshenie liberal'noy i sotsialisticheskoy demokratii v Rossii* (*Historical Situation and Mutual Relationship of Liberal and Socialist Democracy in Russia*), Geneva, 1898.

— — *Rabochii klass i revolutsionnoe dvizhenie w Rossii* (*The Working Class and the Revolutionary Movement in Russia*), St. Petersburg, 1907.

AVRICH, P., *The Russian Anarchists*, Princeton, 1967.

AVTORCHANOV, A., *Proiskhozhdenie partokratii* (*The Origins of Partocracy*), 2 vols., Frankfurt, 1973.

BARON, S. H., *Plekhanov. The Father of Russian Marxism*, Stanford, 1963.

BERDYAEV, N., *The Origin of Russian Communism*, London, n.d.

BILLINGTON, J., *Michailovski and Russian Populism*, Oxford, 1958.

BOGDANOV, A., *Empiriomonizm*, 3 vols., St. Petersburg, 1905.

— — *Vera i nauka* (*Faith and Science*), Moscow, 1910.

— — *Kratkii kurs ekonomicheskoy nauki* (*Short Course of Economic Science*), Moscow, 1897.

— — *Osnovnye elementy istoricheskogo uzglyada na prirodu* (*Essential Elements of the Historical View of Nature*), St. Petersburg, 1899.

CONQUEST, R., *Lenin*, London, 1972.

DAN, F., *Proiskhozhdenie bolshevizma* (*The Origin of Bolshevism*), New York, 1946.

DEUTSCHER, I., *The Prophet Armed. Trotsky 1879–1921*, London, 1954.

FOMINA, V. A. *Filosofskie vzglyady G. V. Plekhanova (Philosophical Views of Plekhanov)*, Moscow, 1955.

GRILLE, D., *Lenins Rivale. Bogdanov und seine Philosophie*, Cologne, 1966.

HAIMSON, L. H., *The Russian Marxists and the Origins of Bolshevism*, Cambridge, Mass., 1955.

HARE, R., *Portraits of Russian Personalities between Reform and Revolution*, London, 1959.

Iz glubiny. Sbornik statey o russkoi revolutsii (From the Depths. A Collection of Essays on the Russian Revolution), Paris, 1967 (1st edn. 1918)

KINDERSLEY, R., *The First Russian Revisionists. A Study of 'Legal Marxism' in Russia*, Oxford, 1962.

KLINE, G. L., *Religious and Anti-religious Thought in Russia*, Chicago, 1968.

KUCHARZEWSKI, J., *The Origins of Modern Russia*, New York, 1948.

LENIN, V. I., *Sochinenia (Works)*, 55 vols., 5th edn., 1959–65; English translation, London, 1960–70.

— — *Essentials of Lenin*, London, 1947.

LOSSKY, N. O., *History of Russian Philosophy*, New York, 1969.

LUNACHARSKY, A. W., *Sobranie sochinenii (Collected Works)*, 8 vols., Moscow, 1963–7.

MARTOV, L., *Zapiski sotsial-demokrata (Notes of a Social-Democrat)*, Berlin, 1922.

— — *Istoria rossiiskoi sotsial-demokratii (The History of Russian Social-Democracy)*, Moscow, 1923.

— — *Mirovoy bolshevizm (World Bolshevism)*, Berlin, 1923.

MEYER, A., *Leninism*, New York, 1962.

Ocherki po filosofii marksizma. Filosofskii sbornik (Essays on the Philosophy of Marxism. A Philosophical Collection), St. Petersburg, 1908.

Ocherki filosofii kollektivizma (Essays on the Philosophy of Collectivism), St. Petersburg, 1909.

PARVUS (A. L. Helphand), *Rossia i Revolutsia (Russia and Revolution)*, St. Petersburg, 1906.

PIPES, R., *Social Democracy and the St. Petersburg Labor Movement 1885–1897*, Cambridge, Mass. 1963.

— — 'Narodnichestvo: A Semantic Inquiry', in *Slavic Review*, Sept. 1964.

— — *Struve. Liberal on the Left 1870–1905*, Cambridge, Mass., 1970 (with a complete bibliography).

— — (ed.), *Revolutionary Russia*, Cambridge, Mass., 1968.

PLEKHANOV, G. V., *Sochinenia (Works)*, 26 vols., Moscow, 1922–7.

— — *Essays in the History of Materialism*, London, 1934.

— — *Selected Philosophical Works*, Moscow, 1961– .

— — *In Defence of Materialism*, trans. A. Rothstein, London, 1947.

— — *The Role of the Individual in History*, London, 1950.

— — *Art and Social Life*, ed. A. Rothstein, London, 1953.

Problemy idealizma (*Problems of Idealism*), St. Petersburg, 1903.

ROSENBERG, A., *A History of Bolshevism from Marx to the First Five-Year Plan*, London, 1934.

SCHAPIRO, L., *The Communist Party of the Soviet Union*, London, 1960.

— — and REDDAWAY, P. (eds.), *Lenin: the Man, the Theorist, the Leader*, London, 1967.

SCHEIBERT, P., *Von Bakunin zu Lenin*, vol. i, Leiden, 1956.

SHUB, D., *Lenin. A Biography*, New York, 1949 (New ed., London, 1966).

STRUVE, P. B., *Kriticheskie zametki k voprosu ob ekonomicheskom razvitii Rossii* (*Critical Remarks on the Question of Russia's Economic Development*), St. Petersburg, 1894.

TREADGOLD, D. W., *Lenin and his Rivals, 1898–1906*, London, 1955.

TROTSKY, L. D., *Sochinenia* (*Works*), 21 vols., Moscow, 1925–7 (incomplete).

ULAM, A. B., *Lenin and the Bolsheviks*, London, 1965 (2nd edn., 1969).

VALENTINOV, N., *Filosofskie postroenia marksizma. Kriticheskie ocherki* (*Philosophical Bases of Marxism. Critical Essays*), Moscow, 1908.

— — *E. Makh i Marksizm* (*E. Mach and Marxism*), Moscow, n.d.

— — *Vstrechi s Leninym* (*Encounters with Lenin*, with a foreword by L. Schapiro), London, 1968.

Vekhi. Sbornik statey o russkoi inteligentsii (*Signposts. A Collection of Essays on the Russian Intelligentsia*), Moscow, 1909 (reprinted Frankfurt, 1967).

VENTURI, F., *Roots of Revolution*, London, 1960.

WALICKI, A., *The Controversy over Capitalism. Studies in the Social Philosophy of Russian Populism*, Oxford, 1969.

— — *Rosyjska Filozofia i myśl społeczna od Oświecenia do marksizmu* (*Russian Philosophy and Social Thought from the Enlightenment to Marxism*), Warsaw, 1973.

WOLFE, B. D., *Three Who Made a Revolution. A Biographical History*, New York, 1948.

YASSOUR, A., *Bogdanov et son œuvre*, in *Cahiers du monde russe et soviétique*, vol. x, 1969 (bibliography of Bogdanov's works)

— — 'Leçons de la révolution de 1905. La Controverse Lénine–Bogdanov', thesis, Paris, 1967 (not published except in Hebrew).

YUSHKEVICH, P., *Stolpy filosofskoy ortodoksii* (*The Pillars of Philosophical Orthodoxy*), St. Petersburg, 1910.

ZEMAN, Z. A. B. and SCHARLAM, W. B., *The Merchant of Revolution. The Life of A. L. Helphand (Parvus) 1867–1924*, London, 1965.

ZENKOVSKY, V. V., *A History of Russian Philosophy*, trans. G. L. Kline, 2 vols., New York, 1953.

Index

Abramowski, E., 18
Accumulation and concentration of capital, 66 ff., 105 f., 111 f.
Adler, F., 3, 16, 240, 256, 423
Adler, M., 2, 16, 111, Ch. XII *passim*
Adler, V., 2, 16, 19, 111, 255, 389
Aesthetics and Marxism: Mehring's views on, 57–60; Plekhanov's theory of, 345 ff.
Akimov, 394
Aksakov, K., 309
Akselrod, L. ('Orthodox'), 422 f., 449 ff., 454
Akselrod, P. B., 330, 332, 350, 379, 394, 413, 417, 470
Aleksinsky, G., 434
Alexander II, 306, 310, 333
Alexander III, 310
Amiel, H., 217
Anarchism and its critique, 8–10, 19–21, 170 ff., 198
Aristotle, 291
Askoldov, S., 421
Auer, I., 100
Avenarius, R., 215, 217, 218 ff., 420, 424 ff., 450 ff., 458, 504, 517
Azev, Y., 218

Bakay, M., 218 f.
Bakunin, M. A., 170 f., 319, 331
Ballanche, P., 212
Baron, S. H., 352
Bauer, O., 2, 16, 39, 71, 90, Ch. XII *passim*, 343
Bazarov, V. A., 432, 444, 454
Bebel, A., 2, 10, 18, 25, 32, 63 f., 101, 108, 111, 113
Belinsky, V., 309
Bentham, J., 1, 48, 127
Berdyaev, N. A., 363, 368 ff., 420 f., 432, 449
Bergson, H., 117, 150, 153, 161, 167, 216, 221, 228, 235, 420

Berkeley, G., 450 ff., 457
Berman, I. A., 434
Bernstein, E., 2, 11, 32, 44, 47, 56, 62, 77, Ch. IV *passim*, 135, 137 f., 166, 190, 196, 249, 276, 340, 347 f., 366 f., 378, 382, 394, 470
Białobłocki, B., 195
Bismarck, O. von, 11
Blanc, L., 32, 137
Blanqui, L., 115
Bloch, J., 102
Blok, A., 420
Böhm-Bawerk, E. von, 2, 243, 290–4, 368
Bogdanov, A. A., 414, 419, 432–45, 448 ff., 457
Bonald, L. de, 212
Bonnafous, M., 120
Brentano, L., 101, 200
Bruno, G., 175, 179
Bryusov, V., 420
Brzozowski, S., 3, 18, 153, Ch. XI *passim*, 343
Bukharin, N., 490 f.
Bulgakov, S. N., 69, 327, 363, 365, 370 f., 378
Bunin, I., 420
Burtsev, V., 218
Byely, A., 420

Cabanis, G., 143
Cabet, E., 518
Calvin, J., 48
Chernov, V., 432
Chernyshevsky, N. G., 195, 313 ff., 346, 357, 420, 464
Chicherin, B. N., 305, 420
Classes and class struggle: Kautsky on, 38, 42 ff.; Rosa Luxemburg on, 80 ff.; class content of socialism in Kantian Marxists, 247 ff.; Lenin on, 405 f.; Sorel's view on, 162 ff.
Clausewitz, K. von, 495
Clemenceau, G., 487

Cohen, H., 39, 245 f., 270, 428
Comte, A., 115, 211, 446
Condillac, E., 143
Condorcet, M. J. de, 157
Consciousness and social processes: Kautsky's views on, 40 f., 53; Rosa Luxemburg on, 75; Jaurès on, 122 f.; Austro-Marxists on, 262 ff., 272 ff.; Lenin on, 386–92
Copernicus, N., 338
Crises: Bernstein's view on, 106, 111; Hilferding's theory of, 299–301
Croce, B., 2, 15, 155, 177 f., 190, 213, 340

Dal Pane, L., 178
Danielson, N. F., 316, 326 f.
Darwin, C., and Darwinism, 36, 51, 56 f., 250, 338
Daszyński, F., 19
David, E., 79, 99, 213
Denikin, H., 483 f.
Descartes, R., 157, 161, 427
Determinism: Kautsky's views on, 35–7, 52; Rosa Luxemburg on, 75; Bernstein's critique of, 103; Lafargue on, 144 f.; Labriola on, 180 f.; Brzozowski on, 225; Adler on, 272; Lavrov on, 320; Plekhanov on, 338 f.; 450; Lenin on, 454, 456
Deutsch, L., 330, 332
Dialectic: Kautsky on, 52; Bernstein's critique of, 102 ff.; Adler's theory of, 271 f.; Plekhanov on, 337, 340 ff.; Lenin on, 461 ff.
Dictatorship of the proletariat: Kautsky on, 45, 50; Rosa Luxemburg on, 86 f.; Austro-Marxists on, 279 ff.; Lenin's and Trotsky's view on, 485 ff., 498 ff., 509 ff.; Martov's critique of, 581 f.
Diderot, D., 143, 157
Dilthey, W., 258
Dobrolyubov, N. A., 315, 420
Dollfuss, E., 257
Dostoevsky, F. M., 216, 218, 420
Dreyfus case, 21 ff., 26, 118 f., 135 f., 155
Dühring, E., 100
Duhem, P., 287
Dzerzhinsky, F. E., 402, 486, 490

Eckstein, G., 16 f.
Engels, F., *passim*

Ferri, E., 177
Feuerbach, L., 143, 313, 340, 446 f., 464
Fichte, J. G., 115, 132, 219, 228, 249, 262, 269 f., 280, 452
Fischer, R., 96
Fontenelle, B. de, 157
Fourier, C., 130, 137, 148
Frank, S. L., 363, 370 f., 420 f.
Frederick the Great, 58
Freedom: 4, 11, 129 ff., 180 f., 252, 339, 360, 513 ff.
Freiligrath, F., 60
Fritsche, V., 433

Galliffet, G., 23
Gapon, G. A., 414
Garibaldi, G., 175
Gentile, G., 2
Gippius, Z., 347, 420
Gobineau, J. A., 197, 285
Goethe, J. W. von, 58, 249
Gorky, M., 218, 344, 433, 446 f., 460, 486
Gramsci, A., 149, 156, 176, 225, 236
Guesde, J., 1 f., 12 ff., 18, 22 ff., 26, 28, 119, 136 f., 141 f., 470
Guizot, F., 338

Haase, H., 28, 102
Hauptmann, G., 60
Hegel, G. W., 36, 102 ff., 122 ff., 133 f., 139, 175, 180, 182, 186, 215, 244, 250, 262, 309, 337 ff., 420, 461–9
Heine, H., 58
Heine, W., 77, 100
Helvétius, C. A., 337, 378
Henry VIII, 33
Herbart, J. F., 175, 178, 180 ff.
Herder, J. G. von, 249
Hervé, G., 26, 28
Herzen, A. I., 311 ff., 322
Hilferding, R., 2, 240, 243, 254, 257 f., 290–304, 471, 490
Historical materialism: Vandervelde's view on, 15; Kautsky's theory of, 40 ff.; Bernstein's critique of, 103; Jaurès's view on, 126 ff.; Labriola on, 184–91; Krzywicki on, 199–205; Kelles-Krauz on, 209ff.; Adler on, 272 ff., Plekhanov on, 338 ff.; Struve's critique of, 367
Hitler, A., 173
Hobbes, T., 146
Hobson, J. A., 491
Höchberg, K., 100

Hoffman, P., 234
Holbach, P. H., 337, 378
Hume, D., 452
Husserl, E., 420, 428
Hyndman, H. N., 491

Ibsen, H., 58
Imperialism: Hilferding's theory of, 297–304; Lenin's and Bukharin's views on, 491 ff.
Ivan the Terrible, 306
Ivanov, V., 420

James, W., 229, 420
Jaurès, J., 2, 9, 13 f., 16, 21 f., 24, 26, 28, 35, 82, 98, 111 f., Ch. V *passim*, 146

Kalecki, M., 74
Kaledin, A. M., 174
Kamenev, L. B., 475, 490 f., 522
Kant, I., 39 ff., 115, 133, 180 f., 209, 215, 276, Ch. XII *passim*, 365, 368, 378, 420, 427, 437, 449, 455 f., 462
Kareyev, N. I., 213, 336
Kautsky, K., 2, 11, 24, 28, Ch. II *passim*, 63 f., 71, 82–6, 95, 99 f., 101 f., 108, 111 f., 137, 150, 162, 196, 198, 200, 210, 214, 223, 260, 282, 328, 340, 342 f., 382, 387, 389, 398, 470, 492, 508 f., 517, 520, 523
Kelles-Krauz, K., 2, 17, 94, Ch. X *passim*
Kelsen, H., 278, 280
Khomyakov, A., 309
Kindersley, R., 363
Kireyevsky, I., 309
Kline, G. L., 446
Klinger, W., 237
Klopstock, F. G., 58
Knowledge, experience, perception: Jaurès on, 121 ff.; Lafargue on, 146 f.; Brzozowski on, 220 ff.; Adler's transcendental approach, 258 ff.; Adler on epistemological realism, 269 ff.; empiriocritical views on, 427 ff., 432 ff., 435; Lenin on, 452–5
Kolchak, A. V., 482 ff.
Kollontay, A., 488
Kon, F., 218
Kornilov, L. G., 475
Krafft-Ebing, R. von, 205
Kremer, J., 217
Kropotkin, P. A., 19 f., 115
Krupskaya, N., 358

Krzywicki, L., 2, 17, Ch. IX *passim*, 208
Krzhizhanovsky, G., 358
Kursky, D. I., 507
Kuskova, E. D., 349, 378, 387

Labour: division of l., according to Kautsky, 37 f.; Brzozowski's philosophy of l., 223 ff.
Labriola, A., 2, 25, 105, 111, 150, 155, Ch. VIII *passim*, 207, 209, 223
Lachelier, J., 120 f.
Lafargue, P., Ch. VI *passim*, 193, 214
Lagardelle, H., 14, 155, 190
La Mettrie, J. O. de, 143
Lange, A., 244
Lassalle, F., 4, 9, 59, 102, 115, 118, 134, 276
Lavrov, P. L., 18, 318 ff., 331
Le Bon, G., 170, 206
Ledebour, G., 256, 470, 525
Lenin, V. I., 2, 16, 18, 26 ff., 42, 50, 63, 71, 75 f., 78 f., 82, 86 ff., 90, 93, 95 ff., 113, 155, 162, 173 f., 193, 242, 269, 281, 288, 290, 303 f., 314, 316 ff., 325, 327, 340, 347 ff., Chs. XV–XVIII *passim*
Leninism, essential characteristics, 381–384, 412
Le Play, P., 144
Lessing, G. E., 58, 249
Lévi-Strauss, C., 80
Liebknecht, K., 26, 28, 62, 65
Liebknecht, W., 10, 18, 32, 135
Liebmann, O., 244
Limanowski, B., 90
Lloyd George, D., 487
Locke, J., 143, 427
Loisy, A., 216
Lombroso, C., 155, 197 f.
Longuet, J., 256
Lukács, G., 84, 225, 236, 254, 375
Lunacharsky, A. V., 218, 414, 419, 432 ff., 445 ff., 458, 472
Luther, M., 133
Luxemburg, R., 2, 16 f., 26 f., Ch. III *passim*, 101, 111, 150, 162, 193, 208, 213, 255, 282, 288 f., 304, 348, 376, 384, 396, 399 f., 403 f.

MacDonald, R., 470
Mach, E., 420, 424 ff., 435, 437, 450, 453, 457 f.
Maine de Biran, M. F., 143

Maistre, J. de, 212
Malatesta, E., 19
Malinowski, R., 390, 468 f., 522
Malon, B., 126
Marchlewski, J., 17, 62 f., 64
Martov, Y. O., 350, 356, 358, 365, 368, 379, 394, 413, 468, 470, 517 ff.
Martynov, A., 387
Marx, K., *passim*
Marx, L., 140
Masaryk, T., 2, 178, 190, 213
Maslov, A., 96
Materialism: Lafargue on, 143 ff.; Krzywicki's view on, 201 ff.; Kelles-Krauz on, 209; Brzozowski on, 227 f., Adler's critique of, 260 ff., 268 ff.; Chernyshevsky on, 315; Plekhanov on, 337, 340; Lenin's defence of, 452 ff.
Mathiez, A., 119
Matter: empiriocritics' concept of, 427; L. Akselrod's view on, 479 f.; Lenin's theory of, 453 f., 465
Maupertuis, P. L. de, 429
Mazzini, G., 177
Mehring, F., 2, 57–60, 63 f., 111, 252, 260, 401
Mendelson, S., 19
Menzhinsky, V., 419, 434
Meredith, G., 228
Merezhkovsky, D., 347, 420
Merlino, S., 169
Michelet, J., 115, 126
Michels, R., 281
Mignet, F. A., 338
Mikhailovsky, N. K., 319 ff., 325, 336, 359
Mill, J. S., 1
Millerand, A., 13, 21, 23, 118, 136 f.
Minsky, N., 420
Miriam-Przesmycki, Z., 217
Moleschott, J., 143
Morals, moral judgements, moral factors in history, moral meaning of socialism: Vandervelde on, 15; Kautsky on, 38f., 49; Jaurès on, 116 ff.; Jaurès on ethics and necessity, 127; Sorel on, 164 ff.; Labriola on, 181 f.; ethical socialism, 245 f.; Austro-Marxists on ethics, 252 ff., 244 ff.; morals and history in Russian populism, 321 f.; Plekhanov's view on, 342 ff.; Lenin's views on ethics, 350, 373 f., 515 f.
More, T., 33
Morgan, L. H., 212

Morris, W., 19
Münsterberg, H., 258
Mussolini, B., 174

Nation, national question, nationalism, patriotism: Rosa Luxemburg on, 88–94; Bernstein on, 110; Jaurès on, 132 f.; Labriola on, 184; Kelles-Krauz on, 213; Brzozowski on, 234 ff.; Leninist theory of, 398–405
Natorp, P., 245 f., 270, 428
Nature and society: Kautsky's view on, 36 ff.; Jaurès's view on 123–5
N.E.P., main features, 482–5
Newman, J. H., 216
Nicholas I, 309 f., 313
Nietzsche, F., 150, 169, 172, 216, 219, 221 f., 420 ff., 446
Norwid, C. K., 218

Ordzhonikidze, G. K., 402, 490
Ostwald, W., 432
Owen, R., 1, 432

Pacifism, Lenin's view on, 459 f.
Pannekoek, A., 2, 18, 71, 304
Pareto, V., 155
Parmenides, 122
Party, theory of: Kautsky on, 42; Rosa Luxemburg on, 83 ff.; Sorel on, 162; in relation to Leninism, 349 ff., 384–98
Parvus (Helphand, A.), 104, 156, 407 f.
Pascal, B., 157
Peasant problem and socialism: Kautsky on, 44, 49; in relation to revisionism, 99; Kelles-Krauz on, 213; Leninism on, 405 ff., 502 f.
Pelloutier, F., 155
Perl, F., 94
Perovskaya, S., 328
Pestel, P., 307
Peter the Great, 306
Petrashevsky, M., 310
Pilsudski, J., 484
Pipes, R., 317, 327, 363
Pisarev, D. I., 315
Plato, 33, 144, 179
Plekhanov, G. V., 2, 15, 28, 105, 142, 214, 252, 271, 306, 323, 327 f., Ch. XIV *passim*, 355 ff., 361, 365 f., 374 f., 379 f., 395, 410, 413, 422 f., 446 f., 457, 465, 468 f., 523
Pokrovsky, M., 419

Posadovsky, 395

Postnikov, N. Y., 358

Potresov, A. N., 358, 365, 373, 376, 379, 413, 468 f.

Praxis in cognitive process: Labriola on, 191 f.; Brzozowski on, 225 f.; Lenin on, 455

Progress: Kautsky on, 37; Jaurès's concept of, 120 ff.; Labriola on, 182, 186; neo-Kantians on, 250

Prokopovich, S. N., 349, 378

Proletariat: its historical mission, 5, 43, 137, 152, 162 ff., 231, 234 ff.; proletarian culture, 441 ff.

Proudhon, P., 150, 152, 163, 168, 170, 172, 216

Przybyszewski, S., 347

Pyatakov, G., 490

Rabelais, F., 148

Rationalism, Sorel's critique of, 157 ff.

Reclus, E., 19

Religion and Marxism, religion and socialist movement: in Erfurt Programme, 11; Jaurès's view on, 124; Lafargue on, 143 f.; Sorel on, 151, 159 f., 167; Labriola on, 181 f., 185 f.; Brzozowski on, 223, 238; Austro-Marxists on, 282–5; in relation to legal Marxism, 368 f.; Lenin on, 458–61; in relation to Russian God-builders, 446 f.

Renan, E., 152, 285

Renner, K., 16, 90, 240, 243, 254 ff., 276, 288

Revolution and reforms: their relationships, 5, 8, 11; Kautsky's view on, 44, 47, 55 f.; Rosa Luxemburg on, 76–82; in debate on revisionism, 105 ff., 110 ff., Jaurès on, 136 ff.; Sorel on, 165 ff.; Kelles-Krauz on, 213; Plekhanov on, 333 f.; Lenin's theory of revolution, 495; Trotsky's permanent revolution, 408 ff.

Rickert, H., 258 ff.

Rodbertus, J. K., 106, 200, 298, 300

Rodzyanko, M., 522

Roland-Holst, H., 2

Rousseau, J.-J., 115, 280, 322

Rozanov, V. V., 420

Saint-Simon, H. C. de, 115, 125, 130, 322

Samarin, Y., 309

Sand, G., 32

Schiller, F. von, 58, 249

Schippel, M., 77, 100

Schmidt, K., 78, 251 ff., 340

Schulze-Gävernitz, G., 101

Shlyapnikov, A., 488

Sienkiewicz, H., 217

Simmel, G., 2, 209

Sismondi, J. C., 106, 317

Śniadecki, J., 217

Socialism and Communism: general concept of, 4–5; views of various socialists on: Vandervelde, 16; Kautsky, 49; Bernstein, 106 f.; Lafargue, 145 ff.; Labriola, 189; Brzozowski, 231; Adler, 247 ff.; debate on socialism and capitalism in Russia, 311 f., 318 ff., 332 ff.; War Communism, 482 f.

Socrates, 179 f.

Solovyov, V., 420

Sombart, W., 2, 101, 104, 213, 370, 373

Sorel, G., 3, 14, Ch. VII *passim*, 186, 190 f., 216, 221, 223, 231 f., 235

Spaventa, B., 177

Spencer, H., 36, 192, 196 f., 215, 250, 321, 419, 429

Spinoza, B., 177, 179, 339

Stalin, J. V., 90, 247, 289, 306, 390, 402, 411, 458, 477 ff., 490 f., 516 f., 521

Stammler, R., 2, 258, 343, 365, 367

State, its functions and its future: Rosa Luxemburg on, 73; Jaurès on, 130 f.; Adler on, 276 ff.; Lenin's and Trotsky's theory of, 498 ff., 509 ff.

Staudinger, F., 251

Stawar, A., 233

Stirner, M., 20, 322, 420

Stolypin, P. A., 466 f.

Struve, P. B., 69, 317, 327, 356, 358, 362–9, 371, 373 f., 398, 421, 449, 522 ff.

Suvorov, S. A., 434

Syndicalism, 163 ff.

Taine, H., 152, 217

Tarde, G., 206

Teilhard de Chardin, P., 123

Thierry, A., 338

Tikhomirov, L., 328

Tkachev, P., 307, 319, 324 f., 396

Tocqueville, A. de, 150, 152

Togliatti, P., 149, 183

Tolstoy, L., 358, 515

Tosca, A., 149

Trotsky, L. D., 16, 85 ff., 97, 162, 407–11, 418, 434, 444, 470, 472, 477 f., 485, 488, 490, 509–13, 520, 522

Truth: Kautsky on, 37; Brzozowski on, 229; Adler on, 264 f.; Bogdanov on, 436 f.; Lenin on 454 f.

Tugan-Baranovsky, M. I., 69, 71, 210, 327, 363, 370 f.

Turati, F., 2, 9, 17, 82

Ulyanov, A., 357

Ulyanov, I. N., 357

Utilitarianism, in Chernyshevsky, 314 f.

Utopia, Sorel's critique of, 157 ff.

Vaillant, E., 13, 18, 26

Valentinov (Volsky), N. V., 431 f., 464

Value, theory of, surplus value, rate of profit: Rosa Luxemburg on, 67 ff., 70; Bernstein's critique of, 104; Jaurès's view on, 138; Hilferding's defence of, 290–7; legal Marxists' critique of, 368, 370

Vandervelde, E., 2, 15, 25, 168 f.

Venturi, F., 317

Vera, A., 177

Vico, G., 144, 152, 155, 162, 178, 211

Vollmar, G. von, 77, 99

Vorländer, K., 39, 249–52

Vorontsov, V. P., 326 f.

Vorovsky, V., 414

Vvedensky, A. I., 420

Waldeck-Rousseau, P., 21, 118

Walicki, A., 317

Warski, A., 62

Waryński, L., 195

Weber, M., 281

Weitling, W., 518

Wilson, W., 487

Windelband, W., 258 ff., 420

Wundt, W., 187, 420

Xenophon, 179

Yushkevich, P., 432, 434, 441, 457

Zasulich, V., 323 f., 330, 332, 379, 413

Zeller, E., 177, 179

Zeno the Stoic, 144

Zeromski, S., 217

Zetkin, K., 2, 101, 111

Zetterbaum, M., 423

Zhdanov, A. A., 445

Zhelyabov, A. I., 328

Zinoviev, G. E., 468, 475, 490 f., 522

Zubatov, S. V., 414